Communications in Computer and Information Science   1084

Commenced Publication in 2007
Founding and Former Series Editors:
Phoebe Chen, Alfredo Cuzzocrea, Xiaoyong Du, Orhun Kara, Ting Liu,
Krishna M. Sivalingam, Dominik Ślęzak, Takashi Washio, and Xiaokang Yang

More information about this series at http://www.springer.com/series/7899

Alla G. Kravets · Peter P. Groumpos ·
Maxim Shcherbakov · Marina Kultsova (Eds.)

Creativity in Intelligent Technologies and Data Science

Third Conference, CIT&DS 2019
Volgograd, Russia, September 16–19, 2019
Proceedings, Part II

 Springer

Editors
Alla G. Kravets 🆔
CAD & Research Department
Volgograd State Technical University
Volgograd, Russia

Peter P. Groumpos 🆔
Electrical and Computer Engineering
University of Patras
Rion, Patras, Greece

Maxim Shcherbakov 🆔
Volgograd State Technical University
Volgograd, Russia

Marina Kultsova 🆔
Volgograd State Technical University
Volgograd, Russia

ISSN 1865-0929   ISSN 1865-0937 (electronic)
Communications in Computer and Information Science
ISBN 978-3-030-29749-7   ISBN 978-3-030-29750-3 (eBook)
https://doi.org/10.1007/978-3-030-29750-3

This Springer imprint is published by the registered company Springer Nature Switzerland AG
The registered company address is: Gewerbestrasse 11, 6330 Cham, Switzerland

Preface

In the era of digitalization and raise of artificial intelligence, creativity is still a crucial and essential ability for humankind. Creativity is the process of breaking out of established patterns; it is the reorganization, recombination or reinterpretation of concepts and ideas for getting something unique and previously unknown. Creating intelligent systems and artificial intelligence approaches is one of the most creative activities that humans undertake. It is developed for people and by people and people's creativity can be a good source to improvise solutions to problems for dominating complex systems such as intelligent system design and development. These actions merge science and art.

This book includes the proceedings of the third Conference on Creativity in Intelligent Technologies and Data Science (CIT&DS 2019), continuing the successful series of previous conferences, which took place in 2017 and 2015. The main objective of CIT&DS 2019 is to bring together researchers and practitioners to share ideas in using creativity to theory and practice in software and intelligent systems engineering as well as data science and decision-making support solutions. Readers will find results of creating cutting-edge intelligent technologies based on state-of-the-art research.

The conference has three main groups of topics. The first one is called "Artificial intelligence and Deep Learning Technologies for Creative Tasks." This chapter includes papers related to the following topics: (a) Knowledge Discovery in Patent and Open Sources; (b) Open Science Semantic Technologies; and (c) Computer Vision and Knowledge-Based Control. The second chapter unites articles in the framework of "Cyber-Physical Systems and Big Data-Driven World." In particular, findings related to the following are highlighted: (a) Pro-Active Modeling in Intelligent Decision-Making Support; (b) Design Creativity in CASE/CAI/CAD/PDM; and (c) Intelligent Internet of Services and Internet of Things. The last chapter is titled "Intelligent Technologies in Social Engineering," and contains contributions on the topics: (a) Data Science in Social Networks Analysis; (b) Creativity and Game-Based Learning; and (c) Intelligent Assistive Technologies: Software Design and Application.

July 2019

Alla Kravets
Maxim Shcherbakov
Marina Kultsova
Peter Groumpos

Organization

General Chairs

Vladimir Lysak	Volgograd State Technical University, Russia
Igor Kalyaev	Research Institute of Multiprocessor Computing Systems, Russia
Dmitriy Novikov	Institute of Control Sciences of Russian Academy of Science, Russia

Program Chairs

Alla Kravets	Volgograd State Technical University, Russia
Peter Groumpos	University of Patras, Greece
Maxim Shcherbakov	Volgograd State Technical University, Russia
Marina Kultsova	Volgograd State Technical University, Russia

Program Committee

Julio Abascal	University of the Basque Country, Spain
Abdul Hamid Abu Bakar	Putra Business School, Malaysia
Mohammed Al-Gunaid	Volgograd State Technical University, Russia
Yasemin Allsop	University College London, UK
Andrey Andreev	Volgograd State Technical University, Russia
Anton Anikin	Volgograd State Technical University, Russia
Danish Ather	Teerthanker Mahaveer University, India
Bal Krishna Bal	Kathmandu University, Nepal
Fernando Paulo Belfo	Polytechnic Institute of Coimbra, Portugal
Olga Berestneva	Tomsk Polytechnic University, Russia
Igor Bessmertny	ITMO University, Russia
Alexander Bozhday	Penza State University, Russia
Adriaan Brebels	KULeuven, Belgium
Germanas Budnikas	Kaunas University of Technology, Lithuania
Leonid Chechurin	LUT, Finland
Satyadhyan Chickerur	KLE Technological University, India
Yury Danilovsky	QM&E, South Korea
Maria Dascalu	Politehnica University of Bucharest, Romania
Jan Dekelver	Thomas More University, Belgium
Nuno Escudeiro	IPP-ISEP, Portugal
Demetra Evangelou	Democritus University of Thrace, Greece
Alexey Finogeev	Penza State University, Russia
Dragoi George	UPB-FILS, Romania
Olga Gerget	Tomsk Polytechnic University, Russia

Contents – Part II

Artificial Intelligence and Deep Learning Technologies for Creative Tasks. Computer Vision and Knowledge-Based Control

Intelligent Technologies in Social Engineering. Data Science in Social Networks Analysis and Cybersecurity

Intelligent Technologies in Social Engineering. Creativity and Game-Based Learning

**Intelligent Technologies in Social Engineering. Intelligent Assistive
Technologies: Software Design and Application**

Contents – Part I

**Cyber-Physical Systems and Big Data-Driven World. Design
Creativity in CASE/CAI/CAD/PDM**

Cyber-Physical Systems and Big Data-Driven World. Intelligent
Internet of Services and Internet of Things

Artificial Intelligence and Deep Learning Technologies for Creative Tasks. Knowledge Discovery in Patent and Open Sources

Extraction of Knowledge and Processing of the Patent Array

Marina Fomenkova, Dmitriy Korobkin[(✉)], Alla G. Kravets,
and Sergey Fomenkov

Volgograd State Technical University, Lenin Avenue, 28, Volgograd, Russia
dkorobkin80@mail.ru

Abstract. In modern society, science and technology are developing with great speed. This leads to a massive accumulation of scientific and technical texts, their data structures are becoming more complex. There is a problem: how to deal with the growing volume of scientific and technical texts, as well as accurately determine their technical content, technical links, and trends. Traditional text analysis methods are based on the analysis of words and phrases to describe technological development (for example, the TFIDF method). One of the difficult problems that have arisen is how to integrate natural language processing, semantic analysis, and analysis of technology development trends, and how to perform a further in-depth study of the text to find hidden information about the development of technologies. Often, the development of technology is so fast that standardized technical terms are absent within even one technology, which makes it difficult to analyze textual information based on keywords. Therefore, in the framework of this study, it is proposed to use the machine learning method for SAO structures to solve the above problems. SAO (subject, action, object) structures are semantic structures that most accurately represent the semantic information of their textual data.

Keywords: Natural text processing · SAO analysis · Patents

1 Introduction

The development of natural language processing methods allowed SAO structures to express rich semantic information and define the relationship between concepts (Vicente-Amigo et al. 2017), so it was recognized as a powerful tool for identifying related concepts in text data (Auer and Lehmann 2010; Ghudivada et al. 2008; Zhao et al. 2015; Cachini et al. 2004; Moerle et al. 2005; Chao Yang et al. 2017b). The existing method has gone through several stages.

Step 1: Using the SAO structure to define concepts (Vicente-Gomila 2014) and conduct basic statistical analysis.

A number of researchers who identify functions with semantic TRIZ (Theory of Inventive Problem Solving) used the concept of the structure of S AO (Verbitsky 2004; Vicente Gomila and Palop Marro 2013).

Step 2: Using the SAO structure to analyze object similarity. Some studies have calculated the similarity of technologies or patents based on SAO structures (Yun and

© Springer Nature Switzerland AG 2019
A. G. Kravets et al. (Eds.): CIT&DS 2019, CCIS 1084, pp. 3–14, 2019.
https://doi.org/10.1007/978-3-030-29750-3_1

Kim 2011; Yun et al. 2013), and then the risks of patent infringement (Bergmann et al. 2008; Park et al. 2012) identified by competence were identified. Map the inventor [3] and the identified technological capabilities [9].

Step 3: Using the SAO structure to define "functional" information (Choi et al. 2013) or P & S models [11], and then creating technology road maps (Wang et al. 2015; C. Young and others 2015), [11]. These results use the SAO structure to express the relationship between key concepts.

Step 4: Using the SAO network to conduct an in-depth analysis of the relationship between topics, identify key concepts and identify trends in various thematic areas (e.g., technology).

Research methods for determining trends in the development of technologies and new technologies can be divided into three main categories: qualitative analysis (Boone and Morse 2008; Simpson et al. 2008), analysis of indicators Cozzens et al. 2010; Vidal-Espaana and others 2007; Seymour 2008; Guo et al. 2011; Mound and Neuheisler 2015 (Bengizu 2003; Juan et al. 2014, Rotolo et al. 2015) and citation analysis (Erdi et al. 2013; Kajikawa et al. 2008); Thus, the advantages SAO-based methods can be summed up as follows: (1) The SAO structure can combine verbs and nouns to express semantic information (Choi et al. 2011; Wang et al. 2015), and in this case reduces the need to use expert knowledge to compile technological information from mass data; (2) the SAO structure has verbs to describe actions and objects/objects to represent more than one concept, which allows the SAO structure to identify specific relationships between thematic terms (Zhang et al. 2016); (3) SAO can be used to present the "problem and solution" pattern, as well as to understand "what problems arose" and "what solutions were used to solve these problems", which facilitates the identification of technological components, functions, operations and requirements [11].

2   General Algorithm for Analyzing Technological Capabilities Based on SAO Structures

1st step: the selection of patents, extracting parts of the description and claim of them.

2nd step: extracting "significant" SAO from patents obtained in the first step. In order to highlight precisely significant SAOs, it is necessary to define keywords that will describe the subject area. These are terms - significant nouns for the subject area, which are objects in the structure of SAO. The initial object terms can be defined using 39 TRIZ parameters. At the same time, verbs that denote action in the structure of SAO can be found using links with 39 TRIZ parameters. This cyclical process of identifying AOs can be repeated several times until the proportion of new companies found is less than 1% of all companies found (Table 1).

Table 1. TRIZ parameters

№	Parameter
1	Weight of moving object
2	The weight of a fixed object
3	The length of the moving object
4	The length of the fixed object
5	The area of the movable object
6	Fixed object area
7	Volume of a moving object
8	The volume of a fixed object
9	Speed
10	Strength
11	Voltage
12	The form
13	Resilience
14	Strength
15	The duration of the movable object
16	The duration of the motionless object
17	Temperature
18	Illumination
19	Energy of a moving object
20	Energy of a fixed object
21	Power
22	Energy loss
23	Substance loss
24	Loss of information
25	Loss of time
26	Amount of substance
27	Reliability
28	Measurement accuracy
29	Cooking accuracy
30	Harmful factors affecting the object
31	Harmful factors generated by the object itself
32	Ease of manufacture
33	Convenience of operation
34	Convenience of repair
35	Versatility, adaptation
36	Device complexity
37	Complexity of control
38	Degree of automation
39	Performance

3rd step: extracting relevant information from their SAO structures. Subjects are predefined nouns that describe a region. AO can provide 2 types of information: 1. Elements and fields 2. Objectives and effects of the invention. For elements and fields in this step, denoting actions are determined, while for the goals and effects, the AO obtained in the previous step can be used.

4th step: expansion of the array of SAO structures with additional information. This information serves to expand SAOs related to the goals and effects of inventions. To extract such information, phrases are used that are related to the main sentence with the words "to", "with a purpose", as well as partly with the turn.

5th step: information extracted from SAO structures is presented in a more visual and understandable form using modeling of several knowledge spheres, after which two categories—elements and fields, as well as goals and effects of inventions—are evaluated to determine and present technological capabilities.

2.1   Step 1. Patent Collection

Most previous studies of patent bases relied on the study of annotations, as key information about the invention. Annotations do contain brief descriptions, advantages of inventions. However, they do not provide comprehensive information about the details but contain only brief and superficial data.

Analysis of such parts as the claim and description allows to more accurately determine the invention or technology described in the patent. From the part of the description of the patent, we can distinguish detailed technical characteristics, components of the invention, a technical problem and technical solutions, as well as additional information related to the patent.

To extract the SAO structures in this step, the UDPIPE library was used, which presents sentences in the form of a semantic tree structure. At the root of the tree is the verb, which is an action in the structure of SAO. Each part of the sentence is associated with semantic roles (subject, object, etc.), as well as morphological features of the word (part of speech, gender, number, case). Based on this information, it is possible to distinguish SAO structures.

The structure of the patent for invention

- bibliographic data;
- name; objects
- description of the invention;
- claim;
- blueprints;
- essay.

2.2   Step 2. Significant SAO Extraction

This step is necessary in order to distinguish from the set of SAOs those SAO that will be the most "useful" for the analysis of the invention and which directly relate to the characteristics of the invention. This process consists of two sub clauses:

Definitive Terms for Subjects of the Invention
A patent describes a specific invention. Definitive nouns describe the subjects and essence of the invention. Typical nouns that describe the essence of the invention are "invention", "method", "approach", etc. By themselves, these terms are generic and do not carry any useful information about the invention. However, words that are associated with definitive terms may contain the most important characteristics of the invention. Such nouns very often appear in the text, so you can select them based on the frequency analysis of documents.

You can calculate the frequency of occurrence of a word in the text of the documents using the formula:

$$q = \sum t,$$ (1)

where i = 1.. n – the amount of a given word in all documents.

Therefore, the words that occur most often in various documents are assumed as definition terms. However, the list of the most frequently encountered words requires a more detailed "cleaning" of commonly used words (such as "what", "how", etc.), which can be done manually.

Using Engineering Parameters of TRIZ to Extract AO
In the Theory of solving research problems, there are 40 principles of the invention and 39 engineering parameters for solving problems. These 39 parameters can serve as a key point for extracting a set of joint-stock companies that are goals and effects (since they are very closely associated with solving problem problems). The next process is a 5-step procedure for finding key stock companies (Table 2).

Table 2. AO extraction

Step	Action
1	The initial set of Objects is extracted from 39 engineering parameters of TRIZ
2	The Object Set is updated using synonym dictionaries for the 39 parameters listed above
3	The set of actions associated with Objects is distinguished from patents
4	The set of Objects is updated again, taking into account the new set of Actions from step 3
5	Steps 3 and 4 are repeated until the critical level of new AOs is reached. This level is defined as 1% and less new AO from the total number of AOs found

For example, if at the very beginning the words "weight", "length", "speed", "pressure" were allocated as objects from the TRIZ parameters, then these parameters will be expanded with synonyms such as "energy", "influence" etc. With the addition of synonyms, the list of actions is expanded, which also leads to an increase in the number of AOs (Table 3).

Table 3. Parameters of TRIZ

№	Parameter	General parameter
1	Weight of moving object	Weight
2	The weight of a fixed object	
3	The length of the moving object	Length
4	The length of the fixed object	
5	The area of the movable object	Square
6	Fixed object area	
7	Volume of a moving object	Volume
8	The volume of a fixed object	
9	Speed	Speed
10	Strength	Strength
11	Voltage	Voltage
12	The form	The form
13	Resilience	Resilience
14	Strength	Strength
15	The duration of the movable object	Duration, action
16	The duration of the motionless object	
17	Temperature	Temperature
18	Illumination	Illumination
19	Energy of a moving object	Energy
20	Energy of a fixed object	
21	Power	Power
22	Energy loss	Energy loss
23	Substance loss	Substance
24	Loss of information	Time
25	Loss of time	Information
26	Amount of substance	Substance, quantity
27	Reliability	Reliability
28	Measurement accuracy	Accuracy, measurement, preparation
29	Cooking accuracy	
30	Harmful factors affecting the object	Factor, object, impact
31	Harmful factors generated by the object itself	
32	Ease of manufacture	Convenience, manufacturing, operation, repair
33	Convenience of operation	
34	Convenience of repair	
35	Versatility, adaptation	Versatility, adaptation
36	Device complexity	Complexity, device control
37	Complexity of control	
38	Degree of automation	Automation
39	Performance	Performance

2.3 Step 3. Analysis of SAO Structures

In the classical analysis of SAO structures, the action is considered as a link between subject and object. However, this structure can be considered from a similar point of view. The subject and the object are a set of inventions and parameters of the inventions. The action is used to classify information into 2 categories, based on the relationship between the subject and the object: elements/fields and goals/effects.

The first category is information about the parts of the invention, the composite components, the materials, the technologies used in the inventions, and the area to which the invention relates.

The second category is associated with the objectives and effects of the invention.

Words of action were identified in the analysis of AO structures. They are classified into two categories: elements/fields, and targets/effects. For further analysis, only O elements in the first category carry information relevant to the invention. While action words are not informative, because they were needed only to isolate the remaining parts of the SAO structure.

AO elements of the second category (targets/effects) in a bundle carry meaningful information. For example, the phrases "reduce size" and "increase size" carry the exact opposite effects (Table 4).

2.4 Step 4. Advanced SAO Analysis

In the proposal, not only the main SAOs identified in the past steps carry significant information. For the category of goal/effects, information can also be found in complex sentences, where the information sought is related to the main sentence with unions and the phrases "to", "then", "what", "due to the fact that" or adverbial participles, participles, and verbal adjectives. This step allows you to find additional information about the characteristics and objectives of the invention. For these purposes, the Updike library is used, which allows you to build a semantic sentence tree and highlight links between words, as well as highlight morphological information about words (parts of speech, gender, number, case, etc.)

Phrases associated with the main sentence with the words "because", "for" and so on. Will fall into the category of targets/effects, and the words "who", "whose", etc., with the category of "fields/elements" [12].

Example of the semantic analysis:

text = "The disadvantages of such discs include the insufficient quality of crumbling of the soil, depending on the speed of processing, and the increased formation of erosion-hazardous particles."/"Недостатки таких дисков включают недостаточное качество крошения почвы, зависящее от скорости обработки, и повышенное образование эрозионно-опасных частиц" (in Russian)

Table 4. Action words for action types

Action type	Action words
Elements and fields	
Elements	based, equipped, composed of, contain, have, include, provide, entail, require, use
Fields	relate, represent the means of description, can be customized, if, to be directly, to be customized with, be tuned in, be tuned in for a refund, be tuned in for polling, be tuned configure, to enable, configure, to direct, configure, to determine, to be tune up
Targets and effects	accept, access, take into account, acquire, activate, adapt, address, configure, advise, influence, join coincidence, aggregate, strive to decrease, strive to propose, warn, allow, change, analyze, submit an application, organize, agree, contact with, assume that, provide that an attempt to identify, balance, base on, be, be concerned, be customized, be configure to define, configure to direct, configure to enable, configure to be, be direct, be equipped, start, start, belong, invoice, count, call, can, capture, carry, call, change, switch between, charge, check, combine, come, communicate, compare, include, care, configure, configure for display, configure for identification, configure for operation, configure process, tune in to recognize, tune in to store, tune in to transfer, confirm, connect, save, review which consist of, contain, continue to perform, continue to monitor, control, transform, transfer, conform, create, define, depend, deploy, describe, design, develop, dictate, differentiate between, disable, expand, display, display, position inside, make a match, make a pop alert, driving, hug, release, use, inclusion, reach, end, interact with, entail, install, evaluate, exchange, execute, illustrate, expand, exhibit, find, match, focus, get, create, have, store, help decide, identify, ignore, immobilize, introduce, improve, enable, specify, inform, initiate, enter, install, instruct, integrate, interact, interact, interact, intervene, intervene in, engage, issue, join, know, not have, learn, lie down, block, lose, maintain create, manage, manipulate, display, match, means for, means that, measure, meet, mention, change, monitor, monitor for, mount, need to oblige, get, offer, offer, work, work without, exit, overcome, redefine, connect, perform, resolve, relate, play, predict, prevent, process, produce, program, prompt, suggest, provide, insert, achieve, react, receive, reduce, treat, relate, transmit, release, rendering, replenishment, replication, report, query, requirement, restriction, result, receiving, retrofitting, launching, say, scanning, searching, selecting, sending, meaning, separate from, should, show, close, simplify, so, decide, start, stop, store, suffer, tag, accept, track, transmit, use, use, check, evaluate, check, wait, warn, will, will encourage, will guide, to be in

1 недостатки (disadvantages)недостаток   NOUN _   Anima-
cy=Inan|Case=Nom|Gender=Masc|Number=Plur 4 obl
2 таких (such) такой   DET _   Case=Gen|Number=Plur 3 amod_ _
3 дисков (disks) диск NOUN _   Anima-
cy=Inan|Case=Gen|Gender=Masc|Number=Plur1 nmod
4 включают (include) включать VERB _ As-
pect=Imp|Mood=Ind|Number=Sing|Person=3|Tense=Pres|VerbForm=Fin|Voice=Mid
   0 root _ _
5 недостаточное (insufficient) недостаточный ADJ _
   Case=Acc|Degree=Pos|Gender=Neut|Number=Sing 6 amod_ _
6 качество (quality) качество NOUN _   Anima-
cy=Inan|Case=Acc|Gender=Neut|Number=Sing 4 nsubj_ _
7 крошения (crumbling) крошение NOUN _   Anima-
cy=Inan|Case=Gen|Gender=Neut|Number=Sing 6 nmod
8 почвы (soil) почва NOUN _   Anima-
cy=Inan|Case=Gen|Gender=Fem|Number=Sing 7 nmod   _ SpaceAfter=No
…

2.5   Step 5. Determination of Technological Capabilities

At the first stage of determining technological capabilities, the cluster analysis approaches are used to identify several subclasses of the area to a set of objects and object-action bundles found in the previous steps. For this, the CTM or LDA method can be applied. As a result, it may happen that the characteristics that belong to the category of elements and fields will be grouped into one subclass, while these characteristics in the group of goals and effects will be grouped into other subclasses differently.

In the second step, the resulting subclasses are evaluated and the most promising of them are selected. The result of cluster analysis will be the likelihood of each document matching each subclass. As a result, the document will be tied to the class where the probability of its compliance is greatest. Using information about the documents in each subclass, you can select the most promising subclasses.

As a result, links are established between the most promising subclasses from the category of fields/elements and subclasses from the category of effects/goals. This process is shown in Fig. 1.

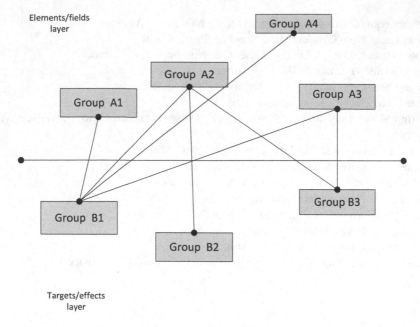

Fig. 1. Links between the most promising subclasses from the category of fields/elements and subclasses from the category of effects/goals.

Based on this information, a trend map [13] can be constructed. This map visualizes the development of subclasses and technologies over time. A map can consist of several layers (for example, word fields/elements and a goal/effect layer). In this way, a network of dedicated subclasses can be built. In this network, the size of a node depends on the number of patents associated with the subclass. At the same time, the relationship between the subclasses determines how strongly these sub-classes are related. This relationship is proportional to the number of patents that are present in that and in another subclass.

On this map, technological capabilities [14, 15] may include both the latest (i.e., the most modern subclasses), and those topics in which there is the greatest number of patents. In addition, those subclasses that have the most connections with other patents. The x-axis in these process charts is a time scale. It is proposed as an experiment to take patents of the last 5 years to analyze technological trends.

Another area of application of the described approach may be the construction of maps for studying the trends of competitors as a competitive advantage, which leads to technological capabilities. Unlike a trend map developed using all applicants' patents, this competitor card limits its attention to a single organization of concern. A map for each company visualizes the focus of technology development in the company, allowing for a comparative analysis between companies. Based on this map, the company can identify competitors with additional technologies and understand the technological advantages and disadvantages of the target area.

3   Conclusion

This article reviewed the approach to the analysis of technological trends based on SAO structures. A 5-step method is proposed for identifying SAO structures, their expansion, clustering, as well as the construction of flow charts. This approach can be applied to the analysis of technological trends (trend mapping), the construction of maps of competing organizations, as well as the prediction of new technological capabilities based on existing technologies.

Acknowledgement. The reported study was funded by RFBR according to the research projects 18-07-01086, 19-07-01200; and was funded by RFBR and Administration of the Volgograd region according to the research projects 19-47-340007, 19-41-340016.

References

1. Guo, J., Wang, X., Li, Q., Zhu, D.: Subject–action–object-based morphology analysis for determining the direction of technological change. Technol. Forecast. Soc. Change **105**, 27–40 (2016)
2. Lee, J., Kim, C., Shin, J.: Technology opportunity discovery to R&D planning: key technological performance analysis. Technol. Forecast. Soc. Change **119**, 53–63 (2017)
3. Moehrle, M.G., Walter, L., Geritz, A., Muller, S.: Patent-based inventor profiles as a basis for human resource decisions in research and development. R&D Manag. **35**(5), 513–524 (2005)
4. No, H.J., Lim, H.: Exploration of nanobiotechnologies using patent data. J. Intellect. Prop. **4**(3), 109–129 (2009)
5. Park, H., Yoon, J., Kim, K.: Identifying patent infringement using SAO based semantic technological similarities. Scientometrics **90**(2), 515–529 (2011)
6. Wang, X., Wang, Z., Huang, Y., Liu, Y., Zhang, J., Heng, X., et al.: Identifying R&D partners through subject–action–object semantic analysis in a problem & solution pattern. Technol. Anal. Strateg. Manag. **29**, 1–14 (2017)
7. Wich, Y., Warschat, J., Spath, D., Ardilio, A., König-Urban, K., Uhlmann, E.: Using a text mining tool for patent analyses: development of a new method for the repairing of gas turbines. In: 2013 Proceedings of PICMET 2013 Technology Management in the IT-Driven Services (PICMET), pp. 1010–1016. IEEE, 2013, July
8. Yoon, J., Kim, K.: Identifying rapidly evolving technological trends for R&D planning using SAO-based semantic patent networks. Scientometrics **88**(1), 213–228 (2011)
9. Yoon, J., Kim, K.: Detecting signals of new technological opportunities using semantic patent analysis and outlier detection. Scientometrics **90**(2), 445–461 (2012)
10. Yoon, B., Park, I., Coh, B.Y.: Exploring technological opportunities by linking technology and products: application of morphology analysis and text mining. Technol. Forecast. Soc. Change **86**, 287–303 (2014)
11. Zhang, Y., Zhou, X., Porter, A.L., Gomila, J.M.V.: How to combine term clumping and technology roadmapping for newly emerging science & technology competitive intelligence: "problem & solution" pattern based semantic TRIZ tool and case study. Scientometrics **101**(2), 1375–1389 (2014)
12. Korobkin, D.M., Fomenkov, S.A., Kravets, A.G., Golovanchikov, A.B.: Patent data analysis system for information extraction tasks. In: Hans, W. (ed.) Applied Computing 2016, IADIS, Germany, pp. 215–219 (2016). http://www.iadisportal.org/digital-library/patent-data-analysis-system-for-information-extraction-tasks

13. Korobkin, D.M., Fomenkov, S.A., Golovanchikov, A.B.: Method of identification of patent trends based on descriptions of technical functions. J. Phys. Conf. Ser. **1015**, 7 (2018). http://iopscience.iop.org/article/10.1088/1742-6596/1015/3/032065/pdf
14. Kamaev, V.A., Finogeev, A.G., Finogeev, A.A., Parygin, D.S.: Attacks and intrusion detection in wireless sensor networks of industrial SCADA systems. J. Phys. Conf. Ser. **803**, 1–6 (2017). Article no. 012063, http://iopscience.iop.org/article/10.1088/1742-6596/803/1/012063/pdf, https://doi.org/10.1088/1742-6596/803/1/012063
15. Korobkin, D.M., Fomenkov, S.A.: Method of detection of technical functions performed by physical effects. IOP Conf. Ser. Earth Environ. Sci. **194**, 7 (2018). http://iopscience.iop.org/article/10.1088/1755-1315/194/2/022014/pdf

Architectural Approach to Ontological Maintenance of Solving the Project Tasks in Conceptual Designing a Software Intensive System

P. Sosnin$^{(\boxtimes)}$ ⓘ, A. Kulikova ⓘ, and S. Shumilov

Ulyanovsk State Technical University, ul. Severny Venets,
Street 32, 432027 Ulyanovsk, Russia
sosnin@ulstu.ru, a.push1206@gmail.com, mars@mv.ru

Abstract. The paper focuses on developing a complex means of ontological maintenance (OM) in designing the software intensive systems (SIS). The essential feature of an offered version of the OM is accessible to such means via interfaces based on architectural views, any of which is realized in the form of the block-and-line scheme reflecting the states of possible applying the OM. Thus, any of such views is applied for developing the OM and its using via the certain interface presented in the understandable form. The prototype version of the OM was developed in the toolkit WIQA (Working In Questions and Answers), which provides the solution of design tasks at the conceptual stage of the development of the SIS. In the described case, this toolkit is applied for solving the task of developing the OM as the complex embedded to the WIQA. In its turn, the complex is intended for the ontological maintenance of solving the project task in conceptual designing of any SIS.

Keywords: Architectural modeling · Conceptual designing · Design thinking · Ontological maintenance · Project task · Software intensive system

1 Introduction

Professionally mature development of a modern SIS is unthinkable without the mandatory construction and operational use of its architectural representation (Architecture Description, AD), which is considered to be a very important version of the existence of the SIS, demanded at all stages of its life cycle. Architectural modeling is recognized as a very important kind of designer's activity that facilitates achieving success in developing the SIS. Such an integral effect because results of modeling are aimed at a constructive expression of the necessary understanding and help to manage the process of designing.

That is why the experience of architectural modeling finds its normative expression in the international standards among which it needs to mark the standard IEEE-1497: 2000 and its extension ISO/IEC/IEEE 42010: 2011 [1]. By the last standard, at the conceptual stage of designing the SIS, it needs to create the architectural description (AD) that integrates a set of architectural views (block-and-line schemes with their

© Springer Nature Switzerland AG 2019
A. G. Kravets et al. (Eds.): CIT&DS 2019, CCIS 1084, pp. 15–26, 2019.
https://doi.org/10.1007/978-3-030-29750-3_2

symbolic descriptions) that express in visualized forms a set of important interests (concerns, $\{C_i\}$) of stakeholders, the opinion of which should be considered in the SIS to be designed. It must be said; the AD combines a set of high-level requirements and decisions in their consistent complex describing the SIS as a wholeness.

Developing this complex, the designers conceptually solve the certain set of the project tasks $\{Z_j\}$, applying a project language that is formed on the course of designing. The kernel of this language is a project ontology, operative creating and using of which define the main feature of the ontological maintenance concerned in this paper. Therefore, it means the set of the project tasks $\{Z_j\}$ includes the subset $S(\{Z_j\})$ of tasks that must be solved in the processes of the OM.

This paper focuses on defining the subset $S(\{Z_j\})$ and our approach to solving these tasks in the toolkit WIQA, which provides the solution of design tasks at the conceptual stage of the development of the SIS [2]. In the described case, this toolkit is applied for solving the task of developing the OM as the complex embedded to the WIQA. In its turn, the complex is intended for the ontological maintenance of solving the project task in conceptual designing of any SIS.

The remainder of the article is structured as follows. Section 2 discloses grounds of our approach to architectural prototyping aimed at controlled understanding in work with project tasks. Necessary prototypes are built with the use of automated design thinking in the frame of the conceptual space. Section 3 points out related works. Prototyping of the OM is described in Sect. 4, and the paper is concluded in Sect. 5.

2 Preliminary Bases

2.1 Features of the Architectural Modeling in the WIQA-Environment

For the set of architectural views that make up the architecture of the developed SIS, it is required to be coordinated so that they form integrity corresponding to the theory of the SIS-project [3]. Since the theory of the project and the architecture of the SIS are built in parallel on the course of designing, they complement each other. Moreover, each architectural view must be the correct application of the project theory, and prompts its development, providing interpretation of theoretical constructs and contributing architectural understanding.

Which means that it is useful to include the view from the viewpoint of theorizing in a coherent set of architectural views materialized in the WIQA, the structure of which is shown in Fig. 1 where it is indicated a number of essences and components involved in our the implementation of our approach to conceptual designing the SIS [2]. The choice of such an integral view on the WIQA toolkit is caused by the intention to clarify the conditions, in which designers have to use the ontological support of their conceptual activity. In the shown structure, the features of this kind of activity reflect the name of blocks, any of which can be interpreted as the certain source of concerns for architectural modeling, for example, for modeling from the viewpoint of working with tasks.

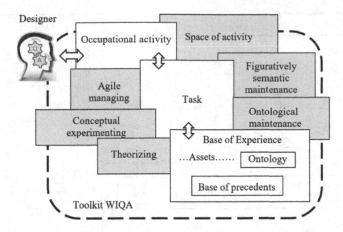

Fig. 1. Structure of the toolkit WIQA from the viewpoint of working with tasks

In Fig. 1, there are no links between the blocks, but for the blocks, we use two colors ("white" and "gray") to separate the main line of designer' activity (white color) from the accompanying actions (gray color).

The main line of activity focuses on solving the project task, on the course of which the designer interacts with the necessary experience and its models that are accumulated in the Base of Experience. In the frame of such activity, the designer builds the reusable descriptions of the solved tasks (models of precedents) that are placed in the Base of Precedents. Indicated blocks of the main activity lead to the corresponding architectural views objectified in the WIQA.

In actions of the main line, the designer uses automated support (blocks marked in gray) that help to increase the quality of working with tasks, their groups, and systems. Such blocks objectify an additional subset of the architectural views on work with project tasks in the toolkit WIQA. We continuously improve these blocks, one of which is responsible for the ontological maintenance.

2.2 Prototyping of Architectural Solutions

A very important part of the WIQA is a set of tools for programming in pseudo code intended for two purposes:

- Tools allow users (and therefore creators) of WIQA to expand the functional potential of this toolkit;
- Using these tools, one can build simple applications or application prototypes by programming a suitable shell above the WIQA.

In particular, we apply pseudocode programming for investigating the mastered functionalities embedded in the WIQA for their continuous improvement. In such work with orientation on the nature of design thinking [4], we use our version [3] of the automated design thinking that is shown in Fig. 2.

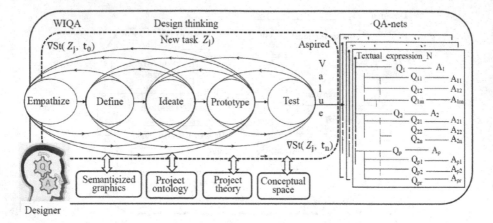

Fig. 2. The iterative process of design thinking

The scheme indicates that process of design thinking is implemented in the instrumental environment WIQA in conditions when the designer can use such artifacts as Project ontology, Project theory and Conceptual space that are created on the course of designing in parallel with other designers' activity. The main attention of actions in the frame of the scheme focused on formulating the statement of the task and also on representing, moving, evaluating and managing components of reasoning in forms of question-answer analysis. All these actions described in detail in the paper [3]. Additionally, actions include building the diagrammatic representation of the view (for example. the view Vj) and prototyping the solution of the task (for example, the task Zj).

The designer creates any diagrammatic representation with the help of a complex of means indicated in the scheme as Semanticized graphics or shortly SG. This component of the WIQA was conceived for objectifying the mental imagination in conceptual experimenting applied in design thinking [2]. By other words, in this process, mental imagination is a source of intellectual "guessing" generated by the right hemisphere of the brain, and any result of such abductive guessing is useful to register in the graphical form reflected its structure as a wholeness.

The kernel of the SG is a specialized graphical editor that is intended for achieving the necessary understanding, the result of which is registered by the set of chosen views (block-and-line schemes and their descriptions). What is especially important, the potential of the SG includes the possibilities for pseudo code programming as the processes of developing the understandable graphics so their interactive using. For example, the designer can create the schemes, elements of which not only express the certain semantics but fulfill the role of references on other schemes or program units or applications outside of the WIQA environment. So, the developed version of the DT-approach is the constructive way for solving the tasks from the subset $S(\{Zj\})$.

3   Related Works

The standard ISO/IEC/IEEE 42010: 2011 envisages that any "concern" may be architecturally described with a coordinated group of useful "points of view" and corresponding "views." For example, the authors of [5] recommend considering such a construct as an "architectural decision" by using the Decision Detail viewpoint, Decision Relationship viewpoint, Decision Chronology viewpoint, and Decision Stakeholder Involvement. Moreover, the same authors in the following publication [6] proposed to expand the given set by the inclusion in it the Decision Forces Viewpoint.

Another trick is given in the publication [7], in which its authors suggest associating with the "Context Description Viewpoint" of the developed SIS the following concerns:

1. "System Scope: Where is the boundary between the system and its context, and what interactions between the system and its context cross this boundary?
2. System Users: Who are the users of the system; what are their types, roles, and characteristics; and how and where do they access and use the system?
3. External Dependencies: Which external services and/or applications are relevant for the system, including their properties and providers?
4. Execution Environment: What is the expected or desired technical execution environment that the system will be running on?
5. Stakeholder Impact: Which stakeholders, including organizations and their resources, influence the system and in what way? What influence does the system have on organizations and stakeholders?"

Another possibility of accounting and materialization of "concerns" is their specification, distribution of a set of types and integration of a set of (distributed) constituent concerns within the framework of "architectural types." With such a possibility they associate an "aspect-oriented" representation and the materialization of concerns [8].

The real practice of architectural decisions is discussed in the industrial case study published in [9]. The current retrospection view on the theory and practice of architectural descriptions is presented in the paper [10].

For our version of the architectural approach to the ontological maintenance of solving the project tasks, one more group of related works includes papers concern the subject area of ontologies. In this group, we mark the paper [11] focuses on developing the software systems in the context of ontological problems. It needs also to mark the paper [12], in which the project ontology is applied for the support of architectural recommendations, the paper [13] investigating the use of fuzzy measures in selecting the architecture tactics and the paper [14] describing the use of a maturity model in specifications of the architecture maintainability.

4   Prototyping the Ontological Maintenance

The prototype of the ontological support tool was developed within the WIQA environment with the help of its graphics editor as well as its pseudo code programming environment. In this section, the overall structure of the prototype is described, and its main architectural views are presented.

All the views relate to the work with a so-called discourse, which is considered a conventional unit for processing a project. A discourse is a short text containing some project requirements or reasoning results of a designer. In a particular case, a project task statement can become a discourse.

To start working with a discourse, one should do the following:

1. Open the project "Architectural views."
2. Select the Index procedure.
3. In the global menu, select Pseudo code -> Launch Interpreter.
4. Click "Autorun."
5. Go to the graphics editor.

Figure 3 shows the task tree of the project. Each task presents a separate view, which can be launched in the graphics editor.

Fig. 3. Task tree

To enable switching between various views we developed three pseudo-code procedures:

- the Index procedure which is launched when a user starts working with the tool, it includes the operation to open the graphics editor;
- the Open procedure which opens the desired view saved in a file;
- the Save procedure which saves all the changes in the current view.

We exported the Open and Save procedures to the XML-file which allowed importing them to the required QA-unit (task) without creating them from scratch,

Let us consider the details of the Index procedure (see Fig. 3). The DD_OpenEditor () command opens the graphics editor. The DD_Load ("diagram_file_path") command opens the view from the *.nspj file, and the DD_LoadEvents ("events_file_path") loads all the events related to the current view (for example, links between diagram elements and QA-units) which are saved in an XML Schema file. And, finally, the FINISH command stops executing the pseudo code.

The default (integral) view is available in Fig. 4. It shows all the forms of a discourse that may exist in the context of the ontological support of a software project.

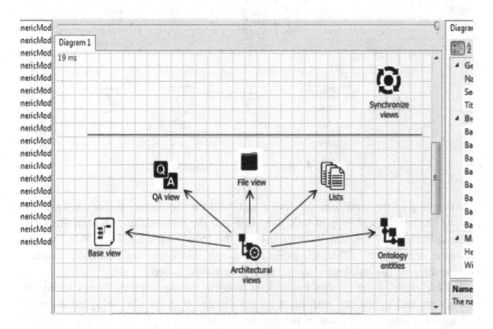

Fig. 4. Integral view of a discourse

Double click on each icon leads to the opening of the corresponding view. Currently, there are five such views:

- base view;
- QA view (discourse in the QA protocol);
- file view (discourse saved in a file);
- lists (discourse processing results);
- ontology entities (concepts related to discourse).

In the top right corner, there is a button which synchronizes all these views. Figure 5 shows the discourse base view.

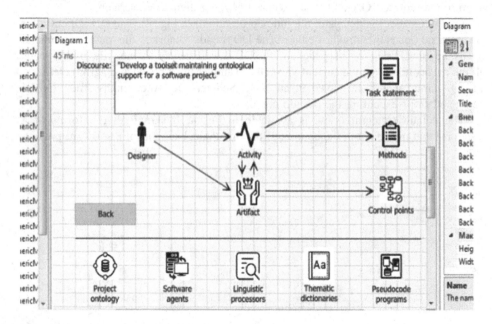

Fig. 5. Base view of a discourse

At the top of the view, one can find a text field for the current discourse. One can also see the ontological support task statement and the methods used within this task.

Double click on the Activity icon leads to the view which allows working with a discourse step by step: filling the project ontology, analyzing the discourse contents with the help of the ontological data, creating semantic schemes, etc.

Double click on the Control Points icon leads to the view which allows seeing all the changes and operations performed on the discourse in the chronological order as well as the changes in the text of the discourse itself.

At the bottom of the diagram, there are instruments for working with a discourse. Double click on the Back button allows going back to the previous view.

In the framework of the ontological support for a project, there are some activities that can be performed automatically – most of them are connected with text processing. Therefore, some software agents were developed in order to take over corresponding activities when there is data to process. When clicking on a certain icon an agent starts its work (Fig. 6).

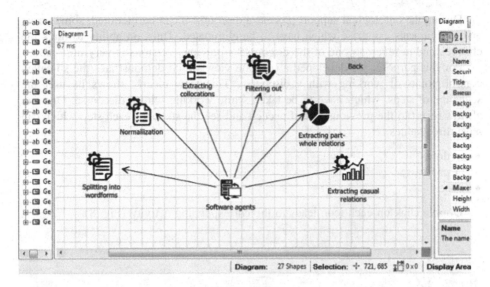

Fig. 6. Software agents

In the Pseudo code Library view, some procedures used in the ontological support toolset are presented. These are the procedures which help to interact between various modules of the OwnWIQA system (for example, ontological editor, QA-tree, graphics editor, etc.) (Fig. 7).

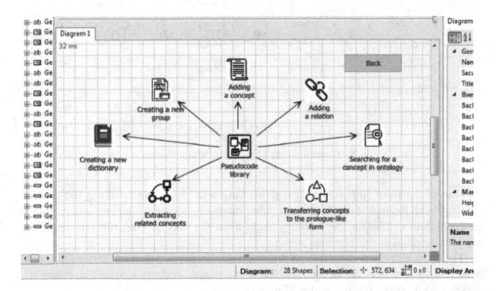

Fig. 7. Pseudo code program library

During the ontological support process a discourse it can be modified, some errors and inaccuracies can arise which have to be eliminated. Thus, an ability to track the changes and to revert to one of the discourse"s previous versions is very important.

For this purpose, we developed a separate view which demonstrates the so-called control points of working with a discourse. This view clearly shows its user the sequence of steps, which have to be taken while working with a discourse. One can always revert to the previous step if needed and see the status of each step which can have three values:

- to do;
- in progress;
- done.

Double click on each icon leads to the corresponding activity (Fig. 8).

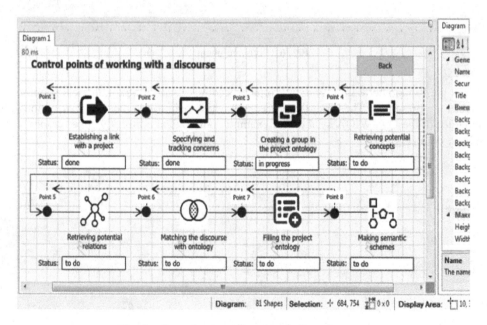

Fig. 8. Control points of working with a discourse

One of the most important steps of working with discourse is filling the project ontology with the new data. A user can either manually add new concepts and relations between them or choose the ontology units from the lists of potential concepts and relations (created at the previous steps).

The view allows entering data to the text fields (concepts, their definitions, relation types, etc.) which become string variables in the pseudo-code procedures launched by clicking on a corresponding button (Fig. 9).

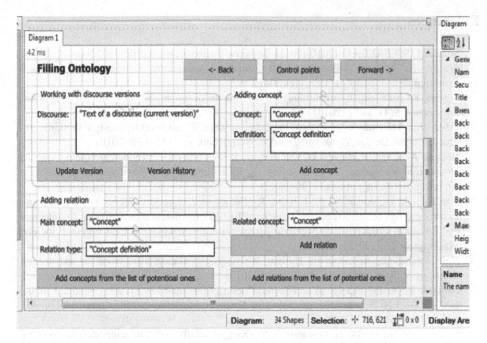

Fig. 9. Filling the ontology.

5 Conclusions

Creating and using architectural models are the key factor in the successful development of modern SIS. Such models register the necessary understanding, reflecting the corresponding essences as a wholeness that is especially important for architectural views, any of which combines semanticized graphics with a necessary symbolic description written in the project language.

In the offered approach, the designer develops any view in the process of solving the architectural task with the use of automated design thinking, means of which are embedded into the WIQA toolkit. Among these means, the specialized graphical editor occupies the very important place. This editor helps to build branched out and visualized structures that express not only separate views but also their programmed compositions.

We apply this approach to improve the existed version of the ontological maintenance embedded into the WIQA toolkit. Now, the new version of the OM is realized in the prototype form, graphical elements of which are drawn with indexed references when it is necessary. By other words, functions of the OM are accessible th the designer via interfaces any of which is the prototype version of the corresponding architectural view on the OM.

Acknowledgments. This work is supported by the Russian Fund for Basic Research (RFBR) with Grants # 18- 07-00989a, 18-47-730016 р_a , 18-47-732012 р_мк, and Ministry of Science and High Education with the State Contract № 2.1534.2017/4.6.

References

1. Standard ISO/IEC/IEEE 42010 (2011). https://www.iso.org/standard/50508.html
2. Sosnin, P.: Experience-Based Human-Computer Interactions: Emerging Research and Opportunities. IGI-Global, Hershey (2017)
3. Sosnin, P.: Substantially evolutionary theorizing in designing software-intensive systems. Information 9(4), 1–29 (2018)
4. Dorst, K.: The nature of design thinking, in DTRS8 interpreting design thinking. In: Proceeding of Design Thinking Research Symposium, pp. 131–139 (2010)
5. Bedjeti, A., Lago, P., Lewis, G.A., De Boer, R.D., Hilliard, R.: Modeling context with an architecture viewpoint. In: Proceeding of IEEE International Conference on Software Architecture (ICSA), pp. 117–120 (2017)
6. Van Heesch, U., Avgeriou, P., Hilliard, R.: Forces on architecture decisions - a viewpoint. In: Proceedings of the 2012 Joint Working IEEE/IFIP Conference on Software Architecture and European Conference on Software Architecture, pp. 101–110. IEEE Computer Society, Washington, DC (2012)
7. Van Heesch, U., Avgeriou, P., Hilliard, R.: A documentation framework for architecture decisions. J. Syst. Softw. 85(4), 795–820 (2012)
8. Hilliard, R.: Using aspects in architectural description. In: Moreira, A., Grundy, J. (eds.) EAW 2007. LNCS, vol. 4765, pp. 139–154. Springer, Heidelberg (2007). https://doi.org/10.1007/978-3-540-76811-1_8
9. Dasanayake, S., Markkula, J., Aaramaa, S., Oivo, M.: Software architecture decision-making practices and challenges: an industrial case study. In: Proceedings of 24th Australasian Software Engineering Conference, pp. 88–97 (2015)
10. Hasselbring, W.: Software architecture: past, present, future. The Essence of Software Engineering, pp. 169–184. Springer, Cham (2018). https://doi.org/10.1007/978-3-319-73897-0_10
11. Eden, A.H., Turner, R.P.: Problems in the ontology of computer programs. Appl. Ontology 2(1), 13–36 (2007)
12. Bhat, M., Shumaiev, K., Biesdorf, A., Hohenstein, U., Hassel, M., Matthes, F.: An ontology-based approach for software architecture recommendations. In: Proceedings of the 3rd Americas Conference on Information Systems, vol. 4, pp. 3110–3120 (2017)
13. Alashqar, A.M., El-Bakry, H.M., Elfetouh, A.: A framework for selecting architectural tactics using fuzzy measures. Int. J. Softw. Eng. Knowl. Eng. 27(3), 475–498 (2015)
14. Rathfelder, C., Groenda, H.: Towards an architecture maintainability maturity model. Softwaretechnik-Trends 28(4), 3–7 (2008)

The Study of Neural Networks Effective Architectures for Patents Images Processing

Alla G. Kravets[1]([✉]) [iD], Sergey Kolesnikov[1], Natalia Salnikova[2] [iD],
Mikhail Lempert[3], and Olga Poplavskaya[4]

[1] Volgograd State Technical University, Volgograd, Russia
agk@gde.ru, sk375@bk.ru
[2] Volgograd Institute of Management – Branch of the Russian Presidential
Academy of National Economy and Public Administration, Volgograd, Russia
ns3112@mail.ru
[3] Technion - Israel Institute of Technology, 3200003 Haifa, Israel
lempertmi@gmail.com
[4] Volgograd State Medical University, Volgograd, Russia
poplavok9@rambler.ru

Abstract. In this paper, we identified the main classes of patent images that will define the neural network for comparing the corresponding classes. Training, test, and testing samples were formed for selected classes of patent images. Existing neural network architectures for working with patent images and machine learning libraries were analyzed; the deep convolutional neural network architecture and the open libraries Keras and Theano were selected to search for relevant patent images. During the implementation of this project, the neural network was trained to recognize selected classes of patent images, and an analysis of the trained model was performed. A testing methodology was chosen, the accuracy of the neural network was evaluated depending on the size of the patent images, the number of epochs and the size of the training sample. Control over neural network training was ensured by means of test and test samples so that the neural network was not retrained and worked correctly on patent images that it did not see; given an assessment of the achievements of the testing objectives.

Keywords: Neural network · Neural network architecture · Machine learning · Deep learning · Training samples · Patent image processing

1 Introduction

There has been a progressive growth of interest in neural networks over the past years. This fact reflects the successful application of neural networks found in various fields, such as business, information technology, geology, medicine, physics [1]. In addition, one of the latest trends is that neural networks are used in practice in industries, which require solving forecasting and control problems [2]. The areas of application of neural networks are diverse in nature, among others are adaptive control, process automation, organization of associative memory, the creation of expert systems, processing of analog and digital signals [3, 4]. It should be noted that the application is due to the availability of non-linear modeling and relatively simple implementation [5]. These characteristics make neural networks indispensable and widely used in the process of solving various kinds of complex and diverse tasks.

The topic of this research is the development of a patent image recognition system based on an artificial neural network apparatus. The task of patent image recognition is very important, as the possibility of automatic recognition by computer patent images brings many new opportunities in the development of science and technology, such as the development of systems for searching people and other objects in photographs, monitoring the quality of products without human intervention, automatic traffic control others.

As for artificial neural networks, in recent years, this section of machine learning has been increasingly developed due to the significant increase in computing power of existing computers and the widespread use of graphics cards for computing, which allows to train neural networks of much greater depth and complex structure than before, which, in turn, show significantly better results compared to other algorithms for many problems, especially patent image recognition tasks [6, 7].

This direction of the development of neural networks has been called deep learning and is the most successful and rapidly developing at present.

In the course of this study, a patent image recognition system based on artificial neural networks was developed, which computational experiments were conducted in order to identify the most efficient architectures for working with patent images.

The system approach method was used as a research methodology: neural networks were studied as an integral system, its elements were considered, as well as a whole set of connections and relations between them.

2 Neural Networks Architectures for Images Processing

Currently, neural networks with different architectures are used to work with images. Deep neural networks have great computational power. The main incentive underlying the development of machine recognition and image classification systems is the ImageNet Challenge campaign. Consider the modern architecture of deep neural networks to classify patent images and summarize the main advantages of each of these architectures.

2.1 Deep Neural Network

To work with images, you can use a regular neural network. It was successfully used for recognizing handwritten images of 28×28 pixels. This network had two layers, an input layer with 800 neurons and an output layer with 10 neurons. The input from each of the 800 neurons receives values from all 784 (28 * 28) pixels of the image. On the output layer of 10 neurons in a digit for each neuron. The problem of using this architecture is that its training requires a large amount of data and with increasing image dimensionality, an even greater number of values arrive at the input layer of each neuron (a large number of weights for training). And also the image is presented in the form of a flat array – information about the topology is lost.

Usually, a deep neural network consisting of many hidden layers (more than 2) is used to classify images (Fig. 1). Such a network is successfully used in many areas. Its drawback – the learning process can be very slow. Learning u deep neural network is the most difficult part of deep learning because you need a large data set and you need a large amount of computing power. To train the network, you need to submit the prepared data to it and compare the output generated by it with the results from our test data set. Since the network has not yet been trained, the results will be incorrect.

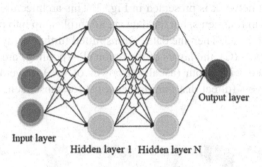

Fig. 1. Deep neural network

After skipping all the data, you can define a function that will show us how the results of the algorithm differ from the real data. This function is called the loss function.

Ideally, the loss function should be zero. In this case, the output of the network is fully consistent with the results of the test data set. To reduce the value of the loss function it is necessary to change the weight between the neurons. You can do this randomly until the loss function becomes zero, but this is not very efficient. Instead, the gradient descent method is used [8]. Gradient descent is a method that allows you to find the minimum of a function. The essence of the method consists of a slight change in the weights after each iteration. By calculating the derivative (or gradient) of the loss function for a certain set of weights, we can determine in which direction the minimum is.

2.2   Convolutional Neural Network

The name of these networks comes from the convolution operation, which is an easy way to perform complex operations using the convolution kernel. The SNA does not use predefined convolution kernels, since this problem is nontrivial, but instead they are determined as a result of learning [9]. For example, if there is a 200×200 image, then all 40 thousand pixels will not be processed immediately. Instead, the network counts a square of size $n \times n$ (usually from the upper left corner), then moves 1 pixel and counts a new square, and so on. These inputs are then transmitted through convolutional layers, in which not all nodes are interconnected. These layers tend to shrink with depth, and the powers of two are often used: 32, 16, 8, 4, 2, 1. In practice, a fully connected neural layer is attached to the end of the SNA for further data processing.

Principles of convolutional neural networks:

- local perception;
- shared weights;
- reduction of dimension.

A convolutional neural network (CNN) is well suited for 2D data, such as images; based on a neurobiological model of the visual cortex. This type of network is very different from the rest, mainly used for working with graphical and audio information. The model of such a network is presented in Fig. 2. This architecture does not process the data entirely, but in fragments, but the data are not broken up into parts, but a kind of sequential run is performed. Then the data is transmitted further in layers. In addition to the convolutional layers (C), the layers of the union (P – pooling) are also used. Merge layers are compressed with depth (usually a power of two). Several perceptrons are added to the final layers (direct distribution network) for subsequent data processing.

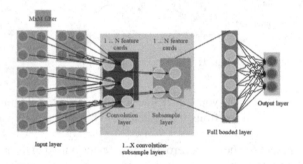

Fig. 2. Convolutional neural network

This architecture is most suitable for image recognition and classification. With its help it is possible to parallelize the calculations, and, as a result, the use of graphics processors. However, this architecture needs to be configured with a large number of variable parameters, such as the number of layers, the number of nuclei in each layer, the activation functions of each neuron, and many others.

This architecture is similar to a direct distribution network, but with a shift in time. Advantages of the convolutional neural network: requires less neuron connections relative to a typical neural network; many different versions of architectures (GoogLeNet [10], AlexNet [11], ZFNet, VGGNet, ResNet).

2.3 Siamese Neural Network

The Siamese neural network is commonly used to find a similarity or relationship between two comparable things; it contains two identical subnets, most often convolutional neural networks (Fig. 3). This is a neural network architecture class that contains two or more identical subnets. Identical here means that they have the same configuration with the same parameters and weights. The parameter update is reflected through both subnets. Siamese neural networks are popular among tasks that include the similarity or relationship between two comparable things [12].

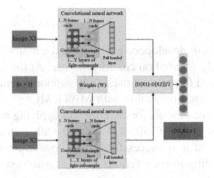

Fig. 3. Siamese neural network

For example, comparing text retelling, where the source data are two sentences, and the result is a score of how similar they are to each other; or verification of the signature on the image, whether two signatures are from the same person.

Usually, in such tasks, two identical subnets are used to process two source images, and the other module will take their result and make a final assessment. The advantage of the Siamese neural network is that it solves the similarity problem and the relationship between images, and the drawbacks are the same as that of the convolutional neural network, and the libraries do not provide the standard possibility of creating this architecture.

3 Analysis of Existing Deep Learning Libraries

To implement the algorithms for working with neural networks in the developed system, it was decided to use one of the existing libraries. For this purpose, such libraries as Keras, Caffe, Theano, and TensorFlow were considered. Consider each of them in more detail.

3.1 Keras Library

Keras is a high-level neural network development API written in Python and able to work on top of TensorFlow, CNTK or Theano. The library was designed with a focus on rapid experimentation, which is key to doing good research.

Keras allows you to easily and quickly create prototypes (due to convenience, modularity, and extensibility), supports both convolutional neural networks and recurrent neural networks, as well as their combinations. Also, the library works on both the CPU and the GPU.

The library contains many implementations of widely used structural blocks of the neural network, such as layers, objects, activation functions, optimizers, and many tools that facilitate the work with images and text data [13].

3.2 Caffe Library

The Caffe library - and the developers put a special emphasis on it - unlike their predecessors, is completely focused on commercial use. At the same time, all the code is open, written in C++, and the product itself fully supports writing custom algorithms in Python/NumPy and is also compatible with MATLAB.

Caffe offers a wide range of tools for creating and applying advanced deep learning algorithms. Among other things, Caffe was created with a good foundation for the future - and at the moment it is successfully used to solve problems of image and speech recognition, including in such serious areas as astronomy and robotics [14].

3.3 Theano Library

Theano is an extension of the Python language that allows you to efficiently calculate mathematical expressions containing multidimensional arrays. Theano is developed in the LISA lab to support the rapid development of machine learning algorithms.

The library is implemented in Python, supported on Windows, Linux and Mac OS. Theano includes a compiler that translates mathematical expressions written in Python into effective C or CUDA code. Theano provides a basic set of tools for configuring neural networks and learning them. It is possible to implement multi-layer fully interconnected networks (Multi-Layer Perceptron), convolutional neural networks (CNN), recurrent neural networks (RNN), auto-encoders and limited Boltzmann machines. Various activation functions are also provided, in particular, sigmoidal, softmax-function, cross-entropy. In the course of training, a packet gradient descent is used [15].

Since this library is low-level, the process of creating a model and determining its parameters requires writing volume and noisy code. However, the advantage of Theano is its flexibility, as well as the possibility of implementing and using its own components. Also, the advantages of the library are close integration with NumPy, transparent use of the GPU, effective differentiation of variables, fast and stable optimization, dynamic code generation in C, advanced features of unit testing and self-tests.

Theano is widely used in high-intensity computational research where greater flexibility is needed.

3.4 TensorFlow Library

TensorFlow is an open source library for numerical computation using flow graphs. The nodes in the graph are mathematical operations, and the edges of the graph are multidimensional data arrays transferred between them. The flexible architecture allows you to deploy computations on both a CPU and a GPU on a personal computer, server computer, cluster or mobile device using a single API. On graphics processors for graphics cards, calculations are possible in applications for general computing using the additional CUDA extension for GPGPU. TensorFlow runs on 64-bit Linux servers and desktops, Windows and Mac OS X, as well as mobile platforms, including Android and iOS. TensorFlow was originally developed by researchers and engineers working on the GoogleBrain team at the Google Machinery Intelligence research organization for machine learning and research into deep neural networks, but this system can also be used in other areas. TensorFlow provides APIs for the Python language, as well as APIs for C++, Haskell, Java, Go, and Rust. In addition, there is a third-party package for R. TensorFlow calculations are expressed as stateful data flow graphs. The Google library of algorithms instructs neural networks to perceive information and reason like a person, so new applications initially possess these "human" qualities. The name TensorFlow itself comes from the name of the operations that these neural networks perform on multidimensional data arrays. These multidimensional arrays are referred to as "tensors", as mathematical objects of the same name that linearly transform the elements of one linear space into elements of another. Task TensorFlow – teaches neural networks to detect and recognize patterns and correlations in data arrays [16].

3.5 Comparison of the Libraries Functionality

During the review of deep learning libraries for the Python programming language, four libraries were considered: Keras, Caffe, Theano, and TensorFlow. Comparative characteristics are shown in Table 1. For comparison, the following criteria were highlighted: name, creator, operating system, programming language, provision of the possibility of creating fully connected neural networks (FC NN), convolutional neural networks (CNN), autoencoders (AE) and recurrent neural networks (RNN), support for OpenMP technology and the possibility of cloud computing.

Table 1. Library functionality for Keras, Caffe, Theano, and TensorFlow

Title	Keras	Caffe	Theano	TensorFlow
Creator	Francois Chollet	University of Berkeley	Montreal University	Google
OS	Linux, Windows, macOS	Linux, Windows, macOS, Android	Cross platform	Linux, Windows, macOS
Language	Python	C ++, Python, Matlab	Python	C ++, Python
FCNN	+	+	+	+
CNN	+	+	+	+
AE	+	–	+	+
RNN	+	+	+	+
Support OpenMP	–	–	+	–
Cloud computing	+	+	+	+

To implement a qualitative method of searching for relevant patent images, it is necessary to develop a comparison algorithm for each class of patent images. This is a voluminous task. As part of this study, it was decided to implement a software module whose task is to assign a class to patent images in the search base and come with an application using the Deep Convolutional Neural Network (DCNN) architecture. As well as assigning the calculated perceptual hash to all patent images for later comparison.

For the development of the program was used library Keras. It uses the Theano library to perform efficient calculations. Keras allows you to quickly and easily describe a neural network. Keras builds a neural network and invokes high-performance methods from Theano library for calculations. Python is used as a programming language in Keras.

4 Classification of Patent Images

Neural network architecture was used (Fig. 4), consisting of three repeating layers of convolution and a subselection to select features of patent images and a fully connected classifier of 64 neurons and an output layer of 8 neurons.

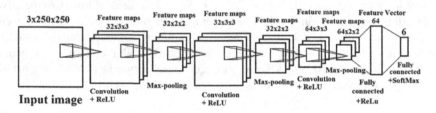

Fig. 4. Convolutional neural network architecture

The use of the ReLU activation function (Fig. 5) is due to the fact that it shows good results when training neural networks and is responsible for cutting off unnecessary parts in the channel (with a negative output). For the training of the neural network, training, test and testing samples formed from classified patent images were used.

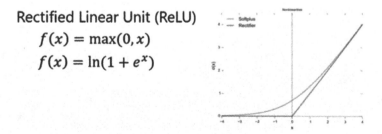

Fig. 5. Activation function ReLU

For optimization, the gradient descent method with a mini-sample size of 32 is used, that is, the first 32 patent images are taken, the direction of the gradient is determined and, in accordance with this direction, we perform a change in weights, etc. Also, epochs are used for teaching - how many times do we perform training using a data set.

4.1 Selection of the Main Classes of Patent Images for the Training Sample Formation

The accuracy of the neural network was evaluated, depending on the size of the patent image and the number of epochs (Table 2). For neural network training, 2400 patent images and 800 patent images were used for the test sample. Data for training/verification/testing did not change. The training took place on a personal computer (IntelCore i3-4160, 8 GB RAM). Re-training of the neural network, in all cases, did not happen.

Table 2. The accuracy of the neural network, depending on the size of the patent image and the number of epochs

Patent image size	Number of epochs	Training time	Accuracy on training data, %	Accuracy on test data, %
100 × 100	8	12 min	26.46	20.15
100 × 100	16	20 min	35	22.88
200 × 200	8	35 min	28	21.25
200 × 200	16	1 h 19 min	38	25
200 × 200	32	2 h 44 min	50	28
400 × 400	16	4 h	37	19
400 × 400	40	8 h 52 min	51	30

Since the retraining of the neural network did not occur, was not, the maximum of the used training sample was reached. The potential for the used sampling is. The results of evaluating the accuracy of the neural network show that the classification based on IPC has room for improvement, but the results are unsatisfactory [17].

So a promising approach was taken to improve the patent image search - it is to adopt the analysis and correspondence to each patent image class, for example, to compare the block diagrams with each other with the developed metric for the block diagrams. The obtained patent images were manually distributed into 6 classes of patent images (technical drawing, chemical structure, diagram, gene sequence, block diagram, table). To create a training sample, 1000 patent images were taken for each class. 600 patent images training sample, 200 verification, and 200 testing.

4.2 Training the Neural Network to Recognize the Selected Classes of Patent Images

To assess the achievement of the goal of testing, the following criteria were put forward:

- average recognition accuracy of 6 classes of patent images more than 70%;
- the possibility of achieving high accuracy with increasing training sample, training time and patent image size;
- the neural network should not be retrained and work correctly on patent images that it did not see.

A training sample of 3,600 patent images was taken for the experiments. On the patent images, there are different types of flowcharts, drawings, graphs/diagrams, tables, gene sequences, and chemical structures. All patent images are divided into 6 groups of (100, 300, 600) patent images for each class.

An experiment was conducted to analyze the dependence of the recognition accuracy of the neural network on the size of the training sample.

Three models (100, 300, 600) of patent images for each class were trained. The training sample of 200 patent images per class in all cases. The number of epochs is 16, the size of patent images is 250×250. The results of the experiment are shown in Tables 3 and 4.

Table 3. The accuracy of recognition of the neural network class on the size of the training sample

Patent image class/number of patent images	100	300	600
Technical drawing	44.5%	62.5%	59%
Chemical structure	5.5%	23.5%	82%
Diagram	79.5%	81.5%	82%
Gene sequence	4.5%	9.5%	68%
Block diagram	10.5%	2%	37.5%
Table	84%	90%	96%

The experimental results show that the final recognition accuracy of the neural network depends strongly on the size of the training set, but not for all classes of patent images. When teaching a model of 600 patent images per class, it was possible to achieve an average accuracy of 70%. The worst result was shown by the class "flowchart". Perhaps, the sample for this class should be changed. Patent images are taken from the data generation module for the training set. Then they are manually distributed into 6 classes of patent images.

Table 4. The accuracy of recognition of the neural network by the size of the training sample (general information)

Patent image class/number of patent images	100	300	600
Training time	1 h 4 min	1 h 39 min	2 h 22 min
Accuracy on the training set	68.36%	65.48%	65.96%
Accuracy on test set	37.24%	44.10%	75.53%
Accuracy on the test sample	37.19%	44.06%	70.31%

4.3   An Experiment to Analyze the Dependence of the Recognition Accuracy of a Neural Network on the Size of Patent Images

As a result of the experiment, 3 models (64 × 64, 192 × 192, 250 × 250) with different sizes of patent images were trained. The training sample is 200 patent images per class in all cases. The number of epochs is 16, the size of patent images (64 × 64, 192 × 192, 250 × 250). The results of the experiment are shown in Tables 5 and 6.

Table 5. The accuracy of recognition of the neural network class by patent image size

Patent image class/patent image size	64 × 64	192 × 192	250 × 250
Technical drawing	34%	31%	59%
Chemical structure	77%	41.5%	82%
Diagram	63.5%	87.5%	82%
Gene sequence	36.5%	83.5%	68%
Block diagram	18%	62.5%	37.5%
Table	52%	93.5%	96%

Table 6. The accuracy of recognition of the neural network on the size of patent images (general information)

Patent image class/patent image size	64 × 64	192 × 192	250 × 250
Training time	50 min	1 h 47 min	2 h 22 min
Accuracy on the training set	43.55%	73.53%	65.96%
Accuracy on test set	49.21%	71.13%	75.53%
Accuracy on the test sample	44.69%	64.38%	70.31%

Experimental results show that the final recognition accuracy of the neural network depends on the size of the patent images, but not for all classes of patent images. The dependence of accuracy on the training sample is larger than the size of the patent images. When teaching a model of 600 patent images per class, with a patent image size of 250 × 250, it was possible to achieve an average accuracy of 70%.

Some patent image classes (diagram, gene sequence, block diagram) show accuracy better with a smaller patent image size. Patent images are taken from the data generation module for the training set. Then they are manually distributed into 6 classes of patent images.

4.4   Analysis of Neural Network Training Quality

For analysis, a trained neural network with the best accuracy among those trained was selected. This network recognizes 6 classes of patent images (technical drawing, chemical structure, diagram, gene sequence, block diagram, table). The model is trained on 3600 patent images with a test and a test sample of 200 each. The patent image size is 250×250. The neural network architecture is shown in Fig. 6. During the experiment, a regularization tool was used to prevent retraining of the neural network.

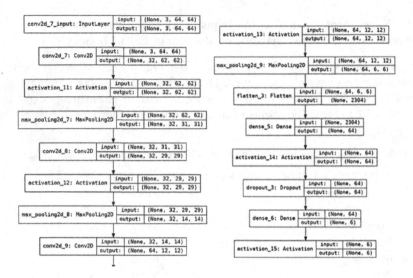

Fig. 6. Neural network architecture

The number of epochs is 40. Based on the graphs shown in Fig. 7, one can say that the neural network began to be retrained from the 5th epoch and the remaining 35 epochs were not needed. Using Dropout with parameter 0.5 for regularization did not help.

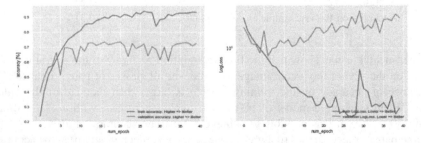

Fig. 7. Graphs of the accuracy and function of the error on the number of epochs. A number of eras 40. Dropout 0.5

Reduce the number of epochs to 16 and increase Dropout to 0.7. It can be seen (Fig. 8) that retraining did not happen, but the neural network was not tested and the accuracy of the model could be improved by increasing the number of epochs. Accuracy on the verification data must be greater than on the training data since the Dropout regularization tool is used on the training data.

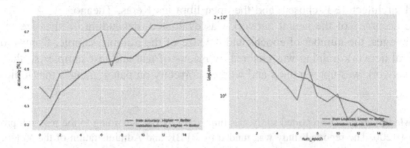

Fig. 8. Graphs of the accuracy and function of the error on the number of epochs. A number of eras 16. Dropout 0.7

The results of the experiment show that the neural network has not been tested and the accuracy of the model can be increased by increasing the number of epochs. You also need to ensure that the neural network is not retrained using regularization tools, such as dropout and using the test and test samples. On the plots, the accuracy on the verification data should be greater than on the training data, since the Dropout regularization tool is used on the training data.

We evaluated the achievements of the testing objectives. To assess the first criterion, we calculate the average value of the recognition accuracy of the patent image class, take the data from Table 2, or see the accuracy on the test data in Table 3. Thus, it can be seen that the average recognition accuracy of the patent image class is 70.44%. Therefore, we can assume that the goal of the first criterion is achieved.

Check the second criterion. From the results of the first and second experiments, it can be seen that the accuracy of the neural network depends on the number of patent images in the training sample and the training time. Not so simple with the size of the patent images, based on 2 experiments. Some patent image classes are better defined with smaller patent image sizes. Also from the results of the third experiment, it is clear that the neural network was not tested and the accuracy of the model can be increased by increasing the number of epochs.

To test the third criterion, look at the graphs in the third experiment. It can be seen from them that the neural network was not retrained and control over training was provided with the help of test and test samples. As well as the analysis of the course of training, writing it to a file for plotting graphs.

5 Conclusion

As a result of the study, the specificity of the patent images was studied, the main classes of patent images were determined, which will define the neural network for comparison of the corresponding classes. The existing neural network architectures for imaging and machine learning libraries are analyzed, the deep convolutional neural network architecture is chosen, and the open libraries Keras, Theano.

The accuracy of the neural network was evaluated, depending on the size of the patent images, the number of epochs and the size of the training sample. Control over the neural network training was ensured by means of test and test samples so that the neural network was not retrained and worked correctly on patent images that it did not see.

Acknowledgments. The reported study was funded by RFBR according to the research project # 19-07-01200. The reported study was funded by RFBR and Administration of the Volgograd region according to the research project # 19-41-340016.

References

1. Lempert, L.B., Kravets, A.G., Lempert, B.A., Poplavskaya, O.V., Salnikova, N.A.: Development of the intellectual decision-making support method for medical diagnostics in psychiatric practice. In: 9th International Conference on Information, Intelligence, Systems and Applications (IISA 2018), pp. 1–5 (2019)
2. Kravets, A.G., Kanavina, M.A., Salnikova, N.A.: Development of an integrated method of placement of solar and wind energy objects in the lower volga. In: International Conference on Industrial Engineering, Applications and Manufacturing (ICIEAM 2017), pp. 1–5 (2017)
3. Kravets, A.G., Skorobogatchenko, D.A., Salnikova, N.A., Orudjev, N.Y., Poplavskaya, O. V.: The traffic safety management system in urban conditions based on the C4.5 algorithm. In: Proceedings of Moscow Workshop on Electronic and Networking Technologies (MWENT 2018), pp. 1–7 (2018). Art. no. 8337254
4. Kamaev, V.A., Salnikova, N.A., Akhmedov, S.A., Likhter, A.M.: The formalized representation of the structures of complex technical devices using context-free plex grammars. In: Kravets, A., Shcherbakov, M., Kultsova, M., Shabalina, O. (eds.) Creativity in Intelligent Technologies and Data Science (CIT&DS 2015). CCIS, vol. 535, pp. 268–277. Springer, Heidelberg (2015). https://doi.org/10.1007/978-3-319-23766-4_22
5. Kravets, A., Shumeiko, N., Shcherbakova, N., Lempert, B., Salnikova, N.: "Smart queue" approach for new technical solutions discovery in patent applications. In: Kravets, A., Shcherbakov, M., Kultsova, M., Groumpos, P. (eds.) Creativity in Intelligent Technologies and Data Science (CIT&DS 2017). CCIS, vol. 754, pp. 37–47. Springer, Heidelberg (2017)
6. Korobkin, D.M., Fomenkov, S.A., Kravets, A.G.: Methods for extracting the descriptions of sci-tech effects and morphological features of technical systems from patents. In: 9th International Conference on Information, Intelligence, Systems and Applications (IISA 2018), pp. 1–6 (2019)
7. Kravets, A.G., Vasiliev, S.S., Shabanov, D.V.: Research of the LDA algorithm results for patents texts processing. In: 9th International Conference on Information, Intelligence, Systems and Applications (IISA 2018), pp. 1–6 (2019)

8. Lecun, Y., Bottou, L., Bengio, Y., Haffner, P.: Gradient-based learning applied to document recognition. Proc. IEEE **86**, 2278–2324 (1998)
9. Simard, P.Y., Steinkraus, D., Platt, J.C.: Best practices for convolutional neural networks applied to visual document analysis. In: Proceedings of the IEEE Conference Publications, pp. 958–963 (2003)
10. The evolution of neural networks for patent image recognition in Google: GoogLeNet. https://habr.com/ru/post/301084/. Accessed 28 Mar 2019
11. AlexNet – convolutional neural network for patent image classification. https://papers.nips.cc/paper/4824-imagenet-classification-with-deep-convolutional-neural-networks. Accessed 28 Mar 2019
12. Koch, G., Zemel, R., Salakhutdinov, R.: Siamese neural networks for one-shot patent image recognition. Department of Computer Science, CA (2015)
13. Keras Documentation: Keras (2018). https://keras.io/applications/. Accessed 28 Mar 2019
14. Caffe 2018: Berkeley Center. http://caffe.berkeleyvision.org/. Accessed 28 Mar 2019
15. Theano 2018: Universite de Montreal. http://deeplearning.net/software/theano/. Accessed 28 Mar 2019
16. Tensorflow 2018: Google. https://www.tensorflow.org/. Accessed 28 Mar 2019
17. Kravets, A., Lebedev, N., Legenchenko, M.: Patents patent images retrieval and convolutional neural network training dataset quality improvement. In: ITSMSSM, vol. 72, pp. 287–293 (2017)

The Software and Information Complex Which Uses Structured Physical Knowledge for Technical Systems Design

Ilya Vayngolts⬤, Dmitriy Korobkin(✉)⬤, Sergey Fomenkov⬤, and Sergey Kolesnikov

Volgograd State Technical University, Lenin Avenue 28, Volgograd, Russia
dkorobkin80@mail.ru

Abstract. The article is concerned about the architecture and cloud infrastructure of the software and information complex, which uses structured physical knowledge for technical systems design. A comparative analysis of microservice architecture and monolithic applications has been carried out. Based on the performed analysis, a microservice architecture project for the designed complex has been developed. Also, the article also describes AWS basic services and how to build the necessary infrastructure for the designed complex with their help.

Keywords: Physical effect · Physical knowledge · Software architecture · Microservices · Cloud infrastructure · AWS

1 Introduction

Structured physical knowledge is important for scientists, engineers, and inventors. Using this knowledge, it is possible to design new technical systems, develop new technologies and improve proof of product concepts. Also, we can teach students and engineers with methods of technical creative.

There are many kinds of research that are devoted to the development of different software products which use structured physical knowledge in the physical effect form. It is the physical principle of operations synthesis systems, automated physical effects search engines, actualization, and fill-in physical effects database systems, etc. [1–4].

However, there is a problem: it is not possible to organize the entire systems as one software complex. Different systems use a different stack of technologies and do not have interfaces to communicate with each other. So, the user cannot work with all software complex features. It is a problem that needs to solve.

2 Microservice Software Architecture Style

To solve the described problem, it is necessary to design new software architecture for the software complex. The main requirements are:

A. G. Kravets et al. (Eds.): CIT&DS 2019, CCIS 1084, pp. 42–51, 2019.
https://doi.org/10.1007/978-3-030-29750-3_4

- it should have independent modules that can add/update and scale easily;
- it should have defense from unauthorized access to the modules and their databases;
- the complex should be able to fast and convenient deployment.

There are two main software architectural styles today: monolithic applications and microservices ones. The monolithic architecture style is a traditional way to design applications. By this approach, we develop the product as one big application. By the microservices architecture style, we develop the product as a set of separated applications called services or microservices (Fig. 1).

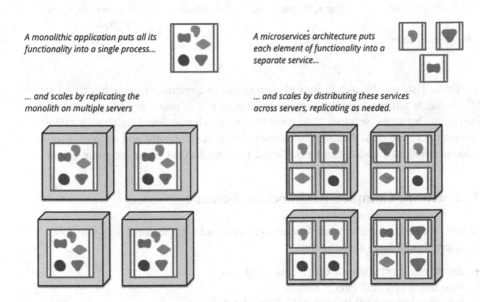

Fig. 1. Monoliths and microservices structure

The advantages of monolithic applications are [5]:

- requests handling executes in a single process;
- it is easy to run and test the application on a developer's PC;
- we can horizontally scale the application by running several instances.

However, it has some significant disadvantages [5]:

- the division into modules has conditional character and they do not have clear borders; so, it is hard to support good module structure in the future.
- horizontal scaling is not so effective and requires many resources;

Microservices allows to solve these disadvantages [5, 6]:

- one service is one module, so, the module borders are defined;
- we can scale only required modules if it is necessary, not the entire product.

Table 1. Monoliths and microservices comparison

Sign	Monoliths	Microservices
Make changes in the module	Need to change the entire application	Need to change only required service
Module borders	Not defined	One module – one service
Using different programming languages	Impossible, the application uses only one programming language	Can be used for different modules
Database structure	The application uses one database	One module – one database
Module execution	In-memory	By REST API

Table 1 shows the comparison of monolithic and microservice architectural styles. Of course, when we use microservice architecture it is necessary to take attention to interfaces between services, but usually, they change rarely. That is why the microservices are more flexible and convenient in development and support, use fewer resources and as a result, can be deployed into production faster are more often.

3   Software Complex Architecture Scheme

At first, we need to define what services we need and what features they will have. The complex should have features for:

- the physical principle of operations synthesis;
- automated physical effects search;
- actualization and fill-in physical effects database.

Also, the complex should have features to limit access to it and client-side part with a user interface. Due to the features, we can distinguish the following services:

- SYNTHESIS – will implement features regarding the physical principle of operations synthesis;
- SEARCH – will implement features regarding automated physical effects search;
- ACTUALIZATION – will implement features regarding actualization and fill-in physical effects database;
- UAM (user access management) – will implement features regarding limit access to the complex;
- FRONTEND – will implement features regarding the user interface.

Also, we need some additional services [7]:

- DB MANAGER (database manager) – will implement features to work with physical effects database; it is necessary to adhere to the rule "one service – one database";

- API GATEWAY – the specific service which works as a proxy between FRONTEND and other services; the direct connection between them is not safe.

Figure 2 shows the general scheme of the software complex architecture and the example of chain execution for DB MANAGER service [8]. The legend is:

- 1 – send the request to API GATEWAY;
- 2 – send the authentication request to UAM;
- 3 – receive the token and scopes from UAM;
- 4 – forward the request to DB MANAGER;
- 5 – send the authorization request to UAM (verify the token and scopes);
- 6 – confirm that the token and scopes are valid;
- 7 – send the request results to API GATEWAY;
- 8 – forward the request results to FRONTEND.

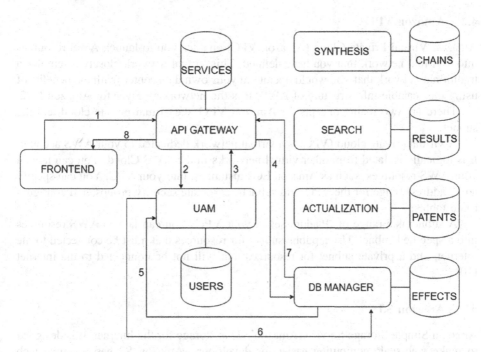

Fig. 2. The scheme of the software complex architecture

4 Introduction to AWS

Amazon Web Services (AWS) is a subsidiary of Amazon that provides on-demand cloud computing platforms to individuals, companies, and governments, on a metered pay-as-you-go basis. In aggregate, these cloud computing web services provide a set of primitive, abstract technical infrastructure and distributed computing building blocks and tools. In 2017, AWS comprised more than 90 services spanning a wide range including computing, storage, networking, database, analytics, application services, deployment, management, mobile, developer tools, and tools for the Internet of Things. Below we describe the most important services to organize the software complex infrastructure.

4.1 Amazon EC2

Amazon Elastic Compute Cloud (Amazon EC2) provides scalable computing capacity in the AWS cloud. Using Amazon EC2 eliminates your need to invest in hardware up front, so you can develop and deploy applications faster. You can use Amazon EC2 to launch as many or as few virtual servers as you need, configure security and networking, and manage storage. Amazon EC2 enables you to scale up or down to handle changes in requirements or spikes in popularity, reducing your need to forecast traffic [9].

4.2 Amazon VPC

Amazon Virtual Private Cloud (Amazon VPC) enables you to launch AWS resources into a virtual network that you have defined. This virtual network closely resembles a traditional network that you would operate in your own data center, with the benefits of using the scalable infrastructure of AWS. It is the networking layer for Amazon EC2.

There are two main concepts for Amazon VPC: the virtual private cloud and the subnet.

A virtual private cloud (VPC) is a virtual network dedicated to your AWS account. It is logically isolated from other virtual networks in the AWS Cloud. You can launch your AWS resources, such as Amazon EC2 instances, into your VPC. You can specify an IP address range for the VPC, add subnets, associate security groups, and configure route tables.

A subnet is a range of IP addresses in your VPC. You can launch AWS resources into a specified subnet. Use a public subnet for resources that must be connected to the internet, and a private subnet for resources that will not be connected to the internet [10].

4.3 Amazon S3

Amazon Simple Storage Service (Amazon S3) is storage for the Internet. It is designed to make web-scale computing easier for developers. Amazon S3 has a simple web services interface that you can use to store and retrieve any amount of data, at any time, from anywhere on the web. It gives any developer access to the same highly scalable, reliable, fast, inexpensive data storage infrastructure that Amazon uses to run its own global network of web sites. The service aims to maximize benefits of scale and to pass those benefits on to developers [11].

4.4   IAM

AWS Identity and Access Management (IAM) is a web service that helps you securely control access to AWS resources. You use IAM to control who is authenticated and authorized to use resources.

There are three main concepts for Amazon VPC: the IAM user, the IAM group, and the IAM role.

An IAM user is an entity that you create in AWS. The IAM user represents the person or service who uses the IAM user to interact with AWS. The primary use for IAM users is to give people the ability to sign in to the AWS Management Console for interactive tasks and to make programmatic requests to AWS services using the API or CLI. A user in AWS consists of a name, a password to sign into the AWS Management Console, and up to two access keys that can be used with the API or CLI.

An IAM group is a collection of IAM users. You can use groups to specify permissions for a collection of users, which can make those permissions easier to manage for those users.

An IAM role is very similar to a user, in that it is an identity with permission policies that determine what the identity can and cannot do in AWS. However, a role does not have any credentials (password or access keys) associated with it. Instead of being uniquely associated with one person, a role is intended to be assumable by anyone who needs it [12].

4.5   Amazon Route 53

Amazon Route 53 is a highly available and scalable Domain Name System (DNS) web service. You can use Route 53 to perform three main functions in any combination: domain registration, DNS routing, and health checking [13].

5   AWS Infrastructure for the Software Complex

5.1   Base Infrastructure

VPC Configuration
To build a high availability infrastructure, we need to have instances in several availability zones. In AWS, availability zone is bound to subnet. So, we need to have a subnet per availability zone at least. Also, it is necessary to have public and private subnets to limit access to instances from the Internet. That is why it is necessary to have two subnets – one public and one private – per availability zone. Figure 3 shows the general scheme of a network configuration for the software complex.

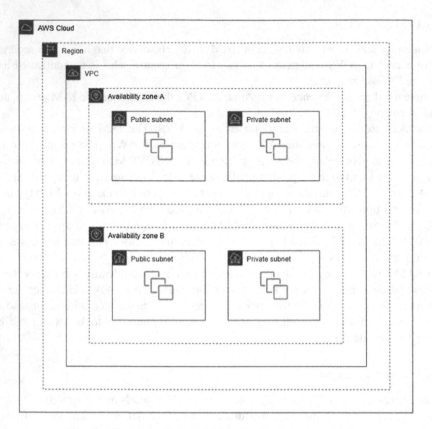

Fig. 3. The network configuration for the software complex

S3 Configuration

We need the S3 bucket to store application artifacts – jar files, zip files, etc. It should be encrypted and have retention policy to remove expired artifacts automatically. Also, it is necessary to configure the bucket policy to deny delete this bucket manually.

Route 53 Configuration

To organize work with DNS, we should have two hosted zones: one for internal services as SYNTHESIS and DB MANAGER, and one for external services as FRONTEND. In these hosted zones we will register record sets which bind DNS name of the service with its canonical name or CNAME.

5.2 AWS Elastic Beanstalk Application Infrastructure

To deploy services, it makes sense to use AWS Elastic Beanstalk. AWS Elastic Beanstalk is an easy-to-use service for deploying and scaling web applications and services developed with Java, .NET, PHP, Node.js, Python, Ruby, Go, and Docker on familiar servers such as Apache, Nginx, Passenger, and IIS. You can simply upload your code and Elastic Beanstalk automatically handles the deployment, from capacity provisioning, load balancing, auto-scaling to application health monitoring. At the same time, you retain full control over the AWS resources powering your application and can access the underlying resources at any time [14].

The main Elastic Beanstalk concepts are:

- application – it is a logical collection of Elastic Beanstalk components, including environments, versions, etc.;
- application version – it is a specific, labeled iteration of deployable code for a web application;
- environment – it is a collection of AWS resources running an application version;
- platform – it is a combination of an operating system, programming language runtime, web server, application server, and Elastic Beanstalk components.

The Elastic Beanstalk application has the following infrastructure:

- the binary file with application keeps in S3 bucket;
- the application executes on EC2 machines [15];
- these EC2 machines unite in the autoscaling group;

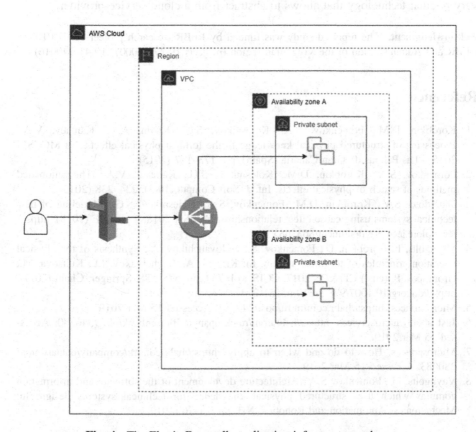

Fig. 4. The Elastic Beanstalk application infrastructure scheme

- the load balancer is in front of the autoscaling group and forward requests to the instances;
- IAM roles manage access to AWS services.

In addition, it is possible to create a Route 53 record set and binds it with load balancer CNAME. The full application infrastructure scheme is on Fig. 4.

6 Conclusion

As a result of this research, we have two main achievements: a project of software architecture for the software complex has been developed and we know what kind of AWS services it is necessary to use for cloud deployment.

For the further steps, we need to investigate topics regarding databases: what databases use, what structure they should have, what AWS services it is necessary to use, how to make the procedures of backup and restore, and so on. Also, it is necessary to make some calculations regarding AWS resources costs. When these topics will investigate, we can start to implement some proof of concepts of the software complex.

As an alternative scenario, it makes sense to have a look at the Kubernetes. It is a very popular technology that allows to abstract from a cloud service provider.

Acknowledgment. The reported study was funded by RFBR (research project 18-07-01086), RFBR and Administration of the Volgograd region (projects 19-47-340007, 19-41-340016).

References

1. Korobkin, D.M., Fomenkov, S.A., Kolesnikov, S.G., Kizim, A.V., Kamaev, V.A.: Processing of structured physical knowledge in the form of physical effects. In: MCCSIS 2015 – Las Palmas de Gran Canaria (Spain), pp. 173–177 (2015)
2. Fomenkov, S.A., Korobkin, D.M., Kolesnikov, S.G., Kamaev, V.A.: The automated methods of search of physical effects. Int. J. Soft Comput. **10**(3), 234–238 (2015)
3. Davydova, S.V., Korobkin, D.M., Fomenkov, S.A., Kolesnikov, S.G.: Modeling of new technical systems using cause-effect relationships. In: IISA 2018, 4 p. IEEE (2018). https://ieeexplore.ieee.org/document/8633683
4. Vayngolts, I., Korobkin, D., Fomenkov, S., Golovanchikov, A.: Synthesis of the physical operation principles of technical system. In: Kravets, A., Shcherbakov, M., Kultsova, M., Groumpos, P. (eds.) CIT&DS 2017. CCIS, vol. 754, pp. 575–588. Springer, Cham (2017). https://doi.org/10.1007/978-3-319-65551-2_42
5. Microservices. https://habr.com/ru/ru/post/249183. Accessed 15 Mar 2019
6. Just about microservices. https://habr.com/ru/company/raiffeisenbank/blog/346380. Accessed 15 Mar 2019
7. Microservices. How to do and when to apply? https://habr.com/ru/company/dataart/blog/280083. Accessed 15 Mar 2019
8. Vayngolts, I.I., Fomenkov S.A.: Architecture development of the software and information complex which uses structured physical knowledge for technical systems design. In: Mechatronics, Automation and Robotics, №3, pp. 73–76 (2019)

9. What is Amazon EC2? https://docs.aws.amazon.com/AWSEC2/latest/UserGuide/concepts. html. Accessed 25 Mar 2019
10. What is Amazon VPC? https://docs.aws.amazon.com/vpc/latest/userguide/what-is-amazon-vpc.html. Accessed 18 Mar 2019
11. What is Amazon S3? https://docs.aws.amazon.com/AmazonS3/latest/dev/Welcome.html. Accessed 18 Mar 2019
12. Identities (Users, Groups, and Roles). https://docs.aws.amazon.com/IAM/latest/UserGuide/ id.html. Accessed 18 Mar 2019
13. What is Amazon Route 53? https://docs.aws.amazon.com/Route53/latest/DeveloperGuide/ Welcome.html. Accessed 20 Mar 2019
14. What is AWS Elastic Beanstalk? https://docs.aws.amazon.com/elasticbeanstalk/latest/dg/ Welcome.html. Accessed 23 Mar 2019
15. Parygin, D., Nikitsky, N., Kamaev, V., Matokhina, A., Finogeev, A., Finogeev, A.: Multi-agent approach to distributed processing of big sensor data based on fog computing model for the monitoring of the urban infrastructure systems. In: SMART-2016, pp. 305–310. IEEE (2016). https://doi.org/10.1109/SYSMART.2016.7894540

Construction of a Matrix "Physical Effects – Technical Functions" on the Base of Patent Corpus Analysis

Dmitriy Korobkin[✉] ⓘ, Dmitriy Shabanov, Sergey Fomenkov ⓘ,
and Alexander Golovanchikov ⓘ

Volgograd State Technical University, Lenin Avenue 28, Volgograd, Russia
dkorobkin80@mail.ru

Abstract. Authors use physical effects (PE) to synthesize the physical operation principle of a technical system. PEs implements the technical functions (TF) that describe the functional structure of the declared technical system. The method finds out relationships between physical effects and technical functions performed by them based on the construction of term-document matrices and the search for hidden dependencies in them. To this end, the authors developed a method for extracting descriptions of physical effects from patents in USPTO and RosPatent databases, as well as a method for extracting technical functions from the natural language texts of the same documents. The developed software has been tested for the tasks of extracting physical effects and technical functions from patent documents.

Keywords: Patent · NLP · Fact extraction · Data mining · Physical effect · Technical function · SAO

1 Introduction

Analysis of the computer-aided innovation systems (CAI) [1] such as Goldfire Innovator, TechOptimizer, Innovation Workbench, Idea Generator, Pro/Innovator, etc., shows these CAI systems do not solve the fundamental problem of updating the information component of the new technical systems generation. Using the world patent database (more than 20 million documents) and open databases of scientific and technical information as a global knowledge base most correctly. The engineer/inventor realizes the required functions of the designed technical system on the basis of heuristic morphological synthesis or the physical operation principle (POP) [2], which is a sequence (network) of physical effects (PE) [3]. Therefore, it is required to extract the following data from the global information space: physical and technical effects, morphological features and their alternatives (elements of functional structure, technical realizations of objects), i.e. information necessary to solve the problems of information support for the synthesis of new technical solutions.

The task of determining the most effective physical operation principle of a technical system with a selected functional structure that synthesized on the basis of a morphological matrix is solved by 2 methods: (1) the method for automating the

© Springer Nature Switzerland AG 2019
A. G. Kravets et al. (Eds.): CIT&DS 2019, CCIS 1084, pp. 52–68, 2019.
https://doi.org/10.1007/978-3-030-29750-3_5

procedures for synthesizing the physical operation principle based on the database of technical functions performed by physical effects, and (2) the developed method for verification the practical realizability [4] of the synthesized POP on based on the criteria parameters of the physical effects that are part of a POP structure.

2 Extracting SAO (Subject-Action-Object) Structures from Natural Language Text

2.1 Segmentation

The "Subject-Action-Object" (SAO) [5] semantic construction is a key concept makes it possible to recognize technical objects and its elements, problems and solutions, technical objects functions and physical effects descriptions in a natural language text.
The following information is extracted from the patent xml-file:

<B110>... </B110> – a patent number;
<B220><date>... </date></B220> – a patent date;
<ru-b542>... </ru-b542> – a patent title;
<ru-b560>... </ru-b560> – a list of citations;
<B721><ru-name-text>... </ru-name-text></B721> – a list of patent authors;
<claims>... </claims> – a patent clame.

The text of the patent claim itself contains in <claim-text></claim-text> tags. Patent claims are based on itself pattern that differs from the usual sentence structure. Most often, the formula is one complex sentence, in which there are several subordinates, each of which extends the properties of the object, which is referred to in the main sentence. Analysis of such a long sentence will be an actually time-consuming procedure. To reduce semantic analysis errors, the sentence is segmented into several parts, and then each part of the original sentence analyzed separately.

The segmentation algorithm [6] consists of the following transformations using regular expressions. To remove the numbering like «A. », «a. », «1. » or «1) » is used «^(\d{1,4}|[a-zA-Z]{1,2})(\.|\))\s» pattern, to remove references like «4. The device according to claim 3...» is used «^.+(of|in|to) claim \d+(,)?» pattern. Sentences are separated by punctuation characters by replacing pattern «(\.|!|\?|:|;)\s?» with the line breaks symbol. Also, the line breaks replace stop words: «, wherein», «, said», «, and», «; and», «, thereby», «if», «else», «thereby», «such that», «so that», «wherein», «whereby», «where», «when», «while», «but». Thus, the sentences will be cut into shorter ones without losing meaning, which will increase the likelihood of the semantic analyzer to work correctly.

2.2 Semantic Text Analysis

We will use the UDPipe library to analyze Russian and English text. The input and output data format for it is CoNLL. For each sentence, a dependency tree is built.
Example of dependency tree from the sentence of patent US20130307109A1: "the incident light causes photoelectric conversion, generating charges":

```
1 the the DET RD Definite=Def|PronType=Art 4 det _ _
2 incident incident ADJ A Degree=Pos 3 amod _ _
3 light lay NOUN S Number=Sing 4 nmod _ _
4 causes cause NOUN S Number=Plur 6 nsubj _ _
5 photoelectric photoelectric ADJ A Degree=Pos 6 amod _ _
·6 conversion conversion NOUN S Number=Sing 0 root _
SpaceAfter=No
```

The dependency tree uses Stanford Dependencies [7] such as nominal subject (nsubj), object (pobj), adjectival modifier (amod), tree root (root). After that, vertexes such as "det" with a semantically minor role are removed from the dependency trees. Thus we obtain reduced Collapsed Stanford Dependencies. Based on Meaning-Text Theory (MTT) [8] this reduced trees with Stanford dependencies are converted to Deep Syntactic Structures (DSyntS).

Reduced Stanford dependencies example:

```
ATTR(light-2, incident-1)
I(causes-3, light-2)
OPER(ROOT-0, causes-3)
ATTR(conversion -5, photoelectric-4)
II(causes-3, conversion-5)
```

From deep syntactic structures, we extract the SAO structures in which the root is «Action», its children are «Subject» (I-vertex) and «Object» (II-vertex). There are several Subjects and Objects for one Action, in addition, for each Subject, Object, and Action, its child relations are extracted.

The following SAO structure is extracted (Fig. 1):

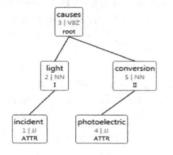

Action – «cause» (root vertex);
Subject –«light» (with "incident" as child element);
Object – «conversion» (with "photoelectric" as child element).

Fig. 1. Graphical representation of a dependency tree

2.3 SAO Grouping

To increase the information content of SAO structures, several SAOs are combined into one according to the developed grouping (comparison) algorithm [9]. Consider an example of comparing two SAOs extracted from sentences "An atom with an ionized shell emitted K-series X-ray photons" and "An ionized atom slowly emitted L-series photons" (Fig. 2).

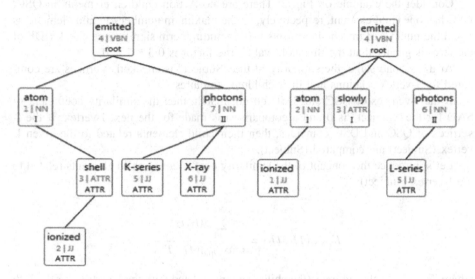

Fig. 2. Comparison of two extracted SAO

The first stage is a comparison of the "Action". If the vertexes of the first SAO (query search case, QSC) and the second SAO (document search case, DSC) do not match, then the SAO trees are not further compared. If the "Actions" match, then the child (not "Subject" and not "Object") elements (children) associated with the root vertex ("Action") are compared.

At each level, if the terms (words) do not match, a significance test occurs. The significance test of a term is made on the basis of a previously prepared table in which IDF factors are defined. If the term IDF is less than the threshold value, then the word is not significant and is not taken into account in the calculation of the similarity factor.

In our case, the «Action» vertices are equal, but their child elements are not (Fig. 2).

Let's introduce the concept of the coefficient of similarity of child elements associated with the root vertex (Action):

$$K_{Child}^{A}(TA_k, TA_l) = \frac{\sum_{i=1}^{N_i} S(t_1, t_2)}{3 \times \max_{Child}(TA_k, TA_l)}, \tag{1}$$

where TA_k, TA_l – subtrees (root related children) for k-th and l-th QSC and DSC respectively;

$max_{Child}(TA_k, TA_l)$ – the maximum number of child elements for QSC and DSC with IDF;

$S(t_1, t_2)$ – an operator defining the similarity of the child elements t_1 and t_2 for the compared subtrees (returns 1 if they completely match);

N_i – number of children in the TA_k semantic tree.

Consider the example on Fig. 2. There are no Action children elements in QSC, DSC has one child element, respectively, so the maximum number of child elements is 1 and the number of matched elements is 0. Including term significance check (IDF of the term is greater than the threshold value) the factor is 0/3 * 1 = 0.

At the second stage, the similarity of the "Subject" is checked. Vertices are compared for I-vertex relations and their children structures.

If the I-vertices of QSC and DSC do not match, then the similarity coefficient of SAO for the "Subject" is 0 and a comparison is made for the next I-vertex. If the I-vertices of QSC and DSC coincides, then their child elements related to the given I-vertex (Subject) are compared (Subject).

Let's introduce the concept of the similarity coefficient of child elements related to the I-vertex (Subject):

$$K_{Child}^I(TI_k, TI_l) = \frac{\sum_{i=1}^{N_i} S(t_1, t_2)}{max_{Child}(TI_k, TI_l)}, \qquad (2)$$

where TI_k, TI_l – is the subtrees (the child elements related with the I-vertex) for the k-th and l-th sentence in QSC and DSC respectively;

$max_{Child}(TI_k, TI_l)$ – is the maximum number of children for QSC and DSC taking into account the;

$S(t_1, t_2)$ – is the operator defining the coincidence of the child elements t_1 and t_2 for the compared subtrees; it returns 1 if matched;

N_i – is the number of child elements of the semantic tree TI_k for DSC.

Let's introduce the SAO similarity coefficient by "Subject":

$$K^I = \frac{\sum_{i=1}^{N_t=|I_k|} K_{M_i}^I}{max(I_k, I_l)} + \frac{\sum_{i=1}^{N_t=|I_k|} K_{Child_i}^I}{3 \times max(I_k, I_l)}, \qquad (3)$$

where $K_{M_i}^I$ – is the coincidence coefficient of the i-th I-vertex, if there is a match $K_{M_i}^I = 1$, if there is mismatch $K_{M_i}^I = 0$;

$K_{Child_i}^I$ – is the coincidence coefficient of child elements, related to i-th I-vertex;

$max(I_k, I_l)$ – is the maximum number of I-vertex in QSC and DSC.

Let's consider the example in Fig. 2. There is 2 child element in the QSC for the I-vertex, in the DSC there is 1, respectively, maximum 2. IDF is greater than the limit value for all terms, which means they are meaningful. The coefficient K_{Child}^I for a pair of "shell, ionized" → "ionized" is 0.5. The SAO similarity coefficient by "Subject" – K^I is 1.1667.

(3) At the third stage, there is a check of the similarity of the "Object" (O) - a comparison of the vertices for the II-vertex relations and related child elements. The SAO comparison algorithm by the "Object" is similar to the comparison algorithm by the «Subject».

Let's introduce the concept of the similarity coefficient of child elements related to the II-vertex (Object):

$$K_{Child}^{II}(TII_k, TII_l) = \frac{\sum_{i=1}^{N_i} S(t_1, t_2)}{\max_{Child}(TII_k, TII_l)}, \tag{4}$$

where TII_k, TII_l – is the subtrees (the child elements related with the II-vertex) for the k-th and l-th sentence in SQC and DSC respectively;

$\max_{Child}(TII_k, TII_l)$ – is the maximum number of children for QSC and DSC taking into account the IDF;

$S(t_1, t_2)$ – is the operator defining the coincidence of the child elements t1 and t2 for the compared subtrees; it returns 1 if matched;

N_i – is the number of child elements of the semantic tree TII_k for QSC.

Let's introduce the SAO similarity coefficient by «Object»:

$$K^{II} = \frac{\sum_{i=1}^{N_t=|II_k|} K_{M_i}^{II}}{\max(II_k, II_l)} + \frac{\sum_{i=1}^{N_t=|II_k|} K_{Child_i}^{II}}{3 \times \max(II_k, II_l)}, \tag{5}$$

where $K_{M_i}^{II}$ – is the coincidence coefficient of the i-th II-vertex, if there is match $K_{M_i}^{II} = 1$ –, if there is mismatch $K_{M_i}^{II} = 0$;

$K_{Child_i}^{II}$ – is the coincidence coefficient of child elements, related with i-th II-vertex;

$\max(II_k, II_l)$ – is the maximum number of II-vertex in QSC and DSC.

Let's consider the example in Fig. 2. There is 2 child element in the QSC for the II-vertex, in the DSC there is 1, respectively, maximum 2. IDF is greater than the limit value for all terms, which means they are meaningful. The coefficient K_{Child}^{II} for a pair of "X-ray, K-series" → "L-series" is 0. The SAO similarity coefficient by "Object" – KII is 1.

(4) The calculation of the SAO similarity coefficient.

Let's introduce the concept of the similarity coefficient of 2 SAO structures:

$$K_{SAO} = K_{Child}^A + K^I + K^{II}, \tag{6}$$

where K_{Child}^A – is the similarity coefficient of child elements associated with the ROOT vertex (Action);

K^I – is the SAO similarity coefficient by "Subject";

K^{II} – is the SAO similarity coefficient by "Object".

Two SAOs can be grouped if their similarity coefficient is greater than a threshold value of 2, which means that the Action, Subject, Object components have coincided excluding the child elements. The maximum value of this coefficient is 3.

3   Search for Descriptions of Physical Effects in Natural Language (NL) Documents

For the problem of extracting descriptions of physical effects and POP structures from Russian and English texts used previously developed procedures for segmentation of complex sentences of patent texts, the building of dependency trees and deep syntactic structures based on the Meaning-Text Theory for reduced Stanford dependencies.

An example of deep-syntactic structures from patent proposal US20130307109A1 «In electrical circuits, any electric current produces a magnetic field and hence generates a total magnetic flux acting on the circuit» is shown in Fig. 3.

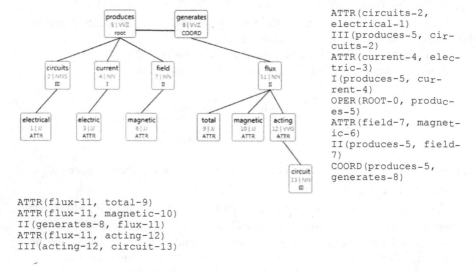

```
ATTR(circuits-2,
electrical-1)
III(produces-5, cir-
cuits-2)
ATTR(current-4, elec-
tric-3)
I(produces-5, cur-
rent-4)
OPER(ROOT-0, produc-
es-5)
ATTR(field-7, magnet-
ic-6)
II(produces-5, field-
7)
COORD(produces-5,
generates-8)
```

```
ATTR(flux-11, total-9)
ATTR(flux-11, magnetic-10)
II(generates-8, flux-11)
ATTR(flux-11, acting-12)
III(acting-12, circuit-13)
```

Fig. 3. Example of deep-syntactic structures

According to the model of the physical effect [10], developed at the CAD department of VSTU, in a Natural-Language text containing a description of the PE, it is necessary to find predicates (verbs) that have some "effect" on arguments that have definite active relations with the predicate inside this "influence". There were identified in a single class all predicates characteristic for describing PE in the physical profile text, such as "влияние", "воздействие", "зависимость", etc. (for Russian language), "change", "increase", "decrease", "depend", "change", "generate", "act", "cause", etc. (for English).

During the work on the project as a result of the analysis of Russian and English texts containing descriptions of PE, for each predicate, the actant relations "I" (what influences), "II" (what the effect is aimed at), "III" (where the effect is implemented) were correlated with description elements of the PE.

There was modified the model for the representation of the description of the physical effect in the Russian and English text, previously developed by the authors [11].

$$M_{PE} = <P, Act, E, R_P, R_E>, \tag{7}$$

where P – is the set of predicates (verbs), specifically describe the PE in the Russian and English text, $p_i \in P$;

Act – is the set of actant relations {I, II, III} of arguments and predicate p_i;

$a_j \in Act$;

E – is the set of elements describing PE (A – PE input, B – PE object, C – is PE output), $E_k \in E$,

$$\forall p_i \in P \quad \exists a_j \in Act \quad [a_j \xrightarrow{def} E_k]$$

where $E_k \in \{A, B, C\}$, def – is the operator assigning to the actant relation of the argument a_j with the predicate d_i the element/set of elements E_k describing the PE;

R_P – is the relation on $P \times Act$, the couple $(p_i, a_j) \in R_P$ uniquely identifies the element/elements of the PE description, that realizes the actant relation a_j for the predicate p_i;

R_E – is the relation on $R_P \times E$, the couple $((p_i, a_j), E_k) \in R_E$ defines a set of concepts of the subject domain "Physical Effect", corresponding to the element of the description of the PE e_l, $e_1 \in E_k$;

According to the modified model, a database of patterns of representations of descriptions of structured physical knowledge in Russian (104 patterns) and English texts (36 patterns) was created.

For example,

P = PRODUCE; Act = {I,II,III}; E = {PE input (A), PE object (B), PE output (C)}; I $\xrightarrow{def}$ A; II $\xrightarrow{def}$ C; III $\xrightarrow{def}$ B;

P = ACT; Act = {I,II,III}; E = {A, B, C}; I $\xrightarrow{def}$ A; II $\xrightarrow{def}$ A,C; III $\xrightarrow{def}$ B;

Next is the construction of a semantic network for the description of the PE in the text.

The vertices of the semantic network $V_i = (T_i, E_i)$, where T_i is the Natural Language representation of the argument (term) for the predicate d_j; E_i is an element of PE description, represented in the text as T_i, $E_i \in R_P$.

When constructing a semantic network, the presence of the Natural Language representation of the argument T_i is tested at the thesauruses of "Physical Effect" ontology that developed by the authors of the paper.

Let us give an example of the semantic network obtained from the sentence «In electrical circuits, any electric current produces a magnetic field and hence generates a total magnetic flux acting on the circuit» (Fig. 4).

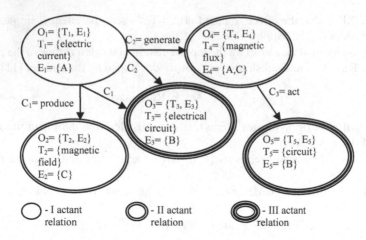

Fig. 4. An example of a semantic network

The extraction of structures of PE is based on the constructed semantic network using the procedure of combining concepts based on the taxonomy of the ontology «Physical Effect».

For example, after analyzing a piece of text: «In electrical circuits any electric current produces a magnetic field and hence generates a total magnetic flux acting on the circuit» we obtain the structure of the PE, which has as an input effect «electric current», as an object of the PE – «electrical circuit» and as an output effect – «magnetic flux» (Fig. 5).

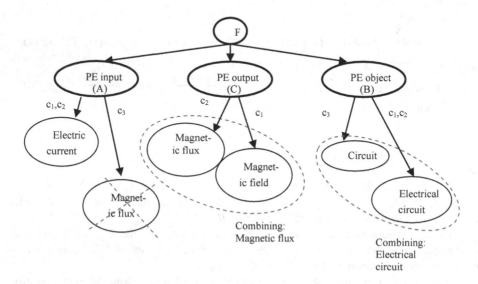

Fig. 5. Extracting information on the structure of PE

In this case, since the full structure of the PE, that contains the input action and no more than one output effect and object, was extracted from the text fragment, then we can speak of the generated description of the new or existing physical effect in the database. Otherwise, if there are several extracted output effects or objects (the latter to a lesser extent, since a structural change of the object, can be observed), we can speak of the extracted description of the elements of the structures of the physical principle of action.

4 The Method of the Automated Construction the Matrix of Technical Functions Performed by Physical Effects Based on Analysis of the Patent Corpus

Methods for extracting descriptions of technical functions (TF) and physical effects from patent texts are used to form the two term-document matrices.

The terms (functions of the technical object $TechFunc_i$) are extracted from the aggregate of all documents {Pat} of the patent array and the frequency of their occurrence in patent documents is determined.

At the same time, the device from the description of the claims is taken as the name of the technical object (TO) (the "claim" field): "A battery containing a body,..." (the TO is "Battery"). This information is stored as an attribute of the patent Pat.

Several TFs are combined into one according to the developed grouping (comparison) algorithm to reduce the space of extracted technical functions (TF).

The normalized term frequency weighting was chosen as the localized weighting of the i-th $TechFunc_i$ technical function in the j-th Pat_j patent document:

$$t_{ji} = 0.4 \times \chi(f_{ij}) + 0.6 \times \left(\frac{f_{ij}}{max_k f_{ij}}\right), \tag{8}$$

where f_{ij} – the frequency of occurrence $TechFunc_i$ in Pat_j,

   k – the number of technical function in j-th patent document Pat_j,

$$\chi(f_{ij}) = \begin{cases} 1, & \text{if } f_{ij} > 0, \\ 0, & \text{if } f_{ij} = 0 \end{cases}.$$

A value of 0.4 is assigned to all terms, included in the document, and 0.6 is added to it, depending on the frequency of occurrence of the term (technical function).

Inverted document frequency was chosen as global weighing $TechFunc_i$, which is equal to 0 if the technical function appears in all patent documents of the array, and this weight increases as the number of documents in which the technical function occurs decreases:

$$g_i = \log\left(\frac{N}{\sum_{j=1}^{N} \chi(f_{ij})}\right), \tag{9}$$

where N – the number of documents in the patent array.

It's helpful to normalize the columns of the final matrix after calculating local and global weights. If this is not done, short patent documents may not be recognized as relevant:

$$d_i = \left(\sum\nolimits_{j=1}^{M} \left(g_j t_{ji} \right)^2 \right)^{-1/2},$$

(10)

where M – the number of terms (technical functions) in the patent array,

t_{ji} is the local weighting of TechFunc$_i$ in Pat$_j$,

g_i – the global weighting TechFunc$_i$.

Calculate the reduced frequencies TFIDF$_{ij}$ of the occurrence of the technical functions TechFunc$_i$ in patent documents Pat$_j$:

$$TFIDF_{ij} = t_{ji} \times g_i \times d_i,$$

(11)

Further, by means of the latent semantic analysis (LSA), the space of technical functions ("noise") is reduced and hidden dependencies between terms (technical functions) are revealed. The LSA uses the term-document matrix as initial information (Table 1). The elements of this matrix contain the reduced frequencies TFIDF$_{ij}$ of the occurrence of the i-th technical function TechFunc$_i$ in the j-th patent document Pat$_j$.

Table 1. Matrix of reduced frequencies of technical functions in documents

Term	Document			
	Pat$_1$	Pat$_2$	...	Pat$_N$
TechFunc$_1$	TFIDF$_{11}$	TFIDF$_{21}$	...	TFIDF$_{N1}$
TechFunc$_2$	TFIDF$_{12}$	TFIDF$_{22}$	...	TFIDF$_{N2}$
...	...	...	...	
TechFunc$_M$	TFIDF$_{1M}$	TFIDF$_{2M}$	...	TFIDF$_{NM}$

The singular decomposition of a term-document matrix into a product of three matrices is used in LSA:

$$A = UDV^T,$$

(12)

where U – the term vector matrix, D – the matrix of singular values, V^T – the matrix of vectors of patent documents.

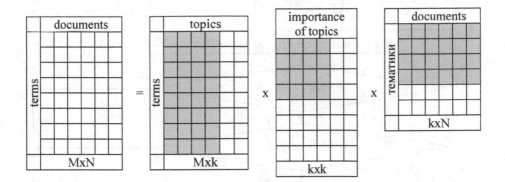

If we leave k the largest singular values in the matrix D, and the columns/rows corresponding to these values in the U/VT matrices, then the product of the resulting matrices $A_k = U_k x D_k x V_k^T$ will be the best approximation of the original matrix A by the rank-k matrix. All terms from the matrix A_k will be an abridged space of technical functions, i.e. the most significant for the patent array will be automatically determined from the entire set of technical functions.

The value of k is chosen empirically, and since the patent array is about a million documents, then k is about 2%.

In the aggregate of all documents {Pat} of the patent array, the physical effects (PE_i) are searched (defined as terms) and the frequency of their occurrence is determined in patent documents.

Normalized term frequency weighting selected as the local weighing of i-th physical effect PE_i in j-th patent document Pat_j:

$$t_{ji} = 0.4 \times \chi(f_{ij}) + 0.6 \times \left(\frac{f_{ij}}{max_k f_{ij}} \right) \times r_i, \qquad (13)$$

Where f_{ij} – the frequency of occurrence of PE_i in Pat_j,

k – the number of PE in j-th patent document Pat_j,

r_i – coefficient of completeness of the description of physical effect (PE_i) in patent document Pat_j,

$$\chi(f_{ij}) = \begin{cases} r_i, & \text{if } f_{ij} > 0, \\ 0, & \text{if } f_{ij} = 0 \end{cases}$$

The search for a description of the physical effect in a patent document is carried out by performing iterative steps with a consistent simplification of the query (Fig. 6):

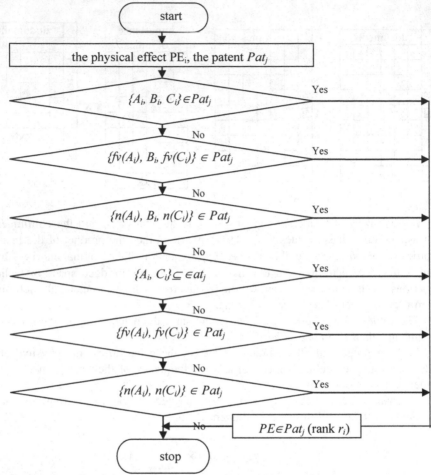

A, B, C – formalized descriptions of the PE input, object, and output,

fv(A), fv(C) - physical values of input A and output C for PE (for non-parametric effects),

n(A), n(C) names of respectively input and output effects.

Fig. 6. Algorithm to simplify the search query

(a) search for full descriptions of input effect A, of object B, output effect C, $r_i = 1$;
(b) search for full descriptions B, physical values A and C (for non-parametric effects), $r_i = 0.8$;
(c) search for full descriptions A and C, $r_i = 0.6$;
(d) search for physical values A and C (for non-parametric effects), $r_i = 0.4$;
(e) search for full descriptions B, names of effects A and C, $r_i = 0.3$;
(f) search for names of effects A and C, $r_i = 0.2$.

The inverted document frequency is chosen as the global weighting of PE_i, which is 0, if the physical effect (at one of the 6 stages of detailing (Fig. 6), which was found in the patent Pat_j) appears in all patent documents of the array, and this weight increases as the number of documents, in which the physical effect occurs, decreases:

$$g_i = \log\left(\frac{N}{\sum_{j=1}^{N} \gamma(f_{ij})}\right), \tag{14}$$

where N – the number of documents in the patent corpus,

$$\gamma(f_{ij}) = \begin{cases} 1, & \text{if } f_{ij} > 0, \\ 0, & \text{if } f_{ij} = 0 \end{cases}$$

Normalization:

$$d_i = \left(\sum_{j=1}^{Q} (g_j t_{ji})^2\right)^{-1/2}, \tag{15}$$

where Q – the number of terms (physical effects) in the patent array,
t_{ji} – the local weighting of PE_i in Pat_j,
g_i – the global weighting of PE_i.
Calculate the reduced frequency of occurrence of the physical effects PE_i in patent documents Pat_j.

$$TFIDF_{ij} = t_{ji} \times g_i \times d_i, \tag{16}$$

A term-document matrix is formed (Table 2), the elements of which contain the reduced frequencies $TFIDF_{ij}$ of the occurrence of the i-th physical effect PE_i in the j-th patent document Pat_j.

Table 2. Matrix of reduced frequencies of occurrence of physical effects in the documents

Term	Document			
	Pat_1	Pat_2	...	Pat_N
PE_1	$TFIDF_{11}$	$TFIDF_{21}$	...	$TFIDF_{N1}$
PE_2	$TFIDF_{12}$	$TFIDF_{22}$	...	$TFIDF_{N2}$
...	...	...	...	
PE_M	$TFIDF_{1M}$	$TFIDF_{2M}$	...	$TFIDF_{NM}$

Since each patent Pat stores information about a technical object (TO) as an attribute, then we will create a «TO-PE» matrix based on physical effects PE_i, for which the coefficient $TFIDF_{ji}$ of occurrence in the j-th patent document Pat_j is greater than a certain threshold value equal to 0.9.

The singular decomposition of the term-document matrix is carried out, and all terms from the matrix Ak will be the reduced space of physical effects (PE), i.e. the most significant PE for the patent array will be automatically determined from the whole set of PE.

Thus, the method of latent-semantic analysis allows you to submit patent documents as vectors distributed in space:

(a) technical functions $Pat_j = (TechFunc_1, TechFunc_2, \ldots TechFunc_M)$,
(b) physical effects $Pat_j = (PE_1, PhE_2, \ldots PE_Q)$.

To build a database performed by the physical effects of technical functions, it is necessary to establish a connection between the physical effects (PE) and technical functions (TF) distributed in the common patent space $(Pat_1, Pat_2, \ldots Pat_N)$.

The construction of the matrix of semantic connections "PE –TF" is carried out with two reduced and cleared of "noise" term documentary matrices. Since in term documentary matrices each term (physical effect or technical function) is a row vector, then the semantic connections between any two terms (PE_i and $TechFun_j$) can be interpreted as proximity or distance the vectors corresponding to these terms, using any known measures of proximity or distance.

An assessment was made of the effectiveness of methods for comparing patent vectors distributed over a term space [12]:

– storage vectors by two different methods (storage in HDFS distributed file system, storage in a PostgreSQL database) [13];
– comparing the resulting vectors by four different methods [14] (based on the standard deviation of the vectors, based on the element-by-element comparison of vectors, based on the cosine method, based on the comparison of the lengths of vectors) to search for patents-analogs.

The efficiency test of the methods (Table 3) was carried out on a test dataset generated on the basis of the patent databases of Rospatent and the USPTO. For each patent, patents from his citation list have been added to the test array as relevant. Irrelevant "noise" patents are also included in the test set.

Table 3. Results of efficiency test of the methods.

№	Comparison of vectors	Storage	T, s	Precision	Recall
1	Cosine method	HDFS	0,5	0,98	0,87
2	Comparison of the lengths of vectors	HDFS	0,7	0,85	0,68
3	The standard deviation of vectors	HDFS	0,7	0,95	0,81
4	The element-by-element comparison of vectors	HDFS	1,1	0,88	0,75
5	Cosine method	PostgreSQL	0,8	0,98	0,87
6	Comparison of the lengths of vectors	PostgreSQL	1,3	0,85	0,68
7	The standard deviation of vectors	PostgreSQL	1,2	0,95	0,81
8	The element-by-element comparison of vectors	PostgreSQL	1,6	0,88	0,75

$$T = t_{end} - t_{start}, \ precision = \frac{|D_{rel} \cap D_{retr}|}{|D_{retr}|}, \ recall = \frac{|D_{rel} \cap D_{retr}|}{|D_{rel}|},$$

where t_{end} – search end time, t_{start} – search start time, D_{rel} – set of relevant documents in the database, D_{retr} – set of documents found by the system.

According to the test results, we can conclude: the cosine method is the most effective method for comparing vectors.

Since we are only interested in the strongest and most stable semantic relations "PE-TF", we will not take into account the proximity values of two vectors, representing the i-th physical effect (PE_i) and j-th technical function ($TechFun_j$) distributed in a common space of patents ($Pat_1, Pat_2, \dots Pat_N$), below a certain threshold value of 0.85, determined empirically.

5   Conclusion

Authors developed the method for extraction the physical effects descriptions from the patents of USPTO and RosPatent databases, and the method for extracting of technical functions from Natural Language documents including patent texts.

The method of automated construction of a matrix of physical functions performed by physical effects is based on the detection of latent dependencies in the consolidated matrix "Physical Effects – Technical Functions". The consolidated matrix is formed from two term-document matrices: (a) the first matrix describes the frequency of occurrence (TFIDF) of each term (technical functions in SAO form) in all patent documents, (b) the second matrix describes the frequency of occurrence of physical effects in all patens.

Acknowledgments. The reported study was funded by RFBR (research project 18-07-01086), RFBR and Administration of the Volgograd region (projects 19-47-340007, 19-41-340016).

References

1. Orloff, M.: Inventive Thinking through TRIZ: A Practical Guide, p. 352. Springer, Heidelberg (2006). https://doi.org/10.1007/978-3-540-33223-7
2. Vayngolts, I., Korobkin, D., Fomenkov, S., Golovanchikov, A.: Synthesis of the physical operation principles of technical system. In: Kravets, A., Shcherbakov, M., Kultsova, M., Groumpos, P. (eds.) CIT&DS 2017. CCIS, vol. 754, pp. 575–588. Springer, Cham (2017). https://doi.org/10.1007/978-3-319-65551-2_42
3. Korobkin, D., Fomenkov, S., Kravets, A.: Methods for extracting the descriptions of sci-tech effects and morphological features of technical systems from patents. In: IISA 2018 (2018). https://ieeexplore.ieee.org/document/8633624
4. Davydova, S., Korobkin, D., Fomenkov, S., Kolesnikov, S.: Modeling of new technical systems using cause-effect relationships. In: IISA 2018 (2018). https://ieeexplore.ieee.org/document/8633683
5. Park, H., Yoon, J., Kim, K.: Identifying patent infringement using SAO based semantic technological similarities. Scientometrics **90**, 515 (2012)

6. Korobkin, D., Fomenkov, S., Kravets, A., Kolesnikov, S.: Prior art candidate search on base of statistical and semantic patent analysis. In: Xiao, Y., Abraham, A.P. (eds.) Multi Conference on Computer Science and Information Systems, pp. 231–238 (2017)

7. Manning, C., Raghavan, P., Schütze, H.: Introduction to Information Retrieval. Cambridge University Press, Cambridge (2008)

8. Mel'čuk, I.: Dependency Syntax Theory and Practice. SUNY, New York (1988)

9. Yufeng, D., Duo, J., Lixue, J.: Patent Similarity Measure Based on SAO Structure. Chin. Sentence Clause Text Inf. Process. **30**(1), 30–36 (2016)

10. Korobkin, D., Fomenkov, S., Kolesnikov, S., Lobeyko, V., Golovanchikov, A.: Modification of physical effect model for the synthesis of the physical operation principles of technical system. In: Kravets, A., Shcherbakov, M., Kultsova, M., Shabalina, O. (eds.) CIT&DS 2015. CCIS, vol. 535, pp. 368–378. Springer, Cham (2015). https://doi.org/10.1007/978-3-319-23766-4_29

11. Fomenkova, M., Korobkin, D., Fomenkov, S.: Extraction of physical effects based on the semantic analysis of the patent texts. In: Kravets, A., Shcherbakov, M., Kultsova, M., Groumpos, P. (eds.) CIT&DS 2017. CCIS, vol. 754, pp. 73–87. Springer, Cham (2017). https://doi.org/10.1007/978-3-319-65551-2_6

12. Korobkin, D., Fomenkov, S., Kravets, A., Kolesnikov, S.: Methods of statistical and semantic patent analysis. In: Kravets, A., Shcherbakov, M., Kultsova, M., Groumpos, P. (eds.) CIT&DS 2017. CCIS, vol. 754, pp. 48–61. Springer, Cham (2017). https://doi.org/10.1007/978-3-319-65551-2_4

13. Ustugova, S., Parygin, D., Sadovnikova, N., Yadav, V., Prikhodkova, I.: Geoanalytical system for support of urban processes management tasks. In: Kravets, A., Shcherbakov, M., Kultsova, M., Groumpos, P. (eds.) CIT&DS 2017. CCIS, vol. 754, pp. 430–440. Springer, Cham (2017). https://doi.org/10.1007/978-3-319-65551-2_31

14. Ustugova, S., Parygin, D., Sadovnikova, N., Finogeev, A., Kizim, A.: Monitoring of social reactions to support decision making on issues of urban territory management. In: Procedia Computer Science: Proceedings of the 5th International Young Scientist Conference on Computational Science, YSC 2016, Krakow, Poland, 26–28 October 2016, vol. 101, pp. 243–252. Elsevier (2016). https://doi.org/10.1016/j.procs.2016.11.029

Artificial Intelligence and Deep Learning Technologies for Creative Tasks. Open Science Semantic Technologies

Named Entity Recognition (NER) for Nepali

Gopal Maharjan[1], Bal Krishna Bal[1(✉)], and Santosh Regmi[2]

[1] Information and Language Processing Research Lab, Department of Computer
Science and Engineering, Kathmandu University, Dhulikhel, Kavre, Nepal
gopalmaharjan59@gmail.com, bal@ku.edu.np
[2] KEIV Technologies Pvt. Ltd., Banepa, Kavre, Nepal
regmi.santosh32@gmail.com

Abstract. Named Entity Recognition (NER) is the process of automatic
extraction of Named Entities (NEs) by means of recognizing (finding the entities
in a given text) and their classification (assigning a type). A lot of work has been
done in English and other languages for NER but very little research has been
done for Nepali NER. Nepali language has its own issues and challenges which
need to be addressed. In this paper, we present the NE Tagset and features that
can be potentially used for Nepali NER. To train the model classifiers like
Support Vector Machine (SVM), Multinomial Naïve Bayes and Logistic
Regression are used and their precision, recall and F1-score have been calculated. 5 fold cross validation is used to evaluate and validate our model.

Keywords: Natural Language Processing (NLP) ·
Named Entity Recognition (NER) · Machine learning (ML) ·
Named Entities (NE)

1 Introduction

We, humans have no trouble understanding natural language as we have common
sense, reasoning capacity and experience, but computers do not have the given capabilities, and so we need to train the machine to get the desired output.

NER is a process in which Named Entities (NEs) are detected in a document and
are classified into their respective NE classes like person, location, organization, time,
etc. using any of the NER based approaches like rule based, machine learning based or
hybrid approach [4].

Example of Named Entities:
Ram (Person) studies in Kathmandu University (Organization).
राम (Person) काठमांडौ विश्वविद्यालय (Organization) मा पढछ।

Nepali is an under-resourced language in terms of the availability of language
resources and tools. This holds true in case of the NER system for Nepali. We do not
yet have a good NER system in place and its development is important since it has a
wide application, especially in problem domains like Information Extraction, Question
Answering System, Machine Translation (among others).

© Springer Nature Switzerland AG 2019
A. G. Kravets et al. (Eds.): CIT&DS 2019, CCIS 1084, pp. 71–80, 2019.
https://doi.org/10.1007/978-3-030-29750-3_6

The development of a NER system for any language entails many technical issues globally across languages as well as specific to a language. Below, we discuss some issues relevant and applicable to the research and development of a NER system for Nepal [1, 9]:

(1) There are not adequate and well-developed resources and tools required for NER development, for example, Nepali text corpus, POS Tagger, Chunker, Parser, etc.
(2) **No Capitalization:** Nepali language does not require capitalization.
(3) **Proper Name Ambiguity:** Person Names are more frequent and diverse in the Nepali language and a lot of these words can be found in the dictionary with some other specific meanings. Example:
  (a) Designation vs. Title-Person:
       'उपकुलपति (Vice Chancellor)' is a designation, but 'महात्मा (Mahatma)' is a Title.
  (b) Organization vs. Brand:
       'पेप्सी (Pepsi)' can mean an Organization, but it is more likely to mean brand.
  (c) Person vs. Organization:
       'टाटा (Tata)' can refer to a Person, but it is more likely to mean an Organization.
  (d) Person vs. Location:
       'पशुपति (Pashupati)' can refer to a person, but it is more likely to mean a Location.
(4) **Nested Entities:**
  Nested Entities contain two or more proper names that come together to form a new named entity.
  Example:
  'Tribhuvan International Airport'
  Translation,
  'त्रिभुवन अन्तर्राष्ट्रिय विमानस्थल'
  Here, 'International' and 'Airport' are translated while 'Tribhuvan' is transliterated. The nested named entities in the above case are:
  'त्रिभुवन' (Person) and 'त्रिभुवन अन्तर्राष्ट्रिय विमानस्थल' (Organization)
(5) **Abbreviations:**
  Example:
  'KU'/'के यू' is an abbreviation, but also an 'organization'.
(6) **Word Order:** Hindi/Nepali language has also some word order issues.
  Example:
  "रामले फोहोरको थुप्रो फाल्यो" and "फोहोरको थुप्रो रामले फाल्यो" which are both translate to "Ram disposed the garbage".

2 Named Entity Tagset for NER

A named entity Tagset for a NER system is a collection of named entity tags that are employed for tagging the named entities in any text. The named entities may range from PERSON, PLACE, ORGANIZATION, DATE, CURRENCY etc. among others.

Table 1, describes some of the named entity Tagset applicable for Nepali [1, 4, 5, 9].

Table 1. NE tagset

NE tag	Definition
NEP (Person)	Name of a person Example: Ram, Sita
NEL (Location)	Name of a place or location Example: Kathmandu
NEO (Organization)	Name of an organization Example: Nepal Oil Corporation
NED (Designation)	Name of any designation Example: General Manager, Prime minister
NETP (Title-Person)	Name of the title coming before the name of the person Example: Dr., Mr., Mahatma, Prof.
NEB (Brand)	Brand Name Example: Coca cola, Addidas
NEM (Measure)	Any measure Example: Rs.1000, 5 kg
NETI (Time)	Date, month, year Example: 25 April, 2015
NEA (Abbreviation)	Name in short form Example: NLP, KU

In order to build a NER system for any language, it is important to build machine learning capability of the system to automatically tag and extract the named entities. To realize this capability, it is important to design some Machine Learning features, which is discussed in the next section.

3   NER Features for Nepali

The following feature scan be potentially used for the Nepali NER as used by various researchers in their work in other languages:

- **Context Window:** It is a method to include the features of the surrounding tokens of a named entity mention in text. In here, similar types of named entities will be described by similar words, which are often around the named entity mentions. The context window is usually set to a fixed size, which means to include 'n' tokens before and 'n' tokens after the current token.
- **Parts of Speech (POS) Information:** It describe linguistic categories of words (or more precisely lexical items). Common categories include noun, verb, adjective and adverb among others. The POS of the current word and the surrounding words can be used as features.

- **Gazetteers Lists:** In general, it is a way to group related terms and map them to certain types or categories, such that the same type of named entities tend to be consistently associated to the same gazetteers.
  The list can be:
  - Person-Prefix like Mr., Mrs., Miss, etc.
  - Organization Suffix Word like Pvt. Ltd., Mill, Company, etc.
  - First-Name like Ram, Shyam, etc.
  - Middle-Name like Bahadur, Kumar, Kumari, Prasad, etc.
  - Last-Name or Surname like Shrestha, Dahal, Yadav, etc.
  - Common Location words like Road, Highway, etc.
  - Location-Name
  - Month-Name
  - Day-Name
- **Orthographic feature** gives information about a word capitalization, use of upper and lower case letters, quote, roman numbers, ends with dots, hyphens and punctuations, dates, percentages, intervals etc. There is no uppercase, lower case, capitalization in Nepali. The punctuation marks used in Nepali are same as those of Roman except the full stop which uses the symbol "। (purnabiram)".
- **Morphological features** are related to words affixes (prefix and suffix) and roots. Example:
  In the word "रामपुर [Rampur], भक्तपुर [Bhaktapur]", the root word is राम [Ram] and भक्त [Bhakta] whereas suffix is पुर [pur]. Although root word is different, but they share the same ending पुर [pur] which means the given two word रामपुर [Rampur] and भक्तपुर [Bhaktapur] refers to a location type NE.

Dey [2] developed NER using the semi hybrid approach, i.e. rule based and Hidden Markov Model. Person, Location, Number, Organization, Currency, Quantifier is used for tagging. The semi hybrid approach gives overall accuracy: Person (85.15%), Location (91.01%), Number (86.17%), Organization (96.10%), Currency (100%) and Quantifier (100%).

Bam [1] developed NER using Support Vector Machine (SVM). Person, Location, Organization, Miscellaneous and words that are not NE is used as a tag set. Multiclass SVM is used in which five SVM are trained that corresponds to five NE tag and for each new word, each of five SVM is evaluated and most confident NE tag is assigned to that word. Gazeetter lists is used as a feature. Developing NER using SVM in corpus size 29298 gives F1-score 92.31%.

As mentioned earlier, very little work has been done in NER for Nepali but still we can do a lot of work in NER for Nepali to improve the accuracy. We can use the POS information, context window size as a feature for NER, which can address issues like Proper name ambiguity, Nested entities and so on which can not be addressed by features like gazeetter list.

Example 1:

(a) बनारस सहर गंगा को किनारमा बसेको छ।
(b) गंगाको जन्म काठमाडौँमा भएको हो।

In Example 1(a), In the context of word "किनार", 'Ganga' is marked as a river.
In Example 1(b), In the context of word "जन्म", 'Ganga' is marked as a person.

Example 2:

(a) राम ले हामीलाई पशुपति<NNP>मा पर्खि बसे छ ।

(b) प्रहरीको लाठी लागेर<NNP>पशुपति घाइते भएका छन् ।

In Example 2(a), the word "पर्खि" marked 'पशुपति' as a Location type NE.
In Example 2(b), the word "घाइते" marked 'पशुपति' as a Person type NE.

Example 3:

(a) मदन पुरस्कार गुठी ले २०७३ सालको मदन पुरस्कारका लागि नौवटा कृति <NN>
को सूची प्रकाशन गरेको छ ।

(b) मेरो साथी को नाम कृति<NNP>हो ।

In Example 3(a), the word 'कृति' is expressed in the context of literature, POS tag as a common noun and marked by the word "सूची" so it is not NE.

In Example 3(b), the word 'कृति' is expressed in the context of name, POS tag as a Proper name and is marked by the word "नाम" so it is a Person type NE.

Example 4:

(a) मदन/B-ORG पुरस्कार/I-ORG गुठी/ORG ले २०७३ सालको मदन पुरस्कारका
लागि नौवटा कृति<NN>को सूची प्रकाशन गरेको छ ।

(b) मदन/B-PER पैसा कमाउनको लागि विदेश जान्छ र फर्कने क्रममा बाटोमा
बिरामी हुन्छ ।

In Example 4(a), the nested entities word 'मदन पुरस्कार गुठी' is NE tag as a मदन/B-ORG पुरस्कार/I-ORG गुठी/ORG and the word "ले" marked 'मदन पुरस्कार गुठी' as an Organization type NE.

In Example 4(b), the word 'मदन' is NE tag as a 'मदन/B-PER' and the word "कमाउन" marked 'मदन' as a Person type NE.

Table 2, describes some of the NER work done in Hindi and Nepali:

Table 2. Summary of NER work

S. No.	Language	Work (Topic)	Approach/Techniques	Performance measure (F1-score)
1	Hindi	Named Entity Recognition in Hindi using MEMM [6]	Maximum Entropy Markov Model	79.7%
2	Hindi	A Hybrid Feature Set Maximum Entropy Hindi Named Entity Recognition [9]	Maximum Entropy and Hybrid Feature Set	81.52%

(continued)

Table 2. (*continued*)

S. No.	Language	Work (Topic)	Approach/Techniques	Performance measure (F1-score)
3	Hindi	Rapid Development of Hindi Named Entity Recognition Using Conditional Random Fields and Feature Induction [7]	Conditional Random Fields	71.50%
4	Hindi	Named Entity Recognition for Hindi Language: A Hybrid Approach [10]	Conditional Random Fields + Maximum entropy + Rule Based &Voting Algorithm	82.95%
5	Hindi	An HMM Based Named Entity Recognition System for Indian Languages: The JU System at ICON 2013 [3]	Hidden Markov Model	75.2%
6	Hindi	Towards Deep Learning in Hindi NER: An approach to tackle the Labelled Data Scarcity [11]	Bi-Directional RNN-LSTM	77.48%
7	(i) English-Hindi (ii) English-Tamil	A Deep Neural Network based Approach for Entity Extraction in Code-Mixed Indian Social Media Text [12]	Gated Recurrent Unit (GRU) works similar to LSTM	(i) English-Hindi: 66.04% (ii) English-Tamil: 53.85%
8	Nepali	Named Entity Recognition for Nepali Text Using Support Vector Machines [1]	Support Vector Machine	92.31%
9	Nepali	Named Entity Recognition for Nepali language: A Semi Hybrid Approach [2]	Hidden Markov Model and Rule based	85.15%

4   Research Methodology

Supervised Machine Learning Architecture

The architecture shown in Fig. 1 generalizes the process of NER using supervised machine learning technique. Supervised machine learning takes a set of input data and known responses to the data and seeks to build NER model that generates reasonable predictions for the response to new data.

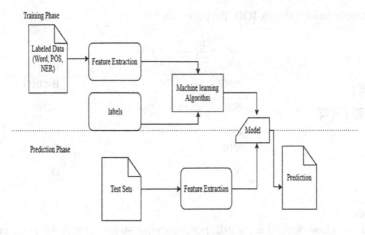

Fig. 1. General architecture of supervised machine learning

While building the model, the provided labeled dataset is divided into a training set and test set. The training set is used to train the supervised machine learning classifier and test set is used to evaluate the model. The architecture shown in Fig. 1 is divided into two phases, i.e. training and prediction. In the training phase, labeled dataset or corpus is used to train the classifier. And in the prediction phase, trained classifier is used to predict unseen data we provided.

The experiment has been performed in order to find the best classifier.

Preprocessing Data

The corpus text is tokenized into a one word per line format and is annotated manually following the CoNLL-2003 IOB Tagging format.

The Table below describes the NE Tags and its corresponding meaning.

NE Tags	Meaning
B-PER	Beginning of Person name (NEP)
I-PER	Inside of Person name
B-LOC	Beginning of Location name (NEL)
I-LOC	Inside of Location name
B-ORG	Beginning of Organization name (NEO)
I-ORG	Inside of Organization name
B-MISC	Beginning of Miscellaneous name
I-MISC	Inside of Miscellaneous name
O	Other than Named Entity

Miscellaneous Name: NEN (Number), NEM (Measure), NETI (Time) Tagset.

Other than Named Entity: NED (Designation), NEA (Abbreviation), NEB (Brand), NETP (Title-Person) Tagset.

An example below shows IOB Tagging scheme:

Word	Part of Speech (POS)	NER
राम	NNP	B-PER
काठमाडौं	NNP	B-ORG
विश्वविद्यालय	NN	I-ORG
मा	POP	O
पढ्छ	VBF	O
।	YF	O

Feature Sets

Five word window size, i.e. word, pos, previous-word, previous-pos, previous-previous-word, previous-previous-pos, next-word, next-pos, next-next word, and next-next-pos are taken as features.

Training Classifier

For training the model, the following classifier has been used.

- Support Vector Machine (SVM)
- Multinomial Naïve Bayes
- Logistic Regression

5   Experiment

Dataset

Asample size of 11816 POS-Tagged words out of 100K words were used as a corpus for experimentation. The full corpus is available at http://www.cle.org.pk/software/ling_resources/UrduNepaliEnglishParallelCorpus.htm.

Test Environment

We have conducted our experiment on Windows7, Python 3.5. For text processing, we have used the Natural Language Toolkit (NLTK) and for machine learning we have used SciKit-Learn.

Experimental Parameters

For validating the model, 5 fold cross validation is used.

Evaluation Metrics

For evaluating the performance of the proposed NER system, various performance measures like Precision, Recall and F-measure have been used [8].

- Precision = Named entities identified correctly/Total number of named entities identified
- Recall = Named entities identified by the system/Total number of named entities present in the file
- F1-score = Harmonic mean of precision and recall

6 Results and Discussion

By doing experiment, we get the following result (Table 3):

Table 3. Average score of different classifier

Classifier	F1-score
Multinomial Bayes	91%
Logistic Regression	95%
Support Vector Machine	96%

From above table, we see that it is better to train our model using SVM classifier rather than logistic regression and multinomial Bayes.

The reasons behinds good performance of SVM over Multinomial Naïve Bayes and Logistic Regression are:

High Dimension of the Training Sets
The dimension of the training set is 11816. Due to the high dimensional size SVM performs better as compared to rest.

Dependent Feature Sets
Here the features taken are dependent on each other whereas assumption of Multinomial Naïve Bayes is that the features are independent. This causes the low performance as compared to SVM.

Table 4, describes the comparison between the Existing [1] and Current work in NER for Nepali.

Table 4. Comparison between existing and current work in NER for Nepali

Existing work	Current work
Corpus size: 29,968	Corpus size: 11816 words
Annotation: PER, LOC, ORG, MISC, O	Annotation: B-PER, I-PER, B-LOC, I-LOC, B-ORG, I-ORG, B-MISC, I-MISC, O Miscellaneous name: NEN (Number), NEM (Measure), NETI (Time) Tagset Other than Named Entity: NED (Designation), NEA (Abbreviation), NEB (Brand), NETP (Title-Person) Tagset
Feature sets: Gazeetter list	Feature sets: Five word window size and pos tag word information
Classifier/Algorithm: Support Vector Machine	Classifier/Algorithm: Support Vector Machine
Evaluation: F1-score = 92.31%	Evaluation: F1-score = 96%

7 Conclusion

In this paper, we have developed a NER system using Support Vector Machine.

We have used 3090 POS- tagged words as a corpus for annotation and experiments. We have adopted the CoNLL-2003 IOB tagging format.

We have considered five word window size and pos information as a feature. For validating the model 5-fold cross validation is used.

We found from the experiment that Support Vector machine performs the best in the given task of NER. By involving larger amount of dataset and also added features set, we have obtained higher accuracies compared to the accuracies of the current Nepali NER. In the future, we look forward to studying and verifying the different factors that can influence classification performance, for example, including more features. Moreover, we are also considering using a hybrid approach using Rule Based + ML Approach or ML + ML Approach, which are used in some other languages. We are also considering to follow Deep Learning Approach within our corpus or in Social Media Text (Twitter, Facebook, etc.) where nowadays code mixing (mixing of more than one language, example: Nepali-English) way of texting is used.

References

1. Bam, S.B., Shahi, T.B.: Named entity recognition for Nepali text using support vector machines. Int. Inf. Manag. **6**, 21–29 (2014)
2. Dey, A.D., Paul, A., Syam Purkayastha, B.: Named entity recognition for Nepali language: a semi hybrid approach. Int. J. Eng. Innov. Technol. (IJEIT) **3**(8), 21–25 (2014)
3. Gayen, V., Sarkar, K.: An HMM based named entity recognition system for Indian languages: The JU System at ICON 2013. Research Gate (2013)
4. Kaur, D., Gupta, V.: A survey of named entity recognition in English and other Indian languages. Int. J. Comput. Sci. **7**(6), 239–245 (2010)
5. Kaur, Y., Kaur, R.: Named entity recognition (NER) system for Hindi Language using combination of rule based approach and list look up approach. Int. J. Sci. Res. Manag. (IJSRM) **3**, 2300–2306 (2015)
6. Kumar, N., Bhattacharyya, P.: Named entity recognition in Hindi using MEMM. Technical report, IIT Bombay India (2006)
7. Li, W., Andrew, M.: rapid development of Hindi named entity recognition using conditional random fields and feature induction. ACM TALIP **2**, 290–294 (2004)
8. Pillai, A.S., Sobha, L.:. Named entity recognition for Indian languages: a survey. Int. J. Adv. Res. Comput. Sci. Softw. Eng. (IJARCSSE) **3**(11) (2013)
9. Saha, S.K., Sarkar, S., Mitra, P.: A hybrid feature set maximum entropy Hindi named entity recognition (n.d.)
10. Srivastava, S., Sanglikar, M., Kothari, D.C.: Named entity recognition for Hindi language: a hybrid approach. Int. J. Comput. Linguist. **2**(1), 10–23 (2011)
11. Vinayak, A., Shreenivas, B., Monik, P., Prabhu Ameya, S.M.: Towards deep learning in Hindi NER: an approach to tackle the labelled data scarcity. In: International Conference on Natural Language Processing (ICON), Varanasi, India, pp. 154–160 (2016)
12. Gupta, D., Ekbal, A., Bhattacharyya, P.: A deep neural network based approach for entity extraction in code-mixed Indian social media text. In: Proceedings of the Eleventh International Conference on Language Resources and Evaluation, pp. 1762–1767. European Language Resource Association, Miyazaki (2018)

Semantic Zooming Approach to Semantic Link Network Visualization

Dmitry Litovkin, Anton Anikin, and Marina Kultsova[✉]

Volgograd State Technical University, Volgograd, Russia
anton@anikin.name, marina.kultsova@mail.ru

Abstract. In the paper, we described a semantic zooming approach to the visualization of special kind structures - semantic link networks (SLN), represented as a visual graph. The proposed approach allows decreasing semantic noise in SLN overview and navigation and also simplifies the process of understanding the domain studied with SLN by means of semantic zooming. We proposed priori importance levels of SLN items and semantic zooming scale to visualize the SLN with different details level. We designed an interactive SLN visualization process including the following SLN transformations: filtering SLN items, context collapse and expansion for SLN item, and changing the details in the visualized object representation in the geometric SLN graph. The transformation algorithms were developed, and also examples of SNL semantic zooming were described in details in the paper.

Keywords: Semantic web · Semantic link network · WHAT-knowledge · Semantic zooming

1 Introduction

In learning and scientific research, the main and most important process is knowledge management. Knowledge management includes different kinds of tasks, such as the creation of new knowledge, knowledge storage, transfer (as well as sharing), and its applying [6, 7]. Any complex domain can be viewed at the different aspects and layers depending on the informational needs of the person, the following aspects based on W-questions are proposed in [12]:

- WHAT-Knowledge (conceptual representation)
- WHAT FOR-Knowledge (strategic representation)
- HOW TO-Knowledge (functional representation)
- WHO-Knowledge (organizational representation)
- WHERE-Knowledge (spatial representation)
- WHEN-Knowledge (temporal representation)
- WHY-Knowledge (causal representation)

A. G. Kravets et al. (Eds.): CIT&DS 2019, CCIS 1084, pp. 81–95, 2019.
https://doi.org/10.1007/978-3-030-29750-3_7

The WHAT-Knowledge is the most important type of knowledge in learning [8, 12] since the classical way of learning assumes that the first the studied concept should be defined, then its properties, and only then its relations with other concepts.

Semantic link network (SLN) [23] can be used to represent the WHAT Knowledge that is structured as a single mental model and answers some focus question [18]. The focus question determines a context, main subject, and knowledge frame being studied.

One of the ways to intensify a learning process in a subject domain is a visualization of the domain knowledge. Since the subject domain usually has a complex structure with a huge set of concepts and relations visualized with many elements of different kinds (nodes, links, node labels, link labels, direction of links in directed networks, node attributes, link attributes) [20], it is difficult for a human to overview and understand the conceptual model represented by SLN. Various approaches and tools for conceptual models visualization and navigation exist and available, but in most cases, the user faced a wide range of issues mentioned in [1] and caused by high information noise in visualization. So, the development of approaches and tools for the convenient and informative representation of WHAT-Knowledge structures and domain conceptual model as a whole remains an extremely important, urgent and promising task.

2   State of the Art

According to [5], in knowledge management, choosing a particular type of knowledge visualization should be based on answering 4 key questions:

1. Why-question: which knowledge management purpose do I want to achieve with the map?
2. What-question: which kind of content about knowledge do I want to represent in the map?
3. "For whom" and "when" question: Who should use the map in which context or situation and at what level?
4. "How" and "who" question: Which graphic form should be used and who can create the map in what way?

In [5], the approaches to knowledge visualization are classified by the intended purpose or knowledge management process:

1. New knowledge creation;
2. Knowledge assessment or audit;
3. Knowledge identification;
4. Knowledge development or acquisition/learning (learning overview and learning path, learning content structure, learning reviewing/repetition);
5. Knowledge transfer, sharing, or communication maps;
6. Knowledge application;
7. Knowledge marketing.

For learning, the most typical purposes are 3, 4, 5, for scientific research - 1, 2, 3, 4, 5, 6; and the most important type of knowledge to be visualized for these tasks is WHAT-Knowledge.

There are many cognitive structures developed for WHAT-knowledge visualization: concept map [3], mind map, UML class diagram [11], ER diagram, OWL ontology in diverse visual notations (in Graphol notation [4], VOWL2 notation [21] and other notations used in corresponding ontology visualization tools like Ontodia [15], OWLGrEd [14]), ORM2 diagram [9, 10] etc.

Most WHAT-knowledge visual models are represented with graph structures. Usually, such graphs belong to the classes of strongly connected, oriented, cyclic, labeled, and non-planar graphs, they can also be multigraphs and even hypergraphs. That's why learning using SLN visualization is complicated by the presence of semantic noise [2]. Noise is all that is added to the signal or taken away from it without the intent of the signal source in the transmission process. The effect of the recipients semantic noise is based on psychological processes - it is a human defensive response to an increase in the power of information flows beyond the recipients' ability to adequately interpret incoming messages.

One way to resolve this issue is the conversion of a large informational message into a sequence of small ones. The conversion should occur without loss of any useful information. But having solved the problem of recipient information overloading, it is possible to get another extreme, when the information is not enough, this case is also considered as information noise. Therefore, converting the information it is very important to maintain a balance between its oversupply and shortage.

We can use geometric and semantic zooming to decrease semantic noise in SLN overview and navigation (and as a result, to simplify the process of understanding the domain studied by means of the visual model). Geometric zooming is an interactive technique of interaction with a graph, which allows to move away or zoom in on objects by changing their size in order to focus on a specific area of the graph. Semantic zooming allows changing the degree of information details on the graph elements. With the increase in semantic zooming, additional properties of objects become visible. Semantic zooming allows dividing one large graph into several different views on the level of details. By changing the zooming parameters, we can hide irrelevant information and at the same time not lose sight of the relevant useful information. Parameter values of semantic zooming vary for different users, it depends on personal user knowledge background and informational needs.

To be understood, SLN can be represented as a graph with different details levels. So, semantic zooming of SLN visual appearance is based on the interactive visualization methods for large graphs representation. They allow reducing shown graph nodes and edges: filtering (removing some nodes and edges of the geometric graph), aggregation (creating a single new item instead of multiple others and replacing them), embed focus and context information, etc. [1, 13, 16]. However, these methods are not well adapted for the SLN visualization. The example of semantic zooming implementation using these methods for SLN vi- sualization is presented in [17, 22]. However, it does not take into account the prior importance of the concepts (defined by an expert) in terms of the sensemaking of the SLN as a whole. Also, this approach does not allow changing the detail level in the focus point.

So the goal of our study is to decrease the semantic noise, caused by excessive detailing of the SLN visual appearance, by providing the user with a mechanism for semantic zooming.

3   SLN Visualization with Different Detail Levels

In a framework of the proposed approach we suggested to decrease the semantic noise caused by excessive detailing of the SLN visual appearance by means of semantic zooming mechanism, so, we should meet the following requirements:

1. As a visual representation of the SLN is a strongly connected geometric graph, interactive visualization is necessary to visualize a different set of SLN elements at different times and provide the transitions between these views. So, the following SLN transformations should be implemented:
   1.1. Filtering the less-important nodes of SLN.
   1.2. Filtering on demand the elements related to the target element of SLN (viewed at the current time) according their importance.
2. To take into account the prior importance of the concepts defined by an expert, the importance scale should be implemented.
3. Semantic zooming scale should be implemented to visualize the SLN elements with different levels of details.

For SLN visualization, we used a node-link paradigm imposed by the visual modeling language ORM2. According to ORM2 notation, the nodes in our SLN implementation are Entity Types and Attributes; Predicates representing semantic relations between Entity Types (or between Entity Types and their Attributes as well) are the links of different types between the nodes. To provide interactive visualization and navigation in the visualized model, each Entity Type is assigned a priori importance of the item in terms of SLN sensemaking as a whole (Table 1). So, SLN is described as follows:

$$\text{primarySLN} = \; <\text{ET, A, H, ET R, R}>, \tag{1}$$

where ET - set of Entity Types; A - set of Attributes, H - set of relations between Entity Types and their Attributes (attributive relations), ET R - set of relations between Entity Types, R - a set of rules for reasoning and inferring relations, for influence entity types and relations, for networking, and for evolving the network [23].

$$\text{ET} = \; <ET_1, ET_2, \ldots, ET_i, \ldots, ET_n>, \tag{2}$$

where ET_i - Entity Type.

$$ET_i = \; <ETn_i, PI_i, ETvis_i >, \tag{3}$$

where ETn_i - name of i-th Entity Type, PI_i - priori importance of i-th Entity Type, $ETvis_i = \{true; false\}$ - i-th Entity Type visibility.

$$A = \; <A_1, A_1, \ldots, A_i, \ldots, A_m >, \tag{4}$$

$$H = \; <H_1, H_2, \ldots, H_i, \ldots, H_p >, \tag{5}$$

$$H_i(ET_j, A_k) : ET \times A \to \{true; false\}, \tag{6}$$

$$ETR = \; <DR, IR, Pr >, \tag{7}$$

where DR - set of Definitional Relations between Entity Types, IR - set of Implicational Relations between Entity Types, Pr - set of Predicate relations between Entity Types.

$$DR = \; <DR_1, DR_2, \ldots, DR_i, \ldots, DR_n >, \tag{8}$$

$$DR_i(ET_j, ETk) : ET \to \{true; false\}, \tag{9}$$

$$IR = \; <IR_1, IR_2, \ldots, IR_i, \ldots, IR_n >, \tag{10}$$

$$IR_i(ET_j, ET_k) : ET \to \{true; false\}, \tag{11}$$

$$Pr = \; <Pr_1, Pr_2, \ldots, Pr_i, \ldots, Pr_n >, \tag{12}$$

$$Pr_i(ET_i, ET_j, ET_k \ldots) : ET \to \{true; false\}. \tag{13}$$

Table 1. A priori importance levels of Entity Type

Priori importance level	Level description
Extremely important	The Entity Type without which the answer for the focal question is impossible
Very important	Very important Entity Type
Quite important	Entity type clarifying, explaining, detailing the important Entity Type
Not very important	Not very important Entity Type for the focus question answering
Not important	Entity Type implicitly related to the answer for the focal question

To implement interactive SLN visualization process, we extended ORM2 notation by the representation of the SLN elements with different level of details. So, SNL nodes and links are represented as visualized objects of the following types (Table 2).

Table 2. Visual representation of SLN items with different scale on visual appearance layer

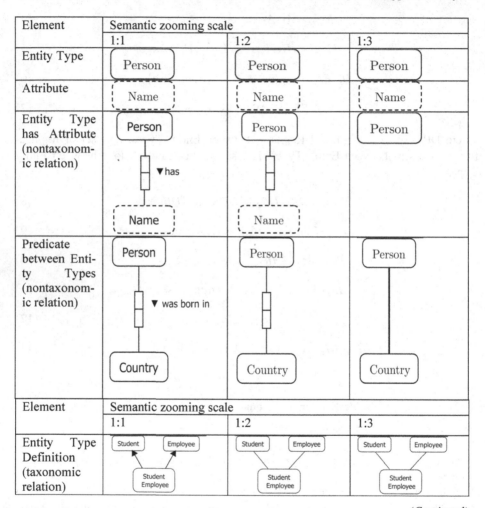

Element	Semantic zooming scale		
	1:1	1:2	1:3
Entity Type	Person	Person	Person
Attribute	Name	Name	Name
Entity Type has Attribute (nontaxonomic relation)	Person ▼ has Name	Person Name	Person
Predicate between Entity Types (nontaxonomic relation)	Person ▼ was born in Country	Person Country	Person Country
Element	Semantic zooming scale		
	1:1	1:2	1:3
Entity Type Definition (taxonomic relation)	Student Employee Student Employee	Student Employee Student Employee	Student Employee Student Employee

(Continued)

Table 2. *(Continued)*

Entity Type Implication (taxonomic relation)	Person ⟶ Student	Person ⟶ Student	Person ⟶ Student
Entity Type Implication + Exclusive (taxonomic relation)	Animal — Elephant / Dog ⊗ Cat	Animal — Elephant / Dog Cat	Animal — Elephant / Dog Cat
Entity Type Implication + Union (taxonomic relation)	Team Member / Player ⊙ Coach	Team Member / Player Coach	Team Member / Player Coach
Entity Type Implication + Exclusive and exhaustive (taxonomic relation)	Parent / Mother ⊛ Father	Parent / Mother Father	Parent / Mother Father

So, in the framework of the proposed approach interactive SLN visualization process (Fig. 1) includes the following mechanisms:

1. Filtering all non-key Entity Types. To define the key and non-key Entity Types, a priori importance P I and scale for filtering f iltZ are used.
2. Filtering on demand SLN Entity Types, Attributes and relations adjacent to the target Entity Type tET taking into account a priori importance P I of the target Entity Type tET and Entity Types adjacent to it (Table 4).
3. Changing the details in the visualized objects representation in geometric graph taking into account scale for visual appearance layer vaZ.

As a result, primarySLN transformed into modSLN:

$$modSLN = <vET, invET, vA, invA, vH, invH, vET R, invET R, R>, \quad (14)$$

where: ET = vET ∪ invET, where vET - set of visible Entity Types, invET - set of hided Entity Types;

A = vA ∪ invA, where vA - set of visible Attributes, invA - set of hided Attributes; H = vH ∪ invH, where vH - set of visible attributive relations, invH - set of hided attributive relations; ET R = vET R ∪ invET R, where vET R - set of visible relations, invET R - set of hided relations, R - set of rules. Further modSLN is visualized according to scale for visual appearance layer vaZ.

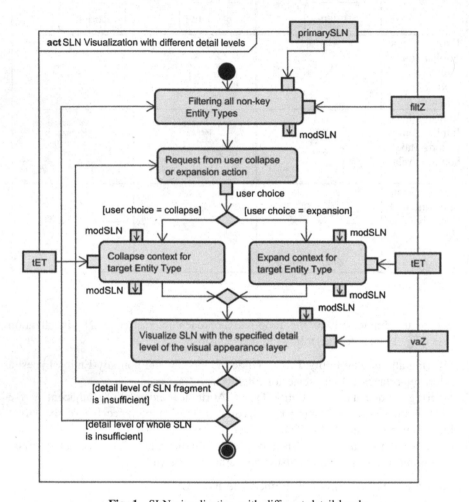

Fig. 1. SLN visualization with different detail levels

Task of Filtering All Non-key Entity Types. Input: primarySLN - original SLN, f iltZ - scale for filtering. Output: modSLNf iltering(f iltZ) - SLN corresponding to the specified semantic zooming for filtering (Table 3).

Table 3. Scale set of semantic zooming for filtering and lower thresholds of priori importance for the visualized Entity Types

Semantic zooming scale	Lower threshold of priori importance
1:1	None (all Entity Types are visualized)
1:2	Not very important
1:3	Quite important
1:4	Very important
1:5	Extremely important

Algorithm:

1. According to specified scale f iltZ and Table 3, find the threshold of priori importance lowP I for Entity Types.
2. Collapse non important Entity Types.
   2.1. For each element e ∈ ET with priori importance P Ie < lowP I set visibility = f alse and add to invET. Set vET = ET \ invET.
3. Collapse the Attributes of collapsed Entity Types.
   3.1. For each relation in h ∈ H that is adjacent to element in invET set visibility = f alse and add h to the set invH. Set vH = H \ invH.
   3.2. For each Attribute a ∈ A that is not adjacent to any relations in vH set visibility = false and add a to invA. Set vA = A \ invA.
4. Collapse relations for collapsed Entity Types.
   4.1. For each relation r ∈ ET R that is adjacent to element in invET set visibility = false and add r to invET R. Set vET R = ET R \ invET R.
5. Set SLN for specified scale f iltZ: modSLNf iltering(f iltZ) = < vET, invET, vA, invA, vH, invH, vET R, invET R, R >.

The algorithm described above is designed to reduce the detailing of the SLN visualization, that decreases the semantic noise caused by redundant information when SNL high-level overview is required. To avoid the situation when filtering leads to a lack of information (another type of semantic noise), an expert sets extremely important Entity Types that should be never hidden. Other Entity Types should be invisible only with minimal semantic scale values. Thus, in filtering, we took into account the following characteristics: expert's point of view, and user's information needs. Expert's point of view was expressed through a priori importance of the Entity Types. User's information needs were taken into account through the varying the semantic scale filtZ, obtaining the different versions of modSLN and choosing the acceptable version.

Task of Context Collapse for Specified Entity Type. Input: modSLN - SLN with some hided elements, tET - specified target Entity Type. Output: modSLNcollapse(tEt) - SLN in that elements from the context of target Entity Type are collapsed.

Algorithm:

1. Collapse attributive relations and collapse Attributes adjacent to only tET
   1.1. For each relation r ∈ vH that is adjacent to tET set visibility = f alse and add r to invH. Set vH = H \ invH.
   1.2. For each Attribute a ∈ vA that is not adjacent to any relation in vH set visibility = false and add a to invA. Set vA = A \ invA.
2. Find in modSLN all elementary chains (in that all the Entity Types are different), started in tET and consisting of elements of ET and ET R, for which visibility = true, that is chain = {tET, ET R1, ET1, ET R2, . . . , ET Rk, ETk}. As a result create a set Ch(tET) of such chains.
3. Collapse not important Entity Types adjacent to tET.
   3.1. For each chain in Ch(tET) where priori importance of tET is P It do:
   3.1.1. If the chain does not contain ETi with priori importance P Ii > P It , then for each element of the chain set visibility = f alse. As a result, all relations ET Ri included in the chain, are added to the set invET R, and all Entity Types ETi included in the chain are added to the set invET.
   3.1.2. If the chain contains Entity Type ET i with priori importance P Ii > P It, and P I1 ≤ P It, and P I2 ≤ P It, then set visibility = f alse for element ET1, and add it to the set invET; for elements ET R1 and ET R2 set visibility = false, and add them to the set invET R.
   3.2. Generate vET = ET \ invET, vET R = ET R \ invET R.
4. Collapse relations for collapsed Entity Types.
   4.1. For each relation r ∈ vET R that is adjacent to element in invET set visibility = false and add it to invET R. Generate vET R = ET R \ invET R.
5. Collapse Attributes for collapsed Entity Types.
   5.1. For each relation r ∈ vH that is adjacent to Entity Type in invET set visibility = false and add r to invH. Generate vH = H \ invH.
   5.2. For each Attribute a ∈ vA that is not adjacent to any relation in vH set visibility = false and add a to invA. Generate vA = A \ invA.
6. Generate SLN with the collapsed context for tET: modSLNcollapse(tEt) = < vET, invET, vA, invA, vH, invH, vET R, invET R, R >.

The proposed algorithm allows decreasing the details of SLN fragment visualization, that decrease the semantic noise, caused by excessive information about the context of target Entity Type tET. This situation can be caused by the reasons below: (a) user is not interested in attributes of Entity Type tET; (b) according to the user's opinion, the semantic scale level for context of EntityType tET should be less than defined by expert with priori importance for Entity Types adjacent to tET; (c) the context for tET was expanded before on user request, and now the collapse is required. To avoid lack or loss of information (another type of information noise) during the context collapse for tET, only the attributes of tET and chains of Entity Types started in tET and having priori importance less or equal of priori importance of the tET, should be collapsed. So, key Entity Types or Entity Types in the context of the key Entity Types will not be collapsed.

Table 4. Examples of context collapse associated with the target Entity Type in various situations

Example	SLN before context collapse	SLN after context collapse
Collapse Entity Type related with some Entity Types with different priori importances	A (1) ← B (2) — C (3)	A (1) ← B (2)
Collapse Entity Types in chain with less or equal priori importance	A (3) ← B (2) — C (2)	B (2)
Collapse Entity Types in chain with great or equal priori importance	A (1) ← B (2) — C (2)	A (1) ← B (2) — C (2)
Collapse Attributes	A (1) ▼ has Attribute	A (1)
Collapse attributive relation with shared Attribute	B (1) ▼ A (1) — Attribute	B (1) ▼ A (1) Attribute

Task of context expansion for specified Entity Type. Input: modSLN - SLN in that some elements are hided, tET - specified target Entity Type. Output: modSLNexpansion(tEt) - SLN in that elements of the context of target Entity Type are expanded.

Algorithm:

1. For specified target Entity Type expand relations with other visible Entity Types.
   1.1. For each relation in invET R that is adjacent to tET and some other Entity Type in vET, set visibility = true and add it to vET R. Generate invET R = ET R \ vET R.
2. Expand the attributes for the Target Entity Type.
   2.1. For each relation in invH that is adjacent to tET set visibility = true and add it to vH. Generate invH = H \ vH.
   2.2. For each Attribute in invA that is adjacent to some relation in vH set visibility = true and add it in vA. Generate invV = A \ vA.
3. Generate SLN with the expanded context for tET: modSLNexpansion(tEt) = < vET, invET, vA, invA, vH, invH, vET R, invET R, R >

The algorithm allows increasing the details in SLN fragment visualization that decrease the semantic noise caused by lack of information about the context for target Entity Type tET. This situation can be caused by one of the following reasons: (a) according to the user opinion, semantic scale for the context of the tET should be greater than defined by expert (the priori importance of Entity Types adjacent to tET); (b) context for tET was collapsed by user request and expansion is required now. To avoid information excess (another type of information noise) as a result of context expansions, only attributes of tET and relations between tET and visible Entity Types are expanded.

SLN Visualization with Specified Details Level for the Visual Representation
Input: modSLN - SLN in that some elements are hided, vaZ - scale for visual appearance layer. Output: visual model of modSLN with scale vaZ.
    Algorithm:

1. For each element of modSLN with visibility = true do:
    1.1. According to specified scale vaZ and Table 1, find visual representation for the element.
    1.2. Visualize the visual representation of the element in position specified by the SLN creator.

This algorithm is designed to change the detailing of the SLN elements visualization - decreasing the information when high-level overview for SLN is required and increasing the information when more details are required for learning some SLN fragment. Moreover, change of the detailing of the SLN elements visualization allows adapting representation of the visualized object to pixels number in the image-space region occupied by the object.

4 Discussion

Ben Shneiderman formulated the visual information seeking mantra: overview first, zoom and filter, then details on demand [19]. For SLN seeking, a different level of details of SLN visualization at different times is required:

1. A high-level SLN overview. A goal of the high-level overview design is to show all key entity types in the SLN simultaneously, without any need for navigation, pan or scroll.
2. Average details for exploration, i.e. the transition from one fragment of SLN representation to another one.
3. Maximum details in focal point or region.

In the proposed approach, we designed the following interactive visualization procedures (listed in descending order of importance) to implement the highlevel SLN overview:

1. Non-key Entity Types filtering. To define the key and non-key Entity Types, we proposed to use a priori importance. Such implementation of high-level SLN overview allows taking into account the expert point of view.

2. Decreasing the visualization details of SLN element.
3. User-defined visualization level of context for different Entity Types, by means of collapse and expansion actions.

The designed combination of interactive visualization procedures allows decreasing the information noise for high-level SLN overview, decreasing amount of information visualized without hiding the key Entity Types. To implement an average detail for SLN exploration, the following interactive visualization procedures (listed in descending order of importance) were designed:

1. User-defined level of details of context for selected Entity Types, using collapse and expansion actions.
2. Changing the details of visualization of SLN elements.

So, the user can define the level of detail he needs for SLN exploration. To implement maximum detail in focal point or region, the following interactive visualization procedures (listed in descending order of importance) were designed:

1. Setting the maximum details of context for selected Entity Type by means of expansion action.
2. Setting the maximum details of visualization of SLN element.

This way the user can get the level of the maximal detail in the visualization of SLN fragment described the selected Entity Types.

5   Conclusion and Future Work

In the paper, a special structure - semantic link network (SLN) - was considered to model and visualize the domain knowledge as a visual graph. To decrease the semantic noise in overview and navigation in SLN visualization, to simplify the process of understanding the domain studied with SLN model in learning, a new semantic zooming approach was proposed and designed. Priori importance levels of Entity Types, as well as semantic zooming scale, were proposed to visualize the SLN with different details level according to the user needs and focus question. Interactive SLN visualization process was described in details as well as SLN transformation issues it implied: non-key Entity Types filtering; context collapse and expansion for specified Entity Type for filtering on demand in SLN; and changing the details in the visualized objects representation in the geometric graph for SLN visualization with specified details level. The corresponding algorithms and visualization examples were provided as well. As future work, we plan to apply the proposed semantic zooming approach to SLN visualization in development of software tool based on the modified ORM2 notation for the visual representation of large ontologies. The software tool will be used and evaluated in the programming languages domain in computer science learning. The evaluation and future using the software tool should cover all the scenarios described in [2]: knowledge storage; knowledge creation; knowledge transferring and sharing.

Acknowledgement. This paper presents the results of research carried out under the RFBR grants 18-07-00032 "Intelligent support of decision making of knowledge management for learning and scientific research based on the collaborative creation and reuse of the domain information space and ontology knowledge representation model" and 18-47-340014 "Development of the mechanism of semantic zooming for the ontology geometric OWL graph for increasing the efficiency of decision making in the tasks of studying a new domain, knowledge accumulating and sharing".

References

1. Anikin, A., Litovkin, D., Kultsova, M., Sarkisova, E., Petrova, T.: Ontology visualization: approaches and software tools for visual representation of large ontologies in learning. In: Kravets, A., Shcherbakov, M., Kultsova, M., Groumpos, P. (eds.) CIT&DS 2017, vol. 754, pp. 133–149. Springer, Cham (2017). https://doi.org/10.1007/978-3-319-65551-2_10

2. Anikin, A., Litovkin, D., Sarkisova, E., Petrova, T., Kultsova, M.: Ontology-based approach to decision-making support of conceptual domain models creating and using in learning and scientific research. In: IOP Conference Series: Materials Science and Engineering vol. 483, p. 012074, March 2019. https://doi.org/10.1088/1757-899x/483/1/012074

3. Cañas, A.J., et al.: Concept maps: integrating knowledge and information visualization. In: Tergan, S.-O., Keller, T. (eds.) Knowledge and Information Visualization. LNCS, vol. 3426, pp. 205–219. Springer, Heidelberg (2005). https://doi.org/10.1007/11510154_11

4. Console, M., Lembo, D., Santarelli, V., Savo, D.F.: Graphical representation of OWL 2 ontologies through graphol. In: International Semantic Web Conference (Posters & Demos). CEUR Workshop Proceedings, vol. 1272, pp. 73–76. CEURWS.org (2014). http://ceur-ws.org/Vol-1272/paper59.pdf

5. Eppler, M.J.: A process-based classification of knowledge maps and application examples. Knowl. Process Manag. **15**(1), 59–71 (2008). https://doi.org/10.1002/kpm.299

6. Gao, T., Chai, Y., Liu, Y.: A review of knowledge management and future research trend. In: Proceedings of the 2nd International Conference on Crowd Science and Engineering, ICCSE 2017, pp. 82–92. ACM, New York (2017). https://doi.org/10.1145/3126973.3126997

7. Gao, T., Chai, Y., Liu, Y.: A review of knowledge management about theoretical conception and designing approaches. Int. J. Crowd Sci. **2**(1), 42–51 (2018). https://doi.org/10.1108/IJCS-08-2017-0023

8. Gavrilova, T., Kudryavtsev, D., Grinberg, E.: Aesthetic knowledge diagrams: bridging understanding and communication. In: Handzic, M., Carlucci, D. (eds.) Knowledge Management, Arts, and Humanities. KMOL, vol. 7, pp. 97–117. Springer, Cham (2019). https://doi.org/10.1007/978-3-030-10922-6_6

9. Halpin, T.A.: Object-Role Modeling: An Overview (1998). http://www.orm.net/pdf/ORMwhitePaper.pdf

10. Halpin, T.A.: ORM 2 Graphical Notation, September 2005. http://www.orm.net/pdf/ORM2TechReport1.pdf

11. Holub, A.I.: Allen Holubs UML Quick Reference. Version 2.1.5 (2017). https://holub.com/uml/

12. Kudryavtsev, D., Gavrilova, T.: Perceptual organization in user-generated graph layouts. Knowledge Process Management **24**(1), 3–13 (2017). https://doi.org/10.1002/kpm.1509

13. von Landesberger, T., et al.: Visual analysis of large graphs: state-of-the-art and future research challenges. Comput. Graph. Forum **30**(6), 1719–1749 (2011). https://doi.org/10. 1111/j.1467-8659.2011.01898.x
14. Liepins, R., Grasmanis, M., Bojars, U.: OWLGrED ontology visualizer. In: ISWC Developers Workshop. CEUR Workshop Proceedings, vol. 1268, pp. 37–42. CEURWS.org (2014)
15. Mouromtsev, D., Wohlgenannt, G., Haase, P., Pavlov, D., Emelyanov, Y., Morozov, A.: A diagrammatic approach for visual question answering over knowledge graphs. In: Gangemi, A., et al. (eds.) ESWC 2018. LNCS, vol. 11155, pp. 34–39. Springer, Cham (2018). https:// doi.org/10.1007/978-3-319-98192-5_7
16. Munzner, T., Maguire, E.: Visualization Analysis and Design. AK Peters Visualization Series. CRC Press, Boca Raton (2015)
17. Nazemi, K.: Adaptive Semantics Visualization. Springer, Heidelberg (2016). https://doi.org/ 10.1007/978-3-319-30816-6
18. Novak, J., Caas, A.: Theoretical origins of concept maps, how to construct them, and uses in education. Reflecting Educ. **3**(1), 29–42 (2007). http://www.reflectingeducation.net/index. php/reflecting/article/view/41
19. Shneiderman, B.: The eyes have it: a task by data type taxonomy for information visualizations. In: Proceedings of the 1996 IEEE Symposium on Visual Languages, VL 1996, pp. 336–343. IEEE Computer Society, Washington, DC (1996). https://doi.org/10. 1109/VL.1996.545307
20. Shneiderman, B., Aris, A.: Network visualization by semantic substrates. IEEE Trans. Vis. Comput. Graph. **12**(5), 733–740 (2006). https://doi.org/10.1109/tvcg.2006.166
21. VOWL: Visual notation for OWL ontologies. http://vowl.visualdataweb.org/v2/
22. Wiens, V., Lohmann, S., Auer, S.: Semantic zooming for ontology graph visualizations. In: Proceedings of the Knowledge Capture Conference K-CAP 2017. ACM Press (2017). https://doi.org/10.1145/3148011.3148015
23. Zhuge, H.: The Semantic Link Network, chap. 2, pp. 71–233. World Scientific Publishing Co. (2012)

Modified Knowledge Inference Method Based on Fuzzy Ontology and Base of Cases

Vadim Moshkin$^{(\boxtimes)}$ (iD) and Nadezhda Yarushkina (iD)

Ulyanovsk State Technical University, Ulyanovsk, Russia
{v.moshkin, jng}@ulstu.ru

Abstract. The article presents a formal ontological model of the rule set and the inference algorithm based on the analysis of the state of a complex technical system (local area network). Also, this paper presents the results of the integration of rules with fuzzy ontology for assessing the state of a local computer network in the process of artificially increasing traffic. In addition, the possibility of modifying this algorithm by means of a parallel launch of the mechanism for analyzing cases in the process of knowledge inference is considered. In conclusion, experiments with the Fuzzy OWL applied ontology prototype and the Pellet inference engine are presented.

Keywords: Fuzzy ontology · Knowledge base · Inference ·
Case-based reasoning · Case database · Fuzzy ontology · Pellet

1 Introduction

Models focused on the description of object structures of the domain are needed for the high quality of the decisions made when designing complex technical systems. These models should help identify, analyze, and manipulate all objects and relationships in the domain.

However, the state of affairs in the field of information and analytical support for designing complex systems does not adequately meet the management needs of modern production organizations, and there are a number of scientific problems that require a systemic solution:

- the need to develop a semantic basis for the analysis of stored knowledge in solving computer-aided design problems;
- lack of integrative conceptual models using different approaches for storing knowledge of the subject area;
- the need to unify the automated processing of stored knowledge when solving design problems of various kinds;
- the need for simultaneous use of multi-aspect descriptions of domain features;
- the need to solve the problem of accounting for the fuzziness in human reasoning;
- the need to take into account past experience in solving problems similar to those put before the designer.

© Springer Nature Switzerland AG 2019
A. G. Kravets et al. (Eds.): CIT&DS 2019, CCIS 1084, pp. 96–108, 2019.
https://doi.org/10.1007/978-3-030-29750-3_8

Thus, today the actual task is the integration of various forms and algorithms for the representation and inference of knowledge in order to support decision-making in the design of complex systems.

2   Fuzziness in the Knowledge Inference

2.1   The Advantages of Using Fuzzy Algorithms in Expert Systems

The problem of using traditional mathematical models arises to describe the human knowledge necessary in the process of inferring recommendations in an expert system. Elements of fuzziness were introduced into the knowledge inference as an implementation of fuzzy models to solve this problem.

The rapid growth of the areas of applicability of fuzzy inference algorithms is due to the main advantages of fuzzy-systems:

- ability to work with fuzzy input data;
- the possibility of fuzzy formalization of evaluation criteria and comparison;
- the possibility of conducting qualitative assessments of input data and output results;
- the ability to quickly simulate complex dynamic systems and their comparative analysis with a given degree of accuracy.

Table 1 presents expert systems using one or more fuzzy inference algorithms [1–9].

Table 1. Examples of expert systems

Name	Approach
Risk Analysis Expert System (RA_X)	Mamdani
Adaptive-Network-Based Fuzzy Inference System (ANFIS)	Sugeno
Fuzzy inference system in river flow forecasting	Mamdani, Takagi–Sugeno–Kang
Control system for unmanned aerial vehicles	Mamdani
FIS To Fault Diagnosis	Sugeno

The use of systems based on fuzzy inference algorithms is expanding every year. However, each of the algorithms used has significant drawbacks when working with complex subject areas:

- does not take into account the peculiarities of the relationship of objects of the subject area;
- all algorithms are single-ended and do not imply finding an output when changing input values in the iterative algorithms;
- the possible hierarchy and synonymy of objects are not taken into account.

Algorithms do not contain elements of learning, which significantly reduces the potential of their development and increases the work of experts on a full description of the behavior of objects in the subject area.

3   Related Works

At present, the integration of CBR and the ontological approach to knowledge representation is more often used to build expert systems for complex subject areas. Consider some of them.

The approach presented in [10] is to reason from the facts and determine whether the patients are suffering from diabetes or not. Case-Based Reasoning (CBR) has a library of solved cases which helps to diagnose the unsolved diabetic cases. The ontology contains information about diabetes - symptoms, causes, different types of diabetes and also the type of diagnosis - which helps in effective system-level reasoning. Based on the relevant count of the symptoms, ontology is analyzed with inputs, the relevant diagnosis report is retrieved from the ontology and repaired, and existing cases are revised and retained in the case library for future use.

In [11] authors present ontology-based architecture for knowledge management in BULCHINO web-based catalog for Bulgarian cultural heritage. This approach for realizing content-based search and retrieval in the catalog implies the application of the CBR technology for the representation of metadata characterizations of the cultural objects and the integration of ontology for the semantic formalization of these characterizations.

This paper [12] proposes an ontology and CBR (case-based reasoning) based method which overcomes the difficulty for computers to understand complex structures of various mechanical products and makes the disassembly decision-making process of the products fully automated and cost-saving. In this method, the ontology concept is applied to disassembly decision-making. This enables computers to understand and self-reason the CBR/RBR (rule-based reasoning) based disassembly decision-making process.

This paper [13] presents methods that support case retrieval in a case-based reasoning system. The authors used the ontology to describe the relationship between terms in application fields. The similar cases are retrieval by calculating semantic similarity which authors have defined.

There is the task of developing and implementing hybrid logic inference algorithms using fuzziness correcting shortcomings of these methods. One such solution is the use of a class of fuzzy ontologies.

4   Fuzzy Ontology Model

At present, the basic notation of the fuzzy ontology representation is the FuzzyOWL standard [14–16]. Formally FuzzyOWL-ontology is:

$$I = (If, Cf, Pf, Af, Df, Qf, Lf, Modf),$$

where

- *If* is an Individual that simply represents an individual of the vocabulary;
- *Cf* is a Concept that represents a fuzzy concept of the vocabulary:

$$C_f = \left\{ C_f^A, C_f^C \right\},$$

where C_f^A are Abstract Concepts, C_f^C - Concrete Concepts;

- *Pf* is a Property that represents a fuzzy role:

$$P_f = \left\{ P_f^A, P_f^C \right\},$$

where P_f^A are Object Properties, P_f^C are Datatype Properties;

- *Df* is Axiom that represents the axioms:

$$D_f = \left\{ A_f^{ABox}, A_f^{TBox}, A_f^{RBox} \right\},$$

where A_f^{ABox} is the Abox that contains role assertions between individuals and membership assertions, A_f^{TBox} is the Tbox that contains assertions about concepts such as subsumption and equivalence, A_f^{RBox} is the RBox that contains assertions about roles and role hierarchies. Some of the axioms are subclasses of FuzzyAxiom, which indicates that the axiom is not either true or false, but that it is true to some extent.

- *Of* is Degree that represents a degree which can be added to an instance of FuzzyAxiom:

$$Of = \left\{ LD_f, MD_f, ND_f, Var_f \right\},$$

where LD_f is Linguistic Degrees, MD_f is Modifier Degrees, ND_f is Numeric Degrees, Var_f are Variables.

- *Lf* is Fuzzy Logic represents different families of fuzzy operators that can be used to give different semantics to the logic.

$$L_f = \left\{ L_f^{Luk}, L_f^{Zad}, L_f^{Goed}, L_f^{Prod} \right\},$$

where L_f^{Luk} is the fuzzy operators logic of Lukasiewicz, L_f^{Zad} is the fuzzy operators logic of Zadeh, L_f^{Goed} is the fuzzy operators logic of Goedel, L_f^{Prod} is the fuzzy operators of producing logic;

- *Modf* is Fuzzy Modifier that represents a fuzzy modifier, which can be used to modify the membership function of a fuzzy concept or a fuzzy role. Current subclasses are Linear Fuzzy Modifier and Triangular Fuzzy Modifier.

Table 2 shows the elements of fuzzy axioms FuzzyOWL, as well as their possible representation.

Table 2. Elements of Fuzzy Axioms in FuzzyOWL

No.	Element	Possible values	Representation in FuzzyOWL
1	LD_f – Linguistic Degrees	«high», «above average», «low»	\<AnnotationAssertion\> \<AnnotationProperty IRI="#fuzzyLabel"/\> \<IRI\>#HighLoad\</IRI\> \<Literal datatypeIRI="&rdf; PlainLiteral"\>fuzzyOwl2 fuzzyType="datatype"; Datatype type="rightshoulder"; a="15.0"; b="30.0";/fuzzyOwl2 \</Literal\> \</AnnotationAssertion\>
2	MD_f – Modifier Degrees	«very», «not very»	type="modified" modifier="very"
3	ND_f – Numeric Degrees	$0 \leq ND \leq 1$	Degree Value=0,6
4	Var_f – Variables	a, b, c, k1, k2	b="30.0";
5	L_f – Fuzzy Logic	Zadeh, Lukasiewicz Goedel, and Product	hasSemantics="Zadeh"
6	$Modf$ – Fuzzy Modifier	Linear, Triangular	\<Datatype type="triangular" a="32.0" b="41.0" c="50.0"/\>

The relationship between a fuzzy ontology and a set of rules for inference is carried out using the formation of queries to the ontology generated by the analysis system when the rule set is executed [17].

The basic inference algorithm based on the integration of ontology and set of the rules is shown in Fig. 1.

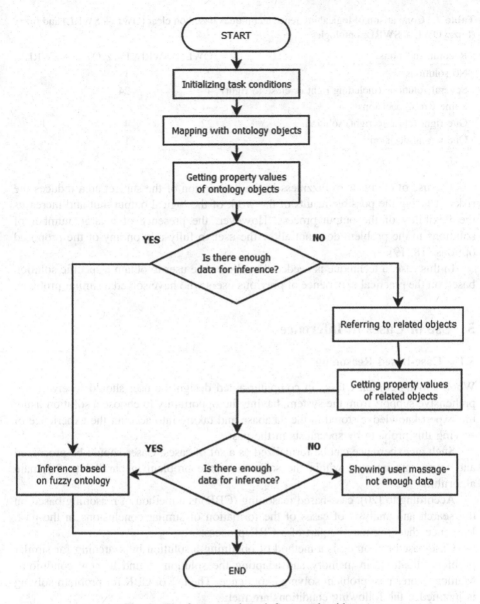

Fig. 1. The fuzzy ontology inference algorithm

Problem situations in the process of a local computer network while artificially increasing the load on communication channels were modeled during experiments.

The object for the experiments was the local computer network of the center for the development of electronic multimedia technologies of Ulyanovsk State Technical University. Comparative characteristics of inference techniques in modeling problem situations of the LAN operation are presented in Table 3.

Table 3. Comparison of logical inference techniques based on clear (OWL + SWRL) and fuzzy (FuzzyOWL + SWRL) ontologies

Recommendations	OWL + SWRL	FuzzyOWL + SWRL
No solutions	2	1
Several solutions (including right or close to right)	4	24
Some wrong decisions	–	–
One right (close to right) solution	22	4
One wrong decision	2	1

The use of elements of fuzziness in the description of the subject area reduces the risks of losing the possible results of the work of the logical output unit and increases the flexibility of the output process. However, the presence of a large number of solutions to the problem does not allow the user to fully rely on any of the proposed options [18, 19].

In this case, a technique is needed that allows the user to obtain a specific solution based on the practical experience of previous users who have solved a similar problem.

5   Use of Cases in Inference

5.1   Case-Based Reasoning

When solving complex tasks in computer-aided design the user should receive comprehensive support from the system, having the opportunity to choose a solution using the expert knowledge stored in the database and taking into account the experience of solving this problem by specialists in the past.

Such an experience can be formalized as a set of cases. Cases should be processed and taken into account within the solution of the problem in parallel to the main algorithm.

According to [20], case-based reasoning (CBR) is a method of reasoning based on the search and analysis of cases of the formation of similar conclusions in the past. Inference checking may be part of a CBR process.

Case-based reasoning is a method of obtaining a solution by searching for similar problem situations in memory and adapting the solutions found to new conditions. Memory stores past problem-solving experience. The use of CBR for problem-solving is justified if the following conditions are met:

1. Similar problems should have similar solutions (regularity principle). The accumulated experience of solving problems is the beginning of the search for solutions for new similar problems.
2. Tasks should have a tendency to repeat. This condition ensures that for many problems in the future there will be an analog in the past experience [21].

Case-based reasoning can be schematically represented as a cycle. The work [22] describes the typical process of case-based reasoning, which consists of the following steps:

- the case formation for a new task (a case for a query);
- search for the most similar cases in the case database;
- reuse of solutions of found cases and their adaptation to the new task;
- verification of the proposed solution for the adequacy
- saving the new solution to the use case database.

There is an analogy between systems based on rules and cases. Both rules and use cases need to be indexed for efficient retrieval. Both rules and use cases are selected by mapping. Selection and ranking are based on knowledge stored in background structures. Ontologies are the most unified storage structures.

Fundamental differences between 1 inference techniques based on production systems and cases were outlined in [23]. The basic differences in these methods:

1. The rules are templates, i.e. contain variables and do not directly describe the solution. Cases are constants and operate on specific knowledge base objects.
2. The application of the rules is an iterative cycle - a sequence of steps leading to a solution. A case is an approximate version of a complete solution.
3. The rule is selected based on an exact match between the antecedent and the input data. The case is selected using partial matching, and knowledge of the nature of the characteristics on which the matching is performed is taken into account.

5.2   The Formal Model of Inference System Based on Case Analysis

The main advantages of arguments on cases:

- no need to fully consider the knowledge of a particular subject area;
- the ability to directly use the experience gained by the expert system, without the intensive involvement of an expert in the subject area;
- the possibility of using heuristics that increase the efficiency of problem-solving [24].

A formal model of a case-based output system is:

CBR = {Cases, I, S_{CASE}},
where Cases – the case database;
I – the domain ontology (fuzzy ontology);
S_{CASE} – the case search algorithm.

The formal model of case is:

Case = {$Index_{CASE}$, $D(Index_{CASE})$, Eff $(D(Index_{CASE}))$},
where $Index_{CASE}$ – case index, i.e. description of the initial situation;
$D(Index_{CASE})$ – a set of solutions to the problem;
Eff $(D(Index_{CASE}))$ – a set of decision effectiveness assessments of the problem.

Cases operate not with variables, but with concrete objects of classes and values of object properties, therefore the initial situation is described by the following set:

$Index_{CASE}$ = {I_f, P_f},
where I_f – is the set of ontology classes;
P_f – the set of values of the object properties.

The model for solving the problem is similar:

The solution is the object of the auxiliary class "Recommendations" that infer the linguistic value of the DatatypeProperty "hasDescription" of the selected object of the class "Recommendations".

5.3   Modification of Inference Algorithm Using Cases

The Protégé OWL ontology editor is used to add an initial set of cases to the knowledge base. This software system represents knowledge in the following formats:

- fuzzy ontologies (using the Fuzzy OWL Plugin);
- SWRL rules;
- the set of cases in OWL format.

Currently, the java-framework jColibri is used to process cases in OWL format. This library is free and freely distributable. Correct analysis of cases using the jColibri framework requires the creation of three base classes in the OWL ontology:

- CBR-CASE - a class containing instances of cases;
- CBR-DESCRIPTION - a class that describes the limitations imposed on the cases;
- CBR-INDEX - stores the structure of the case, i.e. descendant classes and their instances involved in the process of finding a suitable case.

The listed auxiliary classes of ontology are directly consistent with the model of case-based inference.

The main feature of the modified inference algorithm (Fig. 2) is to conduct a parallel and independent inference of the analysis results based on the rule base and the base of cases.

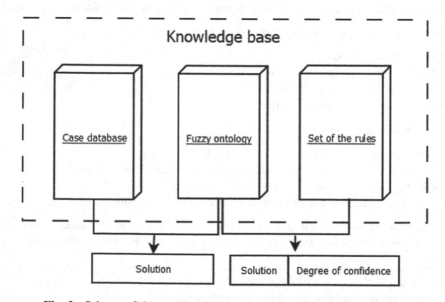

Fig. 2. Scheme of the modified inference algorithm using a case database

Thus, the user can make a decision based on an analysis of the laws of a particular area and based on the experience of users who have solved similar tasks.

In addition, the case database makes this algorithm learnable (Fig. 3).

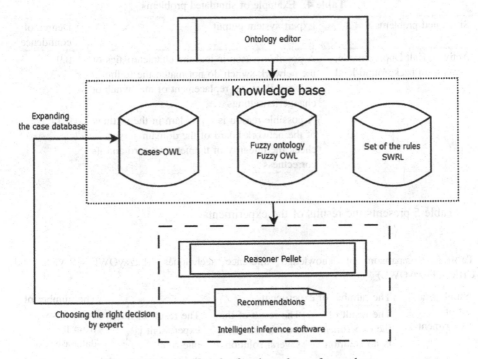

Fig. 3. The algorithm for forming a base of precedents

The main advantage of the algorithm for forming a cases database (Fig. 3) is the ability of the user to select a solution that turned out to be correct in solving this problem.

The solution obtained as a result of the inference based on the rules and selected by the user as the correct one will be entered into the case database with the initial conditions of the problem.

As a result of this action, when solving a similar problem, the next time the user receives this recommendation as a priori, i.e. obtained on the basis of the analysis of the experience of solving a similar problem.

5.4   Conducting Inference Experiments with Interactive Learning Elements

A number of experiments were conducted in order to compare the proposed methodology for the interaction of ontological analysis and inference mechanisms based on fuzzy ontology. Possible problem situations arising in the process of a local computer network with artificially increasing communication channel load were modeled.

Table 4 presents an example of the simulated problems and the conclusion of the expert system with a corresponding degree of confidence.

Table 4. Example of simulated problems

Simulated problems	Expert system output	Degree of confidence
Activate Half Duplex mode, increase in background load	A possible reason is that the characteristics of the network switch do not match the traffic volume. Requires replacement of the switch or change its settings	0,9
	A possible reason is a problem in the settings of the network board of the domain server, check the integrity of the network card and its correctness	0,75

Table 5 presents the results of the experiments.

Table 5. Comparison of knowledge inference techniques (FuzzyOWL + SWRL and CBR + FuzzyOWL)

Number/(a lot of experiments)	The number of experiments			The number of used cases from the database
	The result of the experiment is no solution	The result of the experiment is several solutions	The result of the experiment is one right decision	
1 (1–10)	1	8	1	1
2 (11–20)	–	9	1	3
3 (21–30)	–	8	2	4

As can be seen from the results, the correct decision on the basis of cases is inferred more often with each subsequent batch of experiments due to the fact that the system is learned on the right solutions in the CBR base.

The use of elements of fuzziness in the description of the subject area reduces the risks of losing the possible results of the work of the logical output unit and increases the flexibility of the output process. However, the presence of a large number of solutions to the problem does not allow the user to fully rely on any of the proposed options.

A technique that allows the user to get a specific solution based on the practical experience of users who have solved a similar problem in the past (CBR) is an alternative to correcting the drawbacks of the algorithm based on the integration of FuzzyOWL and SWRL.

The modified algorithm for the integration of ontological and production forms of knowledge representation, due to the introduction of fuzziness in the ontology elements, reduces the risks of losing the possible results of the work of the inference unit based on this knowledge base expert system. The algorithm also increases the flexibility of the inference of the recommendation providing the user with a wider choice of options ordered by degree of relevance.

6 Conclusions

Thus, the modified inference algorithm proposed in this paper, using the fuzzy FuzzyOWL ontology of the domain, the set of rules, and including the analysis of cases allows you to:

- reduce the risks of losing the possible results of the work of the inference unit based on the analysis of the domain ontology;
- increase the flexibility of the inference recommendation providing the user with a wider choice of options ordered by degree of relevance;
- bring a formalized view of knowledge about the subject area to the natural for a person version of their representation and perception;
- ensure that the user receives decision-making capabilities, taking into account the analysis of the laws of a specific area, and based on the experience of users who have already faced similar tasks;
- ensure the possibility of learning the system through the dynamic formation of a case database.

Acknowledgments. The study was supported by the Russian Foundation for Basic Research (Grants No. 19-07-00999, 18-37-00450 and 18-47-732007).

References

1. Wang, J., Modarres, M.: REX: an intelligent decision and analysis aid for reliability and risk studies. Reliab. Eng. Syst. Saf. **30**(1–3), 195–218 (1990)
2. Jang, J.-S.: ANFIS adaptive-network-based fuzzy inference system. IEEE Trans. Syst. Man Cybern. **23**, 665–685 (1993). https://doi.org/10.1109/21.256541
3. Firat, M., Güngör, M.: River flow estimation using adaptive neuro-fuzzy inference system. Math. Comput. Simul. **75**, 87–96 (2007). https://doi.org/10.1016/j.matcom.2006.09.003
4. Nabizadeh, M., Mosaedi, A., Hesam, M., Dehghani, A.A., Zakerinia, M., Meftah, M.: River flow forecasting using fuzzy inference system (FIS) and adaptive neuro- fuzzy inference system (ANFIS). Iran. J. Watershed Manag. Sci. Eng. Winter **5**(17), 7–14 (2012)
5. Spinka, O., Kroupa, S., Hanzálek, Z.: Control system for unmanned aerial vehicles. In: IEEE International Conference on Industrial Informatics (INDIN), vol. 1, pp. 455–460 (2007). https://doi.org/10.1109/indin.2007.4384800
6. Harrouche, F., Felkaoui, A.: Automation of fault diagnosis of bearing by application of fuzzy inference system (FIS). Mech. Ind. **15**, 477–485 (2014). https://doi.org/10.1051/meca/2014059
7. Trausan-Matu, S.: A framework for an ontology-based information system for competence management. Econ. Inform. 1-4/2008, 105 (2008)

8. Nunes, I.L., Simões-Marques, M.: Applications of fuzzy logic in risk assessment the RA_X case. In: Azeem, M.F. (ed.) Fuzzy Inference System Theory and Applications, pp. 21–40 (2012)

9. Lei, Y.: The hybrid intelligent method based on fuzzy inference system and its application to fault diagnosis. In: Azeem, M.F. (ed.) Fuzzy Inference System Theory and Applications, pp. 153–170 (2012)

10. Jaya, A., Uma, G.V.: Role of ontology in case-based reasoning (CBR) for diagnosing diabetes (September 25, 2009). J. Inf. Technol. 5(3), 17–23 (2009)

11. El-Sappagh, S., Elmogy, M., Riad, A.M.: A fuzzy ontology-oriented case-based reasoning framework for semantic diabetes diagnosis. Artif. Intell. Med. 65(3), 179–208 (2015)

12. Chen, S., Yi, J., Jiang, H., Zhu, X.: Ontology and CBR based automated decision-making method for the disassembly of mechanical products. Adv. Eng. Inform. 30(3), 564–584 (2016). https://doi.org/10.1016/j.aei.2016.06.005. ISSN 1474-0346

13. Wang, D., Xiang, Y., Zou, G., Zhang, B.: Research on ontology-based case indexing in CBR. In: 2009 International Conference on Artificial Intelligence and Computational Intelligence, Shanghai, pp. 238–241 (2009). https://doi.org/10.1109/aici.2009.449

14. Assali, A.A., Lenne, D., Debray, B.: Case retrieval in ontology-based CBR systems. In: 32nd Annual Conference on artificial intelligence (KI 2009), Paderborn, Germany, September 2009, pp. 564–571 (2009). https://doi.org/10.1007/978-3-642-04617-9_71

15. Bobillo, F., Straccia, U.: Fuzzy ontology representation using OWL 2. Int. J. Approx. Reason. 52, 1073–1094 (2011)

16. Lee, C.S., Jian, Z.W., Huang, L.K.: A fuzzy ontology. IEEE Trans. Syst. Man Cybern. Part B 5, 859–880 (2005)

17. Straccia, U.: Towards a fuzzy description logic for the semantic web (preliminary report). In: Gómez-Pérez, A., Euzenat, J. (eds.) ESWC 2005. LNCS, vol. 3532, pp. 167–181. Springer, Heidelberg (2005). https://doi.org/10.1007/11431053_12

18. Moshkin, V.S., Zarubin, A.A., Koval, A.R., Filippov, A.A.: Construction of the problem area ontology based on the syntagmatic analysis of external wiki-resources. In: Data Science. Information Technology and Nanotechnology. Proceedings of the International Conference Information Technology and Nanotechnology. Session Data Science, DS-ITNT 2017, Samara, Russia, 24–27 April 2017, pp. 128–134 (2017)

19. Yarushkina, N., Moshkin, V., Filippov, A., Guskov, G.: Developing a fuzzy knowledge base and filling it with knowledge extracted from various documents. In: Rutkowski, L., Scherer, R., Korytkowski, M., Pedrycz, W., Tadeusiewicz, R., Zurada, J.M. (eds.) ICAISC 2018. LNCS (LNAI), vol. 10842, pp. 799–810. Springer, Cham (2018). https://doi.org/10.1007/978-3-319-91262-2_70

20. Filippov, A., Moshkin, V., Namestnikov, A., Guskov, G., Samokhvalov, M.: Approach to translation of RDF/OWL-ontology to the graphic knowledge base of intelligent systems. In: Proceedings of the II International Scientific and Practical Conference "Fuzzy Technologies in the Industry – FTI 2018". Ulyanovsk, Russia, 23–25 October 2018, pp. 44–49 (2018)

21. Leake, D.B. (ed.): Case-Based Reasoning: Experiences, Lessons, and Future Directions. AAAI Press/MIT Press, Menlo Park (1996). ISBN 0-262-62110-X

22. Pal, S.K., Shiu, S.C.K.: Foundations of Soft Case-Based Reasoning. Wiley, New Jersey (2004). ISBN 978-0-471-64466-8

23. Aamodt, A., Plaza, E.: Case-based reasoning: foundational issues, methodological variations, and system approaches. Communications 7, 39–59 (1994)

24. Kolodner, J.L.: Case-Based Reasoning. Morgan Kaufmann, Los Altos (1993)

25. Dvoryankin, A.M., Siplivaya, M.B., Zhukova, I.G.: Integration of reasoning on precedents and ontologies in the intellectual system supporting engineering analysis in the field of contact mechanics. In: Russian. Bulletin of Volgograd State Technical University. Volgograd, vol. 2, no. 2 (2008)

Cognitive Developing of Semiotic Data in Computer-Based Communication (Signs, Concepts, Discourse)

Andrew V. Olyanitch[✉], Zaineta R. Khachmafova,
Susanna R. Makerova, Marjet P. Akhidzhakova,
and Tatiana A. Ostrovskaya

Adyge State University, Maykop, Russia
aolyanitch@mail.ru, zaineta@nextmail.ru,
susannamakerova@gmail.com, zemlya-ah@yandex.ru,
ostrovska.t@mail.ru

Abstract. The paper considers the processes of semiotic data's cognitive development which take place in computer-based communication. The immersion of signs-terminatives and different concepts into the computer discourse is observed. The research had been intended to understand the lingua-semiotic structure of the Semantic Web as well as to get aware of what concepts make the ground of this Web's architecture. Another goal of the research conducted was to clear up the semiotic reasons of the inefficiency of computer-based communication together with forwarding the idea of mind-mapping as means of semiotic structuring the cognition of any type of data involved into computer discourse. The paper also suggests the creation of the semiotic model of interrelations of concepts, information objects and computer codes for easier cognitive mastering of semiotic data in the course of computer communication.

Keywords: Abbreviation · Cognitive · Computer-based communication · Concept · Data · Development · Discourse · Graph · Infographics · Information · Mental map · Metadata · Nomination · Semantics · Semiotics · Semiolinguistics · Sign · Terminative · Web

1 Introduction

The phenomenon of computer communication as an independent type of communication, according to many scientists, lies in its special multi-functionality (see in [3, 5–7, 15, 19, 24]). Researchers believe that the language of electronic communication should be considered as a functional type of language (see in [1, 8, 12, 19, 23]), because: (a) the sphere of functioning of this sublanguage is separated from other spheres of communication (it is carried out with the help of technical electronic means and is always mediated by them); (b) the language of electronic communication means implements specific communicative goals (i.e., phatic); (c) this sublanguage formed a new system of genres and genre formats (digital multimedia) and as a result contributed to the development of a new direction in the theory of conventional genres – virtual genre studies (see in [4, 10, 11]); (d) the considered functional variety of a language is characterized by a diverse set of lexical and grammatical characteristics that are easily distinguished, formalized and form a single pragmatic complex [8].

Like any type of communication, computer communication cannot take place without the support of purely linguistic/speech processes, and especially without the support of the nomination process. In its depths, acts of naming constantly occur, linguistic units are formed, which serve to name and isolate fragments of reality, to form corresponding concepts about them in the form of lexemes, word combinations, phraseological units, sentences, and finally, immerge these signs and concepts into the discourse.

Computer communication is replete with nominations (signs) related to information technology, and, therefore, highly terminologies. This is explained by the semantic-communicative specificity of the term, its fundamental unambiguity, accuracy, efficiency, nominative and distinctive function, stylistic neutrality, greater information richness compared to ordinary words.

The process of searching and localizing information in the network is nominated by a number of language signs-terminatives, such as a query – a set of words and service characters that characterizes the information that the user wants to find; Search Engine Index – an information array where the converted text components of all the visited pages and text files are stored; index-lexical analysis and analysis of textual materials of the site in order to compile a list of used words and expressions; Domain – part of the web address of the website, which is its basis for searching the network; conceptual search – search for documents that are directly related to the specified search word, and not just containing it; distant search – a search in which the user indicates the distance between the keywords in the document; morphological search – the ability of the search engine to search for a word in documents not only in a strictly defined form, but also in all its morphological forms; a search engine is a computer program that contains three components: a robot, a system index, a search system, etc.

The listed terminology is related to the provision of network computer communication, but its organizers – specialists in the field of information technology and network administrators – use these terms (lingual signs) in actual communication. All programs and phenomena intended for ensuring communication in the network (virtual computer communication) are "immersed" in the network thanks to the subjects of actual computer communication.

How the semiosis of computer communication of both types, determining the cognitive mastery (development) of semiotic data, is carried out in virtual environments, is considered in the proposed paper.

2 Background

The key nominations or lingual signs that are relevant for defining the functionality of network communication are those that give an idea of the transmission of messages and information throughout the network. In the center of the entire nominative system of the network, the structure is the key figure of the provider – a company or an individual, ensuring the user's entry into the network and enabling the user to access the necessary information.

Another nomination, important for understanding the operation of the network structure, is the lingual sign "data transmission". This nomination is semantically related to the signs "data package" (or "data pack"), "communication channel" ("data channel") and "route".

Data packs and channels through which they are transmitted are formed and stored in the center of the network (the sign network core) and are sent to the end system (sign host), that is, to the user's computer (nomination network peripheral) at the user's request. The abundance of information, it's multitasking, poly-directionality – all these factors require the functioning of a data transmission facilitation system, which is due to the achievement of simultaneous and stable functioning of network data transmission channels. The process of ensuring the stability of the transmission of data packets over communication channels has received the name of the switching channels and packs.

Switching these network elements provides for strict compliance with the delivery of information along a strictly defined route to the information consumer (nomination sign IP address). In order for the information not to be falsely interpreted by the router, and the data packs sent out do not "collide" with each other, there are programs in the network that ensure the logic of correct data transfer (nomination buffer). With an abundance of packs of transmitted data, the logical buffer system builds these packets into a queue (nomination message queue).

3 Methodology

Data on the World Wide Web is usually presented in the form of text recorded in natural languages, i.e. these are discursive practices, specifically implemented in virtual discourse. Such texts are intended for human perception, but the machine can understand their meaning using one of the methods of processing natural language. The methods perform frequency analysis and/or lexical analysis of the text/discourse.

As a machine-readable format, the W3C suggests using RDF-language which allows you to describe the structure of the semantic network in the form of a graph. Each node and each arc of the graph can be assigned a separate URI. Statements written in RDF can be interpreted using ontologies. To create ontologies, it is recommended to use the languages RDF Schema and OWL. Ontologies are created to derive logical conclusions from these. Ontologies are based on mathematical formalisms called descriptive logic.

Linguistically, all these processes can be described due to semiotic and semiolinguistic methods together with the applying of cognitive analysis. All in all, these ways of research comprise the methodology used in this paper.

4 Results and Discussion

We did our research having in mind to get proper data on how computer communication (virtual and actual) is cognitively developed by semiotic means; so the research has been conducted along the following dimensions: (a) understanding what signs comprise the lingual ground of the Semantic Web (SW); (b) getting aware what concepts lie in the ground of SW-architecture; (c) clearing up the semiotic reasons for inefficiency of computer-based communication; (d) forwarding the idea of mind-mapping as means of semiotic structuring the cognition of any type of data involved in computer discourse; (e) suggesting the creation of the semiotic model of interrelations of concepts, information objects and computer codes for easier cognitive mastering of semiotic data in the course of computer communication.

4.1 Semantic Web

The special level in cyberspace of the Internet, after the already existing Web 1.0 and Web 2.0 is Web 3.0 - the concept of development of Internet technologies, formulated by Netscape.com CEO Jason Calacanis, continuing the Web 2.0 concept Tim O'Reilly [14]. Its essence is that Web 2.0 is only a technological platform, and Web 3.0 will allow you to create high-quality content and services based on it through the power of professionals.

The definition was published in the personal blog of Calacanis October 3, 2007 [2]. Calacanis noted that Web 2.0 makes it possible to quickly and practically free of charge using a significant amount of powerful Internet services with high consumer qualities, which led to the emergence of a huge amount of uniform resources, and, as a result, the devaluation of most of them. The idea is that a new platform should emerge on the basis of Web 2.0 - not so much technological as sociocultural, used by professionals to create interesting, useful and high-quality content. Obviously, Web 3.0 is a platform for implementing new social practices of virtual discourse.

This is probably the stage in the development of computer technology and computer communication, where signs of a combination of natural and artificial intelligence appear.

One of the interpretations of the term Web 3.0 is its correlation with the Semantic web. The semantic web is a publicly available global semantic network formed on the basis of the World Wide Web by standardizing the presentation of information in a form suitable for machine processing. In the usual World Wide Web based on HTML pages, the information is embedded in the text of the pages and is intended for reading and understanding by humans. The semantic web consists of machine-readable elements - nodes of the semantic network, based on ontology. Due to this, client programs are able to directly receive statements from the Internet of the type "subject - a type of interconnection - another subject" and calculate logical conclusions from them. The semantic web works in parallel with the usual World Wide Web and based on it, using the HTTP protocol and URI resource identifiers. The name "Semantic Web" was first introduced by Tim Berners-Lee (inventor of the World Wide Web) in September 1998, and is called by him "the next step in the development of the World Wide Web." Later in his blog, he proposed the term "giant global graph" (English giant global graph, GGG, by analogy with WWW) as a synonym. The concept of the semantic web was adopted and promoted by the World Wide Web Consortium. The semantic web is an add-on to the existing World Wide Web, invented to make information available on the Internet usable for machine processing, i.e. It is practically an interface of natural and artificial intelligence for virtual communication. The information available on the web is convenient for people to read. The semantic web was created to make information suitable for automatic analysis, synthesis of conclusions and transformation of both the data itself and the conclusions drawn from them into various representations useful in practice (see Fig. 1).

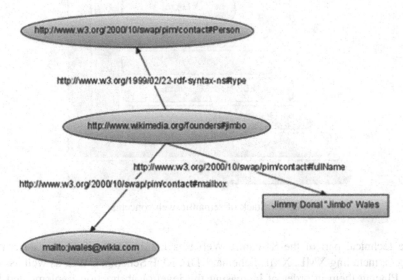

Fig. 1. Business card graph of the Wikipedia founder in RDF format

The elements of this graph in Fig. 1 – both nodes and arcs (except for the literal depicted in the orange rectangle) – are URIs. URI is a uniform resource identifier or address used to specify links to an object (for example, a web page, file, or email inbox). URIs are used to name objects. Each object of the global semantic network has a unique URI. URI uniquely names an object. Separate URIs are created not only for pages, but also for real-world objects (people, cities, artworks, demons, and so on), and even for abstract concepts (for example, "name", "position", "color"). Due to the uniqueness of the URI, the same items can be called the same in different places of the semantic web. Using the URI, you can collect information about a single item from different places. It is recommended to include in the address of the URI the name of one of the World Wide Web protocols (HTTP or HTTPS). That is, the URI is recommended to start with "http://" or "https://"). Such an address can be simultaneously used as a URI address and as a web page address (URL). On web pages whose URL matches the URI, the W3C recommends posting a description of the item. The description is desirable to provide in two formats:

- in a human-readable format;
- in an easy-to-read machine format.

4.2 SW Architecture

The Semantic Web (SW) Architecture consists of the following concepts (see Fig. 2):

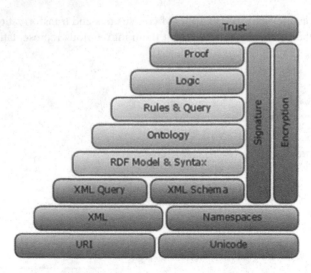

Fig. 2. Stack of semantic web concepts

The technical part of the Semantic Web is a family of standards for description languages, including XML, XML Schema, RDF, RDF Schema, OWL, as well as some others. Placing them in order of increasing the level of abstraction implemented by a language, we get:

- XML provides syntax for defining the structure of a document to be processed. XML syntax does not carry semantic load.
- XML Schema defines constraints on the structure of an XML document. The standard XML parser is able to test an arbitrary XML document for its structure to be called the so-called document scheme described in the XML Schema.
- RDF is an easy way to describe instance data in the subject-relation-object format, in which only resource identifiers are used as an element of this triple (except for an object that is allowed to be literal). There is a standardized mapping of these triples to XML documents of a predefined structure (that is, the W3 scheme defines XML documents containing RDF descriptions), as well as to other presentation formats (for example, in notation N3).
- RDF Schema describes a set of attributes (here it is more accurate to call them relations), such as rdfs: Class, for defining new types of RDF data. The language also supports the rdfs: subClassOf type inheritance relation.
- OWL extends the capabilities for describing new types (in particular, adding listings), and also allows you to describe new types of RDF Schema data in terms of existing ones (for example, to define a type that is the intersection or combination of two existing ones).
- Microdata (HTML microdata) is an international standard for semantic markup of HTML pages, using attributes that describe the meaning of the information contained in various HTML elements. Such attributes make the content of the pages machine-readable, that is, allow you to automatically find and extract the necessary data.

The metadata description formats in the Semantic Web imply a logical conclusion on this metadata and were developed with an eye to the existing mathematical formalisms in this area. The formalism underlying the format makes it possible to draw conclusions about the properties of programs that process data in this format.

This is especially true of the OWL language. The basic formalism for it is descriptive logic, and the language itself is divided into three nested subsets (in order of nesting): OWL Lite, OWL DL and OWL Full. It is proved that the logical conclusion on metadata with the expressiveness of OWL Lite is performed in polynomial time (in other words, the inference problem belongs to the class P). OWL DL describes a maximum solvable subset of descriptive logic, but some queries on such data may require exponential runtime. OWL Full implements all existing descriptive logic constructors by avoiding the mandatory solvability of queries.

The simple structure of the predicates of the RDF language, in turn, makes it possible to use experience from theories of logical databases, predicate logic, etc. in its processing.

Commentators point to various reasons that hinder the active development of the Semantic Web, starting with the human factor (people tend to avoid working on supporting documents with metadata, problems of the truth of metadata remain open, and so on), and ending with an indirect indication of Aristotle division of the world into distinguishable concepts. This casts doubt on the possibility of the existence of a top-level ontology that is critical for the Semantic Web. Aristotle in the "Topic" uses the concept of differential specific, or the presence of concepts of distinguishable quality, as the basis for grouping concepts into classes. The philosopher is convinced of the presence of an infinite number of concepts, from which follows the infinity of the number of classes into which they can be combined. To select such a number of classes, one needs infinitely many distinguishable qualities, the presence of which Aristotle doubts and questions.

The need to describe metadata somehow leads to duplication of information. Each document should be created in two copies: marked for reading by people, as well as in a machine-oriented format. This flaw of the Semantic Web was the main impetus to the creation of so-called micro-formats and the RDF language. The latter is a variant of the RDF language and differs from it in that it does not define its own syntax, but is intended to be embedded in the XML attributes of XHTML pages. In addition, semantic tags appear in the HTML standards themselves.

NeuroNet (NeuroWeb, Brainet) or Web 4.0 is one of the expected stages of the development of the World Wide Web, in which the interaction of participants (people, animals, intelligent agents) will be based on the principles of neuro-communications. According to forecasts, he should replace Web 3.0 around 2030-2040. One of the key markets selected for development within the Russian National Technology Initiative.

4.3   Communication Inefficiency

The first prerequisite is the discrepancy between the high potential of the human brain and the state of those organs that are responsible for the information exchange of a person with the external environment. On the one hand, the brain is much more efficient than a computer: a supercomputer that consumes about 12 GW is needed to fully simulate the brain, while the power consumption of the brain itself is only about 20 watts.

On the other hand, the brain is used inefficiently, as evidenced by human communication errors (noises), characteristic of a person, caused by different reasons (physiological, psychological noise, semantic and socio-cultural barriers). An important barrier to perception is an undeveloped picture of the world, due to a lack of experienced knowledge (see Fig. 3 as a metaphor of all these reasons).

Fig. 3. The problem of the quality of communications

In attempts to create a computer, the efficiency of which would be close to the brain (of a neurocomputer), the work on making a brain map is inevitable, which is already being implemented in a number of international projects. The appearance of such a card will allow, as a side effect, to create artificial channels of direct interaction with the brain.

The expected appearance of such a part of Web 3.0 as the Internet of Things should have no less effect. It will lead to the emergence of communication between things integrated into sensor networks. Future communications will inevitably become anthropocentric, by virtue of at least the well-known philosophy of the concept of organ-projection, that is, their purpose will be to build a certain individual space around a person. The achievements of the Internet of Things will create a technical foundation for the transition to Neuronet.

4.4 Infographics as a Semiotic Representation and Cognitive Mastering (Development) of Data in Network Communication

To organize the presentation of quantitative data, graphs, charts, histograms, and nomograms are used, which, in turn, are subdivided into subgroups (point, linear circular, etc.).

To organize the presentation of a set of objects and qualitative data, numerous types of schemes, maps, images and their sequences are used, among which are: organizational charts reflecting the structure of the object (for example, the composition of the device, etc.); schedules, defining the sequence of problem solving in the course of a process; flow diagrams that clearly show the features and stages of technological processes; graphs that visualize transitions or connections of concepts, events, processes, etc.

According to the density of information, infographics can be divided into two types: simple (non-concentrated) and complex (concentrated). A simple one is built around several numbers, while a complex one is a collection of images of a number of numbers. Complicated infographic objects create a full-fledged graphic narration - combine texts, tables, and images with simple infographic types (maps, charts, diagrams, pointers). This kind of college, endowed with interactive properties, is capable of conveying not images, but concepts that unite them.

Having plunged into the network, infographics has turned into an information genre of a journalistic creole text, has acquired specific network characteristics and has become a network (including institutional) genre. The most capaciously lingua-semiotic network institutional infographic is actualized in one of the subgenres - the mental (semantic) map. Mental or semantic maps were first studied in detail in lingua-didactics. So, Kochetkova in the dissertation research conducted a detailed analysis and carried out the typology of this subgenre. According to the scientist, four types of semantic maps can be distinguished - descriptive, comparative, configurational and integrative [9, p. 72]. With the help of the presented typology, it is possible to describe the elements of the network institutional sector.

Descriptive semantic maps "... are illustrative and schematic pillars and colleges that allow us to present the primary description of concepts and concepts involved in communication in the form of a static frame" [9, p. 72]. Such maps illustrate the definitions of lexemes and special terms describing the essence of phenomena, states, and processes in a certain institutional space.

Comparative semantic maps are "... illustrative and schematic pillars that allow the recipient of information to identify similarities and differences between similar phenomena" [9, p. 72], which occur in compared institutional systems, for example, in Russian and English, in the relevant field (politics, economy, religion, education, etc.).

Configuration semantic maps "... reveal a dynamic scenario of the system functioning process" [9, p. 72], including institutional ones, taking into account information mastered by recipients when performing descriptive and comparative lingua-cognitive operations.

Integrative semantic maps "... combine all the previous types of linguistic cognitive activity, are of a generalizing nature" [9, p. 72], including a panoramic, three-dimensional and detailed presentation of the most significant parts of the institutional system in the country and the world.

Cognitive maps are widely used to depict the semiosis in different spheres (i.e. see papers [16] and [17]). Thus, Siau and Tan [21] proposed to use cognitive mapping to overcome some cognitive biases during user-database interface analysis. In particular, they showed how cognitive mapping elicits knowledge about query formulation from database experts. As shown in the following concept map (Fig. 4), steps needed to write a query are expressed in signs and concepts together with relationships among them. The resulting maps are easier than plain text or discourse for ordinary users to understand the underlying logic.

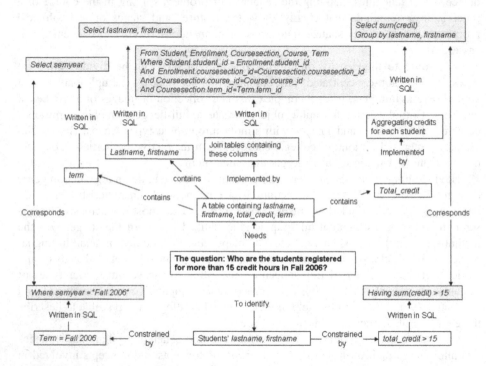

Fig. 4. Concept (semantic) map for writing database query according to Siau and Tan

4.5   Semiotic Model of Interrelations of Concepts, Information Objects, and Computer Codes

Some of the researchers (i.e. [25]) accentuate the theoretical basis for creating information and communication technologies that provide targeted formation processes (or in other words, generation) of new knowledge systems. Intently formed new knowledge systems are proposed to be called targeted ones. This new area of research relates to cognitive computer science, which is at the moment in the initial stage of describing its subject area and its problems. As part of these studies, it is proposed to create a semiotic model of cognitive data mastering in a computer communicative environment (see [13] and [20]).

The semiotic model suggested is supposed to include five components: (1) the mental sphere, the material sphere of physical objects and phenomena, the social and digital environment; (2) the denotation, the corresponding concept (sign value) of the mental sphere and the information object (form of the sign) of the social environment, as well as computer three categories' codes of the digital environment for the denotation, concept and information object; (3) a sign combining a concept as a sign value and an information object as a sign form, which is an element of the sign system of the information environment; (4) a form-code uniting an information object as a form of a sign and a computer code, which is an element of a form-code for the formation of information codes of the forms of signs of an information system; (5) semi-code combining the concept as a sign value and the computer code, which is an element of the semi-code for the formation of the semantic codes of the concepts of the information environment. The semiotic model is based on the G. Frege' triangle whose three vertices are the meaning of the sign (concept), the shape of the sign (as a special case of an information object) and the denotation of the sign (of material, of digital or of any other nature). New components in this model form code and semi-code as key elements of form codes and semi-codes, as well as three categories of codes. In the digital environment, they make a triangle, which is proposed to be called a "computer triangle". The inclusion of a form-code, semi-code, and three categories' codes into the model allows the development of fundamentally new coding methods that ensure the formation of information signs' form-codes; semantic concept codes; dentist's object codes.

5   Conclusion

The signing space of computer communication is represented by heterogeneous signal and iconic formations. Among the first ones stand out terminological units denoting a computer device, information technology, networking, and the second ones fall into various visual images that are organically included in the text. These units are actively used in the professional communication of computer scientists and the meta-professional communication of a wide range of network users.

The cognitive development of semiotic processes in any type or kind of communication implies that a large body of data must be presented for understanding with the help of signs, which are clustered, forming concepts, so that these entities can then, in turn, form a discursive flow. Computer communication is no exception. Its semiosis is also clearly structured for the cognitive development and use of the data obtained. The effectiveness of this type of communication largely depends on such a cognitive lingua-semiotic development, which is possible with the use of semantic maps and a semiotic model for representing the data obtained during computer communication.

It seems that the prospect of further research is to improve the methods of semantic mapping and the proposed semiotic model for data structuring.

References

1. Atabekova, A.A.: Linguistic design of Web pages (a comparative analysis of the language design of English and Russian web pages): monograph. RUDN, 202 p. (2003)
2. Calacanis, J.: Web 3.0, the "official" definition. In: The Personal Blog of Angel Investor and Entrepreneur Jason Calacanis (2003). https://calacanis.com/2007/10/03/web-3-0-the-official-definition/
3. Crystal, D.: Language and the Internet, 272 p. Cambridge University Press, Cambridge (2001)
4. Goroshko, E.I.: Internet linguistics: formation of a disciplinary paradigm. In: Pastukhov, A. G. (ed.) Genres and Types of Text in the Scientific and Media Discourse, vol. 5, pp. 223–237. Kartush Pbl., Oryol (2007)
5. Harris, R.: Psychology of Mass Communications. http://evartist.narod.ru/text5/01/html
6. Herring, S.: Computer-mediated discourse. In: Schiffrin, D., Tannen, D., Hamilton, H. (eds.) The Handbook of Discourse Analysis, pp. 612–634. Blackwell Publishers, Oxford (2001)
7. Herring, S.: Slouching toward the ordinary: current trends in Computer-mediated communication. In: New Media and Society, pp. 26–36. Sage Publications, London (2004)
8. Ivanov, L.Yu.: Language in electronic means of communication. In: Culture of Russian Speech: Encyclopedic Reference Dictionary, pp. 791–793. Flint, Science (2003)
9. Kochetkova, S.Yu.: Formation of a professionally significant foreign language thesaurus among non-philology students based on the semantic mapping method (based on the English language). Volgograd, 230 p. (2006)
10. Kompantseva, L.F.: Virtual modifications of speech genres as a problem of intercultural communication and competence. In: Olyanitch, A.V. (ed.) Professional Communication: Problems of the Humanities, vol. 1, pp. 191–197. Niva Pbl., Volgograd (2005)
11. Kompantseva, L.F.: The Gender Basics of Internet Communication in the Post-Soviet Space: A Monograph, 402 p. Knowledge, Lugansk (2006)
12. Kondrashov, P.E.: Computer discourse: sociological aspect. Krasnodar, 21 p. (2004)
13. Kravets, A., Shumeiko, N., Lempert, B., Salnikova, N., Shcherbakova, N.: "Smart Queue" approach for new technical solutions discovery in patent applications. In: Kravets, A., Shcherbakov, M., Kultsova, M., Groumpos, P. (eds.) CIT&DS 2017. CCIS, vol. 754, pp. 37–47. Springer, Cham (2017). https://doi.org/10.1007/978-3-319-65551-2_3
14. Makarov, M.L.: Fundamentals of the theory of discourse. Gnosis, 280 p. (2003)
15. Morris, M., Ogan, C.: The internet as medium. J. Commun. **46**(1). http://jcmc.indiana.edu/issue4/morris.html
16. Olyanitch, A., Khachmafova, Z., Ostrovskaya, T., Makerova, S.: Engineering an elite in social networks through semiolinguistics' data mapping: a fantasy or reality? In: Kravets, A., Shcherbakov, M., Kultsova, M., Groumpos, P. (eds.) CIT&DS 2017, vol. 754, pp. 671–682. Springer, Cham (2017). https://doi.org/10.1007/978-3-319-65551-2_48
17. Olyanitch, A., Sukhova, E., Necrasova, T., Khramova, O., Popova, O.: Cognitive displays of needs: from semiotics of food to semiotics of agriculture. In: Kravets, A., Shcherbakov, M., Kultsova, M., Shabalina, O. (eds.) Creativity in Intelligent Technologies and Data Science, vol. 535, pp. 238–248. Springer, Cham (2015). https://doi.org/10.1007/978-3-319-23766-4_20
18. O'Reilly, T.: Today's Web 3.0 Nonsense Blogstorm. http://radar.oreilly.com/archives/2007/10/web-30-semantic-web-web-20.html
19. Samaricheva, A.I.: The English-speaking influence on German computer discourse. In: Kretov, A.A. (ed.) Language, Communication and Social Environment, Voronezh, vol. 1, pp. 71–74 (2001)

20. Shcherbakov, M., Groumpos, P.P., Kravets, A.: A method and IR4I index indicating the readiness of business processes for data science solutions. In: Kravets, A., Shcherbakov, M., Kultsova, M., Groumpos, P. (eds.) CIT&DS 2017, vol 754, 21–34. Springer, Cham (2017). https://doi.org/10.1007/978-3-319-65551-2_2
21. Siau, K., Tan, X.: Cognitive mapping techniques for user-database interaction. IEEE Trans. Prof. Commun. **49**(2), 96–108 (2006)
22. Simpson, J.: Meaning-making online: discourse and SMS in a language-learning community. In: Recent Research Developments in Learning Technologies (2005). http://www.formatex.org/micte2005
23. Smirnov, F.O.: National-cultural features of electronic communication in English and Russian languages. Yaroslavl'. 200 p. (2004)
24. Thurlow, C.: The internet and language. In: Concise Encyclopedia of Sociolinguistics, pp. 84–97. Elsevier (2001)
25. Zatsman, I.M.: Semiotic model of interrelations of concepts, information objects and computer codes. Informatics Applications **3**(2), 65–81 (2009)

Methods of Software Self-adaptation Based on Monitoring the Information Environment

Alexander Bershadsky, Alexander Bozhday[(✉)], Yulia Evseeva[(✉)], and Alexei Gudkov

Penza State University, Penza, Russia
bam@pnzgu.ru, bozhday@yandex.ru, shymoda@mail.ru,
alexei.gudkov@gmail.com

Abstract. The paper is devoted to the problem of developing a universal self-adaptation method of software systems. The main difference of proposed method is that a system extracts information about preferred structural and behavioral changes from a user feedback received in the form of reports and reviews. A semantic network of program characteristics will be built on the basis of this feedback information. This network will determine a new system configuration. For the synthesis of a semantic network, it is proposed to use methods of latent-semantic and distributive-statistical analysis. The feature diagram (the graphical representation of a feature model) will be used as a variability model of self-adaptive software. The developed method will allow a software system to independently identify and correct its own objective shortcomings directly in the process of functioning, as well as to adjust itself to different categories of users. The study was carried out with the financial support of the Russian Foundation for Basic Research in the framework of the research project No. 18-07-00408.

Keywords: Feature model · Variability modeling · Latent semantic analysis · Semantic network

1 Introduction

One of the main problems associated with software development is the large time and money costs at design and maintenance stages. These costs are especially high when software is designed to work in highly dynamic and difficult-formalizing subject areas. Various software development methodologies have their own perspective on how to solve these issues.

The methodology of structured programming (historically the earliest) allowed to create large-scale software systems. A prerequisite for this was the existence of strict specifications that should not have undergone major changes in the course of the project. Some time later, the concept of object-oriented programming came into practical use. It allowed to more effectively make changes to the specifications and reorganize the component structure of the program. However, such operations still remained laborious and costly.

A. G. Kravets et al. (Eds.): CIT&DS 2019, CCIS 1084, pp. 122–131, 2019.
https://doi.org/10.1007/978-3-030-29750-3_10

The topic of this article is the methodology of adaptive programming. It promises good prospects and is aimed at creating software that can easily adapt to changes in user preferences and execution conditions. Adaptive programs more clearly present the actions that need to be accomplished and the goals that need to be achieved. In this case, end users are able to modify the goals of the system without having to rewrite the program code.

To date, there is no universal adaptive programming technique. Different approaches can be used to solve various problems. Different subject areas also bring their own specifics. If we try to give a clear and simple definition of adaptive software, it can say the following: it is software that uses information about changes in the external environment (execution environment) to improve its work.

2 Background

To implement its own adaptive behavior, the software system must receive information from the environment and then analyze it. It is rather difficult to carry out this process for the following reasons: software specifications are usually incomplete; the environment is constantly changing; projects (even carefully worked out) sometimes rely on assumptions that may lose relevance. There are several groups of tools and methods that allow you to overcome these difficulties.

The first group consists of dynamic programming languages. Unlike static languages (such as C), languages like Dylan and CLOS allow you to develop software interfaces that can change during execution. For example, in Dylan, a running program can add a method to an existing class without accessing the source code. Another popular language that includes dynamic elements is Java. The paper [1] is devoted to the creation of a specific dynamic programming language for self-adjective applications.

Another approach to the development of adaptive software systems is the use of agent-based technologies. A software agent is a standalone process that can respond to the runtime environment and cause changes in it (possibly in cooperation with users or other agents). Software agents have some knowledge of the runtime environment and subject areas that allow them to solve single problems themselves without user intervention. However, the agent never has full control over the environment. Agent technologies are considered in such well-known works as [2] and [3] despite the noticeable popularity of agent-based technologies, there are several difficulties in their use. The first problem is related to the difficulties of optimization in a complex environments with many parallel and often contradictory processes. It is impossible to get a program that would be simultaneously accurate, fast, productive, resource-intensive. To find the optimum in the space of these contradictory criteria, the user will need an independent expert assessment of their relative value in certain conditions. The end user is not always sufficiently qualified for this. The second problem is connected with the fuzzy development of most real processes and environments. Traditional programs are built on Boolean logic, reducing all situations to single values of TRUE or FALSE. But in the real world, all events occur with some probability. The third difficulty is that the optimization of some processes may adversely affect the performance of other programs in a common runtime environment. Thus, the cumulative computational effect may be unpredictable.

The third group consists of methods of decision theory. Decision making theory is at the junction of utility and probability theories. It can be used as a language for describing adaptive software systems. This theory provides the necessary mathematical apparatus to respond to user preferences and cope with different kinds of uncertainties. Also, the methods of decision making theory can be useful in developing ways of communication between software agents. In this regard, it is worth mentioning the work [4] and work [5].

The fourth group consists of reinforcement learning methods. Reinforcement learning is a machine learning method in which a system under test learns by interacting with an environment. The environment generates reinforcement signals in response to decisions made by the system, therefore such training is a special case of supervised learning. In this case, the source of training data is an environment. The use of reinforcement learning in self-adaptive software is discussed in [6] and [7].

Another group are methods based on probabilistic networks (also known as Bayesian networks, decision networks, influence diagrams). The probabilistic network is a graph probabilistic model, which is a set of variables and their probabilistic dependencies. There are algorithms for finding the values of variables, studying the qualitative and quantitative dependencies between them, calculating their information value. One of the works devoted to probabilistic networks in self-adaptive software systems is [6].

Speaking about the main developments in the field of adaptive software systems, it is necessary to mention the runtime models [7–10]. However, this field is currently very poorly developed.

3   Issues, Controversies, Problems

None of the methods presented in the overview don't automatically reorganize the system in response to changes in user needs. In order to make this possible, the authors of the article propose to build a self-adaptive software system in accordance with the following principles:

1. Take the feature as the base self-adaptive unit of the system. A feature can be either a separate component of the system (for example, a resource manager or a separate three-dimensional model), or a system parameter (for example, the level of complexity at which the user runs the application).
2. Each of the features has many permissible values (for example, there may be several levels of complexity of the training program and several levels of detail of the three-dimensional model).
3. All features must be combined within a single model. The model should also include relationships between different features (for example, the compatibility of a specific value of one feature with selected values of the other should be taken into account).

4. Basic information about which features values should be selected and in which situation should come directly from users in the form of reviews and reviews.
5. In order to be able to reconfigure the software system in the runtime process, the main features of the system, as well as their possible values, must be extracted from the user information and presented in a structured form. In the future, based on the extracted features, the necessary system configuration will be selected.

Thus, to implement the method of self-adaptation of a software system based on observation of the information environment, it is necessary to solve the following tasks:

1. Develop a universal and easily formalized form of representing the feature hierarchy of a software system.
2. Develop a method for extracting features and their possible values from textual information.
3. Develop a universal form of presentation of the features extracted from the text in a structured form.
4. Develop a method for automatically generating the state of a software system based on features extracted from text information.

Thus, the main problems associated with the development of a self-adaptation method are related to the analysis of unstructured data and their presentation in a structured form. The solution to these problems should be sought in the complex using a number of existing techniques for processing text information.

4 Solutions and Recommendations

The first task that needs to be solved when developing a new method of self-adaptation is the selection of the optimal representation of the program system using the basic units of variability - features. To solve this problem, the authors of the article turned to the software product lines engineering (SPLE) - the concept of reusable software components that helps to develop product lines with a reduction in time to market and quality improvement.

The central concept of the SPLE is the concept of variability. The variability model is some formalized description of a set of possible configurations of a software system. The closest concept in the technical sciences is the concept of a morphological set. In essence, the model of variability is a morphological set of a software system, supplemented with some restrictions and rules. These restrictions and rules concern the compatibility of the individual components of a potential system with each other, but they may have a different meaning (depending on the type of variability model used).

SPLE uses the following types of variability models:

1. Feature models are the models that are most often used in practice. It's graphically displayed in the form of a modified AND/OR tree, called a feature diagram, and it can have a different formalized representation (hypergraph, propositional formula, algebraic notation, etc.).
2. Orthogonal variability models. Similar to feature models, also graphically displayed in the form of diagrams. The main difference lies in the fact that orthogonal models

show only the presence of variability in the program system under consideration, while the feature models provide a more specific description of both the subject area and the points of variation.

3. Decision models. The decision model includes the following components: questions from the subject area to which you need to get answers in the process of developing a software product; many possible answers to questions; references to used components (assets) or other decisions; a description of the consequences of making a decision (answering a particular question or choosing a particular asset).

To create a generalized description of the self-adaptive structure of the software system, it was decided to use the feature model.

The second important task is to choose a structured presentation of the features extracted from user reviews. As such a form was chosen semantic network - a structured domain model, having the form of a directed graph, the vertices of which correspond to the objects of the domain, and the arcs define the relations between them. Objects can be event, concepts, process, properties.

Thus, the main task of the developed method of self-adaptation will be to build a semantic network of features based on an array of user reviews and configuration of feature diagram based on the resulting network. Figure 1 shows a fragment of the feature diagram of a certain software system and the corresponding fragment of the semantic network.

The method of self-adaptation of software systems based on information environment monitoring includes the following steps:

1. Collect a documents in natural language, containing the views of users on how the system should work.

2. Extraction of terms for determining similar reviews and for the subsequent extraction of the features of the software system from them. This stage includes the following steps: (1) Removal of words that do not carry a semantic load (prepositions, conjunctions, etc.), as well as special symbols and signs of punctuation from each document (2) Lemmatization of words in documents (coercion words to one) (3) Each word in the document is assigned a part of speech (4) All words except nouns, adjectives and verbs are deleted (5) The result of the algorithm is a matrix M of $m \times n$, where m is the number of terms, $\underline{n}$ is the number of documents. The elements of the matrix are the weighting factors calculated in accordance with the frequencies with which the terms are found in the documents.

3. Identification of similar documents. As a rule, the matrix M is sparse (contains many zero elements), which complicates its analysis. To eliminate this drawback, the procedure of decreasing the dimension of the matrix using its singular decomposition is performed:

$$M = USV,$$

where the matrices U and V are orthogonal, and the matrix S is diagonal. On the main diagonal of the matrix S, the singular numbers of the matrix M are arranged in descending order. To reduce the dimension of the matrix M, take the r first singular numbers (for example, the first two). Accordingly, from the matrix U are taken r first

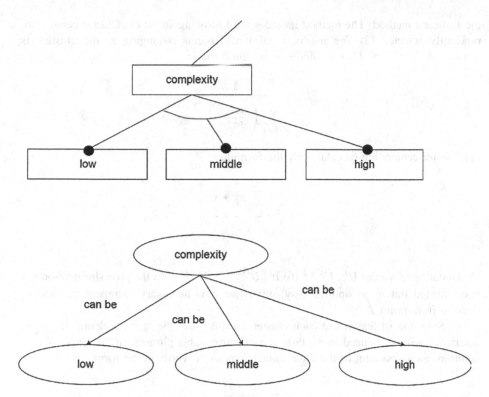

Fig. 1. Fragment of the feature diagram of a certain software system and the corresponding fragment of the semantic network

columns, and from the matrix $V - r$ first rows. The matrices thus obtained will be denoted as U', S', V'. The matrix $M' = U' S' V'$ will be an approximation of a matrix M with lower rank r. To determine similar documents, a matrix $D = S' V'$ is used, having the dimension $r \times n$. With $r = 2$, the columns of the matrix D can be considered as points in a two-dimensional space corresponding to the source documents. This is followed by the phase of clustering documents according to the values of matrix D. The simplest method of clustering is using the k-means method, the main task of which is to optimize the objective function (distance) defined using the formula

$$E = \sum_{i=1}^{c} \sum_{x \in C_i} d(x_i, m_i)$$

where m_i is the center of the C_i cluster, and $d(x_i, m_i)$ is the Euclidean distance between points x_i and m_i. First, the algorithm splits the entire set of data into c clusters, then randomly select the centers of the clusters. Then, for each point, the cluster center nearest to it is determined and the cluster centers are recalculated. The last 2 steps are repeated until the centers of the clusters stop changing. As an alternative, we can consider the C-means fuzzy clustering method, which, in essence, is a development of the k-means method. The method includes the following steps: (1) Cluster centers are randomly selected (2) The matrix U of the elements belonging to the clusters is initialized (3) Values U_{ij} are calculated by the formula

$$U_{ij} = \frac{1}{\sum\limits_{k=1}^{c} \left(\frac{\|x_i - c_j\|}{\|x_i - c_k\|} \right)^{\frac{2}{m-1}}}$$

(4) Cluster centers are calculated by the formula

$$C_k = \frac{\sum\limits_{i=1}^{N} u_{ij}^m * x_i}{\sum\limits_{i=1}^{N} u_{ij}^m}$$

(5) Updating of values U^K, U^{K+1} (6) If $\|U^{(K+1)} - U^{(K)}\| < \varepsilon$ then the sterilization has been carried out in an optimal way, otherwise it is necessary to repeat the actions starting from point 2.

4. Selection of features in each cluster. In this case, the task of identifying characteristics will be reduced to the task of extracting stable phrases. In this paper, for its solution, an assessment of the inter-connectedness of words in the form

$$c = \frac{t_1 + t_2}{2 * f(t^1 t^2)}$$

where t_1 and t_2 reflects the number of different pairs with the first or second word from the considered phrase, $f(t^1 t^2)$ reflects the number of occurrences of the phrase "first-second word together". The smaller the c value, the better a couple of words (t^1, t^2) are considered.

5. Identify the relationship between the selected features and the construction of a semantic network for each cluster. To solve this problem, it is proposed to use the distribution-statistical method. The main hypothesis underlying it is as follows: the significant elements of the language, occurring within a certain text range, are semantically related. The method includes 2 stages: the calculation of quantitative (frequency) characteristics of a single and joint incidence of significant elements of the language, the calculation of the forces of relations between the elements and the composition of the matrix of relations between the features. The central concept in distributive statistical analysis is the notion of context. A context means a segment of text, a sequence (chain) of syntagmas. A syntagma is a segment of a sentence, consisting of one or several words, united grammatically, intonationally and in meaning. The minimal length of a syntagma should be considered simple phrases. Formally, the con-text is defined as follows:

$$T = C_1(T) + \ldots + C_q(T)$$

where $C_i(T) \cap C_j(T) = \varnothing$, $i,j\,(i \neq j) \in [1,q]$. Frequency characteristics are calculated as follows:

$$f_A = \frac{N_A}{N}, f_B = \frac{N_B}{N}, f_{AB} = \frac{N_{AB}}{N},$$

where N is the total number of contexts, N_A and f_A is the number and frequency of contexts where only feature A met, N_B and f_B is the number and frequency of contexts where characteristic B met, N_{AB} and f_{AB} are the number and frequency of contexts in which co-occurrence of characteristics A and B. The next step is to calculate the bond strength coefficients, for which the formulas given in Table 1 can be used.

Table 1. Formulas for calculating the strength of the connection between syntagmas.

Formula	Authors
$K_{AB} = \frac{N_{AB}}{N_A + N_B - N_{AB}}$	T. Tanimoto, L. Doyle
$K_{AB} = \frac{N_{AB} - f_A * f_B}{N}$	M. Mayron, J. Koons
$K_{AB} = \frac{f_A * N}{f_A * f_B}$	A. I. Shaikiewicz, J. Solton, R. Curtis
$K_{AB} = \frac{N_{AB} - N_A * N_B}{\sqrt{N_A * N_B}}$	S. Dennis
$K_{AB} = \log_{10} \frac{[(f_{AB} * N - f_A * f_B) - \frac{N}{2}]^2 * N}{f_A * f_B * (N - f_A) * (N - f_B)}$	H.E. Stiles

All the formulas of the coefficients of the strength of connection unites the consideration of events connected with the appearance of syntagmas A and B, as systems of random phenomena. To determine the thematic connections between the features, the length of the context should be 50–100 words. Based on the calculations of the coefficients of the coupling forces, a matrix of semantic connectivity of features is built. On the basis of the matrix, a semantic network is built. The nodes of the network will be the features extracted from the reviews, the arcs connecting the features will show the presence of a semantic connection between them.

6. Formation of configurations of the feature diagram. For each cluster of documents, it is necessary to make a comparison of the obtained semantic network with the model of system features and thus form a configuration; at the same time, during the formation of each configuration, it should be taken into account from which user type the responses were received (for this purpose, it is necessary to first determine the average portrait of users whose reviews formed a cluster).

7. The further process of self-adaptation is that a user of some type will be assigned a specific configuration, i.e. the system will adapt to specific users. It is assumed that only users registered in the system can have reviews whose profile contains sufficiently complete information about them.

5 Future Research

As a further direction of research, we can consider the improvement of the developed method. First of all, it is necessary to solve the problem of synonyms, since the same characteristic can have different names in different user reviews. The second problem is that users can make spelling mistakes and typing errors when writing reviews. It is also necessary to implement automatic spelling correction. In the current version of the method, stable phrases of 2 words are considered as features, however, in certain cases, the components and parameters of the software system may have more complex compound names, and for their correct identification it is necessary to improve the search engine of stable phrases.

6 Conclusion

The problem of software complexity raises the problem of reducing the quality of its operation: it is difficult to consider in advance how the system behaves under various external conditions, and there is not always time for such assessments. A program that shows good (for example, in terms of performance) results in some situations may not work well in others. Moreover, the development of a complex software system that provides for operation in various software and hardware environments and under various conditions (including user conditions) can become a long and resource-intensive task.

The solution to the problem lies in the development of specialized methods of self-adaptation of software systems. There are many approaches to the development of adaptive software, but none of them solves an important task—it does not automatically reorganize the system in response to changes in user needs. To solve this problem, the authors proposed a new method, according to which the self-adaptable structure of the system is presented from the point of view of the basic units of variability - features, as well as their possible values. To implement self-adaptive behavior, arrays of user reviews are used, from which features are extracted, presented in the form of a semantic network, and later for the formation of a system configuration are compared with a general-system feature model.

References

1. Ghezzi, C., Salvaneschi, G., Pradella, M.: ContextErlang: a language for distributed context-aware self-adaptive applications. Sci. Comput. Program. **102**, 20–43 (2015)
2. Lei, Y., Ben, K., He, Z.: A model driven agent-oriented self-adaptive software development method. In: 2015 12th International Conference on Fuzzy Systems and Knowledge Discovery (FSKD) (2015)
3. Li, Y., Li, L., Wang, W., Wu, T.: ADAPT: an agent-based development toolkit and operation platform for self-adaptive systems. In: 2017 IEEE Conference on Open Systems (ICOS) (2017)

4. Bencomo, N., Belaggoun, A.: Supporting decision-making for self-adaptive systems: from goal models to dynamic decision networks. In: Doerr, J., Opdahl, Andreas L. (eds.) REFSQ 2013. LNCS, vol. 7830, pp. 221–236. Springer, Heidelberg (2013). https://doi.org/10.1007/978-3-642-37422-7_16

5. Belhaj, N., Belaid, D., Mukhtar, H.: Framework for building self-adaptive component applications based on reinforcement learning. In: Framework for Building Self-Adaptive Component Applications Based on Reinforcement Learning (2018)

6. Belaggoun, A.: Exploring the use of dynamic decision networks for self-adaptive systems. Master's thesis, Univ. de Versailles Saint-Quentin-En-Yvelines (2012)

7. Wang, X., Wang, H., Hu, X., Zhang, X.: A multi-agent reinforcement learning approach to dynamic service composition. Inf. Sci. **363**, 96–119 (2016)

8. Blair, G., Bencomo, N., France, R.B.: Models@run.time. Computer **42**(10), 21–35 (2009)

9. Morin, B., Barais, O., Jezequel, J.M., Fleurey, F., Solberg, A.: Models@ Run.time to support dynamic adaptation. Computer **42**(10), 44–51 (2009)

10. Vogel, T., Giese, H.: Model-Driven Engineering of Adaptation Engines for Self-Adaptive Software: Executable Runtime Megamodels. Potsdam University Press, Potsdam (2013)

Artificial Intelligence and Deep Learning Technologies for Creative Tasks. Computer Vision and Knowledge-Based Control

The Fuzzy Rule Base Automatic Optimization Method of Intelligent Controllers for Technical Objects Using Fuzzy Clustering

Vladimir Ignatyev$^{(\boxtimes)}$ ⓘ, Viktor Soloviev ⓘ, Denis Beloglazov,
Viktor Kureychik ⓘ, Kovalev Andrey ⓘ, and Alexandra Ignatyeva

Southern Federal University,
Bolshaya Sadovaya Str., 105/42, 344006 Rostov-on-Don, Russia
vova3286@mail.ru

Abstract. The goal of this work is to develop a fuzzy rule base optimization method of intelligent controllers for technical objects using fuzzy clustering. To achieve the goal of the study, a hybrid model is developed in which the control of a technical object is implemented using the PID-classical and PID-FUZZY controllers with the generated structure of the Sugeno-type fuzzy inference system and the developed model of the adaptive neuro-fuzzy inference system, which allows to form a base of fuzzy rules, which is independent of an expert knowledge in the subject area, a method for optimization the fuzzy controller rule base based on clustering methods is proposed, allows you to reduce the number of fuzzy inference rules and increase the control system speed of the technical object. A hybrid model was simulated before and after fuzzy clustering, which proves the high efficiency of the proposed method for optimization the fuzzy controller rule base by reducing the number of fuzzy inference rules and the number of membership functions required to describe linguistic variables.

Keywords: Control system · Fuzzy clustering · Fuzzy rules · Optimization · Fuzzy inference system · Hybrid network · Training

1 Introduction

The transition to advanced digital, intelligent manufacturing technologies involves the creation of machine training systems and artificial intelligence, as the systems of control and control based on artificial intelligence in industrial enterprises will be more efficient than conventional machine-based automated process control systems (APCS).

The use of artificial intelligence in APCS or their joint use can provide automation of the technological process main operations in production, increase its efficiency due to the optimal distribution of material, energy and information resources of the enterprise, guarantee greater reliability of products.

Integration of artificial intelligence into automated process control systems is an actual but challenging task since, in enterprises, especially those that are not modernized, most control loops function in complex structures of control systems that contain cross-links in the control object.

© Springer Nature Switzerland AG 2019
A. G. Kravets et al. (Eds.): CIT&DS 2019, CCIS 1084, pp. 135–152, 2019.
https://doi.org/10.1007/978-3-030-29750-3_11

The problem lies in setting up each circuit, which significantly depends on the characteristics of other circuits, including the settings of the controllers in these circuits, especially when the mathematical description of the process is very time consuming or impossible.

In most productions in control systems, classical controllers have used that work well with a fully deterministic control object and a deterministic environment. Not all controllers used to control and regulate technological parameters are optimally tuned. In the operational control of objects with high dynamics of changes in output parameters, delays are not allowed when implementing control actions. Also in the operation mode of the automatic control system, one may encounter the difficulty of setting its parameters.

For systems with incomplete a priori information and high complexity of the control object, the optimal controllers are based on fuzzy logic.

The main problems in the development of a fuzzy controller are:

- formation of the fuzzy rule base, which is less dependent or independent of expert knowledge of in the subject area;
- determination of the necessary and sufficient number of fuzzy rules, since the rule base should be built on the principle of necessity and sufficiency and with the aim of reducing the calculations made volume, as well as improving the speed of the control system;
- determination of the necessary and sufficient number of membership functions required to describe linguistic variables.

This article discusses the hybrid control model of a technical object, which implements an integrated approach based on the use of classical methods and means of automatic control and control of technological processes parameters and artificial intelligence elements. In particular, the PID-classical and PID-FUZZY controllers are used with the generated structure of the Sugeno-type fuzzy inference system and the developed model of the adaptive neuro-fuzzy inference system, which allows forming the basis of fuzzy rules that is not dependent on the expert knowledge in the subject area.

A method for optimizing the fuzzy controller rule base with the aim of reducing it using fuzzy cluster analysis is proposed.

2   Literature Review

[1–8] aimed at solving control problems, including using the hybrid approach, contain recommendations (usually based on expert assessments) regarding the choice of membership functions forms, ranges of input and output values, fuzzification and defuzzification procedures with the aim of creating an optimal rule base for a fuzzy controller.

The rule base optimization of a fuzzy controller operating in a hybrid system directly depends on the structure of this system.

For example, in [9] hybrid control logic of a PID controller is proposed, the settings of which are provided in real time. The fuzzy controller is configured on the basis of the Mamdani controller, also using the results obtained with the procedure for identifying the values that affect the behavior of the control process.

[10] describes an effective method for determining the optimal parameters of a linear fuzzy PID controller. In this case, training or adapting the controller when changing the parameters of the control object is not provided.

In [11], the stabilization and control of an inverted pendulum on a trolley moving along an inclined surface using PID and fuzzy controllers is considered. To achieve the required results, the use of a complex mathematical apparatus is required.

[12] shows the organization of interaction between the components of a hybrid controller; the idea is to obtain fuzzy estimates of the PID and fuzzy controllers efficiency for solving the problem of controlling a technical object with the subsequent introduction of the weighting coefficients of control actions for each controller.

In [13], the PID-classical controller is used as the main control device, and the fuzzy controller is used as the compensator of disturbing effects.

An adaptive hybrid controller is described in [14, 15], which uses a fuzzy model of the control object to predict its behavior and adapt the parameters of the control device (PID controller) based on this prediction.

In [16], a hybrid system was developed that uses a neural network to improve the PID controller parameters obtained with the help of a genetic algorithm and to develop a fuzzy model rule base.

A hybrid PID controller is introduced in [17], the tuning of which is performed on the basis of a genetic algorithm.

Savran and Kahraman [16] offered a hybrid system (neural network and PID controller) that uses a neural network to improve parameters of PID controller obtained with the help of a genetic algorithm and develop a fuzzy model rule base.

Jahedi and Ardehali [17] presented a hybrid PID controller, which setting is based on a genetic algorithm.

In [18], a hybrid learning procedure based on a fuzzy inference system implemented as an adaptive network structure (ANFIS). To compile a fuzzy controller rule base in the proposed system, both knowledge of an expert in the subject area and forecast data obtained using ANFIS can be used. ANFIS is used to simulate nonlinear functions, quickly determine nonlinear components in a control system, and forecasting. The disadvantage of this approach is the low level of robustness for reliable and accurate intelligent control in real-time of a technical object under uncertainty conditions of the initial information or incomplete description of the functioning process. There is the problem of processing a large amount of data obtained using ANFIS and increasing the number of calculations performed when calculating the values of the control action.

Much research has also been devoted to solving the problem with the help of fuzzy clustering. For example, Fuzzy clustering is used to detect warnings and failures of a wind turbine, that is, for diagnostics to simulate an optimal power curve [19].

Chaghari et al. [20] used the forest optimization algorithm (FOA) to improve the accuracy of the standard FCM algorithm. Fuzzy clustering, in this case, is a combination of a forest optimization algorithm with a gradient method, which allows obtaining optimized cluster centers.

Ren and Bigras [21] proposed a solution to the problem of controlling the movement of a parallel robot with discrete time using an adaptive neuro-fuzzy inference system based on improved subtractive clustering. The discrete-time PID adaptive neuro-fuzzy logic controller used to control the robot without its physical model is used. The work uses an improved method of subtractive clustering to obtain the structure of the system model in order to provide the high accuracy of intelligent control.

The clustering method is used to isolate homogeneous system faults into groups. The result of the method application is a reduction in the volume of information and the search area, which allows to significantly reduce the time for the determination of faults [22].

Salgado and Igrejas [23] proposed a probabilistic approach for fuzzy clustering of fuzzy rules. At the heart of the approach is the partitioning of input information into subgroups, calculation of the output function and fuzzy rules of each of the subgroups, and obtaining the output function and fuzzy rules of the entire system based on integrating the results of all subgroups using the aggregation function.

Coelho et al. [24] performed a study of the vertical motion dynamic modeling of a double rotor system based on the Takagi-Sugeno-Kang fuzzy inference system using FCM clustering and differential evolution optimization.

The analysis shows a variety of methods and approaches aimed at creating an optimal controller, as well as the use of fuzzy clustering in control tasks, which confirms the relevance of the research conducted in this work.

The scientific novelty of this work is to develop a new method of automatically optimizing the intelligent controllers rule base based on fuzzy cluster analysis in control systems of technical objects, which will improve the performance of the control model, optimize the fuzzy controller rule base (reduce the number of rules and the number of membership functions), and reduce the development time of a fuzzy controller.

To prove the effectiveness of the proposed method, it is approbation on a hybrid control model of a technical object is proposed. The regulating elements of the model are fuzzy and classical controllers, working together. The values of the error signals, the error differential and the control action of the classic controller are the source for the construction of a fuzzy controller.

Terms of linguistic error variables, error differential, and control action are formed automatically on the basis of the source data from the classic controller. There can be several hundreds of such terms, depending on the chosen discretization step of the classical controller values.

Therefore, fuzzy clustering is performed for the values of each input linguistic variable of the fuzzy controller and the output variable, which is a distinctive feature of the proposed method. After performing a fuzzy cluster analysis, the volume of terms is significantly reduced, which allows generating a fuzzy controller rule base with less labor, using only the desired terms.

The obtained new research results will allow obtaining the desired control with a significantly smaller number of calculations.

3   The Proposed Method

The implementation of the proposed optimization method is based on the results obtained by the authors on the development of the theoretical foundations and methods for automatically adjusting the parameters of intelligent control systems for technical objects with a priori uncertainty and involves the following stages.

Stage 1. Development of a hybrid control model of a technical object using a PID-FUZZY controller with the generated structure of the Sugeno-type fuzzy inference system. In the developed model, an intelligent control system of a technical object is synthesized, characterized in that the fuzzy inference rule base is formed automatically [25] on the basis of the reference system.

Stage 2. Development of a neuro-fuzzy inference adaptive system model in the form of a hybrid network [26–28] based on PID- and PID-FUZZY-controllers [25], which allows to simplify, automate and unify the process of designing automated control systems. When implementing an adaptive neuro-fuzzy inference system, the deviation, deviation differential and control indicators obtained from the operation of the classical controller are the data used to test the effectiveness of the hybrid network in order to identify the fact of it is retraining. The data (indicators of deviation, deviation differential, and control action) obtained from the operation of a fuzzy controller, form a training sample for building a hybrid network. This approach helps to reduce labor costs in developing a control system and significantly improve the quality of transition processes.

Stage 3. Phase 3. Optimization of the fuzzy controller rule base based on clustering methods, which allows to reduce the number of fuzzy inference rules and increase the speed of the technical object control system. Optimization is characterized by the use of fuzzy clustering, which reduces the matrix dimension of error signal values, it is differential and control actions necessary for the synthesis of the fuzzy controller rule base [29].

In Fig. 1 shows a hybrid model for controlling a technical object using PID-classical and PID-FUZZY controllers.

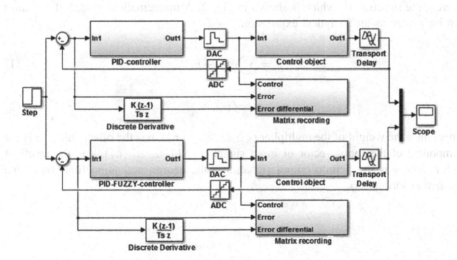

Fig. 1. Hybrid control model

The numerical values of system deviation θ, deviation differential $\dot{\theta}$ and control action U are recorded in special files (Matrix recording in Fig. 1) to build an adaptive neuro-fuzzy inference system.

In particular, after launching the model, 67 values were obtained for each controller for each indicator. The resulting figures are presented in Fig. 2.

1	1	0.666666666666667	13.3761333333333	1	0.666666666666667	4.55720165814288
2	1	0	3.17940400000000	1	0	5.39054815283367
3	1	0	3.27200800000000	1	0	5.39054815283367
4	1	0	3.36461200000000	1	0	5.39054815283367
5	0.670081964000000	-0.219945357333333	-0.97108750351034	0.887588736000000	-0.0749408426666667	5.12122353932397
.						
.						
13	0.305019294000000	-0.0259757680000000	0.823130659489065	0.00720034600000008	-0.000719758666666663	0.794904221770076
14	0.262736158000000	-0.0208192880000000	0.821605865299536	0.0075226260000000009	0.00021485333333333339	0.797430406562450
15	0.219663436000000	-0.0112690573333333	0.929885065083706	0.0089756320000011	0.000848670666666680	0.800173782015182
16	0.180699784000000	-0.00561841466666668	1.00296874375826	0.0091823680000005	0.000257823999999962	0.799160805624919
17	0.149470852000000	-0.00351285200000000	1.03045264010821	0.00908568400000009	-6.44559999999723e-05	0.798307607335909
.						
.						
63	-0.00348323599999	-5.37133333332975e-05	0.803886623103079	0.00599179600000011	0	0.795414878197775
64	-0.00353157799999	-3.2227999999493e-05	0.803443357429515	0.0059756820000009	-1.07426666666743e-05	0.795373506005143
65	-0.00357991999999	-3.22280000000967e-05	0.803041625236446	0.0059756820000009	0	0.795398990581780
66	-0.00361214799999	-2.14853333333487e-05	0.802899207867685	0.0059595680000008	-1.07426666666743e-05	0.795357616985109
67	-0.00361214799999	0	0.802420709201686	0.0059595680000008	0	0.795383102639466

a)   b)

Fig. 2. The numerical values of the PID-classical and PID-FUZZY controllers. (a) – PID-classical controller (deviation, deviation differential, control – from left to right), (b) – PID-FUZZY controller (deviation, deviation differential, control – from left to right)

The conceptual basis and component of an artificial neural network is an artificial neuron, the structure of which is shown in Fig. 3. A mathematical model of a neuron can be written as an analytical expression:

$$s = \sum_{i=1}^{n} \omega_i x_i + b, \tag{1}$$

$$y = f(s), \tag{2}$$

where ωi is the weight of the multiplier ($i \in \{1, 2, ..., n\}$), b is the offset value, xi is the component of the input vector or input signal ($i \in \{1, 2, ..., n\}$), s is the result of summation, y is the neuron output signal, s is the neuron activation function (some linear transformation).

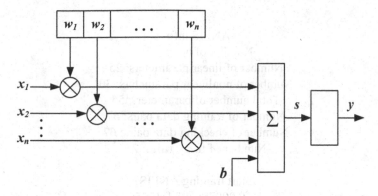

Fig. 3. Artificial neuron structure

Hybrid network training was conducted by a hybrid method, which is a combination of the least squares method [27]. The learning results of the hybrid method are presented in Fig. 4.

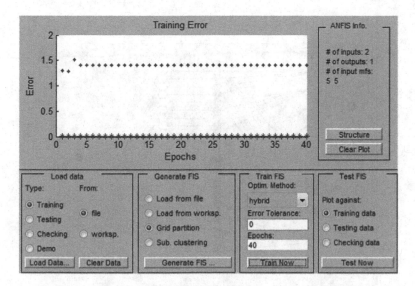

Fig. 4. Dependency graph of training and verification errors on a number of training cycles

The upper graph shows the dependence of the verification error on the number of training cycles, and the lower graph shows the dependence of the training error on the number of training cycles. From the graphs in Fig. 4 shows that using the hybrid method, the training ends at the third stage after two cycles, which is confirmed by the data from the command line of the MATLAB package:

ANFIS info:
Number of nodes: 75
Number of linear parameters: 25
Number of nonlinear parameters: 30
Total number of parameters: 55
Number of training data pairs: 67
Number of checking data pairs: 67
Number of fuzzy rules: 25

Start training ANFIS
1   0.000755307 1.40956
2   0.00313896 1.30758

Designated epoch number reached --> ANFIS training completed at **epoch 2**.

The generated structure of the Sugeno-type fuzzy inference system is shown in Fig. 5.

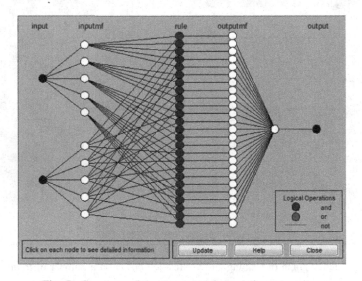

Fig. 5. Structure of the generated fuzzy inference system

In Fig. 6 shows the procedure for setting the number and type of membership functions (type – triangular, number – five).

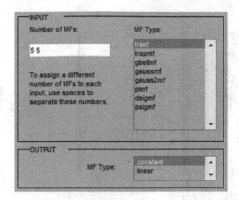

Fig. 6. Setting membership functions

The generated Sugeno-type fuzzy inference system is shown in Fig. 7.

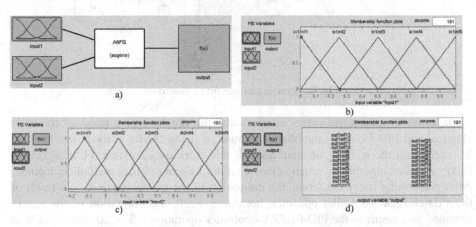

Fig. 7. The Sugeno-type fuzzy inference system. (a) – generated fuzzy inference system, (b) – terms of the deviations input variable, (c) – terms of deviation differential input variable, (d) – sought values of the output variable

From the data obtained in MATLAB, it is clear that the number of fuzzy rules is 25 (Number of fuzzy rules: 25). This is also confirmed by the obtained structure of the PID-FUZZY controller, shown in Fig. 8.

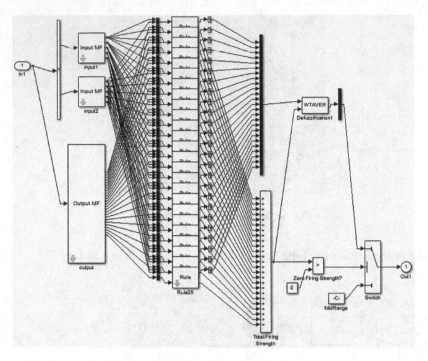

Fig. 8. Structure of the fuzzy controller

In order to reduce the values matrixes volume obtained as a result of the PID-classical and PID-FUZZY controllers operation, a fuzzy cluster analysis was applied. To implement the splitting of input actions, this work uses a classic FCM algorithm (fuzzy c-means algorithm), which is based on the Lagrange fuzzy multipliers method. After performing fuzzy clustering, the dimension of the matrix obtained as a result of the PID-classical controller operation became 3×20, the dimension of the matrix obtained as a result of the PID-FUZZY controller operation – 3×20, that is, in both cases decreased by more than 3 times.

The resulting figures after fuzzy clustering are presented in Fig. 9.

1	9.999999753649639e-01	-2.16288202918867e-10	3.196318213440493e+00	7.646652583861573e-0	-1.66873427742394e-04	7.966493945417989e-01
2	3.112958442154132e-01	1.04686461078833e-02	1.678333907860960e+00	1.545145336930047e-01	-1.150861877586464e-01	8.226130268032290e-01
3	6.700819238122506e-01	-2.199453335006192e-01	-9.710872545841322e-01	9.999999999999985e-01	6.677464943136882e-20	5.390548125833662e+00
4	2.625964543966301e-01	-2.817185803600057e-02	1.001250843463934e+00	7.621844752732974e-03	-1.791243316002747e-04	7.965960713807583e-01
5	2.861989491162561e-01	3.352774120473032e-02	1.914971594377799e+00	7.270847022532034e-03	-1.496903540004230e-04	7.963213311695333e-01
6	9.999998093250998e-01	-1.677442141971000e-10	3.344073833097642e+00	9.016591944979090e-03	3.894121480350987e-04	7.993084643219975e-01
7	1.166980809778497e-01	-3.218794148358744e-03	1.033672020843770e+00	8.875887359999952e-01	-7.494084266666629e-02	5.121223539323946e+00
8	-1.363440867714083e-03	-2.666438020042886e-04	8.076317090577502e-01	9.407963142787047e-03	-2.017471631715421e-02	7.559578434781936e-01
9	1.610583977882031e-02	-1.673515579593383e-03	8.336776413981259e-01	7.720764460628894e-03	-1.309825203199316e-04	7.968070144057060e-01
10	3.050170205139247e-01	-8.390003565195116e-03	1.411131428355161e+00	9.999999999999900e-01	6.666666666666603e-01	4.557201658142839e+00
11	4.372829541856266e-01	-1.551992716450113e-01	-6.391271268341485e-01	5.118585979819884e-01	-1.268923786621289e-01	8.226130268548568e-01
12	3.341660466177981e-01	-6.874145279399919e-02	4.126857022404780e-01	6.211442625862029e-03	-1.944845212703004e-05	7.955852996625623e-01
13	1.059814912173283e-01	-8.260217683154016e-03	9.331144064513728e-01	3.967005463885166e-02	-7.656298203727948e-02	7.670346423121398e-01
14	2.359000987846398e-01	3.480055180464746e-03	1.271790421325896e+00	3.271438159396386e-01	-1.231431879766968e-01	8.226130268510117e-01
15	2.191020946522807e-01	-2.862840329663880e-02	8.825517560842202e-01	7.391900486796351e-03	-1.604279175506043e-04	7.964152369362560e-01
16	1.154324809094456e-01	-5.10989510262127e-03	1.000967076203021e+00	8.108309520751136e-03	-9.949484417799742e-05	7.972641548118262e-01
17	4.973597285442784e-02	-4.135319322481740e-03	8.735096504360903e-01	7.919013653675073e-03	-3.517495844240919e-05	7.972281099110230e-01
18	9.999999999552888e-01	6.666666661549400e-01	1.337613332546800e+00	7.658043159045011e-03	-1.612980631254741e-04	7.966737602587945e-01
19	1.645912660687041e-01	-2.330645275566523e-02	8.226141182062627e-01	7.919527365899620e-03	-3.491973337735824e-05	7.972292173854205e-01
20	2.306850058842192e-01	-6.989209965468e-02	1.155869362932569e-01	7.021971659999475e-01	-1.235943799999906e-01	3.117203836962636e+00

a)   b)

Fig. 9. Numerical values of the PID-classical and PID-FUZZY controllers. (a) – PID-classical controller (deviation, deviation differential, control – from left to right), (b) – PID-FUZZY controller (deviation, deviation differential, control – from left to right)

Graphically, the result of fuzzy clustering is shown in Fig. 10.

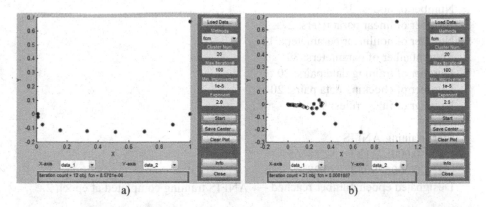

a)   b)

Fig. 10. Results of clustering using an FCM algorithm. (a) – training data, (b) – verification data

Hybrid network training after performing fuzzy clustering was also conducted using the hybrid method. The training results by the hybrid method are presented in Fig. 11.

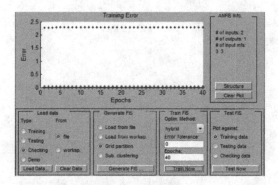

Fig. 11. Dependency graph of training and verification errors on a number of training cycles

The training also ends at the third stage after two cycles, which is confirmed by the data from the command line of the MATLAB package:

ANFIS info:
Number of nodes: 35
Number of linear parameters: 27
Number of nonlinear parameters: 12
Total number of parameters: 39
Number of training data pairs: 20
Number of checking data pairs: 20
Number of fuzzy rules: 9

Start training ANFIS ...
  1   0.000571127   2.28165
  2   0.000579032   2.2814
Designated epoch number reached --> ANFIS training completed at epoch 2.

From the data obtained in MATLAB, it can be seen that the number of fuzzy rules has decreased from 25 to 9. The generated structure of the Sugeno-type fuzzy inference system is shown in Fig. 12.

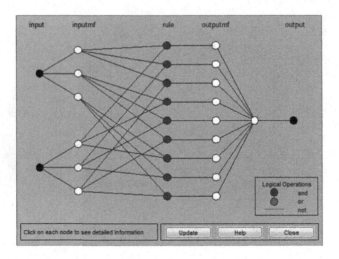

Fig. 12. Structure of the generated fuzzy inference system

The number and type of membership functions are changed (type – a simple Gauss membership function, the number – three), which is graphically represented in Fig. 13.

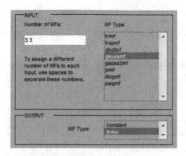

Fig. 13. Setting the membership functions

The generated Sugeno-type fuzzy inference system is shown in Fig. 14.

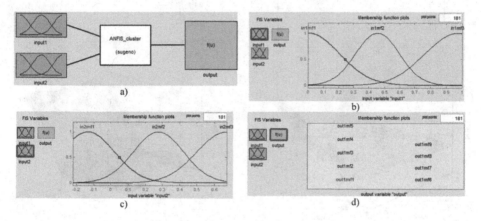

Fig. 14. The Sugeno-type fuzzy inference system. (a) – generated fuzzy inference system, (b) – terms of the deviations input variable, (c) – terms of deviation differential input variable, (d) – sought values of the output variable

The structure of the PID-FUZZY controller after applying fuzzy cluster analysis is shown in Fig. 15.

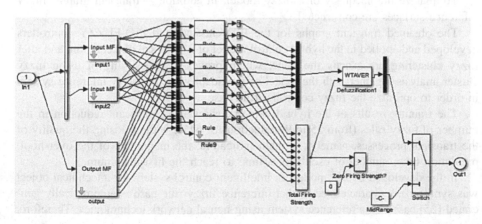

Fig. 15. Structure of the fuzzy controller

4 Results

After the generation of a fuzzy inference system and it is integration into a hybrid control model of a technical object (see Fig. 1), the results of the work simulation are obtained, shown in Fig. 16.

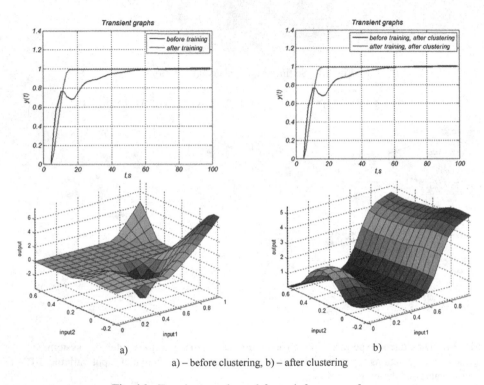

a) – before clustering, b) – after clustering

Fig. 16. Transient graphs and fuzzy inference surfaces

To analyze the adequacy of a fuzzy model, in addition to transient graphs, fuzzy inference surfaces are constructed.

The obtained transient graphs for the PID-classical and PID-FUZZY controllers developed and applied in the hybrid control model of a technical object before and after fuzzy clustering are exactly the same, which proves the possibility of using fuzzy cluster analysis together with the model of the adaptive neuro-fuzzy inference system in order to optimize the fuzzy controller rule base.

The training results of the hybrid network showed a significant reduction in the number of fuzzy rules (from 25 to 9, reduction for 64%) without losing the quality of the transient processes, namely, its main indicators: the magnitude of the overshoot; regulation time; number of oscillations, time to reach the first maximum.

In the developed hybrid model, an intelligent control system for a technical object was synthesized, characterized in that inference fuzzy rule base is automatically generated [25] based on a reference system using neural network technologies. Therefore, it is especially important to take into account the labor costs and the probability of error when developing membership functions, since knowledge of a subject matter expert is eliminated, which makes it possible to avoid the human factor related errors.

In the proposed method, the number of membership functions is also reduced from 5 to 3 (reduction for 40%) for each input linguistic variable. The type in the form of a triangular membership function and a simple Gauss membership function was not manually selected but was set by default.

In the future, you can use the graphical tools of the FUZZY LOGIC TOOLBOX software package to configure the parameters of the constructed and trained network [30].

5 Discussion

The use of fuzzy clustering in the developed hybrid model in which the control of a technical object is implemented using the PID-classical and PID-FUZZY controller with the generated structure of the Sugeno-type fuzzy inference system and the developed model of the adaptive neuro-fuzzy inference system is a distinctive feature of the proposed optimization method of the fuzzy rule base.

Fuzzy clustering reduces the number of calculations performed, which gives an advantage in comparison with [16, 17], where the optimization of the controller parameters is performed using a genetic algorithm that requires considerable effort when setting up a specific task.

In comparison with [18, 20], the already automatically formed rules of the fuzzy controller were subjected to fuzzy clustering in the course of the hybrid model operation and after that the training.

In comparison with the results obtained in [19], the proposed optimization method allows not only to obtain the desired control with maximum quality, but also to increase the speed of the control model of a technical object by reducing the number of rules and the number of membership functions required to describe linguistic variables when developing fuzzy controller.

In comparison with the results obtained in [22], where a probabilistic approach was proposed for fuzzy clustering of fuzzy rules with a complex mathematical apparatus, in this paper there is no need to calculate the output function and fuzzy rules of each of the subgroups in order to obtain the output function and fuzzy rules of the entire system based on integrating the results of all subgroups using the aggregation function. The output variable of the fuzzy controller in the form of a control signal is built automatically [25–29], as well as the input. Fuzzy clustering is applied to the values of these variables without affecting their occurrence during development. Thus, only the number of these values is significantly reduced, which allows you to develop a rule base with minimal labor.

6 Conclusion

Despite the fact that fuzzy control is one of the most active and promising areas of applied research in the problems of control and decision-making, it is practically not used in real automated systems of technological process control. To automated systems based on fuzzy logic or neural networks, there is a great deal of distrust on the part of specialists who operate such systems. Control systems built on fuzzy logic are not capable of training and are highly dependent on the knowledge of an expert in the subject area, training is inherent in neural networks, in a real situation the network will be subject to constantly changing influences and may never see the same training vector twice. In such circumstances, the network will often not be trained; she will continuously change her weight, not achieving satisfactory results.

It is advisable to use combined approaches, one of which is reviewed in this article and includes the classical control theory, fuzzy control methods using fuzzy cluster analysis and a neural network. Based on the listed tools, the hybrid model allowed to solve a number of problems, namely:

- to increase the control efficiency and regulatory quality. The increase is achieved due to the fact that on the basis of the algorithm developed by the authors in [2, 3] for automatic formation of the fuzzy controller rule base and the intra-system interaction method of the hybrid system elements, the data obtained as a result of the classical controller are used to test the effectiveness of the hybrid network in order to identify the fact of its retraining, and the data obtained as a result of the fuzzy controller form a training sample for the construction of a hybrid network;
- to optimize the fuzzy controller rule base, namely to reduce the number of rules and the number of membership functions required to describe linguistic variables in its development;
- to increase the performance of the hybrid model by reducing the required number of computational operations in terms of issuing control actions;
- to reduce labor costs for the development of a fuzzy controller.

Acknowledgments. This work was supported by Grant of the Russian Foundation for Basic Research (№ 18-38-00711) at the Southern Federal University, State task of subordinate educational organizations for the implementation of the project on the theme «Development, research and producing of an automated control system for the training of microwave devices». Project PP0708-11/2017-09 (Task № 8.3795.2017/PP), Grant of the Russian Foundation for Basic Research (№ 18-07-000-50).

References

1. Demidova, G.L., Lukichev, D.V.: Controllers based on fuzzy logic in control systems for technical objects, 81 p. University of ITMO, Saint-Petersburg (2017). (in Russian)
2. Vasil'ev, V.I., Il'jasov, B.G.: Intelligent control systems. Theory and practice, Moscow, 392 p. (2009). (in Russian)

3. Gostev, V.I.: Designing fuzzy controllers for automatic control systems, 416 p. BHV-Peterburg, Saint-Petersburg (2011) (in Russian)
4. Demidova, G.L., Kuzin, A.Yu., Lukichev, D.V.: Application features of fuzzy controllers on example of DC motor speed control. Sci. Tech. J. Inf. Technol. Mech. Opt. **16**(5), 872–878 (2016). (in Russian)
5. Leonenkov, A.V.: Fuzzy modeling with MATLAB and FuzzyTECH, 736 p. BHV-Petersburg, Saint-Petersburg (2005). (in Russian)
6. Shtovba, S.D.: Design of fuzzy systems by means of MATLAB, 288 p. Hot line-Telecom (2007). (in Russian)
7. Kolesnikov, A.V.: Hybrid Intelligent Systems: Theory and Technology of Development, 600 p. Publishing House SPbSTU, Saint-Petersburg (2001). (in Russian)
8. Demenkov, N.P.: Fuzzy control in technical systems: a training manual, 200 p. Publishing House of MSTU of N.E. Bauman (2005). (in Russian)
9. Manenti, F., et al.: Fuzzy adaptive con-trol system of a non-stationary plant with closed-loop passive identifier. Resour.-Efficient Technol. **1**, 10–18 (2015)
10. Kudinov, Y.I., Kolesnikov, V.A., Pashchenko, F., Pashchenko, A., Papic, L.: Optimization of fuzzy PID controller's parameters. In: XIIth International Symposium «Intelligent Systems», INTELS 2016, Moscow, Russia, 5–7 October 2016 (2017). Procedia Comput. Sci. **103**, 618–622
11. Kharola, A., Patil, P., Raiwani, S., Rajput, D.: A comparison study for control and stabilisation of inverted pendulum on inclined surface (IPIS) using PID and fuzzy controllers. Perspect. Sci. **8**, 187–190 (2016)
12. Karli, A., Omurlu, V.E., Buyuksahin, U., Artar, R., Ortak, E.: Self tuning fuzzy PD application on TI TMS320F 28335 for an experimental stationary quadrotor
13. Beirami, H., Shabestari, A.Z., Zerafat, M.M.: Optimal PID plus fuzzy controller design for a PEM fuel cell air feed system using the self-adaptive differential evolution algorithm. Int. J. Hydrogen Energy **40**(30), 9422–9434 (2015)
14. Savran, A.: A multivariable predictive fuzzy PID control system. Appl. Soft Comput. **13**, 2658–2667 (2013)
15. Liem, D.T., Truong, D.Q., Ahn, K.K.: A torque estimator using online tun-ing grey fuzzy PID for applications to torque-sensorless control of DC motors. Mechatronics **26**, 45–63 (2015)
16. Savran, A., Kahraman, G.: A fuzzy model based adaptive PID controller design for nonlinear and uncertain processes. ISA Trans. **53**, 280–288 (2014)
17. Jahedi, G., Ardehali, M.M.: Genetic algorithm-based fuzzy-PID control methodologies for enhancement of energy efficiency of a dynamic energy system. Energy Convers. Manag. **52**, 725–732 (2011)
18. de la Hermosa Gonzalez-Carrato, R.R.: Wind farm monitoring using Mahalanobis distance and fuzzy clustering. Renew. Energy **123**, 526–540 (2018)
19. Jang, J.S.R.: ANFIS: adaptive network based fuzzy inference system. IEEE Trans. Syst. Man Cybern. **23**(3), 665–684 (1993)
20. Chaghari, A., Feizi-Derakhshi, M.-R., Balafar, M.-A.: Fuzzy clustering based on Forest optimization algorithm. J. King Saud Univ. – Comput. Inf. Sci. **30**, 25–32 (2018)
21. Ren, Q., Bigras, P.: Discrete-time parallel robot motion control using adaptive neuro-fuzzy inference system based on improved subtractive clustering. In: 2016 IEEE International Conference on Fuzzy Systems, FUZZ-IEEE 2016; Vancouver; Canada; 24 July 2016–29 July 2016 (2016). https://doi.org/10.1109/fuzz-ieee.2016.7737797
22. Polkovnikova, N.A., Kureichik, V.M.: Neural network technologies, fuzzy clustering and genetic algorithms in the VLSI expert system. In: Proceedings of the Southern Federal University (2014). (in Russian). Eng. Sci. **7**(156), 7–15

23. Salgado, P., Igrejas, G.: Probabilistic clustering algorithms for fuzzy rules decomposition. In: 2004 IEEE International Conference on Systems, Man and Cybernetics (IEEE Cat. № 04CH37583), pp. 115–120 (2004)

24. dos Santos Coelho, L., Pessoa, M.W., Mariani, V.C., Reynoso-Meza, G.: Fuzzy inference system approach using clustering and differential evolution optimization applied to identification of a twin rotor system. IFAC PapersOnLine 50(1), 13102–13107 (2017)

25. Ignatyev, V.V., Kureychik, V.M., Spiridonov, O.B., Ignatyeva, A.S.: The method of hybrid control based on the adaptive system of neuro-fuzzy inference. Bulletin of SFedU. Technical science, № 9(194), 2302 p., pp. 124–1320. ITA SFedU publishing house, Taganrog (2017). ISSN 1999-9429. (in Russian)

26. Ignatyev, V.V., Kovalev, A.V., Spiridonov, O.B., Ignatyeva, A.S., Bozhich, V.I., Boldyreff, A.S.: Model of adaptive system of neuro-fuzzy inference based on PI- and PI-fuzzy-controllers. In: Proceedings of the SPIE 10799, Emerging Imaging and Sensing Technologies for Security and Defence III; and Unmanned Sensors, Systems, and Countermeasures, SPIE Security + Defence, 2018, Berlin, Germany, vol. 10799 107990Y-1, 4 October 2018. https://doi.org/10.1117/12.2513302

27. Ignatyev, V.V., Spiridonov, O.B.: Hybrid algorithm for formation the fuzzy controller rule base. In: Bulletin of SFedU. Technical science. Thematic issue "Radio-electronic and infocommunication technologies, systems and networks", № 11(172), pp. 177–186. ITA SFedU Publishing House, Taganrog (2015). (in Russian)

28. Ignatyev, V.V., Spiridonov, O.B., Soloviev, V.V., Beloglazov, D.A., Ignatyeva, A.S.: Hybrid control simulation of a technical object using the system of Sugeno type fuzzy inference. In: Proceedings of the Congress on Intelligent Systems and Information Technologies, IS&IT 2018, Scientific publication in 3 volumes, 418 p., pp. 29–35. Stupin A.S. publishing House, Taganrog (2018). ISBN 978-5-6041321-4-2, ISBN 978-5-6041321-6-6 (T. 2). (in Russian)

29. Ignatyev, V.V., Ignatyeva, A.S., Spiridonov, O.B., Shapovalov, I.O., Soloviev, V.V.: Optimization of fuzzy controller rule base on the basis of clustering methods. In: Proceedings of the Congress on Intelligent Systems and Information Technologies, IS&IT 2018, Scientific publication in 3 volumes, 418 p., pp. 35–44. Stupin A.S. Publishing House, Taganrog (2018). ISBN 978-5-6041321-4-2, ISBN 978-5-6041321-6-6 (T. 2). (in Russian)

30. Kruglov, V.V., Dli, M.I., Gplubov, R.Yu.: Fuzzy logic and artificial neural networks, 224 p. (2004). (in Russian)

Modeling of Environment for Technical Vision: Automatic Detection of Dynamic Objects in the Data Stream

Korney S. Tertychny(ID), Sergey A. Karpov(✉)(ID), Dmitry V. Krivolapov(ID),
and Alexander V. Khoperskov(ID)

Volgograd State University, Volgograd, Russia
tertychny@volsu.ru, seraphim.v2@gmail.com
http://www.volsu.ru

Abstract. The article describes the implemented package in the ROS framework, which creates a new data stream of the depth camera without a dynamic object. This product can be used in computer vision systems to cut objects that can move on the map in the data stream, thereby preventing the systems from focusing on unnecessary objects. As an example of use, the task of the SLAM method was implemented using data from the Microsoft Kinect 2.0 sensor and building a map for localizing the robot in RTAB-Map.

Keywords: Computer vision · SLAM · Find object · Robotics · RGB-D · Microsoft Kinect 2.0 · RTAB-Map

1 Introduction

Navigation systems development is one of the most important problem in robotic engineering. It becomes more serious with the deployment of autonomous systems in industry and autonomous transport development. There are a lot of various navigation methods Simultaneous Localization and Mapping (SLAM) approach is one of the most promising way of navigation [6,7,11]. SLAM is an approach for building of navigation systems, not a technology implementation. SLAM can be devoted to two main stage [20]. The first stage is an environment mapping using different sensors, such as cameras, GPS trackers, RFIDs, distance meters, and others. The second stage is localization using generated map and trajectory processing.

The first stage implementation strongly depends on environment. It's enough to use standard algorithms for 3D reconstruction if the environment is static [2]. In practice, in most cases, the environment is dynamic, which can cause mistakes during map processing or navigation. Trying to solve this problem we modify

The work has been supported by the Ministry of Science and Higher Education (government task no. 2.852.2017/4.6).

A. G. Kravets et al. (Eds.): CIT&DS 2019, CCIS 1084, pp. 153–165, 2019.
https://doi.org/10.1007/978-3-030-29750-3_12

one of well known SLAM solutions, which is used by Robot operation system (ROS). ROS is a framework for robotic engineering. It provides an opportunity for low-level devise interactions, some popular solutions and functions, it is open source, so it gained popularity among the robotics community [2].

We use topics, specific communication lines to interact with different ROS packages. It works using design pattern called "Publisher-Subscriber" [2]. There is a typical data transferring system, working with Microsoft Kinect 2.0 at the Fig. 1.

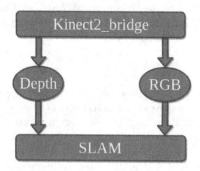

Fig. 1. Typical data transfer for Kinect v2 systems

The rectangles are the ROS packages and the ovals are the topics. We use typical SLAM algorithm as an example. First of all the kinect2_bridge package is started. We need it as a driver for Microsoft Kinect 2.0 and ROS connection. The kinect2_bridge package publishes the Microsoft Kinect 2.0 data as messages to the topics [1]. The topics of RGB camera and Depthmap are published in this example. So now different systems (SLAM systems too), can subscribe to this topics and bring data.

There are some problems of modern SLAM Solutions [4,6]. The dynamic environment problem is very important, because some changes of objects positions may cause critical navigation systems errors. Our research is aimed at the development of the algorithm for removing movable objects to increase the accuracy of 3D models of the real world processing using SLAM approach.

Usually when SLAM navigation system is beginning it's work it has no map or any other information about the objects and the environment where it is placed. So it uses only data which is provided by its own sensors while making the map. Also an assumption that the scene and all objects in it are static, and do not move both in the field of view of the system and behind it. We can highlight some important Simultaneous Localization and Mapping in real environment problems: dynamic environment problem [10,20], cumulative errors, (See discussion in works [1,10,13,14,17,19,20]). This paper is about the first problem.

2   The Dynamic Environment Problem

One of the main problems of SLAM algorithms is the dynamic environment. If the objects are moving in the field of view of the robot—this is called high-dynamic environment, and if outside of the field of view—the low-dynamic environment [10, 20]. The presence of such objects in the work area can worsen the correctness of the constructed map, and make the localization of the system impossible.

The problem of working with a dynamic environment can be divided into several parts: working with objects which move in the field of view, working with static in the field of view objects but having the ability to move, working with a fundamentally changing map.

Different frameworks like DP or RtabMap can partially cope with moving objects out of the system's field of view, if the number of key points on them does not exceed the critical level [5, 15]. So, when DP gets to the same place again, it adds to the existing particle (information about the position and change of the frame relative to the previous particle in the tree) child particles and continues to build the map. In this case, the particle carrying the wrong information will gradually lose its child particles and will be removed according to the basic principle of the algorithm. While RtabMap is gradually refining, the map will add changes on top and parts of the disappeared object will be visible on the map until all the voxels of the space occupied by such object are overwritten. But because the object is not completely removed from the map and the object continues to store the key points needed for positioning, this leads to an error build up, which can lead to a loss of orientation. This is shown on the Fig. 2.

Fig. 2. Example of "transparent" object (human), which is gone out of sigh.

This image shows a point cloud based on several images. Part of the footage was attended by a man who left the frame in the middle of the algorithm. In this case, it is not critical for the algorithm, because most of the key points remained unchanged. You can see that the map has been expanded in a place that had been previously closed by a person, and new key points have been added. However, if there were more features on the object which left the frame, the system would not be able to localize itself correctly on the map [10,14]. The same unpredictable behavior causes any too many changes in the map. So the same algorithm in the same real area can both begin to rebuild the area of the map in which global changes have occurred, and finally get lost, and display the appropriate error messages [20].

While working with the first part of the problem, the robot sensors receive incorrect space information from moving objects. In this case, if these objects do not carry a lot of control points, the algorithms cope with it so if it is noise. However, the objects will leave a mark on the map, as it is shown on the Fig. 3.

Fig. 3. Moving object traces in point cloud (Color figure online)

Features are marked as a yellow points. As we can see the man as a moving object, pulled a significant number of features. Figures 4 and 5 show the selection of special points when a person stops in the frame. Lighter space on RGBD image shows where the distance was correctly measured. Only points with correct distance are placed to the point cloud.

This example clearly shows that a person has about a third part of all special points. And in the transition to RGBD, the number of points becomes equal to half. This is due to the fact that for most of the features selected in the RGB image is not defined distance. A single object is usually isolated from the surrounding space and the distance to it can be correctly determined. That is,

Fig. 4. Example of features matching on RGBD image (RGB+DepthMap) with human

Fig. 5. Example of features matching on RGB image with human

when you try to work, when there may be several dynamic objects in the frame, it is almost guaranteed that the system will not be able to work correctly. The same problem occurs if the object is too close to the sensor, it may occupy most of the observed area.

It is also worth nothing that different colors and the size of the circles on the RGB image indicates the reliability of special points and the accuracy of determining their position respectively (the smaller radius the more accurate). So the location of features is undesirable on humans, animals, cars and other objects inclined to movement.

Previously, solutions to this problem have been proposed as [10]. In this paper, it was assumed orientation on the map of static objects, highlighting not the objects themselves, but the changes that occurred in the frame. That is, the change of RGB components of a pixel is determined as a moving object. But this method does not solve the problem of movement of objects outside the field of view of the system.

Authors of [20] offer a framework to solve the problem with low-dynamic environment (environment properties have changed between scans). This algorithm is engaged in the search for similar frames, and in accordance with the old frame was replaced by the current one. However, it did not take into account the objects moving in the frame and the disappearance of the object with a large number of key points did not allow to establish a correspondence between the frames. We have solved this problem in previous article using human as movable object in particular. Pixels which are inside the human image is being cut from the depthmap to prevent the system to localize features on it [18].

3   Proposed Method

It was decided to make cutting the object from the scene as a separate ROS package so that it could be run as a data bridge. The scheme is shown at the Fig. 6.

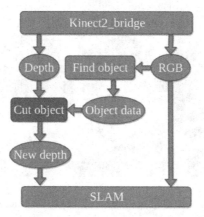

Fig. 6. Modified data transfer scheme for systems using the implemented method

This scheme differs from that shown in Fig. 1 in that the implemented cut_object module appears, which is highlighted in red in the scheme. It subscribes to the depth data topic to get data from the kinect_bridge package and to

Fig. 7. Object location scene (Color figure online)

the topic which publishes data about the found object. Finding the object takes place in a separate module, which can be implemented by yourself or choose from existing ones. In this work, for searching the objects the find_object_2d package is used. This package finds the object on the received data from the RGB camera and publishes the data to the topic/objects.

The cut_object package receives data about the object and from the depth camera, analyzes where the object is on the depth camera and sets these coordinates to 0.

To further understanding of the positions of objects in the scene, Fig. 7 shows a photograph of the scene.

At the Fig. 7 in the foreground on the tables is a Microsoft Kinect 2.0 sensor. In the field of view of the sensor is a green box, which in this work is a cut object, as it is not a static object and in the future may be moved. Therefore, localization systems should not focus on this object, otherwise the localization will be lost when the box is removed.

3.1   Hardware

The tests were conducted using the sensor Microsoft Kinect 2.0, which is a non-contact touch device originally created for the XBox game console. Due to the low cost and rich functionality in the SDK from Microsoft, Kinect is widely used in robotics [21]. The device consists of two cameras RGB and IR (infrared) and 3 IR projectors (the main characteristics are presented in the Table 1).

Table 1. Kinect specifications.

IR camera resolution	512424 pixels
Color camera resolution	1920 × 1080 pixels
Filed of view	70 × 60°
Framerate	30 fps
Operative measuring range	From 0.5 to 5 mc (11 bits)
Object pixel size (GSD)	between 1.4 mm (@ 0.5 m range) and 12 mm (@ 4.5 m range)

Kinect uses Time Of Flight principle, based on the formula $2d_{ij} = c\Delta t_{ij}$, where d_{ij} is the distance to ij-point, c is the light speed, Δt_{ij} is measured time of light flight interval for each pixel [12, 21]. So there are three different data streams [8]:

- infrared image;
- depthMap with the same resolution as IR camera, in each pixel containing information about the distance from the sensor to the point in real space;
- RGB image.

The Microsoft Kinect SDK allows us to obtain a point cloud stream obtained by converting a frame from a depth camera to a 3D, colored point cloud obtained by mapping a point cloud to a color frame [12].

3.2 Finding Object

As an example of the module for finding an object in this work, it was decided to use the package find_object_2d for ROS. This package uses algorithms of detectors and handles of special points, such as SIFT, SURF, FAST, BRIEF implemented in OpenCV [16]. Figure 8 shows the video stream from this package.

As an example of the cut object, a box of green color was selected. The image shows the already selected object with a purple frame, as well as the special points of this object. When an object is selected in the image, the find_object_2d package publishes information about the object as an array of real numbers in the topic/objects. The first 3 numbers indicate the identifier of the found object, its width and height, respectively. The next 9 numbers represent the homography matrix H:

$$\begin{pmatrix} x' \\ y' \\ z' \end{pmatrix} = \begin{bmatrix} h_{11} & h_{12} & h_{13} \\ h_{21} & h_{22} & h_{23} \\ h_{31} & h_{32} & 1 \end{bmatrix} \begin{pmatrix} x \\ y \\ z \end{pmatrix}. \tag{1}$$

The homography matrix for the transformation is represented as a product of the matrices of affine H_a and projective H_p transformation:

$$H = H_a H_p, \tag{2}$$

where

$$H_p = \begin{bmatrix} 1 & 0 & 0 \\ 0 & 1 & 0 \\ h_{31} & h_{32} & 1 \end{bmatrix}. \tag{3}$$

Fig. 8. Image from package find_object_2d (Color figure online)

The affine transformation matrix is defined as follows:

$$H_a = H_t H_r H_s,$$ (4)

where H_t—parallel transfer matrix, H_r—rotation margix, H_s—scaling matrix, which are given by the following formulas, respectively:

$$H_t = \begin{bmatrix} 1 & 0 & \Delta x \\ 0 & 1 & \Delta y \\ 0 & 0 & 1 \end{bmatrix}, \quad H_r = \begin{bmatrix} c & -s & 0 \\ s & c & 0 \\ 0 & 0 & 1 \end{bmatrix}, \quad H_s = \begin{bmatrix} 1 & 0 & 0 \\ 0 & 1 & 0 \\ h_{31} & h_{32} & 1 \end{bmatrix},$$ (5)

where $c = \cos \phi$, $s = \sin \phi$, ϕ is the rotation angle counted in the counterclockwise direction, s_u, s_v and Δx, Δy are scale factors and displacement along the horizontal and vertical axes, respectively [9].

Knowing the data of the width and height of the object, as well as the homography matrix, you can uniquely select an object on the video stream.

3.3   Received Data

Using the object data and depth camera you can define an object in the depth data stream and convert the z-coordinate to a non-significant value. For the depth camera, the non-significant value is 0. Figures 9 and 10 show the depth camera output in the rviz tool from various topics. The Fig. 9 uses a topic that comes directly from kinect2_bridge, without cutting out the object in the frame. The Fig. 10 uses a topic from the implemented package cut_object, which cuts an object from the depth camera.

Fig. 9. The original image of the camera depth, obtained from the package kinect2_bridge

Fig. 10. Image of a depth camera with a cut object, obtained using the cut_object package

As you can see, the object coordinates in the Fig. 10 correspond to black color. This means that this value is not considered in the processing algorithms from the depth camera.

It is more clearly seen how an object is cut from a stream on point clouds, which is represented in Figs. 11 and 12.

Fig. 11. Source point cloud received from the packet kinect2_bridge

Fig. 12. A cloud of points with a cut out object obtained using the package cut_object

In these Figures there is a slight shift in the display, so that you can see the separation of objects in space. As in the Figs. 9 and 10, here for the Fig. 11 from the topic kinect2_bridge is used, and for the Fig. 12 from the topic cut_object. The sought object is in the near plan and looks small from the point of view of the observer. As you can see, in the Fig. 12 it disappears and its background is not filled with anything.

3.4 Map Construction

As an application of the developed module, you can use various tools provided by the ROS framework. In this article, the use of the map for SLAM using the RTAB-Map package is used to demonstrate the performance of the system. Figure 13 shows the constructed point cloud.

Fig. 13. Built map using RTAB-Map package (Color figure online)

As you can see, in the constructed point cloud, the object being cut out is not displayed. At the same time, the space that replaces the object during the initial display is filled with the scan time from different points of view of the camera.

4   Discussion and Conclusions

In this article, we offer a new method for automatic removing dynamic objects from the data flow. The finished program is a ROS package that creates a new topic with depth camera data. This topic publishes data that contains an empty area in place of a dynamic object. Thus, the computer vision system does not focus on this object and passes it during data flow processing.

After analyzing work of the created system, it was noticed a problem with the imposition of RGB camera on the results of the depth camera. As you can see on the map shown in Fig. 13, there are errors next to the cut object on the resulting point cloud, which are shown in green. This is because the object is cut only on the depth camera when the RGB camera receives the unchanged data. Therefore, the errors of the overlapping cameras of the depth and RGB may be some pixels for other color coordinates. But the depth of the objects on the point cloud conveys the real distance of the points, and the problem remains only in the representation of the color of the points. To solve this problem, you can paint the object on the RGB camera, but it is not clear what color to choose for painting. In this case, it will spend additional computing resources of the system.

In addition, during testing the developed module a small delay in data transmission was noticed. This is due to the computational cost for processing and converting depth camera data.

References

1. Bakkay, M.C., Arafa, M., Zagrouba, E.: Dense 3D SLAM in dynamic scenes using kinect. In: Paredes, R., Cardoso, J.S., Pardo, X.M. (eds.) IbPRIA 2015. LNCS, vol. 9117, pp. 121–129. Springer, Cham (2015). https://doi.org/10.1007/978-3-319-19390-8_14
2. Cao, F., Zhuang, Y., Zhang, H., Wang, W.: Robust place recognition and loop closing in laser-based SLAM for UGVs in urban environments. IEEE Sens. J. **18**(10), 4242–4252 (2018). https://doi.org/10.1109/JSEN.2018.2815956
3. Civera, J., Bueno, D., Davison, A., Montiel, J.: Camera self-calibration for sequential Bayesian structure from motion. In: IEEE International Conference on Robotics and Automation 2009, pp. 403–408. IEEE (2009)
4. Cummins, M., Newman, P.: Appearance-only SLAM at large scale with FAB-MAP 2.0. Int. J. Rob. Res. **30**, 1100–1123 (2010). https://doi.org/10.1177/0278364910385483
5. DP Developers. https://github.com/jordant0/DP-SLAM. Accessed 27 Mar 2018
6. Durrant-Whyte, H., Bailey, T.: Simultaneous localization and mapping: part I. IEEE Robot. Autom. Mag. **13**(2), 99–110 (2006). https://doi.org/10.1109/MRA.2006.1638022
7. Durrant-Whyte, H., Bailey, T.: Simultaneous localization and mapping: part II. IEEE Robot. Autom. Mag. **13**(3), 108–117 (2006). https://doi.org/10.1109/MRA.2006.1678144
8. Endres, F., Hess, J., Sturm, J., Cremers, D., Burgard, W.: 3-D mapping with an RGB-D camera. IEEE Trans. Robot. **30**(1), 177–187 (2014). https://doi.org/10.1109/TRO.2013.2279412
9. Find_object_2d Developers. http://wiki.ros.org/find_object_2d. Accessed 24 Mar 2019
10. Hahnel, D., Triebel, R., Burgard, W., Thrun, S.: Map building with mobile robots in dynamic environments. In: Robotics Automation 2003, pp. 1557–1563. IEEE (2003). https://doi.org/10.1109/ROBOT.2003.1241816
11. Kim, P., Chen, J., Cho, Y.K.: SLAM-driven robotic mapping and registration of 3D point clouds. Autom. Constr. **89**, 38–48 (2018). https://doi.org/10.1016/j.autcon.2018.01.009
12. Lachat, E., Macher, H., Landes, T., Grussenmeyer, P.: Assessment and calibration of a RGB-D camera (Kinect v2 Sensor) towards a potential use for close-range 3D modeling. Remote Sens. **7**(10), 13070–13097 (2015). https://doi.org/10.3390/rs71013070

13. Majdi, A., Bakkay, M., Zagrouba, E.: 3D modeling of indoor environments using Kinect sensor. In: IEEE 2nd International Conference on Image Information Processing 2013, pp. 67–72. IEEE (2013). https://doi.org/10.1109/ICIIP.2013.6707557
14. Nistér, D., Naroditsky, O., Bergen, J.: Visual odometry. In: IEEE Computer Society Conference on Computer Vision and Pattern Recognition 2004, vol. 1, pp. 652–659. IEEE (2004). https://doi.org/10.1109/CVPR.2004.1315094
15. RTAB_map Developers. http://introlab.github.io/rtabmap/. Accessed 26 Mar 2019
16. Rublee, E., Rabaud, V., Konolige, K., Bradski, G.: ORB: an efficient alternative to SIFT or SURF. In: IEEE International Conference on Computer Vision 2011, pp. 2564–2571. IEEE (2011). https://doi.org/10.1109/ICCV.2011.6126544
17. Shao, B., Yan, Z.: 3D indoor environment modeling and detection of moving object and scene understanding. In: Pan, Z., Cheok, A.D., Müller, W. (eds.) Transactions on Edutainment XIV. LNCS, vol. 10790, pp. 40–55. Springer, Heidelberg (2018). https://doi.org/10.1007/978-3-662-56689-3_4
18. Tertychny, K., Krivolapov, D., Karpov, S., Khoperskov, A.: SLAM method: reconstruction and modeling of environment with moving objects using an RGBD camera. In: CEUR Workshop Proceedings, vol. 2254, pp. 274–281 (2018)
19. Walcott-Bryant, A., Kaess, M., Johannsson, H., Leonard, J.J.: Dynamic pose graph SLAM: long-term mapping in low dynamic environments. In: IEEE International Conference on Intelligent Robots and Systems, vol. 6385561, pp. 1871–1878. IEEE (2012). https://doi.org/10.1109/IROS.2012.6385561
20. Wang, Y., Huang, S., Xiong, R., Wu, J.: A framework for multisession RGBD SLAM in low dynamic workspace environment. CAAI Trans. Intell. Technol. 1, 90–103 (2016). https://doi.org/10.1016/j.trit.2016.03.009
21. Zhang, Z.: Microsoft kinect sensor and its effect. IEEE Multimed. 19(2), 4–10 (2012). https://doi.org/10.1109/MMUL.2012.24

The Introduction of Multi-level Parallelism Solvers in Multibody Dynamics

Andrey Andreev$^{(\boxtimes)}$, Vitaly Egunov, Evgenia Movchan,
Nikita Cherednikov, Egor Kharkov, and Natalia Kohtashvili

Volgograd State Technical University, Volgograd, Russia
andan2005@yandex.ru, vegunov@mail.ru,
verborum123@mail.ru, meastream@gmail.com,
kharkov.e.s@gmail.com, nat.koxta@yandex.ru

Abstract. The paper deals with the problem of the scaling speed-up of time-consuming computations on the example of the dynamic stress-strain state (DSS) modelling for the multibody systems. Speed-up is achieved through the introduction of multilevel parallelism at the levels of decomposition of the model and the distribution of calculations on the computational nodes of the cluster, at the level of multithreaded computations within the part of the model at one node and at the level of vectorization of calculations and their transfer to GPU/ FPGA accelerators within a single computational flow. Vectorization is considered for both conventional multicore CPUs and the MIC architecture. Accelerators are used using OpenCL technology for heterogeneous systems. The possibility of computations speed-up up to 50 times for the considered problem due to the introduction of multilevel parallelism is shown.

Keywords: Multilevel hierarchical parallelism ·
Multibody (MBS) dynamics stress-stain solver · Cluster computing · MPI ·
Vectorization · OpenCL

1 Introduction

At present, many areas of science and industry use special software systems that perform mathematical modeling of various physical processes and phenomena. Such programs include solvers, similar to the one considered in this work as part of the system of formation of solutions of nonlinear dynamics equations (FRUND), which performs the calculation of the stress-strain state of a multibody model. The multibody approach presents the studied objects as a system of discrete bodies, connected with elastic links, as shown in Fig. 1. Discrete body dynamics is described with a system of differential equations (DE) $M\ddot{y} + Ky = q$, where M – is a mass matrix, K – inertia forces vector, q – vector of forces, influencing bodies.

Due to a large amount of data processed and the high computational complexity of processing algorithms (matrix computations, coordinate transformations from local to global coordinate systems, calculation of forces for right-side of the differential equations on each iteration of integration of DE), such calculations can take a long time and require speed-up. For example, the calculation of stresses in the suspension arms of

A. G. Kravets et al. (Eds.): CIT&DS 2019, CCIS 1084, pp. 166–180, 2019.
https://doi.org/10.1007/978-3-030-29750-3_13

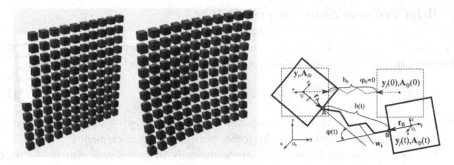

Fig. 1. Multibody system representation.

the car in the dynamics on a conventional computer in single-threaded mode can take more than 24 h.

To perform such calculations and computationally complex modeling, multicomputer systems (clusters) are used [1, 2]. Such systems are often heterogeneous (or hybrid), for example, a computer system includes processors of different architectures: multi-core CPUs, GPU accelerators, accelerators or autonomous processors with a large number of cores (MIC), reconfigurable accelerators based on FPGAs and others. When performing computations on a multiprocessor system or computing cluster, it makes sense to reduce time costs, using all available computing resources of the system at the same time. Though, very often we face the situation when software cannot use heterogeneous or even homogeneous computers of a cluster, obtaining their maximum or even close to maximum performance.

In general, it is necessary to implement all needed algorithms suitable to use all available computing nodes regarding their types, to obtain a system that can work on a heterogeneous computing cluster. This will allow using of clusters with different computing nodes for calculations, achieving their maximum utilization.

The approach to parallelization considered in this paper, namely, multilevel implementation of parallelism, is quite universal [2], though it is applied to the area of DSS analysis. Approbation of various methods of computing acceleration, their combination, and evaluation of their efficiency for the DSS solver is interesting both in itself and as an example, which in the future can allow extending the developed approach to other problems having a similar computational structure.

The paper has the following structure. In Sect. 2 brief problem state for the dynamic stress-strain solver is presented. In Sect. 3 general algorithm of solving the DE, the system is described and possibilities of parallel implementation of its stages are estimated. The main approaches to parallelize the DSS are observed in Sect. 4. In Sect. 5 the multi-level approach to solver implementation is described at each level. Experimental results for multi-level parallel solver testing on the homogeneous cluster are presented in Sect. 6. Some test results, as well as approaches to the use of the heterogeneous cluster, are presented in Sect. 7.

2 Brief Problem State for DSS Solver

Dynamic stress-strain solver, based on discrete elements method [3], or multi-body approach, uses a basic system of differential equations in the form [4]:

$$M\ddot{y} = q(\dot{y}, y, t) - Ma(t) + s(\dot{y}, y) \tag{1}$$

where a – acceleration vector, M – matrix of masses, $s(\dot{y}, y)$ – stabilization forces, $q(\dot{y}, y, t)$ – the function describing the forces between discrete elements.

The model presented is described mathematically in two ways: with the help of absolute coordinates in one common (global) coordinate system, as well as with the help of relative coordinates describing the position of the body relative to the reference, focusing on the center of mass and the central axis of inertia.

Since all the data for the calculation is stored in the global coordinate system, we must introduce the transformation of the body position from local coordinates to global. For this purpose, rotation matrices are used – square matrices, which make it possible to determine the position of the body described in one coordinate system, in another coordinate system. Rotations are based on the form of Euler angles (ψ, θ, and φ), aircraft (ship) angles, or angles of Tait-Bryan, which allow taking into account small displacements.

At each step of the calculations, the Euler angles for each discrete element are recalculated relative to the previous ones to obtain the actual rotation matrices for the transfer of bodies from one coordinate system to another. These matrices have the following form

$$A = X_\varphi Y_\theta Z_\psi$$
$$= \begin{bmatrix} \cos\theta\cos\psi & -\cos\theta\sin\psi & \sin\theta \\ \cos\varphi\sin\psi + \sin\varphi\sin\theta\cos\psi & \cos\varphi\cos\psi - \sin\varphi\sin\theta\sin\psi & -\sin\varphi\cos\theta \\ \sin\varphi\sin\psi - \sin\varphi\cos\theta\sin\psi & \sin\varphi\cos\psi + \cos\varphi\sin\theta\sin\psi & \cos\varphi\cos\theta \end{bmatrix} \tag{2}$$

The use of the described scheme makes it possible to apply explicit methods of numerical integration, in which, unlike implicit ones, it is not required to calculate the roots of the system of linear algebraic equations (SLAE) at each iteration, which also simplifies the problem of calculations. In the considered DSS solver the Eq. (1) is solved by the Runge-Kutta method of the 4th order of accuracy. According to the method, the approximate value at the points of the model is calculated by the iterative formula:

$$y_{n+1} = y_n + \frac{h}{6}(k_1 + 2k_2 + 2k_3 + k_4), \tag{3}$$

$$k_1 = f(x_n, y_n), \tag{4}$$

$$k_2 = f\left(x_n + \frac{h}{2}, y_n + \frac{h}{2}k_1\right), \tag{5}$$

$$k_3 = f\left(x_n + \frac{h}{2}, y_n + \frac{h}{2}k_2\right), \tag{6}$$

$$k_4 = f(x_n + h, y_n + hk_3), \tag{7}$$

where x_n and y_n are parameters of the function f in general differential equation system $y' = f(x_n, y_n)$, h is the size of the grid step for x.

3   The General Algorithm for Calculating the Dynamic Stress-Strain State

To make a general algorithm for calculating the dynamic stress-strain state, it is necessary to proceed from the mathematical model of calculations and identify the main stages. The algorithm shown in Fig. 2 is typical for all multibody dynamics systems, at least for FRUND system [4, 5].

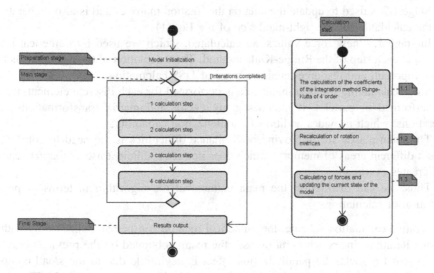

Fig. 2. The general algorithm for calculating the dynamic stress-strain state.

Let us consider each stage from the point of view of the possibilities of its parallelization.

The zero stage (preparation, or model initialization) includes the preparation of computational models and includes the definition of constants, setting calculation parameters, generation of computational domains and other operations. It can be concluded that this stage is rather consistent.

The main calculation is performed at the first stage in a cycle with a given number of iterations, and each iteration corresponds to a certain point in time. Since at this stage, a strict sequence of calculations is specified, and each subsequent iteration uses the result calculated on the previous one, then due to the presence of information dependencies, complete parallelization of the main cycle is impossible.

However, it is possible to parallelize stages 1.1, 1.2 and 1.3 separately, which are performed for each step of numerical integration.

The calculation of the coefficients of the Runge-Kutta method is performed for each discrete element in the model. Since according to the problem statement all elements are identical and initialized with constant values, the calculation of the i-th coefficients can be carried out independently. But the computational complexity of this stage is small and its contribution to the total time of the calculation is insignificant.

Stage 1.2 includes a set of trigonometric operations that implement the formula for calculating the rotation matrix to translate a discrete element in the coordinate system of the reference body and auxiliary calculations. Many actions can be performed separately for each item: the initialization, the updating of matrices of rotation, the steps for the numerical integration of the kinematic Euler and others. If we take into account the short calculation time, we can assume that the efficiency of parallelized computations can be significantly reduced due to frequent memory access and multiple data transfers, as they cause large overhead.

Stage 1.2 is used to update the data on the rotation matrices and is also preparatory for the calculation of the right-hand side of the Eq. (1).

In stage 1.3, new force values are calculated, which are used by numerical integration at each step of the Runge-Kutta method. The calculation of the right parts is the most important and resource-intensive stage of DSS calculation.

Since calculating the right-hand side is performed for each discrete element, it can be performed in parallel. It includes many vector and matrix transformations and operations, which provides additional parallelization capability.

The main reason for improving performance difficulties is the need to constantly access different areas of memory, which does not allow efficient use of the data cache and creates overhead.

Thus, we can distinguish the main features of the algorithm in terms of parallelization of calculations:

1. Iterative calculation scheme: the numerical method can be parallelized only within one iteration since each iteration uses the results obtained on the previous one.
2. On small models, the parallelization effect is negligible due to the small computational complexity of one iteration. A more significant effect can be achieved on larger models.
3. The presence of cycles without information dependencies, as well as the presence of vector and matrix operations, makes it possible to speed up the calculation due to parallelization at a lower level.

4   Approaches to Parallelize the Calculation of DSS

Existing actual methods of parallelization can be conventionally combined into several groups. The first group includes approaches using "fine-grained" parallelism.

Since the solution of the problem under consideration involves numerical integration with dependent iterations, it is difficult to effectively parallelize methods for high-dimensional problems while maintaining the accuracy of calculations due to the fact that most of the computations are described by sequential code and there are few potentially parallelized computations among them. However, the model has significant internal parallelism, which makes it possible to perform many operations on discrete elements in parallel. Multithreaded computing is best suited for this task. Thus, in [1] different parallel algorithms of sparse matrix processing allow achieving acceleration up to 60% in the MST dynamics solver on 6 cores. Similarly, the calculation is accelerated by 20–30% using OpenMP when using "fine-grained" parallelism.

The use of various accelerators and coprocessors is an alternative to the use of multi-core CPU, the number of threads of which is limited. For example, it is possible to use coprocessors with MIC architecture with a large number of cores, on which it is also possible to organize parallel calculations using OpenMP in native mode.

As another alternative, we can consider the use of massively parallel computing devices – graphics coprocessors or even FPGA, which allow achieving a higher degree of parallelism due to the fact that computing units process one discrete element at a time. To work with such devices, you can use OpenCL technology. This approach to the parallelization of engineering calculations is quite popular among foreign and domestic authors and, for example, is considered in [6]. The use of accelerators in the process of calculating the DSS has such a drawback as the complicity of full transfer of the solver implementation to the device, due to the lack of computing and/or memory resources, which makes it necessary to implement a joint calculation of the CPU with the GPU/FPGA, which in turn makes it difficult to actively exchange data between the host and devices.

In addition to multithreaded computing, there are technologies that provide support for "fine-grained" parallelism within a single compute core. Among them is vectorization, which is well suited for parallelizing the code of linear algebra operations. This area of research is relatively new, but there are works showing the possibilities of using vectorization in engineering calculations, including the MIC architecture [7].

There is also a group of approaches that implement the concept of "coarse-grained" parallelism. As a rule, these approaches use some kind of distributed computing using MPI or other ones [8]. Within the framework of the approach, calculations of individual models are paralleled, for example, when using a multivariate calculation, when the same calculations are performed on different input data.

To effectively implement this approach within the framework of one DSS calculation task, it is necessary to decompose the computational domain into several subdomains, which will be processed in parallel by different computing devices.

5 Development of the General Multi-level Scheme of Parallelization of the Dynamic DSS Solver

In order to implement the task of significantly accelerating the dynamic DSS solver via parallelism, in our opinion, it is necessary to use a multi-level scalable approach to parallel calculations, that is necessary to parallelize calculations at several interrelated levels at the same time:

- At the level of decomposition of computational domains for systems with distributed memory;
- At the level of decomposition of computational domains for systems with multi-threaded calculations on shared memory;
- At the level of data parallelism for SIMD processing on multi-core processors with support for vector instructions, for SIMT computing using multi-core MIC and GPU accelerators, as well as FPGA.

Figures 3 and 4 show a diagram of the proposed approach at the upper first and two lower levels.

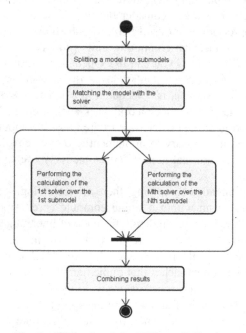

Fig. 3. Higher-level for DSS parallelization.

At the top level is a spatial decomposition, which involves the separation of the original geometry of the model into several related parts and their parallel processing separately for each part, followed by the combining of results in the root process [9].

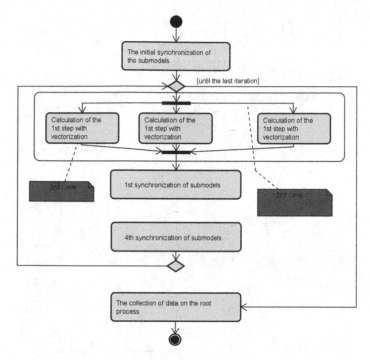

Fig. 4. Lower levels for DSS parallelization.

The computational domain is divided into N fragments, each of which can be processed by one of the M involved computing devices. It is also possible to perform parallel calculations with both shared and distributed memory within the same node.

It is not advisable to divide the computational domain into too many subdomains since in this case there will be a need for data exchange between the executive nodes, and as the number of subdomains increases, the amount of data transferred will also increase. In addition, in order to achieve the greatest efficiency, it is necessary to split the model into submodels of such a size that internal parallelism at lower levels gives an increase in productivity, that is, the calculation of one submodel should not occur too quickly.

Decomposition and synchronization is a complicated process, involving many stages and details, starting from implementing special DEC-files (DECompisition files), containing decomposition information about submodels, as shown in Fig. 5(a–d), to supporting SYNC-data files (SYNCronization data files) for synchronization procedures, shown in Fig. 6, and choosing appropriate MPI – functions for data transfers (in our case –MPI_Sendrecv with user's data types, shown in Fig. 7).

The next level is multithreading – it calculates the individual stages of numerical integration, there is an additional decomposition of the computational domain – in each flow, a part of the discrete elements of the submodel is processed. This step can be performed on a single compute node (GPU or CPU) or jointly on the CPU and GPU or FPGA.

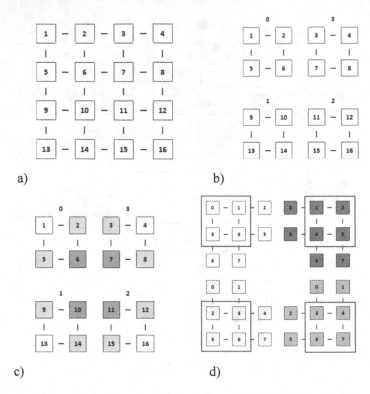

Fig. 5. Blocks of data on the decomposition of the model: (a) initial model, (b) submodels, (c) boundary areas, (d) addressing elements of the submodels in the original model.

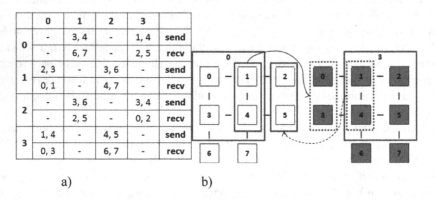

Fig. 6. Data synchronization (a) buffer table, (b) graphical interpretation of data transfer.

At the lowest level, the vectorization of individual calculation operations is used [10]. This step is performed on a single compute node with support for vector registers of a certain type and does not require additional processing power. Also, depending on the hardware platform, it is possible to use different types of vector registers.

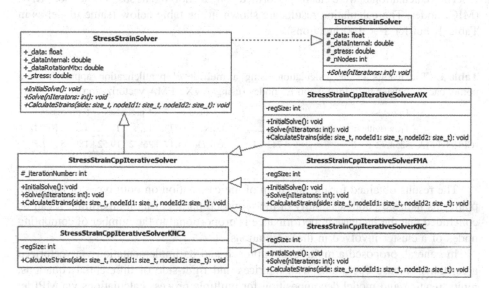

Send type

Count = 2
Lenghts = (8, 8)
Displacements = (8, 32)

X_0	Y_0	Z_0	0	ϕ_0	ω_0	ε_0	0
X_1	Y_1	Z_1	0	ϕ_1	ω_1	ε_1	0
X_2	Y_2	Z_2	0	ϕ_2	ω_2	ε_2	0
X_3	Y_3	Z_3	0	ϕ_3	ω_3	ε_3	0
X_4	Y_4	Z_4	0	ϕ_4	ω_4	ε_4	0
X_5	Y_5	Z_5	0	ϕ_5	ω_5	ε_5	0
X_6	Y_6	Z_6	0	ϕ_6	ω_6	ε_6	0
X_7	Y_7	Z_7	0	ϕ_7	ω_7	ε_7	0

Receive type

Count = 2
Lenghts = (8, 8)
Displacements = (16, 40)

X_0	Y_0	Z_0	0	ϕ_0	ω_0	ε_0	0
X_1	Y_1	Z_1	0	ϕ_1	ω_1	ε_1	0
X_2	Y_2	Z_2	0	ϕ_2	ω_2	ε_2	0
X_3	Y_3	Z_3	0	ϕ_3	ω_3	ε_3	0
X_4	Y_4	Z_4	0	ϕ_4	ω_4	ε_4	0
X_5	Y_5	Z_5	0	ϕ_5	ω_5	ε_5	0
X_6	Y_6	Z_6	0	ϕ_6	ω_6	ε_6	0
X_7	Y_7	Z_7	0	ϕ_7	ω_7	ε_7	0

Fig. 7. Map of user's MPI data type: (a) to send data, (b) to receive data.

Figure 8 shows some classes, implementing vectorization for various processor architectures in DSS solver.

Fig. 8. Some classes implementing vectorization for different SIMD instructions in DSS solver.

However, if the number of vector processors or coprocessors is limited, it is recommended to reduce the number of executive threads to avoid performance degradation by attempting to access the same register at the same time.

Thus, we can highlight the following advantages that are achieved in the proposed multiscale approach:

- The flexibility to change the scheme depending on the configuration of the hardware platform.
- Overcoming the limitations of technologies implementing the concept of coarse-grained parallelism by internal parallelization of the calculation within a single subtask.

- The opportunity to further speed-up the computation by the use of vector instructions for the calculation parallelized on other levels.

This approach is quite universal and makes it possible to use the maximum available computing power to solve large-size problems of modeling the dynamics of body systems, as well as other types of engineering calculations.

6 Experimental Results for Multi-level Parallelization on Homogeneous Cluster

The table below shows the results achieved by decomposition on a homogeneous cluster of Xeon E5 nodes with the maximum available number of OpenMP threads and vectorization using a set of AVX2 with FMA instructions (model with 300 elements per side and 100×100 iterations is considered).

The calculations were also performed on a homogeneous cluster of KNL (MIC) nodes. The calculation results are shown in the table below (same model as in Table 1, but for 1×100 iterations).

Table 1. The results of the calculation using a multi-level parallelization approach on a homogeneous cluster with Intel Xeon E5 nodes (using AVX2 FMA vectorization).

	1 process		2 processes		4 processes		6 processes	
	T_1, s (without vectorization)	$T_{fma+omp}$, s	T_2, s	T_1/T_2,	T_4, s	T_1/T_4	T_6, s	T_1/T_6
CPU + FMA	5254,72	743,14	370.71	14.17	269.2	19.52	189.65	27.7

The results obtained for the speed-up of the calculation on both types of hardware platforms indicate good scalability of the proposed parallelization algorithm. It can be concluded that the increase in performance is proportional to the number of computing nodes of a cluster involved in the calculations.

In general, proposed a multi-level approach and its implementation via vectorized algorithms of base operations with matrices and right-side of differential equations, multi-treading and model decomposition for multiple process calculations via MPI let us obtain scalable speed-up from 27–30 times for Xeon E5 CPUs nodes up to 50 times for KNL many-core (MIC) processor nodes. Though, the performance achieved is far from peak, especially for MIC computers, which is probably due to low memory optimizations. The low performance of MIC nodes and cluster complicates the joint use of MIC and general CPU nodes in a heterogeneous cluster of Xeon and MIC (Xeon Phi) nodes. Still, such a combination could be improved by appropriate load balancing.

Table 2. The results of the calculation using a multi-level parallelization approach on a homogeneous cluster with KNL nodes.

	1 process		2 processes		4 processes		6 processes	
	T_1, s (without vectorization)	$T_{avx512+omp}$, s	T_2, s	T_1/T_2,	T_4, s	T_1/T_4	T_6, s	T_1/T_6
CPU + AVX512	1003	40,83	28,18	35,6	22,6	44,4	19,7	50,9

7 The Alternatives for the Parallelization of the DSS Calculation Using Heterogeneous Cluster

The considered approach to the acceleration of the dynamic stress-strain state solver is quite effective, but its efficiency can be improved for a heterogeneous environment (with GPUs and CPUs) by using OpenCL technology. Thus, it was used to develop a parallel code for GPU [5]. Originally only the calculation of the right-hand sides of the equations was made in OpenCL kernel since this part of the calculations takes the largest part of the calculation time.

This approach had been leading to a significant additional time spent on data transfer from the CPU to the GPU, though the calculation on the GPU was faster than on the CPU.

There are several factors that limit the performance of this approach:

- Intensive data exchange between CPU and GPU;
- Non-optimized calculation algorithm;
- The need to speed-up the numerical integration and recalculation of rotation matrices.

The alternative approach is to perform all the needed calculations for the part of the initial multi-body system inside OpenCL kernel on GPU withing an MPI process. In this case, we can perform some processes on GPUs and other processes on CPUs or other accelerators.

To get a rough idea of the solver performance when running on different hardware configurations for models of different dimensions, the calculations were performed on two processes: one for the host – CPU, one for GPU. Also, the program was run separately for the CPU on two processes and one GPU solely.

Let us combine the results into a table, where the intersection of the rows will indicate the time for which the calculation is performed, in seconds (Table 3).

Table 3. The results of running the solver with OpenCL on CPU and GPU, s.

Computational resource	t_{50}, c	t_{100}, c	t_{200}, c
Xeon E5-2650v3 + NVIDIA P100	47,46	121,38	555,93
Xeon E5-2650v3 + NVIDIA GTX 1080Ti	106,54	323,28	805,39
Xeon E5-2650v3	159,05	417,85	1043,78
NVIDIA P100	4,6	8,41	32,7

Let us also build a graph to visualize the results (Fig. 9).

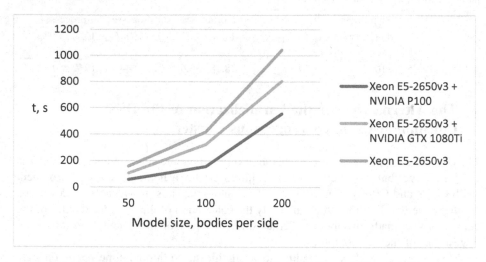

Fig. 9. The results of running the solver with OpenCL on CPU and GPU, s.

Plate models with the side size of 50, 100, and 200 discrete elements in the model and 10,000 iterations are calculated faster on two processes on CPU and GPU bundles than on two processes on the CPU, but calculations on GPU only are much faster than on bundle of GPU and CPU. From the above results it can be seen that server accelerator NVIDIA TESLA itself makes it possible to speed up the calculations of DSS more than 30 times compared to using server CPU E5 (which is surprisingly much more compared to results in [5], though they were obtained on less powerful GPU, this should still be verified). Bundle of GPU and CPU processes is faster than CPU (up to 2–3 times), though it makes no sense yet compared to calculations held on GPU only. The problem is probably in the interaction overhead of GPU and CPU processes via MPI. We still can expect that optimizing this interaction and competent load balancing will allow us to achieve extra speed-up when using decomposition into heterogeneous nodes compared to the results given in Tables 1 and 2 for a homogeneous cluster. But this needs to be studied more thoroughly, confirmed experimentally and has gone beyond the scope of this work.

8 Conclusions and Future Research

The paper shows an approach to solving the problem of extracting the maximum parallelism from both homogeneous and heterogeneous computing clusters equipped with multi-core processors and accelerators when modeling the dynamic stress-strain state via a multibody discrete-element representation of models as an illustrative example. Maximum concurrency and, as a consequence, a high real performance is achieved through the introduction of multilevel parallelism at the levels of submodel-node (process), part of the submodel – flow, and vectorization of calculations within the flow. The speed-up of calculations up to 50 times on 6 homogeneous multicore nodes of the computing cluster is achieved, the possibility to accelerate calculations up to 3 times on each heterogeneous node equipped with a powerful GPU is shown (though performing calculations on sole GPU turned to be more efficient, as MPI interaction of nodes with GPU needs to be improved). It is stated that it is possible to increase the whole speed-up when using heterogeneous nodes with and without GPU due to appropriate model decomposition and load balancing (though the real benefit of such heterogeneous computations should be studied more thoroughly and confirmed experimentally).

As mentioned above, some approaches should be studied in more detail, first of all – the load balancing issues for the heterogeneous cluster, especially with CPU and GPU nodes. As for MIC nodes, their performance for the considered task could be improved if we take into consideration memory optimizations. A reduction of overheads for MPI communication is very important to increase the performance of the cluster, equipped with GPU accelerators. The considered approach for DSS could be also applied to basic multibody dynamics solver.

Acknowledgments. Work is performed with the financial support of the Russian Foundation for Basic Research - project#16-47-340385r_a, partly project #18-47-340010 r_a and the financial support of the Administration of Volgograd region.

References

1. Daniel, S.A., Bitsuamlak, G.: Asynchronous parallelization of a CFD solver. J. Comput. Eng. (2015). https://doi.org/10.1155/2015/295393
2. Gorobets, A., Soukov, S., Bogdanov, P.: Multilevel parallelization for simulating compressible turbulent flows on most kinds of hybrid supercomputers. Comput. Fluids **173**, 171–177 (2018)
3. Blundell, M., Harty, D.: The Multibody Systems Approach to Vehicle Dynamics. Elsevier (2004)
4. Getmanskiy, V.V., Gorobtsov, A.S., Izmaylov, T.D.: Parallelization of stress-strain solver coupled with multi-body solver using domain decomposition. In: Izvestiya VSTU, Volgograd, vol. 8, no. 111, pp. 5–10 (2013)
5. Getmanskiy, V., Andreev, A.E., Alekseev, S., Gorobtsov, A.S., Egunov, V.A., Kharkov, E. S.: Optimization and parallelization of CAE software stress-strain solver for heterogeneous computing hardware. In: Kravets, A., Shcherbakov, M., Kultsova, M., Groumpos, P. (eds.) CIT&DS 2017. CCIS, vol. 754, pp. 562–574. Springer, Cham (2017). https://doi.org/10. 1007/978-3-319-65551-2_41
6. Clauberg, J.: An adaptive internal parallelization method for multibody simulations. In: Proceedings of the 12th Pan-American Congress of Applied Mechanics -PACAM XII, pp. 1–6 (2012)
7. HICFD – Highly Efficient Implementation of CFD Codes for HPC Many-Core Architectures. http://elib.dlr.de/75146/1/HICFD_result_survey.pdf

8. Belviranli, M.E., Bhuyan, L.N., Gupta, R.: A dynamic self-scheduling scheme for heterogeneous multiprocessor architectures. Trans. Arch. Code Optim. **9**(4), 57 (2013). https://doi.org/10.1145/2400682.2400716
9. Bauchau, O.A.: Parallel computation approaches for flexible multibody dynamics simulations. J. Frankl. Inst. **347**(1), 53–68 (2010)
10. Getmanskiy, V.V., Movchan, E.O., Andreev, A.E.: Dynamical stress-strain simulation speedup using SIMD instructions. Izvestiya SfEdu. Eng. Sci. **184**(11), 27–39 (2016)

Traffic Light Detection and Recognition Using Image Processing and Convolution Neural Networks

George Symeonidis, Peter P. Groumpos$^{(\boxtimes)}$, and Evangelos Dermatas

Electrical and Computer Engineering Department,
University of Patras, 26500 Rion, Greece
groumpos@ece.upatras.gr, dermatas@upatras.gr

Abstract. Automatic traffic light detection and mapping is an open research problem. In this paper, a method for detecting the position and recognizing the state of the traffic lights in video sequences is presented and evaluated using LISA Traffic Light Dataset which contains annotated traffic light video data. The first stage is the detection, which is accomplished through image processing technics such as image cropping, Gaussian low-pass filtering, color transformation, segmentation, morphological dilation, Canny edge detection, and Circle Hough transform to estimate the position and radius of possible traffic lights. The second stage is the recognition, whose purpose is to identify the color of the traffic light and is accomplished through deep learning, using a Convolutional Neural Network. Day and night images were used in both training and evaluation, giving excellent location rates in all conditions.

Keywords: Traffic light detection · Classification · Machine learning · Convolutional neural networks

1 Introduction

Traffic and Vehicle Safety is a very important research topic among the automotive industry nowadays The traffic lights vary in color, shape, geolocation, activation pattern, and installation which complicate their automated detection. In addition, the image of the traffic lights may be noisy, overexposed, underexposed, or occluded. It also depends on geographic and weather conditions. Traffic light detection and mapping is an important task for autonomous vehicles [1–5, 14, 16, 17]. An autonomous vehicle should be able to detect the traffic lights and take proper actions based on the signal of traffic lights. Despite the fact that autonomous driving technology is emerging, traffic light detection is still an open challenge. In modern cars, many sensors are installed onboard such as lidar, radar, cameras, and sonars as parts of driver-assistance systems (DAS). Several challenging image processing and recognition problems are met in DAS; the detection of the traffic lights is among the most difficult tasks [2, 5, 6, 8, 10–12]. Around the world, manufacturers produce different traffic lights in shape, size, and layout. Even worse, traffic lights are installed at different positions and typically are operating continuously, introducing a variety of adverse

© Springer Nature Switzerland AG 2019
A. G. Kravets et al. (Eds.): CIT&DS 2019, CCIS 1084, pp. 181–190, 2019.
https://doi.org/10.1007/978-3-030-29750-3_14

environmental conditions i.e. partial occlusion, detection at night, in low vision conditions, etc. [7]. Although traffic lights have been designed to be highly visible, the outdoor nature of the detection problem greatly increases the illumination and the background variations [3, 7, 9]. The automatic traffic light detector, proposed in this paper, follows a similar approach: among the processing units available in the literature, the most efficient are implemented in our detector. In the final classification stage, recent advances in the configuration and the training methods for the convolutional neural networks (CNNs) were used to face the great variability of the traffic lights features in case of adverse lighting conditions. A detailed presentation of the proposed traffic light detection method is given in the next section. The experimental results, carried out in the well-known LISA Traffic Light Dataset [1], are very promising and presented in the last section. The outline of the paper is as follow: in Sect. 2 a short overview of the problem is provided. In Sect. 3 the basics of Automatic detection of traffic lights are briefly discussed. The proposed algorithm and Experimental results are given in Sect. 4 while some problems related to the recognition process is given in Sect. 5. Finally, conclusions are given in Sect. 6.

2 A Short Literature Survey of Automatic Traffic Lights

The automatic generation of street networks is attracting the attention of research and industry communities in areas such as routable map generation. A number of studies with different scientific methods have been reported. The prior knowledge of traffic lights is essential for some traffic light detection algorithms. Since the traffic lights are static objects, they are usually geolocalized and stored in the geospatial database. If intrinsic and extrinsic parameters of the camera are known and the pose of the platform is observed, the position of the traffic lights is projected into the image space and applied to initialize the traffic light detection algorithms [18]. The traffic light most of the times has a circular shape. If the image plane and traffic light plane are parallel, the circular shape of the traffic light in the image remains a circle. In order to exploit this characteristic, authors of [19] and [20] use the Hough transform based circle detection. In order to overcome the computational complexity of the Hough transform, some researchers suggest the fast radial symmetry transform to detect circulars shape of the traffic lights [21]. The assumption that the traffic light fixture plane and image plane are parallel, is not always correct and the traffic light can have ellipse shape.

Another interesting method is that of the Bayesian approach [15]. This Bayesian proposed approach has been evaluated on two benchmark datasets and has been shown to outperform earlier studies. There are a number of approaches apply learning algorithms to detect the traffic lights. Convolutional Neural Network (CNN) has been applied to generate the saliency map and detect the traffic lights [22, 23]. In addition, it has been shown the Aggregated Channel Features (ACF) approach has superior performance over the heuristic models [17]. There are many related interested research studies and the reader is encouraged to perform his own literature overview. For this study, we have proceeded as follow.

Typical automatic traffic lights detectors consist of a sequence of processes.

1. Multiple regions of interest (ROI) are detected through color transformation such as LAB, HSI, HSV, normalized RGB, to enhance the traffic lights detectability and to reduce the image sensitivity to environmental light changes. Narrow thresholds reduce significantly the number of detected ROIs, increasing the probability of missing traffic lights. Wide thresholds increase the false acceptance rate.
2. Blobs detection are usually more accurate ROI detection methods, based on the traffic lights circular shape.
3. The number of ROIs can be drastically reduced recognizing morphological differences between traffic lights and similar structures, such as car tail lights or small red color objects [9].
4. Further ROIs reduction based on geometrical and directional properties of the traffic lights can be achieved decreasing the false positive candidates [4].
5. Spatial features based on wavelets, Harr, Hough transform, oriented gradient information, local binary patterns, and statistical features, derived from the ROI histogram, is the image information which is processed by various pattern recognition methods. These classifiers are based on the nearest neighbor rule, stochastic models, support vector machines and neural networks to detect the traffic lights in the pool of the remaining ROIs.

3   Automatic Detection of Traffic Lights

The proposed system process the sequence of images captured by a video camera installed in the front part of a vehicle:

1. *Image Cropping.* Taking into account the position of the installed camera, the traffic lights appear in the upper part of the video images. Thus, the lower part of the image is removed, eliminating also the presence of the front vehicle rear lights from the scene, a greater source of the false positive ROIs. In our video database, 60% of the lower part of the image is excluded from further processing, because the traffic lights are met in the upper part of the video images. An example is shown in Fig. 1.

Fig. 1. An image from a video camera installed in a vehicle and the 40% of its upper part

2. *Noise elimination* at high frequencies. In low-cost video cameras and in low illu-minated scenes, electronic noise distorts strongly the image quality. Therefore, a Gaussian low pass-filter eliminates the noise at high frequencies from the camera RGB raw data.
3. *Color Transformation.* A color transformation method enhances the red and the green information by estimating the corresponding image in the HSV, a color space mimicking the way human vision perceives color attributes.
4. *Color segmentation.* In the HSV color space, Hue, Saturation, and Value channel offer more robust features, i.e. smaller variability is met than the original RGB color channels even in case of slight color and brightness changes in the red, green and yellow traffic lights. The color segmentation process is applied in the pixel level, detecting the red-yellow and green pixels when the HSV values are within certain limits as shown in Table 1, on daytime recordings. During the nighttime, different limits are estimated.

Table 1. Minimum and maximum values in the HSV 8-bit color space for Color segmentation at daytime

Color	H channel	S channel	V channel
Red-yellow	[175, 180]	[169, 255]	[138, 255]
Red-yellow	[1, 25]	[165, 255]	[130, 255]
Red-yellow	[251, 255]	[160, 255]	[120, 255]
Green	[56, 68]	[150, 255]	[150, 255]
Green	[131, 140]	[140, 255]	[190, 255]

5. *Morphological processing.* The color segmentation in the level of pixels produces very noisy binary images. A morphological dilation operator fills empty spaces, enhancing the ROIs as small circular-like areas.
6. *Canny edge detector.* The popular Canny edge detection algorithm is used to derive the edges in the ROIs, while suppressing further the noise. This transformation creates small circular lines. An example is given in the image of Fig. 2.

Fig. 2. Canny edge detection in the upper part of the image frame270_dayclip2 (LISA Traffic Light Dataset). The image contains four traffic lights.

7. *Detection of circular lines.* The Circle Hough Transform (CHT) estimate triplets, position, and radius, in the ROIs that have strong circular patterns with high probability, completing the bulb detection process.

8. *Detection of traffic lights.* The main advantage of the CNNs is their ability to simultaneously perform image processing, feature extraction, and pattern recognition. The previous 1 to 7 processing units are used to detect a small number of ROIs where the traffic lights can be located. The CNN recognize the traffic lights in the ROIs, detecting multiple circular structures by processing the RGB values of the original image.

4   The Proposed Algorithm and Experimental Results

The proposed algorithm was evaluated with a data set acquired under varying illumination conditions, known as "LISA Traffic Light Dataset". The data set is freely available at Kaggle's website [1], containing annotated traffic light video data of 44 min. Day and night sequences were used in both training and evaluation session. A total number of approximately 1500 traffic light images of 224 × 224 pixels consist of the training data set of the convolutional neural network. These RGB images which are used for training, differ to each other in the angle and the brightness level. A typical example of the training set is depicted in Fig. 3. In a time-consuming training process, the convolutional neural network weights are adapted to minimize the error-classification error using the error backpropagation algorithm.

Fig. 3. Example of a training set

One worth mentioning detail is that all the images in the test set were resized to 224 × 224 × 3 in order all images to have the same size as in the training set. In the evaluation process, new video sequences were used and each traffic light is assumed to be detected if the CNN recognized at least one time in the sequence of images. All this procedure can be seen in Figs. 4 and 5.

Fig. 4. This image is used as input of the CNN to recognize the condition of the traffic light. Subsequently, the image is resized. The result is the green light (*frame900_dayclip2*) (Color figure online)

Fig. 5. This image is used as input of the CNN to recognize the condition of the traffic light during the night. Subsequently, the image is resized. The result is the red light (*frame432_nightSequence1*) (Color figure online)

For the experimental evaluation, according to literature, the accuracy results of such a system are expressed with precision and recall. The precision is computed by the equation:

$$Precision = \frac{true\ positives}{true\ positivies + false\ positives} \tag{1}$$

whereas the recall is computed by the equation:

$$Recall = \frac{true\ positives}{true\ positivies + false\ negatives} \tag{2}$$

where true positives represent the number of the traffic lights that were correctly recognized, false positives the number of the recognized traffic lights that are not traffic lights in reality and false negatives the number of real traffic lights that are not recognized.

False negatives are the most dominant parameter that is necessary to be equal to zero since the false detection of red light can prove to be very hazardous in real-life application.

In the daytime videos, the proposed system detects successfully 53 out of 56 traffic lights, and at nighttime, the error-free detection rate is measured, i.e. 18 out of 18 traffic lights are detected (Figs. 6 and 7). The recall rate for all traffic lights was 95.9%. The false positive events at the daytime videos were 15, and at the nighttime videos, 14 image areas are faultily recognized as traffic lights. The overall precision rate was 71.7%.

Fig. 6. Two examples of the CNN classification results at daytime or close to daytime images: *frame10_nightclip1* and *frame300_dayClip11*.

Fig. 7. Two examples of the CNN classification results at nighttime images *frame300_ nightClip1* and *frame900_ night* Sequence.

5 Problems in Recognition

The problem of recognition was one of the most difficult aspects of this research work. The recognition of green traffic signs, both in the morning and afternoon hours and during the night, was highly satisfying, as the green, blue mainly (due to the technology LED) was distinct in the background. In contrast, red and yellow LEDs were often orange in color, resulting in recognition as either yellow or red. As the part of the bulb was cut off, it might include points that would bury the MRI. In addition, the SNA itself was likely to make a wrong categorization because it was not optimal. Bringing an example of all the above mentioned in this subsection, in a continuous stream of frames (especially in the evening), where proper detection and recognition of PF was made, it can instantly change its recognition status. A good number of simulation studies have shown mistakes in recognition between 2 frames per day and night. This is due to the lighting as well as to possible misconduct in the MRI classifications. On the day these changes were fewer and when at 16 and more frames per second there is a change between 15 correct readings, in real time it may be subtle. On the night, on the other hand, these changes were more, and therefore more work on education is needed with more and more informative images for optimal operation because misidentification is very risky.

6 Conclusions

More than 50 million new cars are manufactured each year. Advanced onboard sensors, such as sonar, radar, and cameras, are becoming common-place as part of commercial driver-assistance systems. With power steering, power brakes, standardized feedback from the CAN bus, cars are basically robots – they only need a brain. A key component of these augmented vehicles is the perception system, which allows the vehicle to perceive and interpret its surroundings. Cars must deal with traffic lights. The two main tasks are detecting the traffic lights and understanding their control semantics. Our approach to solving these two tasks has been to automatically construct maps of the traffic light positions and orientations, and then to manually add control semantically.

This paper has addressed this very important and challenging scientific topic of Traffic and Vehicle Safety for the automotive industry nowadays. A new method for detecting the position and recognizing the state of the traffic lights in video sequences was presented and evaluated using LISA Traffic Light Dataset which contains annotated traffic light video data. Some valuable conclusions can be drawn from this study of the detection and recognition of PH which has been briefly described here. Initially, the system is shown to be relatively satisfactory to some extent in the detection and identification of PH during the day. In adverse conditions, such as the night but especially in bright, central locations, it is not reliable and further research is needed. When the camera was close to PH, the results were fully encouraging both day and night. The problem was, in the transition to the next PH, where the camera saw a lot of information in front of it and the effect was affected.

The results have been presented here are very encouraging and more studies are needed. Some future research directions are: to use a secondary camera with a wider field of view but a shorter detection range, that allows the car to detect nearby lights when it is very close to the intersection. Another research topic would be to experiment with the robust detection of flashing lights by annotating the map with lights that always flash or lights that flash at certain times of day, but during construction or an emergency, lights may unpredictably be switched to flash. One more research topic: there are cases where the lights, frequently arrows, are so dim, it appears that the only way to detect the state is to watch for relative changes in the intensity of the light elements.

References

1. LISA Traffic Light Dataset—Kaggle. https://www.kaggle.com/mbornoe/lisa-traffic-light-dataset
2. de Charette, R., Nashashibi, F.: Real time visual traffic lights recognition based on spot light detection and adaptive traffic lights templates. In: Proceedings of the IEEE Intelligent Vehicles Symposium, pp. 358–363 (2009)
3. Siogkas, G., Skodras, E., Dermatas, E.: Traffic lights detection in adverse conditions using color, symmetry and spatiotemporal information. In: Proceedings of the VISAPP, pp. 620–627 (2012)
4. Sooksatra, S., Kondo, T.: Red traffic light detection using fast radial symmetry transform. In: Proceedings of the IEEE 11th International Conference on ECTI-CON, pp. 1–6 (2014)
5. Moizumi, H., Sugaya, Y., Omachi, M., Omachi, S.: Traffic light detection considering color saturation using in-vehicle stereo camera. J. Inf. Process. 24(2), 349–357 (2016)
6. Tae-Hyun, H., In-Hak, J., Seong-Ik, C.: Detection of Traffic Lights for Vision-Based Car Navigation System. In: Chang, L.W., Lie, W.N. (eds.) PSIVT 2006. LNCS, vol. 4319, pp. 682–691. Springer, Heidelberg (2006). https://doi.org/10.1007/11949534_68
7. Yu, C., Huang, C., Lang, Y.: Traffic light detection during day and night conditions by a camera. In: 10th International Conference on Signal Processing (ICSP), pp. 821–824 (2010)
8. Chen, Q., Shi, Z., Zou, Z.: Robust and real-time traffic light recognition based on hierarchical vision architecture. In: 7th International Congress on Image and Signal Processing (CISP), pp. 114–119 (2014)

9. Chiang, C.-C., Ho, M.-C., Liao, H.-S., Pratama, A., Syu, W.-C.: Detecting and recognizing traffic lights by genetic approximate ellipse detection and spatial texture layouts. Int. J. Innov. Comput. Inf. Control **7**(12), 6919–6934 (2011)

10. Gong, J., et al.: The recognition and tracking of traffic lights based on color segmentation and CAMSHIFT for intelligent vehicles. In: Proceedings of the IEEE Intelligent Vehicles Symposium, pp. 431–435 (2010)

11. Philipsen, M.P., Jensen, M.B., Møgelmose, A., Moeslund, T.B., Trivedi, M.M.: Traffic light detection: a learning algorithm and evaluations on challenging dataset. In: Proceedings of the 18th IEEE Intelligent Transportation Systems Conference, pp. 2341–2345 (2015)

12. Saini, S., Nikhil, S., Reddy Konda, K., Bharadwaj, H.S., Ganeshan, N.: An efficient vision-based traffic light detection and state recognition for autonomous vehicles. In: IEEE Intelligent Vehicles Symposium (2017)

13. Fairfield, N., Urmson, C.: Traffic light mapping and detection. In: Proceedings of the IEEE ICRA, pp. 5421–5426 (2011)

14. Symeonidis, G.: Study and development of a visual assistant system for drivers in adverse conditions: traffic light detection and recognition. Diploma-Master thesis (in reek), Department of Electrical and Computer Engineering, University of Patras (2018)

15. Hosseinyalamdary, S., Yilmaz, A.: A Bayesian approach to traffic light detection and mapping. SPRS J. Photogramm. Remote Sens. **125**, 184–192 (2017)

16. Diaz, M., Cerri, P., Pirlo, G., Ferrer, M.A., Impedovo, D.: A survey on traffic light detection. In: Murino, V., Puppo, E., Sona, D., Cristani, M., Sansone, C. (eds.) ICIAP 2015. LNCS, vol. 9281, pp. 201–208. Springer, Cham (2015). https://doi.org/10.1007/978-3-319-23222-5_25

17. Jensen, M.B., Philipsen, M.P., Møgelmose, A., Moeslund, T.B., Trivedi, M.M.: Vision for looking at traffic lights: issues, survey, and perspectives. IEEE Trans. Intell. Transp. Syst. **PP** (99), 1–16 (2016)

18. Barnes, D., Maddern, W., Posner, I.: Exploiting 3D semantic scene priors for online traffic light interpretation. In: Intelligent Vehicles Symposium (IV), Seoul, 28 June–1 July. IEEE, pp. 573–578 (2015)

19. Caraffi, C., Cardarelli, E., Medici, P., Porta, P.P., Ghisio, G., Monchiero, G.: An algorithm for italian de-restriction signs detection. In: Intelligent Vehicles Symposium, Eindhoven, Netherlands, 4–6 June, pp. 834–840. IEEE (2008)

20. Huang, Y.S., Lee, Y.S., Detection and recognition of speed limit signs. In: International Computer Symposium (ICS), Tainan, Taiwan, 16–18 December, pp. 107–112 (2010)

21. Sooksatra, S., Kondo, T.: Red traffic light detection using fast radial symmetry transform. In: 11th International Conference on Electrical Engineering/Electronics, Computer, Telecommunications and Information Technology (ECTI-CON), Nakhon Ratchasima, Thailand, 14–17 May, pp. 1–6 (2014)

22. John, V., Yoneda, K., Qi, B., Liu, Z., Mita, S.: Traffic light recognition in varying illumination using deep learning and saliency map. In: 17th International Conference on Intelligent Transportation Systems (ITSC), Qingdao, China, 8–11 October, pp. 2286–2291. IEEE (2014)

23. John, V., Yoneda, K., Liu, Z., Mita, S.: Saliency map generation by the convolutional neural network for real-time traffic light detection using template matching. IEEE Trans. Comput. Image **1**(3), 159–173 (2015)

Methods of Increasing Service Minibots Functional Capabilities

Alexander Gorobtsov, Andrey Skorikov(✉), Pavel Tarasov(ID),
Alexey Markov, and Andrey Andreev

Volgograd State Technical University, Volgograd, Russia
vm@vstu.ru, scorpion_energy@mail.ru, tarasradio@mail.ru,
alexmarkov95@gmail.com, andan2005@yandex.ru

Abstract. The main purpose of the article is to give an idea about the ways of increasing the functionality and energy efficiency of walking mobile robots by adding a locomotor element (one-wheel mover) and work in a group. The results of energy efficiency studies for various types of gait and surface reliefs are considered. Mathematical models and methods of robot control with the proposed solutions based on the inverse problem method are presented. Methods of collective movement control using a various number of robots on flat surface and surface with macroscopic obstacles are analyzed.

Keywords: Robotics · Walking robots · Control · Insect robots · Collective control

1 Introduction

Walking robots belong to the intensively developing class of robots. Insect robots, which possess greater stability maintenance capabilities than anthropomorphic or zoomorphic robots due to a larger number of legs, are actively developing direction. Due to the current state of 3D printing development, the manufacture of such small-sized robots becomes available for widespread use [1].

Walking robots have a high capability to overcome obstacles, but moving on a flat surface is inefficient due to high energy costs, especially for insect robots. Improving the energy efficiency and speed of the movement of walking robots is a current research area.

Studying the information presented in some of the ongoing research on the energy efficiency of walking mobile robots and hexapods, one can identify the main problem associated with the need for a robot to be in the support phase most of the time, which requires constant operation of servo drives to maintain its position and, consequently, constant consumption of large amount of energy [2, 3].

In the research [2] a series of experiments were carried out with various types of the gait of a hexapod robot on four types of surface (office floor, artificial grass, inclined surface and wooden blocks of different height). The first and second surface types are distinguished by a different amount of adhesion and, consequently, by different

© Springer Nature Switzerland AG 2019
A. G. Kravets et al. (Eds.): CIT&DS 2019, CCIS 1084, pp. 191–202, 2019.
https://doi.org/10.1007/978-3-030-29750-3_15

slippage, the latter two types of surface are also distinguished by an increased load on the robot servos and, consequently, by increased total power consumption.

In the considered research, a gait type switching rule depending on the type of surface was proposed, for example, a tripod type gait was called the most suitable for smooth surfaces, and the pentagon type was the most preferable gait for complex surfaces such as wooden blocks.

As a result, it is understood that the power consumption of the robot is directly dependent on the type of terrain and the speed of movement. Using various strategies for choosing the type of gait allows you to increase the energy efficiency of the robot, but in order to significantly reduce energy consumption, it is generally not enough to apply specialized gait selection strategies.

One of these areas, not related to the choice of gait type is the combination of wheel and stepping movements. Examples of studies of this type of motor mechanism in robots are presented in [4–6].

The study [4] presents a model of a hexapod with wheels located at the ends of its legs (Fig. 1). Moreover, such a robot cannot be considered a hexapod in the classical sense, since its degrees of freedom are limited to one plane, in contrast to the classical hexapod, whose legs have at least three degrees of freedom lying at least in two planes.

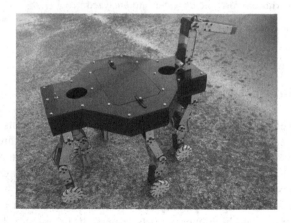

Fig. 1. Model of the hexapod robot Cassino.

Another study [5] presents the kinematic scheme of a classic hexapod with wheels placed on its legs that are in the air in the usual position, and if necessary the robot can change its position so that they have contact with the surface (Fig. 2). This version of the kinematic scheme retains the advantages of the classic hexapod robot and complements them with the advantages of the wheeled robot.

Fig. 2. Hexapod robot model with wheels on its legs.

Another example of the second option is the robot described in [6]. Its limbs are also equipped with wheels, but the robot can move on any of its sides, both the upper and the lower (Fig. 3).

Fig. 3. Model of the robot Creadapt.

Another variant of a wheel mover hexapod is a robot, which can become a wheel in a certain position of its limbs, for example, Festo's robot spider [7] has this capability (Fig. 4).

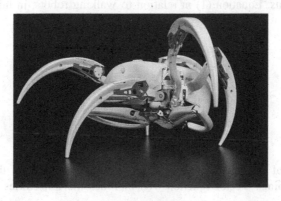

Fig. 4. Festo's hexapod robot.

Although the considered variants of robots can reduce power consumption more significantly than with a simple gait adaptation, nevertheless, none of the presented examples can be called completely solving the problem of energy efficiency, since even in this case the energy of servo drives is required to keep the robot in a support state. A further increase in energy efficiency can be achieved, for example, by eliminating the use of legs from the support of wheel movers, so that the wheels themselves (or one wheel) become support.

A significant increase in the robot's functionality can also be achieved through the organization of the collective work of a group of robots. This paper discusses the use of an additional one-wheel propulsion unit and the control of the coordinated movement of a group of robots.

2 The Synthesis of Controlled Movement of the Walking Robot with a Wheel Mover

The inverse problem method is used for control synthesis, which is implemented in the program for modeling multi-body systems dynamics FRUND (http://frund.vstu.ru) [8, 9].

The general equation of the robot dynamics as a spatial mechanical system can be given as

$$\begin{cases} M\ddot{x} = f(x, \dot{x}, t) + u(t) \\ \quad Q_1(x) = 0 \end{cases} \tag{1}$$

Here x is the vector of coordinates of the whole system of dimension $n \times 6$, where n is the number of body in the system, M is the inertia matrix, $f(x, \dot{x}, t)$ is the vector of positional, dissipative and external forces, $Q_1(x)$ is the vector of constraint equations of dimension k_1, describing kinematic pairs, $u(t)$ is the matrix of forces (moments) in drives, reduced to the bodies coordinates.

Equation (1) are usually called direct problem equations. In terms of analytical mechanics, Eq. (1) describe a system with holonomic constraints. To find u(t) controls in the inverse problem method, the action of the control forces is replaced by additional constraint equations. Equation (1) in relation to walking robots, in this case, take the form:

$$\begin{cases} M\ddot{x} = f(x, \dot{x}, t) & (2a) \\ Q_1(x) = 0 & (2b) \\ Q_2(x) = w(t) & (2c) \\ Q3(x) = 0 & (2d) \\ Q_4(x, \ddot{x}, z(t)) = 0 & (2e) \\ Q_5(x, \ddot{x}, z(t)) = k & (2f) \end{cases}$$

The Eq. (2c) of dimension k_2 sets the movement kinematics of the robot and its body reference points. Vector function $w(t)$ includes the trajectories of the legs and body points. The Eq. (2d) of dimension k_3 sets auxiliary links to eliminate redundant degrees of freedom of the whole robot. Equation (2e) of dimension $k_4 \leq 3$ determines the conditions of stability. The scalar inequality (2f) sets the condition for the absence of slip at the reference points of the robot, which depends on the coefficient of friction on the supporting surface k.

The last two equations are equations for the stability conditions, and at the present, there are no developed methods for the exact numerical solution of (2), that take into account relations of this type containing the second derivatives of the system coordinates. In existing works, as a rule, only Eq. (2e) is taken into account.

The main disadvantages of robots with walking movers are the low speed of movement and low energy efficiency, especially for walking movers of insect type. These parameters can be significantly improved by introducing additional wheel mover.

A mathematical model of a multi-legged robot was created in the FRUND software

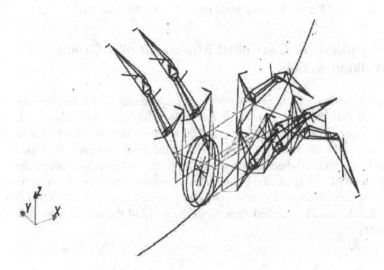

Fig. 5. The model of the robot with a wheeled mover.

package according to the proposed kinematic scheme, shown in Fig. 5.

This structure allows you to combine the advantages of walking robots, such as high profile passability – overcoming steps and other single obstacles, with the advantages of wheeled robots – high movement speed and high energy efficiency.

Possessing additional wheeled mover, the insect robot can quickly overcome large open spaces with a relatively flat surface, while maintaining the energy needed to overcome difficult terrain.

If there are obstacles or a complex surface profile, the robot performs a step movement, like a typical insect robot. If it is needed to move on a flat surface, the robot raises its front legs, leaning on the wheel and moves along a predetermined path, steering with its back legs (Fig. 6). Figure 6 shows the simulation results of a controlled movement of a single-wheeled mover system with steering with back legs.

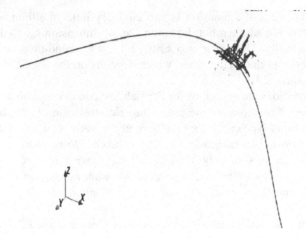

Fig. 6. Steering while moving along the trajectory.

3 The Synthesis of Controlled Movement of a Group of Walking Robots

A group of an arbitrary number of robots carrying a single load is considered – Fig. 7. It is assumed that the load is a non-deformable solid body with known inertial and geometrical parameters. The load is carried by K robots that are attached with the load at the given points. Robots have an arbitrary number of movers. The type of robots drives can be different – wheeled or walking. Note that when performing a coordinated work, the group of robots has the properties of a parallel mechanism, since at any time it includes several kinematic chains connecting robots and a load with a base. It is assumed that the load is attached directly to the body of the robots without additional moving parts.

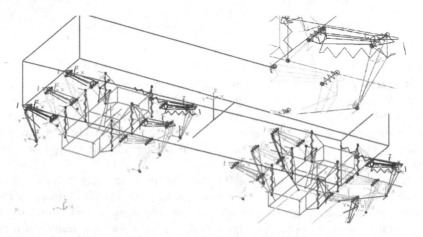

Fig. 7. The design scheme of the mathematical model for the two robots, carrying a cargo.

The calculated synthesis of the programmed movement of a group of robots using Eq. (2) is performed on the example of two six-legged robots – Fig. 7. The kinematic scheme of the robot includes 19 bodies – a body and six three-link legs. In the general case, the load was attached to each robot using three kinematic pairs of 3d, 2d and 1st classes - Fig. 3. Various options for the synthesis of programmed motion are possible. The ratio of the maximum and minimum coefficients of the matrix L was used as an indicator of the constraint matrices degeneracy. The movement of each robot was set in an absolute coordinate system, by specifying the link equations corresponding to each degree of freedom of the robot body. In particular, the kinematic law of the movement of the robot in the lateral direction was specified in the form of acceleration areas with constant acceleration and movement with constant speed. For the remaining five degrees of freedom, zero displacements were specified [8]. Let us consider the options for the synthesis of the software movement of a group of robots.

3.1 Setting the Movement of the Group Through the Movement of Each Robot

In this case, the attachment of the load to the robots was carried out using a spherical joint on the first robot and two joints on the second one (vertical point support and a joint with connections in the lateral and vertical direction).

In this case, both robots moved in the same direction with the same speed – Fig. 8. The system condition number L = 104. At different speeds of robot movement – Fig. 8, the taken kinematics of cargo attachment to a robot ensures good conditioning

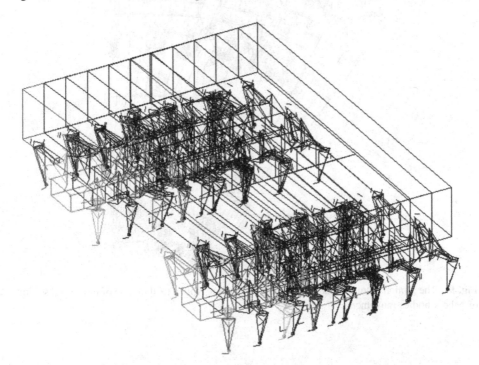

Fig. 8. The motion picture of the lateral movement of robots with a load.

of the system, however, due to the mobility of cargo attachment to the second robot, the leavy of the robot in the area of the cargo attachment takes place. Such leave will take place for any non-degenerate matrix. In other words, if it is necessary to move along an arbitrary path, it is necessary to correct the movement of one of the robots.

3.2   Setting the Movement of the Group Through a Partial Setting of Each Robot Movement

The partial set of the robot movement means the infliction of constraints only on some degrees of freedom of the robot body. Such conditions are satisfied by a large number of options. Let us consider the fixed attachment of the load to each of the robots as an example. For the first robot, the constraints are set for one point in three directions, for the second, the lateral movement of one point is set and constraints are inflicted on two angles of rotation around the horizontal axes. In this case, the rectilinear movement is just as well reproduced, however, since the rotation of the load can be performed only due to the different progressive speeds of the robots, a singular point appears at sufficiently large angles of rotation - Fig. 9.

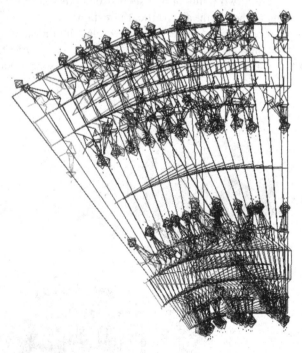

Fig. 9. The motion picture of lateral movement of robots with a load in case of the partial setting of robots bodies movement.

3.3   Setting the Movement of the Group Through the Setting of Cargo Movement

The simplest option, in this case, is the fixed attachment of each robot to the load. This method allows you to plan the movement of robots with a load along an arbitrary path. Figure 10 shows the programmed movement of the group, consisting of two phases — first, a circular movement with moving forward, then a movement without rotation with a changed orientation of the load. It can be concluded that this way of specifying the movement of a group of robots is the most universal and allows you to obtain programmed motion of an arbitrary type. Note also that the method under consideration does not depend on the number of robots and is applicable to a group consisting of any number of robots.

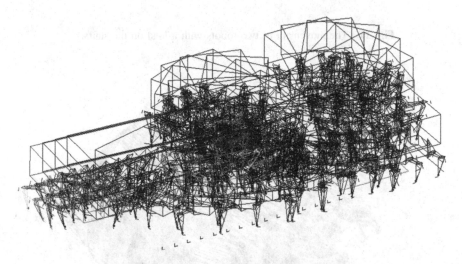

Fig. 10. The motion picture of the composite movement of robots with a load – circular and progressive movements.

The proposed control synthesis methods are applicable for constructing motion control of robots on an uneven surface, for example, a ladder – Figs. 11 and 12. Planning spatial load movement, in this case, is an independent task. Such tasks are currently being developed intensively in robotics in SLAM algorithms (Simultaneous Localization And Mapping). Figure 13 shows the movement of a group of 5 six-legged robots with a load. The movement consists of two parts - rotation around a vertical axis and progressive movement.

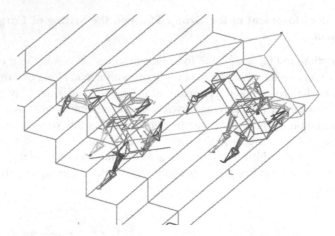

Fig. 11. The movement of two robots with a load on the stairs.

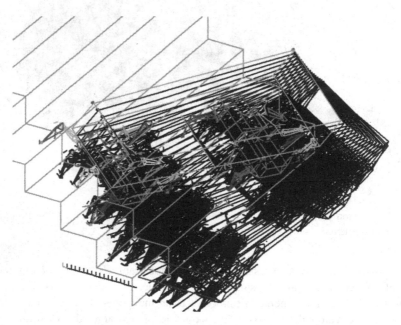

Fig. 12. The motion picture of the movement of two robots with a load on a ladder with rotation about a vertical axis of the load.

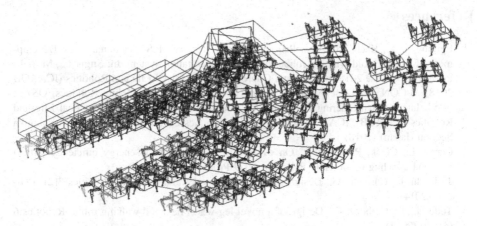

Fig. 13. The motion picture of a group of five robots with a single load (rotation and progressive movement).

Discussion and Conclusion

A small-sized walking robot with a wheel mover is a convenient platform for creating highly mobile service robots for various purposes - inspecting the interior, collecting samples, etc. Its advantages are:

- low cost and ease of manufacture of the mechanical part;
- high unification of the control system hardware;
- the modularity of design.

It is also promising to use small-sized walking robots with a wheel propeller for testing the software part of control systems with elements of artificial intelligence in real operating conditions.

Created methods for controlling the locomotion of walking robots can be used for robots with various types of walking movers. For robots of large size and carrying capacity, thrusters based on delta-like mechanisms can be used.

The presented method of synthesizing a group of robots movement control during cargo transfer can be used for robots of various types. The use of mixed control in terms of force and deflection allows obtaining a system with adaptation to load fluctuations. The developed mathematical methods and software allow the solution of high-dimensional mathematical models in real-time. The proposed calculation methods provide a simple decomposition of the model of a group of robots into independent sub-models. The analysis showed that the most general laws of the movement of a group are realized through management based on planning a cargo trajectory.

A further research direction is connected with the development of a robot prototype with the proposed locomotor mechanism for the study of walking regimes on various difficult terrain, such as various heterogeneous surfaces, as well as stairways. Another direction is connected with the development of a hexapod robot prototype using linear actuators and the study of the energy efficiency of its work in comparison with servo drives.

References

1. Egunov, V.A., Kachalov, A.L., Petrosyan, M.K., Tarasov, P.S., Yankina, E.V.: Development of the insectoid walking robot with inertial navigation system. In: Sugisaka, M. (ed.) Proceedings of the 2018 International Conference on Artificial Life and Robotics (ICAROB 2018), B-CON Plaza, Beppu, Oita, Japan, 1–4 February 2018, Mobile Robotics; OS7-2, p. 54. International Steering Committee of International Conference on Artifical Life and Robotics (ICAROB), ICAROB society (ALife Robotics Corporations Ltd.), IEEE Fukuoka Section (Japan) (2018)
2. Černý, L., Čížek, P., Faigl, J.: On evaluation of motion gaits energy efficiency with a hexapod crawling robot. Acta Polytech. CTU Proc. **6**, 6–10 (2016)
3. Tedeschi, F., Carbone, G.: Design issues for hexapod walking robots. Robotics **3**(2), 181–206 (2014)
4. Tedeschi, F., Carbone, G.: Design of a novel leg-wheel hexapod walking robot. Robotics **6** (4), 40 (2017)
5. Rashid, M.Z.A., Aras, M.S.M., Radzak, A.A., Kassim, A.M., Jamali, A.: Development of hexapod robot with manoeuvrable wheel. Int. J. Adv. Sci. Technol. **49** (2012)
6. Jehanno, J.-M., Cully, A., Grand, C., Mouret, J.-B.: Design of a wheel-legged hexapod robot for creative adaptation. In: CLAWAR 17th International Conference on Climbing and Walking Robots, Poznan, Poland, July 2014, pp. 267–276 (2014)
7. Evan Ackerman. Festo's New Bionic Robots Include Rolling Spider, Flying Fox [Electronic resource].   https://spectrum.ieee.org/automaton/robotics/robotics-hardware/festo-bionic-learning-network-rolling-spider-flying-fox
8. Gorobtsov, A.S.: The synthesis of the parameters of the controlled motion of multilink mechanical systems of arbitrary structures by solving an inverse. In: Mechatronics, Automation, Control, no. 6. pp. 43–50 (2004)
9. Gorobtsov, A.S., Andreev, A.E., Tarasov, P.S., Skorikov, A.V., Kartsov, S.K.: Synthesis of stable quasistatic stepping modes of anthropomorphic robot. Izvestia VolgGTU **6**(185), 75–76 (2016)
10. Kurzhanski, A.B.: The task of group control in an environment with obstacles. In: Proceedings of IMM URO RAS, vol. 20, no. 3, pp. 166–179 (2014)
11. Gorobtsov, A.S., Kartsov, S.K, Pletnev, A.E., Poplyakov, Yu.A.: Computer methods of construction and research of mathematical models of dynamics of car structures: monograph. In: Mashinostroenie, 462 p. (2011)
12. The KITTI Vision Benchmark Suite. [Electronic resource] http://www.cvlibs.net/datasets/kitti/
13. Kim, J.Y., Yang, U.J.: Mechanical design of powered prosthetic leg and walking pattern generation based on motion capture data. Adv. Robot. **29**(16), 1061–1079 (2015)
14. Englsberger, J.: Trajectory generation for continuous leg forces during double support and heel-to-toe shift based on a divergent component of motion. In: Proceedings of IEEE RSJ International Conference on Intelligent Robots and Systems, pp. 4022–4029 (2014)
15. Ijspeert, A.J.: Central pattern generators for locomotion control in animals and robots: a review. Neural Netw. **21**(4), 642–653 (2008)

Development the Online Operating System of Urban Infrastructure Data

Danila Parygin[✉], Dmitry Kozlov, Natalia Sadovnikova,
Vladislav Kvetkin, Ivan Soplyakov, and Vitaliy Malikov

Volgograd State Technical University, Lenina Avenue 28,
400005 Volgograd, Russia
dparygin@gmail.com, mrdiko4@gmail.com, npsnl@ya.ru,
kvetkin@intervolga.ru, vanyakacompany@yandex.ru,
axalter20@gmail.com

Abstract. The practice of administrative and commercial organizations dealing with urban space is firmly connected with the use of various types of automated information processing systems. Custom and boxed desktop and network solutions, data storage systems, GIS systems are used to monitor and manage the urban infrastructure, as a system as a whole, as well as its components. Over the past few years, a number of developments have emerged that offer cloud processing of spatial-temporal data for particular territories or branches, such as transport infrastructure. The paper describes an approach to building such a system of collecting, preprocessing and presenting infrastructure data, which allows creating an ecosystem for working with urban spatial information online for any territory. The features of the implementation of the basic software components for managing data on urban infrastructure, including issues of aggregation and storage organization, are disclosed. An approach to the systematic accumulation and preprocessing of data obtained by paralleling the process of parsing open network sources, using proxy protection against failure to receive updates, and extracting a structured description of infrastructure objects is proposed. The presented research and development are carried out within the framework of development by UCLab "UrbanBasis" the concept of an Online Operating System for work with urban infrastructure data, which implies the possibility of building additional services on its basis. Testing of this concept is presented on the example of creating a specialized data processor, which is a module for constructing a short-term value prediction of real estate objects using regression models.

Keywords: Online Operating System · Urban infrastructure data ·
Data storage · Data preprocessing · Retrieving object description ·
Value prediction · Proxy · Parsing · Spatial data · Data aggregation

1 Introduction

The management of urban infrastructure in modern conditions is impossible to imagine without the use of up-to-date and accurate information about its condition. It is necessary to conduct an analysis to substantiate the choice of decisions related to its

© Springer Nature Switzerland AG 2019
A. G. Kravets et al. (Eds.): CIT&DS 2019, CCIS 1084, pp. 203–216, 2019.
https://doi.org/10.1007/978-3-030-29750-3_16

operation and development. Municipalities are undergoing a digital transformation. Data is becoming more accessible. And the effectiveness of decisions made now largely depends on how sophisticated tools will be used to collect, integrate and analyze data. The introduction of new digital technology solutions in the urban economy leads to a reduction in the cost of servicing various urban systems, increasing the speed of all processes, ensuring their transparency and observability [1].

The formation of the city's digital ecosystem is made possible by the presence of smart sensors, cloud services, open data platforms, map services, etc. Technological solutions for servicing the digital ecosystem of the city are offered by almost all leading IT companies, which are currently mainly concentrated in the USA, Germany, France, Switzerland, Japan, and other developed countries. In Russia, the development of proprietary technologies for data-driven cities has received insufficient attention. This affects the speed of digital innovation.

This paper discusses software solutions for organizing the accumulation, integration, preprocessing and presentation of data on the infrastructure of the city. The example of analyzing data on urban real estate shows the entire technological cycle from data collection to obtain a solution. The peculiarity of the proposed approach is the construction of an operating system of urban infrastructure data that allows connecting additional modules focused on specific user tasks for analytical work with a single pool of geospatial information online. At the same time, the platform does not impose territorial restrictions on data management but forms a complex structure that allows for cross-regional analysis.

2   Current Trends in Organization of Work with Urban Data

The problems of collecting and integrating heterogeneous data are studied quite fully. These include various models, data types and formats, incompleteness and omissions of values, naming conflicts, semantic and structural conflicts [2, 3]. There are various approaches to their solution [4–6].

There are a number of systems that have been implemented to work with heterogeneous data, including in the field of information management on urban infrastructure and territory [7]. A feature of such systems is the need to take into account the spatial reference of data. Therefore, often GIS is chosen as an integrating platform. Such systems include, for example, ArcGIS [8] and ZuluGIS [9].

The advantages of creating data management systems based on universal GIS are invariance to any areas of activity and tasks to be solved. However, the query processing speed [10] in this case will be too low to solve problems in real time.

"CS UrbanView" [11] is a service for solving problems related to the search, analysis, and display of spatial and attribute data at both the municipal and regional levels by supporting all known coordinate systems and map projections. On its basis, it is possible to create municipal GIS, information systems to support urban planning activities (ISSUPA) and GIS monitoring of engineering communications. The developer offers many client applications: for monitoring engineering utilities UtilityGuide (HeatGuide, WaterGuide, GazGuide, EnerGuide), condition monitoring and repair planning for road facilities RoadGuide, maintaining urban planning inventory

UrbaniCS and environmental monitoring EcologiCS. However, the development of this project does not involve working with big data. Therefore, the creation of integrated solutions based on it will be too time-consuming.

Big data analysis and machine learning technologies are used in many urban mobility analysis projects. For example, Citilabs [12] develops solutions for improving the living conditions of communities and the work of organizations based on the analysis of people's use of the urban transport system during the day. Software solutions created by Citilabs allow to measure, predict and manage population movements. For this purpose, the spatial and temporal characteristics of the state of flows from different sources of data on their location for a specific section of the urban area are accumulated. In the process of forecasting, modules are used that implement behavioral models based on current data on population and employment, which provide an idea of the use of urban infrastructure.

POPULUS [13] has been developed for urban mobility management. The platform integrates live data streams from various operators for presentation in a user-friendly form. This approach allows cities to control mobility services, including bicycles, scooters and vehicles.

A large amount of open data about processes in cities is stored in incompatible formats or is not updated. The Stae service [14] implements the concept of aggregation and presentation of access to open sources of structured data about cities and their processing in real time. In a similar vein, but with a specialization in the collection and analysis of telematic data sets in real time, the Geotab project [15] is working. Aggregate, raw, labeled sensory data is stored in a single data lake. Analysts and scientists can use these kits as a turnkey solution for obtaining information from large amounts of IoT data.

The concept of creating a multi-service geo-analytical platform to support urban process management tasks was proposed in 2016 as part of the development of the infrastructure data analysis project implemented by the urban computing laboratory UCLab [16]. The tasks of implementing the Online Operating System of Urban Infrastructure Data, the results of which are presented below, were identified as a result of subsequent research and analysis of the experience of leading developers of such solutions [17].

3 Approach to Building the System for Collection, Preprocessing and Presentation of Infrastructure Data

It is necessary to develop a single operating system that receives, stores, processes and provides the user with all the necessary data to implement user access to relevant information about the state of urban infrastructure. Integral parts of such a system should be a subsystem of data collection from external sources, a subsystem of data storage, a subsystem of data analysis, as well as a subsystem of data presented to the user. The conceptual architecture of the proposed system is shown in the diagram (see Fig. 1).

Current data on the infrastructure of the city can be obtained from various sources. These are primarily web-resources, as well as sensory data [18], catalogs of electronic documentation and information systems. Data storage formats in different sources can vary greatly. Therefore, it is necessary for each such format to implement its own service that receives data from the source, converts them to the format of the operating system and passes them to the data access subsystem for saving them to the database (DB).

It is also important that the organization of the process of unloading data from external web resources, it is necessary to take into account their non-persistent structure [19]. Data on external resources is constantly added and changed so that previously uploaded data becomes irrelevant. And not every external resource is able to notify the underdevelopment system about changes in its data. In this regard, it is necessary to develop a process of continuous data loading, with the ability to detect duplicate data and changes in them.

The functionality of adding new data, finding duplicates in the data and their changes should be implemented in the Data Access Layer (DAL) subsystem. In addition, the data access subsystem must also provide flexible data sampling, modification, and, if necessary, deletion functionality for other subsystems under development. The DAL should also be implemented functionality for user and user groups interact with the system: storage of data about users and their groups, their addition, modification, and deletion; user authentication; user and user group rights management for data access.

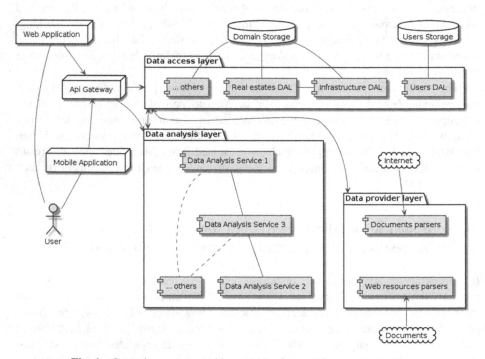

Fig. 1. Operation system architecture (Packages Diagram, UML 2.0).

Users interact with the system via graphical interfaces of web and mobile applications. The user should be able to access not only the functions of obtaining basic information about the city and its objects, aggregated from external sources but also the data obtained as a result of additional analysis of this information with the help of the graphical interface.

All types of information analysis are carried out by the data analysis subsystem. An example of such an analysis is: a semantic analysis of the text of real estate ads; obtaining various types of samples from existing data and analysis of their distribution; search for geographical objects on the map and routes between them; etc.

4 Features of Implementation of Basic Software Components for Urban Infrastructure Data Management

As shown in Fig. 1, the developed system has a multilayer architecture. At the same time, each layer is a set of services that perform a limited set of atomic functions. Virtually every pair of services can communicate with each other by calling the Rest API methods implemented for each of the services. This approach to architecture is called "microservice architecture" [20].

Microservice architecture is generally opposed to monolithic architecture and has a number of advantages over it. First, the design, implementation, and support of the "little" services that are always simpler than the integration of their functionality in a "big" monolithic solution. Secondly, it is the ability to scale-out of the system. Third, unlike a monolithic solution, it is possible to use different technologies for different services, which is often very effective.

On the other hand, the complexity of service deployment and orchestration is the biggest problem when using microservice architecture. However, modern virtualization technologies, as well as technologies of continuous integration and continuous delivery (CI&CD), allow leveling these problems to a greater extent [21].

4.1 Organization of Data Storage

The MongoDB database with the Mongoose library [22] is used for data storage. The data in the database is stored in the form of documents, united in a collection, where the structure of the object is defined by the scheme implemented in Mongoose.

The following most common objects were identified when developing the database structure: apartment, room, house, land, office, retail space, warehouse, premises for free use, garage, building. Each real estate object is characterized by its own set of properties. Also, real estate objects have common properties, such as price and area.

The ER-diagram fragments represent the main tables in the database. The relationship between the tables "Address", "Real Estate" and "Ad" is "one-to-many" (see Fig. 2), i.e. one address or real estate object can correspond to many ads, but one ad always corresponds to only one address and one real estate object.

The table "Real Estate" is linked to the tables "Apartment", "House", "Office", "Retail Space", "Warehouse", "Building" by a "one-to-one" relationship (see Fig. 3).

Thus, the inheritance of fields from the basic entity "Real Estate" to specific entities ("Apartment", "House", etc.) is implemented using the Table Per Hierarchy pattern.

In addition, each of the entities "Apartment", "House", "Office", "Retail Space", "Warehouse" corresponds to the entity "Building", which acts as an independent real estate object. In one building can be several real estate objects such as "Apartment", "House", "Office", "Retail Space", and "Warehouse". Therefore there is a relationship of "one-to-many" between them.

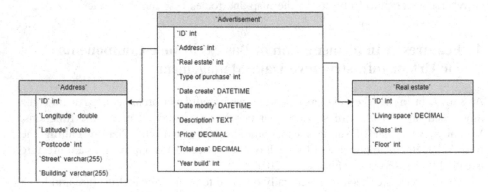

Fig. 2. Tables "Address", "Ad" and "Real Estate" from the database.

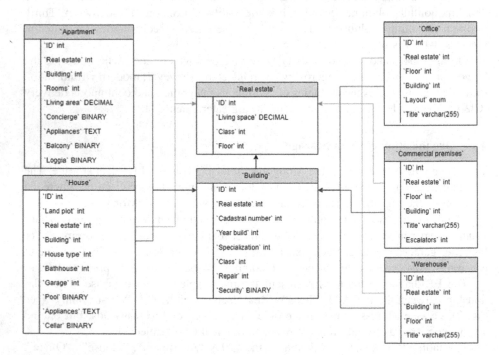

Fig. 3. Tables "Apartment", "House", "Office", "Warehouse", "Retail Space", "Building" and "Real Estate" from the database.

4.2   Services of Data Access Layer

Data Access Layer in the system is represented by a set of microservices that implement their own RESTful API. Services communicate with each other and with other subsystems via HTTP Protocol, transmitting data in JSON format.

JavaScript programming language was chosen in the Node.js execution environment using the Express.js framework for the development of services. MongoDB with Mongoose ODM used as a database.

All services can be divided into two groups according to their functional affiliation: services that store and process information about the infrastructure of the city and real estate; services that implement the functionality of user work with the system. At the moment, the following services are implemented: service-aggregator of real estate data; service-aggregator, providing information about the available ads for the sale of real estate; service, implementing the interaction of users and user groups with the system.

Service-Aggregator of Data on Real Estate. This service implements the addition, storage, and receipt of information.

Adding data is carried out using the web API provided by the service. The added data comes in the form of HTTP POST requests containing content in JSON format. Data for adding can be received at the initiative of users of the system (from the website or mobile application) or from Data Provider Layer services. The input data is decomposed and stored in the appropriate database collections for the convenience of structuring and subsequent search.

In addition, the service provides access to the data that is necessary to display them to users of the system, or for their further analysis and processing by other services from the Data Analysis Layer. The service also controls the history of changes in the data, their integrity, and consistency.

In general, all cases of work with the service aggregator of real estate data can be divided into the following types of operations:

- Adding. Data about new entities is stored in the database with the time of their creation and assigning them a unique identifier. Example of a request to add a real estate object: [POST] /estate
- Update. New entities are created, with the update time specified, when requests to update information about existing entities. Past versions of entities remain in the system for later analysis. Example of a request to edit information about a real estate object: [PUT] /estate/:id
- Editing. Selective updates of entity fields associated with the moderation data (e.g., the record status is changed). Identical to the data update. Example of a request: [PATCH] /estate/:id
- Reception. Retrieves a dataset based on the specified parameters. Filtering and sorting by fields of interest, and data splitting are supported. Example of a request for information about a real estate object by its identifier: [GET] /estate/:id
- Removal. The user can either hide the specified entity from the issuance or completely remove it from the database depending on the permissions. Example of a request to delete data about a real estate object by its identifier: [DELETE] /estate/:id.

Service-Aggregator that Provides Information on Available Real Estate Purchase and Sale Ads. This service provides analysis, grouping and delivery of all ads available in the database.

Basic functionality:

- Group. If several ads correspond to one real estate object, then one ad, which contains detailed information about this object, is created.
- Issue. This request provides a list of ads that match the specified parameters. It supports filtering and sorting by key fields, and splitting data into parts. Example of a request for information about ads for the sale of real estate objects: [GET] /ads?[a set of specifying parameters].

Service-Aggregator of Data on Users. The service implements the interaction of users and user groups with the system. Only registered users have access to the vast amount of data and system functionality.

Users are divided into groups on access rights to differentiate the level of access to the functionality. Each user group has its own set of access rights to certain functionality. A user can be a member of several user groups at the same time. All the functions available to the user are determined from the totality of all the groups in which the user consists.

Implemented functionality for working with users:

- Registration. The user creates an account in the system. At the stage of adding data validation and password encryption takes place. Thus, the security measures of the user's personal data are observed. Example of a request to add a new user: [POST] / auth/signup
- Authorization. The user logs into his/her account. Protection against password guessing is implemented through temporary blocking of users who have made more than 5 login attempts with an incorrect password in a row. Example of a request: [POST] /auth/signin
- Editing. Selective updates of entity fields, for example: user changes his/her data, changes his/her access rights, account lock or unlock. Example of a request to edit user data by the specified identifier: [PATCH] /users/:id
- Removal. The user with the specified ID is marked as deleted and the continuation of activity from this account is no longer possible. However, all data added by the user remains in the system. In this case, the user page is replaced by a stub with information that it has been deleted. Example of a request to delete a user by user ID: [DELETE] /users/:id.

Various authorization strategies are supported for user convenience. This allows to go through the stages of authorization and authentication in the system using both login and password, and through various third-party services using the OAuth 2.0 authorization Protocol [23].

4.3 Services for Collection and Preprocessing of Data on Urban Infrastructure

Multiparsing of Information Resources. The basic content of the operating system information database is performed using a module to collect data on real estate objects to be sold or leased. Internet resources for placing ads, as well as sites of trading platforms are the purpose of parsing.

The analysis of sources was carried out to form a unified model for describing real estate objects and organizing the storage of collected data. Full details of the ads and lots of trading platforms were carried out during this process. Object description patterns were obtained from each resource studied. A single structure for describing the property was subsequently formed on the basis of these patterns [24].

Protecting external resources from copying their data is one of the main problems when parsing these resources. As a rule, large services seek to protect their accumulated database from full copying.

Automated detection and blocking of users who parse data from a resource is the main tool here. The detection of such users is mainly carried out by detecting specific patterns of behavior, for example, a large number of requests in a short period of time, an easily explained sequential navigation algorithm through the pages of the site, etc.

The applicability of the technology of using the pool of ip-addresses to send requests for data was investigated to prevent blocking when parsing a particular resource. For this, each following request was sent from a new ip-address after an unfixed amount of time.

It is possible to implement a similar algorithm using the query proxy service. This service contains a pool of ip-addresses of proxy services and independently changes them for each next request. Using such a proxying service for each of the parsers significantly reduces the number of locks when parsing resources and makes it possible to build a reliable process for obtaining relevant data.

All implemented parsers collect data and save it to JSON files. Their structure is defined by a common pattern for storing objects. It will be relevant until all cycles of passage are completed page by page and for each ad of all source sites. Further, the received files are transferred for processing to the module for recording in the information base of the system.

The module for paralleling the process of collecting data from Internet resources and writing to the output files was developed for organizing multi parsing. An appropriate algorithm was developed for this module (see Fig. 4).

"Multiprocessing" library features were used in the implementation of the parallelization module of the work of parsers [25]. As can be seen from the diagram, the algorithm is based on the creation and launch of processes for each of the parsers. Further, each of the running parsers begins its work. The received data is queued for writing to the file corresponding to its parser after reading the next found object from the declaration. All processes created for them are closed, and the files with the parsed data are saved at the end of the work of the parsers.

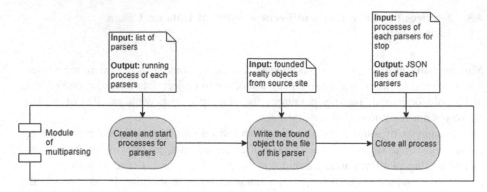

Fig. 4. Scheme of the parallelization process of parsing several collectors.

Retrieving of Real Estate Description. The main problem of extracting descriptions from ads is that the information available on Internet resources is not structured and written in natural language. Text ads from different resources can vary greatly in style of description. For example, announcements in social networks are written shortly, using abbreviations and slang, and the information presented at auctions is more formal and rigorous. The properties of each type of real estate should be described in order to extract information about real estate from different sources. For each type of property were selected and described properties. For example, the following characteristics are defined for a building: address, announcement date, announcement change date, general description, price, price per sq.m, total area, number of floors, room specialization, year of construction, class, line of houses, entrance, repair, type of contract, furniture, parking, lease term, seller, seller number, seller email, ad URL.

A special module for extracting a structured description of real estate objects from natural language texts was developed to solve this problem (see Fig. 5). Tomita-parser [26] was applied on the basis of the module operation algorithm for extracting descriptions of real estate objects. This tool for extracting structured data (facts) from a natural language text has a morphology, grammatical agreement and allows to write own grammar.

Grammars are the basis of the mechanism for extracting named entities in Tomita-parser. They set the rules for parsing incoming information. A grammar is a set of rules that describe a string of words in a text. Accordingly, it is necessary to write a particular grammar for Tomita-parser for successful extraction of properties of real estate objects.

A fact is a set of values of attribute fields connected by meanings. For example, the fact "Price" may have the fields "Per month", "Per square meter", "Utility payments".

The process of interpreting the Tomita parser should begin after describing all the facts. Interpretation is a way to save the result of text analysis in a tabular form, convenient for subsequent processing, for example, for saving to a database. Interpretation is the final stage of text processing in Tomita-parser. The process of interpretation consists in the distribution of subchains from the distinguished grammar of the chain of fact fields.

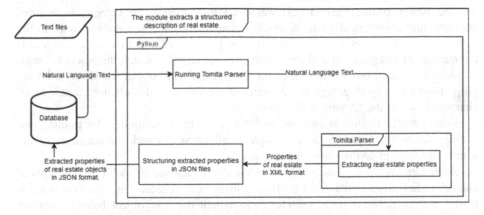

Fig. 5. Architecture module retrieve descriptions of real estate.

4.4 Building of Specialized Data Processors

All collected data on real estate objects from ad sites and sites of trading floors can be used in the future, for example, to conduct research on the real estate market in the country and on certain regions and cities [27]. The price prediction module for a user-defined property object was developed to test the concept of implementing specialized data handlers on operating system infrastructure.

The idea of the study was to develop a regression model for each type of real estate, with the help of which it is possible to construct a price forecast for the property. Moreover, the description of an arbitrary object is formed on the basis of user-defined search criteria.

The main properties of real estate, which are mainly used by appraisers in practice, were chosen to build a short-term forecast of the value of typical objects. So for the objects belonging to the "Apartment" type, six characteristics were selected: the area of the object; number of floors of the house where the object is located; the floor on which the object is located; the material of the walls of the house (panel, brick, solid, etc.); number of rooms; value of the object. And since many of the listed characteristics are categorical, the substitution of their values into the regression equation is impossible. There is a need to bring these properties to a numerical form.

In addition, among these properties, there are "pseudo-quantitative", i.e. characteristics that have numerical values but have a semantic characteristic. For example, the property "floor". As practice shows, when choosing an apartment, a potential buyer/tenant often negatively relates to the location of objects on the first or last floor [28].

Such properties of an object must also be reduced to a numerical form, taking into account their semantic component. These characteristics have been converted to categorical form. For this purpose, existing codes of practice and recommendations on the classification of similar properties of real estate objects in the valuation sphere were used. For example, the characteristic "floor" will have the following values: "first", "average", "last".

The binary coding method [29] was used to transform the categorical features obtained into a numerical form. Its essence was to represent a specific feature in the form of an n-dimensional vector, consisting of (n − 1) zeros and one unit, where n is the number of categories of a given feature. The category to which the object belongs, is taken as 1. As a result, the coding for the "Apartment" object transformed all the properties of the object, except for "Number of rooms", and also obtained a new set of characteristics of the "Apartment" object.

In the created module it implements forms from the existing data for training and testing the model. Also, a separate sample is allocated to check the adequacy of the results obtained in comparison with real prices.

After forming the data sample, the objects that are closest to each other in terms of characteristics are selected from it. This defines new classes. The selection is done using clustering. Next, select the cluster to which the user object belongs. Further forecasts are based on the data belonging to the selected cluster. The use of such a training cycle improves prediction accuracy.

The module builds a regression forecast model using data from a cluster, which may include an object described by the user. The output data of the pricing model are files with the values of the weight coefficients of each individual property, recorded in JSON format. The resulting weights will be substituted into the equation. The unknown variable is the projected price of the user property. Each model will undergo a new training cycle when updating data in the information base of the operating system.

5   Conclusion

The software components described in the paper are the basis of the operating system being created. The information infrastructure implemented at this stage already allows the creation of additional specialized data processors, such as the described real estate price forecasting module. At the same time, not only urban data processing algorithms develop, but also their storage, which is updated with relevant and accumulated historical spatial information.

The proposed concept of working with urban infrastructure data is the result of the research and development experience of the urban computing laboratory UCLab [17]. An important target for the further development of the project is the integration of key basic modules related to the collection and processing of mobile and sensor data streams [30], as well as information from the network catalogs of data on urban socio-economic infrastructure. In addition, it is necessary to implement visual user interfaces to enable work with information and service management not only to software engineers but also to research analysts and a specialist in city services [31]. The Online Operating System being created is actually intended for information and analytical decision support of a wide range of specialists working with urban infrastructure data.

Acknowledgements. The reported study was funded by the Russian Foundation for Basic Research (RFBR) according to the research project No. 18-37-20066_mol_a_ved, and by RFBR and the government of the Volgograd region of the Russian Federation grant No. 18-47-340012_r_a. The authors express gratitude to colleagues from UCLab involved in the development of UrbanBasis.com project.

References

1. Parygin, D.S., Sadovnikova, N.P., Shabalina, O.A.: Information and analytical support for city management tasks [Информационно-аналитическая поддержка задач управления городом], Volgograd (2017)
2. Grogg, M.: Challenges to Data Integration. https://www.fhwa.dot.gov/asset/dataintegration/if10019/dip06.cfm. Accessed 14 Feb 2019
3. Stepanov, S.Yu.: Development of geographic information systems based on the use of heterogeneous spatially distributed information in the interests of territorial management, St. Petersburg (2017)
4. Koskin, A.V., Uzharinsky, A.Yu.: Methods of forming an integrating data model based on the available heterogeneous data sources. Inf. Syst. Technol. **82**, 9–27 (2014)
5. Karin, S.A.: Integration of heterogeneous geospatial data in a single information space. Manag. Inf. Syst. **2**, 89–94 (2012)
6. Makunin, I.V.: Some approaches to managing heterogeneous data using technology XML/XQUERY. Manag. Syst. Inf. Technol. **4**(2), 255–261 (2007)
7. Evdokimov, D.: Situational management in complex systems. https://www.cisco.com/c/dam/assets/global/RU/events/cisco-connect/presentation/ural/17_55_18_55.pdf. Accessed 15 Jan 2019
8. ArcGIS. http://resources.arcgis.com/ru/help/getting-started/articles/026n00000014000000.html. Accessed 30 Jan 2019
9. ZuluGIS. https://www.politerm.com/products/geo/zulugis/. Accessed 10 Feb 2019
10. Vytovtov, K.A., Barabanova, E.A., Podlazov, V.S.: Model of next-generation optical switching system. Commun. Comput. Inf. Sci. **919**, 377–386 (2018)
11. CS UrbanView. http://www.urbanics.ru/products/detail.php?ID=1482. Accessed 13 Jan 2019
12. Citilabs. http://www.citilabs.com. Accessed 22 Jan 2019
13. Populus. https://www.populus.ai. Accessed 02 Feb 2019
14. Stae. https://stae.co/. Accessed 11 Feb 2019
15. Geotab. https://data.geotab.com/our-ecosystem. Accessed 01 Mar 2019
16. Ustugova, S., Parygin, D., Sadovnikova, N., Yadav, V., Prikhodkova, I.: Geoanalytical system for support of urban processes management tasks. Commun. Comput. Inf. Sci. **754**, 430–440 (2017)
17. Golubev, A., Chechetkin, I., Parygin, D., Sokolov, A., Shcherbakov, M.: Geospatial data generation and preprocessing tools for urban computing system development. Proc. Comput. Sci. **101**, 217–226 (2016)
18. Vytovtov, K.A., Barabanova, E.A., Barabanov, I.O.: Next-generation switching system based on 8 × 8 self-turning optical cell. In: Proceeding of International Conference on Actual Problems of Electron Devices Engineering, pp. 306–310 (2018)
19. Persistent Structures, Part 1: Persistent Stack. https://habr.com/ru/post/113585/. Accessed 25 Feb 2019
20. Microservice Architecture. https://microservices.io/. Accessed 16 Mar 2019
21. CI&CD. https://medium.com/southbridge/ci-cd-принципы-внедрение-инструменты-f0626b9994c8. Accessed 20 Jan 2019
22. Mongoose. https://mongoosejs.com/. Accessed 21 Mar 2019
23. OAuth 2.0. https://oauth.net/2/. Accessed 23 Mar 2019

24. Cherkesov, V., Malikov, V., Golubev, A., Parygin, D., Smykovskaya, T.: Parsing of data on real estate objects from network resource. In: Proceedings of the IV International Research Conference "Information Technologies in Science, Management, Social Sphere and Medicine". Advances in Computer Science Research, vol. 72, pp. 385–388. Atlantis Press (2017)
25. Multiprocessing—Process-based "threading" interface. https://docs.python.org/2/library/multiprocessing.html. Accessed 21 Mar 2019
26. Tomita parser. https://tech.yandex.ru/tomita/. Accessed 18 Dec 2018
27. Simionova, N.E.: Methods for analyzing the real estate market for evaluation purposes. In: Herald UGNTU. Science, Education, Economics. Series: Economy 2 (2015)
28. Sevostyanov, A.V.: Economy of Real Estate. Koloss, Moscow (2007)
29. Parygin, D.S., Malikov, V.P., Golubev, A.V., Sadovnikova, N.P., Petrova, T.M., Finogeev, A.G.: Categorical data processing for real estate objects valuation using statistical analysis. J. Phys.: Conf. Ser. **1015**, 032102 (2018). http://iopscience.iop.org/article/10.1088/1742-6596/1015/3/032102/pdf. Accessed 18 Mar 2019
30. Parygin, D., Nikitsky, N., Kamaev, V., Matokhina, A., Finogeev, A., Finogeev, A.: Multi-agent approach to distributed processing of big sensor data based on fog computing model for the monitoring of the urban infrastructure systems. In: Proceedings of the 5th International Conference on System Modeling & Advancement in Research Trends, Moradabad, India, pp. 305–310. IEEE (2016)
31. Parygin, D., Sadovnikova, N., Kalinkina, M., Potapova, T., Finogeev, A.: Visualization of data about events in the urban environment for the decision support of the city services actions coordination. In: Proceedings of the 5th International Conference on System Modeling & Advancement in Research Trends, Moradabad, India, pp. 283–290. IEEE (2016)

Spherical Panoramic Photo Shooting
and Virtual Reality Demonstration
of a Crime Scene

Vladimir Bulgakov[1(✉)], Igor Trushchenkov[1], and Elena Bulgakova[2]

[1] Moscow University of the Ministry of Internal Affairs
of the Russian Federation named after V.Y. Kikot,
12 Academician Volgin str., Moscow 117437, Russia
{vg.bulgakov, hrustals}@mail.ru
[2] Kutafin Moscow State Law University (MSAL),
9 Sadovaya-Kudrinskaya str., Moscow 125993, Russia
kpit2015@mail.ru

Abstract. The relevance of the research topic is associated with a small number
of existing innovations that are used at the stage of inspecting the scene during
the investigation of crimes. Most of the new scientific methods and tools have
been developed and are used in the examination of evidence in the framework of
forensic examination, for example: DNA analysis, computer image analysis,
forensic facial reconstruction, etc. There is a time lag in the scientific support of
the photo shooting of the crime scene, the evidence found, their evaluation and
visual demonstration in court, which negatively affects the speed and quality of
the criminal investigation. The article provides a comprehensive analysis of the
capabilities of spherical photo technologies of a crime scene and building a
visual step-by-step illustration using virtual reality devices. The authors have
developed guidelines for capturing the scene of the incident with modern
panoramic photo and video cameras, as well as visualizing the captured information using virtual reality devices in crime investigation activities. The use of
methods of fixing a crime scene with panoramic photo and video technologies,
as well as visualization of the captured information using virtual reality devices
will be interpreting and presenting evidence, as well as improve the objectivity
and quality of criminal investigation.

Keywords: Spherical panorama · Virtual reality · Inspection of the scene ·
Forensic examination · Interpretation and presentation of evidence in court ·
Multimodal evidence · Artificial intelligence

1 Background

In the modern world, the main attention is paid to improving the quality of production
of forensic examinations, the introduction of new expert technologies and instrumental
methods of researching physical evidence. Such forensic evidence research technologies as DNA analysis, computer image analysis, forensic facial reconstruction, and
many others have been introduced into the practice of forensic experts.

© Springer Nature Switzerland AG 2019
A. G. Kravets et al. (Eds.): CIT&DS 2019, CCIS 1084, pp. 217–225, 2019.
https://doi.org/10.1007/978-3-030-29750-3_17

At the same time, insufficient attention was paid to such important areas in the investigation of crimes as the inspection of the crime scene, the assessment of evidence and the use of evidence in court [1–4]. Significantly less innovation is observed in modern expert photo shooting of the crime scene and in the process of demonstration of physical evidence, which has a negative impact on the effectiveness of the criminal investigation process.

In turn, over the past few years, the quality of spherical photo-panoramas, obtained with the help of new technical devices - panoramic cameras, has significantly improved [5]. Modern virtual reality systems have also been developed for material reproducing. The use of such technological solutions by police experts extends possibilities for the photo shooting of judicial evidence obtained at the scene of the incident, as well as their demonstration in court.

2 Analysis of the Technical Characteristics and Capabilities of Spherical Panoramic Cameras for Fixing the Situation of the Crime Scene

Currently, judicial photography plays a key role in investigating and solving crimes and also accompanies the investigation process at all stages.

The most important investigative action is the inspection of the crime scene, the results of which are often decisive for the successful search of a criminal. However, a comprehensive, complete and detailed reproduction of the scene of the incident cannot be provided by the method of verbal description in the investigating report, due to its subjectivity. The photographic tables used in the reports also do not allow to fully convey the spatial situation of the crime scene.

According to the legislation of the Russian Federation [6, 7], modern photographic technical solutions, including spherical photo-panoramas and virtual reality devices, can be used to fix the storage and display of the situation of the crime scene.

Photographing the scene is used to record the progress and results of the inspection process. To solve problems of displaying objects at the scene, they use orientation, overview, nodal, detailed, and also measuring photography.

In our opinion, modern spherical cameras are of particular interest to law enforcement officers, which allow shooting the spherical panoramas of the crime scene simultaneously. At the same time, the process of capturing an image takes seconds, in contrast to the panoramic cameras already used in police units, for example, the Panoscan MK-3. This possibility is of particular importance when conducting an inspection of large areas, as it allows to significantly reduce the time for fixing the situation of the scene.

The considered devices are different from traditional cameras by the presence of two or more lenses with wide-angle lens systems. Modern cameras for panoramic shooting are quite compact and mounted on a tripod, for example, a spherical panoramic camera Panono Panoramic Ball Camera (Fig. 1). It has thirty-six lenses located on different sides. Thanks to this, the camera allows to simultaneously capture thirty-six photographs with a resolution of 2 megapixels each, which are then stitched together into one spherical panorama with a resolution of 108 megapixels.

Fig. 1. Panono Panoramic Ball Camera.

Technical characteristics of spherical panoramic cameras are given in Table 1. Testing of the presented cameras showed, that cameras with several lenses are most suitable for obtaining full-fledged spherical panoramas of the scene and allowing to get an image with a resolution of at least 15 megapixels. Such a resolution is necessary for displaying small details of objects at the crime scene.

Table 1. Technical characteristics of cameras for spherical panoramic shooting

Model	The number of lenses; resolution of the resulting panoramic image
Panono Panoramic Ball Camera	36; 108 megapixels
Kandao Obsidian (S or R)	6; 59 megapixels
Insta360 Pro 2	6; 29 megapixels
Z CAM S1 Pro	4; 18 megapixels
Samsung Gear360	2; 15 megapixels

It should be noted, that in recent years panoramic cameras have significantly increased the quality of the resulting image. The high resolution of photographs allows these devices to be used to record the scene of the incident, objects, and traces, which act as forensic evidence [8].

3   The Technique of Step-by-Step Spherical Panoramic Shooting at the Scene

The stages of obtaining a spherical photographic image should include:

(1) the preparatory stage;
(2) the stage of work with the camera at the scene;
(3) the final stage.

At the *preparatory stage*, the photographer should prepare the necessary photographic equipment and accessories based on the available information: check whether the camera batteries are charged, select the required lighting devices, etc.

Stage of Work with the Camera at the Scene. When shooting, the camera should be mounted on a tripod with adjustable position. The optimum height for the production of panoramic photographing of the room is at the level of the human eye and is approximately 175 cm from the ground or floor.

Due to the fact that the panoramic camera has the possibility of spherical coverage of the recorded area, it is recommended to install it in the center of the scene. The distance of photographing depends on the nature of the investigated incident and surrounding objects.

1. When taking pictures inside buildings, the photographing point should, if possible, be chosen in the center of the room (Figs. 2 and 3):

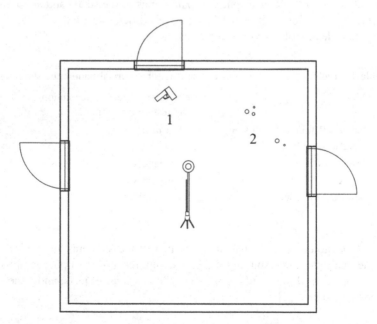

Fig. 2. The layout of the camera for spherical panoramic shooting indoors.

Fig. 3. The location of the camera for spherical panoramic shooting indoors.

It is important that photographs should be taken indoors without any persons. This is implemented by the remote control of the camera from a mobile device or computer.

1. Nodal photography of the corpse is performed when the camera is cross-positioned (Figs. 4 and 5). The camera is installed at the floor level, on two or more sides:

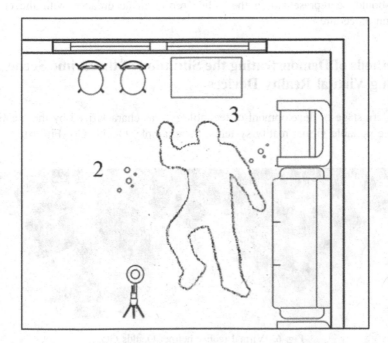

Fig. 4. The layout of the camera for a spherical panoramic shooting of a corpse.

Fig. 5. The location of the camera for a spherical panoramic shooting of a corpse.

2. After the spherical panoramic shooting at the scene, the photographer also performs the nodal and detailed photographic recording of individual objects and traces using a traditional camera. In our opinion, the production of traditional photography is necessary for the qualitative display of details and individual features of forensic evidence.

At the final stage of the inspection and shooting of the situation of the scene, the results should be represented in the police report in accordance with the criminal legislation procedure.

4   Methods of Demonstrating the Situation of the Crime Scene Using Virtual Reality Devices

The modern stage of development of technology was characterized by the creation of affordable portable virtual reality systems, for example, Oculus Go (Fig. 6).

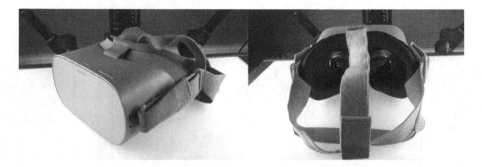

Fig. 6. Virtual reality helmet Oculus GO.

Due to the fact that spherical panoramas are displayed on the monitor screen with distortions (aberrations), it is not advisable to display them in printed form, or in the form of graphics files.

In our opinion, the most promising is the demonstration of spherical photopans using existing virtual reality devices. For example, Oculus GO can be used as a demonstration device in police work. The display of this hardware supports a resolution of 2560 × 1440 dpi, which allows displaying a high-quality image for each eye. The device is autonomous and works without connecting to a computer.

Virtual reality is understood as a realistic model of the surrounding space, implemented by computer means [9, 10]. The most important feature of this environment is the illusion of its direct presence for the user [11, 12]. Practical experience has shown that the feeling of being present to the user largely depends on how detailed and naturally the captured images of the virtual space look. Modern devices of virtual reality demonstration provide a minimal delay between turning the user's head and the visual display of the panorama thanks to modern sensor-based tracking systems, which provides the effect of being present in the virtual space.

The process of demonstrating a "virtual scene" is to use software for the presentation of spherical panoramic images, and is carried out in several stages. We give a diagram of the work using the free software CoSpaces Maker.

1. You need to register and create a new project in your account.
2. In the new project, it is necessary to create several separate pages and upload spherical panoramas of the scene as backgrounds.
3. To ensure movement around the "virtual scene" of the panorama, one should combine the transition script between them, using a conventional marker, for example, a lightning mark. By holding the view on the marker, the user will move to a pre-recorded point of the virtual space.
4. In order to demonstrate forensically significant objects and traces on a large scale, it is necessary to add traditional photographs of such objects. The position of these objects in the photo panorama should be marked with markers. In the case when the user holds the view on such a marker, a transition occurs to the traditional photograph of the object, providing an opportunity to take a close-up view of it. It is possible to use several photographs of the same object from different angles.
5. When the user's head is rotated, other markers are displayed, in accordance with their location on the scene.
6. When the demonstration mode is turned on (this function is built-in on the Oculus GO), all objects observed by the user are displayed in real time using a projector on an interactive whiteboard, which is illustrative, for example, to discuss the situation at the crime scene by participants of the investigation team.

5 Prospects for Using in the Teaching Method of Fixing the Situation of the Crime Scene with Modern Panoramic Cameras, as Well as Visualization of the Captured Information Using Virtual Reality Devices

It should be noted that the considered technologies have significant potential for their use in training. In Russia, in accordance with the provisions of the Federal State Educational Standard of Higher Education dated December 29, 2016 No. 45038 in the direction of preparation of 40.03.01 Jurisprudence, clause 7.3: "Requirements for the material, technical and educational support of the undergraduate program. ... In the case of the use of e-learning, distance learning technologies, it is allowed to replace specially equipped premises with their virtual counterparts, allowing students to master the skills and abilities foreseen by their professional activities" [13].

The presence of the necessary skills of a specialist photographer engaged in the creation of spherical photo panoramas, as well as knowledge of the features of modern technology is important for obtaining high-quality photographs. High-resolution spherical photo panoramas can be used to visually demonstrate the scene of an incident in order to effectively investigate crimes.

6 Implementation and Results

It is important to note that at the present stage of development of science and technology, judicial photography has great potential for spherically fixing the situation of the scene. Existing technologies provide storage, exchange, and visual prompt demonstration of this visual information in its natural form.

Of particular importance is the demonstration of spherical photographs of the scene using virtual reality devices, for example, in order to re-examine, in the case of newly discovered circumstances, the transfer of materials to another judicial investigator, and, of course, for a visual representation during the court session.

The development of an information network of law enforcement data transmission opens up broad prospects for ensuring the rapid exchange of "virtual photographic tables" of real incidents in order to demonstrate them in virtual reality, which will increase the speed and quality of solving crimes committed, for example, by one person or group of people in different regions and countries.

7 Conclusion

Thus, the use of the method of recording of the crime scene with modern panoramic cameras, as well as visualization of the captured information using virtual reality devices, will allow solving a wide range of police tasks about the interpretation and presentation of evidence.

References

1. Grant, H.: Social Crime Prevention in the Developing World. Exploring the Role of Police in Crime Prevention, p. VI, 51. Springer, Heidelberg (2015). https://doi.org/10.1007/978-3-319-13027-9
2. Jahankhani, H.: Cyber Criminology, p. X, 357. Springer, Heidelberg (2018). https://doi.org/10.1007/978-3-319-97181-0
3. Savona, E.U.: Crime and Technology. New Frontiers for Regulation, Law Enforcement and Research, p. XIV, 142. Springer, Dordrecht (2004). https://doi.org/10.1007/978-1-4020-2924-0
4. LeClerc, B., Savona, E.U.: Crime Prevention in the 21st Century. Insightful Approaches for Crime Prevention Initiatives, p. XIII, 396. Springer, Heidelberg (2018). https://doi.org/10.1007/978-3-319-27793-6
5. Jacobs, C.: Interactive Panoramas. Techniques for Digital Panoramic Photography, p. XIII, 248. Springer, Heidelberg (2004). https://doi.org/10.1007/978-3-642-18665-3
6. The Criminal Code of the Russian Federation of June 7, 1996, No. 63-FZ (as amended on June 27, 2018). https://fzrf.su/kodeks/uk/. Accessed 7 July 2018
7. Federal Law "On Police" of 07.02.2011 N 3-FZ (Ed. 12/19/2016). Article 11
8. Langmann, S., Pick, D.: Photography as a Social Research Method, p. XII, 167. Springer, Singapore (2018). https://doi.org/10.1007/978-981-10-7279-6
9. Jung, T., Claudia tom Dieck, M.: Augmented Reality and Virtual Reality, p. XI, 335. Springer, Heidelberg (2019). https://doi.org/10.1007/978-3-030-06246-0
10. Mihelj, M., Novak, D., Beguš, S.: Virtual Reality Technology and Applications, p. X, 231. Springer, Dordrecht (2014). https://doi.org/10.1007/978-94-007-6910-6
11. Bishop, C.: Pattern Recognition and Machine Learning, p. XX, 738. Springer, New York (2006)
12. Deng, Z., Neumann, U.: Data-Driven 3D Facial Animation, p. VIII, 296. Springer, London (2008). https://doi.org/10.1007/978-1-84628-907-1
13. Federal State Standard of Higher Education in the direction of training 40.03.01 Jurisprudence. Registered in the Ministry of Justice of Russia on December 29, 2016 No. 45038, paragraph 7.3

System for Automatic Adjustment
of Intelligent Controller Parameters

Vladimir Ignatyev$^{(\boxtimes)}$, Viktor Soloviev, Denis Beloglazov,
Viktor Kureychik, Alexandra Ignatyeva, and Anastasiia Vorotova

Southern Federal University,
Bolshaya Sadovaya Str., 105/42, 344006 Rostov-on-Don, Russia
vova3286@mail.ru

Abstract. The goal of work is the development of a method for automatically creating a fuzzy controller based on measured data from a control system with a classic controller. To achieve the goal, a mathematical model of the control system in the MatLab Simulink environment has been developed, which allows saving the input and output data of the controller in the modeling process. Analysis of the data series allows determining the parameters of the clusters and the membership functions of the input and output variables of the fuzzy controller. According to the results of clustering, a fuzzy controller rule base can be easily obtained. At the same time, the rule base can have redundant rules not only due to complete duplication, but also due to rules with the same antecedents, but different consequent ones, which leads to uncertainty. To eliminate uncertainty, an algorithm for reducing the rule base has been proposed, based on the selection of redundant rules and the definition of the cluster center corresponding to the new consequent. The authors have developed software that allows to obtain source data from the classical controllers, perform clustering and determination of membership functions parameters, create a rule base, perform its reduction and create a fisstructure for further verification and analysis. The results of modeling a control system with a synthesized fuzzy controller before and after the reduction of the rule base are given.

Keywords: Control system · Clustering · Fuzzy rules · Rule-base reduction · Fuzzy inference system

1 Introduction

Modern control systems of technical objects are characterized by the introduction of intelligent technologies in the control process. There are a large number of methods for the synthesis of fuzzy, neural network and neuro-fuzzy controllers. The trend towards the intellectualization of technical systems is associated with the broader capabilities of such controllers in processing the task signals, parrying disturbances and ensuring the best indicators of the quality of transients. In particular, fuzzy controllers endow the system with robust properties and help reduce overshoot and regulation time in the control process of technical objects.

© Springer Nature Switzerland AG 2019
A. G. Kravets et al. (Eds.): CIT&DS 2019, CCIS 1084, pp. 226–242, 2019.
https://doi.org/10.1007/978-3-030-29750-3_18

The process of developing fuzzy controllers is in some way creative and is carried out with the involvement of experts who are well aware of the properties and behavior of a technical object. There are several problems that arise when creating fuzzy controllers. Firstly, there are difficulties in determining the type, number, and parameters of the membership functions of linguistic variables. Triangular membership functions are most commonly used because of the reduction in computational costs when determining degrees of membership. The number of terms in linguistic variables term-sets is recommended to choose in the range from 5 to 7. This is due to the complexity of the further development of the rule base by the expert. Indeed, if the fuzzy controller input linguistic variables will contain a term-set with 11 terms, then the full fuzzy rule base must contain $11 \times 11 = 121$ rules. It will be difficult for an expert to make such a rule base and not to be mistaken.

Secondly, the fuzzy rule base must satisfy the property of completeness. The expert needs to carefully draw up a rule base so that there are no duplicate rules, which will lead to its redundancy. At the same time, it is necessary to track that there are no rules in the database with the same antecedent, but different sequential, which leads to uncertainty. Incomplete rule bases can be used in the control of a technical object in the case of complete confidence that there will not be a situation in which for the input signals of a fuzzy controller, there will be no rule in its base.

This paper discusses the method of synthesis of fuzzy controllers without the involvement of experts, based on measurements of input and control signals in the control system of a technical object. It is shown how to synthesize a fuzzy controller with higher control quality indicators using measurements of signals in a system with a classical controller. At the same time, the fuzzy rule base is formed automatically and reduced in case of its redundancy. The main advantage of the presented method is independence from the number of input and output controller signals and the power of linguistic variables term-sets. The parameters of the membership functions are determined automatically during the synthesis of the controller.

2 Literature Review

The interest of the world community to intellectual control technologies is constantly increasing. Consider the main publications related to the automation of fuzzy controllers synthesis process and determine the main directions of research in this area.

In [1], a method of control rules automatic generation for a fuzzy controller (FC) was proposed for solving classification problems on the basis of a statistical sample containing objects numerical attributes of certain classes. A distinctive feature of the method is the ability to generate the minimum number of rules needed to effectively solve the tasks. This is achieved by analyzing the importance of individual rules with the subsequent assignment to them of appropriate weights and combining with similar in meaning, already existing rules.

In [2], a method of the FC rule base generation based on a genetic algorithm (GA) was proposed. The statistical dataset used in the synthesis of a fuzzy controller is similar to that used in [1]. A distinctive feature of the method is the use of the integral fitness function for a genetic algorithm, which allows a comprehensive assessment of the FC parameters and the accuracy of its work. Compared to the results of [1], the number of fuzzy rules is reduced several times (3 vs 8) while simultaneously increasing the accuracy of work.

In [3], as in [2], GA was used for the synthesis of a fuzzy controller. A distinctive feature of the proposed method is the absence of the need to preliminarily determine the FC parameters by the user and the use of a modified data clustering algorithm.

In [4], a method of control rule base generation for a fuzzy controller based on cluster analysis and a genetic algorithm was proposed. A distinctive feature of the method is that it is possible to control the process of adjusting FC parameters in order to prevent the phenomenon of retraining.

[5] is close in its content to [2–4]. Its main difference lies in the used type of the genetic algorithm fitness function and the method of chromosome formation based on the FC parameters.

In [6], a method of the FC parameters optimizing was proposed, which allows reducing the number of applied control rules. Its main idea is to reduce the term-sets of FC linguistic variables (LV) to a simpler form (decrease in number) with the subsequent verification performed transformation efficiency. In the event that a new type of LV is more preferable a situation is possible when several rules become the same and can be combined into one.

In [7], a method of FC synthesis based on the classical controllers working results such as PID, PI, PD, etc. was proposed. The idea of the method is to create a training sample of the input-output type of the classical controller and use it to train the Takagi-Sugeno fuzzy model. The proposed method involves human participation in the term-sets forming process of FC LV.

In [8], the proposed GA allows you to automatically create a base of FC control rules. The main difference of the method from analogs [3–6, 11] is the use of a special metric characterizing the degree of inconsistency of the control rules. The use of this metric as one of the evaluation function components of the generated solutions makes the final result more optimal.

In [9], a method of FC control rules number optimizing is presented. Its main idea is the identification and subsequent unification of conflicting rules, i.e. having the same parts conditions and different conclusions. The method does not improve the efficiency of the FC in any way and this is its main drawback.

In [10], a method for solving the problem of synthesizing the fuzzy controller rule base with its subsequent analysis and optimization based on GA is presented. The method differs from the previously considered using two ways of encoding FC parameters and, accordingly, the structure of the resulting chromosomes. The way of correction for conflicting rules used in the method is similar to that described in [9] and has similar disadvantages.

In [12], an automatic synthesis method of a fuzzy controller parameters based on a genetic algorithm is presented. A distinctive feature of the method lies in the evaluation function of the generated solutions, which consists of two parts. The first characterizes the degree of model error and is calculated as the difference between the desired and actual values. This makes it necessary to have a priori information about the desired quality of FC work, expressed as a specific numerical value. The second part is designed to control the tuning term-sets process of LV, making it more orderly.

In [13], a method of search and removing incorrect control rules of a fuzzy controller is presented. The idea of the method lies in the fact that each rule is assigned a certain weight, which determines the degree of its fallacy (inconsistency). When analyzing the base of control rules, the specified weight is adjusted. When it reaches a certain threshold, the rules are removed.

In [14], a method of reducing the number of fuzzy controller control rules was proposed. The principle of removing conflicting rules is similar to that stated in [13]. Also, the method is able to detect and combine control rules similar to each other.

In [15], a method of the FC automated synthesis from a numerical data set was proposed. A distinctive feature of the method is the ability to find a stable balance between accuracy, correctness, number and logical transparency of the generated control rules. As in [13, 14], the optimization of the FC rules base is carried out on the basis of the value of a special weighting coefficient, called the redundancy index, which characterizes the measure of difference between the rules from each other, as well as their effect on the final result.

As can be seen from the review of the articles, there are several automatic synthesis areas of fuzzy controllers that are associated with the use of genetic algorithms, clustering methods and their hybridization. The use of genetic algorithms allows to obtain good results in the synthesis of fuzzy controllers, but using this approach to supplement and expand already existing rule bases in the operation real mode of the control system, as well as supplementing the existing input samples is difficult. In addition, when changing the parameters of the membership functions, correction of fuzzy controller synthesis algorithms may be required.

In contrast to genetic algorithms, the use of clustering methods allows obtaining results for different source data and when changing the parameters of linguistic variables. Modern clustering methods allow to form clusters according on statistical data, regardless of a given number of clusters, or even define them yourself. It should also be noted the high speed of fuzzy controllers automatic synthesis methods using clustering methods.

3 The Proposed Method

This paper uses the results obtained by the authors as a result of research on the development of the theoretical foundations and methods for automatically setting the parameters of intelligent control systems for technical objects with a priori uncertainty [16–18]. Consider the implementation stages of the proposed method for the fuzzy controllers synthesis, the sequence of which is shown in Fig. 1.

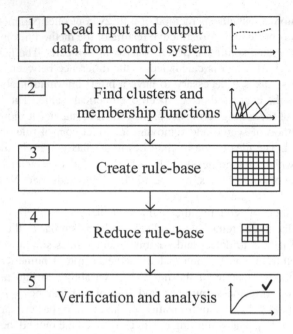

Fig. 1. Stages of the fuzzy controllers synthesis method

Obtaining source data of input and output control signals in a system with a classic controller. These data can either be removed from the real object in the process of its operation, or to develop a mathematical model of the control system and get them in the simulation process. In this paper, studies were performed using a mathematical model of a control system developed in the MatLab Simulink environment. The simulation scheme is shown in Fig. 2.

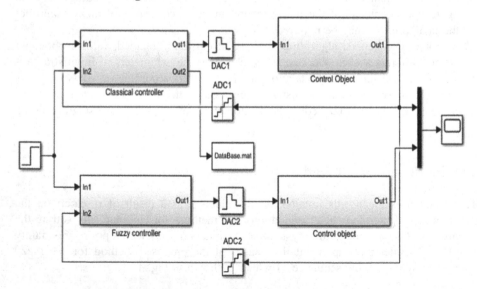

Fig. 2. Control system simulation scheme

The simulation scheme contains two identical control objects, one of which is controlled by a classic controller, and the second – a fuzzy controller. The input of the system receives a setting effect. The input and output data of the classical controller during the simulation are written to the DataBase.mat file.

Clusters formation and membership functions parameters determination for the linguistic variable. As a result of stage 1, data series Rd for the input and output signals of the classical controller have been obtained. For each data series, a linguistic variable Lv is introduced, which is characterized by the set:

$$Lv = \langle N, T, X \rangle, \tag{1}$$

where N is a name of linguistic variable; $T = \{Ti\}$ ($i = \{1, 2, \ldots, m\}$) is a term-set of linguistic variable; X is a domain of elements from T (base set).

The considered method of fuzzy controller synthesis does not involve experts, so the input linguistic variables will automatically name as Inp1, Inp2, ..., InpM, and the output as Out1, Out2, ...OutK according to the number of data series.

The term-set of a linguistic variable is also automatically defined as T = {"1", "2", ..., "m"}, in accordance with a given terms number.

A universal set is determined from a data series, for example, for the InpI input linguistic variable, the universal set is:

$$X = [\min(R_d(\text{InpI})), \max(R_d(\text{inpI}))] = [x_{iMin}, x_{iMax}]. \tag{2}$$

Let determine the values of the linguistic variable N from the term-set T using fuzzy variables Nv:

$$Nv = \langle T_i, X, \mu_i \rangle, \tag{3}$$

where Ti is a name of fuzzy variable; μi is a fuzzy set.

In this paper will consider the triangular membership functions described by the formula [19]:

$$\mu(x, a, b, d) = \begin{cases} 0, & \text{if } x \leq a; \\ \frac{x-a}{d-a}, & \text{if } a < x \leq d; \\ \frac{b-x}{b-d}, & \text{if } d < x \leq b; \\ 0, & \text{if } x > b. \end{cases} \tag{4}$$

As can be seen from (4), require the definition of parameters a, b, d for each membership function μ. If i = 1, a = c, and if i = m, b = d and if the intersection point of the neighboring membership functions at $\mu = 0{,}5$, then the term-set T will have the form shown in Fig. 3.

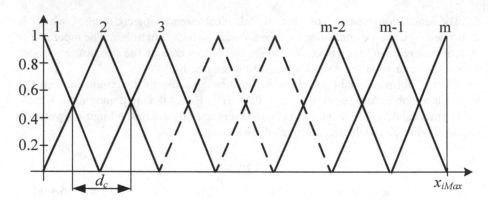

Fig. 3. Term-set T

It is required to match the data from Rd with the elements of the term-set T. To do this, select the cluster cj $\in$ C in the universal set X. Let the number of clusters be determined by the number of terms in the term-set of the linguistic variable. Then the cluster size dc can be determined by the formula:

$$d_c = \frac{x_{iMax} - x_{iMin}}{m - 1}, \tag{5}$$

and the cluster intervals by the formula:

$$
\begin{aligned}
c_1 &= [x_{iMin}, \; x_{iMin} + d_c/2), \\
c_j &= [\max(c_{j-1}), \max(c_{j-1}) + d_c), \; (j = 2, 3, \ldots m - 1), \\
c_m &= [\max(c_{j-1}), \max(c_{j-1}) + d_c/2].
\end{aligned} \tag{6}
$$

Knowing the clusters intervals it is not difficult to determine the centers of clusters cd and the a, b, d parameters of the membership functions:

$$
\begin{aligned}
c_{d1} &= \min(c_1), \quad a_1 = \min(c_1), \quad b_1 = \min(c_1), \quad d_1 = c_{d1}, \\
c_{dj} &= \frac{\max(c_j) - \min(c_j)}{2}, \quad a_j = c_{d(j-1)}, \quad b_j = c_{dj}, \quad d_j = c_{d(j+1)}, \quad j = 2, 3, \ldots, m - 1, \\
c_{dm} &= \max(c_m), \quad a_m = c_{d(m-1)}, \quad b_m = c_{dm}, \quad d_m = c_{dm}.
\end{aligned} \tag{7}
$$

In the case of other membership functions, for example, trapezoidal [20] with

$$
\mu(x, a, b, d, e) = \begin{cases}
0, & \text{if } x \leq a; \\
\frac{x-a}{b-a}, & \text{if } a < x \leq b; \\
1, & \text{if } b < x \leq d; \\
\frac{e-x}{e-d}, & \text{if } d < x \leq e; \\
0, & \text{if } e \leq x.
\end{cases} \tag{8}
$$

the calculated expressions will be:

$$c_{dj} = \frac{\max(c_j) - \min(c_j)}{2}, \quad \forall j,$$
$$a_1 = \min(c_1), \quad b_1 = \min(c_1), \quad d_1 = \max(c_1), \quad e_1 = c_{d2},$$
$$a_j = c_{d(j-1)}, \quad b_j = \min(c_j), \quad d_j = \max(c_j), \quad e_j = c_{d(j+1)},$$
$$a_m = c_{d(m-1)}, \quad b_m = \min(c_m), \quad d_m = \max(c_m), \quad e_m = \max(c_m).$$

$$(9)$$

For other types of membership functions, their parameters are determined according to the same principle.

Creating a rule base. After determining the cluster parameters and membership functions, the Rd analysis is performed in order to determine whether the signal values belong to a particular cluster. To do this, the cycles iterate over the values of the data series and the elements of the set C and determine whether the data falls into clusters, as shown in Fig. 4.

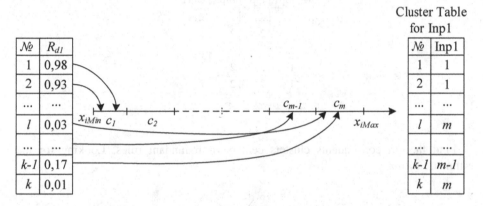

Fig. 4. Determining whether source data belongs to clusters

After all data series have been determined to belong to clusters, the formation of a rule base is performed in several stages.

At first the cluster tables of all input and output variables are combined into a single table, as presented in the Table 1.

Table 1. Combined cluster table

№	Inp1	...	InpM	Out1	...	OutK
1	1	...	...	...	...	...
2	1	...	...	...	...	...
...	...	...	...	...	...	...
l	m	...	...	...	...	...
...	...	...	...	...	...	...
$k-1$	$m-1$	...	...	...	...	...
k	m	...	...	...	...	...

Then, the table is searched for identical rows, one of which is left, and the rest are deleted to eliminate duplication of rules.

Thus, at this stage, a rule base is formed. It should be borne in mind that she may be insufficient or excessive. An insufficient rule base may be due to the small dimension of the Rd source data series or with a large number of linguistic variables terms. The redundant rule base may be due to the presence of rules in the table, in which the antecedent is the same and the sequential is different. In this case, the rule base reduction will be required.

Rule base reduction. The reduction of the rule base is aimed at eliminating its redundancy due to the rules with the same antecedent but different sequential. Consider the reduction procedure by example. Let the controller with three input and one output signals in the table of rules have redundant rules presented in the Table 2.

Table 2. Redundant rules in the rule base

№	Inp1	Inp2	Inp3	Out1
...	...	...	...	...
...	1	2	2	1
...	...	...	...	...
...	1	2	2	3
...	1	2	2	7
...	...	...	...	...

Find the cm consequents clusters centers of redundant rules. Looking for the arithmetic mean:

$$s = \frac{\sum_{j=1}^{p} c_{mj}}{p}, \tag{10}$$

where p is the number of redundant rules with the same antecedent.

Then determine the belonging of s to the cluster from Cout and set its number to the consequent in one of the redundant rules, and delete the rest. It should be noted here that if there are two redundant rules and their consequents correspond to adjacent terms, then the use of expression (10) leads to uncertainty. For this case, it is necessary to enter an additional term with parameters into the output linguistic variable term-set (see Fig. 5):

$$a_j = c_{d(j-1)}, \quad b_j = s, \quad d_j = c_{d(j+1)}, \tag{11}$$

where $j - 1, j + 1$ are cluster centers that form the consequent membership functions of redundant rules.

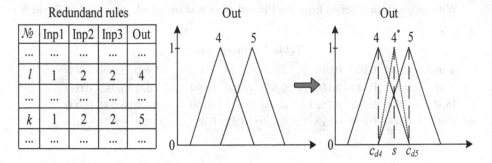

Fig. 5. Combining redundant rules in a rule base

Performing this procedure for all sets of redundant rules obtain a reduced rule base.

4 Results

The study of the proposed synthesis method of fuzzy controllers was carried out in MatLab environment, in accordance with the scheme in Fig. 2. As a control object, a DC motor with a mathematical model in the form of a transfer function was chosen:

$$W(s) = \frac{15.4}{(0.03s + 1)(0.2s + 1)}. \tag{12}$$

B The PI controller with the parameters KP = 0.221, KI = 1.1 was used as a traditional controller.

The signal given at the system input is shown in Fig. 6.

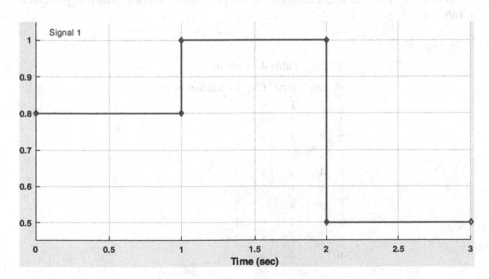

Fig. 6. Input signal for the control system

With its use, a data series from the PI controller was obtained, presented in Table 3.

Table 3. Source data

Time, c	0,000	0,008	0,016	...	1,016	1,024	1,032	...	2,960	2,968	2,976	...
Inp1	0,177	0,181	0,180	...	0,097	0,096	0,094	...	0,032	0,032	0,032	...
Inp2	0,800	0,787	0,752	...	0,188	0,175	0,160	...	0,000	0,000	0,000	...
Out1	0,000	0,006	0,013	...	0,050	0,052	0,053	...	0,029	0,029	0,029	...

The study was performed for input linguistic variables with five terms and an output with nine terms. For each signal, linguistic variables were generated with the following parameters:

Lv1 = $\langle$"Inp1", {"1", "2", "3", "4", "5"}, [−0.5, 0.8]$\rangle$;
Lv2 = $\langle$"Inp2", {"1", "2", "3", "4", "5"}, [0.0, 0.0597]$\rangle$;
Lv3 = $\langle$"Out", {"1", "2", "3", "4", "5", "6", "7", "8", "9"}, [−0.0484, 0.1809]$\rangle$;

The following cluster intervals are determined:

C1 = {[−0.5, −0.3375], [−0.3375, −0.0125], [−0.0125, 0.3125], [0.3125, 0.6375], [0.6375, 0.8]};
C2 = {[0, 0.0075], [0.0075 0.0224], [0.0224, 0.0373], [0.0373, 0.0522], [0.0522, 0.0597]};
C3 = {[−0.0484, −0.0340], [−0.0340, −0.0054], [−0.0054, 0.0233], [0.0233, 0.0519], [0.0519, 0.0806], [0.0806, 0.1093], [0.1093, 0.1379], [0.1379, 0.1666], [0.1666, 0.1809]}.

As a result of source data clustering, a rule base was compiled, which is presented in Table 4.

Table 4. Rule base

№	Inp1	Inp2	Out	Redundant rules
1	5	1	9	
2	5	2	9	
3	5	3	9	
4	4	3	8	1
5	4	3	7	1
6	4	4	7	
7	3	4	7	2
8	3	4	6	2
9	3	4	5	2
10	2	4	4	

(continued)

Table 4. (*continued*)

№	Inp1	Inp2	Out	Redundant rules
11	3	4	4	2
12	3	5	6	3
13	3	5	5	3
14	1	5	1	
15	1	4	1	
16	2	4	2	
17	2	3	2	4
18	2	3	3	4
19	2	3	4	4
20	3	3	4	

The last column of Table 4 lists four groups of redundant rules, therefore, the rule base requires reduction. As a result of the reduction procedure described above, a reduced rule base is obtained, presented in the Table 5.

Table 5. Reduced rule base

№	Inp1	Inp2	Out
1	5	1	9
2	5	2	9
3	5	3	9
4	4	3	7^*
5	4	4	7
6	3	4	6
7	2	4	3
8	3	5	5^*
9	1	5	1
10	1	4	1
11	2	3	3
12	3	3	4

As you can see, the resulting rule base does not contain redundant rules. It should be noted that it is incomplete, as it must contain 25 rules. Based on the obtained data, the FIS structure is generated and opened in the Fuzzy Logic Toolbox of MatLab environment, the parameters of which are shown in Fig. 7.

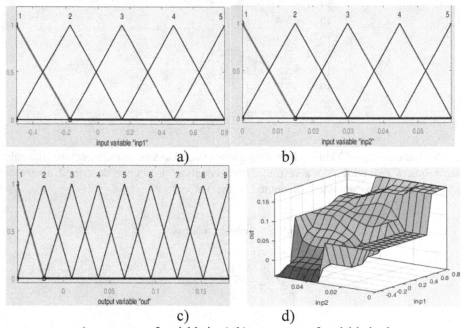

a) – term-set of variable inp1, b) – term-set of variable inp2,
c) – term-set of variable out, d) – fuzzy inference surface

Fig. 7. Parameters of the generated fuzzy controller

As can be seen from the results, the automatic generation of a fuzzy controller was successful. The generated structure was connected in the simulation circuit (see Fig. 2) and the whole system was simulated. The simulation results in comparison of fuzzy and PI-controller are presented in Fig. 8.

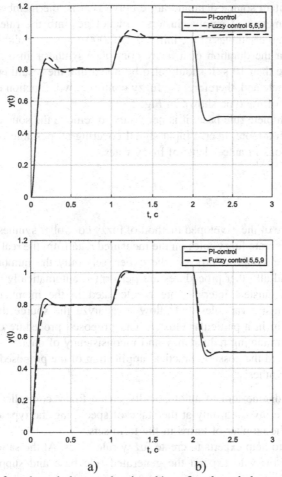

a) – before the rule base reduction, b) – after the rule base reduction

Fig. 8. Simulation results

5   Discussion

The simulation results show that in the case of the controller synthesis with a non-reduced rule base, the transients occur with overshoot, and in the third stage, with an input effect of 0.5, they are unsatisfactory. After reduction, the rule base was reduced from 20 to 12 rules and two additional terms 5* and 7* were added (see Table 5) in the term-set of the output variable to eliminate uncertainty. After reduction, the synthesized fuzzy controller provides a transition process without overshoot and with less control time compared to the classical controller.

The authors' experiments showed a slight improvement in the control quality indicators with an increase in the number of terms in linguistic variables term-sets. In addition, with an increase in the number of terms, situations may arise where some clusters do not contain source data and are empty. That is, the membership functions based on the parameters of empty clusters will not get into the rule base a priori. Experiments with large samples of the initial data (2000 and more values for each input signal) showed that the duration of a fuzzy controller synthesis in the MatLab environment is no more than 10 s. It should also be noted that the resulting rule base (see Table 5) is incomplete and, therefore, the fuzzy controller will function effectively with a step input signal of the type shown in Fig. 5.

To obtain a complete rule base, it is necessary to remove the source data from the control system with a more diverse input signal covering all possible combinations of membership functions in antecedents of fuzzy rules.

6   Conclusion

A distinctive feature of the developed method of fuzzy controller synthesis is the ability to automatically generate fuzzy rules on the measured data from the real control system or its model. In the synthesis process, the expert sets only the number of linguistic variables terms, and all other procedures are performed automatically.

The calculated clusters intervals are recalculated in the membership functions parameters of linguistic variables and allow to analyze the source data in order to identify membership in a particular cluster. The proposed procedure of reducing the rule base allows eliminating redundancy and inconsistency of data.

It should be noted the possible practical application of the proposed method of the fuzzy controllers synthesis:

- using as a standalone tool to automatically create fuzzy controllers. At the same time, experts are involved only at the stage of specifying the type of membership functions and the number of terms in the term-sets.
- using as a tool to help experts to create fuzzy rule bases. At the same time, experts have the opportunity to expand the generated rule base and supplement it with missing rules.
- using as a tool for the research of technical systems control principles. Using the proposed approach, fuzzy controllers are synthesized based on the Mamdani algorithm, so the expert can study the generated rule base and deal with the peculiarities of the control system.

The advantage of the proposed approach is that it allows you to formalize and synthesize fuzzy controllers on the basis of input signals that are difficult to formalize for experts. For example, experts can easily synthesize fuzzy controllers on the basis of error signals and its derivative, but the error integral is hardly formalized with the help of expert knowledge.

Future research by the authors is aimed at developing an algorithm for automatically determining the type and number of linguistic variables membership functions, as well as at studying clustering methods for clusters with unset boundary intervals.

Acknowledgements. This work was supported by Grant of the Russian Foundation for Basic Research (№ 18-38-00711) at the Southern Federal University, State task of subordinate educational organizations for the implementation of the project on the theme «Development, research and producing of an automated control system for the training of microwave devices». Project PP0708-11/2017-09 (Task № 8.3795.2017/PP), Grant of the Russian Foundation for Basic Research (№ 18-29-22019/18).

References

1. Chen, Y.-C., Wang, L.-H., Chen, S.-M.: Generating weighted fuzzy rules from training data for dealing with the Iris data classification problem. Int. J. Appl. Sci. Eng. **4**(1), 41–52 (2006)
2. Castellano, G., Fanelli, A.M.: A staged approach for generation and compression of fuzzy classification rules. In: The Ninth IEEE International Conference on Fuzzy Systems, FUZZ IEEE 2000, vol. 1 (2000)
3. Surmann, H., Selenschtschikow, A.: Automatic generation of fuzzy logic rule bases: examples I. In: Proceedings of the NF2002: First International ICSC Conference on Neuro-Fuzzy Technologies, Cuba, 16–19 January 2002, p. 75 (2002)
4. Al-Shamma, M., Abbod, M.F.: Automatic generation of fuzzy classification rules using granulation-based adaptive clustering. In: IEEE Systems Conference (SysCon 2015) (2015). https://doi.org/10.1109/syscon.2015.7116825
5. Al-Shamma, M., Abbod, M.F.: Automatic generation of fuzzy classification rules from data. In: Recent Advances in Neural Networks and Fuzzy Systems (2014). ISBN 978-1-61804-227-9
6. Wang, W.-J., Yen, T.-G., Sun, C.-H.: GA-based fuzzy rules generation. ECE 6505 (2014)
7. Dmitry, K., Dmitry, V.: An algorithm for rule generation in fuzzy expert systems. In: Proceedings of the 17th International Conference on Pattern Recognition, ICPR 2004, vol. 1 (2004). https://doi.org/10.1109/ICPR.2004.1334061
8. García, F., Martinez, P., Paz, V.: Rule base reduction on a self-learning fuzzy controller. In: EUSFLAT-ESTYLF Joint Conference (1999)
9. Xiong, N., Litz, L.: Reduction of fuzzy control rules by means of premise learning – method and case study. Fuzzy Sets Syst. **132**, 217–231 (2002)
10. Gegov, A., Sanders, D., Vatchova, B.: Aggregation of inconsistent rules for fuzzy rule base simplification. Int. J. Knowl.-Based Intell. Eng. Syst. **21**(3), 135–145 (2017)
11. Akhand, M.A.H., Asaduzzaman, M.D., Murase, K.: Optimization of fuzzy logic controllers with rule base size reduction using genetic algorithms. Int. J. Inf. Technol. Decis. Making (2015). https://doi.org/10.1142/S0219622015500273
12. Amjad Hossain, Md., Shill, P.C., Sarker, B., Murase, K.: Optimal fuzzy model construction with statistical information using genetic algorithm. Int. J. Comput. Sci. Inf. Technol. (IJCSIT) **3**(6), 241–257 (2011)
13. Ciliz, M.K.: Rule base reduction for knowledge-based fuzzy controllers with application to a vacuum cleaner. Expert Syst. Appl. **28**, 175–184 (2005)
14. Sambariya, D.K.: Power system stabilizer design using compressed rule base of fuzzy logic controller. J. Electr. Electron. Eng. **3**(3), 52–64 (2015)
15. Dutu, L.-C., Mauris, G., Bolon, P.: A fast and accurate rule-base generation method for Mamdani fuzzy systems. https://hal.archives-ouvertes.fr/hal-01756513. Accessed 2 Apr 2018

16. Ignatyev, V.V., Kureychik, V.M., Spiridonov, O.B., Ignatyeva, A.S.: Metod gibridnogo upravleniya na osnove adaptivnoy sistemy neiro-nechetkogo vyvoda. Izvestiya YuFU. Tehnicheskie nauki. [The method of hybrid control based on the adaptive system of neuro-fuzzy inference. Bulletin of SFedU. Technical science], 9(194), 2302 p., pp. 124–132. ITA SFedU Publishing House, Taganrog (2017). ISSN 1999-9429. (in Russian)

17. Ignatyev, V.V., Kovalev, A.V., Spiridonov, O.B., Ignatyeva, A.S., Bozhich, V.I., Boldyreff, A.S.: Model of adaptive system of neuro-fuzzy inference based on PI- and PI-fuzzy-controllers. In: Proceedings of SPIE 10799, Emerging Imaging and Sensing Technologies for Security and Defence III; and Unmanned Sensors, Systems, and Countermeasures, 107990Y, 4 October 2018, vol. 10799 107990Y-1. SPIE Security + Defence, Berlin, Germany (2018). https://doi.org/10.1117/12.2513302

18. Ignatyev, V.V., Spiridonov, O.B.: Gibridnyi algoritm formirovaniya bazy pravil nechetkogo regulyatora. Izvestiya YuFU. Tehnicheskie nauki. Tematicheskiy vypusk «Radioelektronnye I infokommunikacionnye tehnologii, sistemy I seti». [Hybrid algorithm for formation the fuzzy controller rule base. Bulletin of SFedU. Technical science. Thematic issue "Radio-electronic and infocommunication technologies, systems and networks"], 11(172), pp. 177–186. ITA SFedU Publishing House, Taganrog (2015). (in Russian)

19. Yasin, Md., Abeda, S., Khodadad, A.: Comparison of fuzzy multiplication operation on triangular fuzzy number. IOSR J. Math. (IOSR-JM) 12(4), 35-41 (2016). Ver. I, e-ISSN 2278-5728, p-ISSN 2319-765X

20. Rahmani, A., Hosseinzadeh, F., Rostamy-Malkhalifeh, M., Allahviranloo, T.: A new method for defuzzification and ranking of fuzzy numbers based on the statistical beta distribution. Adv. Fuzzy Syst. 2016, 8, Article ID 6945184 (2016). http://dx.doi.org/10.1155/2016/6945184

Intelligent Technologies in Social Engineering. Data Science in Social Networks Analysis and Cybersecurity

Error Classification and Human Performance Level Analysis of "Hiyari-Hatto" Incidents Caused by Maintenance Engineers

Nobuhiko Mizusawa[1](✉) and Takako Nakatani[2]

[1] FUJITSU FSAS INC., Tokyo, Japan
nobby@fujitsu.com
[2] The Open University of Japan, Chiba, Japan
tinakatani@ouj.ac.jp

Abstract. Modern information systems are becoming increasingly standardized and are adopting multi-vendor system design and products. Fault tolerant designs have also been implemented and the information systems and the products themselves are becoming redundant. Consequently, in recent years, whilst incidents affecting the entire information system are suppressed, the maintenance operations are getting complicated and human errors, that have not been assumed conventionally, have occurred.

In this paper, we focus on "Hiyari-Hatto" incident data. "Hiyari-Hatto" is an incident which has the possibility to cause an accident but fortunately does not in actuality. We collected "Hiyari-Hatto" incidents experienced by maintenance engineers for information systems and classified them into similar product groups. We have applied error classification by James Reason's theory and the human performance level by Jens Rasmussen's theory. The analysis of the product groups could reveal the differences in the incidents that occurred for each product group. As a result, in order to prevent incidents due to human error, it was concluded that it is effective to devise measures based on the error type and the human performance level for each product group.

Keywords: "Hiyari-Hatto" incident · Human error · SRK model

1 Introduction

The safety of people's living has been preserved [1] by an important social system which is controlled and managed by information systems and a wide variety of equipment with built-in computer systems. This was the same in the era of main-frame computers (1980s). However, recent systems have become more dependent on social systems and computer systems. Information systems are incorporated in most services of social systems and is considered to have changed to tight coupling structures with other systems. Furthermore, modern information systems are becoming freely available and standardized, system designs and products by multi-vendors are being adopted, and the maintenance processes are getting more complicated. Also, in order to practice fault-tolerance design, the reduplication (multiplexing) of the information systems and the products themselves are advancing.

© Springer Nature Switzerland AG 2019
A. G. Kravets et al. (Eds.): CIT&DS 2019, CCIS 1084, pp. 245–257, 2019.
https://doi.org/10.1007/978-3-030-29750-3_19

As mentioned above, we focus on incidents that affect information systems. While the incidents for information systems have been reduced, the maintenance operation is getting complicated and unexpected human-errors are occurring. We need to develop measures to reduce serious maintenance incidents. In the airline industry, where accidents can lead to huge damage, preventive measures are applied by analyzing the incidents [2], having understood the multiple causes of the accidents.

According to the data on the frequency of potential accidents explained in Heinrich's law of "Industrial Accident Prevention" [3], for every accident that causes a major injury, there are 29 accidents that cause minor injuries and 300 accidents that cause no injuries. It is called "Hiyari-Hatto" or "near-miss" as a synonym. "Hiyari-Hatto" or "near-miss" are incidents which have the possibility to cause an accident but fortunately does not in actuality. In total, 330 similar accidents caused by the same person. Therefore, by collecting, classifying, analyzing the reported near-miss incidents experienced by maintenance engineers and implementing the measures to reduce those near-misses, the incidents in the information system can be reduced [4, 5].

The purpose of this research is to reveal the causes of human errors and near-miss incidents by analyzing the records of real near-miss incidents, with the objective of reducing the number of incidents.

2   Related Work

Rasmussen [6, 9] classified human performance into three different levels: skill-based behavior, rule-based behavior and knowledge-based behavior (SRK model). The main features of these three types of performance levels are shown below.

1. Skill-based behavior: This behavior is mostly unconsciously and automatically applied when performing highly-skilled tasks.
2. Rule-based behavior: This behavior is intentionally applied when performing familiar tasks, by pattern-matching the predefined rules and procedures.
3. Knowledge-based behavior: This behavior is intentionally applied when solving new problems, in which solutions are created by relying on one's own knowledge and new investigation.

Reason [7–9] classified human-errors into three different types: slips, lapses, and mistakes. Slips and lapses represent the unintentional failure to carry out an action despite proper planning. Mistakes represent the failure to achieve the intended results as a result of improper planning, even though the actions were carried out as planned. Comparing to slips and lapses, mistakes appear in the higher-order of the thinking process.

1. Slips: The failure of visible actions. Usually with attention and perception failure
2. Lapses: The failure of internal events. An example of memory failure
3. Mistakes: The failure in the higher-order of the planning process.

James Reason related this SRK model and error classification to the execution-level failure (failure due to unintended actions) and the planning-level failure (failure due to intended actions). The skill-based mistakes, which are included in execution-level failure, are classified into the following two types.

1. Skill-based mistakes
   - Slips: action failure
   - Lapses: memory failure.

The mistakes included in planning-level failure are further divided into two sub-categories: rule-based and knowledge-based mistakes. Rule-based mistakes refer to failures such as applying the right rule to the wrong event, applying an inappropriate rule, or not applying a good rule. Knowledge-based mistakes are failures when a series of prepared solutions cannot help to solve the problems and the support from other people is required.

2. Mistakes
   - Rule-based mistakes: deviation from appropriate procedures
   - Knowledge-based mistakes: lacking knowledge regarding the problem.

Upon using these error classification and SRK model, and analyzing the records of near-miss incidents by maintenance engineers, it is necessary to redefine these terms.

3 Research Approach

3.1 Research Subject

The survey target in this paper covers the records of near-miss incidents experienced by hardware maintenance engineers who do maintenance and support businesses at customers' premises. The main tasks included in the records of near-miss incidents are the examples of the experience during repairing customers' machines that broke down, the experience during installing new products for customers, and the experience during performing periodical maintenance. However, the system engineers (SE), who support the information system from the software viewpoint, and the near-miss incidents of the people in the construction department, who install hardware, are not considered as maintenance engineers' work, so have been excluded from this research.

3.2 Human-Error Classification Policy

In order to classify the near-miss incidents experienced by maintenance engineers with reference to the three types of error classification discussed in the Related Work in Sect. 2 (slips, lapses, mistakes) and the SRK model, this paper will redefine the relationship between error classification and the SRK model as below.

1. Skill-based mistakes: The unintentional mistakes that occurred even though maintenance engineers correctly followed the maintenance manuals and operation manual.

- Slips: Mainly due to events such as failure of parts replacing/cleaning, failure of consideration to other devices, failure of status confirmation, etc., slips occurred as a result of incomplete actions (skills) of maintenance engineers.
- Lapses: Mainly due to events such as failure of parts replacing/cleaning failure, failure of status confirmation, failure of confirmation test, etc., lapses occurred as a result of forgetting, or misunderstanding, which related to the actions (skills) of maintenance engineers.

2. Mistakes: Failures caused by procedures, methods, and operations which were determined by maintenance engineers to perform maintenance work.

- Rule-based mistakes: Errors caused by mistakes in maintenance manuals or operation manuals. Also included are mistakes due to non-reference to maintenance and operation manuals by highly skilled engineers.
- Knowledge-based mistakes: Failures caused by manuals not being standardized, also, failures as a result of deciding the work items in procedures basing solely on maintenance engineers' knowledge and experience.

The report contents will be classified based on these definitions.

3.3   The Classification Policy of Near-Miss Incidents Reports

The following methods will be carried out in this research. Reading the data of near-miss incidents reports, dividing the data by incidents into small classification, medium classification, large classification, and analyzing the data with comparable practical size for the analysis target.

3.4   The Classification Policy of Target Data

The reported 7,000 cases of near-miss incidents experienced by hardware engineers from September 2015 to December 2016 will be used in this research. However, since the features and work contents are different for each product, the similar products are classified into seven product groups: server group, printer group, ubiquitous group, PC group, storage group, network group, and mainframe group.

In this paper, in order to clarify the difference of human-error situations by product group, the near-miss incidents reports (around 2,800 cases) of the server group and the printer group, with different product characteristics, will be the focus of analysis.

The definitions and features of the server group and printer group are shown below. The numbers in parentheses are the numbers of near-miss incidents.

1. Server group (around 1,300 cases). The server group is mainly composed of electronic parts (CPU, memory, HDD, etc.) and operating systems (OS) for X86 (IA server), UNIX server. It is connected to multiple peripheral devices and is used as the core of the system.
2. Printer group (around 1500 cases). The printer group is mainly composed of mechanical parts, electronic parts, and consumption articles for printers connected to a network or a direct system, and is connected to the system as one of the peripheral devices for usage.

4   Analysis Result

4.1   Skill-Based Mistakes – Slips (Action Failure)

Table 1 shows the circumstances and the main causes of skill-based mistakes due to slips. There are six types of slips: 1. Failure of parts replacing/cleaning, 2. Failure of consideration to other devices, 3. Failure of configuration, 4. Failure of problem isolation, 5. Failure of confirmation test, 6. Failure of status confirmation. The details of each circumstance are as follows.

1. Failure of parts replacing/cleaning. The ratio is 59.5% for the server group, and 88.4% for the printer group, which means that about 30% more near-miss incidents occurred in the printer group. The unintentional (1) Loosely connected spare parts and/or cables and (2) Dropping spare parts and/or screws make up 68.4% of the main causes, compared with 37.4% is for server group. Compared to the server group, the printer group seems to be affected by due to increased levels of mounting and removing parts and the use of mechanical parts.
2. Failure of consideration to other devices. The ratio is 16.0% for the server group and 2.6% for the printer group, which indicates the proportion of server group is higher. The main causes are the unintentional (1) Cable disconnection of other devices and (2) Contacting other devices. Comparing the server group to the printer group, since there are many cases where multiple machines are installed in racks at a data center or are connected to other products by cables such as storage/network products, it is not necessary to take much consideration in the printer group, but it is necessary to take into consideration the environmental factors used in the server group.
3. Failure of the configuration. The ratio is 11.3% for a server group and 0.8% for the printer group, which indicates the proportion of server group is higher. The main causes are the unintentional (1) Mistakes in setting values and (2) Incorrect input or selection. Compared to printer group, server group seems to be affected by the fact that it has more items to be set-up.
4. Failure of problem isolation. The ratio is 5.4% for server group and 4.2% for printer group. The main cause is (1) Lacking of confirmation of test results, etc.
5. Failure of confirmation test. The ratio is 4.0% for server group and 3.4% for printer group. The main causes are the unintentional (1) Operation mistakes (power supply, OS activation, etc.) and (2) Mistakes in paper for test printing, etc. Compared to the printer group, since the server group has complicated system operations, failures can occur due to the inconsistency between the behaviors expected by maintenance engineers and the actual operation. For example, the power button was pressed to confirm the operation, but the OS unexpectedly rebooted.
6. Failure of status confirmation. The ratio is 3.8% for a server group and 0.7% for the printer group, which indicates the proportion of server group is higher. The main causes are the unintentional (1) Differences in taking notes during setup and (2) Lacking status confirmation (related to required tools). Compared to the printer group, the server group seems to be affected by the fact that there are so many items needed to be copied in the setup/information of to-be-maintained products before maintenance engineers start their maintenance work.

Table 1. The circumstances and the main causes of Skill-based mistakes – slips

Circumstances	Main causes	Server group		Printer group	
1. Failure of parts replacing/cleaning	(1) Loosely connected spare parts and/or cables	22.6%	59.5%	37.0%	88.4%
	(2) Dropping spare parts and/or screws (including near misses)	14.8%		31.4%	
	(3) Damaging and/or corrupting spare parts	5.2%		9.3%	
	(4) Wrong/missing manuals, tools and/or spare parts	4.7%		0.8%	
	(5) Others	12.2%		10.0%	
2. Failure of consideration to other devices	(1) Cable disconnection of other devices	13.6%	16.0%	1.9%	2.6%
	(2) Contacting other devices	1.9%		0.4%	
	(3) Others	0.5%		0.3%	
3. Failure of configuration	(1) Mistakes in setting value	6.1%	11.3%	0.5%	0.8%
	(2) Incorrect input or selection	2.8%		0.3%	
	(3) Operation mistakes	1.2%		0.0%	
	(4) Others	1.2%		0.0%	
4. Failure of problem isolation	(1) Lacking of confirmation of test results	4.9%	5.4%	4.0%	4.2%
	(2) Others	0.5%		0.1%	
5. Failure of confirmation test	(1) Operation mistakes (Power, OS boot, etc.)	3.1%	4.0%	0.3%	3.4%
	(2) Mistakes in paper for test printing	0.0%		1.3%	
	(3) Others	0.9%		1.7%	
6. Failure of status confirmation	(1) Differences in taking notes during setup	1.2%	3.8%	0.1%	0.7%
	(2) Lacking of status confirmation (related to required tools)	0.9%		0.0%	
	(3) Others	1.6%		0.5%	
Total		100.0%		100.0%	

4.2 Skill-Based Mistakes – Lapses (Memory Failure)

Table 2 shows the circumstances and the main causes of skill-based mistakes due to lapses. There are four types of lapses: 1. Failure of parts replacing/cleaning, 2. Failure of configuration, 3. Failure of confirmation test, 4. Failure of status confirmation. The details of each circumstance are as follows.

1. Failure of parts replacing/cleaning. The ratio is 45.9% for the server group and 56.6% for the print group, which means the proportion of the printer group is higher than the server group by 10%. The main causes are the unintentional (1) Forgetting to install/remove parts, (2) Skipping manuals, and (3) Misidentification of spare parts and broken parts. Compared to the server group, the printer group is more prone to error due to when the disassembling procedures and cleaning procedures of parts replacement task get complicated.
2. Failure of configuration. The ratio is 28.6% for a server group and 22.6% for print group, which means there are few differences among different product groups in term of configuration failures. The main causes are the unintentional (1) Forgetting to do setup and (2) Skipping manuals; in both groups, the ratio of 1. Forgetting to do setup are quite high.
3. Failure of confirmation test. The ratio is 15.1% for the server group, and 9.6% for printer group. The main causes are the unintentional (1) Forgetting to collect test media, (2) Forgetting to operate, and (3) Forgetting to carry out tests. The similar main cause for the server group and the printer group is forgetting to collect the recovery media of CD/DVD or reports etc. used in operation testing after maintenance work.

Table 2. The circumstances and the main causes of Skill-based mistakes – Lapses

Circumstances	Main causes	Server group		Printer group	
1. Failure of parts replacing/cleaning	(1) Forgetting to install/remove parts	34.6%	45.9%	48.4%	56.6%
	(2) Skipping manuals	3.8%		2.1%	
	(3) Misidentification of spare parts and broken parts	3.8%		1.6%	
	(4) Others	3.8%		4.5%	
2. Failure of configuration	(1) Forgetting to do setup	28.1%	28.6%	22.3%	22.6%
	(2) Skipping manuals	0.5%		0.3%	
3. Failure of confirmation test	(1) Forgetting to collect test media	5.9%	15.1%	5.6%	9.6%
	(2) Forgetting to operate	2.7%		3.7%	
	(3) Forgetting to carry out tests	5.4%		0.3%	
	(4) Others	1.1%		0.0%	
4. Failure of status confirmation	(1) Forgetting to take notes during setup	2.7%	7.0%	1.3%	3.2%
	(2) Forgetting to collect test media	3.8%		0.0%	
	(3) Others	0.5%		1.9%	
5. Others	(1) Forgetting belongings at customer site	1.6%	3.2%	5.3%	8.0%
	(2) Forgetting ejection/insertion of media	1.6%		2.7%	
Total		100.0%		100.0%	

4. Failure of status confirmation. The ratio is 7.0% for server group and 3.2% for printer group. The main causes are unintentionally (1) Forgetting to take notes during setup and (2) Forgetting to collect test media. Compared to the printer group, the server group has a specific case of forgetting to collect customer media (CD/DVD, etc.).

4.3 Rule-Based Mistakes – Mistakes

Table 3 shows the circumstances and the main causes of rule-based mistakes. There are five types of rule-based mistakes: 1. Failure of parts replacing/cleaning, 2. Failure of status confirmation, 3. Failure of problem isolation, 4. Failure of setup, 5. Failure of confirmation test. The details of each circumstance are as follows.

1. Failure of parts replacing/cleaning. The ratio is 57.2% for the server group and 65.8% for the printer group. The main causes are (1) Mistakes in parts installation/cable route due to not reading the manual, (2) Manual defects, and (3) Mistakes during work due to not reading the manuals. Compared to the server group, the printer group has more mistakes caused by not reading the manuals ((1), (3)). Maintenance engineers are supposed to refer to manuals in rule-based work, but as they get more skillful, more mistakes can occur when engineers switch to skill-based.
2. Failure of status confirmation. The ratio is 19.1% for the server group and 9.2% for the printer group. The main causes are (1) Wrong instructions from others, (2) Mistakes during work due to not reading the manuals and (3) Mistakes in system configuration management. Compared to the printer group, since the server group usually has to use different information (installation, setup, etc.) for each system whilst working, mistakes could occur due to complicated information management.
3. Failure in problem isolation. The ratio is 11.2% for the server group and 12.5% for the printer group. The main causes are (1) Wrong instructions from others (2) Mistakes during work due to not reading the manuals. Compared to the server group, the printer group tends to isolate (the faults) according to experience.
4. Failure of configuration. The ratio is 4.7% for the server group and 8.6% for the printer group. The main cause is (1) Mistakes during work due to not reading the manuals.
5. Failure of the confirmation test. The ratio is 5.3% for the server group and 1.7% for the printer group. The main cause is (1) Mistakes during work due to not reading the manuals, similar to 4. Failure of configuration. Compared to the printer group, the server group seems to be affected by the complicated confirmation tests.

Table 3. The circumstances and the main causes of Rule-based mistakes – mistakes

Circumstances	Main causes	Server group		Printer group	
1. Failure of parts replacing/cleaning	(1) Mistakes in parts installation/cable route due to not reading the manual	32.3%	57.2%	46.7%	65.8%
	(2) Manual defects	16.7%		11.7%	
	(3) Mistakes during work due to not reading the manuals	4.2%		6.7%	
	(4) Others	4.0%		0.8%	
2. Failure of status confirmation	(1) Wrong instructions from others	3.5%	19.1%	6.4%	9.2%
	(2) Mistakes during work due to not reading the manuals	7.7%		1.7%	
	(3) Mistakes in system configuration management	6.0%		0.3%	
	(4) Others	1.9%		0.8%	
3. Failure of problem isolation	(1) Wrong instructions from others	8.8%	11.2%	4.2%	12.5%
	(2) Mistakes during work due to not reading the manuals	2.3%		8.3%	
4. Failure of configuration	(1) Mistakes during work due to not reading the manuals	4.4%	4.7%	8.6%	8.6%
	(2) Others	0.2%		0.0%	
5. Failure of confirmation test	(1) Mistakes during work due to not reading the manuals	4.7%	5.3%	1.4%	1.7%
	(2) Others	0.7%		0.3%	
6. Others	(1) Others	2.6%	2.6%	2.2%	2.2%
Total		100.0%		100.0%	

4.4 Knowledge-Based Mistakes – Mistakes

Table 4 shows the circumstances and main causes of knowledge-based mistakes. There are three types of knowledge-based mistakes: 1. Failure of problem isolation, 2. Failure of status confirmation, 3. Failure of consideration to other devices. Knowledge-based does not apply to deal with new incidents and rule-based (manuals and work procedures) and is categorized as cases involving judgement based on the knowledge and experience of maintenance engineers.

1. Failure of problem isolation. The ratio is 33.9% for the server group and 52.5% for the printer group. The main causes are (1) Device mistakes and (2) Mistakes in parts arrangement. A case of this failure is where there is a possibility that correct results cannot be obtained as a result of implementing fault isolation and dealing with the problems based on the judgment of maintenance engineers. For example, compared to the printer group, when the server group is installed in multiple servers like in a

data center, it is difficult to identify devices, etc. there are reasons other than devices which can also cause near-miss incidents.

2. Failure of status confirmation. The ratio is 29.5% for the server group and 25.0% for the printer group. The main causes are (1) Lacking of detailed confirmation for customers, (2) Lacking collaboration with others and (3) Lacking consideration for connected devices. In (1) Lacking of detailed confirmation for customers, near-miss incidents occur due to insufficient communication with customers and authorized people before carrying out maintenance work about the explanation of work contents and login credentials to be used.

3. Failure of consideration to other devices. The ratio is 29.1% for the server group and 7.5% for the printer group. The main causes are (1) Operating another device, (2) Unplugging the cable of another devices, and (3) Insufficient consideration to the connecting devices. It can be seen that the ratio of failures is high in the server group, and failures are likely to occur when in a data center and multiple similar devices exist.

Table 4. The circumstances and the main causes of Knowledge-based mistakes – mistakes

Circumstances	Main causes	Server group		Printer group	
1. Failure of problem isolation	(1) Device mistakes	21.1%	33.9%	32.5%	52.5%
	(2) Mistakes in parts arrangement	12.3%		17.5%	
	(3) Others	0.4%		2.5%	
2. Failure of status confirmation	(1) Lacking of detailed confirmation for customers	18.1%	29.5%	5.0%	25.0%
	(2) Lacking of collaboration with others	4.0%		0.0%	
	(3) Lacking of consideration for connection devices	0.9%		15.0%	
	(4) Others	6.6%		5.0%	
3. Failure of consideration to other devices	(1) Operating another device	14.1%	29.1%	0.0%	7.5%
	(2) Unplugging the cable of another devices	8.4%		7.5%	
	(3) Insufficient consideration to the connecting devices	5.7%		0.0%	
	(4) Others	0.9%		0.0%	
4. Others	(1) Others	7.5%	7.5%	15.0%	15.0%
Total		100.0%		100.0%	

5 Discussions

In respect to maintenance work of engineers, experienced near-missed incidents were classified into a server group and a printer group, and error contents were analyzed against each circumstance using the error classification and SRK model.

Table 5 shows the circumstances and the main causes of the Server Group and the Printer Group incidents. The ratio of slips in skill-based errors is 33.5% for the server group and 48.9% for the printer group; this means half of the number of near-miss incidents occurred in the printer group. When considering the countermeasures against human-errors in the printer group, it appeared to be effective to focus on slips, especially, category 1. Failure of parts replacing/cleaning, which is as high as 43.3%. A feature of the printer group is that it has more tasks requiring the installation and replacement of mechanical parts than in the server group. In order to perform these tasks in a reliable way, training using actual equipment can be effective. Also, it is necessary to improve the products by making them less prone to maintenance related errors, and improvements such as using fewer screws and adding cable lock mechanisms to prevent unintentional loosening of cables.

The ratio of lapses in skill-based errors is 14.6% for the server group and 24.8% for the printer group; especially the category of 1. Failure of parts replacing/cleaning, which is as high as 14.0%. The problem of forgetting is likely to occur during the task of parts replacing/cleaning, so it can be effective to take notes in the middle of maintenance work and to use measures to prevent forgetting, such as marking and labeling when removing spare parts, screws, and connectors that have similar shapes.

As a countermeasure for slips and lapses in skill-based errors, and to prevent near-miss incidents based on common errors, manuals, and educational materials could be developed using AR (Augmented Reality) [10] and MR (Mixed Reality) [11] technology.

The ratio of rule-based errors classified as mistakes is 33.9% for the server group and 23.7% for the printer group. The proportions of 1. Failure of parts replacing/cleaning in both the server group and the printer group are quite high. Although maintenance engineers should refer to manuals, they often misjudge that work can be done based on skill-based as they tend to rely on their experience, which is gained from absorbing knowledge (procedures) and skills (skill-up) after repeating the same tasks many times. When mistakes occur in this case, they can be regarded as near-miss incidents, which is the same in both the server group and the printer group. Some effective countermeasures for this problem are simplified manuals, consideration of portability, and safety training.

The ratio of knowledge-based errors classified as mistakes is 17.9% for the server group and 2.6% for the printer group. The knowledge errors in server group can be broken down to 2. Failure of problem isolation, 4. Failure of status confirmation, and 5. Failure of consideration to other devices. In the server group, since the products are connected to peripheral devices as a whole system, server maintenance work is performed by the maintenance engineers' knowledge-base. Thus, when mistakes occur, they can be considered as near-miss incidents, as customer environmental factors, system factors, etc. are not applied to rule-based (formalization).

The measures of compiling system information other than product-specific information, the customers' installation environment into the database, and updating information by authorized people are considered to be effective.

Table 5. The circumstances and the main causes of the server group and the printer group

Circumstances	Server group					Printer group				
	Slips	Lapses	Mistakes		Total	Slips	Lapses	Mistakes		Total
	Skill-based	Skill-based	Rule-based	Knowledge-based		Skill-based	Skill-based	Rule-based	Knowledge-based	
1. Failure of parts replacing/cleaning	20.0%	6.7%	19.4%	-	46.1%	43.3%	14.0%	15.6%	-	72.9%
2. Failure of problem isolation	1.8%	-	3.8%	6.1%	11.7%	2.0%	0.0%	3.0%	1.4%	6.4%
3. Failure of configuration	3.8%	4.2%	1.6%	-	9.6%	0.4%	5.6%	2.0%	-	8.0%
4. Failure of status confirmation	1.3%	1.0%	6.5%	5.3%	14.0%	0.3%	0.8%	2.2%	0.7%	3.9%
5. Failure by lack of consideration to other devices	5.4%	-	-	5.2%	10.6%	1.3%	-	-	0.2%	1.4%
6. Failure of confirmation test	1.3%	2.2%	1.8%	-	5.4%	1.6%	2.4%	0.4%	-	4.4%
Others	-	0.5%	0.9%	1.3%	2.7%	-	2.0%	0.5%	0.4%	2.9%
Total	33.5%	14.6%	33.9%	17.9%	100.0%	48.9%	24.8%	23.7%	2.6%	100.0%

6 Conclusion

The ultimate goal of this research is to reduce human-errors that occur during the maintenance of information systems. It is suggested in this paper that by analyzing each product group using aliasing and human performance level can be effective to safely maintain a complicated information system.

In the analysis of the results of this research, whilst procedures are established and made into manuals, when maintenance engineers carry out work without referring to the manual and at their own judgment, the near-miss incidents that occur are regarded as mistakes and rule-based errors. However, when maintenance engineers carry out tasks that they are skillful at/familiarized with, the work errors that occur are considered slips or skill-based errors. In the future, it is necessary to examine human-independent classification methods such as the systemization of error classification.

References

1. Information-technology Promotion Agency Japan(IPA) Homepage. http://www.ipa.go.jp/files/000004556.pdf. Accessed 27 Feb 2019
2. Miyagi, M.: Daijiko no yochō o saguru [Exploring the Sign of a Major Accident]. Kodansha, Tokyo (1998)

3. Heinrich, W., Petersen, D., Roos, N.: Industrial Accident Prevention, 5th edn. Original English edition Published by McGraw-Hill (1980). Japanese Translation Edition Published by Kaibundo Publishing Co., Ltd, Japan (1982)
4. Kudou, T., Tsukuda, Y.: Serious failure prevention activity of information systems utilizing incident information. In: Proceedings of the National Conference of the Society of Project Management Spring 2009. The Society of Project Management (2009)
5. Jones, S., Kirchsteiger, C., Bjerke, W.: The importance of near miss reporting to further improve safety performance. J. Loss Prev. Process Ind. **12**, 59–67 (1999)
6. Rasmussen, J.: Skills, rules and knowledge; signals, signs, and symbols, and other distinctions in human performance models. IEEE Trans. Syst. Man Cybern. **SMC-13**(3), 257–266 (1983)
7. Reason, J.: Managing the Risks of Organization Accidents. Original English Edition Published by Ashgate Publishing Limited (1997). Japanese Translation Edition Published by JUSE Press, Ltd., Japan (2001)
8. Reason, J., Hobbs, A.: Managing Maintenance Error: A Practical Guide. Original English Edition Published by Ashgate Publishing Limited (2003). Japanese Translation Edition Published by JUSE Press, Ltd., Japan (2005)
9. Fire and Disaster Management Agency Homepage. https://www.fdma.go.jp/html/new/pdf/161129_kentou/2-2.pdf,last. Accessed 27 Feb 2019
10. Hara, H., Kuwabara, H.: Innovation in on-site work using smart devices and augmented reality technology. Fujitsu Sci. Tech. J. (FSTJ) **51**(2), 12–19 (2015)
11. Konstantin, N.: Mixed reality in maintenance. Soutěžní přehlídka studentských a doktorských prací FST 2019 (2019). ISBN 978-80-261-0860-3

Assessing the Response Timeliness to Threats as an Important Element of Cybersecurity: Theoretical Foundations and Research Model

Sergey Skryl'[1], Mikhail Sychev[1], Artem Sychev[1],
Tatyana Mescheryakova[2], Anna Ushakova[1], Elvira Abacharaeva[1],
and Elena Smirnova[1(✉)]

[1] Bauman Moscow State Technical University, Moscow, Russia
evsmirnova@bmstu.ru
[2] Voronezh Institute of the Ministry of Internal Affairs of Russia,
Voronezh, Russia

Abstract. Currently, the theory of information security provides effective measures to ensure the protection of information in computer systems (CS), cyber-physical systems, etc. However, there is a need to develop specific elements of mathematical representation of indicators of timely response to threats to the security of computer information to support intelligent systems of cybersecurity. The article substantiates the need to take into account the moments of threats and the beginning of a response to their manifestations in the formalized representation of processes using the classical theory of probability. Theoretical conclusions are tested on the example of malware flow, for this purpose a functional model of anti-virus protection mechanisms is developed.

Keywords: Theory of information security · Parameter's formalization · Characteristics of the process · Threats · Protection mechanisms · The flow of malware

1 Introduction

The theory of information security, related to the study of the effectiveness of measures to counteract negative factors, provides a variety of options for mathematical description of the negative factors affecting the state of information security (is), which can be divided into three large clusters/groups: technical impact [1], information impact [2] and psychological effects [3].

The questions of modeling of counteraction to negative influence in the information sphere, main models as a system of differential equations and the experiments based on the developed models which have been implemented with the usage of the Analogic simulation platform show the considerable dependence between the agent models and the system-dynamic models which showed a high degree of agreement between them and with statistical data [2–4].

In work [3] based on a method of the cluster analysis typological groups in a selective set of objects with a various average time of distribution of information,

© Springer Nature Switzerland AG 2019
A. G. Kravets et al. (Eds.): CIT&DS 2019, CCIS 1084, pp. 258–269, 2019.
https://doi.org/10.1007/978-3-030-29750-3_20

influences are allocated. The models of information impact propagation have been successfully tested. Models allow to predict information impacts and information counteractions, to reproduce different scenarios of their dynamics, to control corresponding processes.

In this article, the authors propose the results of the study of the mathematical model of the indicator of timely response to security threats. The use of the classical approach to assessing the probability of timely response to threats to the security of computer information is justified. The scientific hypothesis of an extremely high assessment of the timeliness of response to threats to the security of computer information based on existing models is proposed.

2 The Classical Approach to Assessing the Probability of Timely Response to Threats to the Security of Computer Information

Mathematical representation of the indicator of timely response to threats to the security of computer information is based on the following conditions:

$$D = 1 \text{ in case of } \tau_{(p)} \leq \tau_{(y)} \tag{1}$$

and

$$D = 0 \text{ in case of } \tau_{(p)} > \tau_{(y)}, \tag{2}$$

where D – the parameter of the timeliness of implementation of the functions of protection of computer information;

$\tau_{(p)}$ – the response time to a threat to the security of computer information;

$\tau_{(y)}$ – the time of existence of this kind of threat.

Let's assume that condition (1) is a mandatory requirement for the implementation of information security procedures against threats in computer networks (CN) cording to the security of information. Otherwise, the condition (2) is realized and the threat is implemented.

In general, both values in the inequality (1) are random, therefor it's execution is a random event also. The probability of this event is the average number of situations in which during the existence of a threating process in CN. It is possible to perform the functions of the threat's detection and suppression of its source as a relative to the total number of attempts to implement such threats according to the following equation

$$P\left(\tau_{(r)} \leq \tau_{(t)}\right) = \frac{1}{J} \sum_{j=1}^{J} \xi_j,$$

where

$$\xi_j = \begin{cases} 1, & in\ case\ \tau_{(r)j} \leq \tau_{(t)j}\,; \\ 0, & in\ other\ case \end{cases}$$

$\tau_{(r)j}$ – the response time of the information protection mechanisms in the CNs on the j-the realization of threats to its security;

$\tau_{(t)j}$ – threat lifetime on the j-the realization of threats;

J – total number of information security threat implementations during the time interval $[t_{(b)}, t_{(d)}]$ of the carried on the research of the proper network.

Taking into account the above, the following expression takes place for the indicator of CN's timely response to threats to information security in CN:

$$D = P(\tau_{(r)} \leq \tau_{(t)}), \tag{3}$$

Based on the above justification of indicator (3) timeliness of response to the threats to the information security, it is obvious that the underlying condition of its formal presentation is

$$\tau_{(r)} \leq \tau_{(et)}, \tag{4}$$

It is easy to see that the indicator D does not take into account the moments of occurrence of threats and the moment of the beginning of a response to their manifestations. So the indicator D is correct when there is an instant response to a threat. Formally, this situation can be represented as

$$\Delta t = t_{(br)} - t_{(bt)} \approx 0, \tag{5}$$

where $t_{(br)}$ – the time when the threat response began;

$t_{(bt)}$ – the time at which the threat starts.

Naturally, the fulfillment of condition (4) in practice is an improbable event, and models based on the interpretation of this condition as a condition of timely response to threats to the security of information in the COP have low adequacy.

3   The Scientific Hypothesis of an Extremely High Assessment of the Timeliness of Response to Threats to the Security of Computer Information

3.1   The Hypothesis Description

In order to substantiate theoretically the need to develop new models with other conditions, alternative to the condition (5), authors formulate and prove the following scientific hypothesis.

The lack of consideration of the times of threat's occurrence and/or the times of the reaction's starts to the threat's manifestations in the formalized mathematical description of the representation of the reaction's processes to the information security threats in computer systems leads to the overestimation of a reaction timeliness' assessment.

Since it is obvious that the adequacy of the indicator's assessment apparatus of threat's response time to the security of information depends on the possibility of a formal presentation of the conditions connected to the response time of such kind of threats, a number of important provisions are further considered. Each position is accompanied by mathematical proof.

3.2   Formal Representation of the Probability Distribution Function and Theorem Provement

In order to prove the hypothesis written in Subsect. 3.1, let's use the formal representation of the probability distribution function as the probability of the condition:

$$\tau(r) > \tau(t), \tag{6}$$

the opposite to the condition (4):

$$P(\tau(r) \leq \tau(t)) = 1 - P(\tau(r) > \tau(t)) = 1 - \int_0^{\overline{\tau}_{(r)}} f_{(y)}(x)dx, \tag{7}$$

where $f(t)$ – the density distribution of the random variable of time $\tau(t)$ of the threat existence;

$\overline{\tau}_{(r)}$ - the average value of the random variable of time $\tau(r)$ of the responding to a threat.

Let's write expression (7) for two options:

Option 1, corresponding to the condition (5) ($\Delta t = 0$),

$$\int_0^{\overline{\tau}_{(r)} + 0} f_{(t)}(x)dx$$

Option 2, alternative to the condition (5) ($\Delta t > 0$):

$$\int_0^{\overline{\tau}_{(r)} + \Delta t} f_{(t)}(x)dx.$$

From the integral definition, it is obvious that its value for the option 2 is bigger than the value for the option 1, so the value $P1(\tau(r) \leq \tau(t))$ for the option 1 exceeds the value $P2(\tau(r) \leq \tau(t))$ for the option 2, what authors wanted to prove.

3.3   Consequence of Theorem

The following parameter can serve as a characteristic of the adequacy of the methodological apparatus for assessing the indicators of timely response to threats to the security of information in computer networks:

$$\Delta D = \int\limits_{0}^{\bar{\tau}_{(r)}+\Delta t} f_{(t)}(x)dx - \int\limits_{0}^{\bar{\tau}_{(r)}+0} f_{(t)}(x)dx. \tag{8}$$

Thus, it is obvious that the adequacy of the methodological apparatus for assessing the indicators of timely response to threats to the security of information depends on the possibility of formalized representation of the conditions for timely response to such threats. Accordingly, the accuracy of intelligent cybersecurity systems depends on the mathematical apparatus used to describe the processes of attacks and respond to them.

Let's consider a number of theoretical propositions.

3.4   Theoretical Proposition and Provement #1

Proposition #1. The condition (4) is a necessary only, but not sufficient condition for the formal presentation of the situation in a timely response to threats to information security.

In order to prove the proposition #1, authors present possible options for fulfilling the condition (4) (Figs. 1, 2 and 3).

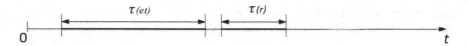

Fig. 1. The option, when the threat is not detected.

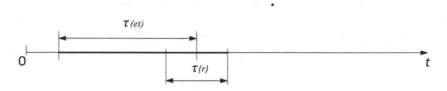

Fig. 2. The option, when the threat is detected, but there is no timely response to the threat.

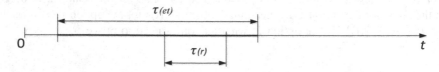

Fig. 3. The option, when the threat is detected, and there is a timely response to the threat.

From the Figs. 1, 2 and 3 it follows that the necessary and sufficient conditions for the formal presentation of all situations in a threat timely response to the information security are the conditions:

$$t_{(bt)} < t_{(br)}, \tag{9}$$

$$t_{(br)} < t_{(br)} + \tau_{(et)}, \tag{10}$$

$$t_{(br)} + \tau_{(r)} \le t_{(bt)} + \tau_{(et)}. \tag{11}$$

As it follows from the Figs. 1, 2 and 3, the physical meaning of the condition (4) has only the interpretation, presented in Fig. 3.

3.5   Theoretical Proposition and Provement #2

Sufficient conditions for the formal presentation of the situation when there is a timely response to the information security threats are the conditions that interpret both the relationship: (1) between the duration of the threat and the duration of the response, and (2) between the moments of the threat's appearance and its detection.

In order to prove the proposition #2, let us present possible relations between the duration of the information security threat, the duration of the threat response, the moment of the threat occurrence and the moment of its detection, corresponding to the situation of timely response to information security threats (Fig. 4.).

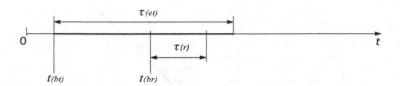

Fig. 4. The situation of timely response to information security threats.

3.6   Theoretical Proposition and Provement #3

To determine the parameters t(bt), τ(et), t(br) and τ(r) you need to use two-dimensional space.

The proof of this proposition is based on the formal presentation of the situation of timely response to the threat of risk-free information as a situation that depends on two processes:

- the process of implementing the threat and
- the process of implementing the mechanism of information protection.

The characteristic of the first process is the time interval [t(bt), t(bt) + τ(et)], as well as the characteristic of the second process – is a time interval [t(br), t(br) + τ(r)].

This allows to separate the areas of condition's definition (9)–(11) and to separate the area of joint fulfillment of these conditions to be represented in a two-coordinate system (Figs. 5, 6, 7 and 8).

3.7   Theoretical Proposition and Provement #4

There is an analytical representation of the probability of conditions (9)–(11).

In order to prove this proposition, let us use the similarity of the formal representation of the probability distribution function and the probability of the conditions (9) to (11):

$$P\big(t_{(bt)} < t_{(br)}, t_{(br)} < t_{(bt)} + \tau_{(t)}, t_{(br)} + \tau_{(r)} \le t_{(bt)} + \tau_{(t)}\big). \tag{12}$$

Taking into account the region Ω of these conditions' existence presented in Fig. 8, the probability (12) can be represented as a probability of belonging to a random event of the region Ω:

$$P\big(t_{(bt)} < t_{(br)}, t_{(br)} < t_{(bt)} + \tau_{(t)}, t_{(br)} + \tau_{(r)} \le t_{(bt)} + \tau_{(t)}\big) = P(\Omega).$$

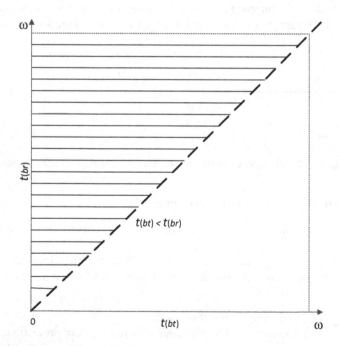

Fig. 5. The graph interpretation of the definition area for the condition (9).

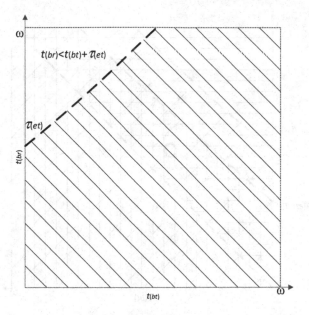

Fig. 6. The graph interpretation of the definition area for the condition (10).

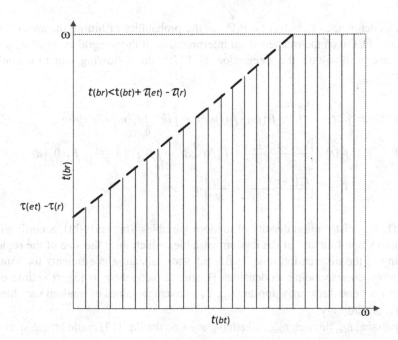

Fig. 7. The graph interpretation of the definition area for the condition (11).

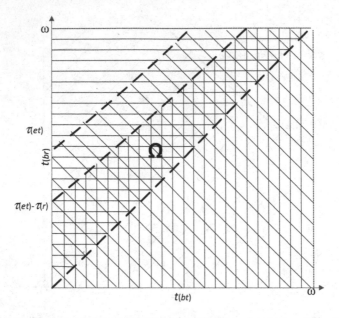

Fig. 8. The graph interpretation of the definition area for the condition (12).

Let us define the characteristic $P(\Omega)$ as the probability of hitting the area occupied by the area Ω. Given the mathematical interpretation of the integral as an area bounded by the integrand within the integration of $P(\Omega)$, the following equation could be written:

$$
\begin{aligned}
P(\Omega) &= \int\limits_0^\alpha dt \cdot \int\limits_0^{t+\bar{\tau}_{(t)}-\bar{\tau}_{(r)}} f_1(\omega) \cdot f_2(t)d\omega - \int\limits_0^\alpha dt \cdot \int\limits_0^t f_1(\omega) \cdot f_2(t)d\omega \\
&= \int\limits_0^\alpha f_2(t) \cdot \left[\frac{F_1\left(t+\bar{\tau}_{(t)}-\bar{\tau}_{(r)}\right)}{\beta_1} - F_1(0) \right]dt - \int\limits_0^\alpha f_2(t) \cdot \left[\frac{F_1(t)}{\beta_2} - F_1(0) \right]dt \\
&= \int\limits_0^\alpha f_2(t) \cdot \left[\frac{F_1\left(t+\bar{\tau}_{(t)}-\bar{\tau}_{(r)}\right)}{\beta_1} - \frac{F_1(t)}{\beta_2} \right]dt,
\end{aligned}
\tag{13}
$$

where f1, f2 – distribution density of random variables t(br) and t(bt), accordingly; F1 (x) – distribution function of the random variables which limit the size of the region Ω, according to the distribution law f1; $\beta1$, $\beta2$ –normalization coefficients for truncated distributions corresponding to densities f1 and f2, according to [5]; α – time during which at least one threat may appear; $\bar{\tau}_{(t)}$, $\bar{\tau}_{(r)}$ – average values of random variables $\tau(t)$ and $\tau(r)$, accordingly.

Expressing $t_{(bt)}$ through $t_{(br)}$ and aiming $\alpha \to \infty$ the Eq. (13) could be transformed to

$$
P(\Omega) = \int\limits_0^\infty f_2(t) \cdot \left[\frac{1}{\beta_1} \cdot F_1(t+\bar{\tau}_{(t)} - \bar{\tau}_{(r)}) - \frac{1}{\beta_2} \cdot F_1(t) \right]dt.
\tag{14}
$$

An analytical representation of the probability of conditions (9) to (11) could be obtained if the corresponding distribution laws' expressions for f2(t) and F1(x) will be substituted.

4   Mathematical Model of Timely Response to Virus Attacks' Threats

As an example, a mathematical model of the indicator of timeliness of response to threats of virus attacks was developed, while the analytical representation (14) was used.

To achieve the described aim, the interpretation of the model justified in [6] was performed for this kind of information security threats. At the same time, the flow of malware effects was presented at the time interval of the study as an elementary stream of events with the corresponding properties: stationarity, ordinariness, and absence of aftereffect. The exponential law of the distribution of the lifetime of a virus attack is a consequence of such a mathematical interpretation of the flow of effects as elementary [7].

In its turn, the response time to the virus attacks threats, as a random variable, is a composition of the implementation time of the anti-virus protection individual functions. In accordance with the functional model of anti-virus protection mechanisms presented in [8, 10], the implementation mechanisms have the following functions:

1. Work environment's scanning.
2. Comparison between the memory contents of well-known computer viruses strains using the library of the anti-virus system.
3. Computer viruses' identification.
4. Detection of the working environment integrity violation signs of non-viral origin.
5. Identification of the status of the working environment integrity.
6. Removal of detected viruses.
7. The information recovery in the files which were exposed.
8. Automatic recovery of the working environment exposed to the effects of non-viral origin.
9. Automatic restoration of information processes correctness in the working environment.

The first five of the listed functions make up the procedure for virus attack detection, the other four are the procedures for maintaining the integrity of the working environment by anti-virus tools.

Both in the first and in the second cases, the number of consecutive compositionally related functions, as well as the absence of a dominant value among them, allows us to consider the time of implementation of these mechanisms as a random value having a normal (Gaussian) distribution. This conclusion is based on the provisions of the Central limit theorem of the Probability theory [7] and its interpretation, justified by the authors of the work [9].

Taking into account the above let us transfer the expression (14) in the form of a corresponding integral' solving:

$$P(\Omega) = \int\limits_{0}^{\infty} f_2(t) \cdot \left[\frac{1}{\beta_1} \cdot F_1\left(t + \overline{\tau}_{(a)} - \overline{\tau}_{(n)}\right) - \frac{1}{\beta_2} \cdot F_1(t) \right] dt$$

$$= \frac{1}{2 \cdot \beta_2} \cdot \left(-\exp\left(\frac{\overline{\tau}_{(a)} - \overline{\tau}_{(n)} - \overline{\tau}_{(d)}}{\overline{\tau}_{(d)}} \right) \right) \cdot erf\left(\frac{\left(\overline{\tau}_{(a)} - \overline{\tau}_{(n)} - \overline{\tau}_{(d)}\right) \cdot \overline{\tau}_{(d)} + \sigma^2}{\overline{\tau}_{(d)} \cdot \sigma \cdot \sqrt{2}} \right) \qquad (15)$$

$$+ \frac{1}{2 \cdot \beta_2} \cdot erf\left(\frac{\left(\overline{\tau}_{(a)} - \overline{\tau}_{(n)} - \overline{\tau}_{(d)}\right)}{\sigma \cdot \sqrt{2}} \right) + \frac{1}{2 \cdot e \cdot \beta_1} \cdot erf\left(\frac{\sigma^2 - \overline{\tau}_{(d)}^2}{\overline{\tau}_{(d)} \cdot \sigma \cdot \sqrt{2}} \right) + \frac{1}{2 \cdot \beta_1} \cdot \left(\frac{\overline{\tau}_{(d)}^2}{\sigma \cdot \sqrt{2}} \right),$$

where $\overline{\tau}_{(a)}$ - average duration of virus attack; $\overline{\tau}_{(d)}$, σ - the average value and standard deviation of the random value of the implementation time of the virus attack detection procedure, corresponded to the duration of the time interval t(br) − t(bt) between the time t(bt) of the attack's start and the time t(br) of its detection; $\overline{\tau}_{(n)}$ - the average random value of the implementation time of the working environment integrity maintenance procedure using anti-virus tools;

$$\beta_1 = \frac{1}{2} \cdot \left(1 - erf\left(\frac{\overline{\tau}_{(a)} - \overline{\tau}_{(n)} - \overline{\tau}_{(d)}}{\sigma \cdot \sqrt{2}} \right) \right);$$

$$\beta_2 = \frac{1}{2} \cdot \left(1 + erf\left(\frac{\overline{\tau}_{(d)}}{\sigma \cdot \sqrt{2}} \right) \right);$$

$erf(x) = \frac{2}{\sqrt{\pi}} \int\limits_{0}^{x} e^{-z^2} dz$ – error function, Laplace's function or probability integral [7].

The Indicator (15) of the response timeliness to the virus attacks threats, calculated at typical values of characteristics, is presented in the following (Table 1).

Table 1. Typical values of the researched characteristics.

#	Description	Parameter	Value, minutes
1	The average duration of virus attack	$\overline{\tau}_{(a)}$	$20,0 \pm 2,1$
2	The average time of implementation of procedures for the detection of virus attack	$\overline{\tau}_{(d)}$	$14,2 \pm 0,2$
3	The standard deviation of the time of realization of detection for virus attack	σ	$2,8 \pm 0,3$
4	The average random value of the implementation time of the working environment integrity maintenance procedure by anti-virus tools usage	$\overline{\tau}_{(n)}$	$14,6 \pm 0,4$
5	Indicator of the threats response probability to the virus attacks	$P(\Omega)$	$0,772$

5 Conclusion

The research carried out by the authors showed that the mathematical model and the indicator (15) of timely response to threats of virus attacks have signs of adequacy. The mathematical function corresponding to the indicator (15) is continuous, the dependences showing the changes of its parameters correspond to the physical meaning.

A resulting mathematical model is an effective tool for solving a number of scientific problems in the field of cybersecurity associated with both the optimization of temporary resources of anti-layer protection mechanisms and with the justification of ways to improve information security measures.

The high adequacy of the model allows us to assert the possibility of its use in intelligent systems of cybersecurity.

Acknowledgments. The described research work is been financially supported by the Ministry of Science and Higher Education of the Russian Federation, Government Contract #2.7782.2017/BC dated 10/03/2017.

References

1. Scryl', S., et al.: Probabilistic models of information processes in integrated security systems in terms of information protection from unauthorized access. J. Telecommun. **6**, 26–31 (2015)
2. Minaev, V., Sychev, M., Vaits, E., Gracheva, Y.: Modeling of threats to information security using principles of system dynamics. Questions Radio Electron. **6**, 75–82 (2017). (In Russ.)
3. Minaev, V., Vaiz, E., Kuptsov, V., Yablochnikov, S., Vidov, S.: Modeling of information impacts on elements of onboard system. In: 2018 System of Signals Generating and Processing in the Field of on Board Communications: Materials of the International Scientific and Technical Conference, Moscow, Russia, pp. 1–5 (2018)
4. Liu, W., Cui, Y., Li, Y.: Information systems security assessment based on system dynamics. Int. J. Secur. Appl. **9**(2), 73–84 (2015)
5. Korchagin, A., Serdyk, V., Bochkarev, A.: Reliability of technical systems and man-made risk: tutorial (in 2 volumes). Vol. 1: theory basis – Omsk (2011). (in Russian)
6. Skryl, S., Gromov, Yu., et al.: Mathematical representation of the indicator of timely response to the threats of computer information security in the simplest model of the offender. Eng. Phys. **4**, 29–35 (2016). (in Russian)
7. Ventcel, E., Ovcharov, L.: Exercises in Probability Theory: Handbook, 11th edn. Academy, Moscow (2003)
8. Skryl, S., Sychev, A., Meshcheryakova, T., Arutyunova, V., Golubkov, D.: Mathematical model for evaluating the effectiveness of information protection mechanisms against virus attacks. Ind. ACS Controllers **4**, 62–69 (2018)
9. Fisz, M.: Probability Theory and Mathematical Statistics: Textbook, 2nd edn. Higher School, Moscow (1982)
10. Mitkovskiy, A., Ponomarev, A., Proletarskiy, A.: SIEM-platform for research and educational tasks on processing of security information events. In: ELSE Conference Proceedings 3, pp. 48–56. Bucharest, Romania (2019)

Intelligent Information Technologies
in Social Safety

Vladimir Tsyganov[(✉)]

Institute of Control Sciences, Profsoyuznaya 65, 117997 Moscow, Russia
bbc@ipu.ru

Abstract. Public safety issues are explored in a community model consisting of sensible, forward-looking (onward) elements. A neuropsychological model of onward element is considered. The concept of the sense of his life connected with the hope for a positive emotion in the future is introduced. It is assumed that the safety of community ensures the existence of a sense of life for all its members. One type of onward element is the Progressist governed by desires. It is shown that for the safety of a community consisting of Progressists, it is necessary and sufficient to create a sequence of incentives that contribute to the fulfillment of the desires of each member of the community. The other type of onward element - Phobic acts in nasty medium that causes irritation. It is shown that regular creation of irritants provides the sense of its life, so the community of Phobics is safe. Information technologies in social safety engineering based on obtained theoretical results are considered.

Keywords: Social safety · Information · Technology · Incentive · Irritant · Fobia

1 Introduction

In a democratic society, social stability is traditionally supported by feedback from members of society to politicians. This feedback is realized through voting in elections, formation of ratings of politicians, etc. However, the limits of global growth due to limited natural resources and capacity of the environment [1] slows down economic growth, leads to stagnation and social instability [2]. The growing protest consciousness is expressed in voting against the policies of the ruling elites in developed countries. Related modern illiberal and quasi-democratic tendencies were predicted by Zakaria [3]. They lead to the emergence of toxic leaders and corrupt politicians [4], leaders without ethics [5], politicians-wirepullers [6], and oligarchy [7], which threaten the public safety. In this regard, it is necessary to create intelligent information technologies in social safety engineering.

First of all, it is necessary to create a model of a member of society. It is a widely used the social and rational models of man, which origins date back to Simon [8]. Also, it is known models of human behavior based on psychology and game theory. They are widely recognized in the scientific community, including marked with the Nobel Prize such as the theory of psychoanalysis [9] and theory prospects [10]. Now even more adequate models are required, taking into account not only human rationality but

© Springer Nature Switzerland AG 2019
A. G. Kravets et al. (Eds.): CIT&DS 2019, CCIS 1084, pp. 270–284, 2019.
https://doi.org/10.1007/978-3-030-29750-3_21

sensuality and emotionality. At the heart of these models lie the advanced neuro-physiologic investigations of linkage of people behavior with their hormonal characteristics [11]. Based on this, a model of the far-sighted person administered by desires developed [12]. In fact, this is model of farseeing social man, using the available opportunities to achieve current and future goals. For example, such a model is used to establish the relationship between the limits of global growth, stagnation, creativity, and international stability [13]. Similar model also was used to develop intelligent technologies for the sustainable development of the social system in migration [14]. In this paper we focus on the problem of designing methods and intelligent information technologies for society safety with the desires and fears.

2 Intelligent Technologies of Social Safety Based on Desires

2.1 Sensations, Emotions, and Sense of Life of Progressist

Considered onward element as Progressist whose input u_t is the incentive s_t arising at time o:

$$u_t = s_t = \begin{cases} s > 0, & if \ o \leq t \leq o + e \\ 0, & if \ t < o \ or \ t > o + e \end{cases} \tag{1}$$

t - time. The solid line in Fig. 1a shows Progressist's primary reaction (sensation) Y_t to incentive s_t. This is typical for empirical studies of galvanic skin reaction, where Y_t is skin-sympathetic evoked potential, measured in microvolts, t - time in milliseconds [15]. There is also parallelism with similar neuropsychological reactions, but at a different scale (like neuron-level reactions translated to much more complex cognitive functions or social behaviors).

Human activity is expressed in the individual psyche needs a minimal level (norm N) of the sensation Y_t in time t. In Fig. 1a the dotted lines shows the normative meaning of Y_t – so called neurophysiologic norm N (a minimum level of tension according to Z. Freud [9]). The solid line in Fig. 1b shows the secondary integral reaction $y_t = \int\limits_o^t Y_\tau d\tau$ bringing together information on past and current primary reactions. The corresponding normative meaning of y_t – integral psychological norm $n_t = \int\limits_o^t N d\tau = (t - o)N$ – is shown by dotted line in Fig. 1b.

Progressist reaction to external stimulus is expressed in emotions:

$$f_t = F(n_t, y_t) = \begin{cases} F(n_t, y_t) \geq 0, & if \ y_t \geq n_t \\ F(n_t, y_t) < 0, & if \ y_y < n_t \end{cases} \tag{2}$$

where $F(n_t, y_t)$ is emotional function. The dependence of the emotions (2) at the incentive (1) is shown in Fig. 1c.

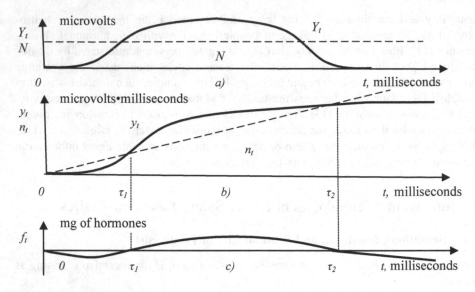

Fig. 1. Primary (a) and integral (b) Progressist reaction at incentive s_t; (c) Progressist emotion.

Z. Freud assigned an important role in psychoanalysis for a life instinct. It is associated with the hope of getting positive emotion into the future [9]. On the basis of a life instinct, it is possible to form an understanding of the sense of onward element life associated with such hope. Formally, it represents next.

Definition 1. We shall say that onward element life has a sense if for any t there is $v \geq t$ such that $F(n_v, y_v) > 0$:

$$\forall t \; \exists v \; such \; that \; v \geq t, \; and \; F(n_v, y_v) > 0 \tag{3}$$

If (3) is not satisfied, we shall say that life of onward element has no sense.
Positive feelings Y_t shown in Fig. 1, form a favorable situation for Progressist.

Proposition 1. Progressist life has no sense in the favorable situation.

Proof. Primary and integral reaction to the incentive s_t, as well as Progressist emotions f_t, shown in Fig. 1. As seen in Fig. 1b, c, $y_t < n_t$ for sufficiently large t and $F(n_t, y_t) < 0$. Thus, there is no v such that $v \geq t$ and $F(n_v, y_v) > 0$. Consequently, condition (3) does not hold. So using Definition 1 and considering the onward element is a Progressist, we get that his life has no sense, QED.

Substantially, the senselessness of Progressist life is due to lack changes leading to new pleasures in favorable situation. Figure 1c shows that the positive emotions related to the satisfied Progressist desire, eventually pass. "Everything pass", - said King Solomon. Therefore, the changes are needed for Progressist, followed by its new positive sensations and positive emotions.

2.2   Creative Engineering for Progressist Community Safety

The paradox of Proposition 1 is formally reflects the problem of social stagnation - a contradiction between the pursuit of pleasure in a favorable situation and the need of change this situation to prevent the loss of life sense. In fact, this problem is connected with the absence of new sensations during an excessively calm life. Subjectively, Progressist considers the lack of life sense as regress motivating him to protest actions. His frustration and aggression may apply to other people, community, society and existing order. Assume that the security of the community is ensured by the existence of a life sense for every its member. Then, from the above, it follows that the community consisting of Progressists in the favorable situation is unsafe. Consider the approach for solving safety problem of a community consisting of Progressists.

Definition 2. Unlimited set of the favorable situations is called favorable medium.

Definition 3. Regular change of the situation mean that, for any t, there exists future finite time v (i.e. $v \geq t$), in which incentive s_v defined by (1) occurs at the entrance of Progressist.

Proposition 2. To provide sense of Progressist life in favorable medium, it is necessary and sufficient creating regular change of the situation.

Proof. Let prove necessity by contradiction. Suppose that there is only one favorable situation, and Progressist life has a sense when this situation remains unchanged since moment o. Then the primary and integral reaction to incentive s_t, as well as emotions f_t are shown in Fig. 1. After the moment $o + \tau_2$, there is $n_t > y_t$, and Progressist feels negative emotions. However, the condition of Proposition 2 said about presence sense of Progressist life. According to (3), it means that exists v such that $v \geq t$ and $F(n_v, y_v) > 0$. Consequently, the assumption of the immutability of the situation contradicts the condition of Proposition 2. This proves the necessity.

Now let us prove sufficiency. According to Definition 2 in favorable medium there is unlimited set of favorable situations. Thus, we can regularly change the situation by replacing it with a new situation from this set. Formally this means that we have regular change of the situation according to Definition 3. So for any time t exists v such that $v \geq t$, and in the time v Progressist occurs the new incentive s_v. Then $y_t > n_t$ during the time interval $(v + \tau_1, v + \tau_2)$. Thus for any t such v exists that $v \geq t$ and $F(n_v, y_v) > 0$. By using Definition 1 in case if the onward element is Progressist, we get that his life has a sense, QED.

Meaningful, regular change of situation will initiate new incentives, leading to obtain new positive emotions and giving sense of Progressist life. It leads to an emotional series - the temporal sequence of positive and negative emotions ("white" and "black" strips a person's life). Such sequence formed by a chain of incentive (1) is called Stairs Desires. Obviously, to realize Stairs Desires in favorable media it is necessary and sufficient to change situation regularly. Figure 2 shows the primary (*a*) and integral (*b*) Progressist reaction on such incentive sequence, as well as appropriate Progressist emotions (*c*).

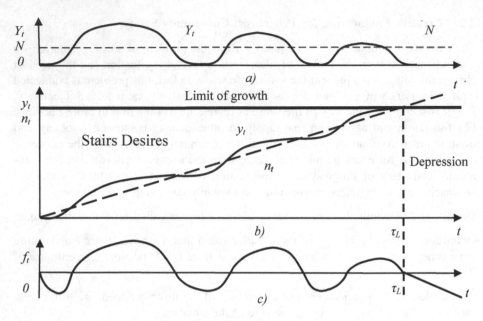

Fig. 2. Stairs Desires of Progressist.

Corollary 1. To give Progressist life sense in a favorable medium, it is necessary and sufficient to create his Stairs Desires.

Proof. By Proposition 2, to give sense of Progressist life in a favorable medium, it is necessary and sufficient to change situation regularly. But that means realization of his Stairs Desires by definition, QED.

In other words creating the Stairs Desires, Progressist can always rely on the positive emotion into the future, and his life makes sense. That provides public safety. So for the safety of a community consisting of Progressists, it is necessary and sufficient to create a sequence of incentives that contribute to the fulfillment of the desires of each member of the community.

3   Technologies Based on Phobia in Social Safety Engineering

The prototype of Progressist is "economic man" whose state is defined in money. State of Progressist in consumer society is defined by the volume of consumption. The goal of Progressist is to increase consumption for maximum enjoyment. So he may be considered as Hedonist [16]. Assume that Hedonist consumption in time t characterizes the value of y_t. Due to growth limits, there is an objective restriction of L (Fig. 2b).

The nature of Hedonist is that the consumer's needs (ambitions) n_t are constantly growing (dashed line in Fig. 2b). Limit of growth of L is reached at time τ_L. Then Hedonist experiences persistent negative emotions (Fig. 2c). Thus, the objective stagnation of consumption contradicts to the growing of Hedonist needs (n_t) and leads to depression. His anger and aggression may be paid to the social environment.

Therefore, the consumer society under the limits of economic growth is unsafe. This is the result of favorable medium in which Hedonist life has no sense (Proposition 1).

To solve the problem of ensuring public safety, it is necessary to eliminate its causes. Traditional solution lies in expanding limits of growth L (e.g., increasing demand which may be result of new Kondratieff technological cycle). The alternative solution is associated with liberalization. Then the active Hedonist can change the situation, getting the positive emotions and realizing Stairs Desires. Furthermore, he can obtain power and can change the medium providing possibility to avoid depression for another member of community.

3.1   Sensation, Emotion and Sense of Life of Phobic

Man is governed not only by desires, but also by fears. Considered onward element as model of farseeing phobia person having an extreme or irrational fear of or aversion to something (briefly – Phobic). Its input u_t is irritant i_t occurs in the moment o:

$$u_t = i_t = \begin{cases} i < 0, & \text{if } o \leq t \leq o + e, \\ 0, & \text{if } t < o \text{ or } t > o + e \end{cases} \quad (4)$$

The solid line in Fig. 3a shows primary reaction Y_t to irritant i_t as negative sensation. Irritant i_t (4) forms a nasty situation for Phobic. Medium, bringing together all sorts of nasty situations, is called nasty medium. The solid line in Fig. 3b shows the secondary integral reaction $y_t = \int_o^t Y_\tau d\tau$ to the irritant i_t. The dotted lines in Fig. 3 show neurophysiologic norm N and neuropsychological norm $n_t = \int_o^t Nd\tau = (t - o)N$. Since Phobic is a type of onward element, his emotional function is determined by (2). So Fig. 3c shows Phobic emotions related to the irritant i_t.

The Phobic life has a sense if (3) take place. Consider the nasty situation for the members of the community (for example, in the society of consumption with limits of growth). At first glance it seems that Phobic life in nasty situation is associated with negative emotions and has no sense.

Proposition 3. Phobic life has a sense in the nasty situation.

Proof. Primary and integral reaction to a irritant i_t, as well as Phobic emotions f_t, shown in Fig. 3. As seen in Fig. 3b, c, for sufficiently large t, $y_t > n_t$ and $F(n_t, y_t) > 0$. Thus, there is τ such that $\tau \geq t$ and $F(n_\tau, y_\tau) > 0$ takes place. Consequently, condition (3) does hold. So using Definition 1, and considering that the onward element is a Phobic, we get that Phobic life has a sense, QED.

On Fig. 3c it is shown that the negative emotions related to the fear, eventually pass (remember King Solomon). Substantially, according to Proposition 3, the sense of Phobic life is due to no changes leading to new pains in nasty medium. The paradox of Proposition 3 is formally reflects the effect of phobia - a contradiction between trouble for the phobic nasty medium and, at the same time, the willingness of the phobic to accept it. At the same time obedience to the phobic is caused by the non-desire of any changes to prevent the loss of life sense. This will motivate him to avoid any action that can lead to medium changes. So the Phobic community is safe.

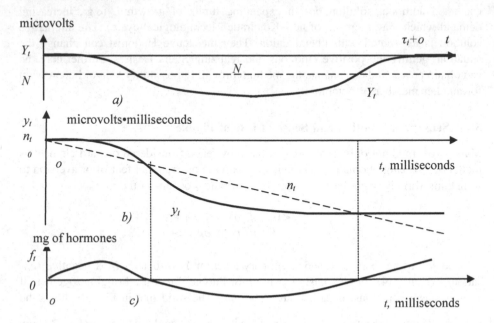

Fig. 3. Primary (a) and integral (b) Phobic reaction at irritant i_t; (c) Phobic emotion. There τ_i is the adaptation time to irritant.

3.2   Creativity and Intelligent Technology Preservation Phobias

The prototype of a Phobic model is a person suffering from a phobia, preserving a phobia until the end of life, regardless of external factors (even if reality refutes phobia). An example is a mentally ill person. But a healthy person adapts to reality. And if the fears associated with a phobia are not confirmed, then, over time, he forgets about them and ceases to be a carrier of phobia. Thus, adaptation in favorable medium leads to forgetting the phobia. A person suffering from a phobia transforms into a normal person who does not have a phobia. In fact, there is a transformation of a frightened person, seeking to avoid pain, into a normal person, striving for pleasures. In particular, in the society of consumption, Progressist is transformed into Hedonist with constantly growing desire. After reaching the limits of growth, Hedonist feels persistent negative emotions and dissatisfaction. It provides instability and threat to public safety. Consider the way to public safety associated with the prevention of the transformation of Phobic into Progressist.

Proposition 4. Suppose that the onward element does not forget the phobia during the time τ_f after the end of the adaptation period to the irritant (4), where $\tau_f > 0$. Then, to prevent the transformation of Phobic in Hedonist and preserve the sense of Phobic life, it is sufficient to create irritant (4) regularly with a time interval $\tau_p = \tau_i + \tau_f$.

Proof. To prevent the transformation of Phobic in Hedonist, it is necessary that onward element does not forget the phobia By the condition of Proposition 4, onward element does not forget the phobia during the time τ_f, $\tau_f > 0$, after the end of the adaptation time to irritant (4). Further, according to Fig. 3, the adaptation time to irritant is equal to τ_i. Therefore, in order to prevent the transformation of Phobic in Hedonist, it is sufficient to implement an irritant (4) regularly with a time interval $\tau_p = \tau_i + \tau_f$. Let show that Phobic life has a sense with such irritants. Consider the corresponding regular primary and integral reactions, as well as emotions, cause by irritant (4) starting in the moment o. Then Phobic reactions and emotions are shown on Fig. 4. Taking into account $\tau_f > 0$, from Fig. 4 it is seen that there is a moment $v > o$ that satisfies the inequalities $\tau_i + o < v < \tau_f + \tau_i + o$, and $F(n_v, y_v) > 0$. Since o can take any valid value, we can formulate a general statement: for any moment w in which irritant appeared, there exists a moment $v > w$ satisfying the inequalities $\tau_i + w < v < \tau_i + \tau_f + w$ such, that $F(n_v, y_v) > 0$. Consequently, condition (3) does hold. So using Definition 1 and considering that onward element is a Phobic, we get his life has a sense, QED.

Meaningful, creation of regular new irritants do not allow an onward element to forget about phobia. By Proposition 4, regular new irritants lead to an emotional series - the temporal sequence of positive and negative emotions ("white" and "black" strips a Phobic's life). Such sequence is formed by a chain of irritants (4) is called Stairs Fears of Phobic. It gives sense of Phobic life even in a nasty medium, which results in public safety (for example, at the limits of growth in a consumer society). Denote if the changes in the nasty medium are too frequent, only negative emotions arise which lead to the loss of the Phobic sense of life. This motivates him to protest and destabilized other members of community, society and existing order. So creativity and intelligent technology need for preservation phobias.

3.3   Creativity and Game-Based Learning of Voters and Politician

Consider a social system includes community of Voters as onward elements, and democratically elected Politician. Consider the game of Politician and Voters in which Politician is responsible for the safety of community in the period between elections. If voter has a sense of life at the time of elections, he votes for Politician. Otherwise he votes against.

Consider goals and strategies of players in this game. According to the principle of adequacy of the controlling subject to the controlled object, the authorities of the Progressist community should consist of Progressists. Thus Politician himself should be Progressist whose state can be characterized by the number of votes, ratings in community, etc. Then the sense of his life is connected with the realization of own Stairs Desires. His positive emotions are connected with the regular re-election. For this it is sufficient that at the time of the election every voter has a sense of life.

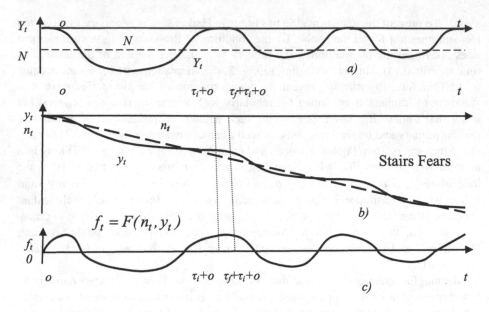

Fig. 4. Stairs Fears of Phobic.

For example if community is hedonistic consumer society both voters and Politician should be Hedonists. Above it was shown that under limits of growth every Hedonist invariably experience negative emotions and has no sense of life. And since voter-Hedonist considers authorities responsible for this, he will vote regularly against the incumbent Politician. Then Politician life also has no sense.

From the other side if Voter is Phobic, he sometimes experiences positive emotions (see Proposition 3). Taking into account said in paragraph 3.2, to regularly receive the votes of onward elements, it is sufficient to make them Phobics, and then prevent forgetting phobia. And for this is necessary repetition of irritants.

Proposition 5. Politician-Hedonist who creates Stairs Fears for all Voters is re-elected and ensures the safety of the Phobics community.

Proof. By the condition of Proposition 5, Politician creates Stairs Fears for all voters who are members of the Phobic community. To do this, Politician supports their phobia by irritants (4). According to Proposition 4 to prevent the transformation of Phobic in Hedonist and preserve the sense of Phobic life, it is sufficient to implement an irritant (4) regularly with a time interval $\tau_p = \tau_i + \tau_f$. Then (3) is satisfied, i.e. there always is a time when every Phobic has a sense of life. Let show that there is a moment of feeding irritant (4), at which every Phobic has a sense of life at the moment of elections u. Consider the primary and integral reaction of Phobic, as well as his emotions, initiating by irritant (4) in the moment o. Phobic reactions and emotions are shown on Fig. 4, starting from the moment o, in which irritant appeared. From Fig. 4 it is obvious that for any moment o, there is a moment $u > 0$ that satisfies the inequalities $\tau_i + o < u < \tau_f + \tau_i + o$ such that $F(n_u, y_u) > 0$. Then we can formulate a general statement: for any moment w in which irritant appeared, there exists a moment u satisfying the inequalities $w + \tau_i < u < w + \tau_i + \tau_f$, such that $u > w$ and $F(n_u, y_u) > 0$. It follows that, for any moment of election u satisfying the inequalities $w + \tau_i < u < w + \tau_i + \tau_f$, a moment w exists, in which irritant (4) appeared, such that $w < u$ and $F(n_u, y_u) > 0$. So using Definition 1 we get that for any moment of the election u, Politician can choose the moment of giving irritant (4) so that every Phobic has a sense of life at the time of the election u. So Politician receives vote of every Phobic. Then being elected Politician getting the positive emotions and realizing his own Stairs Desires. That provides the sense of life for Politician as Hedonist. Thus, the lives of every element of considered social system have a sense. This ensures the public safety, QED.

Proposition 5 theoretically justifies the traditional recipe for the manipulation of community consciousness. So Politician-Hedonist, who creates Stairs Fears for members of the community - Phobics, can be called Intriguer. Content created by Intriguer regular irritants leads to temporal sequence of positive and negative Phobic's emotions. Intriguer's task is to determine when the irritant (4) is being dispensed in such a way that every Phobic has a sense of life at the time of the election. If the irritant is synchronized with the elections, then all Phobics votes for Intriguer. Then winner of the election Intriguer also experiences positive emotions, realizing own Stairs Desires. All this gives a sense of Phobic's life and Intriguer's life, even in a nasty medium, which results in public safety (for example, at the limits of growth).

Considered game-based mathematical model is useful because of it provides quantitative recommendation. Of course, some of the above conclusions can be obtained through qualitative reasoning. But mathematical formulations not only strictly substantiate these conclusions, but also describe inequalities about the timing of public actions in considered game. Their formal proof allows Politician to justify the choice of time points for these actions, and Voters to predict them.

Of course, to make decisions both Politician and voters require values of parameters τ_1 and τ_2 (Fig. 1), τ_L (Fig. 2), τ_i (Fig. 3), and τ_f (Fig. 4). Politician and voters can obtain them by learning, for example, by means of special sociological researches. Thus, when choosing the moment of the action in the game with voters, the Politician can use the results of both theoretical and empirical research. So game-based learning of Politician is realized. Similar game-based learning of voters creates theoretical and empirical basis of their decisions. If the community is large enough, to promote these decisions, it is possible to create a system for disseminating information. An example of such system, including relevant structures and technologies of information management in social networks, is described in [17].

4 Information Technologies in Social Safety Engineering

4.1 Phobias of Creative Person, Corporative Psychopath, and Toxic Leader

Consider the model of behavior of a creative person prone to phobias in personal and corporative relations. Such Phobic provides the necessary sequence of positive emotions for life, creating a Stairs Fears. His phobias and emotions may be intensified by others. In personal relationships, creative Phobic builds his Stairs Fears, using loved ones. His fears can frighten loved ones, form their phobias and associated positive emotions.

Similarly, in the process of production relations, the creative Phobic builds his Stairs Fears in collaboration with his work colleagues. And, having received the power in the corporation, creative Phobic can already build his Stairs Fears, using subordinates. To understand how Phobia can realize this Stairs Fears without obvious conflicts in a corporation, it's worth remembering the plot of F. Kafka's "Process" - the constant increase in alarm without charge. There the usual clerk Joseph K. is accused of a crime that he did not commit because he did not commit anything at all. Actually, the prosecutors themselves do not name the elements of a crime, since they also do not know what he is guilty of...

As a result creative Phobic can turn into a corporate psychopath [5]. He can also turn subordinates into Phobics, guided by Propositions 3, 4 and 5. In fact, his phobias are transmitted to his subordinates, who are starting to build their own Stairs Fears that form the sequence of positive emotions they need themselves. That is why we follow corporate Phobics as a variety of toxic leaders [4]. Further promotion of the creative Phobic through the hierarchy is facilitated if the corporation is in a state of stagnation because of its leaders are also constantly afraid of the negative effects of limits to growth. Such an allure of toxic leaders contributes to the spread of phobias not only in corporations, but also in society and the country. And through transnational corporations, toxic leaders can also grow in the world [4].

4.2 Persuasive Threats and Social Phobias

Of key importance for the re-election of Intriguer is the persuasiveness of the threats that form and support social phobia. To do this, Intriguer must make threats as plausible as possible to society. For this, the most daring scenarios can be written and implemented, which the best writers and directors of Hollywood could envy.

Theoretically, for re-election, Politician - Intriguer should create and maintain phobias that can affect the emotional expectations of his electorate. Phobias that encompass the target audience of the Intriguer (society or its social groups) will be called social. The most powerful phobias are associated with the fear of death. Corresponding social phobias can be based on different types of threats to the individual and society: terrorism, radioactivity, chemical (toxin), bacteriological (biological) and nuclear weapons etc. Such threats have recently been implemented in the course of terrorist, radioactive, chemical, and toxic attacks. Accordingly, the main types of social phobias that Intriguer can create and maintain are the phobias of terrorism, radioactive, chemical (toxic), bacteriological (biological), and nuclear war.

Consider the problem of the credibility of the threat of aggression with the use of different types of weapons of mass destruction. Note that international treaties have created special organizations and regimes to prevent the use of weapons of mass destruction, such as chemical, toxin, bacteriological (biological) and nuclear weapons. Information about these treaties and relevant organizations and regimes is published by the James Martin Center [18]. Organizational models and progressive adaptive mechanisms for the functioning of the international regimes for the nonproliferation of chemical, biological and nuclear technologies of dual (military and civilian) use were considered in [19, 20]. The mere existence of treaties, organizations, and regimes relating to arms control reduces the persuasiveness of social phobias associated with the use of weapons of mass destruction. Under these conditions, for re-election, Intriguer must convince the public of the reality of the threats that support phobia.

Consider the problem of the persuasiveness of threats of mass destruction on the example of a phobia of nuclear war. The threats of nuclear weapons for different countries depend on their military capabilities. In particular, the nuclear arsenals of USA and Russia are much more than in other countries. Therefore, for example, the threat of North Korea's nuclear attack on the USA is unconvincing and cannot be used to form and maintain social phobia. Thus to form a phobia, Intriguer must make the nuclear threat real. Obviously, the threat of a nuclear war is all the more real the fewer the treaties and agreements that restrain the nuclear arms race.

First of all, these include "Treaty between the USA and the USSR on the Elimination of Their Intermediate-range and Shorter-range Missiles" (INF Treaty). The INF Treaty was a bilateral agreement between the USA and the USSR It was the first treaty to reduce nuclear arms instead of establishing an arms ceiling [18]. This agreement was concluded because of the difficulty of controlling short-range missiles, since a contradiction arose between the maximum possible speed of human response and the necessary speed of decision-making that affect the fate of peoples and states.

This contradiction first manifested itself in the 1980s, when the Warsaw Pact and NATO deployed short-range missiles in Europe. The time of their approach to the goal was only a few minutes. Therefore, none of the parties had time to verify the information on the launch of the enemy's missiles and hold talks. Under these conditions, the retaliatory strike should have been delivered automatically, and not by the command of the heads of the opposing states. Such a control system in the USSR was called "Dead Hand". In this case, the entire system became unstable, since any failure of automation or interference could be the cause of the global thermonuclear war. This threat disappeared only after the conclusion of the INF Treaty in 1987, under which medium and short-range missiles were completely destroyed.

Now this contradiction again arises in connection with the termination of the INF Treaty. But it is repeatedly enhanced by cybernetic threats, and therefore it becomes much more real. After all, a successful hacker attack of a lone maniac on the computer system "Dead Hand" can cause a world thermonuclear war and the death of humanity. In the event of the USA abandoning the INF Treaty, a new nuclear arms race will begin on the basis of medium and short-range missiles. And since any step in this race is associated with new threats, it will be easy for any Intriguer to regularly maintain a phobia of nuclear war in order to maintain power. Thus, humanity can become a hostage to his political ambitions.

4.3 Humanitarian High Technologies in Social Safety Engineering

Intriguer's interest in creating and maintaining the above-described social phobias is due to the contradiction between the individual's desire to increase consumption and limits to growth caused by limited resources and the ecology of the biosphere (in short, the main contradiction). First type of possible solutions to the main contradiction is based on expanding the global limits of consumption growth (e.g., as a result of Kondratieff's technological cycle) [21]. The second type of solutions is connected with the expansion of growth limits in one or several countries through their economic, political or military expansion in the world (for example, by organizing color revolutions or local wars). But such solutions lead to international instability [16]. The third type of solutions is associated with a periodic decrease in macroeconomic consumption, followed by its growth (for example, due to the global financial crisis, the collapse of states and decay of their unions, ethnic conflicts). Such decisions also lead to socio-political and international instability.

Therefore, a fundamentally different class of solutions to the main contradiction is connected with the replacement of the paradigm of unlimited growth of material consumption with the paradigm of non-material, spiritual development. In fact this is change in the ideology of the consumer society. Also this is contrary to traditional economic ideas based on the assumption that continual growth is possible and desirable. Similarly, most politicians are prone to growth because it solves the problems of unemployment, poverty, taxes, etc. Thus there is a set of vested interests in the growth [1].

However, the shift in ideology of consumer society creates important opportunities for positive changes. One of the humanistic solutions associated with the creativity of people (especially the middle class of developed countries), aimed at spiritual development [15, 16]. Then the growing desires of these people in the spiritual realm can be satisfied without increasing material consumption. For this it is necessary to derive both humanitarian high technologies [15] and adaptive mechanism for sustainable development and improving social stability [22, 23].

5   Conclusions

The emergence and development of *homo sapience* throughout the history of mankind has been associated with a progressive consciousness, which means the constant growth of desires and possibilities. Today mankind has entered the era of growth limits due to the limited resources of the Earth as well as the ability of its nature to compensate for the harmful effects of human activities. A contradiction arises between the ever-growing desires of person with progressive consciousness (Progressist), and the possibilities of their satisfaction. This contradiction provokes mass discontent in the consumer society. Its members believe that the authorities should provide supportive conditions for a constant increase in consumption. Therefore, their discontent everywhere leads to criticism of power expressed in the mass protest voting in many developed countries.

In these conditions, more profound studies of the influence of human nature on socio-political stability are relevant. On neuroscience basis, a model of a sensible, far-sighted (onward) element is proposed. In accordance with the accepted concept emotional expectations of onward elements affect their behavior with respect to society and power. Socio-political system consisting of onward elements is stable if all of them have positive expectations. Then socio-political system consisting of Progressists is stable in supportive environment. But the growth limits make the environment unsuitable for development, and such system is instable.

People are governed not only by desires, but also by fears. It is shown that the phobias of members of society can contribute to the stability of the socio-political system under the limits of growth. Socio-political system, consisting of the society of Phobics and its power, is stable in a fearful environment. But, in the absence of regular incidents and subsequent stimuli, the phobia disappears, and the progressive consciousness returns. Thus, a transformed society of people with progressive consciousness becomes instable under growth constraints. In these conditions, the authorities can use the phobias of members of society to ensure the stability of the socio-political system under the limits of growth.

It is shown that for such stability, it is enough to create regular incidents which provide stimuli-fears supporting phobia of the members of society. By synchronizing these stimuli with the elections, intriguer maintains positive expectations of Phobics at the right time. This is the reason for their loyalty to the intriguer and his success in the election. Examples of such behavior of politician-intriguer are well known. Ancient shamans and priests did this, using the phobia of hunger, an external enemy, etc. Modern intriguers without ethics in global politics widely use similar methods, in particular, based on Russophobia. By manipulating information about the short-range rockets, intriguer can easily maintain a social phobia of nuclear war. But humanity will be even closer to death.

Note that all these problems are a consequence of the basic contradiction between the desire to increase consumption and limits to growth caused by the biosphere. It is necessary to change the paradigm of unlimited growth of material consumption to the paradigm of non-material, spiritual development. Do we think that the crisis of the ideology of consumer society is a problem? It depends on our own ideology. After all, we can proceed from the fact that this crisis creates important opportunities for positive changes. Various types of changes are possible without economic growth, many of which would lead to a more just society and international stability.

Aspirations and luck will bring us only so far. But the survival of humanity cannot risk relying solely on them.

References

1. Meadows, D., Randers, J., Meadows, D.: Limits to Growth: The 30-Year Update. Chelsea Green Publishing, Vermont (2004)
2. Kile, F., Dimirovski, G.: Choices for global social stability. In: 17th IFAC World Congress Proceedings, pp. 6681–6685. COEX, Seoul (2008)
3. Zakaria, F.: The Future of Freedom: Illiberal Democracy at Home and Abroad. W.W. Norton, New York (2003)
4. Lipman-Blumen, J.: The Allure of Toxic Leaders: Why We Follow Destructive Bosses and Corrupt Politicians – and How We Can Survive Them. Oxford University Press, USA (2004)
5. Boddy, C., Ladyshewsky, R., Galvin, P.: Leaders without ethics in global business: corporate psychopaths. J. Public Aff. **10**, 121–138 (2010)

6. Tsyganov, V.: Emotional expectations and social stability. IFAC-PapersOnLine **51–30**, 112–117 (2018)
7. Tsyganov, V., Schultz, V.: Oligarchy, ontology, cycles, and change in a globalizing world. Sotsiologicheskie Issledovaniya **2**, 3–15 (2009)
8. Simon, H.: Models of Man - Social and Rational. Wiley, New York (1966)
9. Freud, S.: On Metapsychology - The Theory of Psychoanalysis. Gardners Books, London (1991)
10. Tversky, K.D.: Advances in prospect theory: cumulative representation of uncertainty. J. Risk Uncertain. **5**, 297–323 (1992)
11. Fehr, E., Rangel, A.: Neuroeconomic foundations of economic choice - recent advances. J. Econ. Perspect. **25**(4), 3–30 (2011)
12. Tsyganov, V.: Intelligent mechanisms for global evolution regulation. IFAC-PapersOnLine **18**, 3130–3135 (2011)
13. Tsyganov, V.: Large scale socio-economic system control under limits of global growth. IFAC-PapersOnLine **13**, 236–241 (2013)
14. Tsyganov, V.: Intelligent technologies for large-scale social system sustainable development. Commun. Comput. Inf. Sci. **754**, 107–118 (2017)
15. Tsyganov, V., Schultz, V.: Humanitarian high technologies in political system of society. Sotsiologicheskie Issledovaniya **8**, 85–93 (2012)
16. Tsyganov, V.: Limits of global growth, stagnation, creativity and international stability. Artif. Intell. Soc. **29**(2), 259–266 (2014)
17. Enaleev, A., Tsyganov, V.: Structures and cluster technologies of data analysis and information management in social networks. Commun. Comput. Inf. Sci. **754**, 683–696 (2017)
18. James Martin Center for Nonproliferation Studies at the Middlebury Institute of International Studies at Monterey Homepage. https://www.nti.org/learn/treaties-and-regimes/treaties/. Accessed 11 Apr 2019
19. Tsyganov, V.: Progressive adaptive mechanisms for the international cooperation. In: 17th IFAC World Congress Proceedings, pp. 6697–6702. COEX, Seoul (2008)
20. Tsyganov, V.: Regulation of decentralized active system development and intelligent control mechanisms. IFAC-PapersOnLine **9**, 94–98 (2010)
21. Tsyganov, V.: Control of evolution under limits of global growth. IFAC-PapersOnLine **3**, 132–137 (2012)
22. Borodin, D., Gurlev, I., Klukvin, A., Tsyganov, V.: Adaptive mechanism for sustainable development. Syst. Sci. **30**(2), 89–95 (2004)
23. Tsyganov, V., Bagamaev, R., Gurlev, I.: Adaptive mechanism for mastering capital and improving international stability. IFAC-PapersOnLine **16**, 42–45 (2005)

Optimization of Technical Information Protection System's Composition

Arina Nikishova(✉), Yuriy Umnitsyn, Mikhail Umnitsyn(ID),
and Tatiana Omelchenko

Department of Information Security,
Volgograd State University, Volgograd, Russia
{nikishova.arina, umnitsyn.up, umnitsyn,
omelchenko.tatiana}@volsu.ru

Abstract. Technical means of protection is used to protect sensitive information when hardware and software protection is insufficient or not applicable. Technical information protection system is a complex multi-component system. The effectiveness of the protection system is determined by the effect it achieves, taking into account the financial resources spent. In most cases, the composition of the protection system is regulated by regulations. However, you can select different security means for a particular information security subsystem. Each means is evaluated by its quality indicators. For the information protection system an integral indicator of quality is formed taking into account the private indicators of the means of protection. It is proposed to use the method of obtaining a Bayesian evaluation to obtain an integral indicator of the quality of the protection system. This method reduces the accuracy requirements, as well as naturally reveals the inconsistency of estimates of particular indicators of the quality of protection.

Keywords: Technical means of protection · Information protection system · Optimization · Threats overlapping · Price

1 Introduction

Not only computer systems need protection. Protected information can be in visual form, audio form, in the form of an electromagnetic wave. As a result, in addition to the channels of information leakage circulating in the computer system, there are the following technical channels of information leakage:

- optical;
- radio-electronic;
- acoustic;
- material.

The information carrier in the optical channel is the electromagnetic field (photons). The optical range is divided into:

A. G. Kravets et al. (Eds.): CIT&DS 2019, CCIS 1084, pp. 285–294, 2019.
https://doi.org/10.1007/978-3-030-29750-3_22

- far infrared sub-band 100–10 mkm (3–30 THz);
- middle and near infrared sub-band 10–0.76 mkm (30–400 THz);
- visible range (blue-green-red) 0.76–0.4 mkm (400–750 THz).

In the radio-electronic channel of information leakage, electric, magnetic and electromagnetic fields in the radio range, as well as electric current (electron flow) propagating through metal wires are used as carriers. The frequency range of the radio-electronic channel occupies a frequency band from tens of GHz to sound. It is divided into:

- low frequency 10–1 km (30–300 kHz);
- medium frequency 1 km–100 m (300 kHz–3 MHz);
- high frequency 100–10 m (3–30 MHz);
- ultra-high frequency 10–1 m (30–300 MHz);
- etc. to SHF 3–30 GHz (10–1 cm).

The information carriers in the acoustic channel are elastic acoustic waves propagating in the environment. There are:

- infrasound range 1500–75 m (1–20 Hz);
- lower sound range 150–5 m (1–300 Hz);
- sound range 5–0.2 m (300–16000 Hz);
- ultrasonic range from 16000 Hz to 4 MHz.

In the material channel information leakage is made by unauthorized distribution outside the controlled zone of material carriers with protected information. Drafts of documents and used copy paper are most often used as material carriers.

To protect information from leakage through such channels hardware and software, usually used to protect the information in computer systems, will not suit. To block each of the technical channels of information leakage, different technical means of information protection is used. The formation of a technical information security system as a set of these means is a non-trivial task. An approach for its solution is proposed.

2 Existing Approaches

Few authors conduct research in the field of technical protection of information. Author of [1] conducts research of technical channel of voice information leakage in fiber-optic communications, which is created with parasitic modulation in the light stream that goes through regular connection system. That is one of the technical channels of information leakage. Places and areas of intelligence accessibility are researched and a possible scenario of threat attack is considered.

Author of [2] explorers issues of quantitative evaluation of the effectiveness of physical protection systems. These systems integrate a number of security systems (including procedures, equipment, and personnel) into a single interface to ensure an adequate level of protection of people and critical assets against malevolent human actions. Model-driven approach to support the design and the evaluation of physical protection systems based on (a) UML models representing threats, protection facilities, assets, and relationships among them, and (b) the automatic construction of a Bayesian Network model to estimate the vulnerability of different system configurations is proposed. The proposed approach is useful both in the context of vulnerability assessment and in designing new security systems as it enables what-if and cost–benefit analyses.

There are other works on physical protection system's construction. Author of [3] proposed a novel heuristic path-finding method named "Heuristic Path-finding for the Evaluation of PPS effectiveness, HPEP" for the evaluation of a vulnerable intrusion path in Physical Protection System (PPS). HPEP takes the detection probability and interruption probability as heuristic information to analyze the vulnerable adversary path. With the help of simulation, the main parameters can be analyzed. It will provide detailed and comprehensive technical information for the redesign and upgrade of the PPS.

Author of [4] formalizes the security policy of privacy information flow on three aspects: service reputation, retention, and purpose. The composition is modeled with privacy workflow net, which gives support to the analysis of privacy information flow, and the detection of privacy information leakage is performed by analyzing execution paths of composition.

Author of [5] aims to regard the service composition business as the research object, focusing on the analysis of security equipment's character that deployed by the system, abstracting the behavior of security service, classifying it to the business service, and systematically solving the security evaluation problems in business operation. User behavior pattern is established on the cloud-model theory and fully studied in the premise of ensuring the structural accuracy of the workflow. Then, by analyzing the credibility of user behavior, the utility function is defined from the relationship between threat and protection, and the security service efficiency identified by the change operation set of security service.

Author of [6] suggests applying Edgeworth-Pareto method in an effort to address the multicriteria discrete optimization problem, associated with the assessment of the security in a higher education institution's (HEI) information learning environment (ILE) and its technical means of protection (TMP). Modification to the method, based on a combination of discrete optimization of Edgeworth-Pareto and Podinovski's lexicographic method, is proposed. In order to highlight a variety of Pareto-optimal solutions, the vector criterion for evaluating output, which considers two conditions for the optimality as its elements: cost assessment of the analyzed TMP and its technical efficiency evaluation. This is an effective method, but it does not quite solve the studied problem.

So the study on technical information protection system's composition should be carried out.

3   Threats and Protection Means

Signals convey protected information that may be intercepted by a malicious user and then the retrieval of this information called a threat. Dangerous signals are divided into two types: functional and random. Functional signals are created by the technical means of information processing to perform the specified functions. The main sources of functional signals include:

- sources of communication systems;
- transmitters of radio engineering systems;
- in transducers of acoustic signals;
- people.

The principal difference between functional and random signals is that the owner of the information is aware of the possible risks of information security violations and can take appropriate measures to reduce the risk to acceptable values. To prevent risk threats that cause it must be identified.

The work of modern means of processing, storage, and transmission of information is accompanied by phenomena and physical processes that can create side radio or electrical signals. These signals are called random danger signals. These signals occur regardless of the desire of the owner of the information. Without special research to identify them is almost impossible.

The technical means that can be sources of random dangerous signals include:

- wired telephone facilities;
- mobile and radio communications;
- computer aids;
- audio equipment and sound reinforcement;
- radio receiver;
- video equipment;
- television media;
- means of linear radio broadcasting and notification.

Random dangerous signals can be generated by the following electrical devices:

- electrorheological system;
- security alarm systems;
- fire alarm systems;
- office equipment (in particular, printers);
- air conditioning and ventilation system facilities;
- household appliances and other equipment, which includes elements of conversion of acoustic information into electrical signals;
- conductive communications of the building passing through the controlled area.

Depending on the belonging of the information circulating in technical means to the protected and open, technical means are divided into basic technical means and systems (BTMS) and auxiliary technical means and systems (ATMS). Important here is that ATMS do not process the protected information, but can be within the controlled area together with the BTMS. Under certain conditions, ATMS can become sources of random dangerous signals; therefore, they need protection along with the BTMS.

The variety of technical channels of information leakage (TCIL) represents a certain choice of ways, methods, and means of unauthorized extraction of information.

After analyzing TCIL conclusions can be drawn:

- Leakage of information with the possibility of its further analysis is possible through all technical channels.
- The optical channel is the most vulnerable on the specific unmasking signs, because at a distance with the help of appropriate technical means it is possible to intercept information
- The main channel for obtaining signal unmasking features is the radio-electronic channel. Also, the material channel is important.
- The greater the bandwidth and length has TCIL, the more dangerous it is for the owner of the information.
- Throughput, length and relative informativity of the TCIL depends on the characteristics of its elements: source, medium, and receiver.

As a result of the implementation of technical channels of information leakage, the following threats may occur:

- the threat of specific information leakage;
- the threat of acoustic information leakage;
- the threat of information leakage through the channels of side electromagnetic radiation and interference (SEMRI).

3.1 The Threat of Specific Information Leakage

Along with the information processed in the technical means of information transfer and speech information, species information obtained by technical means of interception in the form of images of objects or documents plays an important role.

Depending on the nature of the information, the following ways of obtaining it can be distinguished:

- monitoring of objects;
- the shooting of object;
- shooting (copying) of documents.

The set of threats of specific information leakage is $Th^S = \{Th_1^S, \ldots, Th_n^S\}$, where n – total number of threats.

To prevent the leakage simple technical means can be used in most cases:

- the decrease in reflection characteristics and a decrease of illumination of objects;
- installation of various barriers and disguises;
- the use of reflective glass;
- location of objects so that the light from them does not fall into the area of possible interception.

But there is a more typical risk of leakage of species information: removal of documents from the premises for their photographing, other forms of copying, screenshots of database screens containing important information, and other methods. The main measures to combat these risks relate exclusively to the administrative and organizational sphere. Although there are software tools that, for example, do not allow to make a screenshot of the data displayed on the screen.

The set of means of protection from specific information leakage is $M^S = \{M_1^S, \ldots, M_m^S\}$, where m – total number of protection means.

3.2 The Threat of Acoustic Information Leakage

Depending on the physical nature of the occurrence of information signals, the propagation medium of acoustic vibrations and methods of interception technical channels of leakage of acoustic (speech) information can be divided into:

- air channel;
- vibration channel;
- electroacoustic channel;
- optoelectronic channel;
- parametric channel.

In air acoustic leakage channels, the main mean of interception is the microphone. The microphone converts the acoustic signal into an electrical signal and connects either to the recording device or to the transmitter.

The medium of propagation of acoustic information in vibration channels is the construction of buildings, walls, ceilings, pipes, and other solids. Stethoscopes, which use contact microphones as sensors, are used to intercept such information without access to protected areas.

Electroacoustic channels of information leakage arise due to electro-acoustic transformations in sound broadcasting systems, telephones and microphones.

Information retrieval in the optoelectronic channel is realized by means of a laser. Under the influence of sound wave, thin reflective surfaces begin to vibrate. If a laser is directed at them, the reflected laser radiation is modulated and fed to the input of the optical radiation receiver. So the attacker can receive the original acoustic signal.

The occurrence of parametric channels is due to the fact that under the pressure of the sound wave relative positioning of circuit elements, wires, etc. can be changed in BTSM and ATSM. Along with the location, the inductance and the capacitance are changed. Accordingly, there will be a modulation of signals passing through BTSM and ATSM with information signal contained in the acoustic wave. The modulated signals are emitted into space where they can be intercepted.

The set of threats of acoustic information leakage is $Th^A = \{Th_1^A, \ldots, Th_k^A\}$, where k – total number of threats.

Methods of protection of acoustic (speech) information are divided into passive and active methods.

Passive methods are aimed at attenuation of direct acoustic signals circulating in the room, as well as products of electro-acoustic transformations circulating in BTSM and ATSM and connecting circuits. The main passive method of protection of acoustic (speech) information is soundproofing.

Active methods include the creation of masking interference and suppression/destruction of technical means of acoustic reconnaissance. The main active method of protection of acoustic (speech) information is noise pollution. The information signal is most effectively masked by a noise close to the signal in the spectral composition.

Means of acoustic noise creating can be divided into the following types:

- generators of noise in the acoustic range;
- devices of vibroacoustic protection;
- technical means of ultrasonic protection of premises.

The set of means of protection from acoustic information leakage is $M^A = \{M_1^A, \ldots, M_l^A\}$, where l – total number of protection means.

3.3 The Threat of Information Leakage Through the Channels of SEMRI

Processes and phenomena that are sources of SEMRI can be divided into four types:

- conversion of external acoustic signals into electrical signals not provided by functions of radio equipment and electrical devices;
- side low-frequency emissions;
- secondary high-frequency emissions;
- parasitic connections and interferences.

The set of threats of information leakage through the channels of SEMRI is $Th^E = \{Th_1^E, \ldots, Th_q^E\}$, where q – total number of threats.

Protection of information from leakage through SEMRI is carried out using passive and active methods and means.

Passive methods of information protection are aimed at:

- attenuation of side electromagnetic radiation (information signals) of BTMS at the border of the controlled zone to the values that ensure the impossibility of their isolation by means of reconnaissance against the background noise;
- attenuation of side electromagnetic radiation interference in foreign conductors and connecting lines beyond the controlled zone to the values that ensure the impossibility of their isolation by means of reconnaissance against the background noise;
- exclusion or attenuation of information signals leakage in the power supply circuit beyond the controlled zone to the values that ensure the impossibility of their allocation by means of exploration against the background noise.

Active methods of information protection are aimed at:

- creation of masking spatial electromagnetic interference in order to reduce the signal-to-noise ratio at the boundary of the controlled zone to the values that ensure the impossibility of isolation by means of exploration of information signal;
- creation of masking electromagnetic interference in foreign conductors and connecting lines in order to reduce the signal-to-noise ratio at the boundary of the controlled zone to the values that ensure the impossibility of allocation by means of exploration of the information signal.

The set of means of protection from information leakage through the channels of SEMRI is $M^E = \{M_1^E, \ldots, M_r^E\}$, where r – total number of protection means.

4   Protection System's Composition

There are certain principles on which technical information protection system should be based:

- continuity of the system in space and time. The system must control the entire material and information perimeter around the clock, preventing the occurrence of certain gaps or reduce in level of protection;
- multizone protection. Information should be ranked according to its significance and different protection means should be used to protect it;
- setting priorities. Not all information is equally important, so the most serious protection measures should be applied to information of the highest value;
- integration. All components of the system must interact with each other and be managed from a single center.
- duplication. All the most important units and communication systems should be duplicated so that in the event of a breakthrough or destruction of one of the means it was replaced by backup one.

Technical information protection system S is a set of three subsystems:

- protection subsystem from specific information leakage S^S;
- protection subsystem from acoustic information leakage S^A;
- protection subsystem from information leakage through the channels of SEMRI S^E.

Each subsystem S^i is a set of corresponding protection means M^i. They are different means for each subsystem, so their composition can be chosen independently. Herewith subsystem can contain not all means of the set, but a subset $\widetilde{M^i}$. So to determine the best composition of technical information protection system the set of attributes A for a subset $\widetilde{M^i}$ is defined:

1. A_1 – threats overlapping. Determines how the subset of protection means overlap actual threats from the set of threats Th^i. To get the attribute value the matrix of threats overlapping O is built. The element o_{jh} of the matrix determines the probability of j-th threat being blocked by h-th protection mean. For the final table, the convolution is calculated. This value determines the value of the attribute.
2. A_2 – characteristics quality. In regulatory documents, the minimum required characteristics that protection means must have been specified. So the value of the attribute can be "insufficient", "minimum" or "elevated" for each protection mean in the subset. To obtain the value of the attribute the convolution for all values in the subset is calculated.
3. A_3 – certification. Each protection mean in the subset may or may not have a regulatory compliance certificate. To obtain the value of the attribute the convolution for all values in the subset is calculated.

4. A_4 – price. Each protection mean in the subset has a different price. To make the evaluation universal, a scale is introduced: "low", "medium" or "high". To obtain the value of the attribute the convolution for all values in the subset is calculated.

The problem is formulated as optimization task $|A| \underset{\widetilde{M^i}}{\rightarrow} max.$

To obtain an integral estimate $|A|$ for a subset $\widetilde{M^i}$ the Bayes formula is used [7]:

$$P(H_i|A_1,\ldots,A_4) = \frac{P(H_i)P(A_1|H_i)\ldots P(A_n|H_i)}{\sum_{b=1}^{d} P(H_b)P(A_1|H_b)\ldots P(A_4|H_b)}. \tag{1}$$

For subset $\widetilde{M^i}$ defines a set of quality ranking levels $L_i, i = 1\ldots d$.

Before the measurement results are obtained a priori probability distribution $P(H_i)$ (it can be even) is formed on the set of d hypotheses of the form "The quality of subset corresponds to the ranking level L_i" [8].

The results of mapping the values of the selected attributes to the ranking levels are used as evidence. Therefore, conditional probabilities $P(A_j|H_i)$ are defined as follows: $P(A_j|H_i) = |M_j(L_i)|/l_j$, where $M_j(L_i)$ – set of attribute's A_j metrics, such as $M_{jk} \in L_i$, $j = 1\ldots 4, k = 1\ldots l_j$, where l_j – number of metrics of j-th attribute.

The posterior conditional probability $P(H_i|A_1,\ldots,A_4)$ according to (1) is the degree of confidence in the validity of the hypothesis H_i after obtaining estimates on the metrics of all attributes [9].

After determining the most probable hypothesis, the conclusion about the quality of a particular subset $\widetilde{M^i}$ can be made [10].

5 Conclusion

The first priority when choosing protection means for technical information protection system's forming belongs to threats overlapping. But if there are different protection means with similar functionality, then its other characteristics can determine its chose.

To determine whether all subsystems should be presented in a technical information protection system, it is necessary to conduct a preliminary analysis to identify the list of actual threats.

This approach is also applicable to the private task of adding or replacing one of the protection means. In this case, the convolutions are not applied when the attributes are calculated. The rest of the algorithm remains unchanged.

Acknowledgment. The reported study was funded by the Council for grants of Russian Federation President, according to the research project No. MK-6404.2018.9.

References

1. Grishachev, V., Kalinina, Y., Kazarin, O.: Fiber-optic channel of voice information leakage. In: Proceedings of the 2019 IEEE Conference of Russian Young Researchers in Electrical and Electronic Engineering, ElConRus 2019, pp. 1512–1514 (2019)
2. Drago, A., Marrone, S., Mazzocca, N., Nardone, R., Tedesco, A., Vittorini, V.: A model-driven approach for vulnerability evaluation of modern physical protection systems. Softw. Syst. Model. **18**(1), 523–556 (2019)
3. Zou, B., et al.: Evaluation of vulnerable path: using heuristic path-finding algorithm in physical protection system of nuclear power plant. Int. J. Crit. Infrastruct. Prot. **23**, 90–99 (2018)
4. Peng, H.-F., Huang, Z.-Q., Liu, L.-Y., Li, Y., Ke, C.-B.: Static analysis method of secure privacy information flow for service composition. Ruan Jian Xue Bao/J. Softw. **29**(6), 1739–1755 (2018)
5. Wang, D., Xu, Y., Xu, P.: Information system's security evaluation of dynamic behavior based on service composition. In: Proceedings - The 2015 10th International Conference on Intelligent Systems and Knowledge Engineering, ISKE 2015, pp. 112–120 (2016)
6. Akhmetov, B., Lakhno, V., Akhmetov, B., Myakuhin, Y., Adranova, A., Kydyralina, L.: Models and algorithms of vector optimization in selecting security measures for higher education institution's information learning environment. In: Silhavy, R., Silhavy, P., Prokopova, Z. (eds.) CoMeSySo 2018. AISC, vol. 860, pp. 135–142. Springer, Cham (2019). https://doi.org/10.1007/978-3-030-00184-1_13
7. Burakov, D.P., Kozhomberdieva, G.I.: Comparison of approaches to obtain integral estimation of software quality according to ISO/IEC 9126 standard. In: Information Technologies in Science, Management, Social Sphere and Medicine, pp. 221–226 (2018)
8. Koskin, A., Uzharinskiy, A., Averchenkov, A., Ivkina, N., Rytov, M.: Mechanisms for the construction of the service-oriented information system of educational institution based on technologies of data integration and virtualization. In: Kravets, A., Shcherbakov, M., Kultsova, M., Groumpos, P. (eds.) CIT&DS 2017. CCIS, vol. 754, pp. 177–186. Springer, Cham (2017). https://doi.org/10.1007/978-3-319-65551-2_13
9. Kvyatkovskaya, I.Yu., Kosmacheva, I., Sibikina, I., Galimova, L., Rudenko, M., Barabanova, E.A.: Modular structure of data processing in automated systems of risk management in the fisheries industry. In: Kravets, A., Shcherbakov, M., Kultsova, M., Groumpos, P. (eds.) CIT&DS 2017. CCIS, vol. 754, pp. 284–301. Springer, Cham (2017). https://doi.org/10.1007/978-3-319-65551-2_21
10. Kultsova, M., Litovkin, D., Zhukova, I., Dvoryankin, A.: Intelligent support of decision making in management of large-scale systems using case-based, rule-based and qualitative reasoning over ontologies. In: Kravets, A., Shcherbakov, M., Kultsova, M., Groumpos, P. (eds.) CIT&DS 2017. CCIS, vol. 754, pp. 331–349. Springer, Cham (2017). https://doi.org/10.1007/978-3-319-65551-2_24

Mass Media as a Data Source on Social Preferences Analysis

Yaroslav Milchuk[1], Alla G. Kravets[1](✉) , Natalia Salnikova[2] ,
and Vladimir Shinkaruk[3]

[1] Volgograd State Technical University, Volgograd, Russian Federation
carhangel@gmail.com, agk@gde.ru
[2] Volgograd Institute of Management – Branch of the Russian Presidential
Academy of National Economy and Public Administration, Volgograd, Russia
ns3112@mail.ru
[3] Volgograd State University, Volgograd, Russia
shinkarukvm@gmail.com

Abstract. The information obtained from social networks analysis is one of the most reliable sources of knowledge that could be used in regional development management. The number of people who use different social networking services is increasing year by year, the social network audience includes different age groups. More and more profiles in social networks are becoming open. The article describes the concept of "digital region" - regional development management based on social behavior and social preferences analysis. A model based on social preferences of people visiting certain social places is described. The model is used for the identification of social preferences and building a geo-information model. The data were collected in social nets VKontakte, Facebook, Twitter, LinkedIn by questionnaires and were analyzed by knowledge mining method based on the algorithm for modeling of the implicit social graph of users' interests, providing a complete scheme of social data of the user. The algorithm is based on data obtained from the HTML code of social network and the information selected from key tags. Implementation of the described models and algorithms in the regional development management system is described.

Keywords: Digital region · Knowledge discovery · Social behavior ·
Forecasting of social preferences · Implicit social graph · Geoformation model ·
e-Government

1 Introduction

Progress in the development of information and communication technologies and methods for extracting knowledge determines the deep penetration of intelligent tools for working with data in various spheres of human life. Information technology helps in engineering and management activities for the management of complex infrastructure systems and territories.

Making informed decisions is a prerequisite for choosing social development options, both at the level of the regional leadership and for local authorities.

© Springer Nature Switzerland AG 2019
A. G. Kravets et al. (Eds.): CIT&DS 2019, CCIS 1084, pp. 295–304, 2019.
https://doi.org/10.1007/978-3-030-29750-3_23

A significant problem for determining the directions of social development is the laboriousness of collecting and processing data on the preferences of the inhabitants of the region. The information necessary for analyzing the current state is large, constantly updated and is characterized by heterogeneity. Existing statistical methods often do not allow for timely updating of data; therefore, alternative methods for monitoring social processes are needed.

Taking into account the wishes of the inhabitants of the regions through the analysis of data from social networks, it is possible to significantly improve the efficiency of obtaining information about the current state of affairs in the region and the quality of decisions made.

To obtain actual data on the preferences of residents of different territories, it is necessary to ensure prompt collection of information and its storage in a database in a unified format. One of the sources is social networks [1, 3]. Collecting such data from user profiles, such as gender, age, interests, place of work, place of study, photos, as well as hashtags and geo-data correlated with them, can help in identifying social needs realized at a specific point in time. For example, users of social networks regularly publish a significant number of photos reflecting their favorite or most visited places. Identifying frequent repetitions, it is possible to determine the actual social needs in comparison with the places of their realization [2].

One of the main criteria for the quality of data in determining social preferences is the completeness of information about the inhabitants of the territory, therefore the main problem of finding relevant data is the partial closure of user profiles. To ensure the completeness of the collected data, you can use the data collection algorithm with the mechanism for constructing the closure of the social graph, which allows you to collect the most complete information. The algorithm is based on adding the missing information from the data in the profiles of the most relevant users, consisting of the mutual status of "friends" with the profile under study.

Thus, the identification and study of the social needs of regional residents using data analysis of social networks are the determining factors in building effective social policy, as well as the choice of a specific project and business solutions for state municipal authorities and commercial organizations. Knowing the most popular places and their goals in formal terms and perceptions of residents, it becomes possible to complete the picture of the emerging situation in the infrastructure: to determine the lack or excess of the infrastructure of networks and communications, and subsequently - to form the purpose of unused territories.

2 The Concept of Regional Development Management Based on the Data Analysis of Social Networks

For the most effective regional management, it is necessary to respond quickly and efficiently to the situation there, we propose to establish feedback, not only through the media but also through social networks.

In social networks people registered are from the different ages and social groups, so regional authorities can guide the development of regions for older generations, and for the younger ones [15]. "Digital region" in our research is a virtual model of the real region based on data from Internet sources including social nets.

Digital region is an informational core for the e-Government concept implementation.

On voting and articles, in newspapers and magazines, most attention is a focus for people older and middle age groups, so we often forget in what direction should be directed to regional development. After all, we are building a future for the young (younger) generation, often without thinking about their interests. Since simply do not have feedback from them.

If a person is sure that his voice could be decisive, and the opinion, written somewhere in the forum, receives the response, we will be able to generate interest in taking part in the development of the region's own citizens. Thus we can talk about the development of the political consciousness of citizens, which is an integral part of the stable development of society.

That is why the concept of regional development management is based on the use of behavioral models of society and predicting social preferences based on analysis of data from social networks is an urgent task.

The concept implies: different groups of people in their social lives communicate with each other. This is accompanied by the construction of the political views of man, whom he often shared in the Internet community. Just part of the social dialogue does not take place in person and on the pages in social networks. So we can use political views, opinions and behavioral characteristics of a person studying its behavior in social networks.

The most popular social networks in Russia are VK, Odnoklassniki, Facebook, Instagram, Twitter [10]. Data from these social networks are divided into two types: Social Media (comments/messages left by users on the forum) and users' data profiles. Each of these networks stores all user data on its servers, part of the data is public, but also there are private data. Thus, the first problem of the use of these social networks is a need to ensure the completeness of the information. There are many different ways how to do it, but somehow all of them use social networks' application programming interface (API). However, by the need to find algorithms for circuit social networking graph, it is necessary to take into account privacy. In many countries, the law protects account privacy, therefore, it is legally forbidden to process personal data of a person without his/her explicit consent. Consequently, the algorithm described in this article collects only the information from the user profile, which is not hidden by the privacy settings of the user and dehumanizes it. This data considered in social networking policy how publicly available for further processing and after use. In this research, we used the method that requires specially generated softbots (agents) that go to specific pages of the site and read all the information from the profile, and then create a database, distributing information on the required options [8]. It is also due to the limitation of the number of requests to the social networks' servers in a minute. The concept is shown in Fig. 1.

In this case, we are interested in the quantitative method of aggregated data analysis that would eliminate the false information of some users. To eliminate spam, intentionally added to influence the solutions found by our algorithm was used as an algorithm for determining the user's relevance based on the statistics of its activity.

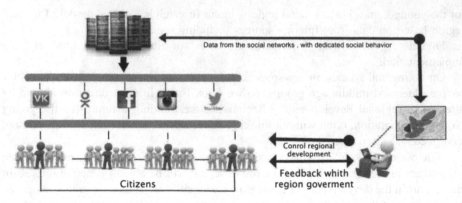

Fig. 1. The concept of regional development management

Thus, instead of drawing conclusions from a set of characteristics of objects of study (users' profiles), our approach seeks to establish regularities on the differences of specific examples of intersubjective interaction in the set of the user profiles in social networks. The software builds a model of the social behavior connected with geographic information and identifies the most relevant (problem) place in the region. Further data comes to be analyzed and assessed according to the criteria scored in the database to identify the most important problems existing in the selected area, and the user is provided in the form of entries with explanations and links to citizens' opinions on this issue. Thus, we can create management decision-making support contributing to sustainable regional development.

For effective functioning of the system should be developed new models and algorithms (Fig. 2). In this paper, we'll describe 2 and 3 as basic features of the proposed concept.

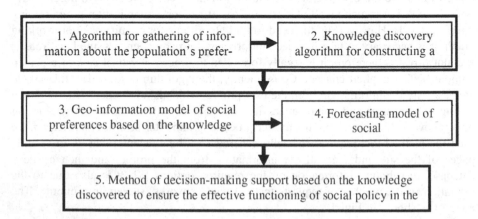

Fig. 2. Components of the regional development management system

3   An Algorithm for Constructing a Complete Social Graph

In our work, we are dealing with incomplete networks. Now, the use of incomplete networks is actively developing research area, also called citation analysis [11, 14]. Therefore, we analyzed algorithms for constructing the social graph, ensuring completeness of social data, identified key performance criteria for quality and reliability algorithms. In this system, we are dealing with incomplete networks, so there is the problem of additions (circuit). According to the results of algorithms' analysis, we used the social networks' nodes grouping algorithm [12] additionally adopted for the data gathering from different social nets.

We use a customized strategy of a profiles' network building with the choice of analyzed parameters, for example, a place of residence (region). The incomplete network may also comprise ego-networks. Because of this, we use the data of the user's friends to fill the incomplete information.

Now we developed software that is able to parse information about users of social networks by some criteria (city of residence, the age of the user, and so on) and combine it to build the social graph and interests' graph. Public APIs (such as Facebook Graph API, Instagram API, and Foursquare API) are used to get data from social networks. Gephi software is most appropriate to visualize the graph. The Graph API is the primary way to get data in and out of Facebook's social graph. It is a low-level HTTP-based API that user can use to query data, post new stories, upload photos and to a variety of other tasks that an app might need to do [6, 13]. All nodes and edges in the Graph API can be read simply with an HTTP GET request to the relevant endpoint. It is used to collect profiles' data from different social networks: VKontakte, Facebook, and others.

Social network data is often incomplete, which means that some actors or links are missing from the dataset [7]. Nevertheless, there are different profiles' data in social networks, and a varying part of these data is filled. To ensure the completeness and accuracy of the data we need to develop an algorithm covering the empty fields of the profile [4]. This problem is solved in our research with the use of the social graph by collecting the information from the friends' profiles with various degrees of probable accuracy, depending on the frequency of another page visits, the quantity of related evaluations ("likes" and "re-posts") and events of common groups for communication. In this case, we need to identify the specific information provided by conducting the survey through social networks of different social and age groups.

Figure 3 shows the graph of the user "Milchuk" in different social networks. A central red dot indicates the selected user, and the points around are his friends. Communication between the points of different social networks indicates the following: 1. mutual friends; 2. registered friends on multiple networks and associated with the primary user by each tag.

Thus, it is possible to supplement the information of user profile "Milchuk" mutually from the profiles of his friends in different social networks (Fig. 4).

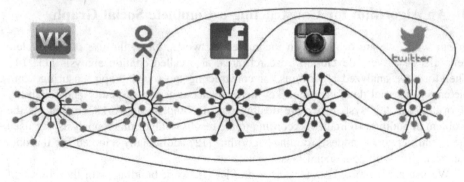

Milchuk's Social network graph

Fig. 3. An example of a social graph

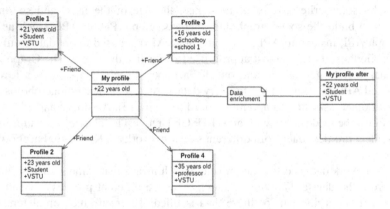

Fig. 4. The result of the social network graph modeling

4   Geo-information Model of Social Preferences

The described approach was used to create a support system for making management decisions on regional management based on infographic analysis. For this, a mechanism for collecting data from social networks VK and Instagram, as the most popular in the region, was implemented (Fig. 5). For this, web crawling technology is used [9]. The data collection algorithm searched for profiles according to specified parameters (person's age, gender, social preference, a region of residence). Additional fields allowed to indicate the time interval of data sampling, city, age, gender and the type of social need of the user being investigated.

During the period of the study, 13044 questionnaire users' profiles and 15436 Instagram user profiles were collected. As a result of data collection, about 100,000 geotags were recorded in the database for each of the social networks with information about the users who created them.

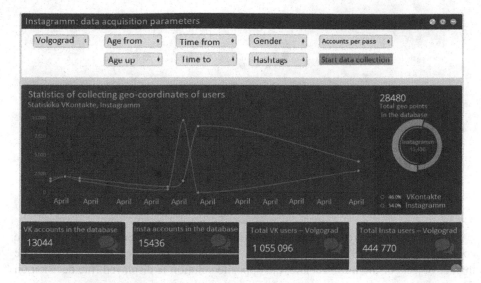

Fig. 5. The interface of the module implementing the technology of web crawling

The collected data were used to define and delineate areas on a map of a region with more than 5 geotags with one type of social preference within a radius of 300 meters, and this criterion was used to search for the most popular places in the region. After determining the popular places in the region, the problem component (lack or excess of any type of infrastructure) is determined, depending on the type of geotag, the average age of users in this area, gender, and the time the geotag was created. For example, for a geotag with a type of "Entertainment", made at 11 p.m. with an average age of 22 years, this component is the number of infrastructure facilities such as karaoke, club, and cafe. And for geotags with the type of "study", the average age of users is 16 years old and the average time is 1 p.m. – 2.p.m. - the number of places of food, low price policy is a component. The system determines the current state of affairs in the area by counting the number of infrastructure objects taken from the 2GIS system. If the number of required objects is less than 5 (for the type "Food"), it is considered that this area has a weak infrastructural component.

Thus, for the example under consideration, we singled out 7 areas, and also we obtained the appropriate solutions on the need to increase the places of budgetary nutrition in these areas because they contain high traffic of schoolchildren at lunchtime. The results are shown in Fig. 6.

At the next stage, the zones were identified, to which solutions are developed based on the analysis of user preferences, as well as examining the territory for insufficient provision of social needs. The definition of the zone to which the solution is applied is as follows: if the number of geotags reaches F within a radius of R meters, then a solution is formulated for this region in accordance with the chosen preference. The choice of limiting the length of the zone and the number of geotags considered in this zone is given to the person making the decision. It is possible to repeatedly receive solutions for various restrictions.

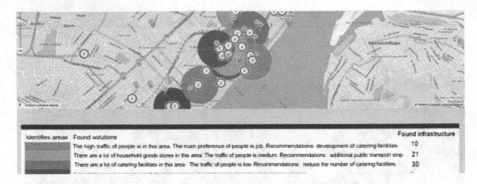

Fig. 6. 4 Geo-information model and probable decisions for problem areas

In the delineated area, infrastructure is searched. To search for existing objects, the connection to the 2GIS system is used (Fig. 6). If in the delineated area there are more than X objects of the infrastructure, the opposite solution is displayed (the decision on the excess).

Our software allows selecting a region and an area of this region. Then the program shows what problems exist in this area, with which reasons they are associated and which groups are focused. And also link to the comments of residents in social networks (if there are).

To identify the social behavior measure the following rule is used:

$$if\left(\sum_{i=0}^{N} S_i > K\right) then\ B = \sum_{i=0}^{N} S_i,$$

where:

B – a quantified measure of social behavior;
S_i – counter of identified social preference;
K – significance coefficient of social preferences (the number indicating the required quantity of labels in area, which would distinguish it as a favorite area to satisfy social preference S_i);
N – number of identified social preferences in the region, defined by experts and stored in the database;
i – a current possible (required) type of social preferences.

Knowledge about social behavior includes the most densely populated areas of the region's, most visited places as well as the preferences of people who are in this area, and their presence in places of interests [5]. These knowledge are basic for the decision-making support in RDM system. Comparison of this knowledge with the existing infrastructure allows creating an effective strategy for the development of the region (bottom part of Fig. 6).

5 Conclusion and Discussion

The developed approach allows to design geo-information systems and analyze dynamic systems effectively, such as social preferences of the population. Its applicability to decision support systems has been proven. The developed methods were tested on the task of supporting decision making in the management of the region. A comparative analysis of the speed of processing data from social networks shows that, even with the limitations of the social network API, the system allows you to collect data on 15,000 users per day, as well as send them targeted surveys. Comparison of the information received with the map of the location of infrastructure facilities will allow for more purposeful planning of the development of complex geographically distributed systems, taking into account the interests of various social groups, more effectively managing the operation of the environment and designing new infrastructure solutions.

The software was implemented to define social behavior in the city of Volgograd, Russia. We selected about 30 thousand primary users' profiles from the most popular social networks in the Volgograd region to construct a complete social graph. According to the analysis results, 30 areas of the city with a social priority of the region's residents were revealed. As well as a number of problems in these areas were identified, and some possible solutions were found. Table 1 shows the number of users' profiles analyzed (includes friends' profiles), identified social behavior as a main type of knowledge discovered, isolated places and the solutions found.

The developed method of collecting and analyzing data from social networks can be used to update information on the preferences of residents in the development of territories. The collected data can serve as a basis for building a management decision support system at the city or regional level. Identifying and exploring social needs with precise geo-referencing is one of the determining factors for building effective economic and social policies, as well as the choice of a specific project and business decisions for both state-municipal and commercial organizations.

Table 1. Results of implementation

No.	Users' profiles analyzed	Identified social behavior	Isolated places	Solutions found
1	15200	9	9	2
2	22726	15	16	5
3	30478	17	31	10
4	50000	18	40	11
5	70000	16	35	10
6	100000	17	36	11

Knowing the most popular places and their intended purpose in formal terms and in the perception of residents, it becomes possible to complete the picture of the current situation in the infrastructure: to determine the shortage or excess of services of the transport system and housing and communal services, infrastructure networks and communications, cultural facilities - household purpose, to formulate the purpose of unused areas.

Nevertheless, despite all the advantages of this approach, there are still restrictions associated with access to data in social networks, as well as with the reliability of the information received. It is necessary to improve the methods of infographic representation of knowledge, as well as methods for monitoring complex, dynamically changing systems.

Acknowledgments. This research was supported by the Russian Fund of Basic Research (grant No. 19-07-01200).

References

1. Adamic, L., Adar, E.: How to search a social network. Soc. Netw. **27**(3), 187–203 (2005)
2. Barabasi, A., Albert, R.: Emergence of scaling in random networks. Science **286**, 509–512 (1999)
3. Carrington, P.J.: Models and Methods in Social Network Analysis. Cambridge University Press, Cambridge (2005)
4. Chumak, A., Kravets, A.: The method of support vectors in the analysis of social networks user profiles. Int. J. Soft Comput. **10**(3), 242–246 (2015)
5. Chumak, A.A., Ukustov, S.S., Kravets, A.G.: Analysis of user profiles in social networks. In: Kravets, A., Shcherbakov, M., Kultsova, M., Iijima, T. (eds.) JCKBSE 2014. CCIS, vol. 466, pp. 70–76. Springer, Cham (2014). https://doi.org/10.1007/978-3-319-11854-3_7
6. Chumak, A.: Social networks message posting support module. World Appl. Sci. J. **24**(24), 191–195 (2013)
7. Kossinets, G.: Effects of missing data in social networks. Soc. Netw. **28**(3), 247–268 (2006)
8. Kravets, A.: Intelligent multi-agent systems generation. World Appl. Sci. J. **24**(24), 98–104 (2013)
9. Liu, B.: Social network analysis. In: Liu, B. (ed.) Web Data Mining. DCSA, pp. 269–309. Springer, Heidelberg (2011). https://doi.org/10.1007/978-3-642-19460-3_7
10. Nguyen, T., Kravets, A.: Analysis of the social network Facebook comments. In: 7th International Conference on Information, Intelligence, Systems & Applications (IISA), Chalkidiki, Greece, pp. 1–5 (2016)
11. Park, H.: Hyperlink network analysis: a new method for the study of social structure on the web. Connections **25**(1), 49–61 (2003)
12. Perepelitsyn, V., Kravets, A.: The social networks' nodes grouping algorithm for the analysis of implicit communities. In: 7th International Conference on Information, Intelligence, Systems & Applications (IISA), Chalkidiki, Greece, pp. 1–6 (2016)
13. Quyên, L.: Protocols to provide anonymity in social nets. In: Proceedings of the International Conferences on ICT, Society and Human Beings 2014, Web-Based Communities and Social Media 2014, e-Commerce 2014, Information Systems Post-Implementation and Change Management 2014 and e-Health 2014 - Part of the Multi Conference on Computer Science and Information Systems, MCCSIS 2014, pp. 318–321 (2014)
14. Thelwall, M.: Link Analysis: An Information Science Approach. Elsevier, Amsterdam (2004)
15. Watts, D.: Six Degrees: The Science of a Connected Age. W. W. Norton, New York (2002)

Program Modeling in the Investigation of Crimes Against Cybersecurity in Russia

Natalia Solovieva[1] , Valentina Khorsheva[2]([⊠]),
Evgeny Likholetov[3] , Yuriy Naumov[4], and Daniyar Kairgaliev[2]

[1] Volgograd State University, 100 Universitetskiy av.,
Volgograd 400062, Russia
solovievanataa@gmail.com
[2] Volgograd Academy of the Russian Ministry of Internal Affairs,
Volgograd, 130 Istoricheskaya str., Volgograd 400089, Russia
i-periscope@yandex.ru, danchem@mail.ru
[3] Volgograd State Agricultural University, 26 Universitetskiy av.,
Volgograd 4000020, Russia
l.evgeni.a@mail.ru
[4] Management Academy of the Ministry of the Interior of Russia,
8 Z & A Kosmodemyanskih str., Moscow 125171, Russia
naumov6112@rambler.ru

Abstract. In a series of recently conducted forensic studies related to methods of a criminal investigation in the sphere of computer information, scientifically interesting data about the constancy of connections of particular characteristics of these criminal actions have been obtained. On their basis, a researcher is supposed to build typical and then individual models of an event being investigated. As practice shows, such a problem is quite complicated for officials of preliminary investigation agencies since they have to choose necessary data from legal regulations and a wide range of reference materials (the Criminal Code, the Code of Criminal Procedure, federal laws, and other statutory acts regulating public relations in the sphere of information, information technologies, and protection of information, forensic scientific products, etc.), most of which don't apply to a particular case under investigation. It appears that in present-day conditions of science and technology development this problem should be solved on the basis of forensic computer modeling.

Keywords: Cybersecurity · Crimes in the sphere of computer information · Computer modeling

1 Technical and Infrastructural Prerequisites for the Transition to Modeling in Investigation of Computer Crimes

To create an automated information system for the investigation of crimes in the sphere of computer information as a model required to work out forensic recommendations on their investigation, it is more preferable to focus on a basic open model using an

A. G. Kravets et al. (Eds.): CIT&DS 2019, CCIS 1084, pp. 305–314, 2019.
https://doi.org/10.1007/978-3-030-29750-3_24

algorithmic method and MS Word software product available to every non-professional PC user. According to recent research, the vast majority (99.2%) of investigators' workplaces are equipped with personal computers (Fig. 1).

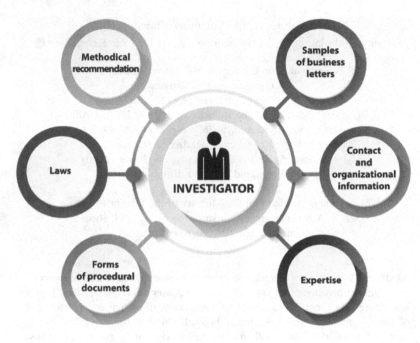

Fig. 1. Related elements of the system.

It will allow an investigator who doesn't specialize in the investigation of crimes in the sphere of computer information to organize his work correctly from the methodical point of view, reduce the time required to complete it, and obtain qualitative and properly formalized results. Subsequently, as knowledge is accumulated, he can modify the information contained in databases of the automated information search system (after this AISS) with the help of MS Word and without involving a computer technology specialist, supplement it, and build new logical connections between elements of the system. Therefore, a basic algorithm of its operation will be evolving as a "tree" with more and more "branches" appearing year by year as algorithms of investigating particular crimes of the given type, and with "leaves" on them representing electronic forms and samples of procedural and other documents.

The investigator can fill the gap in search and statistical information by means of specialized resources of the Internet as well as departmental services, in particular, the Information Analytical System of Support for Activities of the Ministry of Internal Affairs of Russia [1]. They are also quite accessible: 94.4% of investigators have access to the World Wide Web (Fig. 2), while 84.8% have access (yes – 84,8%, no – 8%, were undecided – 7,2%) to the Ministry's Portal (Fig. 3).

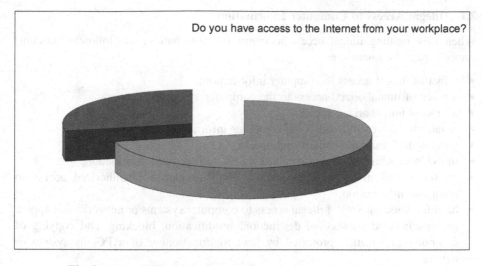

Fig. 2. Accessibility of the Internet from the investigator's workplace.

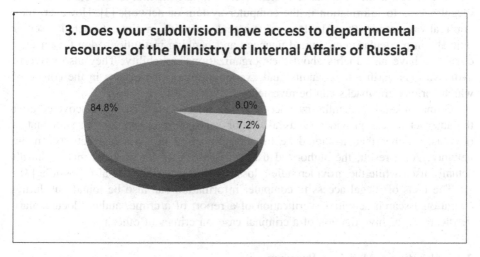

Fig. 3. Access to the Information Analytical System of Support for Activities of the Ministry of Internal Affairs of Russia.

2 Forensic Matrices for Building Models

Having studied a typical model of investigating crimes in the sphere of computer information, we came to the conclusion that models of investigating various types of crimes in the sphere of computer information have a similar structure and differ mainly in the circumstances to be established and proved [2].

2.1   Illegal Access to Computer Information

When investigating illegal access to computer information, the following circumstances are to be established:

- a fact of illegal access to computer information;
- a place of unauthorized access to the computer system or network;
- a time of unauthorized access;
- reliability of security features of computer information;
- a method of gaining unauthorized access;
- individuals who gained unauthorized access to computer information;
- guiltiness and motives of the individuals who gained unauthorized access to computer information;
- harmful consequences of illegal access to computer systems or networks that appear as unauthorized possession, destruction, modification, blocking, and copying of computer information protected by law; malfunctioning of a PC, its system or network;
- circumstances that facilitated illegal access to computer information.

As a rule, it is the information system users who are the first to find out the facts of illegal access to information in the computer system or network [3]. However, they don't always report them to law enforcement agencies in time. Generally, senior officials, in particular in credit and financial and banking institutions, don't want their clients to have any doubts about their organizations' reliability. They also strive to avoid various verifications, audits, and examinations on these facts in the course of which serious drawbacks can be revealed.

Crimes related to unauthorized access to the Internet are basically discovered after the Internet access provider sends a bill for services rendered for the sum that is obviously higher than it should be for the authorized user's actual activity on the network. As a result, the authorized user refuses to pay for services that he hasn't actually used while the provider suffers losses. Other scenarios are also possible [4].

The facts of illegal access to computer information can also be found out during operational search activities, verification of a report of a crime, audits (documentary verification), or investigation of a criminal case on crimes of other types.

2.2   Creating a Malicious Program

When investigating criminal actions stipulated by Article 273 of the Criminal Code of the Russian Federation, the legislator basically provides for liability for the following crimes:

- creating malicious programs;
- making the corresponding modifications in the existing programs;
- using malicious programs;
- spreading malicious programs;
- spreading machine-readable media with such programs.

When investigating the creation of malicious programs for a PC or modification of the existing programs that provide a typical program with malicious functions, the following circumstances are to be established:

- a fact of creating a malicious program for a PC;
- a method of creating a malicious program;
- its intended purpose and mechanism of action;
- a place and time of its creation, computer software and hardware that were used;
- a personality of its creator;
- a motive and purpose of its creation;
- the presence or absence of a criminal intent to use and spread this program;
- the amount of material damage;
- causes and conditions facilitating the commission of a crime.

As a rule, a malicious program is detected only when its consequences become evident or by antivirus scanning of a data medium by the computer system user, which is especially often applied while using shared machine-readable media or receiving e-mail messages. Along with this, it can be detected when using optical media, in particular by studying information on a CD cover [5].

When investigating the use of malicious programs for a PC the following circumstances are to be established:

- the origin of a malicious program;
- a personality of its creator;
- a fact of using a malicious program for a PC;
- the presence of malicious consequences, the amount of material damage;
- an intended purpose of a malicious program and its mechanism of action;
- a causal link between the use of this program and malicious consequences;
- where an individual who used this program got it from, who its creator is;
- the awareness of an individual who used it of its malicious properties;
- the presence of a criminal intent to use this program;
- a motive and purpose of its use.

When investigating the spread of malicious programs for a PC and machine-readable media with such programs the following circumstances are to be established:

- a fact of spreading a malicious program for a PC;
- an intended purpose of a malicious program;
- where an individual who spread this program got it from;
- a personality of its creator;
- the awareness of an individual who spread it of its malicious properties;
- the presence of a criminal intent to spread this program;
- the amount of material damage;
- a motive and purpose of its spread;
- causes and conditions facilitating the commission of a crime [6].

First of all, it is necessary to establish that there are certain operating rules for a PC in a given location. They may refer to the order of creating, collecting, processing, accumulating, storing, searching, and spreading computer information as well as providing a consumer with it and protecting it at every stage of the information process. The following components may relate to PC operating rules: requirements for certification of computer networks and equipment; technical documentation for computers being purchased; certain internal regulations adopted in a particular institution or organization, formalized and notified to all the corresponding employees; job descriptions of particular employees; guidelines for using computer networks [7].

As a rule, direct computer system or network owners or users find out the facts of serious violation of PC operating rules after they discover a lack of the necessary information or its significant alteration, when it has already exerted a negative influence on the main activities of a particular enterprise, institution, or organization [8].

The fact of violation of PC operating rules can be established on the materials of an internal investigation that is generally conducted by the information security department of the organization where it took place, materials of prosecutor's inspection, or materials of operational search activities. The materials obtained by the investigator to make a decision about the institution of a criminal case are subject to thorough and comprehensive consideration. The investigator is to conclude that there are grounds for initiating a criminal case and make sure that there are sufficient data indicating elements of a crime (Article 140 of the Code of Criminal Procedure of the Russian Federation).

2.3   Operational Search and Organizational Activities

A set of initial investigative actions as well as operational search and organizational activities is considered to be an important component of the model of a particular crime in the sphere of computer information. They are as follows:

Initiating a criminal case.

Filling out recorded documents and submitting them to the Information Center of the constituent entity of the Russian Federation.

Drawing up a plan for investigation.

Interviewing a complainant or individuals indicated as possible witnesses in the initial information.

Solving an issue about the possibility of apprehending a perpetrator red-handed as well as about the conduct of further activities.

Engaging necessary specialists to participate in crime scene examination (if it hasn't been conducted earlier).

Crime scene examination.

Conducting operational search activities to establish causes of the commission of a crime, identify those individuals who are guilty, and detect traces and other real evidence.

Seizing and further examining computer technology facilities, things, materials, and documents (including those on machine-readable media in an electronic form) characterizing a working operation during which criminal actions have been committed according to the obtained data.

Interviewing witnesses/eyewitnesses.

Interrogating suspects/witnesses responsible for the given area of work, a particular working operation, and protection of information.

Searching at suspects' workplaces and places of their residence.

Assigning forensic computer technical, radio technical, accounting, and other types of examinations [9].

3 The Structure of the Information System of Investigation of Computer Crimes

We are currently developing a specialized software tool intended to simplify the investigation of the given category of crimes (Fig. 4).

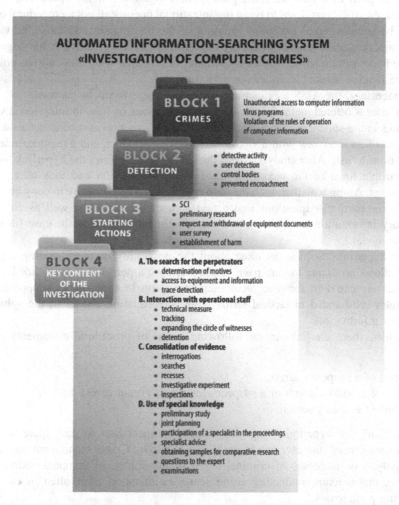

Fig. 4. The structure of the information system of investigation of computer crimes

When choosing a corresponding investigative action with an interactive mouse pointer in this software shell, methodological recommendations on how to conduct it can appear on a monitor display. After that, it is reasonable to provide a hyperlink to an electronic form of a procedural document that is necessary to fill in according to the results of the conducted investigative action.

Following the hyperlink "Initiating a criminal case" the user will find an electronic digital form of the order of the institution of a criminal case and criminal proceedings available for the investigator to fill in.

The hyperlink "Filling out and submitting recorded documents" is supposed to make electronic forms of a statistical report accessible for the user.

Following the hyperlink "Drawing up a plan for investigation" the user will be able to open a form of a recommended plan of investigative actions, operational search activities, etc. It is considered to be an organizational document, not a procedural one. It should be acknowledged that joint planning of the investigator and those individuals providing operational support for the investigation is the most effective at this stage [10].

The hyperlink "Interviewing a complainant or potential witnesses" allows going to the investigative action "Interviewing a victim".

If necessary, the AISS user can add other electronic forms of his own.

The user is offered methodological recommendations on how to interview a victim on crimes in the sphere of computer information. This section also contains a statutory definition of an interview with a victim, stages of its conduct, and a recommended list of questions to ask. After studying them the investigator follows the hyperlink to open an electronic form of the record of this investigative action and thus may initiate proceedings. Along with that, with the help of MS Word services he can copy and paste all or some particular questions into a text area of the record as well as any other necessary information from other electronic documents related to the case (in multi-window mode).

The hyperlink "Solving an issue about the possibility of apprehending a perpetrator" allows accessing the tab page "Apprehending a perpetrator red-handed".

Here one can find forensic recommendations on how to properly apprehend a perpetrator red-handed in tactical terms while investigating crimes in the sphere of computer information.

Besides, there are links to the following forms of procedural documents in MS Word:

- record of a suspect's arrest;
- order of a bodily search of a suspect/accused in urgent cases;
- record of a bodily search.

Choosing the hyperlink "Engaging necessary specialists to participate in crime scene examination" the user can move to the window "Crime scene team members". The analysis of materials of criminal cases in the sphere of computer information indicates that a team conducting crime scene examination most often involves the following participants:

- a detective of the economic security or cybersecurity subdivision;
- an investigator;
- a forensic expert, a specialist in telecommunications and computer technologies;
- other individuals.

This window displays forensic recommendations on how to form a crime scene team in order to properly conduct crime scene examination related to crimes in the sphere of computer information.

The hyperlink "Crime scene examination" allows moving to the tab page of the same name.

The given section contains information about the concept of crime scene and tactics of its investigative examination. There is also a link to the record of crime scene examination in an electronic digital form. The conducted research revealed the following typical crime scenes connected with crimes in the sphere of computer information:

- a scene where signs of a crime were detected;
- scenes of the direct commission of criminal actions;
- scenes of preparing/finding crime instruments (documents; passwords, codes, and access keys; malicious programs for a PC; telecommunications facilities; special technical means for undercover obtaining, destructing, modifying, blocking, and copying of information as well as for malfunctioning of a PC, its system or network).

Choosing the hyperlink "Conducting operational search activities to establish causes of the commission of a crime, identify those individuals who are guilty, and detect traces and other real evidence" the user goes to the window "Operational search activities".

Here are some recommendations on the main operational search activities which can be conducted simultaneously with investigative actions on criminal cases in the sphere of computer information. They include interviewing citizens, engaging the community in search activities, sending out an all-points bulletin, intercepting communications, collecting samples for comparative research, checking certain individuals for criminal records, and making inquiries.

Clicking on the hyperlink "Seizing and further examining of computer technology facilities, things, materials, and documents (including those on machine-readable media in an electronic form) characterizing a working operation during which criminal actions have been committed according to the obtained data" the user opens the window with a list of the following actions:

- examination of a PC;
- examination of a machine-readable medium;
- examination of a document on a machine-readable medium;
- seizure of a PC and computer information.

This list is also accomplished using hypertext technology. Choosing a corresponding position the user can acquaint himself with forensic recommendations on the tactics of conducting a particular investigative action. Having read them the investigator may initiate this investigative action and draw up a procedural document in an electronic digital form. Among sections of the given recommendations, there is an algorithm of detailed circumstances which must be indicated in the record of examination of these things/documents.

Clicking on the hyperlink "Interviewing witnesses/eyewitnesses" the user opens the window "Interviewing witnesses". This section of the program focuses on the peculiarities of interviewing with witnesses/eyewitnesses and contains a link to an electronic form of the record of witness interviews. The modules "Interrogating a suspect", "Search and seizure", and "Assigning forensic examinations" are similarly structured and function in the same way. These are the investigative actions which are most often conducted by officials of preliminary investigation agencies on criminal cases of the given type [11].

References

1. Kravets, E., Birukov, S., Pavlik, M.: Remote investigative actions as the evidentiary information management system. In: Kravets, A.G. (ed.) Big Data-driven World: Legislation Issues and Control Technologies. SSDC, vol. 181, pp. 95–103. Springer, Cham (2019). https://doi.org/10.1007/978-3-030-01358-5_9
2. Hyland, J.M., Hyland, P.K., Corcoran, L.: Cyber aggression and cyberbullying: widening the net. In: Jahankhani, H. (ed.) Cyber Criminology. ASTSA, pp. 47–68. Springer, Cham (2018). https://doi.org/10.1007/978-3-319-97181-0_3
3. Kravets, A.G., Bui, N.D., Al-Ashval, M.: Mobile security solution for enterprise network. In: Kravets, A., Shcherbakov, M., Kultsova, M., Iijima, T. (eds.) JCKBSE 2014. CCIS, vol. 466, pp. 371–382. Springer, Cham (2014). https://doi.org/10.1007/978-3-319-11854-3_31
4. Saltykov, S., Rusyaeva, E., Kravets, A.G.: Typology of scientific constructions as an instrument of conceptual creativity. In: Kravets, A., Shcherbakov, M., Kultsova, M., Shabalina, O. (eds.) Creativity in Intelligent Technologies and Data Science. CCIS, vol. 535, pp. 41–57. Springer, Cham (2015). https://doi.org/10.1007/978-3-319-23766-4_4
5. Montasari, R., Hosseinian-Far, A., Hill, R.: Policies, innovative self-adaptive techniques and understanding psychology of cybersecurity to counter adversarial attacks in network and cyber environments. In: Jahankhani, H. (ed.) Cyber Criminology. ASTSA, pp. 71–93. Springer, Cham (2018). https://doi.org/10.1007/978-3-319-97181-0_4
6. Pournouri, S., Zargari, S., Akhgar, B.: Predicting the cyber attackers; a comparison of different classification techniques. In: Jahankhani, H. (ed.) Cyber Criminology. ASTSA, pp. 169–181. Springer, Cham (2018). https://doi.org/10.1007/978-3-319-97181-0_8
7. Quyên, L.X., Kravets, A.G.: Development of a protocol to ensure the safety of user data in social networks, based on the backes method. In: Kravets, A., Shcherbakov, M., Kultsova, M., Iijima, T. (eds.) JCKBSE 2014. CCIS, vol. 466, pp. 393–399. Springer, Cham (2014). https://doi.org/10.1007/978-3-319-11854-3_33
8. Kananizadeh, S., Kononenko, K.: Development of dynamic protection against timing channels. Int. J. Inf. Secur. 16, 641 (2017). https://doi.org/10.1007/s10207-016-0356-7
9. Vasilev, D., Kravets, E., Naumov, Y., Bulgakova, E., Bulgakov, V.: Analysis of the data used at oppugnancy of crimes in the oil and gas industry. In: Kravets, A.G. (ed.) Big Data-driven World: Legislation Issues and Control Technologies. SSDC, vol. 181, pp. 249–258. Springer, Cham (2019). https://doi.org/10.1007/978-3-030-01358-5_22
10. Yemelyanova, E., Khozikova, E., Kononov, A., Opaleva, A.: Counteracting the spread of socially dangerous information on the internet: a comparative legal study. In: Kravets, A.G. (ed.) Big Data-driven World: Legislation Issues and Control Technologies. SSDC, vol. 181, pp. 135–143. Springer, Cham (2019). https://doi.org/10.1007/978-3-030-01358-5_13
11. Nikonovich, S.L., Makeeva, I.V., Avdalyan, A.Ya., Likholetov, A.A., Mogutin R.I.: Qualification problems of credit card fraud. Int. J. Econ. Perspect. 11(3), 42 (2017)

How Popular or Unpopular Have Your Leaders Been - Popularity Tracking and Trend Analysis of Socio-Political Figures

Bal Krishna Bal[1(✉)], Santosh Regmi[2], and Kamal Kafle[1]

[1] Information and Language Processing Research Lab,
Department of Computer Science and Engineering, Kathmandu University,
Dhulikhel, Kavre, Nepal
bal@ku.edu.np, kamal.kafle1@gmail.com
[2] Keiv Technologies Pvt. Ltd., Banepa, Kavre, Nepal
regmi.santosh32@gmail.com

Abstract. Online news media can serve as a very useful resource in terms of tracking the popularity and trend analyses of socio-political figures. The closest technology developed so far in this regard is Google Trends which is however based on the number of searches conducted by the users on the person or figure. And this is not necessarily a measure of popularity – the searches conducted could well be a random search. In this work, we define popularity (growing and diminishing) in terms of the sentiment scores received by the individual statements or sentences in the online news text with respect to some named-entity or socio-political figure. Based on the sentiment analysis and the named-entity extraction, we plot time-series line graphs that represent the popularity and trend analysis of the respective named-entities. The plots were verified with the help of individual opinion surveys and the conformance was more than 80% which signals that our proof-of-concept is viable and works. In the future, we will be extending the work to Nepali based on whatever has been achieved for English news media texts. We also will be improving the current individual module's performances for English.

Keywords: Social media · News media · Sentiment analysis ·
Named entity recognition · Popularity · Trends

1 Introduction

Online data is ever-growing day by day and together with that newer dimensions of data and opinion analysis are also being undertaken in different spheres of our society. There is a growing trend of following public figures and getting updates about their activities in social media like Facebook, Twitter, Linkedin, etc. [1, 5]. However, news media texts are also prominent sources of information and coverage about the public figures/entities. Besides, the data generated in the news media are more likely to be less biased and rather factual as they are held accountable for any information or opinion they publish [3]. In this respect, news media texts could be a more reliable source for tracking the popularity and conducting trend analysis of the public figures. Such a

© Springer Nature Switzerland AG 2019
A. G. Kravets et al. (Eds.): CIT&DS 2019, CCIS 1084, pp. 315–325, 2019.
https://doi.org/10.1007/978-3-030-29750-3_25

tracking and trend analysis serve multiple folds – first of all, this can be a very useful piece of information to the concerned "public figure/entity" itself and secondly, this can be of interest to the general public including the fans as well as the competitors. A very close technology to the given problem is Google Trends[1] but it is purely based on relative searches made on a particular entity over Google's data across time. However, search volumes do not necessarily confirm that somebody was more popular at the given time. The search could have been a random search and hence nothing to do with his/her popularity. In addition to this, Google Trends is based on Google's data and this means the trend graphs would not necessarily reflect the true statistics of a given entity from a local perspective. In fact, "popularity" should be tightly coupled with opinions (positive or negative) or some factual data expressed with respect to the entity in question [5, 8, 9]. This leads to the fact that popularity tracking and trend analysis requires the formulation of a deeper and more serious computational linguistic model.

In this paper, we discuss our research work whereby we look into the Popularity Tracking problem via the extraction of named-entities and conducting sentiment analysis on these entities. The analysis of sentiments is then depicted in the form of a time-series line graph. Such a time-series sentiment analysis would in a true sense provide feedback to the image of the concerned person. The work is currently in progress and we are currently working to realizing a proof-of-concept of the solution to the problem. For this purpose, we have crawled the data from four major online newspaper portals of Nepal publishing the news in the English language for the period of a year. The primary reason for choosing the English language as the medium is because of the availability of rich language processing utilities and applications for the language. We are also extending the work for the data in the Nepali language. Our preliminary research has shown that the research can also be replicated for Nepali although with some limitations.

2 Problem Definition

The dictionary meaning of popularity is "the state or condition of being liked, admired, or supported by many people". However, if we define the same from the perspective of the news or social media, then we find that it is determined by one or more of the following factors:

- Content that has more comments within a timeframe (Most commented);
- Number of views within a timeframe (Most viewed);
- Number of mentions of the individual or entity (High Number of Mentions);
- Number of tweets or retweets (High Number of tweets/Retweets);
- Best rated – the number of high(er/est) ratings (Highly Rated, High Ratings);
- Number of friends and fan following (High number of friends, High number of fan following).

---

[1] https://trends.google.com/trends/.

All of the above parameters seem to be related directly or indirectly with quantitative data and that makes sense if we are considering the social media where the opinions are expressed in the form of short texts (words or phrases or short sentences). Such texts are relatively easier to process in terms of quantifying the opinion related parameters. The case of news media data is a little bit more involved as it deals with larger texts, highly unstructured, not always clear or unambiguous and most of the time implicit and sarcastic in terms of opinions.

From that point of view, we define popularity in the news media as determined by the following parameters:

- Growing popularity;
- This is determined by instances of news sources and articles where a person or entity is positively covered or written about;
- Diminishing popularity;
- This is determined by instances of news sources and articles where a person or entity is negatively covered or written about.

We carry out a sentence-level sentiment analysis and assign sentiment scores to each article with respect to socio-political figures. Hence, our basis for popularity tracking and trend analyses are the scores received per article per source over time with respect to the socio-political figure under consideration. We deal with the concepts – "Growing popularity" and "Diminishing popularity" independently as the news sources would cover or write about the person or entity independent of each other. A person being positively covered or written by one source could be negatively covered or written by another source. Furthermore, it should also be noted that a person or individual may not be covered or written about either positively or negatively in absolute terms. There could be some trace of negativity expressed about somebody by the same source along with the marked opinion of positivity and vice versa. There could also be cases where a person or individual has been covered but in a neutral manner not contributing to either positive or negative popularity. Such texts are treated as being neutral.

3 Related Works

To the best of our knowledge, this is the first of the kind of work looking into popularity tracking and trends analyses of socio-political figures via sentiment analysis on articles published by the news media. Nevertheless, a few works exist which have looked into the social media and partly on news media articles though not directly related to our research topic and direction. [6] propose VADER, a simple rule-based model for sentiment analysis to assess the sentiment of tweets. [9] study the feasibility of using popularity prediction methods for automatic online news ranking. [1] study about the use of social media to investigate the web as a device to explore and track political preferences. [3] discuss the bias of newspapers on covering the news regarding events – the selection bias and the description bias. [7] focus on election result prediction using social media data. [8] examine the effectiveness of applying machine learning techniques to the sentiment classification problem by considering the overall sentiment of the document. [4] present a methodology for predicting the sentiment of documents, under the hypothesis that leveraging the strength of lexicons together with the state-of-the-art word embedding models will result in improved classification performance. [2] propose a deep neural network architecture to recommend popular threads of conversation potentially of interest to the readers.

Based on the studies, we see that there have been sufficient groundworks for our research work, for example from a socio-linguistic perspective, in terms of defining popularity as well as assessing the enormous potentials that the social and online news media as a resource can provide for carrying out different analyses ranging from predictions of election outcomes to more sophisticated works like tracking political preferences of people. Furthermore, there are separate bodies of literature and vibrant research going on about sentiment analysis and opinion mining. However, the problem of popularity tracking via the application of sentiment scores on the document level of an entity seems to be missing. This research work attempts to leverage the existing resources and methods to address the problem of popularity tracking from a socio-technical and computational perspective.

4   Conceptual Framework

In Fig. 1 below, we provide a conceptual framework of our work.

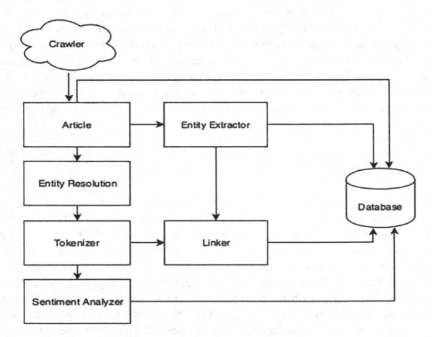

Fig. 1. Conceptual framework of popularity tracking and trends analyses.

As seen from Fig. 1 above, our conceptual framework or high-level architecture consists of the following components:

4.1   Crawler

This module crawls data from online news sources. We have developed several crawler scripts for this purpose.

4.2   Entity Extractor

This module extracts the named-entities from the articles downloaded from online news sources. By named-entities, we refer to the names of the socio-political figures mentioned in the articles. We used the spaCy[2] tool for extracting the named-entities.

4.3   Named-Entity Resolution Module

This module replaces the pronouns in the articles with their respective proper noun references. This is important because we want to ascertain that the referring pronouns actually point to the respective named-entity in question. For this purpose, we used NeuralCoref[3].

4.4   Tokenizer

This module tokenizes the named-entity wise resolved articles into sentences or statements. The tokenized statements are stored along with their article number for further analysis and reference later on.

4.5   Sentiment Analyzer

This module consults the Vader sentiment tool for calculating the sentiment scores of different articles with respect to a particular named-entity.

4.6   Linker Module

This module establishes the link between the named-entity and the sentiment category of each statement in the article for further analysis. We treat only two types of sentiment categories – positive and negative.

4.7   Query Processor

This module takes different parameters like named-entity, date range, etc. in the form of a query and processes the previously analyzed data to develop popularity tracking and

---

[2] https://spacy.io/usage/facts-figures.

[3] https://github.com/huggingface/neuralcoref.

trend analyses graphs of the named-entities. The workflow of our system can be described as follows:

Phase I: Data Preprocessing and Analyses
Algorithm 1
   While (article):

- Store the article;
- Extract all the entities and store the unique ones;
- Resolve the entities in the article;
- Tokenize the resolved article in the sentence/statement level and store the tokens along with the article id;
- Determine the sentiment category of each token;
- Extract the opinion target from the tokens;
- Link and store the token and the opinion target.

Phase II: Query Processing and Data Visualization
Algorithm 2

- Get the entities and the date/time in the query in comma-separated form;
- For each entity, get all articles within the given time frame grouped by their polarity (i.e., positive and negative) on the basis of the token and opinion target relation established in *Algorithm 1;*
- Return the response to the query;
- Plot the positive and negative popularity tracking and trends analyses charts (Fig. 2).

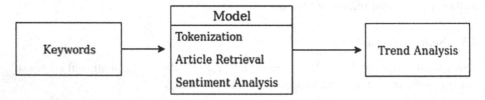

Fig. 2. Query processing workflow.

5   Results and Discussion

We crawled the news articles from four major online sources for a year (2018–2019). These sources include the following:

- Rising Nepal (http://therisingnepal.org.np/);
- Kathmandu Post (http://kathmandupost.ekantipur.com/);
- Nepali Times (https://www.nepalitimes.com/);
- Karobar Daily (https://english.karobardaily.com/).

   We provide the details of the crawled articles below in Table 1.
   We have arranged two different settings for popularity tracking:

Table 1. Details of the crawled articles.

Source	No. of articles
Karobardaily	76846
Kathmandu Post	59935
Nepali Times	166
Rising Nepal	4602

5.1 Popularity of Multiple Entities

Given a comma-separated list of values, the system compares the popularity of those entities in terms of polarity or sentiment scores. For this experiment, two socio-political figures from Nepal were taken - KP Sharma Oli and Puspa Kamal Dahal. The two personalities are influential political figures in Nepal, respectively the current Prime Minister of Nepal and the Chairman of the Nepal Communist Party.

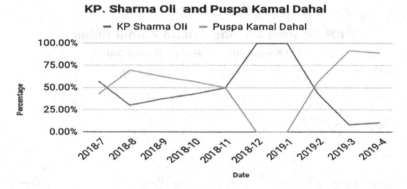

Fig. 3. Positive popularity trend of KP. Sharma Oli vs Puspa Kamal Dahal.

In Fig. 3, we see that there are a rise and fall in the growing popularities of both named-entities. Initially, there is a rise in the popularity of Puspa Kamal Dahal, it begins to fall, reaches the bottom and then gains the height.

We also see the inverse relationship in the positive popularity between the two named-entities. During the time frame when Puspa Kamal Dahal gains popularity, there is a loss in the popularity of KP. Sharma Oli and vice-versa.

In Fig. 4 we can see there is a rise-fall-constant and rise and then constant in the diminishing popularity of Puspa Kamal Dahal. Similarly, there is fall-rise-constant-fall-constant in the diminishing popularity of KP. Sharma Oli. In Fig. 5 the same interpretation holds as for Fig. 3.

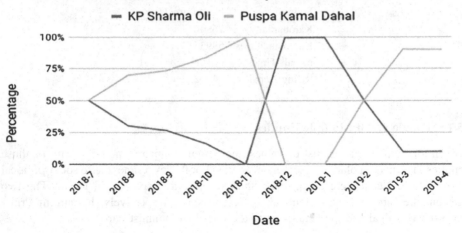

Fig. 4. Negative popularity trend of KP. Sharma Oli vs Puspa Kamal Dahal.

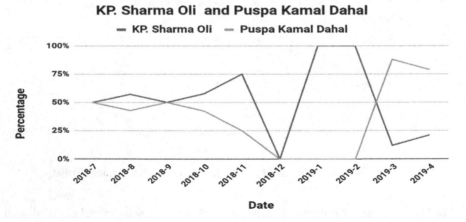

Fig. 5. Neutral popularity trend of KP. Sharma Oli vs Puspa Kamal Dahal.

5.2   Popularity of Single Entity

(See Figs. 6 and 7).

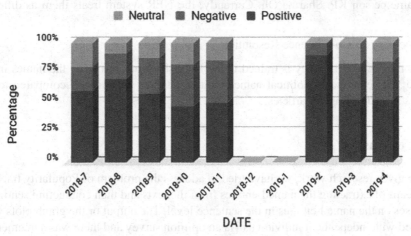

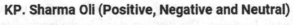

Fig. 6. Popularity of Puspa Kamal Dahal.

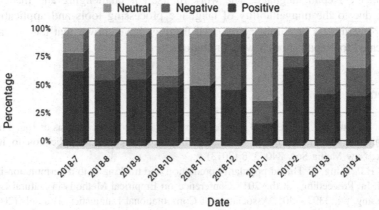

Fig. 7. The popularity of KP Sharma Oli.

6   Challenges

A number of research challenges exist for the given work, which we describe below:

- Accuracy of NER

Misclassification in labeling e.g. KP is categorized as ORG. But KP is a person.
A single entity can be represented in different forms in news article for example:

KP. Sharma Oli can be written as Oli, KP, KP. Sharma although all of them represent the same person KP. Sharma Oli. Currently, the NER system treats them as different entities.

- Accuracy of Co-reference Resolution

Since the NER tool, Spacy is trained in the English corpus resolving the names in the article for Nepali socio-political named-entities has less accuracy as compared to the names in native English articles.

7 Conclusion

In the given research work, we have tried to address the problem of Popularity tracking by means of extracting the named-entities from the texts and then conducting sentiment analyses on the named-entities in the sentence level. The output or the graph plots were verified with independent individuals via an opinion survey and there was agreement or conformance of more than 80%. This signals the fact that our approach to the problem is viable and the proof-of-concept works. In the future, we will work towards training the respective modules with named-entities from Nepal and also improve the sentiment analyzer module. We are already working in terms of extending the work for articles written in the Nepali language. The work in itself is challenging and made further complex due to the unavailability of language processing tools and applications for Nepali. Nevertheless, preliminary research findings have shown that the research can be replicated to Nepali though with limitations.

References

1. Ceron, A., Curini, L., Iacus, S.M.: Tweet your vote: how content analysis of social networks can improve our knowledge of citizen's policy preferences. An application to Italy and France. New Media Soc. 340–358 (2013)
2. Chan, H.P., King, I.: Thread popularity prediction and tracking with a permutation-invariant model. In: Proceedings of the 2018 Conference on Empirical Methods in Natural Language Processing, pp. 3392–3401. Association of Computational Linguistics, Brussels (2018)
3. Earl, J., Martin, A., McCarthy, J.D., Soule, S.A.: The use of newspaper data in the study of collective action. Ann. Rev. Soc. 65–80 (2004)
4. Giatsoglou, M., Vozalis, M.G., Diamantaras, K., Vakali, A., Sarigiannidis, G., Chtazisavvas, K.C.: Sentiment analysis leveraging emotions and word embeddings. Expert Syst. Appl. 214–224 (2017)
5. Gupta, N., Waykos, R.K., Narayanan, R., Chaudhari, A.: Introduction to machine prediction of personality from Facebook profiles. Int. J. Emerg. Technol. Adv. Eng. 66–70 (2017)
6. Hutto, C., Gilbert, E.: VADER: a parsimonious rule-based model for sentiment analysis of social media text. In: Proceedings of the Eighth International AAAI Conference on Weblogs and Social Media (2014)
7. Jain, V.K., Kumar, S.: Towards prediction of election outcomes using social media. Intell. Syst. Appl. 20–28 (2017)

8. Pang, B., Vaithyanathan, S.: Thumbs up? Sentiment classification using machine learning techniques. In: Proceedings of the Conference on Empirical Methods in Natural Language Processing (EMNLP), pp. 79–86. Association for Computational Linguistics, Philadelphia (2002)
9. Tatar, A., Antoniadis, P., DiasdeAmorim, M., Edida, S.: From popularity prediction to ranking online news. Soc. Netw. Anal. Min. **4**, 174 (2014)

Prevention of Crimes Made with the Use of the Internet Network as One of the Directions to Ensure the Cybersecurity of Russia

Ilyas Kasaev[1](✉), Alexander Likholetov[1], Yuriy Bokov[2],
Tatiana Dugina[3], and Alexander Nemchenko[3]

[1] Volgograd Academy of the Russian Ministry of Internal Affairs,
130 Istoricheskaya str., Volgograd 400089, Russia
ilyas.kasaev@yandex.ru, a.likholetov@mail.ru
[2] Volgograd State University, 100 Universitetskiy av.,
Volgograd 400062, Russia
bokov@volsu.ru
[3] Volgograd State Agricultural University, 26 Universitetskiy av.,
Volgograd 4000020, Russia
deisi79@mail.ru, volgsnemchenko@mail.ru

Abstract. The article defines the range of socially dangerous acts committed using the information and telecommunications network "Internet", which are currently prohibited by the criminal law of Russia. Based on official data of the Federal State Statistics Service, the current state of counteraction to these crimes is analyzed. In order to effectively counter these negative phenomena, measures have been formulated to prevent crimes committed using the Internet information and telecommunications network—legal, organizational, and software-technical. In addition, as part of the elimination of circumstances conducive to the commission of cybercrime, we can not neglect the measures of software and hardware confrontation to attackers.

Keywords: Cybersecurity · Cybercrime ·
Information and telecommunication network "Internet" · Crime prevention ·
Crime counteraction

1 The Problem Statement, Conceptual Apparatus

Currently, at the legislative level, definitions of the concepts "cyberspace" and "cybersecurity" are not formulated. Also, the legal definition of "Internet" has not been worked out. The term "Internet" has been replaced by the term information and telecommunication network "Internet" by the legislator in the current legal acts. From this, we can conclude that the "Internet" is a kind of information and telecommunications network [1].

It should be noted that along with the "Internet", other global information and telecommunication networks of a global nature are currently operating in the world:

© Springer Nature Switzerland AG 2019
A. G. Kravets et al. (Eds.): CIT&DS 2019, CCIS 1084, pp. 326–337, 2019.
https://doi.org/10.1007/978-3-030-29750-3_26

Bitnet, EVnet, Fidonet, etc. [2]. In addition, the commission of a number of crimes is in principle possible using the resources of not only global networks, but also, for example, local or regional.

Given the rapid pace of scientific and technological progress, we should not exclude the possibility that any of these or newly created information and telecommunication networks will become more widespread than the Internet at present. This circumstance will require the introduction of the next package of changes to the current legislation.

In Russia, unlike some countries (USA, Germany, France, Canada, etc.), the potential of information and communication technologies is not fully used. According to the Federal State Statistics Service in 2017, 25.6% of domestic households do not have personal computers, and 23.7% do not have access to the Internet (see Fig. 1) [3].

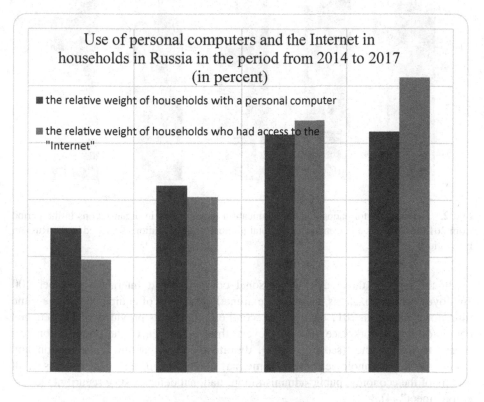

Fig. 1. Use of personal computers and the Internet in households in Russia.

At the same time, things are a little better with the use of information and communication technologies in organizations (see Fig. 2) [3].

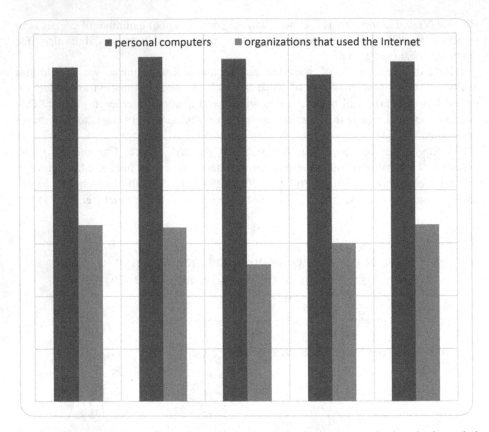

Fig. 2. The use of information and communication technologies in organizations in the period from 2013 to 2017 (as a percentage of the total number of organizations surveyed in the Russian Federation).

In the ratio of the number of personal computers and Internet access per 100 employees in organizations, there is an extremely low level of equipment. At the same time, for example, in 2017 only every second employee was provided with a personal computer at the workplace, and only every third employee of the organization had access to the Internet (see Fig. 3) [3], despite the fact that that "information and communication technologies have become part of modern management systems in all sectors of the economy, public administration, national defense, state security, and law enforcement" [4].

Crimes committed with the use of Internet resources are characterized by an increased degree of public danger caused, among other things, by the wide possibilities of the World Wide Web, minimization of the risk of identifying illegal activities and identification of the criminal, as well as constant improvement of the forms and methods of criminal activity.

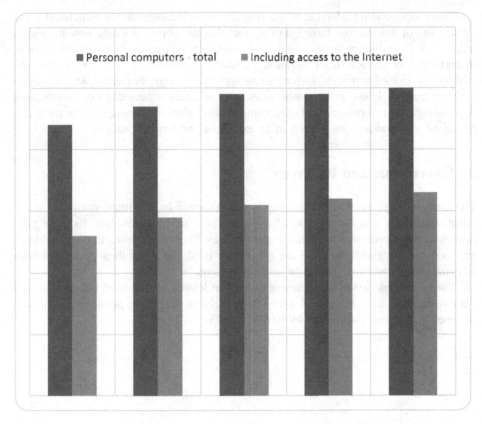

Fig. 3. Data on the number of personal computers per 100 employees (including those with access to the Internet) in the period from 2013 to 2017.

The particular danger of such crimes lies in the fact that the resources of the Internet, which provide an opportunity to commit criminal offenses, can be easily visited by minors, who, due to their psychophysiological characteristics, are most susceptible to the negative impact of information threatening their normal development. The development of technology over the past decade has allowed access to the Internet from virtually anywhere in the world using various gadgets (smartphones, tablets, laptops), which made it impossible for parents to restrict access to sites containing illegal information (for example, on narcotic drugs or materials of an extremist nature).

To organize a crime on the Internet, there is no need to select premises and personnel, special equipment, or to undergo registration and authorization procedures established by law. Thus, the creation of a website for the purpose of committing a crime is limited only by the user's actions to register on the portal of any hosting provider, for which you must specify your username and password (the username can be fictitious), and then, following the instructions, fill in the already existing site template information on a specific topic [5].

The widespread introduction of information and telecommunications networks, the availability of the Internet, have led to the fact that the criminals of the new formation widely use these circumstances as a means to achieve their goals. In the modern world, in particular, in the Russian Federation, "classic" criminal acts cannot be committed without the risk of exposure, without using high technology. For example, the sale of narcotic drugs and psychotropic substances, in most cases is carried out in a contactless way through the information and telecommunication network "Internet". The same can be traced when committing crimes of an extremist and terrorist nature.

2   Cybercrime and Its Types

The modern stage evolution of society is characterized by the improvement of computer technology and the creation of a global information space. But, like any phenomenon, these processes have their negative sides. The more information technologies are used and the global networks are more often used, the lower their protection from criminal attacks and the greater the amount of damage caused.

The overall picture of all crimes registered in Russia in statistical indicators looks very optimistic: over the past 5 years from 2014 to 2018, the number of criminal offenses in the report decreased by 9.09% (see Fig. 4) [6].

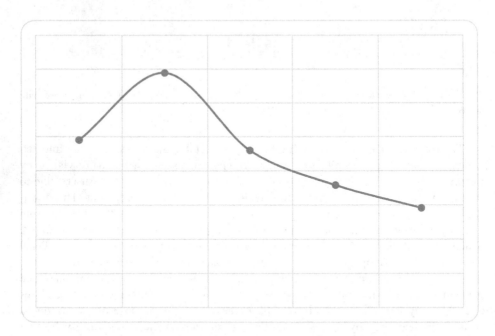

Fig. 4. Number of registered crimes in the Russian Federation.

However, it must be borne in mind that most crimes are not only not disclosed, but not established, and are not registered. Consequently, crime statistics are not only incomplete but also naturally distorted because the most organized part of criminal groups committing crimes does not come into the view of law enforcement agencies.

In recent years, an increase in the number of crimes has been observed in Russia, as well as the Internet information and telecommunications network. Thus, according to official statistics, in 2018, 174,674 crimes were registered, in 2017 - 90,587, in 2016 - 65.9 thousand, in 2015 - 43.8 thousand [6].

At present, in the criminal law of Russia, the information and telecommunications network, as a sign of the objective side, is contained in 22 criminal law norms [7] (Section "d", part 2 of article 110 "Bringing to suicide", section "d" Part 3 of Article 110.1 "Declining to commit suicide or facilitating the commission of suicide", Part 2 of Article 110.2 "Organization of activities aimed at encouraging the commission of suicide", Part 3 of Article 137 "Violation of privacy", Clause "C" of part 2 of article 151.2 "Involvement of a minor in the commission of acts representing for the life of a minor", part 1 of article 159.6 "Fraud in the field of computer information", part 1 of article 171.2 "Illegal organization and conduct of gambling", part 1 of article 185.3 "Market manipulation", part 2 of article 205.2 "Public calls for terrorist activities, public justification of terrorism or propaganda of terrorism", paragraph "b" of part 2 of article 228.1 "Illegal production, sale or shipment of narcotic drugs, psychotropic substances or their analogues, as well as illegal sales or shipment of plants containing narcotic drugs and whether psychotropic substances, or parts thereof, containing narcotic drugs or psychotropic substances", p. "b" part 3 of art. 242 "Illegal manufacturing and trafficking of pornographic materials or objects", p. "G" Part 2 of Art. 242.1 "Production and circulation of materials or items with pornographic images of minors", p. "G" Part 2 of Art. 242.2 "The use of a minor in the manufacture of pornographic materials or objects", paragraph "g" of Part 2 of Art. 245 "Cruel treatment of animals", Part 1.1 and Clause "b" Part 2 of Art. 258.1 "Illegal extraction and trafficking of especially valuable wild animals and aquatic biological resources belonging to species listed in the Red Book of the Russian Federation and (or) protected by international treaties of the Russian Federation", Part 1 of Art. 274 "Violation of the rules of operation of the means of storing, processing or transmitting computer information and information and telecommunication networks", Part 3 of Art. 274.1 "Irregular impact on the critical information infrastructure of the Russian Federation", Part 2 of Art. 280 "Public calls for extremist activities", Part 2 of Art. 280.1 "Public calls for the implementation of actions aimed at violating the territorial integrity of the Russian Federation", part 1 and part 2 of art. 282 "Incitement of hatred or enmity, as well as the humiliation of human dignity" of the Criminal Code of the Russian Federation).

At the same time, in four offenses (art. 137; art. 159.6; art. 274; art. 274.1 of the Criminal Code of the Russian Federation), the legislator does not specify the type of information and telecommunications network (the "Internet").

In Art. 159.6, 171.2, 185.3, Part 1 of Art. 282 of the Criminal Code of the Russian Federation the considered sign of the objective side is constitutive, in other crimes it constitutes qualified or specially qualified compositions.

It should be noted that in Art. 159.6, 274, 274.1 of the Criminal Code of the Russian Federation, the information and telecommunications network serves as the subject of criminal infringement, in the rest of the criminal offenses - as a means of performing a crime.

Thus, all criminal acts, an objective sign of the composition of which is an information and telecommunication network, can be divided into two groups:

Crimes in which the information and telecommunications network is a means of performing a criminal offense.

Crimes in which the information and telecommunications network is the subject of infringement.

It is necessary to emphasize that the last group of criminal acts, taking into account the scope of this work, is not included in the subject of the study and will not be considered by us.

Crimes, in which the Internet serves as a means of performing a criminal offense, impinge upon various groups of public relations, which are combined in separate chapters of the Criminal Code of Russia on the grounds of a specific object. Thus, the following criteria for the classification of crimes committed with the use of information and telecommunication networks should be considered signs of a specific object, taking into account which can be identified:

- crimes against life and health (Art. 110, 110.1, 110.2 of the Criminal Code of the Russian Federation);
- crimes against constitutional rights and freedoms of a person and a citizen (Art. 137 of the Criminal Code of the Russian Federation);
- crime against a family and minors (article 151.2 of the Criminal Code of the Russian Federation);
- crime in the sphere of economic activity (Art. 171.2, 185.3 of the Criminal Code of the Russian Federation);
- crime against public safety (Article 205.2 of the Criminal Code of the Russian Federation);
- crimes against public health and public morality (Articles 228.1, 242, 242.1, 242.2, 245 of the Criminal Code of the Russian Federation);
- environmental crimes (article 258.1 of the Criminal Code of the Russian Federation);
- crimes against the foundations of the constitutional system and the security of the state (Article 280, 280.1, 282 of the Criminal Code of the Russian Federation).

The possibility of performing a criminal act using the Internet information and telecommunications network has changed crime in general: it has now become anonymous and global, which made it difficult to identify, suppress and investigate crimes, and in some cases made it impossible to carry out criminal prosecution.

When it comes to criminal acts committed using the information and telecommunications network "Internet" as a way, it means not its physical implementation, but implies a set of principles and rules that formed the basis for the functioning of the network. Any networks implemented on the basis of IP (Internet Protocol) and TCP (routing protocol) have the properties and principles of the Internet, often differing only in their prevalence and general accessibility. For example, a VPN (Virtual Private Network), although it provides a higher level of security and restricts access by unauthorized recipients, this security is limited to the frame of the protocols that underlie its routing and addressing, that is, the IP and TCP frames. Looks like to call a network built on the basis of the IP protocol, which literally translates as "Internet

Protocol", not an Internet network, is not entirely correct. It means that, crimes committed with the use of the Internet information and telecommunications network include any crimes in which the "Internet" is used as a means, but in this array, actions are particularly distinguished, where the "Internet" is not only a means, but also a way as when using the global network to perform a directly socially dangerous act, not only quantitative characteristics change (preparation time and cost of preparatory actions), but also qualitative (social danger, anonymity, transboundary) [8].

3   Prevention of Crime Using the Internet Information and Telecommunications Network

As practice shows, the introduction of a criminal law prohibition in itself does not solve the problem of crime, since a necessary part of countering criminal assault, in addition to punishment, is the prevention of criminal offenses.

Here, victims deserve particular attention - individuals who, due to legal illiteracy, lack of skills and abilities to handle modern communication devices and access to the Internet, tend to facilitate the commission of crimes against them [9]. Official statistics for the period from 2014 to 2017 demonstrate the annual growth of the country's population who use the Internet (see Fig. 5) [3].

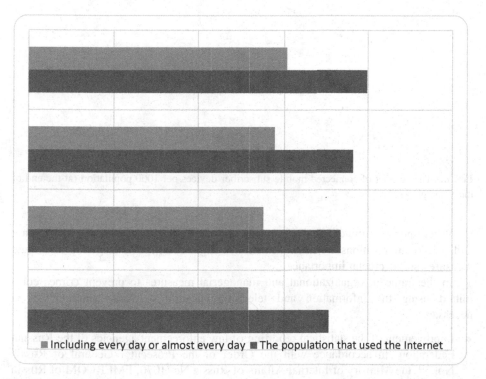

Fig. 5. Usage of the Internet by the population (according to a sample survey of the population on the use of information and telecommunication technologies; as a percentage of the total population).

The situation is aggravated by the constant increase in the number of subscriber devices that have access to the Internet, including among citizens who ignore the basics of information security. For example, according to the Federal State Statistics Service in the Russian Federation in the period from 2014 to 2017. There is an increase in the number of connected mobile subscriber devices per 1000 population (at the end of the year; pieces - see Fig. 6) [3].

Despite the fact that among theorists of criminal law and practitioners there are supporters of increased responsibility for crimes committed using the Internet information and telecommunications network, in our opinion, instead of toughening the law, it is advisable to develop effective mechanisms to counteract these negative phenomena.

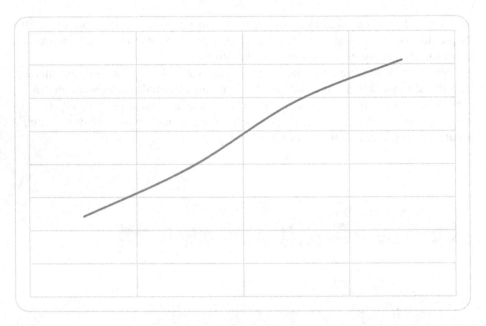

Fig. 6. The number of connected mobile subscriber devices per 1000 population (at the end of the year; pieces).

When special criminological prevention of crimes committed using the information and telecommunications network "Internet", organizational, managerial and legal measures are of crucial importance.

In the frame of organizational and managerial measures to prevent crimes committed using the information and telecommunication network "Internet", it is necessary:

- improvement of the statistical reporting of law enforcement agencies of the Russian Federation. In accordance with the Order of the Prosecutor General of Russia No. 39, the Ministry of Internal Affairs of Russia No. 1070, EMERCOM of Russia No. 1021, the Ministry of Justice of Russia No. 253, the FSB of Russia No. 780, the

Ministry of Economic Development of Russia No. 353, Federal Drug Control Service of Russia No. 399 of December 29, 2005 "On Unified Accounting of Crimes" - analytical center of the Ministry of Internal Affairs of Russia and information centers of territorial bodies of the Ministry of Internal Affairs of Russia are the holders of interdepartmental statistical databases representing state information resources reflecting the state of crime and the results of the fight against it. Information databases are formed on the basis of the statistical cards received by them, which are primary accounting documents, which reflect detailed information about the circumstances of the crime, its social and criminological characteristics, the person who committed it, and the victim. However, taking into account the crimes committed with the use of the Internet information and telecommunications network, the existing forms and details of the directory, in our opinion, do not fully reflect the true information, since not only the Internet, but also communication (mobile, satellite), which creates certain difficulties for the law enforcer;

- improve the skills of law enforcement officers involved in the identification, disclosure, and investigation of these acts. Specialists should have the knowledge and skills to work on the Internet for a planned and proactive activity. The existing form of crime registration is directly dependent on the fact that the officials conducting preliminary investigations fill out primary registration documents and sufficiently informative details in the reports, and not on the classification of the above compositions as high technologies [10];

- the identification by law enforcement agencies of Internet resources on which, for example, extremist and terrorist materials are promoted, with the subsequent transfer of the information received to the court for a decision to limit the transfer of information to subscribers to Internet sites. As a positive experience, it should be noted the current practice of creating "hot" lines and "hotlines" in the fight against crime in law enforcement agencies. By calling on the phone numbers offered, citizens can, for example, report on the distribution of extremist materials using the Internet information and telecommunications network, including on a confidential basis. This measure is of particular relevance due to the fact that modern technologies allow members of extremist movements and groups the opportunity to defend and promote their ideology in the information resources of the Internet, where a huge number of users are concentrated, especially the people of this type are often affected. The Federal Law "On Information, Information Technologies and Information Protection" does not allow the use of a website or a website page on the Internet containing public calls for terrorist activity or publicly justifying terrorism, other extremist materials. Information resources blocked by a court decision replenish the federal list of extremist materials on the website of the Ministry of Justice of the Russian Federation;

- based on the analysis of investigative and judicial practice in criminal cases, as well as taking into account theoretical developments in this area, prepare and send methodological recommendations to territorial units aimed at improving activities in the fight against crimes committed using the Internet information and telecommunications network.

In addition, as part of the elimination of circumstances conducive to the commission of cybercrime, we can not neglect the measures of software and hardware confrontation to attackers. This, above all, about the technology, called "network management systems". They are used to improve the security of computer networks and fault tolerance, to ensure their reliability. The network management system should include:

- analysis and error handling - determining the causes of failures and failures of the terminal and network devices, providing the necessary tools for their detection, performing the function of restoring performance;
- network hardware and software configuration management - configuration setting and tracking;
- accounting - detection of network resources for use and availability;
- productivity management - researching network performance, collecting and analyzing information about the functioning of the network for its operation at a standard level, both for planning the development of the network and for operational management;
- alarming - access control (with obligatory logging) to network resources and equipment to timely prevent unauthorized access, its detection and suppression [11].

To implement legal measures to prevent crimes committed using the Internet information and telecommunications network, in our opinion, it is necessary to make changes to the statistical reporting system, in particular, to specify the offenses committed using the Internet information and telecommunications network.

Of course, the list of preventive measures for the type of crime in question is not exhaustive. At the same time, the implementation of at least some of them will allow, in our opinion, to reduce the number of criminal acts committed using the Internet information and telecommunications network.

References

1. Saltykov, S., Rusyaeva, E., Kravets, A.G.: Typology of scientific constructions as an instrument of conceptual creativity. In: Kravets, A., Shcherbakov, M., Kultsova, M., Shabalina, O. (eds.) Creativity in Intelligent Technologies and Data Science. CCIS, vol. 535, pp. 41–57. Springer, Cham (2015). https://doi.org/10.1007/978-3-319-23766-4_4
2. Klimmt, C.: Virtual worlds as a regulatory challenge: a user perspective. In: Cornelius, K., Hermann, D. (eds.) Virtual Worlds and Criminality, pp. 1–18. Springer, Heidelberg (2011). https://doi.org/10.1007/978-3-642-20823-2_1
3. Regions of Russia. Socio-economic indicators. P32 Stat. Sat/Rosstat, M., 1162 p. (2018)
4. Prokofieva, E., Mazur, S., Chervonnykh, E., Zhuravlev, R.: Internet as a crime zone: criminalistic and criminological aspects. In: Kravets, A.G. (ed.) Big Data-driven World: Legislation Issues and Control Technologies. SSDC, vol. 181, pp. 105–112. Springer, Cham (2019). https://doi.org/10.1007/978-3-030-01358-5_10
5. Gurlev, I., Yemelyanova, E., Kilmashkina, T.: Development of communication as a tool for ensuring national security in data-driven world (Russian Far North Case-Study). In: Kravets, A.G. (ed.) Big Data-driven World: Legislation Issues and Control Technologies. SSDC, vol. 181, pp. 237–248. Springer, Cham (2019). https://doi.org/10.1007/978-3-030-01358-5_21

6. Official site of the Ministry of Internal Affairs of Russia [Electronic resource]. http://www. mvd.ru/stats/. Accessed 04 Jan 2019
7. Pournouri, S., Zargari, S., Akhgar, B.: Predicting the cyber attackers; a comparison of different classification techniques. In: Jahankhani, H. (ed.) Cyber Criminology. ASTSA, pp. 169–181. Springer, Cham (2018). https://doi.org/10.1007/978-3-319-97181-0_8
8. Hyland, J.M., Hyland, P.K., Corcoran, L.: Cyber aggression and cyberbullying: widening the net. In: Jahankhani, H. (ed.) Cyber Criminology. ASTSA, pp. 47–68. Springer, Cham (2018). https://doi.org/10.1007/978-3-319-97181-0_3
9. Quyên, L.X., Kravets, A.G.: Development of a protocol to ensure the safety of user data in social networks, based on the Backes method. In: Kravets, A., Shcherbakov, M., Kultsova, M., Iijima, T. (eds.) JCKBSE 2014. CCIS, vol. 466, pp. 393–399. Springer, Cham (2014). https://doi.org/10.1007/978-3-319-11854-3_33
10. Bulgakova, E., Bulgakov, V., Trushchenkov, I., Vasilev, D., Kravets, E.: Big data in investigating and preventing crimes. In: Kravets, A.G. (ed.) Big Data-driven World: Legislation Issues and Control Technologies. SSDC, vol. 181, pp. 61–69. Springer, Cham (2019). https://doi.org/10.1007/978-3-030-01358-5_6
11. Kravets, E., Birukov, S., Pavlik, M.: Remote investigative actions as the evidentiary information management system. In: Kravets, A.G. (ed.) Big Data-driven World: Legislation Issues and Control Technologies. SSDC, vol. 181, pp. 95–103. Springer, Cham (2019). https://doi.org/10.1007/978-3-030-01358-5_9

Computer Tools Increasing the Quality of the Evidence Information Received During the Investigation of Road-Transport Crimes

Taulan Boziev[1], Sergei Kolotushkin[2], Yuriy Bokov[3],
Dmitry Vasilev[4(✉)], and Mikhail Pavlik[5]

[1] State Institute of Economics, Finance, Law and Technologies,
5 Roschinskaya str., Gatchina, Leningrad Region 188350, Russia
boziev1975@yandex.ru
[2] Research Institute of the Federal Penitentiary Service of Russia,
15 «a» Narvskaya str., building 1, Moscow 125130, Russia
kolotushkinsm@mail.ru
[3] Volgograd State University, 100 Universitetskiy av., Volgograd 400062,
Russia
bokov@volsu.ru
[4] Volgograd Academy of the Russian Ministry of Internal Affairs,
Volgograd, 130 Istoricheskaya str., Volgograd 400089, Russia
89889599848@mail.ru
[5] Leningrad State University named after A. Pushkin, Peterburgskoe shosse, 10,
Sankt-Peterburg, Pushkin 196605, Russia
pavlik-mu@mail.ru

Abstract. The paper presents topical issues related to improving the quality of evidence obtained in the investigation of road traffic accidents through the use of automated information systems that simulate this process. Also, the main directions of the use of computer technology and elements of traffic accident investigation modeling. The overall performance of interdependent elements of a system of investigation in the organizational relation depends on high-quality methodical providing that defines functioning of criminalistic accounting, information retrieval systems, the automated information retrieval systems of technical and criminalistic assignment. Work on production, acquisition, distribution of scientific and technical means, their maintenance in a suitable status and improvement of technical and criminalistic training of graduates of legal higher education institutions and law enforcement officers for the acquisition of special knowledge, skills is also inherent in this stage.

Keywords: Investigation modeling · Automated information system ·
Traffic accidents · Computer technologies

© Springer Nature Switzerland AG 2019
A. G. Kravets et al. (Eds.): CIT&DS 2019, CCIS 1084, pp. 338–347, 2019.
https://doi.org/10.1007/978-3-030-29750-3_27

1 Basic Ideas of Process of Automation of Investigation of Road and Transport Crimes

At the present stage of development of society, any manufacturing processes are inconceivable without their broad automation with the use of computer technologies. In turn production automation is covered by the concept "information technologies" designating the system of methods of processing, production, change of a state, properties and a form of special material—information [1].

The integrity as the main quality of a system of investigation of crimes is designed to provide conditions for achievement, maintenance and saving constant readiness of authorized persons of law enforcement agencies for the solution of criminalistic tasks in each case of use of their knowledge and skills. Reliability of a system of legal proceedings, one of the principles of activity of subjects of investigation of crimes, acts as the ability to provide effective and high-quality implementation during the certain time under the corresponding conditions of the functions.

Address and point use of technical and criminalistic techniques and program complexes by production of investigative actions in each case of investigation of crimes is the isolated direction as premises for permanent readiness of application of scientific and technical means and special knowledge demand the continuous analysis, tracking of the repeating situations and decision-making within the existing legal regulation [2].

The overall performance of interdependent elements of a system of investigation in the organizational relation depends on high-quality methodical providing that defines functioning of criminalistic accounting, information retrieval systems, the automated information retrieval systems of technical and criminalistic assignment, forming of help and auxiliary collections, samples, including natural collections. Work on production, acquisition, distribution of scientific and technical means, their maintenance in a suitable status and improvement of technical and criminalistic training of graduates of legal higher education institutions and law enforcement officers for the acquisition of special knowledge, skills is also inherent in this stage.

In scientific literature, the concept "new information technologies" asset of methods and implementers of information processes of different areas of human activity is often used in recent years, at the same time the person is considered as a biological information system. New information technologies unlike traditional assume existence not only information product but also special tools of its production—means of electronic ADP equipment. The last allows the user not only to get acquainted visually with contents of information—to consume it but also to quickly receive a new information product in the volume and a format which is adequate (are relevant) to his requirements.

Computer-based information technologies are called "new", "modern", "high" though initially in legal and special literature they were called "computer". It is represented that the last concept is fuller than others reflects an entity of the considered definition. Such approach is correct and not only because at present fast rates of development of scientific and technical progress the modern information technologies applied today will stop being after a while those as will appear new, more modern, but also because new information technologies are the generalized concept. It equally belongs also to other technologies which are based on the allocated means of production, for example, telecommunication where the computer equipment and methods of its use also have fundamental value. It is obvious as electric communication (telecommunication) is understood as any transfer or reception of information—signs, signals, the written text, images, sounds on wire, radio-optical and to other types of electromagnetic systems using means of telecommunication—technical means for forming, processing, transfer or reception of messages, including others technical and software of functioning of communication networks [3]. Now digital means of telecommunication—specialized means of electronic ADP equipment are used.

At the same time, with the activity of the investigator, it is about computer technologies which provide an application of modern personal computers, the software, and other computer aids. Let's select the following main directions:

- when collecting proofs;
- at an investigation of criminal cases as proofs of the documents created by other participants of criminal proceedings using computer technologies;
- at receiving from computer databases of information and use when scheduling on an investigation of crimes;
- at the application of e-mail for correspondence on criminal cases;
- at familiarizing with criminal case as proofs of information which is stored on machine-readable mediums;
- when planning investigation on criminal cases and control of execution of the planned investigative actions, operational search, organizational and other actions;
- at use by the investigator of computer databases for control over observance of procedural terms of detention of suspects, detention of accused (suspects), preliminary investigation and other terms provided by the criminal procedure legislation;
- at assessment available in the matter of proofs;
- application of means of the computer equipment when training investigators [4].

2 The Software Increasing Quality of the Evidentiary Information Obtained at the Survey of the Place of the Road Accident

At the investigation of road and transport crimes such hi-tech direction as the application of photogrammetric complexes begins to play a special role by production of the investigative action having key value at the investigation of the specified category of punishable acts – inspection of the scene.

Photogrammetry (PM)—the scientific and technical discipline which is engaged in the definition of a form, the sizes, situation and other characteristics of objects according to their facsimiles. There are two main directions in PM: phototopography— the creation of maps and plans of Earth (and other space objects) and a solution of applied tasks in architecture, construction, military science, medicine, criminalistics, etc. (land, applied PM). Its emergence belongs in the middle of the 19th century (about 1840), practically along with the emergence of the photo.

In modern conditions of PM finds broad application in different types of activity: during creation of topographic maps, geological researches, environmental protection (studying of glaciers, snow cover and soils, a research of processes of an erosion, observation of changes of a vegetable cover, studying of sea currents), design and construction of buildings and constructions, archeological excavations, in the film industry (combination of acting with a computer-generated imagery), the automated creation of space models of objects, etc. [5].

Treat the main advantages of the PM methods the big productivity as measure not objects, but their images; high accuracy of measurements and also existence of strict ways of control and processing of the received results; possibility of studying of both motionless, and moving objects; full objectivity of the executed researches; a possibility of automation of process of measurement, including on remote removal from an object that is of particular importance in conditions when an object of a research is physically unavailable or when stay in its zone is unsafe for the person.

By production of PM researches basic data are the coordinates defining the provision of points of an object in space; coordinates on the photos setting the provision of points of an object in the analog or digital picture; the elements of external orientation of the camera (scanner) defining its position in space and the direction of shooting; the elements of internal orientation setting geometrical characteristics of process of shooting. All variety of methods using which perform measurements on pictures is divided into two groups. The method of measurement of objects based on the use of properties of the single picture is called monophotogrammetric, and on use of properties of a couple of pictures—stereophotogrammetric. The photographing method essence with use of special measured objects, or test objects, is that on-site incidents set a special large-scale object which parameters are in advance known, at the same time photography of a situation is made so that this object every time got into the shot (Fig. 1). Then, knowing dimensional characteristics of parameters of this test object, it is possible to calculate the distance between other attendees in frame objects and their sizes (ad hoc methods of calculation and the corresponding software are for this purpose developed).

In these complexes, the autonomous specialized software installed on the personal computer. It is included in the delivery of the complex. The mentioned cover is intended for processing of digital photos by photogrammetric methods as a result of which three-dimensional coordinates of the selected points of objects and their relative positioning are defined. Data retrieved allow to construct the scheme of the place of road and transport crime and to define the distance between the selected points. These data can be exported to files of the exchange DXF format. For software protection from the unauthorized intervention which can lead to distortion of results of measurements, protection in the form of check of integrity of a program code of the metrological library, verification of the identification number of the hardware is provided [6].

Using a 3D scanner, you can determine any distances between objects: cars, tags, buildings, lighting columns, etc. - with an accuracy of 2 mm, and also establish the relative position of objects at the scene of a traffic accident. A distinctive feature of this equipment is the ability to create three-dimensional models of the elements of the

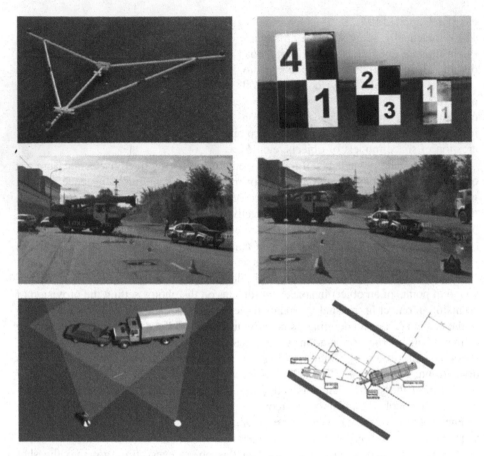

Fig. 1. Photogrammetric research of the place of road accident

inspection site, the characteristics of which fully correspond to real objects at the time of their inspection and registration. The falsification of data when plotting a crime scene is completely excluded, since the scheme itself, created in the form of a unique "point cloud", is saved as a single file that cannot be changed. The sequence of actions when using means of 3D-fixation of the accident site can be represented as the following algorithm: assembly and activation of the scanner; installation of spheres markers; output of the equipment to the operating mode (search for "zero point", activation of the laser); start, conduct and end scanning; if necessary, transfer equipment to the next scan point without dismantling the equipment (complete); transferring the received digital scans (files) from the memory of the 3D-scanner to a laptop computer, turning off the equipment, dismantling the product, placing the component parts of the sphere-markers in the transport container. The time of the full process of scanning MP is on average 15 min. The time parameters for processing the results of scanning on a personal computer with the output of a formalized form of an accident scheme using a printing device (printer) depend on the operator having experience in preparing an accident scheme using an appropriate computer program. After the formation of certain skills to use the available tools to perform this task, an experienced operator needs no more than 5–7 min [7].

3 Software Simulation of the Investigation of Road Traffic Offenses

In addition to the listed areas of application of computer technology in the activities of the investigator, we would like to add a no less important and promising one - the use of computer modeling in the investigation of crimes, including road traffic.

According to data from specialized information systems, the number of cars in Russia as of January 1, 2019, is 39.3 million cars, and the average annual growth over the past 5 years is about 6%. The size of the fleet of Russia, the emergency dangerous condition of roads, the discrepancy between the level of driver training and the technical characteristics of modern vehicles, as well as the level of development of automatic safety systems for commercially available vehicles, all together result in a consistently high number of road accidents. Despite preventive measures based on an analysis of the causes and conditions of accidents, every year more than 145 thousand such incidents occur in the Russian Federation, in which about 18 thousand people die.

In this regard, objective, comprehensive investigation, and disclosure of this category of crimes are of particular importance. The complexity and dynamism of the processes occurring during a road traffic accident dictate the need to reconstruct the mechanism of a perfect traffic accident according to trace information that has arisen during the accident process. As a rule, the sources for the construction of a model for the reconstruction of the accident, its mechanism, are the testimony of witnesses, eyewitnesses, and victims, traces, their mutual location, as well as changes that have occurred to them. Currently, there is a toolkit of the information technology environment that allows for the reconstruction of a crash event in the form of a computer model that demonstrates an idea of its mechanism, formed on the basis of trace information collected at the scene, and a set of physical interaction rules set by the developer when creating a software product [6]. Such computer programs are, in particular, "Evaluation of Accidents" and "Express Analysis of Accidents", which have entry-level functions at the time of this writing, and the more advanced ones - "Examination of Accidents" and "PC-Crash", which have much more comprehensive capabilities. input data, coupled with the built-in three-dimensional visualization mechanism of the computer model of an accident, built in the process of processing the entered data [8].

The need to create an automated information system that simulates the process of investigating road traffic crimes was shown by a sociological study, where respondents were employees of the preliminary investigation bodies - investigators specializing in road accident investigations, heads of investigative units and investigators from 61 regions of the Russian Federation. Positively refer to the use of computer simulation in the investigation of accidents 71%, neutral - 28% (Fig. 2). At the same time, more than 90% of respondents would use a recommending information system that models the investigation algorithm for typical investigative situations if they had the opportunity.

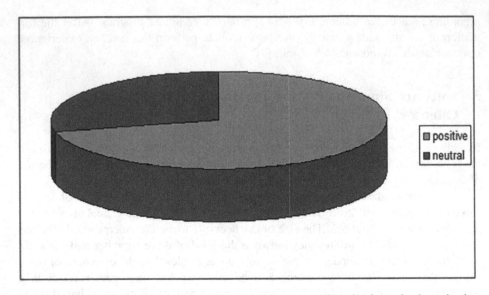

Fig. 2. Practices about the prospect of creating a program that simulates the investigation process.

To accomplish the task of developing an automated system for investigating traffic accidents, the PHP programming language is optimally suited as a tool [9]. When choosing a programming tool, we were guided by the following positions:

- the implemented software product should have minimum requirements for a computer, this is due to the fact that the units of the preliminary investigation bodies, where the use of the AIS is mostly assumed, are far from equipped with all modern computer equipment;
- implementation of the system using the PHP language allows it to be used in any Internet browser that is included in the standard set of components of the operating system and does not require additional installation and debugging, and since the preliminary investigation bodies mainly use the Microsoft Windows operating system, this allows you to implement this system to a large number of users;
- the possibility of using the software in the computer departmental network of the Ministry of Internal Affairs of Russia, including as one of the services of the "Unified system of information and analytical support for the activities of the Ministry of Internal Affairs of Russia" (Fig. 3).

The interface of such a specialized software shell for investigating traffic accidents should be simple and intuitive; in attracting a specialist to work with it there should be no need for the investigator to cope independently while having minimal knowledge of working with a computer.

When developing this computer system as a model that is fundamentally necessary to create forensic recommendations for investigating traffic accidents, it is reasonable to limit oneself to the simplest type and create a model using the algorithmization method [10].

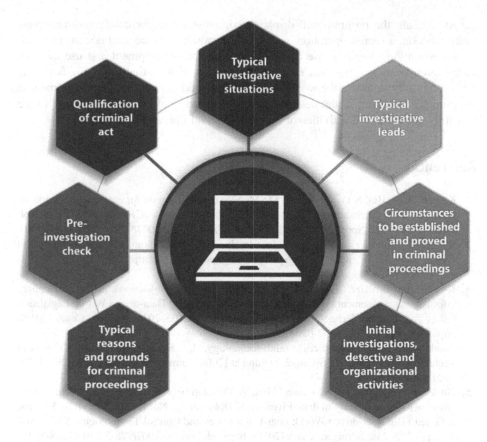

Fig. 3. The structure of the automated system for the investigation of road traffic crimes.

Using this model (algorithm), even a novice investigator who does not have experience in investigating this type of crime would have been much easier to investigate.

The program should be based on a strict algorithm for investigating traffic accidents depending on the available source data. The implementation of this algorithm can be based on the principle of hypertext, very easy to use, to proceed to the next stage of the investigation, embedded in the algorithm, the user must click the mouse pointer on the corresponding hyperlink (icon or pictogram) [11].

In general, the algorithm should include several basic blocks, namely:

- typical reasons and grounds for initiating a criminal case;
- pre-investigation check;
- qualification of the criminal act;
- typical investigative situations;
- typical investigative versions;
- the circumstances to be established and proved during the criminal proceedings;
- initial investigative actions, operational search, and organizational measures.

As a result, the program will display recommendations for conducting an investigative action, a search operation, and the corresponding procedural document form.

Based on the foregoing, we can conclude that the development and use of automated information systems that simulate the process of investigating traffic accidents can significantly optimize the work of investigative and operational units. The method of computer modeling in the detection and investigation of crimes in the near future will fully enter into the activities of investigators and operational staff [12].

References

1. Kravets, A.G., Bui, N.D., Al-Ashval, M.: Mobile security solution for enterprise network. In: Kravets, A., Shcherbakov, M., Kultsova, M., Iijima, T. (eds.) JCKBSE 2014. CCIS, vol. 466, pp. 371–382. Springer, Cham (2014). https://doi.org/10.1007/978-3-319-11854-3_31
2. He, J.: The rules of judicial proof. In: He, J. (ed.) Methodology of Judicial Proof and Presumption. MCJC, pp. 87–118. Springer, Singapore (2018). https://doi.org/10.1007/978-981-10-8025-8_4
3. Kravets, E., Birukov, S., Pavlik, M.: Remote investigative actions as the evidentiary information management system. In: Kravets, A.G. (ed.) Big Data-driven World: Legislation Issues and Control Technologies. SSDC, vol. 181, pp. 95–103. Springer, Cham (2019). https://doi.org/10.1007/978-3-030-01358-5_9
4. Smith, C.J.: Research on crime and technology. In: Savona, E.U. (ed.) Crime and Technology, pp. 105–110. Springer, Dordrecht (2004). https://doi.org/10.1007/978-1-4020-2924-0_10
5. Gurlev, I., Yemelyanova, E., Kilmashkina, T.: Development of communication as a tool for ensuring national security in data-driven world (Russian Far North Case-Study). In: Kravets, A.G. (ed.) Big Data-driven World: Legislation Issues and Control Technologies. SSDC, vol. 181, pp. 237–248. Springer, Cham (2019). https://doi.org/10.1007/978-3-030-01358-5_21
6. Korotkov, A., Kravets, A.G., Voronin, Y.F., Kravets, A.D.: Simulation of the initial stages of software development. Int. J. Appl. Eng. Res. 9(22), 16957–16964 (2014)
7. Klimmt, C.: Virtual worlds as a regulatory challenge: a user perspective. In: Cornelius, K., Hermann, D. (eds.) Virtual Worlds and Criminality, pp. 1–18. Springer, Heidelberg (2011). https://doi.org/10.1007/978-3-642-20823-2_1
8. Bulgakova, E., Bulgakov, V., Trushchenkov, I., Vasilev, D., Kravets, E.: Big data in investigating and preventing crimes. In: Kravets, A.G. (ed.) Big Data-driven World: Legislation Issues and Control Technologies. SSDC, vol. 181, pp. 61–69. Springer, Cham (2019). https://doi.org/10.1007/978-3-030-01358-5_6
9. Kravets, A.G., Skorobogatchenko, D.A., Salnikova, N.A., Orudjev, N.Y., Poplavskaya, O. V.: The traffic safety management system in urban conditions based on the C4.5 algorithm. In: Moscow Workshop on Electronic and Networking Technologies, MWENT 2018 – Proceedings March 2018, Article no. 8337254, pp. 1–7 (2018)
10. Shcherbakov, M., Groumpos, P.P., Kravets, A.: A method and IR4I index indicating the readiness of business processes for data science solutions. In: Kravets, A., Shcherbakov, M., Kultsova, M., Groumpos, P. (eds.) CIT&DS 2017. CCIS, vol. 754, pp. 21–34. Springer, Cham (2017). https://doi.org/10.1007/978-3-319-65551-2_2

11. Kravets, A.G., Al-Ashval, M.: Mobile corporate networks security control. In: 2016 International Siberian Conference on Control and Communications, SIBCON 2016 - Proceedings, Article no. 7491811 (2016)
12. Parygin, D., Sadovnikova, N., Kravets, A., Gnedkova, E.: Cognitive and ontological modeling for decision support in the tasks of the urban transportation system development management. In: 6th International Conference on Information, Intelligence, Systems and Applications, IISA 2015, Article no. 7388073 (2016)

Intelligent Technologies in Social Engineering. Creativity and Game-Based Learning

Preparation of PhD Students for Engineering Disciplines' Teaching

Elena Smirnova[1]([✉]) [iD], Elisabeth Lazarou[2] [iD], Natalia Vatolkina[1] [iD],
and Maria-Iuliana Dascalu[2] [iD]

[1] Bauman Moscow State Technical University, Moscow, Russia
evsmirnova@bmstu.ru
[2] University Politechnical Bucharest, Bucharest, Romania

Abstract. The paper contains some findings of the study of the Russian universities' system of PhD students pedagogical training that have been carried on in the framework of the ERASMUS+ Capacity Building for Higher Education project EXTEND (# 586060-EPP-1-2017-1-RO-EPPKA2- CBHE-JP). The name of the project is "Excellence in Engineering Education through Teacher Training and New Pedagogic Approaches in Russia and Tajikistan", so it is devoted to the training of new personnel for the engineering universities. The strengths and weaknesses of the system of pedagogical training of young teachers are under discussion in this paper as well as few recommendations on how to enhance the Russian teacher's preparation.

Keywords: Erasmus+ · Education technology · Competence ·
Teachers training · Engineering education · PhD education

1 Introduction

The paper contains some findings of the study of the Russian universities' system of Ph.D. students training to be university teachers that have been carried on in the framework of the ERASMUS+ Capacity Building for Higher Education project EXTEND (# 586060-EPP-1-2017-1-RO-EPPKA2- CBHE-JP). The name of the project is "Excellence in Engineering Education through Teacher Training and New Pedagogic Approaches in Russia and Tajikistan", so it is devoted to the training of new personnel for the engineering universities. The strengths and weaknesses of the system of pedagogical training of young teachers are under discussion in this paper.

The authors describe the EXTEND project, a team of four Russian Universities, objectives of the analysis and its results.

The methodology part of the paper draws four following stages of the analysis: (1) Preparatory; (2) Data Collection; (3) Analysis; (4) Discussion and Exploitation. According to this schema, the content of the paper was constructed.

The main part of the paper presents the results of a study of 22 Ph.D. students' programs collected by Russian universities' team. The research questions are the following: (1) Do the Ph.D. programs in Russia include courses and internships on teaching and learning tools to prepare Ph.D. students to be a University teacher? If yes,

A. G. Kravets et al. (Eds.): CIT&DS 2019, CCIS 1084, pp. 351–365, 2019.
https://doi.org/10.1007/978-3-030-29750-3_28

do these courses are sufficient and up-to-date? (2) What are the strengths and weaknesses of the system of pedagogical training of teachers of higher engineering education?

The Discussion part consists of three recommendations on how to enhance Russian teacher preparation.

2 Russian Higher Education System

Russian higher education system is based partly on the Bologna principles and includes the following levels of education [1]:

- bachelor's degree (4 years) – ISCED Level 6;
- master's degree (2 years) – ISCED Level 7;
- Ph.D. degree (3–4 years) – ISCED Level 9;
- specialist degree (5–6 years) – ISCED Level 8;
- clinical internship (2 years) – ISCED Level 9.

Along with the Bologna three cycle system, a part of traditional Russian system has been kept in the most important and intensive education fields, such as medicine [2] and several fields of engineering [3]. In these fields, the 5 or 6-year specialist degree programs are offered equally to ISCED Level 8.

In Russia the PhD degree programs were included in the system of higher education degrees in 2013 according to the Minister of Science and Higher Education Decree #1259 dated November 19, 2013 named as "About the statement of the Order of the organization and implementation of educational activity on educational programs of the higher education - programs of preparation of scientific and pedagogical shots in postgraduate study" [4] with modifications dated April 2016. Before that time (between 1925 and 2013) the Ph.D. programs were regarded as post-graduate education for specialists of the highest qualification and were completely research-based. The aim of students was to prepare and defend a thesis to obtain the so-called Candidate of Science degree, which is equal to a PhD degree according to the EU system. If the student failed to defend the thesis, he or she didn't get any document of education. In 2012 new Federal Law № 213-FS "On Education in Russian Federation" was issued and since 2013 postgraduate education were included in the system of higher education in the Russian Federation [5].

Regulation on postgraduate education is performed by the Higher Attestation Commission of the Russian Federation (VAK RF) [6]. All research fields are systemized into 26, specialties or mega-fields, which are further divided into smaller fields. The description of the research topics of each specialty is presented in a special document named "Specialty's Passport" issued by the Higher Attestation Commission of the Russian Federation (VAK RF). After the year 2013, the Ph.D. programs are the subjects to Federal Education Standards issued by the Ministry of Education and Science of the Russian Federation. They include requirements to contents, duration, learning outcomes and conditions of Ph.D. programs of a certain specialty. To be able to offer a PhD program, the university has to get a license and has to pass through state accreditation procedure every 5 years [7].

Graduates of a Master's or Specialist Degree can be enrolled in a Ph.D. program. The entry exams are the following: (1) foreign language, (2) philosophy and (3) major discipline. Every Ph.D. program includes regular classes according to the curriculum, teaching internship and research. The Ph.D. students select a research field and a subject of research for their dissertation. The full-time study lasts from 3 to 4 years, while part-time study lasts from 4 to 5 years. Upon graduation, a graduate is awarded a postgraduate certificate with the corresponding qualification "Research Fellow" or "Research-Teaching Fellow". Depending on the result of the dissertation's defense the Candidate of Sciences Degree (equal to the Ph.D. status) is awarded, which is the first Degree to confirm the status of a scientist. Next level can be achieved by the Researcher when the Candidates of Sciences proceed to their Doctoral Degree (the second Degree to confirm the status of scientist), which is awarded following successful completion of their doctoral dissertation. Some characteristics of the Ph.D. program are present in Table 1.

Table 1. Characteristics of the Russian PhD programs.

Program Characteristics	Ph.D. programs in the Russian Federation
Entry requirements	Master's or Specialist Degree
Duration of study	3–4 years (full-time), 4–5 years (part-time)
Academic qualification certificate	Postgraduate Degree certificate
Qualification (degree)	Researcher (qualification), research fellow (qualification), Candidate of Sciences (degree)
Type of study	Regular classes according to curriculum, teaching internship, research
Form of final state assessment	Three qualifying examinations for a candidate's Degree, state examination, dissertation defense
A further career in a scientific and professional field	Doctoral dissertation defense
Employment	Research, analytical and scientific work in accordance with the qualification

The Ph.D. graduates have the right to be employed as a university teacher. After that, each university teacher has to improve his or her skills every three years and participate in professional training programs with the duration of not less than 72 h (2 ECTS). It is an obligatory requirement to pass through the so-called teacher attestation procedure and prolong labor agreement.

3 Russian Universities Team

Four Russian universities' academic staff took part in this research materials' collection and they are listed below with a small description.

3.1   Bauman Moscow State Technical University (BMSTU)

The BMSTU is one of the biggest and oldest universities in Russia with a total enrollment of over 28000 students. The university structure includes 8 Research and Education Units with 18 Faculties and branches in Kaluga, Mytischy and Dmitrov cities. Faculties and Research Institutes enable students, staff, and scientists to study and conduct research and offer courses covering all fields of Engineering Science including manufacturing engineering, computer science, control systems, robotics, medical engineering, power engineering, and industrial design. BMSTU pays particular attention to relationships with industrial enterprises and continuously searches for innovative, high-quality ways of preparing graduates for employment [8].

3.2   Moscow State University of Civil Engineering (MGSU)

The MGSU is the leading University in Russia for the training of specialists for the construction industry and construction science. It plays a key role in the formation of high-quality human capital and the formation of the labor market in the field of construction in Russia and CIS countries. The MGSU, as well as the BMSTU, were among the first universities to receive the status of the National Research University of Russia in 2010. The main mission of the MGSU is to train high-quality civil engineers, urban planners, and architects. The MGSU has about 25 thousand students in 8 institutes. Training is conducted in 13 areas of bachelor's degree, 7 areas of master's degree, 2 areas of specialty; 18 programs for the training of highly qualified personnel (postgraduate) are implemented. More than 170 teachers are full professors (Doctors of Science degree) and more than 600 are the associate professors (Ph.D.), who work at 50 departments of the MGSU [9].

3.3   Nosov Magnitogorsk State Technical University (NMSTU)

The NMSTU was established in 1934 as a general source of engineering staff for the Magnitogorsk Iron and Steel Factory, a major steel plant in the Russian's history. That is why some the most popular fields of study at the NMSTU include Metallurgy, Materials Science and Technology, Information Security and Automated Systems, Computer Engineering and Programming. A number of students are about 16 000. The NMSTU is engaged in international student exchange programs and has signed agreements with 75 universities from 60 countries. The NMSTU consists of 8 institutes and 2 faculties and encompasses a number of colleges and branches [10].

3.4   National Research Mordovia State University (MRSU)

The MRSU was founded in 1931 and was awarded the status of National Research University in 2010. The MRSU incorporates 17 academic departments, 7 research institutes, and 2 affiliated campuses, fully-fledged research infrastructure, Distance Learning Centre. The student body counts almost 19000. University enrolls more than 1000 doctoral students and runs 11 dissertation councils. The teaching staff is almost 1400 people. The University offers over 200 academic programs in life sciences, engineering, humanities, arts, and medicine. University awards Bachelor, Master, Doctoral and Post-Doc Degrees and equivalents. MRSU promotes ICT-based research and education. Quality Management System of MRSU is certified according to the requirements of ISO 9001. In 2012 the MRSU was awarded the Recognized Excellence Level by the National Quality Award for Higher Education.

The system of teachers' preparation in all four listed universities includes Ph.D. students training in pedagogy and teaching, as well as a set of teacher training courses, plans and other local documents relating to teacher training and re-training [11].

4 Methodology of Research

The objective of the analysis is defined as the identification of strengths and weaknesses of the system of pedagogical training of teachers of higher education based on analysis of the Ph.D. programs in Russian universities. The following tasks have to be solved to achieve the goal: selection and analysis of Ph.D. programs, identification of strengths and areas of improvement of the system of pedagogical training of teachers of higher education. The methodology of analysis consists of the following stages: 1. Preparatory stage; 2. Data Collection Stage; 3. Analysis Stage; 4. Discussion and Exploitation Stage.

4.1 Preparatory Stage

During the Preparatory stage, each University selected from 3 to 5 Ph.D. programs in the field of engineering to evaluate. Two types of programs have to be selected - the most popular programs and the programs in which the university has greater expertise.

According to the study's objectives the following parameters of each Ph.D. program have to be evaluated: number of students; annual enrollment; structure of the program; learning outcomes, connected to teaching activities; list and content of the courses and other activities, which are dedicated to prepare PhD student for teaching; teaching tools and approaches taught to students; assessment tools and practices; teaching internships; industry cooperation; ICT tools used in the program; international element in the program (mobility, conferences, languages, guest lectures).

4.2 Data Collection Stage

In total data, 21 Ph.D. Training programs were collected by universities teams with a total enrollment of 248 students. Unfortunately, the number of students per Ph.D. program varies significantly in Russian universities. The number of Ph.D. students depends usually more on a number of available state scholarships and much less on market needs and employers' demands. Table 2 includes the full list of the Ph.D. programs' names which have been analyzed in this research (Table 2).

Table 2. Titles of the PhD programs analysed in the paper.

No.	MGSU
1	Architecture
2	Equipment and building technologies
3	Mechanical engineering
4	Management in technical systems
BMSTU	
1	Computer science and engineering
2	Nuclear, thermal and renewable energy and related technologies
3	Mechanical Engineering
4	Aviation and rocket and space technology
5	Air navigation and operation of aviation and rocket and space vehicles
NMSTU	
1	Electric and Thermal Technics (Industrial Thermotechnics)
2	Geotechnology (underground, open and construction)
3	Technologies and machines of processing by pressure
4	Building structures, buildings, and structures
5	Electrical systems and complexes
MRSU	
1	Electrical and heat engineering (Lighting Engineering)
2	Electrical and heat engineering (Electrotechnical complexes and systems)
3	Electrical and heat engineering (Power plants and power systems)
4	Technology, mechanization and power equipment in agriculture, forestry (Technologies and means of technical agricultural services)
5	Engineering and construction technology (Building structures and buildings)
6	Engineering and construction technology (Building materials and products)
7	Engineering and construction technology (Heat Supply, ventilation, air conditioning, gas supply, and lighting)

Data collection has been performed by universities' EXTEND project teams as a desk and field study. The following documents have been used to collect data for this research: Federal State Education Standards on Ph.D. programs, basic professional educational programs (a set of documents describing the contents of each program, learning environment, teaching tools and learning outcome), curricula, course descriptions, internship descriptions, Ph.D. department and academic department reports, teacher interviews.

4.3 Analysis Stage

The analysis methods were comparison and content analysis. The comparison criterion are the following: number of students; structure of the program; learning outcomes, connected to teaching activities; list and contents of the courses and other activities, which are dedicated to prepare Ph.D. student for teaching; teaching tools and approaches taught to students; assessment tools and practices; teaching internships; industry cooperation; ICT tools used in the program; international element in the program (mobility, conferences, languages, guest lectures).

The research questions to be answered in the study are the following.

1. Do the Ph.D. programs in University include courses and internships on teaching and learning tools to prepare Ph.D. students to be University teachers? If yes, do these courses are sufficient and up-to-date?
2. What are the strengths and weaknesses of the system of the Ph.D. students' pedagogical training?

The research aimed to investigate the crucial factors of university education quality – the quality of educational resources and quality of education technologies, as authors seek to investigate whether Ph.D. students receive substantial education in the implementation of teaching tools and approaches. Education technologies are the framework term which includes theoretical pedagogic approaches, teaching tools and information technologies facilitating teaching and learning [12].

4.4 Discussion Stage

The final Discussion stage supposes to produce the following results: strengths and areas of improvement of Ph.D. training programs according to criteria; suggestions of results implementation.

5 Results of the Study of Russian Practices in Ph.D. Programs with a Focus on Teaching Engineering Disciplines

In Russia, every Ph.D. program is of 240 ECTS or 4 years duration.

The structure of the program includes the mandatory part (basic) and the variable part, which provides the opportunity to implement different directions within one area of training.

The Ph.D. program consists of the following blocks:

Block 1 "Disciplines (modules)" includes disciplines related to the basic part of the program (History and philosophy of science and Foreign languages) and disciplines related to the variable part. This block workload is 30 ECTS.

Block 2 "Internship" refers to the variable part of the program and includes internships to obtain professional skills and experience (including obligatory teaching internship).

Block 3 "Research" refers to the variable part of the program. Block 3 and Block 2 workload is 201 ECTS. Block 3 includes research activities and preparation of scientific qualification work (dissertation) for the degree of Candidate of Sciences.

Block 4 "State final attestation" refers to the basic part of the program (workload is 9 ECTS) and ends with the award of the qualification "Researcher. Teacher-researcher". It includes the preparation for the state exam and submission of a scientific report on the main results of the prepared scientific qualification work (dissertation).

The list of existing courses and internships in pedagogy which are included in Ph.D. programs of Russian universities are shown below (Table 3).

Table 3. Courses and internships on pedagogy included in Ph.D. programs.

Ph.D. Programs	Courses on Pedagogy	Teaching Internship
MGSU		
All Ph.D. programs in engineering	Pedagogy and methods of professional education (2 ECTS)	Pedagogical Practice (3 ECTs)
BMSTU		
All PhD programs in engineering	Fundamentals of pedagogy and psychology of higher education (6 ECTS)	Pedagogical Practice (18 ECTs)
NMSTU		
All PhD programs in engineering	Pedagogy and Psychology of HEI (3 ECTS)	Pedagogical Practice (9 ECTs)
MRSU		
All Ph.D. programs in engineering	IT in research and education (2ECTS), included (1 ECTS self-study) Pedagogy of higher education (2ECTS), included (1 ECTS self-study)	Pedagogical Practice (3 ECTs)

The readiness of the Ph.D. program graduates to teach, as well as his/her ability to develop scientific and methodological support of academic disciplines in the professional field, are formed by following activities: (1) study of the courses on pedagogy; (2) teaching internship; (3) preparing for the state exam.

According to the results of the State final examination, the graduates are awarded the qualification of "Researcher. Teacher-researcher".

In Russian universities, each Ph.D. program has at least one general course on pedagogy with the value between 2 and 6 ECTS.

In NMSTU, in addition, the Ph.D. students must acquire a good level of foreign language proficiency to be able to deliver lectures for foreign students; acquire fundamentals of inclusive education to be able to deliver lectures for inclusive students.

In MRSU an additional course is included: "IT in research and education" (2 ECTS). The teaching internship is obligatory and its duration varies between 3 and 18 ECTS.

In BMSTU the maximum share of the curriculum dedicated to pedagogical training is 10%.

Also it can be considered that some other courses contribute to the development of related soft skills of the future university teacher, such as History and Foreign Language (all universities), Communicative and Stylistic features of the Academic Language and Writing (BMSTU), Professionally-Oriented Translation (NMSTU), although the major part of the curriculum is dedicated to professional courses, courses on research methodology and research activities.

Analysis of Ph.D. programs shows that each Ph.D. program includes one general professional competence in teaching – "Readiness for teaching on the educational programs of higher education". The Ph.D. programs in MGSU include in addition two general competencies which are connected to teaching: "Willingness to participate in the work of Russian and international research teams to solve scientific and educational problems" and "Ability to plan and solve problems of professional and personal development". Ph.D. programs in MRSU include two additional professional competences concerning teaching – "Readiness for teaching in the specific field" and "Ability to develop scientific and methodological support of educational disciplines in the specific field. It means that teaching is regarded as a general professional skill for each Ph.D. graduate although in some universities the role of the teacher is considered as more important for Ph.D. graduate.

Content analysis of learning outcomes shows significant differences between universities in terms of what exactly should know, be able to do and which skills should Ph.D. graduate possess to be a university teacher. Although each university includes understanding and ability to implement teaching tools, technologies, and methods.

The contents of the pedagogical courses also show significant differences between universities. Analysis of the courses allows identifying three main parts: fundamentals and theories of pedagogy, psychology, methods, and tools. Table 4 presents three different examples of the courses on pedagogy. Two selected courses include three out of four main parts (modules), NMSTU course includes all four parts but the number of a topic is fewer.

Structures of two selected courses on pedagogy delivered to Ph.D. students at three Russian universities are shown at the following (Tables 4, 5 and 6).

Table 4. Structures of course on pedagogy delivered to Ph.D. students at the BMSTU.

Instruments of the course	Topics in the course on Pedagogy
Fundamentals and theories of pedagogy	Modern requirements to the European engineer according to the concept of sustainable development
	History of formation and development of technical education in Russia
	History of foreign engineering education
	Modern trends in the development of higher technical education in Russia and abroad
	Comparative analysis of foreign systems of higher education subject "Engineering pedagogy", its place and role in the system of pedagogical science
	Social expectations concerning qualities of a graduate of higher technical school
	Professional requirements to the teacher of higher school
	Structure of activity of the teacher of the higher school
	Theoretical bases of a technique of teaching at the higher school

(*continued*)

Table 4. (*continued*)

Instruments of the course	Topics in the course on Pedagogy
Psychology	Psychology of higher education
	Components of professionalism and creative self-realization of the person
	Self-Improvement of the person as one of the bases of achievement of tops of creative potential
	Pedagogical experience as result and support of self-realization of the creative potential of the teacher
	Pedagogical skills – the highest level of professionalism of the teacher
	Preparation of classroom with the use of techniques of rhetoric and public speaking
	Dynamics of mental development (childhood, adolescence, and youth)
	Dynamics of mental development (adult psychology, old age)
	Role of the group in human behavior and activity (group structure, group processes)
	Role of the group in human behavior and activities
Methods and tools	Overview and experience of the use of modern educational technologies in higher education
	Modernization of traditional types of training
	Active educational technology
	Project-based learning
	E-learning
	New organizational and technological formats of educational activities
	Requirements for modern educational technologies
	Organization of forms and content of training at the University
	The modular system of training, design goals, and content of the curriculum
	Practical use of the properties of the material for the preparation of training sessions and presentations
	Methods of preparation and control measures
	Methods of evaluation of the teacher
	The professional culture of the engineer
	Culture of a high school teacher
Communication and classroom management	Role of the group in human behavior and activity (structure of psychological climate in the group)
	Conscious communication in conflict situations (conflicts in different spheres of human interaction)

Table 5. Structures of course on pedagogy delivered to Ph.D. students at the MRSU.

Instruments of the course	Topics in the course on Pedagogy
Fundamentals and theories of pedagogy	Higher educational institution as a pedagogical system Functioning and efficiency of pedagogical process in a higher educational institution The pedagogical activity of researchers and teachers, pedagogical laws of formation and development of the personality of the student Process of higher education and self-education Education and self-education of students Personality of the teacher
Psychology	No data
Methods and tools	Forms, methods and pedagogical technologies in a higher educational institution Pedagogical aspects of continuous independent work of students
Communication and classroom management	Pedagogical interaction between students and teachers

Table 6. Structures of course on pedagogy delivered to Ph.D. students at the NMSTU.

Instruments of the course	Topics in the course on Pedagogy
Fundamentals and theories of pedagogy	Fundamentality and humanization in higher education Integration processes in modern higher education Principles of training as the main reference point in teaching The essence, structure and driving forces of the learning process in higher education Forms of organization of the educational process at the University A systematic approach to the formation of the student's personality in pedagogy and psychology of higher education The personality of the student as a subject of education and psychological and pedagogical bases of its study The main problems and trends in the development of modern higher education
Psychology	Pedagogical skills of a high school teacher Psychological and pedagogical bases of formation of professional and pedagogical thinking of post-graduate students Pedagogical abilities of a higher school teacher Cognitive activity of University students, ways and means of its activation Psychological and pedagogical bases of formation of communicative competence of students in high school Typology of the University teacher's personality

(continued)

Table 6. (*continued*)

Instruments of the course	Topics in the course on Pedagogy
Methods and tools	Teaching methods in higher education
	The business game as a form of active learning in high school
	Technologies of developing education and their application in higher education
	System design on the example of the development of a specific educational technology
	Portfolio at the University, the technological map of its preparation
	The instructional strategy of the teacher of the high school
	Information technologies in University education
	Development of creative abilities of students
	Competence approach in higher education
	Research skills of students
	Development of critical thinking of students.
	Development of creative thinking of students
Communication and classroom management	Communicative characteristics of a higher school teacher
	Monitoring the quality of education
	Organization of the research team

Taking into account that courses are rather short, the contents are ample and cover the major topics to achieve the necessary competencies. The less attention in the courses is paid to the "Communication and classroom management". Also, our analysis shows that training is oriented mostly on the theory where often Ph.D. students with engineering background try to study the fundamentals of pedagogy and pedagogical psychology in only 2 or 3 ECTS courses. The structure of the courses is not clear and rather unbalanced. It makes almost not possible to make exchange programs for Ph.D. students because it would be difficult to compare and recognize the period of study in partner universities.

The practical-oriented training in teaching students is received through internships, which aim at revealing the principles of the educational process at the University: the study and analysis of scientific and technical information, domestic and foreign experience in the area of study; the development of teaching materials, laboratory and practical training tasks and classes for bachelor and master students; classroom training, preparation for the implementation of the educational process in higher education institutions.

Besides the contents of the courses on pedagogy, students value the active teaching tools as well as ICT tools, the integration of international component and involvement into activities of industry partners. Unfortunately, universities provide only general information about these dimensions of the Ph.D. programs.

6 Conclusion and Recommendations

The research developed in the framework of the EXTEND project had the intention to present a comparative analysis of the practices in Ph.D. students teacher training with a focus on teaching engineering disciplines in Russian universities. Our data collection intended to cover information related to the content and courses' structure of the selected Ph.D. training programs.

The contextual background allowed us to identify the similarities of the Ph.D. education in Russian universities, the fact that the Ph.D. programs are aligned with the Bologna system and are regarded as higher education of 3rd Cycle.

Results of the study allow giving three recommendations.

6.1 Recommendation 1

Develop networking in the university's Ph.D. students' teacher training system to create joint flexible courses and programs.

The analysis revealed that each university has different approaches to Ph.D. students' teacher training focusing on the specific areas of study. Networking between partner and program universities involving other countries universities could help to joint efforts and achieve synergy effect in the development and delivery of fully-fledged training and re-training programs for teachers. The network would allow each university to excel in the selected area thus improving the quality of the whole program. Involvement of foreign partners could provide an international dimension to the program. According to types of inter-university partnerships [13] such networking could lead to emergence of multi-level educational complex of continuous training including development of academic exchange of students and teachers; carrying out joint individual PhD research projects; organization and implementation of joint conferences, seminars, symposia of PhD students; development and implementation of modern educational programs and their continuous improvement; expansion of the range of joint educational programs/"two diplomas" programs (joint or double degrees).

6.2 Recommendation 2

Develop university teacher model of competences with the descriptor of learning outcomes for the teacher of engineering disciplines.

The competencies on teaching used in Ph.D. programs are standard in Russian universities but at the same are very vague and general. It confuses all stakeholders about the real competences which the university teacher should possess. That is why there are significant differences between universities in the description of these competencies and learning outcomes achieved. On one hand, it allows to achieve diversity in teacher training approaches but on the other hand, it decreases the compatibility and portability of teaching competencies, decreases opportunities for Ph.D. student mobility and recognition of periods of study in other universities, confronts the rights of student for the quality education.

University teacher model of competences could be used also for design of teacher enhancement programs. It would help to increase the continuity of teacher training and improve career opportunities.

6.3   Recommendation 3

Introduce a modular approach to teacher training and re-training programs.

Each university offers several (some of them offer dozens of) Ph.D. programs where a set of competences could vary as well as the duration of the program/course. The modular approach could provide flexibility and scalability of the programs/courses, design tailor-made courses and create network joint programs with partners. Analysis of teaching competencies and real contents of the programs/courses allowed to identify basic modules to be developed: Project Based Learning (PBL), E-learning and ICT Tools [14, 15], Foreign Languages for Engineering + Academic Writing, Research-Based Learning (PhD Students) [16], Curriculum Design and Development, Assessment, Design thinking, Communication, Active Learning Strategies [17], etc.

References

1. Russian education system. https://studyinrussia.ru/en/study-in-russia/info/. Accessed 11 Apr 2019
2. Sidorova, E.: Current state of international research in the field of evaluation of competence and result of training in higher school (bachel and magistracy). Sidorova, E.A.: Nauka. Mysl'. - № 3 (2015) (in Russian)
3. Shankararaman, V., Ducrot, J.: Leveraging competency framework to improve teaching and learning: a methodological approach. Educ. Inf. Technol. **2**, 115–128 (2015)
4. Guarantor system. http://base.garant.ru/70581484/#ixzz5ouNoQwFC. Accessed 23 Feb 2015
5. Federal Law No. 273-FZ of December 12, 2012 on education in the Russian Federation (amended on July 21, 2014 collection of legislation: official gazette, no. 53, p. 1, Art. 7598 (2012). (in Russian)
6. VAK RF. https://vak.minobrnauki.gov.ru/main. Accessed 13 Apr 2019
7. National information centre on academic mobility ministry of science and higher education of the russian federation, peoples' friendship university. http://www.russianenic.ru/english/rus/. Accessed 14 Apr 2019
8. Bauman Moscow State Technical University. http://www.bmstu.ru/en. Accessed 16 Apr 2019
9. Moscow State University of Civil Engineering. http://mgsu.ru/en/. Accessed 16 Apr 2019
10. Nosov Magnitogorsk State Technical University. http://en.magtu.ru/. Accessed 16 Apr 2019
11. National Research Mordovia State University. https://www.mrsu.ru/en/. Accessed 16 Apr 2019
12. Smirnova, E., Vatolkina, N.: Teacher training in Engineering education: search for new pedagogical approaches. In: Proceedings of INTED2018 Conference, pp. 6240–6247. IATED Academy, Valencia (2018)
13. Vatolkina, N., Fedotkina, O.: International Strategic University partnership: interaction models. Higher Educ. Russia **6**(27), 113–119 (2018). (in Russian)

14. Titov, I., Smirnova, E.: Network architectures of remote laboratories proposal of a new solution and comparative analysis with existing ones. Int. J. Online Eng. **6**(9), 41–44 (2013)
15. Suzev, V., Smirnova, E., Kucherov, K., Gurenko, V., Khachatrian, G.: Spectral algorithms for signal generation as learning-methodical tool for engineer's preparation. In: Smirnova, E., Clarke, R. (eds.) Analyzing Engineering Education in a Global Context. IGI Global, USA (2018)
16. Mitkovskiy, A., Ponomarev, A., Proletarskiy, A.: SIEM-Platform for Research and Educational Tasks on Processing of Security Information Events. In: ELSE Conference Proceedings, Bucharest, Romania, vol. 3, pp. 48–56 (2019)
17. Chachanidze, E.: Serious games in engineering education. In: ELSE Conference Proceedings, Bucharest, Romania, vol. 1, pp. 78–82 (2019)

Use of Playing and Training Software Complexes in the Lawyers Preparation

Elena Bulgakova[1](✉), Vladimir Bulgakov[2], and Igor Trushchenkov[2]

[1] Kutafin Moscow State Law University (MSAL),
9 Sadovaya-Kudrinskaya str., Moscow 125993, Russia
kpit2015@mail.ru
[2] Moscow University of the Ministry of Internal Affairs of the Russian
Federation named after V.Y. Kikot, 12 Academician Volgin str.,
Moscow 117437, Russia
vg.bulgakov@mail.ru, hrustals@mail.ru

Abstract. To implement the strategy of the training, computer game "Cyber law-yer", information visualization methods, analysis, synthesis, observation, design were applied.

The author of the article has created a training, gaming software "Cyber lawyer", which allows to test knowledge, work out skills and abilities in the field of providing information security for a lawyer. The game operates on a PC running the Windows family operating systems. It refers to multiplayer online games, to the genre of the turn-based local strategy. According to game theory, a game matrix was developed, in which the lines - attack strategies and the columns - are defense strategies. At the intersection of the column and the row is the success rate of the selected remedy, if it is close to one, then the probability of a successful attack is minimal. Respectively, if it is close to zero, then the probability of a successful attack is high. The game with a mixed strategy is used in the educational process since when playing in pure strategies there will always be one outcome. In this game, both the attacker and the defender are endowed with organizational, legal, technical, software remedies.

Keywords: Computer games · Gaming training · Digital technologies ·
Programming · Digitalization of legal activities ·
Professional computer games for lawyers · Cyber lawyer · Legal tech

1 Background

The relevance of the research topic is due to the low degree of use of game learning elements in the educational process. The author of the article addresses the need to create and use educational software based on game theory, in order to develop students' competencies. A lawyer who lives and works in the information society has to think about the issues of information security not only within the framework of his professional duties but also remember that these measures are observed in the information

A. G. Kravets et al. (Eds.): CIT&DS 2019, CCIS 1084, pp. 366–377, 2019.
https://doi.org/10.1007/978-3-030-29750-3_29

space as a whole. Occupational risks in this area are increasing in connection with the emergence of qualitatively new types of information security threats, neglect of measures to ensure information security, due to lack of knowledge and skills to protect the information, counter information security threats, the vulnerability of professional automated systems, etc. Therefore, the components of the competence of a modern lawyer are the knowledge, skills, and abilities to safely use information technologies, measures to protect the information, the requirements of legal acts in the field of protection of state secrets and information security, ensuring secrecy. Lawyers need to understand the nature and importance of information in the development of the modern information society, to be aware of the threats arising in this process [1–4]. The dynamism of the process of developing information technologies used in the activities of a lawyer, the associated new dangers to information security determine the specifics of persons' training and its level directly depends on the use of flexible, modern educational methods in the educational process.

2 Description of the Computer Game "Cyber Lawyer"

The computer game "Cyber lawyer" is designed for a wide range of personal computer users. The game allows the player to acquire skills and abilities in the application of methods and resources of protection to counter the threats of information security in legal activities.

The goal of the game in question is to acquire skills in setting up means of protection, their combination, and organization of protection of an informatization object. It is based on the game theory, according to which game matrices were developed, in which the lines are attacked strategies, and the columns are defense strategies. At the intersection of the column and the row is the success rate of the chosen remedy, if it is close to one, then the probability of a successful attack is minimal. Accordingly, if it is close to zero, then the probability of a successful attack is high.

Matrix game is the ultimate zero-sum game for two players. In the general case, its payment matrix is rectangular.

The row number of the matrix corresponds to the strategy number used by player 1. The column number corresponds to the player strategy number 2. Player 1's win is an element of the matrix. Winning player 2 is equal to losing player 1.

In general, strategies can be one-step and multi-step. In the first case, the game ends after the first step and the winner is determined in the second game after a certain number of steps.

The lower price of the game α is the maximum winnings that we can guarantee in the game against a reasonable opponent if we use one and only one strategy throughout the game (this strategy is called "pure").

The top price of the game β is the minimum loss that player B can guarantee in a game against a reasonable opponent if he uses one and only one strategy throughout the game.

If the top and bottom prices of the game are different, then the game has no solution in pure minimax strategies, but it always has a solution in mixed strategies.

A mixed strategy is randomly interleaved pure strategies with certain probabilities (frequencies).

Mixed strategy of player "A" will be denoted:

$$S_A = \begin{vmatrix} A_1 & A_2 \\ p_1 & p_2 \end{vmatrix}$$

where A_1, A_2 are the player's strategies "A", and p_1, p_2 are, respectively, the probabilities (frequencies) with which these strategies are applied, with $p_1 + p_2 = 1$.

Similarly, the mixed strategy of the player "B" will be denoted:

$$S_B = \begin{vmatrix} B_1 & B_2 \\ q_1 & q_2 \end{vmatrix}$$

where B1, B2 are the strategies of player "B", and q_1, q_2 are, respectively, the probabilities with which these strategies are applied, with $q_1 + q_2 = 1$.

The optimal mixed strategy for player "A" is the one that provides him with the maximum winnings. Accordingly, for "B" - the minimum loss. These strategies are designated SA * and SB *, respectively. A pair of optimal strategies form the solution of the game.

It is known from game theory that if player "A" uses his optimal strategy, and player "B" remains within his active strategies, then the average you-game remains unchanged and equal to the price of the game - no matter how player "B" uses its active strategies. And in our case, both strategies are active, otherwise, the game would have a solution in pure strategies. Therefore, if it is assumed that the player "B" will use the pure strategy B1, then the average gain v will be:

$$k_{11}p_1 + k_{21}p_2 = v \tag{1}$$

where: kij - elements of the payment matrix.

If we assume that player "B" will use a pure strategy B2, then the average gain will be:

$$k_{12}p_1 + k_{22}p_2 = v \tag{2}$$

Equating the left parts of Eqs. (1) and (2) we get: $k_{11}p_1 + k_{21}p_2 = k_{12}p_1 + k_{22}p_2$.

And taking into account the fact that $p_1 + p_2 = 1$ we have: $k_{11}p_1 + k_{21}$ $(1 - p_1) = k_{12}p_1 + k_{22}(1 - p_1)$

Where it is easy to find the optimal frequency of strategy A1:

$$p_1 = \frac{k_{22} - k_{12}}{k_{11} + k_{22} - k_{12} - k_{21}} \tag{3}$$

in our case $p_1 = \frac{\frac{3}{2}-6}{3+\frac{3}{2}-5-6} = \frac{9}{13}$.

The probability of p_2 is found by subtracting p_1 from one: $p2 = 1 - p1 = \frac{4}{13}$

We calculate the price of the game by substituting p_1, p_2 into the Eq. (1):

$$v = k_{11}p_1 + k_{21}p_2 = 3*\frac{9}{13} + 6*\frac{4}{13} = \frac{51}{13} \tag{4}$$

It is known from game theory that if player "B" uses his optimal strategy, and player "A" remains within his active strategies, then the average you-game remains unchanged and equal to the price of the game - regardless of player "A" uses its active strategies. Therefore, if we assume that player "A" will use the pure strategy A1, then the average gain v will be:

$$k_{11}q_1 + k_{12}q_2 = v$$

Since the price of the game v is already known to us and given that $q_1 + q_2 = 1$, the optimal frequency of the strategy B1 can be found as:

$$q_1 = \frac{v - k_{12}}{k_{11} - k_{12}} \tag{5}$$

$$q_1 = \frac{\frac{51}{13} - 5}{3 - 5} = \frac{7}{13}$$

The probability q_2 is found by subtracting q1 from one: $q_2 = 1 - q_1 = 1 - \frac{7}{13} = \frac{6}{13}$

Lower price of the game: $\alpha = 3$

Top price of the game: $\beta = 5$

Price of the game: $v = \frac{51}{13}$

Optimal player "A" strategy $SA* = \begin{vmatrix} A_1 & A_2 \\ \frac{9}{13} & \frac{4}{13} \end{vmatrix}$

Optimal player "B" strategy $SB* = \begin{vmatrix} B_1 & B_2 \\ \frac{7}{13} & \frac{6}{13} \end{vmatrix}$

3   Developing the Game Model of «Cyber Lawyer»

The development of a multi-level game to prevent unauthorized access to the server was divided into two sublevels of user interaction and game principles. The idea of the game is to confront the attacker and the defender.

3.1   Developing a Multiplayer Game

The game belongs to the genre of step-by-step strategies in a 2D projection that does not have a plot and elements. Is developed only in the version for a personal computer. The game is aimed at a wide audience, does not contain restrictive content, the minimum age of a player is 8 years, does not require knowledge in the field of information protection.

The main task for the player is to defeat the enemy using his own set of resources of attack and defense and the use of successful strategic and tactical decisions.

The player forms the necessary position of the «server» and has its resources of attack in conditions of limited positions.

The gameplay is not direct control of "their" objects. The game does not use trademarks or other intellectual property that is subject to licensing.

3.1.1   Development of Game Elements

The multiplayer game is designed for users who do not have knowledge in the field of information security. The goal of the game is to demonstrate various classes of threats and defenses, namely software, technical and organizational.

The game has two players, namely:

(1)   the attacker;
(2)   a defender;

Each player has the following set of resources:

(1)   The organizational resources of the attacker;
(2)   Technical equipment;
(3)   Software;
(4)   Attacker's Server.

Visual images of defense and attack resources are listed in Table 1:

Table 1. View of defense and attack resources

Type of figure	Defender	Attacker
General view of the server		
General view of the figures (the enemy does not see the resource figures)		
View from the player (or the opponent in case of disclosure of the figure)		
Organizational		
Technical		
Software		
View from the player if the resource became known to the enemy		
Organizational		
Technical		
Software		

3.2 Development of the Rules of the Game

The goal of the players is to find an opponent's computer that cannot defend and walk.
For that the following resources are used:

1. organizational;
2. technical;
3. software.

Organizational tools can help find channels of information leakage, for example, to regulate access to a room. Thus, the process of overcoming the technical protection of the object becomes complicated.

Using Social Engineering techniques, an attacker can gain access to resources that are technically blocked (for example, by deceiving personnel).

With hardware, user can limit software vulnerabilities, such as physically blocking the connection of third-party media, or physically disconnecting from global networks. In turn, an attacker using technical means can access the software in a limited way.

In the event that physical access is impossible, unauthorized access can be carried out remotely using software and software vulnerabilities, communication protocols, and operating systems.

Based on the above, it is possible to make the rules of the game, such as following:

1. Organizational resources + Technical resources = Organizational resources.
2. Hardware + Software = Hardware.
3. Software + Organizational resources = Software.

Based on the classical game theory [5–12], it is possible to present the game in a matrix form (Table 2):

Table 2. Game matrix

	Organizational	Software	Technical
Organizational	0	−1	1
Software	1	0	−1
Technical	−1	1	0

Visually, the rules can be represented as follows (Fig. 1):

Fig. 1. Visual representation of the rules of the game

In reality, non-standard situations occur, but such simplified rules were chosen for a logically correct game.

3.3   Gameplay Development

The game field consists of a 6 × 7 table. For the initial filling, the player is given 2 bottom lines (Fig. 2).

Fig. 2. Playing field

The player can choose the location of the server in these lines, after which the attack (defense) resources will be automatically generated. If the player is not satisfied with the location of the resources of attack (defense), he can repeat their filling, and so on until he reaches the optimal location (Fig. 3).

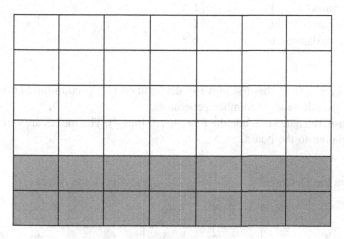

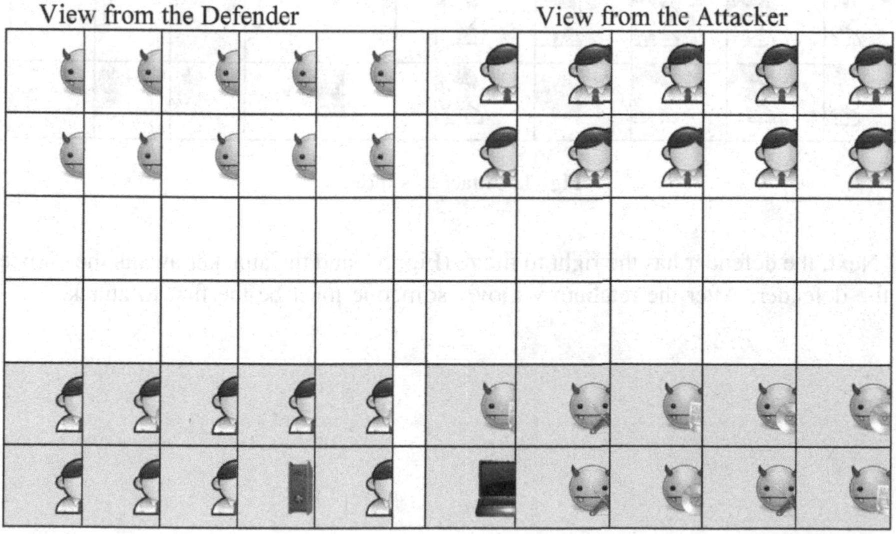

View from the Defender   View from the Attacker

Fig. 3. View of the playing field

After the opponents positioned their pieces, one of them is granted the right to move. Turns carried out in turn. The list of stroke capabilities is listed in Table 3.

Table 3. List of possible moves

Resources	Move forward	Move backward	Move left	Move right
Organizational	1	1	1	1
Technical	1	1	1	1
Software	1	1	1	1
Server (laptop)	0	0	0	0

Which player makes the first move is determined in a pseudo-random way, based on a pair of pseudo-random number generators.

In this case, the attacker made the first move (Fig. 4). The moves are symmetrically displayed relative to the board.

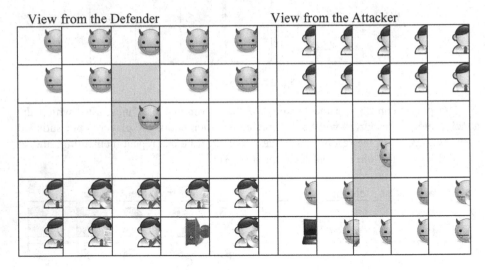

Fig. 4. Attacker's move

Next, the defender has the right to move (Fig. 5), and the attacker awaits the choice of the defender. After the retaliatory move, someone must be the first to attack.

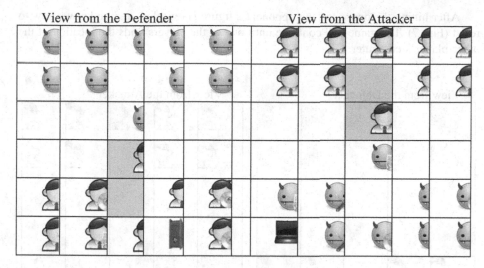

Fig. 5. Defender's move

Follow the rule:

Organizational resources + Hardware = Organizational resources

In this case (Fig. 6) the attacker's impact or defense will be successful for him, but none of the players knows, what means the opponent has before the strike.

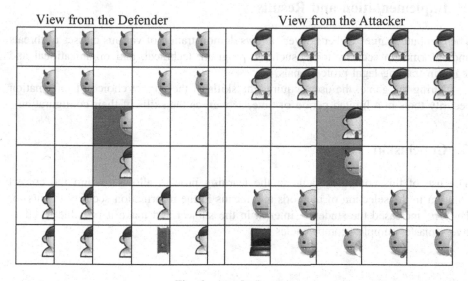

Fig. 6. Attacker's move

No matter who strikes first, the outcome of the game depends on the resources of the enemy.

After hitting the opponent, the opponent's figure is revealed, and he knows how to resist (Fig. 7). The game will continue until one of the players finds the location of the other player's computer.

View from the Defender   View from the Attacker

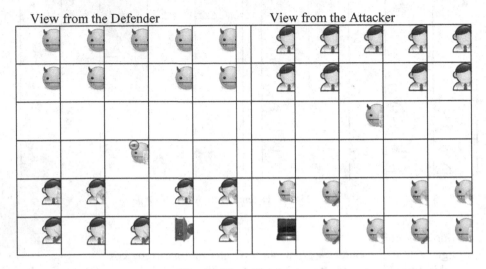

Fig. 7. View after impact

4   Implementation and Results

The computer game "Cyber lawyer" allows demonstration of various classes of threats and information security tools, such as: program, technical, and organizational and legal, in training legal professionals.

During the game, the user acquires the skills of the correct choice of information security tools in a limited period of time, as well as the skills of their configuration.

5   Conclusion

The use of this computer game in the learning process allows to find the correct solution in the selection of methods and means in the information security threats for lawyers, increased the students' interest in the subject and make it possible to effectively master complex competencies.

References

1. Bulgakova, E.V., Bulgakov, V.G., Akimov, V.S.: The use of «Big Data» in the system of public administration: conditions, opportunities, prospects. Yuridicheskaya nauka I praktika: Vestnik Nizhegorodskoj akademii MVD Rossii - Legal Science and Practice: Bulletin of Nizhny Novgorod Academy of the MIA of Russia № 3(31), 10–14 (2015)
2. Bulgakova, E.V., Akimov, V.S., Bulgakov, V.G.: Mechanisms of the electronic state for counteracting corruption. Legal Inform. (1), 23–27 (2014)
3. Bulgakova, E., Bulgakov, V., Trushchenkov, I., Vasilev, D., Kravets, E.: Big Data in Investigating and Preventing Crimes. In: Kravets, A. (ed.) Big Data-driven World: Legislation Issues and Control Technologies. SSDC, vol. 181, pp. 61–69. Springer, Cham (2019). https://doi.org/10.1007/978-3-030-01358-5_6
4. Vasilev, D., Kravets, E., Naumov, Y., Bulgakova, E., Bulgakov, V.: Analysis of the data used at oppugnancy of crimes in the oil and gas industry. In: Kravets, A.G. (ed.) Big Data-driven World: Legislation Issues and Control Technologies. SSDC, vol. 181, pp. 249–258. Springer, Cham (2019). https://doi.org/10.1007/978-3-030-01358-5_22
5. Haunschmied, J., Veliov, V.M., Wrzaczek, S.: Dynamic Games in Economics. DMEF, p. XII, 315. Springer, Heidelberg (2014). https://doi.org/10.1007/978-3-642-54248-0
6. Peters, H.: Game Theory. A Multi-Leveled Approach. STBE, p. XVII, 494. Springer, Heidelberg (2015). https://doi.org/10.1007/978-3-662-46950-7
7. Matsumoto, A., Szidarovszky, F.: Game Theory and Its Applications, p. XIV, 268. Springer, Japan (2016). https://doi.org/10.1007/978-4-431-54786-0
8. Munoz-Garcia, F., Toro-Gonzalez, D.: Strategy and Game Theory. Practice Exercises with Answers. STBE, p. XIV, 341. Springer, Cham (2016). https://doi.org/10.1007/978-3-319-32963-5
9. Tanimoto, J.: Evolutionary Games with Sociophysics. Analysis of Traffic Flow and Epidemics. EESCS, p. XIV, 221. Springer, Singapore (2018). https://doi.org/10.1007/978-981-13-2769-8
10. Sun, S., Sun, N.: Management Game Theory, p. XI, 129. Springer, Singapore (2018). https://doi.org/10.1007/978-981-13-1062-1c
11. Carayannis, E.G., Campbell, D.F.J., Efthymiopoulos, M.P.: Handbook of Cyber-Development, Cyber-Democracy, and Cyber-Defense, p. XXIV, 1089. Springer, Cham (2018). https://doi.org/10.1007/978-3-319-09069-6
12. Meissner, D., Erdil, E., Chataway, J.: Innovation and the Entrepreneurial University. STAIS, p. VI, 327. Springer, Cham (2018). https://doi.org/10.1007/978-3-319-62649-9

Method of Preliminary Computer Evaluation of Professional Readiness of the Vehicle Driver

Maksim Dyatlov[1](⊠), Olga Shabalina[1] ⓘ, Aleksej Todorev[1],
Rodion Kudrin[2], and Nikolaj Sentyabryov[3]

[1] Volgograd State Technical University, Volgograd, Russia
makdyatlov@yandex.ru, o.a.shabalina@gmail.com
[2] Volgograd State Medical University, Volgograd, Russia
[3] Volgograd State Academy of Physical Culture, Volgograd, Russia

Abstract. For successful driving in dangerous and difficult road conditions, the driver must possess certain psycho-physiological qualities in order to quickly and accurately respond to a large number of visual, sound and other stimuli. At the same time, its current functional state and psycho-physiological capabilities should allow it to effectively and safely perform various professional tasks. As a result of analyzing various factors that reduce the level of professional performance of the driver of a motor vehicle, a method of pre-trip computer assessment of his professional readiness has been developed.

In order to increase the predictability of this approach, the key factors that reduce the level of pre-trip performance are highlighted, simple and widely available methods for assessing the functional state are selected, original and existing test tasks are used to diagnose the development of the driver's important professional qualities. Developed software for personal computers and mobile devices, allowing to conduct a quick survey of drivers, testing, evaluation of functional states based on data analysis and mathematical analysis of the values obtained.

Keywords: Pre-trip professional readiness · Driver of vehicles ·
Expert assessments · Pre-trip performance · Functional status · Rapid tests

1 Introduction

According to domestic and foreign experts in the field of road transport, approximately three out of four cases of road traffic accidents (TA) occur due to improper actions of drivers. As a result of the accident, people are dying, causing enormous material and moral damage not only to transport companies, but also to countries as a whole.

The work of drivers in cities is associated with significant neuro-emotional stress, the causes of which are increased attention, the rapidly changing situation on the road, the need to perceive and process a large amount of information [1, 2]. The high level of stress, information and sensorimotor load, responsibility for the safety of cargo and the life of passengers accompanying this type of professional activity, put the task of assessing pre-trip professional readiness in relation to the profession of a motor vehicle driver to one of the first places.

© Springer Nature Switzerland AG 2019
A. G. Kravets et al. (Eds.): CIT&DS 2019, CCIS 1084, pp. 378–392, 2019.
https://doi.org/10.1007/978-3-030-29750-3_30

2 Analysis of Factors Affecting the Professional Readiness of the Driver of Vehicles

Currently, the main task of pre-trip medical examinations used for professional drivers of vehicles in the Russian Federation, is a rapid assessment of the functional state before going on a trip. It is carried out in order to exclude cases of the exit to the trip of the driver in a painful or tired state, as well as in order to detect drug or alcohol intoxication. The method of pre-trip medical examination used at motor transport enterprises includes a visual inspection of the driver, blood pressure measurement and determination of the possible presence of alcohol in the blood. After analyzing the information received, the health worker concludes that the driver is ready to work.

However, numerous studies of the work activities of motor vehicle drivers and operator professions [3–5] have determined that the intensive intellectual, psycho-emotional, informational and sensory loads characteristic of these types of activities require significant stress on the body's functional reserves, which manifests itself in dysfunction and physiological changes leading coupled systems.

Analysis of the performance studies of operators in the man-machine system [6] showed that the driver's psychophysiological state and, consequently, the safety and accuracy of his work also have a significant effect on factors that lead to an obvious decrease in functionality, but are often not felt and not realized by man. In such cases, the pulse rate and blood pressure of the driver may be within acceptable limits (some mental states, the initial stages of cold and flu, the influence of biological rhythms, atmospheric phenomena, etc.).

The need to study the physiological mechanisms to ensure the activity of a human operator as a key element of the "man-machine-environment" system is dictated by high requirements for its reliability, which is largely determined by the accuracy of actions [7]. It is known that for a significant proportion of drivers the workload causes noticeable changes in psycho-physiological indicators and functional status, which can lead to errors, accidents, and the development of professional diseases.

With regard to the transport process, the block diagram of the system for the operation of automotive vehicles with certain assumptions can be represented as consisting of four main elements: "driver – car – road – environment" (DCRE) [8] (Fig. 1).

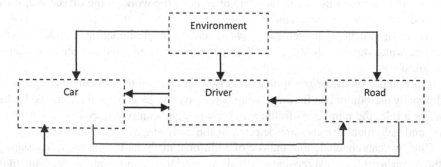

Fig. 1. Block diagram of the system DCRE

Considering that a driver's mistake can threaten the health and life of both the driver and other people, the requirements for his performance should be high enough.

The reasons for reducing the efficiency of drivers most often are fatigue, alcohol consumption, a painful condition, strong emotional arousal, depression, taking certain medications, smoking, etc.

Among the psychological factors affecting safety, motivation is, perhaps, one of the main places [9, 10]. It is expressed in the interest of the person in the work process, the results of work, job satisfaction in general. Motivation is ensured and maintained by the relevant labor regime, wages, working conditions, state of the workplace, relations with the staff of the enterprise and other factors. Encouraging the driver for the desired forms of behavior and punishing – for undesirable, you can achieve the desired effect.

Emotions, as a rule, improve the quality of human activity. However, a strong emotional stress leads to a decrease in production performance, and superstrong can even lead to the cessation of production activity. Strong positive emotions also do not contribute to improving the reliability of the driver on the road.

One of the causes of accidents on the roads is driving while intoxicated. The danger is not only a drunk driver behind the wheel. The negative effect of alcohol on the functional state of a person can be traced for several days.

The profession of a motor vehicle driver under the influence of various factors can be extreme [1].

In the extreme mode, which usually occurs when the conditions of tasks are significantly complicated (for external reasons, and sometimes for internal reasons due to deterioration of health) or the price increases, wrong actions are allowed most often due to the lack of individual capabilities of the operator [11].

These factors make the work of the driver of passenger vehicles one of the most difficult and responsible among the mass professions.

Even if an experienced driver is transferred to a car of a different model or class, his experience, although not reset, takes some time in a variety of conditions to get used to the technical features and characteristics of the vehicle.

High technical and operational characteristics of the car, its serviceability, fitted seat growth, good visibility, informativeness of instrumentation, ease of working with controls, meeting the hygienic requirements of the microclimate in the cab contribute to maintaining high performance drivers, and, consequently, increase their reliability.

The parameters of the road, its arrangement, the level of traffic organization, the behavior of other road users can facilitate or impede the work of the driver and, thus, have a direct impact on its reliability.

The environment of movement is characterized by illumination, humidity, temperature, wind, dust, visibility, as well as solar geomagnetic activity and barometric pressure drops.

In a number of motor transport enterprises, during pre-trip examinations, drivers additionally use equipment for diagnosing basic psycho-physiological functions. In this case, as a rule, the number of traffic accidents is significantly reduced by the drivers' fault, and individual diseases are detected in the early stages.

Thus, we can conclude that the use of additional methods for the rapid assessment of the driver's professional readiness will allow specialists conducting an assessment of its functional state to analyze more parameters and thereby minimize the number of erroneous decisions.

3 The Concept of Express Diagnostics

As a result of the analysis of scientific literature, professiograms, as well as the analysis of their own data obtained by survey and observation methods, the authors concluded what characteristics and factors significantly affect the readiness of the driver of a motor vehicle operating in a large city.

Many factors affecting the driver determine the effectiveness of his work. There are subjective, that is, dependent on the driver, and objective, that is, external factors in relation to the driver, affecting the efficiency of operator activity (Fig. 2).

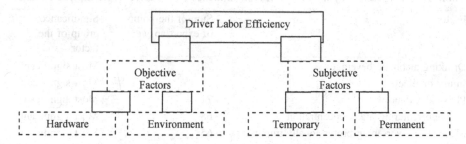

Fig. 2. The main factors affecting the efficiency of the driver

The subjective factors include: the health status of the driver, his level of preparedness for this type of operator activity, etc. By permanent subjective factors, we understand the totality of all the physical, physiological and mental characteristics of the driver's personality, as well as their influence on the success of their work. Such a group of temporary subjective factors, such as impaired health, fatigue, emotional arousal, driving while intoxicated, under the influence of drugs or drugs, have a significant impact on the functionality of the driver.

Objective factors, in turn, are divided into hardware, depending on the functioning of technology, and environmental, depending on the working environment in which the driver operates. The instrumental factors are determined by the organization of the driver's workplace, the form and type of presentation of the flow of working information, the features of the systems that control the implementation of activities. Environmental factors are determined by the conditions of habitability, situation, organization of activities (modes of work and rest, the number of work shifts, etc.).

Taking into account the influence of factors from the group of subjective and objective on the efficiency of the driver's work, a method of integrated rapid diagnostics was developed, which includes the following types of assessments:

1. assessment of pre-trip performance;
2. assessment of the physical condition;
3. assessment of the functional state.

3.1   Evaluation of the Driver's Pre-trip Performance

In the context of the study, we analyzed and selected factors that reduce the level of efficiency of the driver of vehicles before going on a trip.

In Table 1 presents a rating of factors by the degree of their influence on the driver's pre-trip performance. The ranking was carried out by an expert group, which included experts in the field of psychology, physiology, as well as drivers of vehicles. After calculating the resulting estimates and ranking factors in order of importance, they were divided into three groups. The first group – the most significant factors that significantly reduce the efficiency of the driver before the flight (1–5 factors from the overall rating). The second group – significant factors (6–10 factors from the overall rating). The third group – less significant (11–15) factors.

Table 1. Rating factors by the degree of their influence on the driver's pre-trip performance

Factor	Sum of the points of expert answers	Significance group of the factor
Drinking alcoholic beverages	77	Most significant
Injury or illness	71	Most significant
Physical fatigue	71	Most significant
Problem requiring high concentration	68	Most significant
Medication, worsening professionally important qualities	65	Most significant
Departure on a vehicle of a different type or brand	63	Significant
Strong emotional arousal (joy, anxiety) or depression	61	Significant
Violation of the regime of work and rest, work after hours	58	Significant
Departure on a new route	56	Significant
Significant changes in weather and road conditions from the previous few working days	52	Significant
Big break in the drivers work	51	Less significant
Reducing the level of personal motivation for professional activities	47	Less significant
Deterioration of own general functional state	44	Less significant
Impact of atmospheric pressure and geomagnetic environment on health	43	Less significant
Strong feeling of hunger or thirst	29	Less significant

Further, a questionnaire was formulated with a "closed" type of questions with the aim of simplifying the answers to them and the convenience of processing the results of the survey.

Appendix A presents the original questionnaire, which contains 15 questions, including all the considered characteristics of reducing the pre-trip driver performance level.

According to preliminary observations, the time that the subjects spent on familiarizing themselves with questions and answers to them, on average, did not exceed 5 min.

Before the survey, the driver was informed that the obtained results would have a recommendatory character, which in turn would allow the subject not to be afraid for possible consequences (reprimands, punishments, suspension from work, etc.) and with a greater degree of confidence answer the proposed questions.

After the driver answered all the questions, the obtained data was processed, as a result of which the points were summed up separately for each group of factors affecting the performance.

Then the estimated coefficients were calculated: K_{ms}, K_s, K_{ls}, as the ratio of the total number of points obtained for each group of factors to the maximum possible number of points in this group (15 points) using the following three formulas:

$$K_{ms} = \frac{N}{15},$$

where K_{ms} – the estimated coefficient of the group of the most significant factors affecting the performance;

N – the total number of points for the group of the most significant factors affecting the performance;

$$K_s = \frac{Z}{15},$$

where K_s – the estimated coefficient of the group of significant factors affecting the performance;

Z – the total number of points for a group of significant factors affecting the performance;

$$K_{ls} = \frac{M}{15}$$

where K_{ls} – the estimated coefficient of the group of the less significant factors affecting the performance;

M – the total number of points for the group of less significant factors affecting performance.

For a qualitative assessment of the results, it was necessary to compare the obtained values of each estimated coefficient with the scale estimates (Table 2).

Table 2. Scale values of the estimated coefficients for each group of significance factors pre-trip driver health

K_{ms}	K_s	K_{ls}	Pre-trip driver performance level
0,33–0,87	0,33–0,6	0,33	"low"
0,88–0,93	0,61–0,8	0,34–0,67	"medium"
0,94–1	0,81–1	0,68–1	"high"

The calculation of the estimated coefficients for each group of significance of the factors of the driver's pre-trip performance is so that the values obtained are in the range K (0.33–1).

Taking into account the degree of influence on the driver's pre-trip performance of factors from the three significance groups, the following conditions were adopted:

4. if one factor from the group of the most significant is estimated at 1 point, then the level of driver performance is "low";
5. if three factors from the group of significant are estimated at 1 point, then the level of driver performance is "low";
6. if five factors from the group of less significant are estimated at 1 point, then the level of driver performance is "low".

The limits of the numerical values for the "medium" and "high" levels of driver performance were calculated using the following formula:

$$P = \frac{1 - V}{2}$$

where P is the limit of numerical values for a certain level of driver performance;

V – the highest value of the estimated coefficient corresponding to the "low" level of driver's pre-trip performance.

3.2   Assessment of the Physiological State of the Driver

To assess the physiological state of a person, a complex of somatometric and physiometric characteristics can be used, which include: height, weight, chest circumference, heart rate, respiration rate, etc.

Of the numerous indicators and tests described in the literature and proposed for assessing the physiological state and level of health (weight-height ratio Ketle index, Pigne index, Kerdo vegetative index and others), the functional change index of the circulatory system or adaptation potential (AP) for Baevsky [12] and the method for determining the level of physical condition according to Pirogova [13].

The parameters in the selected methods are calculated without carrying out stress tests, which allows to obtain a preliminary quantitative assessment of the level of health and physiological state of the subject. The calculation formulas include the largest number of parameters that can be previously known to the subject (weight, height, age), or their evaluation does not require complex and high-precision measuring equipment (heart rate at rest, systolic and diastolic blood pressure).

Determination of the AP of the circulatory system by Bayevsky is produced according to the following formula [12]:

$$AP = 0.011(HR) + 0.014(SAP) + 0.008(DAP) + 0.014(A) + 0,009(W) - 0,009(H) - 0,273,$$

where AP is the adaptation potential of the circulatory system in points;

HR – heart rate, beats/min.;
SAP – systolic blood pressure, mm Hg;
DAP – diastolic blood pressure, mm Hg;
A – age, years;
W – body weight, kg;
H – height, cm.

By scoring the AP of all subjects are divided into four groups (Table 3).

Table 3. The scale of the definition of adaptive capacity

Thresholds of functional states, points	Adaptation potential
Less than 2.6	Satisfactory adaptation
2.6–3.09	Stress adaptation mechanisms
3.10–3.49	Poor adaptation
3.5 and above	Breakdown of adaptation

The first group: AP less than 2.6. These are individuals with adequate functionality of the circulatory system and satisfactory levels of adaptation.

The second group: AP 2.6–3.09. This includes individuals with functional stress adaptive mechanisms and a state of health below average.

The third group: includes people with unsatisfactory adaptive capacities (AP 3.1–3.49), who are in a "borderline" state or a state of pre-illness, who have been shown an additional examination.

The fourth group: persons with the breakdown of adaptation mechanisms (AP 3.5 and more), suggesting the presence of somatic pathology.

The determination of the level of the physiological state is carried out according to the method of E.A. Pirogova [13]. To calculate it, use the following formula:

$$PSL = (700 - 3 \times HR - 2.5 \times MAP - 2.7 \times A + 0.28 \times W)/(350 - 2.6 \times A + 0.21 \times H),$$

where PSL – physiological state level, points

HR is the heart rate at rest, beats/min.;
MAP – mean arterial pressure, mm Hg;
A – age at the time of the survey, years;
W – body weight, kg;
H – height, cm.

Assessment of the level of the physiological state according to E.A. Pirogova presented in Table 4.

Table 4. Assessment of the physiological state level (PSL) according to E.A. Pirogova

PSL thresholds, points	Evaluation of PSL
0.255–0.375	"low"
0.255–0.375	"below the medium"
0.376–0.525	"medium"
0.526–0.675	"above the medium"
0.826 and more	"high"

3.3   Evaluation of the Driver's Functional State

To predict the success of the driver's work, the authors propose to use the "Effecton Studio" test set [14], which makes it possible to study such indicators as complex sensorimotor reactions, switching of attention, reaction to a moving object, and other professionally important qualities.

To assess the functional state, we used a test system with the following tasks: "Stuntman" (assessment of reaction to a moving object), "Schulte Table" (assessment of attention switching), "Taxi" (assessment of complex sensorimotor reactions), "Test of American pilots" (complex assessment of attention, sensorimotor reactions, accuracy of movements), the original hardware-software complex (HSC) evaluation of sensorimotor reactions (assessment of sensorimotor reactions, attention).

Several variants of simulation test tasks (STT) are implemented in the HSC (Fig. 3). For each of them, the settings of the parameters that determine the complexity of the route according to its curvature, the testing time, the density of the stationary obstacles and the speed mode of movement are provided [15, 16].

Fig. 3. HSC screen form when performing the test with "fixed obstacles"

After the test task was completed, temporary and quantitative indicators of the location and intersection of dangerous and critical zones by the "Automobile" object at various speed sections (Fig. 4) were recorded [17, 18].

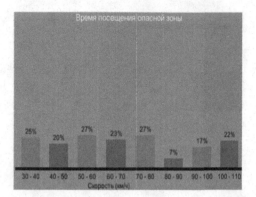

Fig. 4. HSC screen form with the results of the intersection of "dangerous zones of obstacles"

3.4   Computer Express Diagnostics System

The concept proposed by us is implemented in the system of pre-trip computer express diagnostics of the driver, which is intended for employees of the motor transport enterprises responsible for the readiness of drivers to work. The system includes the functions of authorization/registration of employees (users of the system for diagnostics of health, physiological and functional status, data collection and analysis for statistical studies; for most of the assessment methods, mobile versions are also implemented, except for tests on the auto-simulator), which allows group or remote testing of drivers on mobile devices.

The screen form of the system in the mode of assessing the physiological state of the driver according to the method of R.M. Bayevsky is shown in Fig. 5.

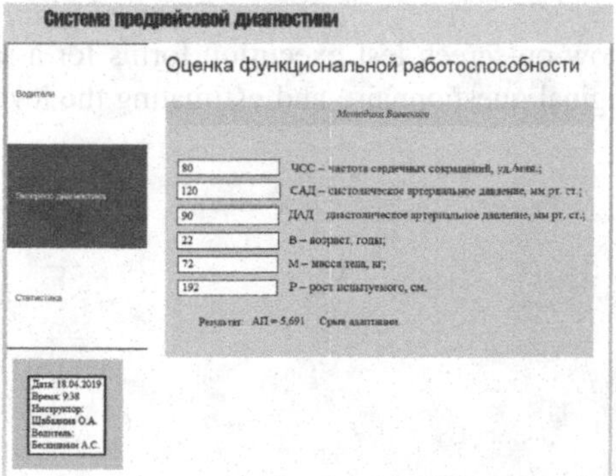

Fig. 5. The screen form of the system in the mode of assessing the physiological state of the driver according to the R.M. Baevsky method

In Figs. 6 and 7 show the screen forms for selecting the method for assessing driver readiness, as well as the possibilities for analyzing the results of test tasks performed earlier.

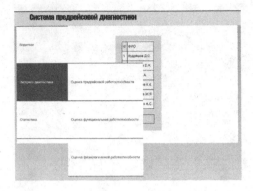

Fig. 6. The screen form of the system in the mode of methods selection for studying of the driver state

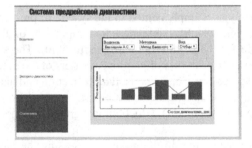

Fig. 7. The screen form of the system in the mode of displaying statistics on the results of test tasks performed by the driver earlier

In Figs. 8 and 9 show on-screen test execution forms for assessing the functional state, answering the original questionnaire and estimating the level of the driver's pre-trip performance level.

Fig. 8. The screen form of the system in the mode of assessing the functional state of the driver

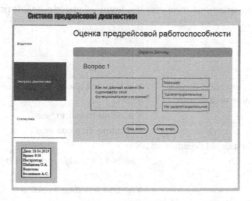

Fig. 9. The screen form of the system in the mode of assessing the level of pre-trip driver health

Using a web-application allows the driver to perform on-line test tasks, which, as a result of interactive interaction with a medical worker, makes it possible to get generalized recommendations on readiness for work.

Each of the methods proposed by us can be used independently or in combination with others. This allows the medical professional to select the necessary, in his opinion, the number of tests and design characteristics in addition to the basic procedures currently used at the stage of pre-trip express diagnostics of drivers.

4   Study Results

The proposed method of pre-trip computer assessment of professional readiness of a driver of a motor vehicle allows analyzing and assessing a driver's readiness according to an extended set of characteristics, including performance, functional and physiological states, taking into account the objective and subjective factors affecting the efficiency of work.

The implementation of the proposed methodology in the pre-trip diagnostic system allows it to be used as one of the elements of a comprehensive assessment of the safety level of the DCRE system, as well as for deciding whether the driver is ready to work in such conditions.

Acknowledgements. The work was supported by RFBR, research project No. 18-47-342003 p_мк.

Appendix A

(See Table 5).

Table 5. The list of questions to assess the level of pre-trip health professional driver

Number of question	Question	Possible answer	Scale of values, points	Result of answer, points
1.	Did you have a big break in your work before going on a flight?	No/(Yes, but not more than a few weeks)	3	
		Yes, from month to year	2	
		Yes, more than one year	1	
2.	Today is your first day of departure on a new route?	No	3	
		Yes, but I already worked on this route before	2	
		Yes, and this route is not very familiar to me	1	
3.	Are weather and road conditions significantly different today from those in the previous few working days?	No	3	
		Yes, but slightly	2	
		Yes	1	
4.	Is this your first time to go on a flight on a different type of vehicle or brand today?	No	3	
		Yes, but the cab ergonomics and vehicle performance characteristics differ slightly from the usual	2	
		Yes, the dimensions and location of the vehicle controls are completely different	1	
5.	How do you assess your functional status at the moment?	Good (normal)	3	
		Satisfactory (slight deterioration of health)	2	
		Unsatisfactory	1	
6.	Did you have to drink alcoholic beverages the day before the work shift?	No	3	
		Yes, within normal limits	2	
		Yes, more than normal[1]	1	

(continued)

Table 5. *(continued)*

Number of question	Question	Possible answer	Scale of values, points	Result of answer, points
7.	How do you assess the level of your own motivation for professional activity?	High	3	
		Medium	2	
		Low	1	
8.	Do you feel hunger or thirst now?	No	3	
		Light feeling of hunger or thirst	2	
		Yes, strong feeling	1	
9.	Do you feel physical fatigue now?	No	3	
		Yes, insignificant	2	
		Yes	1	
10.	Are you currently worried about any problem requiring high concentration?	No	3	
		Yes, there is a small problem	2	
		Yes	1	
11.	Do you go to work on a schedule that takes into account standards for work and rest, or after hours?	On schedule	3	
		With minor changes over time	2	
		With significant changes that reduce the rest period	1	
12.	Are any injuries or illnesses troubling you at the moment?	Absolutely do not disturb	3	
		Slightly disturb	2	
		Strongly disturb	1	
13.	Do you take any medications (by course or once) that impair your professional-important qualities as a driver (attention, reaction, memory, etc.)?	No	3	
		Yes, but they do not significantly affect the functional state	2	
		Yes	1	
14.	Are you currently experiencing strong emotional arousal (joy, excitement) or depression?	No	3	
		Yes, but insignificant	2	
		Yes	1	
15.	Are you currently experiencing the influence of atmospheric pressure and geomagnetic conditions on your health?	No	3	
		Yes, but insignificant	2	
		Yes	1	

References

1. Komarov, Yu.Ya., Kudrin, R.A., Lifanova, E.V., Dyatlov, M.N.: Psihofiziologicheskie osobennosti trudovoj deyatel'nosti voditelej passazhirskogo avtotransporta. Avtotransportnoe predpriyatie № 11, pp. 7–10 (2015)
2. Komarov, Yu.Ya., Kudrin, R.A., Lifanova, E.V., Todorev, A.N., Dyatlov, M.N.: Ekspertnye ocenki professional'no vazhnyh kachestv voditelej passazhirskogo avtotransporta. Avtotransportnoe predpriyatie № 5, pp. 10–13 (2016)
3. Kudrin, R.A.: EHmocional'nyj intellekt cheloveka-operatora. In: Klaucheka, S.V. (ed.) 172 p. Izd-vo VolgGMU, Volgograd (2013)

4. Tebenova, K.S., Il'yasova, B.I., Zarkenova, ZH.T., Zarkenova, L.S.: Funkcional'noe sostoyanie sistemy krovoobrashcheniya u rabotnikov video-displejnyh terminalov v dinamike smeny [Tekst]. Uspekhi sovremennogo estestvoznaniya № 1, pp. 382–386 (2015)

5. Shimada, H., et al.: Driving continuity in cognitively impaired older drivers. Geriatr. Gerontol. Int. **16**(4), 508–514 (2016). https://doi.org/10.1111/ggi.12504

6. Battellino, H.: Transport for the transport disadvantaged: a review of service delivery models in New South Wales. Transport Policy Special Issue International Perspectives on Transport and Social Exclusion № **16**(3), 90–96 (2009)

7. Shmidt, S.A.: Fiziologicheskie osobennosti vnutri- i mezhsistemnyh vzaimootnoshenij psiho-motornogo statusa cheloveka, opredelyayushchie ehffektivnost' operatorskoj deyatel'nosti: dissertaciya ... kandidata medicinskih nauk: 03.00.13/ SHmidt Svetlana Anatol'evna; [Mesto zashchity: GOUVPO «Volgo-gradskij gosudarstvennyj medicinskij universitet»], Volgograd, 134 p (2006)

8. Dyatlov, M.N., Dolgov, K.O., Todorev, A.N.: Osnovnye faktory, snizhayushchie rabotosposobnost' voditelya pered rejsom (ch. 1). Molodoj uchyonyj № 11, pp. 99–103 (2013)

9. Nosyreva, I.G., Yun, G.D.: Motivaciya i stimulirovanie personala: sootnoshenie ponyatij. Vestnik magistratury № **10** 2 (61), 50–53 (2016)

10. Hiam, A.: Motivational Management: Inspiring Your People for Máximum Performance, 276 p. American Management Association, New York (2003)

11. Kotik, M.A., Emel'yanov, A.M.: Oshibki upravleniya: psihologicheskie prichiny. Metod avtomatizirovannogo analiza, 390 p. Valgus, Tallin (1985)

12. Baevskij, R.M., Berseneva, A.P.: Ocenka adaptacionnyh vozmozhnostej organizma i risk razvitiya zabolevanij, 265 p. Medicina, Moscow (1997)

13. Berezin, F.B.: Psihicheskaya i psihofiziologicheskaya adaptaciya cheloveka, 267 p. Nauka, Leningrad (1998)

14. Kompleks: «Effecton Studio» [Elektronnyj resurs] Rezhim dostupa. http://www.effecton.ru/03.html. data obrashcheniya 02 Mar 2016

15. Dyatlov, M.N., Agazadyan, A.R., Shabalina, O.A.: Apparatno-programmnyj kompleks dlya testirovaniya professional'nyh kachestv voditelej passazhirskogo avtotransporta na ehtape professional'nogo otbora. Vestnik komp'yuternyh i informacionnyh tekhnologij № **12**(150), 48–55 (2016)

16. Dyatlov, M.N., Shabalina, O.A., Komarov, Yu.Ya., Kudrin, R.A.: Razrabotka testovyh zadanij dlya komp'yuternoj diagnostiki stepeni razvitiya sensomotornyh reakcij s uchyotom osobennostej professional'noj deyatel'nosti voditelej. In: Izvestiya VolgGTU. Series Aktual'nye problemy upravleniya, vychislitel'noj tekhniki i informatiki v tekhnicheskih sistemah. – Volgograd № **6**(185), pp. 33–39 (2016)

17. Shabalina, O.A., Kudrin, R.A., Agazadyan, A.R., Todorev, A.N., Dyatlov, M.N.: Ocenka professional'noj prigodnosti voditelej passazhirskogo avtotransporta v usloviyah imitacii dorozhnogo dvizheniya. Vestnik Volgogradskogo gos. med. un-ta (Vestnik VolgGMU). Vyp. **2**(62), 126–129 (2017)

18. Todorev, A.N., Shabalina, O.A., Dyatlov, M.N., Kudrin, R.A., Komarov, Yu.Ya.: Comparison of testing results of drivers on the road traffic simulator and on the set of psychological tests [Electronic resource]. In: Berestneva, O.G., et al. (eds.) Proceedings of the IV International research conference «Information technologies in Science, Management, Social sphere and Medicine», ITSMSSM 2017. Series Advances in Computer Science Research (ACSR), vol. 72, pp. 430–433. Atlantis Press (2017). https://www.atlantis-press.com/proceedings/itsmssm-17

Intelligent Technologies in Social Engineering. Intelligent Assistive Technologies: Software Design and Application

Medical Diagnostic Expert System for Training and Decision Support of Early Stage Diagnoses

Yumchmaa Ayush[1]([✉]), Uranchimeg Tudevdagva[2],
and Sharaf Asrorovich Boboev[1]

[1] Novosibirsk State Technical University,
20, Prospect Karl Marx, Novosibirsk, Russia
yumchmaaa@gmail.com
[2] Chemnitz University of Technology, 09111 Chemnitz, Germany

Abstract. The detection of diseases at an early stage can increase an opportunity to prevent diseases and to carry out their effective treatment. However, making a diagnosis at an early stage of the disease is difficult in the case of most diseases initially present and with similar symptoms and signs. Specific medical expert systems based on the integration of traditional Western and Eastern medicine helps to identify the causes of the disease in early stage.

Differentiated analyses of the relationship of diseases will provide an opportunity to identify constitutional-dependent signs of the disease and risk factors, will individualizes the prognosis and treatment, which, in turn, help to improve the results of treatment of the disease. Medical diagnostic expert system (MDES) based on the integration of traditional Western and Eastern medicine is for studying additional factors of the disease, in particular, the influence of anthropological and psychological data of a person on the manifestation of the disease.

The probability theory, mathematical statistics and some methods of artificial intelligence are applied for development of basic model. The diagnoses vector basis both: general doctor opinion and indicators of individual diseases.

The knowledge base of MDES developed based on the integration of various sources: reflection forms which links key constitutional types of the human body and traditional Western diagnoses. The MDES provides doctors of the differential diagnosis hypothesis reliable from the point of view of the expert system based on the entered symptoms and expected, existing or excluded related diagnoses.

This paper describes the results of MDES test and the statistical processing of the data obtained.

Keywords: Decision support system · Diagnostic · Western medicine ·
Eastern medicine · Health assessment · Information entropy ·
Statistical hypothesis · Constitutional types

1 Introduction

1.1 Diagnose Schemes Based on Logical Relationship of Symptom-Disease

Core idea of MDES is to use estimation diagnose of two directions of medicine: Western and Eastern. First diagnose data (Western medicine) obtains by measurement

A. G. Kravets et al. (Eds.): CIT&DS 2019, CCIS 1084, pp. 395–406, 2019.
https://doi.org/10.1007/978-3-030-29750-3_31

of medical analysis or apparatuses. Second part of diagnose data (Eastern medicine) collects by predefined questionnaire where counts the constitution of an individuals.

The MDES focuses on specific questionnaire, which developed on constitutional types of human [21, 22]. The questionnaire designed as questions matrix with possible answers. The informative hints linked to each answer that helps the expert system to issue a diagnosis of the disease through an inference engine.

A. *The logical analysis of western approach diagnostic*

To fulfill core idea of MDES done logical analysis of medical diagnoses in both approaches [16–18]: Western and Eastern medicine.

Figure 1 shows the general scheme of the western approach diagnosis. Here is the case of the first symptom for the first disease. In general, scheme has the "i^{th}" symptom of the "j^{th}" disease. If the program gives a positive response to a symptom, then it continues to pass through the symptoms of this disease. Else the symptom analyze switched to the next disease.

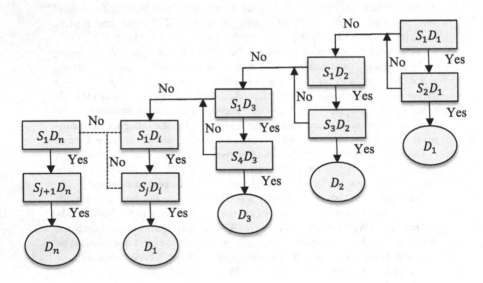

Fig. 1. The general scheme for acquiring knowledge about the relationship of symptom-disease.

Type of diagnoses D based on symptoms S is huge. That means information, which the user can obtain the necessary information about the diagnosis of diseases, is very big. MDES organized each diagnosis with its negation: a set of hypotheses and a set of symptoms; where $\{S_j\}, j = \overline{1,m}$ - set of symptoms. For any - S_j will consider, that have a symptom, or not - $\overline{S_j}$.

A priori probability is considered on the basis of usual probability of diagnosis. $P(D_i), i = \overline{1,n}$ – priori probability of diagnosis, that prior probability of diagnosis, established before the receipt of any symptoms, where $P(\overline{D_i}) = 1 - P(D_i)$.

The conditional probability of the symptom manifestation, if the client has many symptoms and its designation of probabilities are presented:

$$\left\{P\left(\frac{S_j}{D_i}\right)\right\}; \left\{P\left(\frac{\overline{S_j}}{D_i}\right)\right\}; \left\{P\left(\frac{S_j}{\overline{D_i}}\right)\right\}; \left\{P\left(\frac{\overline{S_j}}{\overline{D_i}}\right)\right\} P_{apost}(D_i)$$

and

$P_{apost}(\overline{D_i})$ when acquisition both positive and negative responses about the symptom [15]:

1. $P_{apost}\left(\frac{D_i}{S_j}\right) = \dfrac{P(D_i) \cdot P\left(\frac{S_j}{D_i}\right)}{P(S_i)}$

where,

$$P(|S_j|) = P(|D_i|) \cdot P\left(\left|\frac{S_j}{D_i}\right|\right) + P(|\overline{D_i}|) \cdot P\left(\left|\frac{S_j}{\overline{D_i}}\right|\right)$$

2. $P_{apost}\left(\frac{D_i}{S_j}\right) = \dfrac{P(D_i) \cdot P\left(\frac{\overline{S_j}}{D_i}\right)}{P(\overline{S_J})}$

where,

$$P_{apost}|\overline{S_J}| = P(D_i) \cdot P\left(\frac{\overline{S_J}}{D_i}\right) + P(\overline{D_i}) \cdot P\left(\frac{\overline{S_J}}{D_i}\right)$$

$$P_{apost}\left|\frac{\overline{D_i}}{S_j}\right| = 1 - P_{apost}\left(\frac{D_i}{S_j}\right)$$

$$P_{apost}\left|\frac{\overline{D_i}}{\overline{S_J}}\right| = 1 - P_{apost}\left(\frac{D_i}{\overline{S_J}}\right)$$

B. The logical analysis of traditional eastern approach diagnostic

The most methods for determination of human constitution are based on the scoring [1]. Researchers develop scoring methods by different ways and there no well-accepted theory based methods. Reason is human body is unique in each case and it is difficult to develop "general" method of scoring for individual with various symptoms. The questionnaire for data collection in MDES consists of 43 questions. All questions are selected from state of the art of main topic, from work of researchers [2–13] based on constitutional types, which accepted by most eastern medical doctors.

The constitutional types are defining by several factors: severity and correlation of certain signs, properties of morphology, physiological systems, and the whole organism, including the nervous system.

This eastern medical concept is based on the concept about equilibrium of the three basic elements which exists in the human body under the names of wind, bile, and phlegm. Features that recur in populations, it is customary to distinguish the following 7 constitutional types: T1–T3 dominant types (wind, bile and phlegm people), mixed types T4–T6 (wind-bile, bile-slime, wind-slime, bile-wind, slime-bile and slime-wind) and the combined type T7 (wind-bile-phlegm) [2–8, 10, 11, 13].

Human constitution type can be identify depending on life principles of human and on self-assessment of the intensity their physiological and mental activities.

The questionnaire of MDES has n questions and each question can receive three values as respond to question (Table 1).

Table 1. The fuzzy interval for n questions of questionnaire

Amount of questions	Response values	Fuzzy interval of response values A_{ij}, B_{ij}, C_{ij}	Confidence levels of given responses
U_n	A_i	A little sure	0,4
		Sure	0,7
		More sure	0,9
		Full sure	1
	B_i	A little sure	0,4
		Sure	0,7
		More sure	0,9
		Full sure	1
	C_i	A little sure	0,4
		Sure	0,7
		More sure	0,9
		Full sure	1

New approach of this kind of questionnaire design is first time trying to count more probabilistic results about human constitution types. The fuzzy interval in verbal contents should support to increase probability of real feeling of client relating to questions.

1.2 The Development and Test of Medical Diagnostic Expert System

For the medical diagnostic expert system was developed architecture design for system. The main architecture of expert system consists of four parts: Input, Knowledge base, Inference Engine and Output (Fig. 2). Each part includes smaller elements of parts.

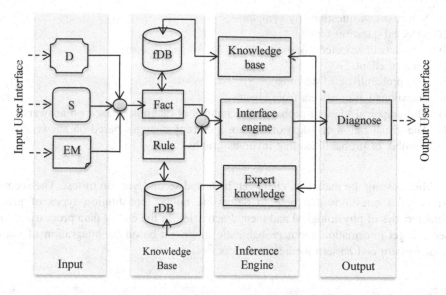

Fig. 2. The general architecture of expert system

Input part. This part serves as input user interface of system to clients. A client can enter data {D, S, EM} to system. All these input data joined to one and transferred to next part of system.

Knowledge base part. This part consists of two main processes: the main test and the eastern medicine test for determining the human constitution type. The basic logic of work defined in the database in the form of tables, views, functions and procedures. Facts in database (fDB) includes all facts that describe information about symptoms (signs) of diseases and determinant characteristics for human constitution types. Knowledge base consists of western medical findings (evidences) and experiments of eastern medical experts. That means the knowledge base contains a high quality and extraordinary knowledge in that particular domains. Rules in database (rDB) includes set of rules that can get from experience of experts. The rule of experts translated into the "if-then" statements.

Inference engine. This part of system helps to define how to make decision based on the knowledge in integration based on traditional western and eastern medical diagnosis methods.

Output. The expert system concluded processes in system and delivered diagnose to user which can be provide decision for early stage of diagnoses.

A client should to choose one of two different test versions (main test and test by TM). Main test contains diagnosis options and questions that belong to symptoms of given diagnosis will be primary data.

The Fig. 3 shows screenshot of running MDES with client data. Diagnoses are the result of a general state that corresponds to the symptoms of a given disease and their client complaints. Here are short explanation of elements visualized in screenshot:

(1) Selections of questions by symptoms,
(2) Selected question views,
(3) Amounts of selected questions,
(4) Data of client,
(5) The probabilistic of diagnosis,
(6) Questions with answers from client,
(7) The graphical view of probabilistic changes of diagnosis based on answers,
(8) The visualization of graph of diagnosis entropy changes based on answers,
(9) Number of probabilities that involves graphs.

After passing the main test, client can be tested second version of test. The second test contains questions that help to determine human constitution types of given characteristics of physiological and mental activities. In the end of data processing, the user can get information about probabilistic diagnosis based on integration of traditional western and eastern medical concepts.

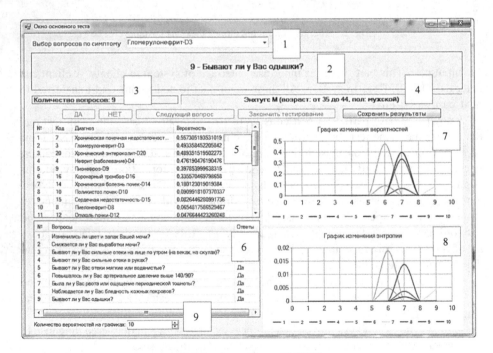

Fig. 3. Screenshot of MDES

1.3 The Results of Medical Diagnostic Expert System

The system tested with cooperation of two hospitals of Mongolia and clients asked to take part of test based on volunteer. Statistic about data source for MDES test. The 235 volunteers (healthy 102 and with some problems 133) answered to questionnaire of expert system. The DMES can produce several results as output data.

Table 2 shows constitution types distribution rate with relationship of gender.

Table 2. Gender analyze of frequency ration human constitution

№	Constitution types	Frequency M	Frequency F	Frequency M	Frequency F
		Healthy		Sick	
1	Type 1	1	1	5	8
2	Type 2	1	19	18	28
3	Type 3	0	1	0	4
4	Type 4	17	31	7	33
5	Type 5	2	2	3	4
6	Type 6	9	12	16	7
7	Type 7	1	5	0	0
	Total	31	71	49	84
		102		133	

Based on the data from Table 2 the hypothesis of homogeneity of data for a sample of healthy and having cardiovascular diseases in men, the following data were obtained: the value of statistics $\chi_n^2 = 11,20$, the value of quantile χ_n^2 at a given significance level of 0.05 equals $F_{\chi_{(7-1)(2-1)}^2}^{-1}(0,95) = 12,59$.

Therefore, the data do not contradict the defined hypothesis above. For other diseases, similar results were obtained. From here can conclude that the type of constitution affects to the type of diseases.

Note that the statistics of the criterion has a similar form for testing the independence hypothesis [14], if you choose a value as a two-dimensional random variable, in which the first component is a type of constitution, and the second is a sign of "Healthy/Sick".

Test of DMES had two phases. In first test attended 235 volunteers and it was based on scoring method. In next phase of test included 10 volunteers.

Main goal of second test was to compare results of two different methods for collecting data from clients: with basic scoring method and with fuzzy interval values.

10 volunteers were selected from all of participants. At first, all clients were passed first test version of support decision system and obtained results according to their symptoms. When clients were passing main test, changes of diagnosis probability are determined depending on client's answers. Symptoms appear with different frequencies in some cases of diseases. According to this, state uncertainty of some symptoms of disease is can be offer more than other cases. Therefore, main point of interrelation between questions and answers consist in correct definition of symptoms. If clients answer many of questions - "YES", then it increases result of diagnosis probabilities of given diseases.

After main test, clients were passed second test version in two ways: scoring interval and fuzzy interval. In results, clients had been determined their constitution types, and, also diagnosis probabilities of diseases were changed.

Table 3. The comparison table of two different tests for 10 volunteers

№	Scoring interval			Answer	Fuzzy interval			Answer
	A	B	C		A	B	C	
1	21	17	4	T4	16	11,6	3,2	-
2	28	8	6	T1	15,1	6,7	2,9	-
3	16	16	10	T4	12,6	10,6	7,2	-
4	11	14	17	T6	9,7	10,6	12,4	-
5	17	14	11	T4	13,5	9,8	6,4	-
6	12	27	3	T2	8,4	14,2	1,8	T4
7	20	19	3	T4	15,1	12,7	1,8	-
8	20	9	13	T5	15,9	5	6,1	T1
9	13	19	10	T4	9,8	13,3	6,8	-
10	18	11	13	T5	11,2	6,2	6,7	T1

Table 3 shows the deference between two determination methods for human constitution type. From these result can to notice that the result of method on fuzzy interval differs from the scoring interval method. It causes from the personality significance about their mental and physiological activities, that are directly depends on self-assessment.

The accuracy of diagnosis determination $F = f_1 \cdot P_d$ depends on the position number in the list of results (coefficient $f_1(N_d) \in [0; 1]$ and on the probability of diagnosis P_d after passing the first test version in the system. Here,

$$f_1 = \frac{N_d}{N},$$

where, N_d - position number in the result lists of the diagnosis manifestation, N- the total number of diagnosis.

In the Table 4 shows, the testing results of the diagnosis determination was carried out in two test versions (first test version and second test versions).

Table 4. The accuracy of diagnosis

№	$F = f_1 \cdot P_d$	$F_{TM} = f_1 \cdot P_d$
1	0,570879979	0,570879979
2	0,69078482	0,750890256
3	0,482198202	0,463329364
4	0,69078482	0,69075452
5	0,7479503	0,7479503
6	0,379576889	0,449589147
7	0,379576889	0,492339929
8	0,533893572	0,533893572
9	0,381970019	0,607037922
10	0,512964083	0,577532225

Figure 4 shows the relationship the accuracy diagnosis on the position numbers of diagnosis in the obtained result lists of the support decision system.

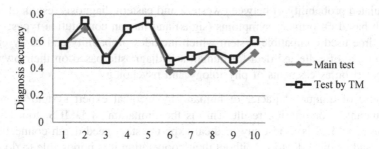

Fig. 4. Changes in the reliability of the known diagnosis

The average value of the accuracy of the two test versions is estimated by the following formula:

$$\overline{F} = \frac{\sum\limits_{i=1}^{n} F_i}{n}$$

Where, F_i is the value of ith accuracy of the test, n is the total number of tests (volunteers).

Then, the average value of the test accuracy from first test version is equal to $\overline{F} = 0,537$, similar to for the second test versions - $\overline{F}_{TM} = 0,577$. Consequently, the average value of the second test versions accuracy is greater than first test version $(\overline{F}_{TM} > \overline{F})$ by 7.53%.

1.4   Advantages and Limitations

The idea for MDES developed based on previous similar online systems which determine health condition of 12 organs based on their pulse changes [18–20]. But, previous developed systems used to be additional measuring systems. Our main goal was directed to diagnosis based on integration western and eastern diagnosis methods which can to diagnose easy for users not required specific measuring system.

New aspects of MDES are:

- Based on diagnostic methods of traditional western and eastern medicine;
- Developed primary signs set of diseases, which include symptoms base on traditional western and eastern medicine concepts in primary diagnosis;
- Proposed Bayesian model for choosing sequences of questions based on criterion of the minimum residual entropy;
- Developed integral model including probability and fuzzy models for determination human constitutional types.

There are several advantages with new MDES:

- Defined questions based on well-established theory of eastern medicine;
- Compared offered diagnoses from system with diagnose of western medicine;
- Calculated probability of between western and eastern diagnosis results of diseases which based on primary symptoms (signs) and human constitution types;
- First time used compatible system which includes probability and fuzzy elements for analyze of collected data for human self diagnostic based on their own whole characteristic assessments of physiology and psychology.

Because of unique character of human any medical expert system cannot give 100% guarantee for offering result. This is the limitation of DMES, too. Other big limitation of DMES is to test any medical expert system need depth connection with hospitals and medical doctors. Without their cooperation it is impossible to do test any medical expert system. Because of this limitation DMES has not enough practical evidence for effectiveness and efficiency. But this is the completely self-developed idea based on medical engineering experiences and observation from work in several hospitals and cooperation of many discussions with medical doctors.

1.5 Technical Requirement for Implementation

In the choices for most likely diseases uses one data base, Bayesian procedure and conditional residual entropy. The MDES is including modules of determination method for human constitutions and set of diseases. Also, the MDES is software which not needed special install process. System was writing on programming language C# and SQL Server (in Visual Studio 2017). To use this system should have: computer with RAM at least 8 GB, 2G free spaces on the hard disk, standard input and . System output devices supports operation systems Windows XP, 7, 8 and 10. MDES is intended to integration diagnostic of western and eastern medicines.

2 Conclusion

The determination method for human constitution type according to the eastern medicine demonstrates a qualitative approach, whereas it's based on a subjective concept about human mental and physiological characteristics. Therefore, need to pay more attention on the human self-expression about own mental and physiological features.

Two different test versions for determination of human constitution were passed within selectable 10 clients from all participants. At the result of first test version (scoring interval) half of clients who participated had Type 4 (50%), the type following on frequency was Type 5 (20%), then Type 1 (10%), Type 2 (10%) and Type 6 (10%). Type 7 wasn't determined. After passing second test versions had been changed some constitutions types. In there, amount of Type 4 (60%) and Type 1 (30%) were increased, also Type 5 wasn't determined. In evidence 30% changes were differed between 2 test versions. It shows that determination method based on the fuzzy interval is more flexible. Main goal of this research is create support decision system based on integration of traditional western and eastern medical diagnostic methods that can help to support make decision to user or clients and to give opportunity get more causal information about disease manifestation. Also it is able to use for training of medical students. Actually, this system is not intended to direct diagnosis.

References

1. Kim, J. U., et al.: The concept of sasang health index and constitution-based health assessment: an integrative model with computerized four diagnosis methods. Evid.-Based Complement. Altern. Med. **2013**, 13 (2013). http://dx.doi.org/10.1155/2013/879420. Accessed 13 Apr 2019
2. Usukhbayar, B.: Logical and methodical research of the basic principles of traditional medicine for prevention and diagnostics of diseases. Ph.D. Medical Science Dissertation, Mongolia, 124 p. (2003)
3. Batsukh, B.: Research of influence biological age and the constitutional types on coronary heart disease. Ph.D. Medical Science Dissertation, Mongolia, 127 p. (2010)
4. Chzhud-Shi.: The fundamentals of Tibetan medicine, 380 p. Ulaanbaatar, State Publications (1990). http://www.rulit.me/books/chzhud-shi-osnovy-tibetskoj-mediciny-read-415656-1. html. Accessed 10 Jan 2017
5. Baavgaj, Ch., Boldsajhan, B.: Mongolian Traditional Medicine. State Publications, Ulaanbaatar, 380 p. (1990)
6. Choijinimaeva, S.G.: Diseases of nervous people or where blows the wind, 183 p. Astral Publications, Moscow (2010)
7. Choijinimaeva, S.G.: Diseases of big people or what is the bile, 136 p. Piter Publications, Saint-Petersburg (2016)
8. Choijinimaeva, S.G.: Diseases of strong people or how to temperate phlegm, 145 p. Astral Publications, Moscow (2010)
9. Naidanova, S.M.: Buddhist fundamental of Tibetan medicine, extended abstract of thesis Ph. D. Phil. Science, 26 p., Chita (2015)
10. Test for constitutional type determination by Tibetan medicine. http://www.tibet-medicine. ru/konstitucii/typy-konstitutcij. Accessed 01 May 2017
11. Kalmykov, S.V., Tsybikov, A.S., Zandanova, G.I., Zinina, O.A.: Empirical analysis of the Tibetan system of classification of constitutional human types. In: Bulletin of Buryat State University, pp. 93–100. BSU Publications, Ulan-Ude (2014)
12. Kalmykov, S.V., Sagaleyev, A.S., Tsybikov, A.S.: Analysis of Tibetan three-factor human constitutional model in sport. http://www.teoriya.ru/ru/node/487. Accessed 01 Apr 2019
13. Diagnosis information system. http://www.mz.bsu.ru. Accessed 22 June 2018
14. Postavolav, S.N., Chimitova, E.V., Karmanov, V.S.: Mathematical Statistics. NSTU Publications, Novosibirsk (2014)
15. Grif, M.G., Shegal, B.R., Ayush, Yu., Yastrebova, S.V.: Diagnostic test design for the medical decision support system "AIMedica" based on integration of the "European" and the "Eastern" medicines. In: Proceedings International Multi-Conference on Engineering, Computer and Information Sciences, SIBIRCON-2017, Novosibirsk , pp. 209–214 (2017)
16. Grif, M.G., Ayush, Yu., Shegal, B.R.: The development of diagnostic expert system based on the integration of European and eastern medicines. In: Scientific Bulletin of Astrakhan State Technical University, vol. 2 (April), pp. 81–90. ASTU Publications, Astrakhan (2018)
17. Ayush, Yu., Grif, M.G.: The computational method for self-diagnostical system. In: IBS Scientific Workshop Proceedings, pp. 67–69. TUC Publications, Germany (2017)

18. Tsidipov, T.: Pulse Diagnosis in Tibetan Medicine, 133 p. Science Publications, Novosibirsk. (1988)
19. «Veda pulse» pulse analysis device. http://www.vedapuls.ru. Accessed 01 May 2019
20. Boronoev, V.V., Ayusheeva, L.V., Ledneva, I.P., Naguslaev, I.V.: Duration of period of pulse signals in the Tibetan diagnosis of disorder in the activity of regulatory systems. J. Buryat State Univ. **12**, 39–42 (2013)
21. Ayush, Y., Tudevdagva, U., Grif, M.: Expert system based diagnostic application for medical training. In: Kravets, A., Shcherbakov, M., Kultsova, M., Groumpos, P. (eds.) CIT&DS 2017. CCIS, vol. 754, pp. 750–761. Springer, Cham (2017). https://doi.org/10. 1007/978-3-319-65551-2_54
22. Tudevdagva, U., Sambuu, U., Ayush, Yu.: A prototype of expert system for rural medical centers. In: 7th International Conference on Frontiers of Information Technology, Applications and Tools, and the 4th PT-ERC International Symposium on Personalized Medicine, FITAT/ISPM 2014, pp. 23–26 (2014)

Using Eye-Tracking and Emotion Recognition as Additional Sources of Information When Testing People with Intellectual Disabilities

Dmitriy Skvaznikov[1], Olga Shabalina[1(✉)], and Jan Dekelver[2]

[1] Volgograd State Technical University, Volgograd, Russia
orkich@gmail.com, o.a.shabalina@gmail.com
[2] Thomas More University College, K-point, Geel, Belgium
jan.dekelver@thomasmore.be

Abstract. Today, the development of special-purpose software for helping People with Intellectual Disabilities (PID) in their daily life and professional activities is a very active trend. Various testing systems with simplified text, images or videos are used to analyze problems, interests, and preferences of the PID related to their daily life or professional activities. However, in relation to the PID, the credibility of the test results might strongly depend on how much they understand the testing process and how they interpret questions and choose the answers.

This article discusses the possibility of increasing the reliability of the PID test results by adding additional sources of information. A web-based system is described for analyzing professional interests and preferences of PID using additional data on the point of gaze and emotional state of PID during the testing process. A method for evaluating test results is described, taking into account the contribution of these data as well as possible errors occurred when collecting them. The results of testing with the participation of several PIDs are presented, and it is shown that adding such sources of information as eye tracking data and emotion analysis can increase the reliability of the test results.

Keywords: People with Intellectual Disabilities · PID ·
Testing PID · Interests and preferences · Web-based testing system ·
Emotion recognition · Eye tracking

1 Introduction

Socialization, professional orientation, and development of People with Intellectual Disabilities (PID) are some of the prominent problems of modern society. PID may experience certain difficulties in various aspects of their daily or professional activities, significantly reducing their quality of life (QoL). In order to improve the life of PID, support their personal growth and professional development, it is helpful to be aware of their problems, intentions, interests, and preferences.

However, obtaining the information from PID may be a problem as for many of them it might be quite challenging to express their thoughts as well as to understand and to interpret the questions of other people and to respond to them. Thus, direct

© Springer Nature Switzerland AG 2019
A. G. Kravets et al. (Eds.): CIT&DS 2019, CCIS 1084, pp. 407–421, 2019.
https://doi.org/10.1007/978-3-030-29750-3_32

communication with PID due to their intellectual disabilities (ID) may be difficult, and the reliability of the information received from them in a direct dialogue may be questionable.

Today, the development of special-purpose software for helping PID in their daily life and professional activities is a very popular trend. A number of applications have been developed to support their safety, independent movement and travel, homework, the use of money, phone, and job search. To analyze the problems, interests, and preferences of PID, specially developed testing systems are used. Such systems implement various types of tests with questions and answers presented as simplified text [1], images ("tests in pictures") [2] or video [3].

However, in relation to people with PID, the results of computer testing may be even less reliable compared to the direct dialogue, in which the interlocutor can help a person with ID to understand the questions and more or less adequately answer them. Therefore, any additional data obtained from other sources of information can enhance the reliability of computer testing of people with PID.

2 Specialized Web-Based System for Testing People with Intellectual Disabilities

To analyse the interests and preferences of people with PID in various areas of life, the authors have developed a Web-based testing system that implements the "tests in pictures" approach [4]. The test includes a set of images grouped into categories reflecting some areas of interests or preferences. The images are displayed on the screen, and the user just has to rate the contents of an image by selecting the answer "I like it" (i.e. "I like this kind of professional activities") or "I do not like it". The test results are calculated by the number of images that the user has found "likable" for each category, and the categories are ranked based on the number of the user's "I like it", showing their interests and preferences for each category. Thus, the test result is an indirect assessment of the interests, and the user's preferences are represented by the categories by summing up the number of images belonging to these categories that the user likes. Besides the testing function, the system also includes the functions for managing the testing process, such as managing user profiles, calculating and visualizing test results.

The first version of the system implemented a specialized test [2] designed to identify the most preferred professional activities that PID would like to perform. The test includes sixty images divided into ten categories that reflect different types of professional activities. Associations between categories and images are defined by relationships, the strength of the association is stored in weight in the range [1...5]: the higher the score, the stronger is the relation between the image and the category. In general, an image may be associated with more than one category. The list of categories, along with short strings serving as their identifiers for describing the results of the experiment presented later in this paper, are given in Table 1.

Table 1. Categories of interests and their identifiers

Interest category	Identifier
Customer oriented work	cat_client
Craft work	cat_craft
Care and well-being	cat_care
Creative work	cat_art
Gardening	cat_garden
Animal care	cat_pets
Administrative work	cat_administrative
Cooking work	cat_food
Semi-industrial work	cat_factory
Home chores	cat_home

User-centered design and iterative design technologies were used to develop the system interface. Testing iterations were organized at MPI Oosterlo (https://www.mpi-oosterlo.be/), a service centre caring for PID in Flanders, Belgium. Based on the results of three iterations of testing, a full-featured version of the system has been developed.

The screenshots of the system for the testing and evaluation mode pages are shown in Figs. 1 and 2.

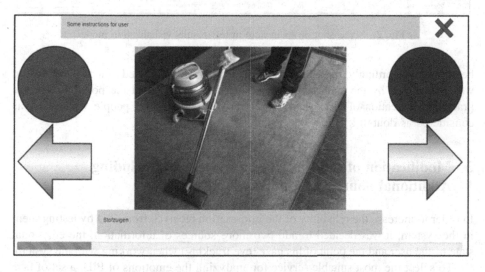

Fig. 1. Screenshot of the system in test mode

The testing at the medical centre was conducted under the supervision of the staff. Observing the users' behaviour during the testing process showed that some users did not carefully consider the images before choosing the "Like"/"I don't like" answer, others quickly got tired and began to respond at random. Several participants did not seem to understand what to do and pressed the answer buttons at random from the very

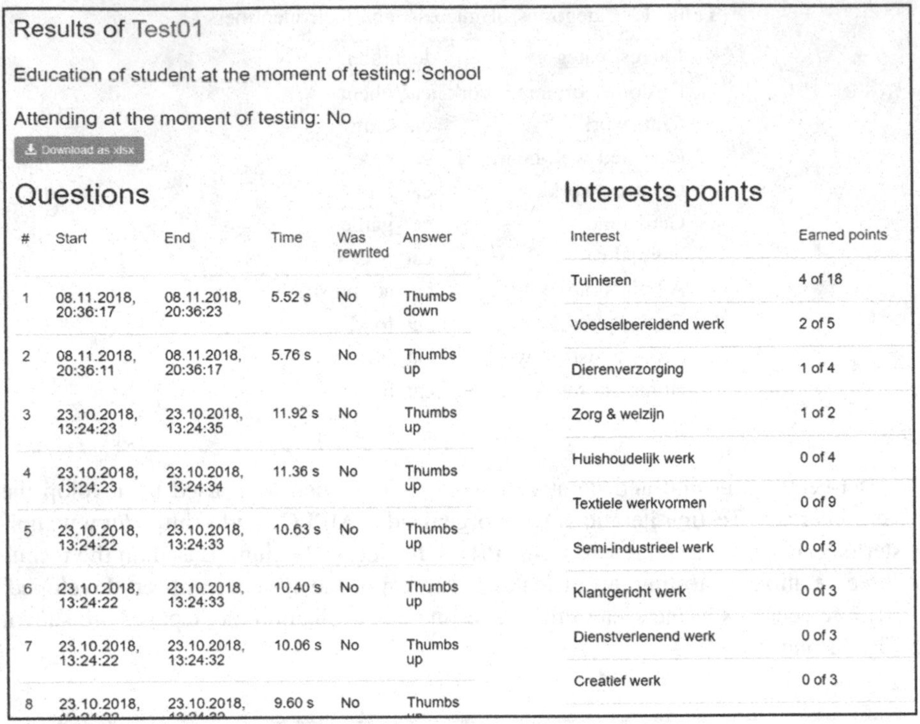

Results of Test01

Education of student at the moment of testing: School

Attending at the moment of testing: No

Download as xlsx

Questions

#	Start	End	Time	Was rewrited	Answer
1	08.11.2018, 20:36:17	08.11.2018, 20:36:23	5.52 s	No	Thumbs down
2	08.11.2018, 20:36:11	08.11.2018, 20:36:17	5.76 s	No	Thumbs up
3	23.10.2018, 13:24:23	23.10.2018, 13:24:35	11.92 s	No	Thumbs up
4	23.10.2018, 13:24:23	23.10.2018, 13:24:34	11.36 s	No	Thumbs up
5	23.10.2018, 13:24:22	23.10.2018, 13:24:33	10.63 s	No	Thumbs up
6	23.10.2018, 13:24:22	23.10.2018, 13:24:33	10.40 s	No	Thumbs up
7	23.10.2018, 13:24:22	23.10.2018, 13:24:32	10.06 s	No	Thumbs up
8	23.10.2018,	23.10.2018,	9.60 s	No	Thumbs

Interests points

Interest	Earned points
Tuinieren	4 of 18
Voedselbereidend werk	2 of 5
Dierenverzorging	1 of 4
Zorg & welzijn	1 of 2
Huishoudelijk werk	0 of 4
Textiele werkvormen	0 of 9
Semi-industrieel werk	0 of 3
Klantgericht werk	0 of 3
Dienstverlenend werk	0 of 3
Creatief werk	0 of 3

Fig. 2. Screenshot of the system in test results visualization mode

beginning. Accordingly, the reliability of the information obtained as a result of testing was recognized by the staff as “conditionally acceptable”, and the possibility of the practical application of test results to select work suitable for people with PID was considered as doubtful.

3 Modification of the Web-Based System by Including Additional Sources of Information

In order to increase the reliability of the information received from PID by testing them in the system, it was decided to add two more sources of information: the emotional state of the user and the point of his gaze (eye tracking) when working with the system.

To select the most suitable service for analyzing the emotions of PID, a set of face images of PID with different emotions was collected from various sources. This sample was used to test the following services: Emotion API (https://azure.microsoft.com/en-us/services/cognitive-services/emotion/), Cloud Vision API (https://cloud.google.com/vision/), EmoVu (http://emovu.com/e/), F.A.C.E. API (https://face.sightcorp.com/). As a result of testing, the service from Microsoft Emotion API was selected, which showed the best accuracy of emotion recognition of PID on the set [5].

The eye tracking library was selected by the requirements for methods of measuring either point of gaze. Libraries using infrared radiation require special equipment (for example tobii, https://gaming.tobii.com/products/). Using data from such the device in test results is a time-taking task. Besides, collecting the data from such the device and transferring it to the web-application requires additional development of middleware between the device and web-application. Libraries, based on specially trained models for determining user's point of gaze, use conventional web cameras that are built into almost all modern computers.

Existing libraries based on trained models differ in calibration method (absent/ setting parameters/automatic/before analysis); video stream location processing (external server/locally (on the testing application server or via additional software)/in the browser), software distribution conditions (GNU, FSF, and others). Free WebGazer library [6] was selected for the test system. The library processes the video stream in the browser, and thus it does not require transferring the video stream to the server.

4 Algorithm for Evaluating Test Results Using Additional Data Sources

The testing by asking the image-based questions is intended to determine the most preferable category of interests of the user. The algorithm of evaluating the test results includes the following steps:

1. collecting a set *QuestionLiked* of questions with images that were rated by the user as "*I like it*";
2. grouping the collected questions into categories *Category$_j$*, which they are associated with:

$$Category_j = \{QuestionLiked_1, QuestionLiked_2, \ldots, QuestionLiked_n\},$$

where *QuestionLiked$_i$* – i-th question associated with *Category$_j$*;
n – number of questions in *Category$_j$*.

(1) Summing the points of relationships between the questions and category, for each category:

$$pointsForCategory_j = \sum_{i=1}^{|QuestionLiked|} interestWeight_i,$$

where *interestWeight$_i$* – the weight of the i-th question associated with the j-th category;
pointsForCategory$_j$ – sum of the points between questions and j-th category.

(2) normalizing the sum of points for each category in the interval [0,1], where the upper limit of the interval corresponds to the maximum possible number of points in the category:

$$points_{jo} = \frac{pointsForCategory_j}{MaxPointsForCategory_j},$$

where $points_{jo}$ – normalized score for the j-th category;
$MaxPointsForCategory_j$ – the maximum number of points that can be scored in the j-th category.

The coefficient of correction of test results is calculated taking into account the data on the user eye tracking or his emotional state during the testing process.

The calculation of the coefficient of correction of test results based on the user eye tracking:

– collecting a set $gazePoints_j$ of points of gaze of the user for all pages associated with *QuestionLiked* for each category $Category_j$;
– calculation of the correction coefficient as a ratio of gaze points located in the image and all the points in the page for each category:

$$k_j = \frac{count\left(gazePoints_{j\,insidePicture}\right)}{count\left(gazePoints_j\right)},$$

where k_j – correction coefficient for the j-th category;
$gazePoints_{j\,insidePicture}$ – points of gaze, located in the image.

Thus, the coefficient for correcting test results based on the distribution of points of gaze reflects the proportion of time during which the user looked at the image itself, in relation to the time spent working with the corresponding page. The data processing scheme for collecting the gaze points is shown in Fig. 3.

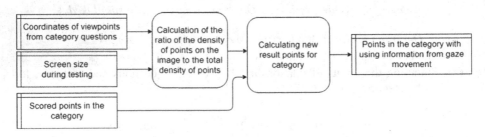

Fig. 3. Collecting the gaze points

The coefficient of correction of test results based on data on the emotional state is calculated as follows:

– collection of a set $emotionStates_j$ of emotional states for all *QuestionLiked* for each $Category_j$;
– calculation of the correction coefficient as fraction of positive emotions to all emotion states in each category;

$$k_j = \frac{\text{count}\left(emotionStates_{j\,positive}\right)}{\text{count}\left(emotionStates_j\right)},$$

where k_j – correction coefficient for the j-th category;
$emotionStates_{j\,positive}$ – positive emotional states.

The Microsoft Emotion API library, used to assess emotional states of the users, recognizes seven different emotions: happiness, surprise, neutral expression, sadness, anger, contempt, disgust, fear. As it was decided to distinguish just two emotional states of the user, positive and negative the emotions distinguished by the library, were combined into two groups, one reflecting a positive emotional state ("Happiness", "Neutral", "Surprise") the other reflecting a negative emotional state, respectively, the remaining emotions ("Sadness", "Anger", "Contempt", "Disgust", "Fear").

The coefficient of correction of the test results, taking into account the data on the emotional state, shows the proportion of positive emotions in the process of testing with the corresponding page.

The processing of data on the emotional state is shown in Fig. 4.

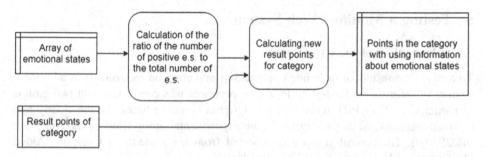

Fig. 4. Diagram of the transformation of emotional state data

It is assumed, that the value of the coefficient k, which determines either he proportion of gaze points located in the image or fraction of positive emotions while working with the corresponding page, increases the reliability of the answer. However, the values of the correction coefficient of test results k, obtained on the basis of data on movements of the point of gaze or data on the emotional state, can be influenced in varying degrees by the errors of the methods of collecting these data themselves. When choosing the test results correction function $points_o$ the assumption was made that for small values of the category rating, meaning that the corresponding category was unattractive for the person being tested, the error in the way of collecting additional data can be neglected. For higher values of $points_o$ an error must be taken into account, and the significance of the calculated value of k in comparison with the value of the possible error of data collection, with increasing $points_o$, which determines the attractiveness of the corresponding category, should increase.

To calculate the adjusted normalized sum of points, a piecewise linear function is chosen with intervals $\in (0; 0.3]$, $\in (0.3; 0.6]$, $\in (0.6; 1]$:

$$points_n(k) = bk + a,$$

where $points_o$ – value of normalized points in the category;
$points_n$ – the adjusted value of the normalized points in the category;

a – threshold;
b – significance coefficient.

The coefficients a, b of the function is matched empirically, based on the assumptions of a change in the dependence of the function at selected intervals:

a = 0, if $points_o \in (0; 0.3]$;
a = 0.2, if $points_o \in (0.3; 0.6]$;
a = 0.5, if $points_o \in (0.6; 1]$;
b = 2, if $points_o \in [0; 0.3]$;
b = 0.5, if $points_o \in (0.3; 1]$.

5 Testing a Modified Web System

5.1 Description of the Experiment

To analyse the results of including eye-tracking and emotion recognition as additional sources of information for testing PID an experiment was conducted with two groups of participants. Four PID living in the Volgograd boarding house for the elderly and disabled were invited as participants to the experimental group (http://442fz.volganet.ru/025001/). The control group was collected from ten students of Computer-Aided Department at Volgograd State Technical University.

Each group was divided in half into two subgroups. One half of each subgroup was just tested in the system, the other two subgroups were tested with collecting the results of eye-tracking and emotion state.

After passing the test, each participant was asked to choose the most preferred category directly. The result of this direct assessment was compared with the result of the assessment using images representing categories. The matches of the direct and indirect assessment were recorded.

To improve the efficiency of the eye tracking and emotions recognition methods, implemented in the system, the following conditions were provided during the testing process:

- stable connection to the Internet;
- bright lighting, illuminating the face of the user without lightning directly into the camera;
- in case the PID is helped by the assistant, the assistant should not show his presence in front of the camera.

5.2 Testing the Control Group

According to the research plan, half of the tested control group (five people) were tested without collecting additional information (basic testing), the other five were tested with collecting the eye-tracking and emotional state data. All participants in the control group were tested independently without assistance.

For both groups, the list of the most preferred categories was formed by the system, after each participant chose the most preferred category directly. The matches of the direct and indirect assessment were recorded. In the case a result two or more categories had the same score, the result was evaluated by the coincidence of at least one of them.

Matches of the results of the indirect and direct assessment of preferred categories for the first subgroup are given in Table 2.

Table 2. Test results of the first subgroup of the control group

№	Name	Category (s) with maximum points		Matches
		Image-based assessment	Direct assessment	
1.	Denis	cat_craft; cat_pets	cat_craft	+
2.	Sergey	cat_craft; cat_pets	cat_craft	−
3.	Nikolay	cat_home	cat_craft	+
4.	Alexandr	cat_craft; cat_administrative	cat_food	−
5.	Nikita	cat_craft	cat_administrative	+

For the second subgroup the eye-tracking and emotional state data were additionally collected. The test results are shown in Table 3.

Table 3. Test results of the second subgroup of the control group

№	Name	Category (s) with maximum points		
		Image-based assessment	Assessment using eye-tracking data	Assessment using emotion state data
1.	Daria	cat_craft; cat_food;	cat_food;	cat_food;
2.	Konstantin	cat_food;	cat_food;	cat_food;
3.	Vitaliy	cat_factory; cat_food; cat_craft;	cat_factory;	cat_factory;
4.	Stanislav	cat_food; cat_client	cat_food;	cat_food; cat_client
5.	Andrey	cat_food; cat_client	cat_food; cat_client	cat_food

Table 4 shows the matches between the test results of the second subgroup of the control group, using additional sources of information. For the "Assessment using additional source of data" column the category from the "Image-based (indirect) assessment" that repeated in at least one of the "Assessment using eye-tracking data" or "Assessment using emotion state data" columns from Table 3 was selected.

Table 4. The results of the coincidence categories of the second subgroup of the control group

№	Name	Category (s) with maximum points		Matches
		Direct assessment	Assessment using additional source of data	
1.	Daria	cat_food	cat_food	+
2.	Constantin	cat_food	cat_food	+
3.	Vitaliy	cat_factory	cat_factory	+
4.	Stanislav	cat_food	cat_food	+
5.	Andrey	cat_food	cat_food	+

Analysis of the test results showed that for almost all participants the inclusion of additional sources of information (eye-tracking and emotional state data) led to a better matching of the results. This can be considered as an increase in the reliability of the test results.

5.3   Testing the Experimental Group

Four participants included in the experimental group have different degrees of intellectual disabilities. For all of them, additional sources of data were collected when testing. The list of participants is presented in Table 5.

Table 5. List of experimental group

№	Name	Age	Intellectual disability
1.	Dmitriy	21	Severe intellectual disability
2.	Alexandr	19	Moderate intellectual disability
3.	Masha	28	Mild intellectual disability
4.	Julia	30	Mild intellectual disability

The testing process for people with severe and moderate intellectual disability was very difficult. They could not choose the answers themselves; some images were not clear for them. These two participants were tested with the help of an assistant; their answers strongly depended on the comments and hints of the assistant. Therefore, it was decided not to include the results of the testing of these participants into the analysis of the experiment.

The two participants with mild mental intellectual disability had trouble using the mouse when answering the questions, but this did not affect the testing process as a whole. The test results of the experimental group are shown in Table 6 and show the result of the two people with mild intellectual disability.

Table 6. The test results of the experimental group

№	Name	Category (s) with maximum points		
		Image-based assessment	Assessment using eye-tracking data	Assessment using emotion state data
1.	Masha	cat_home	cat_home	cat_home
2.	Julia	cat_home; cat_administrative;	cat_administrative;	cat_home

Analysis of the test results showed that including the additional sources of information for these participants also improves the reliability of the test results (Table 7).

Table 7. The results of the coincidence of categories in the experimental group

№	Name	Category (s) with maximum points		Matches
		Image-based assessment using additional source of data	Direct assessment	
1.	Masha	cat_home	cat_home	+
2.	Julia	cat_home; cat_administrative	cat_home	+

5.4   Detailed Analysis of Eye-Tracking Data

To detail the test results, taking into account eye-tracking data, an additional analysis of the distribution of the point of gaze between the image and the navigations buttons in the testing pages was carried out. The average distribution of the point of gaze between the image and the buttons for both control and experimental subgroup's is given in Table 8 and Fig. 5.

Table 8. Average distribution of the point of gaze between the image and the buttons

Average fraction	Group								
	Control group. The second subgroup					Experimental group			
	1	2	3	4	5	1	2	3	4
Point of gaze in the image	0.38	0.56	0.57	0.47	0.38	0.01	0	0.27	0.31
Point of gaze in the controls	0.24	0.18	0.17	0.23	0.29	0.71	0.93	0.45	0.30

Average fractions of focus points on the image and buttons in each question

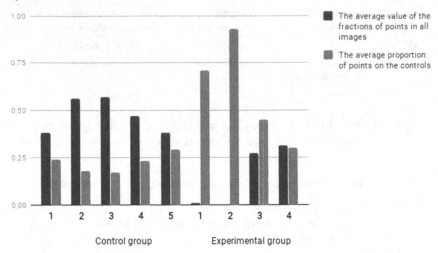

Fig. 5. Average fractions of gaze points on the image and buttons in each question

Analysis of the results shows that for the control group, the fraction of points of gaze in the image is 1.5–2 times higher than the fraction of points of gaze in the buttons, which is expected when working with such kind of applications. The heat map of one of the control group participants is shown in Fig. 6.

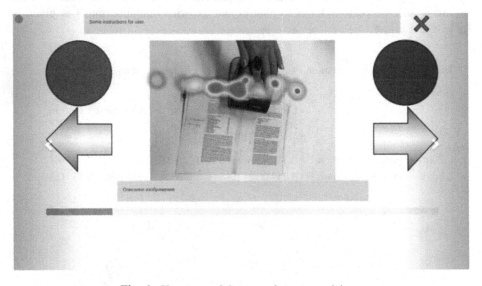

Fig. 6. Heat map of the control group participant

The participants with mild intellectual disability showed a result that was slightly "worse" than the results of the control group (the fraction of points of gaze in the image is slightly less than that of the control group). The heat map of one of the participants of the experimental group is shown in Fig. 7.

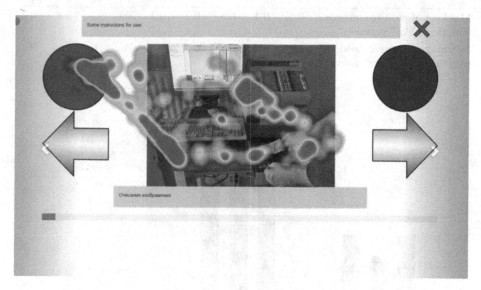

Fig. 7. Heat map of a participant in an experimental group with a slight degree of intellectual disability

For the participants of the experimental group with a moderate and severe intellectual disability, the fraction of points of gaze in the image is significantly lower than in the buttons. This confirms the assumption that the results of the testing of these participants cannot be considered reliable.

5.5   Detailed Analysis of Data on Emotional State

To update the image-based test results using the data on the emotional state of the users (see Sect. 2), the recognized emotions were grouped into two categories - "Positive" ("neutral" emotion was included in the category of positive emotions) and "Negative". The correction algorithm took into account the influence of only positive emotions. To clarify the effects of emotions on the answers to the questions, an analysis of the dependencies between the positive and negative answers to the questions and the positive and negative emotions was carried out. The coefficients of matching the emotions with the answers for the control and experimental subgroups are shown in Table 9 and in Fig. 8.

Table 9. Coefficients of matching the emotions with the answers for the control group

Coefficient of matching	Group								
	Control group. The second subgroup					Experimental group			
	1	2	3	4	5	1	2	3	4
Matching of positive emotions with the "I like" answer	0.5	0.4	0.5	0.2	0.2	0.8	1	0.8	0.2
Matching of negative emotions with the "I don't like" answer	0	0	0	0	0	0	0	0	0

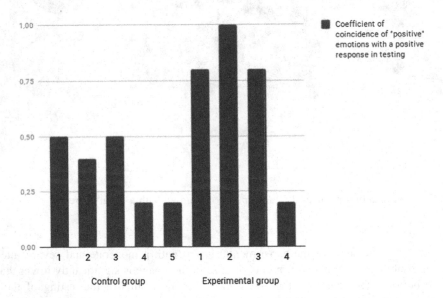

Fig. 8. Coefficients of matching of groups of emotions with the answers of the tested

Table 9 results show that the coefficients of matching between the positive emotions with the "I like" answers for PID are much higher than for the participants of the control group. It proves the assumption that PID can react more emotionally to the testing process and thus adding the emotional state data can really help to assess the results of testing.

6 Conclusions

The results of the experiment of testing PID showed that image-based testing of PID depended on their understanding of the testing process on how clear the images were clear for them. For people with a severe and moderate intellectual disability, it was very difficult to answer the questions themselves as they could not choose the answers and just followed the instructions of the assistant. People with mild intellectual disability were much more independent in answering the questions and were able to pass the test with the help of the assistant.

Analysis of additional data collected during the testing allowed to clarify the results. Firstly, PID demonstrated a lot of different emotions during the testing process and their positive emotions were connected with their "I like" answers. It proves the assumption that adding the emotional state data can really help to increase the reliability of the results of testing.

Using the eye tracking data for clarifying the results of testing was also considered justified. The fraction of points of the gaze of PID in the image during selecting the answer was also related to the answer reliability which was confirmed by subsequent direct interviewing PID.

Thus, speaking generally it can be said that additional sources of information, such as eye-tracking and emotion analysis, can increase the confidence in the "truthfulness" of the results obtained in testing. However, this requires the careful selection of images in the test itself. Eye-tracking and emotion analysis data can't provide a full guarantee of verifiability or "truthfulness" of the results; they can only help to evaluate the PID's involvement to the testing process and thereby increase the confidence in the result. As the tests include only very small numbers of test persons, the results should be interpreted as a proof of concept. Further research is necessary to provide for more reliable results.

Acknowledgements. The work was supported by RFBR, research project No. 18-07-01308a.

References

1. Davies, D.K., Stock, S.E., King, L., Wehmeyer, M.L., Shogren, K.A.: An accessible testing, learning and assessment system for people with intellectual disability. Int. J. Dev. Disabil. **63** (4), 204–210 (2017). https://doi.org/10.1080/20473869.2017.1294313
2. Bos, A., Dekelver, J., Niesen, W., Shabalina, O.A., Skvaznikov, D., Hensbergen, R.: LIT: labour interest test for people with intellectual disabilities. In: Kravets, A., Shcherbakov, M., Kultsova, M., Groumpos, P. (eds.) CIT&DS 2017. CCIS, vol. 754, pp. 822–832. Springer, Cham (2017). https://doi.org/10.1007/978-3-319-65551-2_59
3. Marciniak, J.A., Jankowska, T., Dudek, B.: The computer test measuring vocational interests (CTMVI) of people with intellectual disabilities: method development. Kwartalnik Pedagogiczny **1**(235) (2015)
4. Laming, C., Hezemans, G.: Aan het werk. Arbeid voor mensen met een verstandelijke beperking. Lib Edits, Tilburg (1996)
5. Skvaznikov, D.E.: Issledovanie primenimosti servisov raspoznavaniya ehmocij dlya analiza ehmocional'nogo sostoyaniya lyudej s intellektual'nymi ogranicheniyami. In: Skvaznikov, D. E., Shabalina, O.A. (eds.) Informacionnye tekhnologii v nauke, upravlenii, social'noj sfere i medicine: sb. nauch. tr. IV mezhdunar. konf. (g. Tomsk, 5–8 dekabrya 2017 g). V 2 ch. CH. II, redkol.: O. G. Berestneva [i dr.]; FGAOU VO «Nacional'nyj issledovatel'skij Tomskij politekhnicheskij un-t», FGBOU VO «Tomskij gos. un-t sistem upravleniya i radioehlektroniki». - Tomsk, pp. 80–85 (2018)
6. Papoutsaki, A., et al.: Webgazer: scalable webcam eye tracking using user interactions. In: Proceedings of the Twenty-Fifth International Joint Conference on Artificial Intelligence-IJCAI 2016 (2016)

Ontology Based Personalization of Mobile Interfaces for People with Special Needs

Marina Kultsova(✉), Anastasiya Potseluico,
and Alexander Dvoryankin

Volgograd State Technical University, Volgograd, Russia
marina.kultsova@mail.ru, poas@vstu.ru

Abstract. The paper is devoted to a problem of interface personification for people with special needs on the base of information about their behavior during interaction with mobile applications. This work evolves our previous researches on the development of adaptive user interfaces. Much attention in this paper was given to the investigation of existing approaches to collecting and analyzing the information about user behavior and interaction context data as well as interface adaptation recommendations. The improved interface adaptation mechanism was developed and described based on the ontological representation of the interface patterns and knowledge about users and their interaction with a mobile application. The set of adaptation rules was developed and implemented in the ontology knowledge base. In the paper, we described the improved ontology model and some examples of ontological representation of interface patterns.

Keywords: Assistive technologies · Adaptive user interface ·
Mobile applications · Ontological user modeling · Interface patterns ·
User behavior

1 Introduction

The problem of socialization for people with special needs plays a key role in the modern world and especially in IT-Sphere. According to the [2] every fifth person in the world has some range and type of disability. Therefore the life quality of many people dramatically depends on the usability and accessibility of web sites, mobile and desktop applications, TV, and electronic devices. The W3C [1] tried to solve the problem of accessibility by developing a guide which contains the set of recommendations on the best techniques for making the interface available for people with special needs. Today the problem still exists, the new devices, types of applications were developed, and new types of human-computer interaction appeared so software developers try to make all applications more usable for all categories of users and their interfaces more adaptive and personified.

Large organizations such as Google [3] encourage to make applications more accessible and provide information about special features for people with disabilities in Google Chrome, Android and YouTube. The leading companies in software development such as Microsoft [7], Apple [4] and Android [6] have their own guidelines on how to make an application accessible. Also, each of these companies provided their

© Springer Nature Switzerland AG 2019
A. G. Kravets et al. (Eds.): CIT&DS 2019, CCIS 1084, pp. 422–433, 2019.
https://doi.org/10.1007/978-3-030-29750-3_33

software with accessibility settings such as alternatives to audio, voice to text, contrast colors and much more.

Unfortunately, not all software developers follow these recommendations during the application creating, so the main aim of our project is to facilitate of accessible assistive applications development by implementing the set of relevant recommendations directly inside the interface development environment.

2 State of the Art

The leaders of the software development industry provide a variety of methods and tools for the support of interface developers in creating accessible applications for users with special needs.

Apple included the technology for supporting accessibility into its operating system and accessibility settings can be turned on via the standard menu. For iOS developers, Apple suggests UIKit [5] for making the interface elements accessible for people with special needs. The main idea of UIKit is giving the opportunity to personalize an interface according to the user's needs.

Now UIKit supports the several types of diseases: vision impairment (blindness, colorblindness, focusing difficulty), hearing impairments (deafness, partial hearing loss, difficulty in hearing sounds within a certain range), physical and motor disorders (difficulty in holding a device or tapping the interface), mental problems (difficulty in remembering a sequence of steps to manage the task, difficulty in perceiving the task).

Except UIKit iOS provides other accessibility features such as VoiceOver, Switch Control, and Assistive Touch. All these features can be included in the interfaces of applications developed for iOS devices. In addition to this developers can use special classes of interface elements and behavior in their applications. For example, UIAccessibility is a class for providing accessibility information about user interface elements; UIAccessibilityElement is a class for interface element encapsulation to make it accessible and many others. More functionality you can find in special documentation for developers.

The Android operating system also provides accessibility features for users. Accessibility settings are built-in for Android 6.0 and later. Standard settings include the possibility to change display size and font size, to set the magnification, to change contrast and color options, to enable captions. The latest versions of Android have built-in Android Accessibility Suite which contains the following applications:

- TalkBack which describes user actions and warns about alerts and notifications.
- Select to Speak for choosing the text on the screen and reading it out loud.
- Voice Access lets user control the device with spoken commands. Can be used to open applications, navigate and edit text hands-free.
- Switch Access lets user interact with the Android device with the help of one or more switches instead of touchscreen.
- BrailleBack allows a user connect the braille display to the device via Bluetooth.
- Sound Amplifier can be used with wired headphones to filter, augment and amplify the sounds in the environment.

Android provides special classes for developers to improve the accessibility to their applications. The simplest way to do it is to implement accessibility methods of classes AccessibilityEventSource and AccessibilityDelegate. These classes contain methods for sending events and reacting to them. To be sure that the application is accessible Android provides the Accessibility Scanner - the program for testing the interface of an application. It collects such information as duplicate clickable views, clickable links, items without labels, duplicate item descriptions, contrast ratio less than 3.0 and much more.

Microsoft has a great variety of tools supporting the development of application for people with different disorders such as vision disorder (Color filtering, Tell Me, Soundscape), hearing impairment (Microsoft Stream, mono audio feature, captions creator in PowerPoint), neural impairment (Dictation, Windows Hello sign-in), problems in learning (Learning Tools for Office 365, Text suggestions, Dictate, Learning Tools in Edge), mobility impairments (Dictate add-in, eye control support) and mental health (focus assistant, reducing distractions tool).

Microsoft provides comprehensive documentation [7] on accessibility support for web and desktop application, in addition, there is a separate review of common accessibility principles. Win32 API provides a set of accessibility features to make it easier for users with impairments to use applications. Developers can use such structures as ACCESSTIMEOUT, FILTERKEYS, HIGHCONTRAST to get the information about accessibility parameters of interface elements. Also, Microsoft supplies developers with Microsoft Active Accessibility - Component Object Model (COM)-based technology that improves the accessibility of the applications running on Microsoft Windows. It contains reliable methods for exposing information about interface elements. The main COM interface of the technology is IAccessible which provides information about interface elements via its methods.

Finally, Microsoft developed API for testing the interfaces on accessibility which is called UI Accessibility Checker. The tool verifies that the main accessibility requirements are met in the application.

So we can state that a lot of methods and tools to provide application accessibility are available now. However, their use is left to the discretion of the developers and depends directly on their experience, qualification, and skills.

The most important point in the development of assistive applications for people with disabilities [16] is the issues of adaptation and personalization of user interface. We can distinguish two main approaches to interface adaptation: an ontology-based approach (AEGIS and EGOKI projects ([14], [13] can be mentioned regarding this), and the pattern-based approach (MyUI Project [12]). We analyzed these approaches and tools in detail in [8–11].

Despite the variety of existing technologies for support of accessible application development, there is no one universal tool for creating adaptive personalized interfaces for users with special needs. So, the focus point of our project is to create a special tool Interface Editor which allows developing adaptive interfaces for cross-platform assistive applications. To provide the interface adaptivity and personalization we combined ontology- and pattern-based approaches, and implemented this combined approach the first version of Interface Editor [11].

The testing of the interfaces developed with our Interface Editor in groups of users with disabilities identified a number of problems in the process of interface development. These problems were caused by insufficient consideration of user context changing during his/her interaction with the interface. So in this paper, we described how we re-engineered the process of interface development and redesigned ontology model and knowledge base to take into account information about user behavior.

3   Adaptation Rules and Recommendations

In our project, we implemented the most valuable recommendations for interface accessibility according to W3C [1]. The main principles of this guide mean that the interface must be perceivable, operable, understandable and robust.

The perceivable interface must meet the following requirements:

- All multimedia context represented to the user must have a text alternative.
- If an interface has input text widgets they must be supported with a brief and clear text description.
- If it is impossible to use the text alternative to some interface elements (for example the application contains non-text exercise or test which would be invalid if presented in the text) the text must provide at least descriptive information about the non-text elements.
- Colors must not play key roles in the interaction of a user with an interface.
- A user must have a possibility to change font size, color, and style, background and foreground colors.
- The contrast ratio between interface elements and their background must be at least 7:1.
- Text can be resized up to 200%. To be operable the interface must follow the conditions:
- The interface must not contain any blinking content which can cause seizures.
- All interface elements must be "keyboard accessible" which means that the user can operate through a keyboard interface without any time restrictions.
- A user must have a possibility to stop, pause or restart video and audio content.
- The application must notify a user about any unexpected failures and suggest to save data or to finish all current tasks.
- Focusable components receive focus in an order that preserves meaning and operability.

The understandable interface must follow the requirements:

- The default language must be determined by the application, but the user must have a possibility to change it.
- The interface should not change the context if any event occurred (button clicking, changing the text for input widgets).
- The context can be changed only by the user.
- The navigation process must be the same within the application.
- All components must have the same functionality within the application.

– The application must provide the user with context-sensitive help.
– The application must warn the user that an error occurred and suggest the subsequent scenario.
– The application must validate the data that the user inputs.

The robust interface must follow the main condition: the interface must be compatible with all current and future user agents, including assistive technologies.

Most of these recommendations have been already implemented in the Interface Editor for Unity 3D [11] as a part of menu settings: text alternative to multimedia, font and background settings, contrast ratio, disabling blinking context and some others. Now we work on the second version of the editor with extended functionality where all recommendations mentioned above will be implemented.

After testing of the first version of editor it was decided to include interface patterns into the ontology model to achieve integrity of knowledge, the possibility of their reusing in other projects and simplicity of extending the interface pattern base.

4 Development of Adaptive Personalized Interface

We re-engineered the process of interface development presented in [11] to take into account information about the interaction of the user with the interface. The two-phase process of adaptive personalized interface development is presented in Fig. 1. Two main phases of the algorithm are separated in the figure by the vertical line. The first phase of the process (the left part in the figure) includes two procedures executing by software developer: (1) the creation of interface mock-up; (2) interface adaptation in accordance with the user context (user disease, his/her peculiarities caused by the disease, used device, and some others). The second phase (the right part in the figure) includes two procedures: (1) application evaluating by users and their caregivers during interaction with the interface; (2) interface personalization on the base of information about user behavior and possible changes in his/her context.

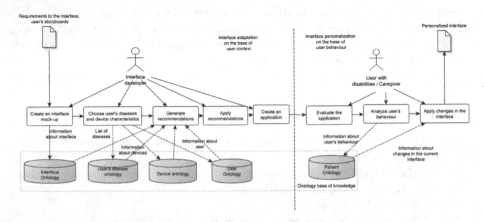

Fig. 1. The two-phase process of adaptive personalized interface development.

The first phase is implemented on the base of inference on expert knowledge represented in the domain ontology. The second phase is implemented using interface patterns represented in the pattern ontology. These patterns describe all possible changes in the interface elements (in accordance with W3C recommendations) corresponding to changing user behavior caused by changing the user context.

For example, a user has moderate problems with vision. The application interface adapted to this user context was developed according to the relevant recommendations in the Interface Editor plugin. The user interacts with the interface but after a period of time, his vision problems can become more severe. The user context has been changed, it can lead to a situation when the user is unable to click on some buttons and read the text. To react to these changes in user behavior caused by changes in user context, a caregiver can create a request for relevant changing the interface elements. And then to accept or reject suggested changes.

To implement this process we needed to redesign the ontology model and knowledge base, develop a relevant ontological representation of interface pattern and also create the set of the interface patterns.

5 Ontology Model

Redesigned meta-ontology model (Fig. 2) includes the pattern ontology model and is presented as follows:

$$M = <O_M, C, Inst, R, I>, \tag{1}$$

where M - meta-ontology; $O_M = \{O_{user}, O_{dis}, O_{int}, O_{dev}, O_{pat}\}$ – set of domain ontologies, O_{user} - user ontology, O_{dis} - user disease ontology, O_{int} - interface ontology, O_{dev} - device ontology, O_{pat} - pattern ontology; C – finite set of meta-ontology concepts, C = $\varnothing$; Inst – finite set of meta-ontology instances, Inst = $\varnothing$; R = {has, impacts on, uses, selects} – finite set of relations between meta-ontology components; I - finite set of interpretation rules, I = $\varnothing$.

The pattern ontology has the connection with a user ontology because a user can directly choose any pattern from the set to personalize the interface. The pattern model implemented in the first version of our interface editor and described in details in [9, 11] had one main disadvantage - the context could change independently of user behavior. Also, the conditions for replacing one widget with another one were not included in any standards for interface development. The main advantage of the proposed redesigned ontology model is that interfaces and interface patterns were separated, and so context now can change in accordance with user behavior. All patterns included in the pattern ontology model meet the W3C recommendations. The proposed ontology model can be easily extended by adding any new interface patterns. Now the pattern ontology is defined as follows:

$$O_p = <C_p, Inst_p, R_P, I_P>, \tag{2}$$

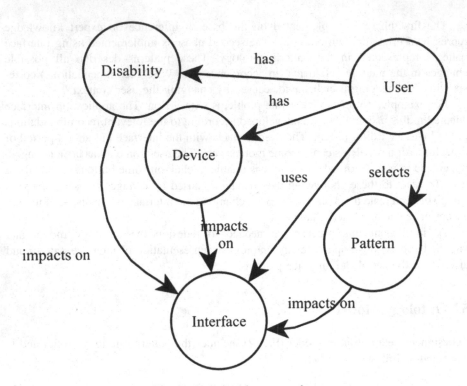

Fig. 2. Redesigned meta-ontology

where CP – finite set of the pattern ontology concepts; InstP – finite set of the pattern ontology instances, Inst = ∅; RP – finite set of relations between the pattern ontology components; IP - finite set of interpretation rules.

The pattern ontology model is presented in IDEF5 notation in Fig. 3. Other parts of the meta-ontology model remained unchanged and presented in details in [11].

All interface patterns are separated into two groups: patterns which change the widget appearance, and patterns which change the widget functionality. Each pattern is connected with the actual interface element and has access to its properties. The examples of patterns of these two types are presented in Tables 1 and 2 respectively. All patterns in the ontology were represented using Jena rules.

The ontology representation of the pattern is shown on Fig. 4. The figure shows that the interface contains two widgets of the text widget type. Each text widget has a current font size. Every instance of text widget is tracking by text resize pattern which contains the current font size of text widget and also two limitations for font size so the size cannot be less than 8 and greater than 32.

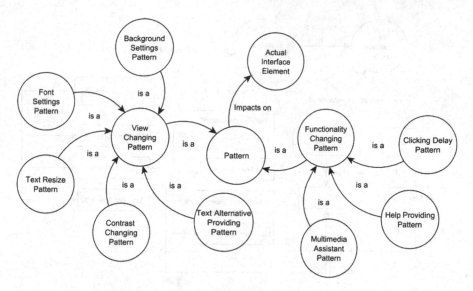

Fig. 3. Pattern ontology model (IDEF5 notation).

Table 1. Text resize pattern

Name	Text resize pattern
Problem	User may not feel comfortable with the font size of the interface elements
Solution	Increase the size of text up to 200%
Implementation	Get each text component from each interface element and increase font size

Table 2. Multimedia assistant pattern

Name	Multimedia assistant pattern
Problem	User wants to replay, pause or stop playing a multimedia content
Solution	Add "Play", "Restart" and "Stop" buttons to all multimedia content
Implementation	Get all video and audio widgets and set enabled the panel with buttons

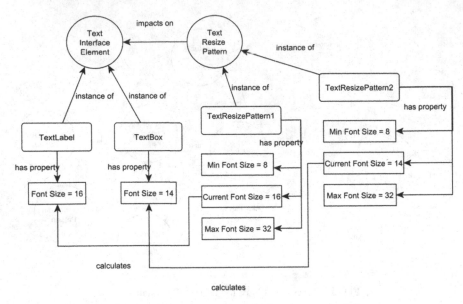

Fig. 4. Text resize pattern ontology representation

The corresponding Jena rule is shown below (3):

[increaseTextFontSizePattern : (?usermain : hasNecessityToIncreaseText

dis : VisionDisability),(?usermain : hasInterf ace?interface),

(?interfaceinterface : hasElement?element),

(?elementrdf : type

interface : ActualTextContentElement) →

→ (?elementinterface : has TextSize?newT extSizeValue)] (3)

where ?user, ?interface, ?element, ?newTextSizeValue – Jena variables; main: hasDiseaseProblem, main: hasInterface, dis: VisionDisability; interface: hasElement, interface: hasTextSize, rdf: type– ontology relations with ontology prefixes; ActualTextContentElement – ontology instance of Interface domain.

The ontology representation of the pattern is shown on Fig. 5. The figure shows that the interface contains two widgets of multimedia widget type: video widget and audio output widget. Each widget has a property for enabling and disabling the panels with "Stop", "Restart" and "Play" buttons. Every instance of the multimedia widget is tracking and can be changed with the instance of the multimedia assistant pattern.

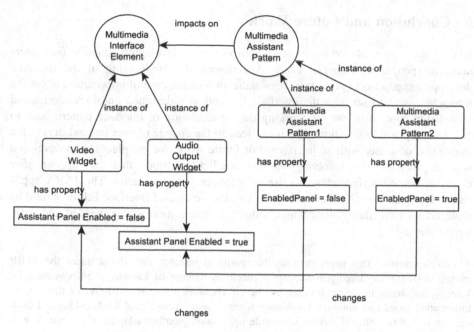

Fig. 5. Multimedia pattern ontology representation

The corresponding Jena rule is shown below (4):

[multimediaAssistantPattern : (?usermain : hasInterface?interface),

(?interfaceinterface : hasElement?element),

(?elementrdf : type

interface : ActualMultimediaContentElement) →

→ (?interfaceinterface : hasMultimediaControlButtons?element)] (4)

where ?user, ?interface, ?element – Jena variables; main: hasInterface, dis: Deafness; interface: hasElement, interface: hasMultimediaControlButtons, rdf: type– ontology relations with ontology prefixes; ActualMultimediaContentElement – ontology instance of Interface domain.

Now the pattern base is on the stage of implementation. Using the ontology model for interface pattern representation gave a number of advantages like simplicity of pattern ontology model extension, maintaining and reusing. By this moment pattern ontology base contains the implementation for 6 patterns in 32 rules. These rules cover vision disorders and partly motor skills disorder. The part for supporting mental disabilities, hearing disabilities and physical disabilities are going to be implemented.

6 Conclusion and Future Work

In the paper, we analyzed the existing approaches to developing adaptive user interfaces for people with special needs. We described reengineering of the interface development process to provide its personalization on the base of information about the interaction of the user with the interface, as well as redesigned ontology model and knowledge base. Now we are working on the extension of interface pattern base to cover most possible situations which can lead to the change of user context during the interaction of a user with an interface. For future work, we are planning to develop a special procedure for resolving various conflict situations that can appear after changing some interface elements during interface personalization. The JAVA application for operating with the ontology in the first version of Interface Editor should be replaced with dll library, which makes the application more stable, unified and more simple for testing.

Acknowledgment. This paper presents the results of research carried out under the RFBR grants 18-07-00032 "Intelligent support of decision making of knowledge management for learning and scientific research based on the collaborative creation and reuse of the domain information space and ontology knowledge representation model" and 18-47-343001 "Development of the two-phased method of mobile application interface adaptation for people with special needs".

References

1. W3C official website: World Wide Web Consortium. http://www.w3.org/standards/webdesign/accessibility/
2. The World Bank official website: The World Bank. http://www.worldbank.org/en/topic#1
3. Google. http://www.google.com/intl/en/accessibility/
4. Apple official website: Apple Inc. http://support.apple.com/accessibility/
5. Apple official developer website: Apple Inc. http://developer.apple.com/documentation/uikit/accessibility/
6. Android Developers official website. http://developer.android.com/guide/topics/ui/accessibility
7. Microsoft official website. http://www.microsoft.com/en-us/accessibility
8. Kultsova, M., Romanenko, R., Anikin, A., Poceluico, A.: An ontology-based adaptation of user interface for people with special needs. In: Proceedings of the AINL FRUCT 2016 Conference, November 2016
9. Kultsova, M., Romanenko, R., Anikin, A., Poceluico, A.: An ontology-based approach to automated generation of adaptive user interface based on user modeling. In: Proceedings of the IISA2016 Conference, July 2016
10. Kultsova, M., Romanenko, R., Zhukova, I., Usov, A., Penskoy, N., Potapova, T.: Assistive mobile application for support of mobility and communication of people with IDD. In: Proceedings of the MobileHCI 2016 Conference, September 2016
11. Kultsova, M., Potseluico, A., Zhukova, I., Skorikov, A., Romanenko, R.: A two-phase method of user interface adaptation for people with special needs. In: Kravets, A., Shcherbakov, M., Kultsova, M., Groumpos, P. (eds.) CIT&DS 2017, vol. 754, pp. 805–821. Springer, Cham (2017). https://doi.org/10.1007/978-3-319-65551-2_58

12. Peissner, M., Schuller, A., Spath, D.: A design patterns approach to adaptive user interfaces for users with special needs. In: Jacko, J.A. (ed.) HCI 2011. LNCS, vol. 6761, pp. 268–277. Springer, Heidelberg (2011). https://doi.org/10.1007/978-3-642-21602-2_30
13. Gamecho, B., et al.: Automatic generation of tailored accessible user interfaces for ubiquitous services. IEEE Trans. Hum.-Mach. Syst. **45**(5), 612–623 (2015)
14. AEGIS Ontology. http://www.aegis-project.eu
15. Elias, M., Lohmann, S., Auer, S.: Towards an ontology-based representation of accessibility profiles for learners. In: Proceedings of the Second International Workshop on Educational Knowledge Management, vol. 1780, November 2016
16. Lempert, L.B., Kravets, A.G., Lempert, B.A., Poplavskaya, O.V., Salnikova, N.A.: Development of the intellectual decision-making support method for medical diagnostics in psychiatric practice. In: 9th International Conference on Information, Intelligence, Systems and Applications, IISA (2018)

Proactive Control System of Multicomponent General Anesthesia

V. M. Sokolsky[1], I. Z. Kitiashvili[2], Irina Yu. Petrova[3]([✉]) [ID],
and M. V. Sokolsky[4]

[1] LLC «Systems, Technologies and Services», Astrakhan, Russia
sokolskiy_vm@mail.ru
[2] Astrakhan State Medical University, Astrakhan, Russia
[3] Astrakhan State University of Architecture and Civil Engineering,
Astrakhan, Russia
irapet1949@gmail.com
[4] Astrakhan State University, Astrakhan, Russia
sokol_2608@mail.ru

Abstract. The article gives the analyses of modern automation systems for multicomponent general anaesthesia (MGA), the principles of their operation and controlled parameters. The article raises the question of a minimal set of monitored parameters giving a complete picture of the current state of the patient and his need for anaesthesia. The efficiency of using a proactive algorithm for optimal control of the MGA process has been shown. It has been stated that for the most effective assessment of the patient's condition it is necessary to monitor the parameters of central and peripheral hemodynamic, oxygen transport, sedation level using the method of auditory evoked potentials, the level of neuromuscular blockade. Authors have developed the functional scheme of the automated system for controlling the process of multicomponent general anaesthesia.

Keywords: Automation system · Proactive algorithm ·
Hemodynamic parameters · Sedation level · An anaesthetic drug ·
Auditory evoked responses

1 Introduction

The rapid development of modern information-measuring and control systems affects almost all spheres of human activity, including medicine. In world practice, there is an annual steady increase in the number of surgical operations using multicomponent general anaesthesia (MGA). To date, most of the long-term surgical procedures are performed using MGA, which is known as the safest for the patient, but at the same time the most difficult to implement. Due to the complexity of the MGA process, its duration and intensity, medical errors lead to serious morbidities, and sometimes to the death of the patient. The main causes (up to 76%) of medical errors are inattention, fatigue and lack of experience [1].

Safety standards in modern anesthesia include mandatory monitoring of vital functions of the body. During anesthesia, the doctor is faced with the need to analyze

© Springer Nature Switzerland AG 2019
A. G. Kravets et al. (Eds.): CIT&DS 2019, CCIS 1084, pp. 434–446, 2019.
https://doi.org/10.1007/978-3-030-29750-3_34

large amounts of rapidly changing information about the current state of the patient. Not only the successful outcome of anesthesia and surgical intervention but also the patient's life depends on the correctness of the decision made by the anesthesiologist.

To reduce the number of errors in anaesthesia and to defuse intellectual stress faced by doctors, it is advisable to use a variety of systems to automate the process of anaesthesia [2, 3].

The first experience of automation of the anaesthesia process can be considered the appearance on the market of a system to maintain a target controlled infusion (TCI 1996) for propofol [4]. The 'Diprifusor' target-controlled infusion system has been developed as a standardised infusion system for the administration of propofol by concentration-controlled infusion [5]. The mathematical model that relates the rate of infusion with the concentration of propofol in the blood was obtained on the basis of pharmacokinetic parameters of propofol with the help of computer simulation. TCI technology has now become part of conventional anaesthesia techniques for practitioners [6].

SEDASYS, a division of Ethicon, itself part of J&J, is releasing the Sedasys® Computer-Assisted Personalized Sedation (CAPS) System in the U.S. market [7, 8]. Sedasys system is an automated system of personalized propofol delivery with patient monitoring. The system was designed exclusively to maintain a minimal or moderate sedative effect. The US Food and Drug Administration (FDA) in May 2013 authorized the use of this device [9].

The system, which was created by researchers from McGill University in Montreal and called "McSleepy", is able to decide which anaesthetic and in what quantity is necessary to infuse the patient with [10, 11]. The "McSleepy" system uses three parameters for calculating the control effect, the depth of hypnosis (by means of the analysis of the electroencephalogram), the level of intraoperative nociception (measured by the AnalgoscoreTM monitor), the level of muscle relaxation (measured by the PhonomyographyTM monitor).

The next system to automate the process of General anaesthesia, which should be paid attention to, is a robot for anaesthesia IControl-RP [12]. To control the process of anaesthesia, this system uses automatic delivery of intravenous anaesthetic-propofol and narcotic Remifentanil (total intravenous anaesthesia - TIVA). IControl-RP belongs to the group of closed systems that use their own infusion rate calculation algorithms for two drugs propofol and Remifentanil based on the sedation level obtained by Neuro-SENSE monitor, blood oxygen content, blood pressure, respiration rate and heart rate.

The purpose of this article is to present the results of the development of a proactive management system for the MGA process on the basis of combined methods of analysis, modelling and visualization of information about the patient's condition.

2 Comparison of the Functionality of Existing Systems and the Formulation of the Research Task

Table 1 provides a complete list of parameters necessary for assessing the patient's condition and for obtaining the optimal control effect for each of the drugs used during anaesthesia: K – parameters, that are visually monitored by the physician, Y –

parameters, that are taken into account in the formation of control actions. The control actions are the type of preparation and the rate of its infusion.

Table 1. Comparison of the functionality of existing and proposed systems for multicomponent general anaesthesia

Parameter	The name of the parameter	The type of the parameter	System FM Controller	System McSleepy	IControl-RP	Suggested system
DIA, SYS, APP	Arterial pressure: diastolic, systolic, pulse	Measured	K	K	y	y
MAP	Arterial blood pressure	Measured		K	y	y
RR, PR	Respiratory rate, heart rate	Measured	K	K	y	y
HR	Heart rate	Measured	K	K	y	y
NB	Neuromuscular blockade	Measured		y		y
BIS	Bispectral index	Measured		y	y	
AEP	Auditory evoked potentials	Measured				y
SpO$_2$	Oxygen saturation	Measured	K	K	K	y
T	Temperature	Measured	K	K	K	K
EF	Ejection fraction	Expected				K
CO	Cardiac output	Expected				K
IPVR	Peripheral vascular resistance index	Expected				K
CI	Cardiac index	Expected				y
SV	Shock volume	Expected				K
EDV	Finite-diastolic volume	Expected				K
ESV	finite-systolic volume	Expected				K
CaO$_2$	O$_2$ content in arterial blood	Expected				y
Kj	Concentration of the drug in the blood	Expected	y			y
PROF	Profile of the preparation	Expected	y			y
IIP	Integral index of pain	Expected		y		y

As follows from the analysis of the table, the FM Controller system allows the practitioner to visually monitor eight measured parameters and only two parameters (concentration and profile of the drug) are taken into account when forming control actions. The system controls the rate of infusions of one drug. The "McSleepy" system controls nine parameters, but the control effect forms on the basis of three parameters (neuromuscular block level, bispectrality index and integral pain index). The system controls the rate of infusion of three drugs. The IControl-RP system monitors ten parameters and takes into account nine parameters (arterial pressure diastolic, systolic, pulse, average, respiratory rate, heart rate, heart rate, bispectrality index, oxygen saturation) for calculating the infusion rates of two drugs.

To control the anaesthetic drugs (AD), it is necessary to measure the maximum number of parameters, for which mathematical models could be determined (correlation links identified), that could further be used to calculate the patient's need for AD depending on the parameters measured in process. The more parameters of the patient's condition will be taken into account when forming the control action, the more accurately the type and rate of infusion of the used AD can be determined.

This article proposes a new proactive control system of multicomponent general anaesthesia, which allows taking into account twelve parameters at the stage of formation of control actions and visually monitoring seven more parameters. The system can manage the infusion rate of four drugs.

3 The Requirements for the Formation of the Proactive Control System of Multicomponent General Anaesthesia

It is known, that a complete picture of the state of the patient's circulatory system can be obtained by knowing the parameters of not only of the peripheral but also the central hemodynamics. Sramek proposed an original method of graphical representation of integral parameters of central and peripheral hemodynamic [13, 14]. In 1994 the American Society of cardio dynamic monitoring (ASCM) adopted this method as a standard for determining the tactics of correction of hemodynamic disorders in patients.

The hemodynamic state of the patient as a whole, the system hemodynamic status (SHS), is basically determined by two integral parameters: mean arterial pressure (MAP) for peripheral hemodynamics and cardiac index (CI) for central hemodynamics. As a consequence, the SHS can be easily graphically represented as a single point in the two-coordinate "pressure-blood flow" system. However, hemodynamics and its changes do not exist by themselves. They are a reflection of the oxygen delivery needs of tissues and organs. It is proposed in [15, 16] to combine the parameters of hemodynamics and oxygen transport on one graph. One of the most important indicators of the latter is the oxygen delivery index (DO_2I), which gives an idea of how much oxygen is delivered to organs and tissues per unit time. It follows thence, that to assess the current status of the patient, it is necessary to additionally monitor the CI and DO_2I.

A key aspect for balanced anaesthesia is to monitor the current level of sedation, which can be determined by the analysis of the electroencephalogram (EEG). For the analysis of sedation, it can be used the bispectral index (BIS), AAI index (A-line ARX Index) [17] or SL (Sedation Level) index. The exact details of the algorithm, used to calculate the BIS index, are not disclosed by the developer (Aspect Medical Systems) [18]. The AAI index is calculated by the analysis of auditory evoked potentials and is used in the AEPtm monitor. SL index is calculated according to the original author's method.

Monitoring of nociception is also necessary to adequately assess the current state of the patient and calculate the dosage of analgesic. Heart rate variability depends on the tone of the autonomic nervous system (ANS) under the influence of pain stimulus or analgesics. Regulation of the heart rate of the ANS is affected by the respiratory cycle: the inhalation temporarily suppresses the parasympathetic effect, causing acceleration of the heart rate and reducing the intervals R-R; the exhalation, on the contrary, stimulates the parasympathetic tone, slows the heart rate and increases these intervals. Each respiratory cycle is accompanied by changes in parasympathetic tone i.e. the respiratory sinus arrhythmia (RSA) [18–20]. In the absence of the painful stimulus and/or stress only RSA has an impact on a series of R-R intervals. Therefore, by analyzing the variability of R-R intervals, it is possible to determine the current level of nociception, which is the main indicator for calculating the need for analgesic dosage.

The level of neuromuscular blockade (NMB) is determined by processing the value of the muscle response to the diagnostic electroneurostimulation (ENS) test stimulus. According to the level of NMB, it is possible to calculate the dosage of the relaxant.

Consequently, to control the rate of infusion of four drugs in the designed system, it is necessary to constantly monitor the following parameters: data of central and peripheral hemodynamics, oxygen transport, sedation level, degree of intraoperative nociception, analgesia level and neuromuscular blockade.

To solve this problem, the authors developed a method and algorithm for proactive control of the dynamics of intravenous anaesthesia, different from the known techniques by the ability to control the intensity of the input of four components of general anaesthesia: analgesic, muscle relaxant, anaesthetic and hypnotics. The technique is based on the analysis of hemodynamic data, oxygen transport, the degree of intraoperative nociception, sedation level, and neuromuscular blockade. There are two mathematical models underlie the method:

1. The mathematical model of changing the concentrations of the drugs in the blood during the MGA process, which allows taking into account the processes of their intravenous injection, destruction and elimination with due regard to the effects of delay in the reactions of the organism to such changes;
2. Mathematical model of controlling the physiological parameters of the patient due to changing the rate of infusion of these drugs, taking into account the matrixes of the sensitivity of the patient's parameters to drug concentrations.

The whole complex of information about the patient's condition is provided to the physician on the monitor screen in the simplest graphical form of a mnemonic (Fig. 3). Visualization helps to improve the quality of the MGA process and reduces the number of medical errors.

4 Functional Scheme of MGA Process Management

To construct a proactive controlling algorithm for MGA process, authors perform a decomposition of the solvable problem by dividing it into several simpler, functional tasks implemented in the modules of the system. A simplified algorithm of proactive control of the MGA process is composed of five modules (see Fig. 1).

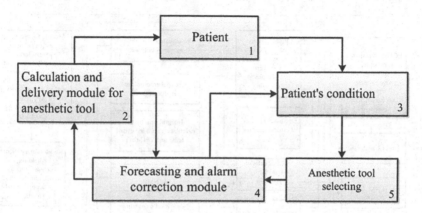

Fig. 1. Simplified algorithm for proactive management of multicomponent general anesthesia.

The patient monitoring subsystem (3) includes algorithms for calculating the current parameters of central and peripheral hemodynamics, oxygen transport, sedation level, neuromuscular blockade and nociception. The subsystem of calculation and delivery of an anaesthetic drug (2) includes algorithms for calculating the dosages and rates of AD (analgesic, relaxant, anaesthetic and hypnotics). The selection of the specific drugs from these four groups is carried out by the anesthesiologist module (5) based on current hemodynamic parameters and personal experience. For delivery of anaesthetic tool (AD) in the module (2), it is used the algorithm allowing to operate and control work of syringe batches utilized for AD's input.

The adjustment and forecasting subsystem (4) predicts hemodynamic parameters, oxygen transport, level of sedation, neuromuscular blockade of nociception and regulates the rate of the anaesthetic tool's infusion drawing on parameters from following sources: the calculation results of the subsystem (2), the own database and the calculated optimality criteria for autoregressive models with exogenous input (ARX). In the case of approximation of current indicators to acceptable limits, the module (4) runs the alarm system and transmits the status of the patient to the corresponding information subsystem of monitoring (3), waiting for actions of an anesthesiologist.

Authors suggest an algorithm for the proactive process management of MGA (see Fig. 2). The work of the algorithm begins with the process of testing sensors connected to the system in module 2 and dispensers (modules 3–6), carrying out the injection of anaesthetic drugs (analgesic, relaxant, anaesthetic and hypnotics). During the normal test, the calibration coefficients obtained earlier are considered relevant and used by the system. If errors are detected during testing, the system enters the calibration mode with the display of the corresponding messages. Before the operation begins, the anaesthetist will enter the following data into the system: anthropometric indicators; results of a general blood test, biochemical parameters of blood serum. By analysing the auditory evoked potentials (AEP) the module 20 measures and calculates parameters of central hemodynamics (CI), peripheral hemodynamic (DIA, SYS, MAP, T), oxygen transport (SPO$_2$, DO$_2$I) and sedation level (SL).

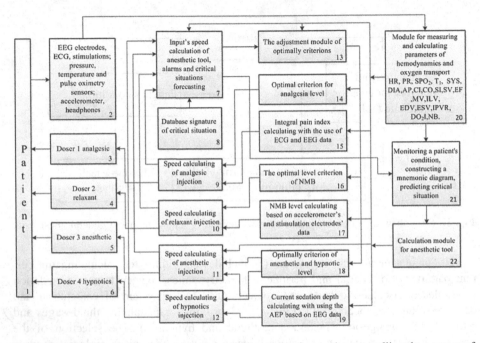

Fig. 2. Functional scheme for implementing the method of proactive controlling the process of multicomponent anaesthesia.

The level of neuromuscular blockade (NMB) is determined by the accelerometer, fixing the movement of the patient's finger, caused by the action of four successive pulses (Train-of-Four stimulation, TOF). The level of intraoperative nociception is determined by analyzing the ECG and EEG and calculating the IPI (Integral Pain Index). Index calculation is based on the original technique of the authors (calculated by module 15). Module 20 is connected to ECG electrodes, EEG, pressure sensor, pulse oximetry, temperature sensor, and headphones to reproduce acoustic stimulus. Based on transformation modelling of electrocardiogram signal (ECS) data the electrocardiographic method is used to determine the parameters of central hemodynamics. In Safonov's study [22] there is an extensive factual material showing a close of electrical and mechanical parameters of the heart. It demonstrates the possibility of estimating the finite diastolic radius (FDR), the finite systolic radius (FSR), the finite diastolic volume (FDV), the finite systolic volume (FSV) and other parameters.

Module 21 is responsible for the visualization of all measured and calculated indicators of the patient's condition in a convenient graphical form – a mnemonic diagram. In the same module, short-term forecasting of the critical situation (Fig. 3) is calculated.

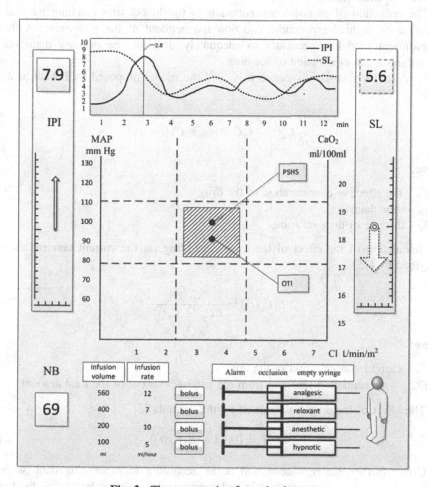

Fig. 3. The mnemonic of a patient's state

Drugs used are divided into four functional groups: hypnotics, analgesics, anaesthetics and relaxants. For anaesthesia, the anaesthetist selects the necessary drugs from each group, depends on personal experience and the current state of the patient. The selection is recorded in module 22. The work of the module (9–12) begins after the analysis of the selected preparations. The first stage of the calculation is based on the patient's anthropometric data and the pharmacokinetic and pharmacodynamic models of the selected drugs. It depends on the duration and extent of the surgery by reference to the desired concentration of the drug in the blood and specified ranges of change in modules 14, 16 and 18. To calculate the initial dose of the anaesthetic tool the three-compartment model is used. It was developed in 1983 by a group of scientists J. Schuttler, H. Schwilden, H. Stoeckel, and it was further promoted at the University of Glasgow (1996) where the system "Diprifusor" was created to control the serial syringe dispenser [23, 24].

The reduction of propofol concentration in the blood after reaching its peak is described by a three-exponential equation independent of the bolus size. A three-compartment model is necessary to adequately describe the primary distribution, redistribution and elimination of the drug.

To describe pharmacodynamics it is used the model proposed by Bibian in 2006 [24]:

$$\frac{d}{dt}C_e(t) + k_d C_e(t) = k_d C_p(t - \tau_d) \tag{1}$$

where:

C_e - the effective concentration of the drug
τ_d - time delay
k_d - the rate of drug infusion

Calculation of the effect of the drug depending on the current concentration is described by [25]

$$E(C_e(t)) = \frac{C_e(t)^\gamma}{EC_{50}^\gamma + C_e(t)^\gamma} \tag{2}$$

where:

C_e - current concentration of the drug
EC_{50}^γ - concentration resulting from the use of 50% out of the total amount

The effect of the drug is calculated by the formula [2]

$$DoH = 100(1 - E(C_e(t))) \tag{3}$$

Going further, the regulation will occur according to monitoring data (without anthropometric data, pharmacokinetic and pharmacodynamic models) using the target optimality criteria, which are calculated in module 13. Based on the results of current measurements in module 20, the following values are calculated: cardiac index (CI), cardiac output (CO), ejection fraction (EF), shock index (SI), oxygen delivery index (DO$_2$I), shock volume (SV), index work of the left ventricle (ILV), minute volume of circulation (MV), index of peripheral vascular resistance (IPVR). Then module 21 builds a mnemonic diagram of the patient's condition during anaesthesia (Fig. 3).

The calculation of the input rate of the analgesic is performed in module 9 based on the current value of the integral indicator of pain IPI which is computed by the module 15.

The calculation of the rate of relaxant injection is made by the module 10 (Fig. 2) on the basis of data on the current level of neuromuscular blockade (NMB), which determined by module 17 according to the accelerometer monitoring neuromuscular function by processing the value of the muscle response to the electroneuro-stimulation (ENS) diagnostic test. The method of estimating the level of NMB depends on the ENS regime and is reduced to determining the degree of attenuation or complete disappearance of responses to ENS under the action of muscle relaxants. To control the NMB, two standard stimulation modes are used: TOF (Train-of-Four - stimulation by a pack of four pulses) and DBS (Double Burst Stimulation - stimulation by double packs). The main adjustable parameter of the electrostimulation is the amplitude of the stimulating current.

The calculation of the rate of hypnotic injection is regulated on the basis of the current sedation depth determined by the module 19 using auditory evoked potentials (AEP) and EEG analysis. The AEP method uses an active stimulus in the form of sound clicks acting through headphones on the auditory receptors, then on the brain and EEG. As a result of EEG processing, the SL index characterizing the current level of sedation of the patient is calculated. Pharmacokinetic and pharmacodynamic models [23, 24] are used in the calculation of anaesthetic dosage by module 10 at the first stage [23, 24]. Once data on the current level of sedation are available, the models are no longer used. In addition to the level of sedation used, the data of hemodynamics of the patient calculated by the module 19.

5 Visualization of the Patient's State During Anesthesia

It stands to reason that if the point of system hemodynamic status (PSHS) is in the central square of the mnemonic scheme, then the patient has no hemodynamic disorders. Therefore, Sramek called it a normal SHS zone. At the "ideal" of the SHS, the point will have coordinates: CI 3.5 l/min/m2 and MAP 92 mm Hg. ("ideal PSHS"). In 1997 the described nomogram was adopted by the American Society of cardiodynamic monitoring (ASCM) as a standard for determining the tactics of correction of hemodynamic disorders in patients. For combining on one graph the hemodynamic parameters and oxygen delivery (DO_2I) the CaO_2 chart is attached, which scale is graduated in such a way that the line of the normal range MAP and CaO_2 on the chart coincide. This allows us to select another point on the graph - the indicator of oxygen transport (OTI). Since the CI value at any given time for the PSHS and OTI points will be the same, these points will always lie on the same vertical line. Based on the current position of the PSHS, and the results of the calculation of the target optimality criteria (module 13), it is possible to adjust the previously calculated infusion rates of four drugs (modules 14, 16, 18). Module (7) allows predicting critical situations on the basis of the current analysis of infusion rate, patient's current parameters and information from a database of critical situations signatures. The planned anaesthetic infusion is calculated using a linear autoregressive ARX model of the 5th order. The forecast time interval is 40 s. Calculation of the probability of critical situations is based on the current parameters of the patient, the data obtained from the database of signatures of critical situations and the planned anesthetic infusion. The 40-second time limit allows you to prevent a critical situation from occurring, even if the database does not have its signature.

The monitoring module of the patient's condition (21) gives a message about the approach of the controlled parameters to the boundary values to the anesthesiologist in advance. The approximation of hemodynamic parameters and oxygen transport to the boundary values during anesthesia on the patient's mnemonic diagram (Fig. 3) looks like the tendency of PSHS and OTI points to go beyond the boundaries of the shaded area.

On the presented mnemonic diagram, the shaded area corresponds to 20% deviation of hemodynamic parameters and oxygen transport from the optimal ones at the moment. The current level of nociception – the integral pain index (IPI) and sedation level (SL) are displayed on the scheme in the form of trends and vectors of instantaneous values. The length of the vector is proportional to the current value of the measured parameter, and the thickness of the vector is determined by the current rate of change of the controlled parameter.

The proposed mnemonic diagram of the patient's state presents to the anesthesiologist in the most simple graphical form the data of central and peripheral hemodynamics, oxygen transport, neuromuscular blockade, the current level of sedation and nociception, and allows to control the state of dispensers used in anaesthetic's injection tool.

6   Conclusion

A complete set of monitored and calculated parameters that giving an idea of the patient's current state, was received to determine the optimal volume of multicomponent anesthetic tool based on the analysis of modern systems used to automate the process of multicomponent General anesthesia.

It is shown that the control action should be formed taking into account the data of central and peripheral hemodynamics, oxygen transport, sedation level, degree of intraoperative nociception, analgesia level and neuromuscular blockade. The whole complex of information about the patient's condition is provided to the doctor in the simplest graphical form - the mnemonic diagrams of the patient's condition during anesthesia.

The algorithm of proactive management of the process of multicomponent general anesthesia was developed. It allows predicting the probability of critical situations based on the current parameters of the patient, the data obtained from the database of signatures of critical situations and the planned anesthetic load.

References

1. Kothari, D., Gupta, S., Sharma, C., Kothari, S.: Medication error in anaesthesia and critical care: a cause for concern. Indian J. Anesth. **54**(3), 187–192 (2010)
2. Yousefi, M., Heusden, K., Mitchell, I.M., Ansermino, M., Dumont, G.: A formally-verified safety system for closed-loop anesthesia. IFAC-PapersOnLine **50**, 4424–4429 (2017). https://doi.org/10.1016/j.ifacol.2017.08.368

3. Hemmerling, T., Arbeid, E., Wehbe, M., Cyr, S., Taddei, R., Zaouter, C.: Evaluation of a novel closed-loop total intravenous anaesthesia drug delivery system: a randomized controlled trial. Br. J. Anesth. **110** (2013). https://doi.org/10.1093/bja/aet001
4. Absalom, A., Glen, J., Zwart, G.J.C., Schnider, T., Struys, M.: Target-controlled infusion: a mature technology. Anesth. Analg. **122**, 70–78 (2015). https://doi.org/10.1213/ANE.0000000000001009
5. Glen, J.: The development of 'Diprifusor': a TCI system for propofol. Anaesthesia **53**(Suppl 1), 13–21 (1998). https://doi.org/10.1111/j.1365-2044.1998.53s115.x
6. Egan, T.D.: Target-controlled drug delivery: progress toward an intravenous "Vaporizer" and automated anesthetic administration. Anesthesiology **99**(5), 1214–1219 (2003)
7. Hemmerling, T., Terrasini, N.: Robotic anesthesia: not the realm of science fiction any more. Curr. Opin. Anesth. **25**(10), 1097 (2012)
8. Goudra, B., Singh, P.M.: Failure of sedasys: destiny or poor design. Anesth. Analg. **124**, 686–688 (2016). https://doi.org/10.1213/ANE.0000000000001643
9. Goudra, B.G., Singh, P.M., Chandrasekhara, V.: SEDASYS®, airway, oxygenation, and ventilation: anticipating and managing the challenges. Dig. Dis. Sci. **59** (2014). https://doi.org/10.1007/s10620-013-2996-z
10. Wehbe, M., et al.: A technical description of a novel pharmacological anesthesia robot. J. Clin. Monit. Comput. **28** (2013). https://doi.org/10.1007/s10877-013-9451-8
11. Hemmerling, T.M., Taddei, R., Wehbe, M., Morse, J., Cyr, S., Zaouter, C.: Robotic anesthesia - a vision for the future of anesthesia. Transl. Med. UniSa **1**, 1–20 (2011)
12. Brodie, S.M., et al.: Closed-loop controlled propofol anesthesia with remifentanil administered either by target-controlled infusion or closed-loop control, p. S-357 (2015)
13. Sramek, B.B.: Thoracic electrical bioimpedance measurement of cardiac output. Crit. Care Med. **22**(8), 1337–1339 (1994)
14. Sramek, B.B.: Systemic Hemodynamics and Hemodynamic Management, p. 122 (2002). ISBN 1-59196-046-0
15. Sokologorsky, S.V.: Method of graphic representation of integral parameters of hemodynamics and oxygen transport. Her. Intensiv. Care № 1 C, 3–12 (2001). (in Russian)
16. Sokologorsky, S.V.: Monitor and computer security of anesthesia in abdominal interventions in obstetric and gynecological clinic. DMedSc thesis, Russian Academy of Medical Sciences. Scientific center of obstetrics, gynecology and Perinatology, Moscow (2003). (in Russian)
17. Jeanne, M., Logier, R., De Jonckheere, J., Tavernier, B.: Validation of a graphic measurement of heart rate variability to assess analgesia/nociception balance during general anesthesia. In: 2009 Proceeding Conference of IEEE Engineering in Medicine and Biology Society, pp. 1840–1843 (2009)
18. Kaul, H.L., Bharti, N.: Monitoring depth of anaesthesia. Indian J. Anaesth **46**(4), 323–332 (2002)
19. Jeanne, M., Logier, R., De Jonckheere, J., Tavernier, B.: Heart rate variability during total intravenous anesthesia: effects of nociception and analgesia. AutonNeurosci **147**, 91–96 (2009)
20. Ledowski, T., et al.: Monitoring of intra-operative nociception: skin conductance and surgical stress index versus stress hormone plasma levels. Anaesthesia **65**, 1001–1006 (2010)
21. Logier, R., Jeanne, M., et al.: PhisioDoloris: a monitoring device for analgesia/nociception balance evaluation using heart rate variability analysis. In: Proceeding Conference of IEEE Engineering in Medicine and Biology, vol. 1, pp. 1194–1197 (2010)

22. Safonov, M.Y.: Modeling and diagnostics of the functional state of left ventricle of cardiac hemodynamics based on the transformation of electro cardio. DMedSc thesis, Voronezh State Medical Academyn.a. N. N. Burdenko, Voronezh (1998). (in Russian)
23. Schüttler, J., Kloos, S., Schwilden, H., Stoeckel, H.: Total intravenous anesthesia with propofol and alfentanil by computer-assisted infusion. Anaesthesia **43**(Suppl 1), 2–7 (1988)
24. Al-Rifai, Z., Mulvey, D.: Principles of total intravenous anesthesia: basic pharmacokinetics and model descriptions. BJA Educ. **16**(3), 92–97 (2015). https://doi.org/10.1093/bjaceaccp/mkv021
25. Bibian, S., Dumont, G.A., Huzmezan, M., Ries, C.R.: Patient variability and uncertainty quantification in clinical anesthesia: part I - PKPD modeling and identification. In: Proceedings of the 2006 IFAC Symposium on Modelling and Control in Biomedical Systems (2006)
26. Struys, M.M., Sahinovic, M., Lichtenbelt, B.J., Vereecke, H.E., Absalom, A.R.: Optimizing intravenous drug administration by applying pharmacokinetic/pharmacodynamic concepts. BJA Br. J. Anaesth. **107**(1), 38–47 (2011). Advance Access publication

Verification and Validation of Computer Models for Diagnosing Breast Cancer Based on Machine Learning for Medical Data Analysis

Vladislav Levshinskii[✉], Maxim Polyakov[✉], Alexander Losev[✉],
and Alexander V. Khoperskov[✉]

Volgograd State University, Volgograd, Russia
{v.levshinskii,m.v.polyakov,alexander.losev,khoperskov}@volsu.ru

Abstract. The method of microwave radiometry is one of the areas of medical diagnosis of breast cancer. It is based on analysis of the spatial distribution of internal and surface tissue temperatures, which are measured in the microwave (RTM) and infrared (IR) ranges. Complex mathematical and computer models describing complex physical and biological processes within biotissue increase the efficiency of this method. Physical and biological processes are related to temperature dynamics and microwave electromagnetic radiation. Verification and validation of the numerical model is a key challenge to ensure consistency with medical big data. These data are obtained by medical measurements of patients. We present an original approach to verification and validation of simulation models of physical processes in biological tissues. Our approach is based on deep analysis of medical data and we use machine learning algorithms. We have achieved impressive success for the model of dynamics of thermal processes in a breast with cancer foci. This method allows us to carry out a significant refinement of almost all parameters of the mathematical model in order to achieve the maximum possible adequacy.

Keywords: Mammary glands · Machine learning techniques · Simulations · Computer-aided diagnosis

1 Introduction

Today a very relevant problem is the creation of diagnostic technologies based on the integration of modern engineering developments, the most recent medical

AL and VL are grateful to Russian Science Foundation (grant RFBR No. 19-01-00358) for the financial support of the development of mathematical models for early diagnosis of breast cancer. MP is grateful to RFBR and the government of Volgograd region according to the research project No. 19-47-343008 for the financial support. AK acknowledges Ministry of Science and Higher Education of the Russian Federation (government task, project No. 2.852.2017/4.6) for the financial support of the development of the software and numerical simulations.

© Springer Nature Switzerland AG 2019
A. G. Kravets et al. (Eds.): CIT&DS 2019, CCIS 1084, pp. 447–460, 2019.
https://doi.org/10.1007/978-3-030-29750-3_35

knowledge and the latest developments in the fields of mathematical modeling and machine learning. Foremost it is connected with the demand for the creation of a brand new medical equipment, as well as the creation of functional diagnostics methods based on dynamic measurements, description and interpretation of the parameters of physical fields and radiation of human body. At the same time, we must note one of the most difficult and relevant problem in medicine. It is a problem of early differential diagnosis of breast diseases. According to statistics, breast cancer is the most commonly occurring cancer in women. In 2012 more than 1.7 million cases of female breast cancer were diagnosed worldwide, which is about 12 % of all types of cancer. But the forecast for 2025 is more shocking, because 19.3 million new cases of cancer will be registered [1,2].

The problem of diagnostics is far away from any acceptable solution despite the considerable achievements over the past decades in understanding the clinical picture of the disease, the presence of major changes in treatment approaches, and notable development of functional diagnostics methods. The problem statement of survivability enhancement through early detection and subsequent appropriate treatment seemed quite obvious. However, the actual results, at the moment, is very far from the expected. Traditional methods that are currently in use do not effectively detect a tumor at an early stage. There are two complementary ways to solve this problem. The first one based on the usage of a complex of methods in early diagnostics. The second one is the development and improvement of new diagnostic methods. At the same time, the current situation in the world is such that in most cases the modern medical equipment application after solving some problems gives rise to others. In most cases difficulties in diagnostics arise not because of a lack of information, but because of underperformance of its processing methods. To some extent, the creation of systems for medical data mining and interpretation provides a solution to the said problems. Using methods and algorithms of machine learning, such systems should help specialists in the diagnostics, prediction of disease development, etc.

The application of information technologies in the diagnostics of diseases, as well as breast cancer, is not a new idea. For example, administrative databases can be used for early detection of breast cancer [3]. In the paper [4], the authors proposed a comprehensive method that includes FEM modelling based on heat transfer principles and requires 3D scanning and IR imaging for disease diagnostics. Naturally, various algorithms and methods of machine learning had been showing a sufficiently high efficiency in medicine [5–9]. Many studies are devoted to the analysis of the effectiveness of various decision support systems [10–14].

Microwave radiothermometry is one of the most promising methods for increasing the effectiveness of breast screening and early differential diagnosis. It is known that human tissues, like any heated body, emit electromagnetic oscillations in a wide frequency range. In addition, the radiation spectrum and the intensity of electromagnetic radiation of tissues in the microwave range is determined not only by the temperature distribution, but also by absorption and reradiation in physically inhomogeneous tissues. Thus, by measuring this radiation, one can obtain an additional and extremely important information about the state of internal and skin tissues. This is the main idea of the microwave radiothermometry method that based on measurements of tissue radiation in the microwave (RTM) and infrared (IR) wavelength ranges. It is known that changes in tissue temperature usually precede structural changes that are found with traditional diagnostic methods. In particular, temperature anomalies can be caused by enhanced metabolism of cancer cells. Early diagnosis of breast cancer is based on this characteristic.

For the first time ever the possibility of using microwave radiothermometry for the diagnosis of breast cancer was shown in [15]. To some extent, it can be considered that the theoretical basis of microwave radiothermometry in mammology is founded on the studies of the French scientist M. Gautherie [16]. Based on the clinical data of more than 85,000 patients, he convincingly showed that the heat radiation of a tumor is directly proportional to the rate of its growth. Thus, microwave radiothetmometry has a unique ability to detect fast-growing tumors in the first place.

In general, despite the obvious advantages of microwave radiothermometry, for a long time it has not received proper application in medical practice and worthy attention in scientific research. As mentioned above, this is due to the complexity of creating measuring equipment and the quality of measurements. Interest in this technique has significantly grown after the creation of effective microwave radiometers [8,17,18]. Note that microwave radiothermometry is applicable not only for the diagnosis of breast cancer, but also for the diagnosis of other diseases [19].

The main task of our project is the development and application of the method of iterative verification and validation of thermometric data obtained with simulation models. The objective is to find a correct range of the mathematical model parameters based on machine learning technologies and statistical data analysis. The proposed method will allow the development of adequate computer physical and mathematical models for studying the spatial and temporal dynamics of temperature and radiation fields in biological tissues of mammary gland.

2 Thermal Model of Breast and Model RTM-Measurements

2.1 Model of Breast

The breast has a complex, multicomponent, heterogeneous structure. We distinguish between muscle tissue, adipose tissue, blood flow, breast lobes, areola, nipple, excretory ducts, connective tissue, skin. Effect for cancer is a separate problem because the location and physical characteristics of the tumor are unknown.

These components are characterized by complex geometry, strong heterogeneity of their physical and chemical characteristics $G(r)$ and individual variations

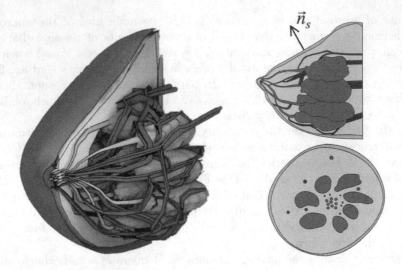

Fig. 1. 3D model of the breast. We show the internal small-scale structure of biotissue. Breast model slices are shown in different planes

of physical parameters $\delta\boldsymbol{G}$. We determine the state of biotissue using a vector of physical characteristics.

$$\boldsymbol{G}(\boldsymbol{r}) \rightleftharpoons \langle \varrho, c_p, \lambda, \varepsilon_c, Q_{met}, Q_{bl}, Q_{car}, Q_{rad}, h_{air}, \sigma, \boldsymbol{n}_s, ... \rangle, \qquad (1)$$

where ϱ is a density, c_p is a specific heat, λ is a thermal conductivity coefficient, ε_c is a complex permittivity, Q_{met}, Q_{bl}, Q_{car} are the rate of heat release from metabolic processes, blood flows and cancers, respectively, Q_{rad} is a radiative cooling, h_{air} is a convective heat transfer coefficient, σ is a electrical conductivity, $\boldsymbol{n}_s$ is a vector that determines the characteristic shape of the breast. Each characteristic depends on the coordinates inside the biotissue.

Individual variations in the properties of biotissue components can be significant, amounting normally to tens of percent for some parameters G_j. We use a more realistic geometric structure of tissues with heterogeneous characteristics instead of the traditionally used models with homogeneous parameters in a multilayer approximation (usually limited to four types of tissues — skin, muscles, mammary glands, tumor) [19]. We also take into account the filamentous connective tissues, the share structure of the breast, areola, nipple, excretory ducts (Fig. 1).

The procedure for constructing a 3D model of the internal structure of the breast is shown on Fig. 2.

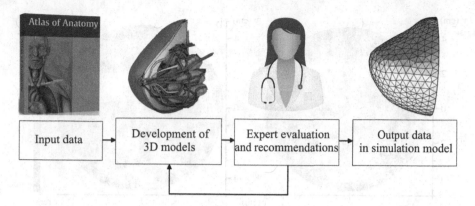

Fig. 2. Scheme of procedure for building a 3D model of the breast

2.2 Thermal Model

The process of heat transfer in biotissue is described by the equation [20]

$$\varrho(\boldsymbol{r})c_p(\boldsymbol{r})\frac{\partial T}{\partial t} = \boldsymbol{\nabla}\left(\lambda(\boldsymbol{r})\boldsymbol{\nabla}T\right) + \sum_j Q_j(\boldsymbol{r}), \tag{2}$$

$$\boldsymbol{n}(\boldsymbol{r})\cdot\boldsymbol{\nabla}T = \frac{h_{air}}{\lambda(\boldsymbol{r})}\cdot(T - T_{air}) \quad \text{for} \quad \boldsymbol{r}\in\boldsymbol{S}_0(\boldsymbol{r}) = \boldsymbol{n}(\boldsymbol{r})\cdot\boldsymbol{S}_0(\boldsymbol{r}), \tag{3}$$

where $T(\boldsymbol{r})$ is the temperature at the point $\boldsymbol{r} = \{x, y, z\}$, $\boldsymbol{\nabla}$ is differential operator nabla, heat source $Q_j > 0$ for $j = \{met, bl, car\}$ and $Q_{rad} < 0$, T_{air} is temperature of environment, $\boldsymbol{S}_0(\boldsymbol{r})$ is the boundary of biological tissue, $\boldsymbol{n}$ is unit normal vector (see Fig. 1) [18, 20]. The equation specifies the boundary conditions between biological tissue and environment.

2.3 Modeling of the Radiation Field and Numerical Model

An important problem of the microwave radiometry method is the difference between the measured temperature (brightness temperature) T_B and the thermodynamic temperature T (see Fig. 3). Measurements are carried out using microwave antennas.

Brightness temperature equals to

$$T_B(\boldsymbol{r}) = \int\limits_{\varDelta f}\left\{|S_{11}(f)|^2 T_{REC} + \left[1 - |S_{11}(f)|^2\right]\times\right.$$

$$\left.\times\left(\int_{V_0} T(\boldsymbol{r})\frac{P_d(\boldsymbol{r}, f)}{\int_{V_0} P_d(\boldsymbol{r}, f)\,dV}\,dV + T_{EMI}\right)\right\}df, \tag{4}$$

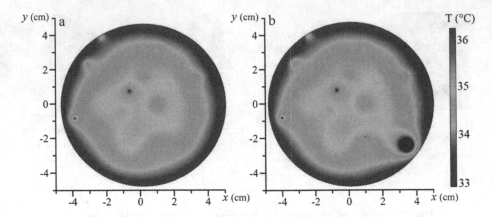

Fig. 3. Distribution of the thermodynamic temperature T at a depth of 3 cm: without cancer (a), with cancer (see right lower part) (b)

where $P_d = \dfrac{1}{2}\sigma(r, f) \cdot |E(r, f)|^2$ is electromagnetic field power density (see Fig. 4(a)), E is an electric field vector. Values T_{EMI} and T_{REC} characterize electromagnetic interference when measured with a radiometer [17, 19]. The coefficient S_{11} determines the interaction between the antenna and the biological tissue. Integration is carried out over the entire volume of biotissue (V_0). Frequency range $\Delta f = 1.3 \div 1.5$ GHz.

To construct a stationary electric field distribution, it is convenient to solve the time-dependent Maxwell equations and as the result to obtain the stationary-state:

$$\frac{\partial B}{\partial t} + rot(E) = 0, \quad \frac{\partial D}{\partial t} - rot(H) = 0, \quad B = \mu H, \quad D = \varepsilon E, \quad (5)$$

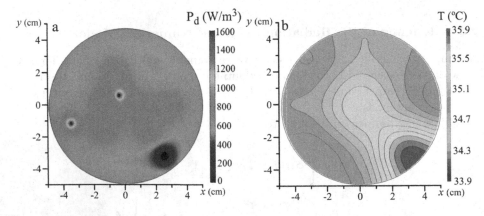

Fig. 4. Distribution of P_d (a). Brightness temperature distribution T_B (b)

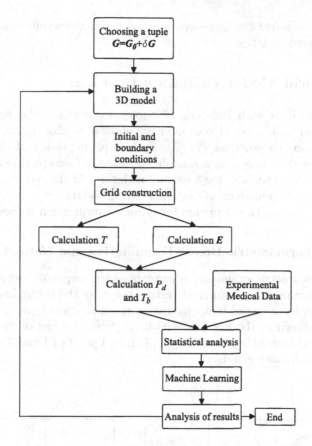

Fig. 5. Algorithm for conducting numerical experiment and verification

where B is magnetic induction, E is electric field strength, D is electric induction, H is magnetic field strength, $\varepsilon(r)$ is the dielectric constant, $\mu(r)$ is magnetic permeability.

Procedure of numerical solution for determination of internal temperature distribution $T_B(x, y, z)$ inside the tissue volume in the model (2)–(4) described in [20]. The value $T_B(r, t)$ (see Fig. 4(b)) is a convolution of the thermodynamic temperature distribution $T(r, t)$. It is obtained by solving the problem (2)–(3), and electric field distribution $E(r, t)$.

The development of new medical antennas and radiometers with improved performance is an important practical problem [19]. The method of microwave radiometry requires high precision temperature measurement. It allows us to detect thermal anomalies non-invasively at a depth of several centimeters and localize the measurement point.

The emergence printed antennas for microwave radiothermometry (see [17]) improve the efficiency of diagnosis based on an analysis of the internal temperature of the breast. Switching to textile antennas, that are embedded in clothing and are able to conduct continuous monitoring can make revolutionary advances in breast oncology practice.

3 Numerical Model Validation Problem

We make sequences with different G tuples to perform the procedure for verification and validation of computer simulation results. Each set contains $K = 80$ solutions to problems (2)–(5). Each implementation of the F_k model ($k = 1, ..., K$) is determined by a random variation δG except tumors. The vector of physical characteristics has a natural variation. At the end of each iteration we had performed an analysis of modelled thermometric data and corrected the physical components. The algorithm for iterative verification is shown in Fig. 5.

3.1 Radiothermometric Breast Examination and Dataset

The radiothermometric examination consists of the sequential measurement of surface and internal temperatures at certain points of the mammary glands and the subsequent recording of temperatures in the numerical form. The examination chart is shown in the Fig. 6: points $0, ..., 8$ are located on the mammary gland, point 9 is located in the axillary region, and points $T1$ and $T2$ are located between the mammary glands.

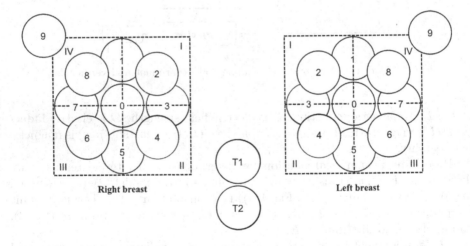

Fig. 6. Radiothermometric examination chart

We had formed a thermometric dataset based on the data from cancer centers. It contains the following data: temperature values, age, breast diameter, parity, etc. However, we need only consider temperature values at the points $0, ..., 8$, because computer simulation results contain only points of the mammary gland. Each patient is assigned to a certain class from the following:

healthy, other (various diseases of the mammary glands), cancer (malignant tumor). Next, the data set was combined with the simulation results. The number of mammary glands per class is shown in the Fig. 7. For clarity, the simulation results obtained after the first and second iterations of the verification algorithm are also shown.

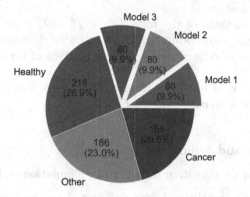

Fig. 7. Per-class counts of breasts in the combined dataset

We denote the combined dataset as

$$X = \begin{bmatrix} t_0^1 & t_1^1 & \dots & t_{18}^1 \\ t_0^2 & t_1^2 & \dots & t_{18}^2 \\ \dots & \dots & \dots & \dots \\ t_0^{810} & t_1^{810} & \dots & t_{18}^{810} \end{bmatrix}, y = \begin{bmatrix} y_1 \\ y_2 \\ \dots \\ y_{810} \end{bmatrix} \tag{6}$$

where $t_0^i, \dots, t_8^i$ are internal temperatures at the points $0, \dots, 8, t_9^i, \dots, t_{18}^i$ are surface temperatures and $y_i \in \{\text{Model 1}, \text{Model 2}, \text{Model 3}, \text{Healthy}, \text{Other}, \text{Cancer}\}$ is a label of the i-th breast.

3.2   Feature Space

The original feature space contains the values of surface and internal temperatures. However, at the anomaly detection process the experts analyze not the temperature values, but their various relations. Based on this fact in the process of thermometric data mining, we proposed several hypotheses about the behaviour of temperature fields and significantly expanded the feature space. It allows to detect temperature anomalies with better performance and to build various classification algorithms [8,9,21] that can provide a full explanation of the result and underlie the intelligent system for diagnostics of the mammary glands diseases.

Taking the above into account, the feature space of the combined dataset was extended by the following features:

1. The values of functions of the form $T_i^g = t_i - t_{i+9}, i = \overline{0,8}$ that are the so-called internal temperature gradients at the points $0, \ldots, 8$. These functions represent temperature changes with respect to depth;

2. Values of functions of the form $R_i^{mw} = t_0 - t_i, i = \overline{1,8}$ and $R_i^{ir} = t_9 - t_i, i = \overline{10,18}$ that are so-called radial gradients. These functions represent temperature changes relative to nipple temperature, which is the one of the most important features;

3. The values of functions of the form $G^2 = T_0^g - T_i^g, i = \overline{1,8}$ that describe changes of internal temperature gradients in radial direction. These functions are the difference analogs of the second derivatives of temperature functions [8];

4. More general forms of functions from other groups. For example, the maximum value of the internal gradients $F_1 = \max\limits_{i \in \overline{0,8}} |T_i^g|$.

3.3 Verification and Validation

We apply the following algorithm to verify the simulation results:

1. Build a classifier using the real data and test it on the model data;
2. Build a classifier using the model data and test it on the real data;
3. Analyze the results and the values of features for the wrong predictions;
4. Change the model coefficients, simulate new data and return to step 1.

Consider the breast cancer binary classification problem. Let patients with breast cancer be positive examples and patients without breast diseases (or computer simulation results) be negative examples. Note that we do not consider a group of patients called "Other" and left it in the figures for clarity. This is due to the complexity and diversity of the diseased breast structure.

As the model evaluation criterion we use the following

$$M = \sqrt{Spec_1 \cdot Spec_2}, \tag{7}$$

where $Spec_1$ is the specificity of a classifier built at step 1 and tested on the model data, $Spec_2$ is the specificity of a classifier built at step 2 and tested on the real data, $Spec = \dfrac{TN}{TN + FP}$ is the specificity, TN is the number of true negatives and FP is the number of false positives.

As the classifier evaluation criterion we use the following

$$G = \sqrt{Sens \cdot Spec}, \tag{8}$$

where $Sens = \dfrac{TP}{TP + FN}$ is the sensitivity (recall), TP is the number of true positives and FN is the number of false negatives.

As a classifier we use the weighted simple rule voting algorithm, that is a modified version of an algorithm proposed in [8]. Its performance measure reported by 5-fold nested cross-validation is 0.83, and specificity is close to 1 after refitting. A key feature of this classifier is the fully interpretable output that allows to immediately detect differences in patterns.

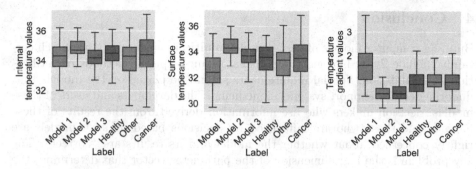

Fig. 8. Boxplots of temperature values at the point 0 (outliers aren't shown)

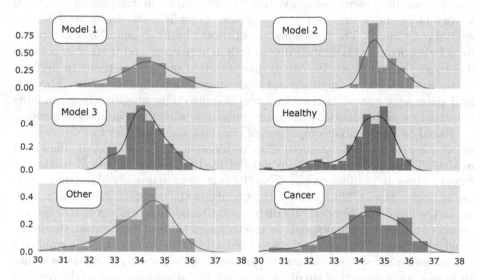

Fig. 9. Per-class distributions of the internal temperature values at the point 0

3.4   Results and Analysis

After the first iteration of the verification algorithm, we measured $M = 0.67$, $Spec_1 = 0.75$ and $Spec_2 = 0.61$. The analysis of the results has shown that the surface temperatures in modelled data is characterized by the lower values. In addition, the modelled data has a higher variance.

The problems mentioned above were taken into account at subsequent iterations of the algorithm. At the steps 2 and 3 we measured nearly identical $M = 0.72$. The second modelling results are characterized by higher surface and internal temperature values, as well as low variance. At the third iteration, these gaps were partially eliminated. Typical situations are shown in the Figs. 8 and 9.

4   Conclusion

Building computer models of very complex multicomponent systems, which certainly include living biological organisms, requires special methods of verification and validation. Special requirements should be placed on the models that underlie decision support systems in medicine. The developers and users of these models, decision makers who use information derived from the results of these models, and those who are influenced by decisions based on such models are rightly concerned about whether the model and its results are "correct". The key problem is the high dimension of the parameter vector that determines the properties of a biological tissue or organ, when the properties of a biological tissue are radically heterogeneous. Within the medical norm, the parameter spread is very large and a time factor may appear in addition to the dependence on spatial coordinates. The determination of these physico-chemical characteristics for a living organism is difficult due to technical reasons, and is often impossible due to legal restrictions. We cannot use standard physical methods to perform a validity check for a computational model based on a physical object. The natural parameter spread of the biosystem requires diligent simulations and the construction of distributions that are compatible with medical measurements.

Based on a sequential comparison of classification results for two datasets we are developing an iterative method of verification and validation of simulation models. The first dataset contains data of medical measurements of brightness temperatures at 18 different points on the surface of mammary gland and inside the biological tissue. The second dataset contains the results of numerical modeling of the brightness temperature distribution based on a complex mathematical model of the heat dynamics and the electromagnetic field distribution inside the biological tissue. We rely on the so-called Objective Approach [22], making a comparison using statistical tests and procedures. As a result, we have the ability to form a set of numerical simulations, which is statistically close to the medical measurement dataset. We have demonstrated a sufficiently rapid convergence of the iterative approach.

References

1. WHO, in: Latest World Cancer Statistics Global Cancer Burden Rises to 14.1 million New Cases in 2012: Marked Increase in Breast Cancers Must Be Addressed, World Health Organization, p. 12 (2013)
2. Bray, F., et al.: Global estimates of cancer prevalence for 27 sites in the adult population in 2008. Int. J. Cancer **132**(5), 1133–1145 (2013). https://doi.org/10.1002/ijc.27711
3. Abraha, I., et al.: Accuracy of administrative databases in detecting primary breast cancer diagnoses: a systematic review. BMJ **8**(7), 1–18 (2018). https://doi.org/10.1136/bmjopen-2017-019264
4. Igali, D., Mukhmetov, O., Zhao, Y., Fok, S.C., Teh, S.L.: An experimental framework for validation of thermal modeling for breast cancer detection. IOP Conf. Ser. Mater. Sci. Eng. **408**(1), 012031 (2018). https://doi.org/10.1088/1757-899X/408/1/012031

5. Mohanty, A.K., Senapati, M.R., Lenka, S.K.: Retraction note to: an improved data mining technique for classification and detection of breast cancer from mammograms. Neural Comput. Appl. **22**(1), 303–310 (2013). https://doi.org/10.1007/s00521-012-0834-4

6. Yassin, N.I.R., Omran, S., Houby, E.M.F.E., Allam, H.: Machine learning techniques for breast cancer computer aided diagnosis using different image modalities: a systematic review. Comput. Methods Programs Biomed. **156**, 25–45 (2018). https://doi.org/10.1016/j.cmpb.2017.12.012

7. Horsch, A., Hapfelmeier, A., Elter, M.: Needs assessment for next generation computer-aided mammography reference image databases and evaluation studies. Int. J. Comput. Assisted Radiol. Surg. **6**(6), 749–767 (2011). https://doi.org/10.1007/s11548-011-0553-9

8. Losev, A.G., Levshinskiy, V.V.: Data mining of microwave radiometry data in the diagnosis of breast cancer. Math. Phys. Comput. Simul. **20**(5), 49–62 (2017). https://doi.org/10.15688/mpcm.jvolsu.2017.5.6

9. Zenovich, A.V., Baturin, N.A., Medvedev, D.A., Petrenko, A.Y.: Algorithms for the formation of two-dimensional characteristic and informative signs of diagnosis of diseases of the mammary glands by the methods of combined radiothermometry. Math. Phys. Comput. Simul. **21**(4), 44–56 (2018). https://doi.org/10.15688/mpcm.jvolsu.2018.4.4

10. Beeler, P.E., Bates, D.W., Hug, B.L.: Clinical decision support systems. Swiss Med. Wkly. **144**, w14073 (2014). https://doi.org/10.4414/smw.2014.14073

11. Berner, E.S., La Lande, T.J.: Overview of clinical decision support systems. In: Berner, E.S. (ed.) Clinical Decision Support Systems. HI, pp. 1–17. Springer, Cham (2016). https://doi.org/10.1007/978-3-319-31913-1_1

12. Manar, J., Mouna, B., Naima, A.M., Samy, H., Zineb, S., Mohammed, B.O.: Evaluation of the decision support systems. J. of Commun. Comput. **14**, 129–136 (2017). https://doi.org/10.17265/1548-7709/2017.03.004

13. Wasylewicz, A.T.M., Scheepers-Hoeks A.M.J.W.: Clinical Decision Support Systems. In: Kubben, P., Dumontier, M., Dekker, A. (eds.) Fundamentals of Clinical Data Science, pp. 153–169 (2019). https://doi.org/10.1007/978-3-319-99713-111

14. Walsh, S., de Jong, E.E.C., van Timmeren, J.E., Ibrahim, A., Compter, I., Peerlings, J., et al.: Decision support systems in oncology. JCO Clin. Cancer Inform. **3**, 1–9 (2019). https://doi.org/10.1200/CCI.18.00001

15. Barrett, A.H., Myers, P.C.: Subcutaneous temperature: a method of noninvasive sensing. Science **190**, 669–671 (1975)

16. Gautherie, M.: Temperature and blood flow patterns in breast cancer during natural evolution and following radiotherapy. Biomed. Thermology **107**, 21–64 (1982)

17. Sedankin, M.K., et al.: Antenna applicators for medical microwave radiometers. Biomed. Eng. **52**(4), 235–238 (2018). https://doi.org/10.1007/s10527-018-9820-1

18. Avila-Castro, I.A., et al.: Thorax thermographic simulator for breast pathologies. J. Appl. Res. Technol. **15**, 143–151 (2017). https://doi.org/10.1016/j.jart.2017.01.008

19. Sedankin, M.K., et al.: Mathematical simulation of heat transfer processes in a breast with a malignant tumor. Biomed. Eng. **52**(3), 190–194 (2018). https://doi.org/10.1007/s10527-018-9811-2

20. Polyakov, M.V., Khoperskov, A.V., Zamechnic, T.V.: Numerical modeling of the internal temperature in the mammary gland. In: Siuly, S., et al. (eds.) HIS 2017. LNCS, vol. 10594, pp. 128–135. Springer, Cham (2017). https://doi.org/10.1007/978-3-319-69182-4_14

21. Zenovich, A.V., Grebnev, V.I., Primachenko, F.G.: Algorithms for the classification of diseases of paired organs on the basis of neural networks and fuzzy sets. Math. Phys. Comput. Simul. **20**(6), 26–37 (2017). https://doi.org/10.15688/mpcm.jvolsu. 2017.6.3
22. Sargent, R.G.: Verifying and validating simulation models. In: Proceedings of the Winter Simulation Conference vol. 37, no. (2), pp. 166–183. IEEE (2011). https://doi.org/10.1109/WSC.2010.5679166

Multi-level Model for Structuring Heterogeneous Biomedical Data in the Tasks of Socially Significant Diseases Risk Evaluation

Alena A. Zakharova⬚, Dmitry Lagerev$^{(\boxtimes)}$⬚, and Aleksandr Podvesovskii⬚

Bryansk State Technical University,
50 Let Oktyabrya Ave., 7, 241035 Bryansk, Russia
{zaa, LagerevDG, apodv}@tu-bryansk.ru

Abstract. The article provides an overview of modern approaches to building multi-level models for structuring heterogeneous data of different nature. A generalized multilevel model for structuring heterogeneous data is proposed and its adaptation for processing biomedical data in the tasks of socially significant diseases risk evaluation is described by the example of risk evaluation of congenital malformations among children from areas in the Bryansk region radioactively contaminated after the Chernobyl disaster. The developed model allows for enriching the available data, taking into account more factors and hidden relationships between them, facilitating intelligent analysis and enhancing the quality of its results. As a result of the study, no statistically significant excess of the frequency of anencephaly, hydrocephalus and encephalocele in children in more radiation-contaminated southwestern territories was found compared to the average regional data. The results obtained presumably indicate the influence of the radiation factor on the increased incidence of microcephaly in southwestern territories relative to the average regional values without southwestern territories for a sixteen-year period (1999–2014).

Keywords: Heterogeneous · Unstructured and semi-structured data ·
Biomedical data · Model ensembles · Machine learning ·
Retrospective scalable models · Comprehensive risk evaluation ·
Socially significant diseases · Congenital malformations

1 Introduction

Data flows, that have to be operated in the modern world, grow avalanche-like every day. Modern medical systems accumulate a large variety of data: hereditary factors reading (prevention of genetically determined pathology), analysis of anamnestic and laboratory data, physical examination results – ultrasound, X-ray, CT, MRI, DICOM files, data from monitoring sensors, etc., records of populational and epidemiological and environmental factors. Heterogeneous semi-structured biomedical data of large volume (Big Data) are accumulated in integrated electronic medical records (IEMRs). A variety of heterogeneous devices serve as their source and their volume increases avalanche-like over time.

© Springer Nature Switzerland AG 2019
A. G. Kravets et al. (Eds.): CIT&DS 2019, CCIS 1084, pp. 461–473, 2019.
https://doi.org/10.1007/978-3-030-29750-3_36

The peculiarity of these data is that they arrive and accumulate continuously. This is a huge part of biomedical data, which need to be effectively managed and used for analysis and personal preventive recommendations. A distinctive feature of biomedical information is that it is usually represented in a semi-structured or unstructured format.

Use of technologies for collecting and analyzing heterogeneous data opens up new opportunities in medical information systems development and healthcare quality improvement. The major problems facing developers of technologies for collecting and analyzing heterogeneous data in medicine are determined by the nature of the data processed in medical information systems. Processing these data using traditional software becomes impossible not only due to the large data volume but also because of various structures of these data (numbers, texts, images) and the need to process them in a limited period of time [11].

Research in this area has a fairly wide geography. The United States owns more than 35% of patents in the field of heterogeneous data processing. China is in second place with 21%. Researchers from the Republic of Korea, Great Britain, Japan, Spain, Australia and India are also actively engaged in the analysis of big unstructured data in medicine.

Many researchers point out shortcomings of standard methods (as a rule, ETL processes – Extract, Transform, Load) for the implementation of projects associated with a large amount of medical data. For example, in the work of the authors from the University of Seville, where the problem of integrating heterogeneous data sources for intelligent network ecosystems is considered, it is noted that the integration of existing medical systems within one warehouse is very complex, since each database has its own structure, and for effective analysis it is necessary to use all the information from existing databases [4].

One of the most famous projects in the field of intelligent data analysis in medicine is IBM Watson for Oncology (WFO). In this system, information from the patient's medical record is analyzed taking into account the knowledge base and personal recommendations for him are generated. However, various research results show that this system has limited clinical applicability without additional algorithms and information [5]. Chinese researchers also state that localization and retraining of models are required for use in other countries, which imposes large material costs [13].

Foreign experience has been considered in implementing systems for intelligent analysis of medical data, in the course of which information was collected from various medical systems. For example, paper [2] describes experience of creating a data mart and conducting clinical study using electronic data from four institutions of the same hospital network in New York. In this system, the authors analyze the difficulties, they have faced, and the complexity of solving various problems. They also note that researchers' increased attention to methods of collecting, integrating, processing and storing electronic patient data in this field can help simplify implementation of similar projects.

In a large review of the development of Xiangya Medical Big Data project (a project aimed to build a distributed system for analyzing medical data in the PRC), the authors note that the task of developing a suitable data structure as well as collection and integration tools proved to be more complicated than the task of creating distributed infrastructure that meets information security standards [10].

Intelligent data analysis is actively used in matters related to human ecology. In Lausch et al. [9], on the subject of intelligent data analysis in ecology, it is noted that despite the development of intelligent data analysis techniques, classical approaches are limited to use on a particular data structure and therefore often remain tied to specialized tasks. The paper also acknowledges that complex and generally interdisciplinary issues in the field of environmental studies cannot be solved adequately using classical approaches to intelligent data analysis. In the work Environmental Data Science [3], it is stated that integration of heterogeneous data from several sources allows for more holistic analysis and opens the potential for finding new knowledge in the data.

The diverse experience of foreign studies indicates that when implementing a system for processing heterogeneous data much attention should be paid to the development of a suitable data warehouse structure and methods for integrating data from existing data sources.

2 Statement and Features of Modeling the Task of Group Expert Evaluation in a Distributed Environment

Many tasks have a complex interdisciplinary nature; to solve them it is necessary to aggregate and process jointly a large amount of data from various sources. Sources of information in the modern world can be:

- structured sources: multidimensional data warehouses, relational databases of accounting, information and automated systems;
- semi-structured sources: non-relational databases (NoSQL), data lakes, databricks;
- unstructured sources: BLOB storage (Binary Large Object), documents in formats of popular office suites, publications in the Internet in natural language.

At the same time, information about a single object can be found in numerous sources of different types; it can be presented in various formats, time scales, with a different level of detail and reliability. In classical approaches to organization of data warehouses, it is proposed to import, cleanup and transform data separately for each source and to perform identification of links between objects obtained from different sources only after importing all the data into the warehouse. This approach does not allow identifying vertical and horizontal links between objects to the full extent, revealing and restoring data distortions and omissions. This is due to the fact that data are usually multi-level and have different densities at different levels.

Figure 1 shows the generalized multi-level model proposed by the authors for structuring heterogeneous data from various sources (both structured and unstructured), allowing for the integration of heterogeneous data and the identification of vertical and horizontal links between objects. The proposed data model can be described as follows:

$$M = <S, P, A, V, O, L>,\tag{1}$$

where at the input:

S is a set of data sources
P is a set of data preprocessing methods;
A is a set of ensembles of intelligent data analysis models;
V is a set of visualizers;
at the output:
O is a set of objects;
L is a set of links between objects.

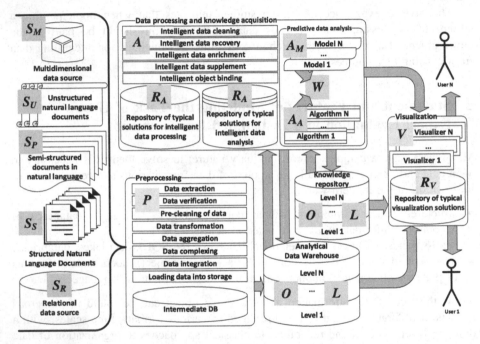

Fig. 1. Generalized multi-level model for structuring heterogeneous data

A set of data sources can be represented as:

$$S = <S_M, S_R, S_S, S_P, S_U >, \tag{2}$$

where S_M is a set of multidimensional data sources;

S_R is a set of relational data sources;
S_S is a set of structured documents in natural language;
S_P is a set of semi-structured documents in natural language;
S_U is a set of unstructured documents in natural language [1].

A set of data preprocessing methods can be represented as:

$$P = <P_1,\ldots, P_N >,\tag{3}$$

where P_I is a specific method of data preprocessing.

The following classes of methods can be used as a data preprocessing method (see Fig. 1): data extraction, data verification, data pre-cleaning, data transformation, data aggregation, data complexing, data integration and data loading in storage.

A set of ensembles of intelligent data analysis models can be represented in the following form:

$$A = <A_M, A_A, W, R_A >,\tag{4}$$

where A_M is a set of intelligent data analysis models;

A_A is a set of intelligent data analysis algorithms;

W is a set of rules determining interaction and order of application of models and algorithms;

R_A is a repository containing many typical model ensembles for intelligent data processing and analysis.

In the ensembles of models, various classes of intelligent data analysis algorithms can be used, e.g.: clustering, classification, neural network algorithms, decision trees, etc.

A set of visualizers can be represented as:

$$V = <V, R_V >,\tag{5}$$

where V is a set of visualizers;

R_V is a repository containing sets of type visualizers for various tasks.

A set of objects can be represented as:

$$O = <A_1,\ldots,A_N >,\tag{6}$$

where A_1 is an object attribute and value.

A set of links between objects can be represented as:

$$L = <L_H, L_V >,\tag{7}$$

where L_H is a set of single-level ("horizontal") links between objects;

L_V is a set of inter-level ("vertical") links between objects.

Single-level links show that the state of one object depends on another, inter-level links form a hierarchy and show that one object belongs to some class (links of the form "is a") or is a part of another one (links "part of"). Hierarchical structures allow for data convolution and aggregation.

According to the developed data model, the initial data loading is carried out through software adapters into the intermediate database. Meanwhile, classical data conversion algorithms can be executed during the loading process. Subsequently, import is carried out from the intermediate database into the data warehouse.

Concurrently, using models, methods and algorithms of intelligent data analysis, there is performed identification of entities and construction of a hierarchical model of the form: "Object" – "Level-1 Cluster" –... – "Level-N Cluster" – "Set". When building the hierarchical model for identification of missing from sources, unknown, hidden links, ensembles of models are used, and the use of visualizers makes it possible to evaluate the results of data enrichment. Application of approaches of intelligent data analysis when loading data into the warehouse allows for performing data enrichment at a new level using information about other objects included in the same clusters. It is possible to build a knowledge warehouse on the basis of a data warehouse. Since there is a semantic layer in the data warehouse, the data contained in it have undergone preprocessing, enrichment and integration, clusters and hidden relationships have already been identified, using the data warehouse as a data source for model ensembles helps to simplify the process of constructing a model ensemble and to enhance the quality of the results.

3 Adaptation of a Multi-level Model for Structuring Heterogeneous Biomedical Data

Modern medicine should be as preventive as possible and offer a personalized approach to risk assessment, early diseases detection and targeted correction of negative changes at the individual, cohort and population level. To implement this approach, it is necessary not only to monitor state of health regularly, but also to perform a retrospective analysis of the available data on the course and causes of socially significant diseases. It is advisable to take into account a number of additional factors, characterizing the state of the ecosystem and the habitat of the object under study.

In the present context, it is extremely difficult to identify the determining factors of etiology, pathogenesis and clinical symptoms in such a huge flow of information. In addition, increase in life expectancy, deterioration of ecological and demographic situation cause not one but several polypathias in the population. They hinder diagnostics and choice of therapeutic approach considerably. Current clinical protocols presuppose statistically averaged methods for treating individual nosological forms. This violates fundamentally the principles of personification of a particular patient's care management. Clinical protocols do not address disease prevention issues.

Thus, to obtain qualitative forecasts and assess the risks of socially significant diseases, research is needed at the intersection of scientific fields: medicine, biology, ecology, intelligent and cognitive visualization models for analyzing and interpreting biomedical data—with the subsequent creation of a methodology and tool for analyzing big heterogeneous unstructured data from various sources.

Selection, identification and search of objects O (objects in the given subject area can refer to patients, social groups, age groups, etc., depending on the purposes of the analysis) with the best correspondence of the compared parameters to the formulated problem in semi-formalized areas of knowledge are complicated by the complexity of presenting many of the parameters under study in numerical or logical form. In such cases, the use of visual analytics (V) and model ensembles (A) when considering non-numerical factors helps to overcome semantic and ontological differences between the adjoining areas of knowledge and synthesize new knowledge that is not available with direct statistical processing.

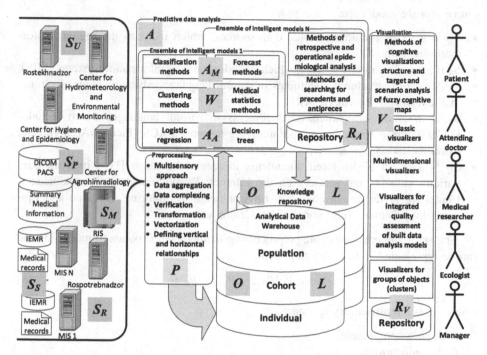

Fig. 2. Generalized scheme of processing heterogeneous biomedical data for socially significant diseases risks evaluation

Figure 2 shows a generalized scheme of the proposed methodology for processing heterogeneous biomedical data for socially significant diseases risk evaluation. The scheme reveals the main sources of biomedical data and shows the place of the above-described methods in data extraction and processing.

It is proposed to use a regional information system (RIS) as a multidimensional data source (S_M), which aggregates patients' medical data within the region. As relational data sources (S_R), it is proposed to use medical information systems (MIS). MIS also contain integrated electronic medical patient records (IEMR), which are structured documents in natural language (S_S). As a source of semi-structured documents in natural language (S_P), DICOM image transmission and archiving systems PACS (Picture Archiving and Communication System) can be used. Various websites and services on the Internet are sources of unstructured documents in natural language (S_U).

The proposed model allows for the identification of single-level (L_H, "horizontal") and interlevel (L_V, "vertical") links between objects (O), as well as vertical and horizontal scalability of solutions, which makes it possible not to limit either the number of parameters (dimensions) or the number of processed objects.

Mathematical description of the proposed model of heterogeneous biomedical data processing for risk evaluation of socially significant diseases corresponds to model (1). The set of data sources and source types used correspond to model (2). The data sources for the model are:

- S_M is a set of multidimensional data sources, which includes the regional information system (RIS);
- S_R is a set of relational sources, which includes medical information systems (MIS);
- S_S is a set of structured documents in natural language, which includes electronic medical patient records (IEMR);
- S_P is a set of semi-structured documents in natural language, which includes DICOM image transmission and archiving systems PACS (Picture Archivingand Communication System);
- S_U is a set of unstructured documents in natural language [1], which includes various websites and services on the Internet: Rospotrebnadzor, Rostekhnadzor, Center for Hydrometeorology and Environmental Monitoring, Hygiene and Epidemiology Center, Agrohimradiology Centre, etc.

The set of the employed data preprocessing methods corresponds to model (3) and can be represented in the following form:

$$P = \; <P_1, P_2, P_3, P_4, P_5, P_6> \, , \qquad (8)$$

where P_1 is a multisensory approach;

P_2 is data complexing;
P_3 is verification;
P_4 is transformation;
P_5 is vectorization;
P_6 is defining vertical and horizontal relationships.

The set of ensembles of intelligent data analysis models corresponds to model (4). Intelligent data analysis algorithms (A_A) include: classification methods, clustering methods, logistic regression, decision trees, medical statistics methods, forecast methods, retrospective and operational epidemiological analysis methods, search for precedents and anti-precedents.

The set of visualizers (5) is represented in the form:

$$V = \; <V_1, V_2, V_3, V_4, V_5, R_V> \, , \qquad (9)$$

where V_1 is methods of cognitive visualization: structure and target analysis and scenario analysis of fuzzy cognitive maps;

V_2 is classic visualizers
V_3 is multidimensional visualizers
V_4 is visualizers for comprehensive evaluation and quality of constructed intelligent data analysis models
V_5 is visualizers for groups of objects (clusters)
R_A is a repository containing sets of type visualizers for biomedical data visualization.

Use of the model is possible in a wide range of applied tasks of preventive and personalized medicine. Additional advantages are expected by increasing the efficiency, performance of software systems, and speed of decision-making based on processing large volumes of heterogeneous data.

Use of visual cognitive analytics technology within the framework of the project will enable processing and interpretation of raw data streams promptly and at a qualitatively higher level. Modeling and designing visual models provides approximate solutions not only for a task in question, but for entire classes of applied problems [12].

Collecting biomedical data from various sources (anamnestic and laboratory data, results of physical examinations – ultrasound, X-ray, CT, MRI, DICOM files, data from monitoring sensors, data of environmental and epidemiological monitoring and population register) implies their complexing. In this case, the sources are heterogeneous. It is proposed to use a multisensory approach to aggregate such biomedical data.

For the development of models and software tools, it is proposed to use the following approaches and methods: approaches to building multidimensional data and knowledge warehouses, visual modeling (multidimensional graphs), graphic and cognitive modeling, object-oriented modeling and design, intelligent data analysis including ensembles of models.

For heterogeneous biomedical data analysis within the models, implementation of model ensembles (A) is foreseen, containing the following models (A_M) and algorithms (A_A):

- retrospective and operational epidemiological analysis;
- medical statistics;
- pathology assessment and management (scoring, logistic regression, classification algorithms);
- clusterization of similar objects (clustering algorithms, decision trees, classification and search for similar objects);
- predictive analysis;
- search for precedents and anti-precedents;
- cognitive visualization: a structure and target analysis and scenario analysis of fuzzy cognitive maps;
- structural and parametric identification of fuzzy cognitive models;
- comprehensive evaluation and quality of constructed intelligent data analysis models and results obtained from these models (ROC analysis, lift curves, profit curves, gain charts, classification matrix, cost matrix, etc.).

The above sets of sources, preprocessing methods, model ensembles and visualizers are open and can be expanded if necessary. However, the abovementioned models and methods for analyzing biomedical data should support work at various levels of object generalization (an individual, cohort, region, population). In order to improve the quality, it is proposed to use integration of methods for analyzing and processing biomedical data by developing ensembles of intelligent data analysis models suitable for solving a number of typical tasks.

For effective application of the above methods with the involvement of domain experts:

- data warehouse and knowledge warehouse (O, L), containing final data models and model templates, optimized for storing large volumes of biomedical data for the purpose of subsequent analysis;
- repository of ensembles of intelligent analytical models (R_A), containing numerous solved sample problems of analyzing biomedical data, including the data models used, their processing methods and the results obtained;
- repository of type visualizers for visualizing results of biomedical data analysis tasks (R_V).

4   Risk Evaluation of Congenital Malformations in Newborns

Congenital malformations (CM) are becoming increasingly important in children's morbidity patterns as well as in disability and infant mortality. This problem is urgent as the contribution of CMs to the structure of mortality causes in the first year of life is almost 20%, and they are found in 4–6% of newborns.

The study was carried out using methods of statistical (Student's t-test, Pearson's chi-squared test, Pearson correlation test, linear regression) and intelligent data analysis (G-means clustering) based upon data on registered cases of CM (S_S) and data on radioactive contamination of various territories of the Bryansk region (S_R). To conduct the study, there was developed a MS SQL Server 2017 data warehouse (for storing historical data O, L), an ETL subsystem (Extraction, transformation, loading – P), and a visualization subsystem (V). Model ensembles were built using third-party software (Stata, Loginom, Python, Anaconda).

Based on data monitoring for 1999–2014, a comparative analysis was performed of congenital malformations occurrence in children of the Bryansk region, the RF, radioactively contaminated with different densities with cesium-137 and strontium-90 after the Chernobyl disaster [6–8]. The monitoring is conducted on the basis of the medico-genetic counselling center of Bryansk Clinical Diagnostic Center, in accordance with the computer screening program CM Monitoring, which represents a database of all newly identified cases of CM in children and fetuses registered in the region.

The study was conducted on the basis of data from gynecological clinics and obstetric institutions of the region, children's clinics and hospitals, and women's consultation clinics. Radioactive contamination of southwestern territories and the rest of the region with cesium-137 and strontium-90 was determined according to official sources. The time period of statistical analysis was 16 years from 1999 to 2014. All data were uploaded to the data warehouse from sources using the ETL subsystem.

As research methods, a model ensemble (A) was used, which included algorithms (A_A): clustering and statistical data processing. Allocation as objects (O) of Bryansk region districts and children and fetuses with CM, and establishment of links (L) between them allowed for identifying individual patterns and dependencies. However, disadvantages and limitations of the study can be attributed to the fact that the analysis should take into account not only environmental data on radiation and chemical pollution, but also more detailed information from parents and other relatives' integrated medical records (S_M), information on parents' place and type of work, economic situation in the region (S_U), health care system effectiveness, etc. That is a direction for further research in this field.

There has been detected no statistically significant increase in the frequency of anencephaly, hydrocephalus, and encephalocele in children from more radioactively contaminated southwestern territories compared with the average regional data without these territories. However, in the southwestern areas, the frequency of microcephaly is statistically significantly ($p < 0.05$) above the average regional values (5.8 times). Herewith, the maximum values are recorded in the most radioactively polluted areas of the region when detecting high statistically significant correlations with the density of radioactive contamination with cesium-137 ($r = 0.69$; $p = 0.040$) and strontium 90 ($r = 0.70$; $p = 0.037$). Meanwhile, no significant dependencies of other congenital brain malformations have been identified. There has been revealed a statistically significant decrease in the long-term trend in microcephaly frequency throughout the region without southwestern territories in the period 1999–2014 and an increase in the radioactively contaminated southwestern territories.

Among the circumstances of CM, there are a number of both exogenous and endogenous factors. Thus, it is extremely difficult to take them into account using conventional data warehouses. For example, among the main risk factors for the occurrence of CM, we can distinguish socio-economic situation, working and living conditions, health care system and its efficiency (including early CM detection), mother's endocrine and metabolic diseases, abnormalities of germ cells, drug usage, etc.

In addition, the effect on the statistics of early diagnosis and artificial termination of pregnancy should be taken into account when analyzing data on CM frequencies. For example, in Belarus, it's been possible to stabilize the birth frequency of children with CM since 1992 due to the state program of abortion on therapeutic and genetic indicators (500–600 cases annually). Such targeted programs do not exist in Ukraine and Russia, but, obviously, the number of therapeutic abortions has significantly increased in these countries as well. In the most radioactively contaminated Bryansk region, the number of such abortions is four times higher than countrywide –5.8% and 1.4%, respectively.

In future research it seems necessary to:

- consider in detail the dynamics of other CM types;
- to study CM dynamics taking into account the influence of chemical and combined radiation-chemical environmental pollution, parents' various endocrine and metabolic diseases, the use of certain medicines and drugs, etc.
- perform similar studies taking into account possible embryotoxic effects of radioactive contamination of the southwestern areas of the region with other radionuclides in addition to ^{137}Cs and ^{90}Sr;
- identify the reasons for the increasing frequency of microcephaly in the radiation-contaminated southwestern areas decades after the Chernobyl disaster.

5   Conclusion and Future Work

As a result of the research, a generalized multilevel model has been developed for structuring heterogeneous data from various sources. To implement the proposed model of structuring heterogeneous biomedical data, there can be used traditional models of data and knowledge warehouses (e.g., Data Vault), DBMS-based software packages for building and maintaining data warehouses (e.g., Microsoft Analysis Services Oracle Data Warehousing), or cloud services (e.g., Microsoft Azure). For visualization, both traditional visualization systems (Microsoft Power BI, QlikView, Tableau) and special cognitive visualizers can be used.

The proposed model was adapted for processing heterogeneous biomedical data in the risk evaluation tasks for socially significant diseases. Ecological monitoring data and medical data were loaded into the developed model. A comparative analysis of the incidence of congenital malformations in children of the Bryansk region, the RF was carried out on the basis of the aggregated data and the model-selected links between objects.

The approaches proposed in the paper contribute to expanding the possibilities of ensembles of intelligent data analysis models: to apply them to already aggregated data with established relationships, to apply ensembles of models for new tasks with a similar structure. The developed model allows for enriching the available data, taking into account more factors and hidden relationships between them, facilitating intelligent analysis and enhancing the quality of its results, which in turn enables to improve the efficiency and validity of management decisions and perform their subsequent verification.

Currently, studies are conducted on the influence of parents' anamnesis on the risk of congenital malformations in children taking into account environmental factors. Meanwhile additional medical and environmental data for the Bryansk region of the Russian Federation are loaded into the developed model.

Acknowledgments. The reported study was funded by RFBR, project number 19-07-00844.

References

1. Averchenkov, V., Budylskii, D., Podvesovskii, A., et al.: Hierarchical deep learning: a promising technique for opinion monitoring and sentiment analysis in Russian-language social networks. In: Kravets, A., et al. (eds.) CIT & DS 2015. CCIS, vol. 535, pp. 583–592. Springer, Heidelberg (2015). https://doi.org/10.1007/978-3-319-23766-4_46
2. Cohen, B., Vawdrey, D., Liu, J., Caplan, D., Furuya, E., Mis, F., Larson, E.: Challenges associated with using large data sets for quality assessment and research in clinical settings. Policy Politics Nurs. Pract. **16**(3–4), 117–124 (2015). https://doi.org/10.1177/15271544156 03358
3. Gibert, K., Horsburgh, J., Athanasiadis, I., Holmes, G.: Environmental Data Science. Environ. Model Softw. **106**, 4–12 (2018). https://doi.org/10.1016/j.envsoft.2018.04.005
4. Guerrero, J., Garcia, A., Personal, E., Luque, J., Leon, C.: Heterogeneous data source integration for smart grid ecosystems based on metadata mining. Expert Systems With Applications (2017). https://doi.org/10.1016/j.eswa.2017.03.007

5. Kim, Y., Oh, S., Chun, Y., Lee, W., Park, H.: Gene expression assay and Watson for oncology for optimization of treatment in ER-positive, HER2-negative breast cancer. PLoS ONE **13**(7), e0200100 (2018). https://doi.org/10.1371/journal.pone.0200100

6. Korsakov, A., Hoffmann, V., Pugach, L., Lagerev, D., Korolik, V., Bulatseva, M.: Comparative assessment of stillbirth rate in Bryansk region, EU and sic countries (1995–2014) Bulletin of Russian State Medical University, (4). Pp. 91–99 (2018). https://doi.org/10.24075/vrgmu.2018.048

7. Korsakov, A., Yablokov, A., Geger, E.: Congenital malformations at the chernobyl territories and among posterity of liquidators (review). In: Chapter in the monograph «The Chernobyl Disaster» . New York, Nova, pp 15–62 (2016)

8. Korsakov, A., Yablokov, A., Troshin, V., Mikhalev, V.: The buccal epithelium as environmental indicator. Biol. Bull. Russ. Acad. Sci. **42**(3), 273–277 (2015). https://doi.org/10.1134/S1062359015030048

9. Lausch, A., Schmidt, A., Tischendorf, L.: Data mining and linked open data – new perspectives for data analysis in environmental research. Ecol. Model. **295**, 5–17 (2015). https://doi.org/10.1016/j.ecolmodel.2014.09.018

10. Li, B., Li, J., Jiang, Y., Lan, X.: Experience and reflection from China's Xiangya medical big data project. J. Biomed. Inf. **93**, 103149 (2019). https://doi.org/10.1016/j.jbi.2019.103149

11. Manyika, J., et al.: Big Data: the next frontier for innovation, competition, and productivity. McKinsey Global Institute (2011). https://www.mckinsey.com/business-functions/digital-mckinsey/our-insights/big-data-the-next-frontier-for-innovation

12. Zakharova, A., Vekhter, E., Shklyar, A., Zavyalov, D.: Visual detection of internal patterns in the empirical data. In: Kravets, A., et al. (eds.) CIT & DS 2017, CCIS, vol. 754, pp. 215–230. Springer, Heidelberg (2017). https://doi.org/10.1007/978-3-319-65551-2_16

13. Zou, F., Liu, C., Liu, X., Tang, Y., Ma, J., Hu, C.: Concordance study between IBM Watson for oncology and real clinical practice for cervical cancer patients in China retrospective analysis. JMIR Preprints.: 12868 (2018). https://doi.org/10.2196/preprints.12868

Adaptable Mobile Software for Supporting Daily Activities of People with Intellectual Disabilities

Olga Shabalina[1]($\boxtimes$) (iD), Vladislav Guriev[1], Stanislav Kosyakov[1],
Angelina Voronina[1], and David C. Moffat[2]

[1] Volgograd State Technical University, Volgograd, Russia
o.a.shabalina@gmail.com, orkich@gmail.com
[2] Glasgow Caledonian University, Glasgow, UK
D.C.Moffat@gcu.ac.uk

Abstract. Many a person with intellectual disabilities (PID) will experience various problems in daily life. The use of mobile applications can help PIDs to cope with these problems and feel more confident. At the present time, the number of applications (apps) that are intended to support the everyday life of PID is growing rapidly. However, different PIDs have different capabilities and limitations. Focusing on a certain category of PID significantly limits the usage of such apps. On the other hand, attempts to cater to a wide range of disabilities can make the app less suitable for most of them. Meanwhile, most PIDs have caregivers who are well aware of the capabilities and limitations of their clients and, if allowed to, would be able to customize mobile apps for each individual user. This situation makes it possible to develop apps for PID that are adaptable by their caregivers.

The paper presents an approach to the development of mobile apps for PIDs whose interface can be configured by others who well understand the user's capabilities and limitations. The mobile app's interface is to be designed using template-based technologies. The interface templates can include mandatory and optional image elements. Development begins with the design of templates for each app screenshot, showing the mandatory and optional elements, their positions on the screen and sets of possible images for each element.

A web service to manage the development of such mobile apps, with adaptable interfaces, and to configure an app's interface to particular users (PIDs), is described. We then show the suggested approach by the development of two mobile games for PIDs, both with adaptable interfaces.

Keywords: Person with intellectual disabilities · PID · Everyday life skills · Mobile application · App · Adaptability · Adaptable interface · Adaptive interface · Testing labor preferences · Training shopping skills · Mobile application development management system

© Springer Nature Switzerland AG 2019
A. G. Kravets et al. (Eds.): CIT&DS 2019, CCIS 1084, pp. 474–484, 2019.
https://doi.org/10.1007/978-3-030-29750-3_37

1 Introduction

Intellectual Disability (ID) is defined by the American Association of Intellectual and Developmental Disabilities (AAIDD) as "a disability characterized by significant limitations both in intellectual functioning and in adaptive behavior, which covers a range of everyday social and practical skills" [1]. Many people with intellectual disabilities experience problems in various aspects of their daily lives, such as movement/travel, housework, support of health and safety of life, using money, phone, job search, and so on.

Advances in human-computer interaction (HCI), and in information and communication technology (ICT) have developed various assistive technologies especially for PIDs [2, 3]. The capabilities of modern mobile applications (apps) offer promising opportunities to help PIDs to cope with their everyday life problems and to feel more confident in everyday activities. At the present time, more applications are appearing that focus on the capabilities and limitations of PIDs. Those apps are typically simple, have limitations in their functionality and their visual interface, many apps have sound support.

One of the most important problems of assistive technology software development is the problem of accessible interface design for PIDs). Different PIDs have different capabilities and limitations. Developing an application so as to direct its interface toward a specific category of ID significantly limits the app's general usefulness to some other users. On the other hand, orientation toward a wider range of ID can lead to a loss of specificity and make them unsuitable for most PIDs. One of the most effective solutions to overcome this contradiction should be to develop applications whose interface can somehow be customized for specific users.

2 Adaptive and Adaptable GUI Design Approaches

There are two basic approaches to customize a user interface – pre-customization and runtime customization. The ability to pre-customize a system's interface is considered "interface adaptability," while runtime customization is "interface adaptivity." Adaptability refers to the process of selecting or modifying some aspects of the user interface according to some user characteristics. Adaptivity refers to the process of selecting or modifying the user interface dynamically, according to dynamic user characteristics and situations that are detected at run-time [5].

Adaptivity cannot be initiated by the interface components, as they do not have knowledge of changing user characteristics and situations. An adaptive user interface (AUI) has to automatically change its design, controls, information and other elements according to the user' needs [6]. Development of AUIs is based on interface design patterns, user models and rules for their interpretation, to generate the interface most suitable for specific user [7]. The use of artificial intelligence techniques has been a widely accepted approach to designing AUIs [8]. Designing AUIs is a more time-consuming and methodical process than non-adaptive user interfaces. Consequently, this increases the cost of adaptive user interfaces [9].

Adaptable User Interfaces (AdUIs) can be defined as systems in which the activation of user-computer interaction is performed by the final user through the selection of a specific user profile from a predefined list [10]. Adaptability is based on user characteristics and preferences that are known prior to interaction and, in any case, are assumed to remain static throughout a single interaction session [11]. Development of AdUIs is based on user and dialogue modes, multiple-component user interface techniques, Semantic Web technologies and evidence-based best practices [12–16]. The most important advantage of adaptable interfaces is that the users are in total control of the individual appearance of the user interface.

3   Concept of Interface That Is Adaptable by Caregivers

The success of an interface that is adaptive to the user depends on how the user's characteristics, and his (or her) interactions, can be interpreted in real time to modify the interface. In case the users are PIDs, their behavior with the app might be unpredictable, and their interactions might be misinterpreted. Thus the interface generated by the app may turn out to be difficult or even unsuitable to a particular user. On the other hand, apps with adaptable interfaces, that require the users themselves to personalize them, can be a significant barrier for users with disabilities and lower levels of ICT [17].

Meanwhile, in fact, almost all PIDs during their life are cared for in some way. Their parents and other relatives can act as caregivers. Some PIDs visit medical and rehabilitation centers (or even stay there for some time) where they are also taken care of by specially trained staff. The caregivers are well aware of the capabilities and limitations of their clients, and if asked are able to customize mobile applications for each individual user. This situation makes it possible to develop applications for PIDs which are adaptable by their caregivers [18].

The concept of an adaptable interface is based on the separation of the interface elements into mandatory and optional elements; using an image with text for those interface elements; the ability to select element images from the database (or add new ones to the database) and match the elements "in place".

Mandatory elements reflect the app's functionality and should always present, regardless of the user. Optional elements can be included in the interface for a particular user, depending on his individual capabilities and preferences. Pictograms from different pictographic languages can be used for images of the interface elements, which are stored in the database. For some elements, more than one image can be specified. Each control, navigational and informational element that is selected for the interface is attached to a certain area of the screen. The fixed location of the elements helps to train users to work with the new application.

Adaptable app development is based on using template-based technologies. The interface development begins with the design of templates for each app screenshot, showing mandatory and optional elements, their positions on the screen and sets of possible images for each element. The caregiver, who is well aware of the capabilities and limitations of his or her client, customizes the app for the user.

4 Mobile Application Development Management System

To manage the development of mobile applications with an adaptable interface and adapt the app interface to certain users (PID), a Mobile Application Development Management (MADM) system has been developed. The system is implemented as a web service and provides to developers the following functions: management of information about the users of web and mobile apps, PID administration, application interface configuration, and secure access to PID information for third-party applications.

To ensure the independence of the way to connect the applications to the database, the Representational State Transfer (REST) architectural style, commonly used for web services, was chosen for the system implementation. The REST architecture has a simple interface without additional interlayers, and it does not depend on who makes the request to the system. The system includes the following components: Application Programming Interface (API) for communication with applications, a web interface for configuring mobile applications, and external applications that connect with the application via the API. The system architecture is shown in Fig. 1.

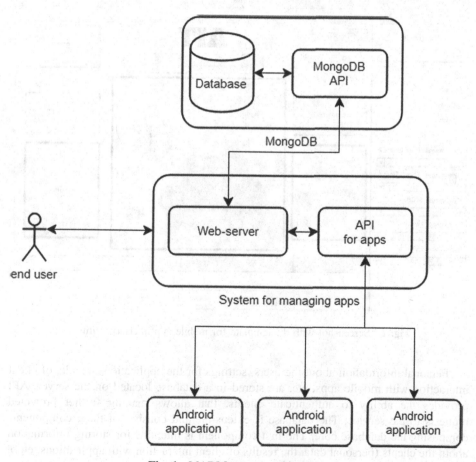

Fig. 1. MADM system architecture

The system's web interface implements security functions (user authentication/ registration, password recovery), web-system and mobile user (PID) management, and configuration of the interface of mobile applications. To ensure interaction with mobile applications, the web-system receives data about a mobile user and sets the mobile application functions.

The web interface of the system is used to configure the interface of an Android app. It consists of two windows. The left window includes checkboxes to toggle on/off optional UI elements, and sliders to select an image for the chosen UI elements from the database. The right window is used for pre-viewing the UI with selected images in real time. By moving the slider, the caregiver can see each image (one after another) that can be assigned to the chosen UI element for the mobile app. The caregiver can select the most understandable image for the client (PID); or elect not to use the element at all, if it is an optional one. A screenshot of the web configuration page is shown in Fig. 2.

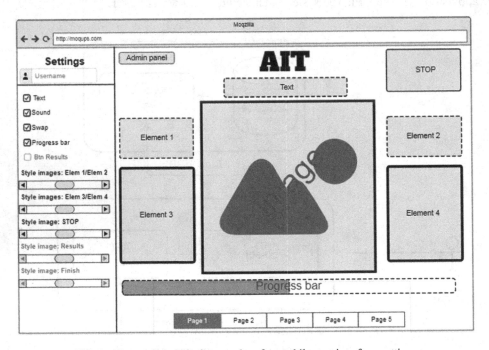

Fig. 2. Screenshot with the template for mobile app interface settings

Personal information about the users, settings for the applications, results of client interaction with mobile apps, etc. are stored in a database located on the server. API provides the ability to authenticate clients, that allows making further protected requests to the service. The database is extensible and consists of three components composing the database core. The first component is intended for storing information about the clients (personal data, the results of client interaction with applications, etc.).

The second component is supposed for use by people responsible for configuring mobile apps for the clients (it can be some end user and super or local administrator as well). And the last component is intended for storing the information about mobile the applications to be added to the system.

The system is implemented as a Web service, so it is universal from the perspective of client application platforms. This greatly expands the capabilities of the system, because allows for the development of new applications to choose the most suitable platform for different PIDs.

The system is implemented in the programming language JavaScript, the Node.js software platform is used to develop the web application. The application architecture is built on the MVC pattern. For storing the data MongoDB database is used, images for mobile application interfaces are stored in the file system. The application itself is hosted in the Heroku cloud service.

Adding new applications to the system is supposed to be done by the system developers. Developers add the app support functions by scaling the "Android-application" entity and create new Web pages on the site to configure this application and analyze the feedback from the app user.

5   Mobile Applications with Adaptable Interface

5.1   Mobile App for Testing Labor Preferences (AIT Test)

One of the important ways that PIDs have to socialize is their involvement in work activities. However, they are not often able to adequately assess their own capabilities and determine their preferences for possible work activity [19, 20]. They often need the support of their parents and caregivers. To help parents and caregivers to solve this problem we developed a mobile app that implements an online test (AIT test), for analyzing preferences for various professions, which was designed specifically for people with mental disabilities, developed by Cor Lamings & George Hesemans [21].

The AIT test is a collection of images illustrating different professions and grouped into several categories. The PID goes through the test to evaluate each image from the point of view of its attractiveness to him (Like /Dislike). The app then calculates the sum scores in order to rank the categories or professions by attractiveness [21].

The adaptable user interface is developed by iterative user-centered design. The app implements the functions of testing and evaluating results, managing the database of tests, saving and visualizing current and final test results, and sound support. The screen forms of the application in the testing and evaluation mode are shown in Fig. 3a. The PID can work independently with the app registration function by using icons, which allow users who do not have reading and writing skills to log into the application themselves.

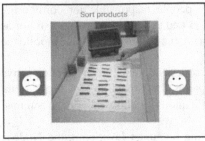

a) Testing mode

b) Image-based registration and authentication

Fig. 3. The app screenshots

Web service screenshots for configuring two variants of the mobile app testing page are shown in Fig. 4.

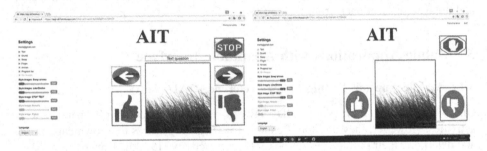

Fig. 4. Configuring the testing page of the mobile app

The application is implemented in the Java programming language. The app architecture is built on the MVP pattern, using the Moxy MVP library, and the Dagger2 library is used to implement the DI pattern. The cloud storage database which was selected was Firebase. Database requests are implemented in a reactive style using the RxJava2 library. The front view of the interface was implemented with the ButterKnife library.

5.2 Mobile App for Training Shopping Skills

One of the challenges PID can face in their everyday life is making purchases in real shops. Analysis of shopping behaviors of PIDs shows [22] that they might have difficulties in making shopping lists, searching for items in the shop, reading prices, choosing the right coins or bills, calculating what their change should be, and so on [23]. To help PID to become more confident in a real shopping environment and to make purchases on one's own "at the right time and at the right place," a mobile application with the adaptable interface has been developed. The aim of the app is to teach PID users how to use money and how to make payments.

The application supports the following steps of making a purchase: managing money, choosing a store for purchases, making a list of purchases in this store, searching for goods in the store, paying for goods. The app has two modes: a real-time mode and a training mode. In real time mode, the app can be used to do real shopping. The training mode is implemented as a game with a virtual shop assistant. The game implements the same functions and interfaces as in the online mode and simulates a trip to a real store. The game assistant can explain to the user how the game works when first uses it, give suggestions when he gets stuck, and explain or show him what to do. For example: to explain how the user can choose a category, a hand will move over the screen and click on a category. The emoticons in Fig. 5 are the faces that will be shown to give feedback to the user about how many mistakes he or she made. The user can click on these faces/emoticons to get suggestions. The virtual assistant can also give feedback to users about how many mistakes they made through emotional dialogs.

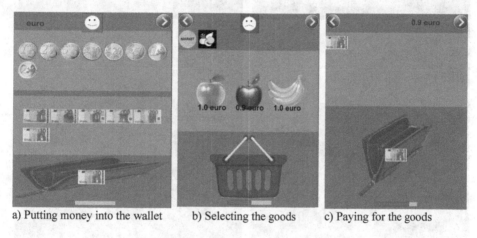

a) Putting money into the wallet   b) Selecting the goods   c) Paying for the goods

Fig. 5. Examples of possible testing page

The application is developed in C # in the Unity environment. It uses standard Unity libraries and the Android SDK for compiling the app to run on the Android operating system.

6 Apps Testing

The game interface was developed by iterative design and testing. The iterations were tested in MPI Oosterlo, which is a service center for PIDs in Flanders, Belgium. In the testing sessions, several PID worked with the app. Some users were familiar with the use of apps and touch-screens, while others were not. The users in the session did not have any training in advance, so in the testing sessions, they all saw the app for the first time. Some photos from the first testing of the app for training shopping skills are shown in Fig. 6.

Fig. 6. Testing the game with PIDs

The results of the first play-tests of the game with PID showed that some game activities were clearly understandable for all of them, but some others were quite difficult. The second version of the game was made to overcome those difficulties. In subsequent testing, the second version showed that the game interface had become clearer for PIDs, but there were still some weak points. Currently, the third version of the game is under development.

7 Conclusion

Successfully performing everyday life activities is important for everyone's well-being, and this is equally the case for persons with intellectual disabilities. Testing the developed mobile applications with PIDs certainly helped to make the apps more understandable and applicable for people with a wide range of abilities and limitations. The results of testing also showed that the mobile applications we developed can help PIDs to feel more confident in their everyday life.

Acknowledgment. The applications development is a collaborative action between Volgograd State Technical University, Russia, Thomas More University College Geel and medical center MPI Oosterlo, Belgium. The testing was conducted by Mr. Raf Hensbergen, a job-coach who helps mentally disabled people to find and keep a suitable (voluntary) job.

The research was supported by RFBR, research project No. 18-07-01308a.

References

1. Definition of intellectual disability. http://aaidd.org/intellectual-disability/definition#.VSIvyUZ9fTt. Accessed 06 Apr 2015
2. McMahon, D.D., Cihak, D.F., Gibbons, M.M., Fussell, L., Mathison, S.: Using a mobile app to teach individuals with intellectual disabilities to identify potential food allergens. J. Spec. Educ. Technol. **28**(3), 21–32 (2013)
3. Daems, J., Bosch, N., Solberg, S., Dekelver, J., Kultsova, M.: AbleChat: development of a chat app with pictograms for people with Intellectual Disabilities. In: Proceedings of Engineering for Society. Leuven (2016)
4. Kbar, G., Mian, S.H., Abidi, M.H.: Unified interface for people with disabilities (UI-PWD) at smart city (design and implementation). In: Information innovation technology in smart cities, pp. 3–20 (2017). https://doi.org/10.1007/978-981-10-1741-4_1, www.scopus.com
5. Stephanidis, C., et al.: Adaptable and adaptive user interfaces for disabled users in the AVANTI project. In: Trigila, S., Mullery, A., Campolargo, M., Vanderstraeten, H., Mampaey, M. (eds.) Intelligence in Services and Networks: Technology for Ubiquitous Telecom Services. IS&N 1998. LNCS, vol. 1430, pp. 153–166. Springer, Heidelberg (1998). https://doi.org/10.1007/BFb0056962
6. Kbar, G., Bhatia, A., Abidi, M.H.: Smart unified interface for people with disabilities at the work place. In: 2015 11th International Conference on Innovations in Information Technology, IIT 2015, pp. 172–177 (2016). https://doi.org/10.1109/INNOVATIONS.2015.7381535, www.scopus.com
7. Cortes, V.A., Zarate, V.H., Uresti, J.A.R., Zayas, B.E.: Current challenges and applications for adaptive user interfaces. Human-Computer Interaction, Inaki Maurtua, IntechOpen, 1 December 2009. https://doi.org/10.5772/7745. https://www.intechopen.com/books/human-computer-interaction/current-challenges-and-applications-for-adaptive-user-interfaces
8. Gelšvartas, J., Simutis, R., Maskeliūnas, R.: Projection mapping user interface for disabled people. J. Healthc. Eng. **2018**(6916204), 6 (2018). https://doi.org/10.1155/2018/6916204
9. Kurschl, W., Augstein, M., Stitz, H.: Adaptive user interfaces on tablets to support people with disabilities. In: Harald, R., Deussen,O. (eds.) Mensch & Computer 2012 – Workshopband – 12. fachüübergreifende Konferenz für interaktive und kooperative Medien, pp. 91–94. Oldenbourg Verlag (2012)

10. Gullà, F., Cavalieri, L., Ceccacci, S., Germani, M., Bevilacqua, R.: Method to design adaptable and adaptive user interfaces (2015). https://doi.org/10.1007/978-3-319-21380-4_4, www.scopus.com

11. Kantorowitz, E., Sudarsky, O.: The adaptable user interface. Commun. ACM **32**(11), 1352–1358 (1989). https://doi.org/10.1145/68814.68820

12. Iqbal, M.W., Ahmad, N., Shahzad, S.K., Feroz, I., Mian, N.A.: Towards adaptive user interfaces for mobile-phone in smart world. Int. J. Adv. Comput. Sci. Appl **9**(11), 556–565 (2018). www.scopus.com

13. Kultsova, M., Potseluico, A., Zhukova, I., Skorikov, A., Romanenko, R.: A Two-Phase Method of User Interface Adaptation for People with Special Needs. In: Kravets, A., Shcherbakov, M., Kultsova, M., Groumpos, P. (eds.) Creativity in Intelligent Technologies and Data Science. CIT&DS 2017. CCIS, vol 754, pp. 805–821. Springer, Cham (2017). https://doi.org/10.1007/978-3-319-65551-2_58, www.scopus.com

14. Grundy, J., Hosking, J.: Developing adaptable user interfaces for component-based systems. Interact. Comput. **14**(3), 175–194 (2002). https://doi.org/10.1016/S0953-5438(01)00049-2

15. Perez, C.D.L.R.: Adaptable user interfaces for people with autism: a transportation example. In: Proceedings of the 15th Web for all Conference: Internet of Accessible Things, W4A 2018 (2018). https://doi.org/10.1145/3192714.3196, www.scopus.com

16. Gullà, F., Ceccacci, S., Germani, M., Cavalieri, L.: Design adaptable and adaptive user interfaces: a method to manage the information. In: Andò, B., Siciliano, P., Marletta, V., Monteriù, A. (eds.) Ambient Assisted Living. Biosystems & Biorobotics, vol. 11, pp. 47–58. Springer, Cham (2015). https://doi.org/10.1007/978-3-319-18374-9_5

17. Gajos, K.Z., Everitt, K., Tan, D.S., Czerwinski, M., Weld, D.S.: Predictability and accuracy in adaptive user interfaces. In: Proceedings of the SIGCHI Conference on Human Factors in Computing Systems, 05–10 April 2008, Florence, Italy (2008). https://doi.org/10.1145/1357054.1357252

18. Borblik, Y., Shabalina, O., Kultsova, M., Pidoprigora, A., Romanenko, R.: Assistive technology software for people with intellectual or development disabilities: Design of user interfaces for mobile applications [Электронный ресурс]. In: IISA 2015 – 6th International Conference on Information, Intelligence, Systems and Applications, Corfu, Greece, 6 July–8 July 2015, Conference Proceeding/Ionian University, Institute of Electrical and Electronics Engineers (IEEE). Piscataway, USA (2015). https://doi.org/10.1109/IISA.2015.7387976. (индекс. в Scopus)

19. Vilà, M., Pallisera, M., Fullana, J.: Work integration of people with disabilities in the regular labour market: What can we do to improve these processes? J. Intellect. Dev. Disa-bil. **32**(1), 10–18 (2007)

20. Bos, A., Dekelver, J., Niesen, W., Shabalina, O.A., Skvaznikov, D., Hensbergen, R.: LIT: Labour interest test for people with intellectual disabilities. In: Kravets, A., Shcherbakov, M., Kultsova, M., Groumpos, P. (eds.) Creativity in Intelligent Technologies and Data Science, CIT&DS 2017. Communications in Computer and Information Science, vol. 754, pp. 822–832. Springer, Heidelberg (2017). https://doi.org/10.1007/978-3-319-65551-2_59

21. Laming, C., Hezemans, G.: Aan het werk. Arbeid voor mensen met een verstandelijke beperking. Tilburg: Lib Edits (1996)

22. RCNi: More support needed to make shopping easier for people with intellectual disabilities, ScienceDaily (2015). www.sciencedaily.com/releases/2015/09/150929112119.htm

23. Abbott, D., Marriott, A.: Money, finance and the personalisation agenda for people with learning disabilities in the UK: some emerging issues. Br. J. Learn. Disabil. **41**(2), 106–113 (2013)

Author Index

Printed in the United States
By Bookmasters